GLEIM® | Aviation

2017 EDITION

PRIVATE PILOT

AND RECREATIONAL PILOT

FAA Knowledge Test

for the FAA Computer-Based Pilot Knowledge Test

Private Pilot - Airplane *Recreational Pilot - Airplane* *Private Pilot - Airplane Transition*

by

Irvin N. Gleim, Ph.D., CFII and Garrett W. Gleim, CFII

Gleim Publications, Inc.
P.O. Box 12848 · University Station
Gainesville, Florida 32604
(352) 375-0772
(800) 87-GLEIM or (800) 874-5346
Fax: (352) 375-6940
Internet: www.GleimAviation.com
Email: admin@gleim.com

For updates to the first printing of the 2017 edition of

Private Pilot and Recreational Pilot FAA Knowledge Test

Go To: www.gleim.com/updates

Or: Email update@gleim.com with **PPKT 2017-1** in the subject line. You will receive our current update as a reply.

Updates are available until the next edition is published.

ISSN 1080-4900
ISBN 978-1-61854-057-7

First Printing: August 2017

YOU CAN HELP

This 2017 edition is designed specifically for private pilots. Please send any corrections and suggestions for subsequent editions to us via the feedback links within the online components or using the form at www.gleim.com/AviationQuestions.

Two other volumes are also available. ***Private Pilot Flight Maneuvers and Practical Test Prep*** focuses on your flight training and the FAA practical test, just as this book focuses on the FAA knowledge test. ***Pilot Handbook*** is a complete pilot ground school text in outline format with many diagrams for ease in understanding.

Save time, money, and frustration--order online at www.GleimAviation.com today! Please bring Gleim books to the attention of flight instructors, fixed base operators, and others with a potential interest in flying. Wide distribution of these books and increased interest in flying depend on your assistance, good word, etc. Thank you.

Environmental Statement -- This book is printed on recyclable, environmentally friendly groundwood paper, sourced from certified sustainable forests and produced either TCF (totally chlorine-free) or ECF (elementally chlorine-free).

GLEIM SUCCESS TIPS

Our answers have been carefully researched and reviewed. Inevitably, there will be differences with competitors' books and even the FAA. If necessary, we will develop an UPDATE for ***Private Pilot and Recreational Pilot FAA Knowledge Test***. Visit our website or email update@gleim.com for the latest updates. Updates for this 2017 edition will be available until the next edition is published. To continue providing our customers with first-rate service, we request that technical questions about our materials be sent to us via the feedback links within the online components. We will give each question thorough consideration and a prompt response. Questions concerning orders, prices, shipments, or payments will be handled via telephone by our competent and courteous customer service staff.

ABOUT THE AUTHORS

Irvin N. Gleim earned his private pilot certificate in 1965 from the Institute of Aviation at the University of Illinois, where he subsequently received his Ph.D. He is a commercial pilot and flight instructor (instrument) with multi-engine and seaplane ratings and is a member of the Aircraft Owners and Pilots Association, American Bonanza Society, Civil Air Patrol, Experimental Aircraft Association, National Association of Flight Instructors, and Seaplane Pilots Association. He is the author of flight maneuvers and practical test prep books for the sport, private, instrument, commercial, and flight instructor certificates/ratings and the author of study guides for the sport, private/recreational, instrument, commercial, flight/ground instructor, fundamentals of instructing, airline transport pilot, and flight engineer FAA knowledge tests. Three additional pilot training books are *Pilot Handbook*, *Aviation Weather and Weather Services*, and *FAR/AIM*.

Dr. Gleim has also written articles for professional accounting and business law journals and is the author of widely used review manuals for the CIA (Certified Internal Auditor) exam, the CMA (Certified Management Accountant) exam, the CPA (Certified Public Accountant) exam, and the EA (IRS Enrolled Agent) exam. He is Professor Emeritus, Fisher School of Accounting, University of Florida, and is a CFM, CIA, CMA, and CPA.

Garrett W. Gleim earned his private pilot certificate in 1997 in a Piper Super Cub. He is a commercial pilot (single- and multi-engine), ground instructor (advanced and instrument), and flight instructor (instrument and multi-engine), and he is a member of the Aircraft Owners and Pilots Association and the National Association of Flight Instructors. He is the author of study guides for the sport, private/recreational, instrument, commercial, flight/ground instructor, fundamentals of instructing, and airline transport pilot FAA knowledge tests. He received a Bachelor of Science in Economics from The Wharton School, University of Pennsylvania. Mr. Gleim is also a CPA (not in public practice).

REVIEWERS AND CONTRIBUTORS

Paul Duty, CFII, MEI, AGI, is a graduate of Embry-Riddle Aeronautical University with a Master of Business Administration-Aviation degree. He is one of our aviation editors and an aviation marketing specialist. Mr. Duty researched questions, wrote and edited answer explanations, and incorporated revisions into the text.

Drew S. Glastetter, CFII, MEI, ASES, ATP - SA227, CA212, B737, is one of our aviation editors. Mr. Glastetter researched questions, wrote and edited answer explanations, and incorporated revisions into the text.

Char Marissa Gregg, CFII, LTA, Glider, ASES, ATP, is the Gleim 141 Chief Flight Instructor and one of our aviation editors. Ms. Gregg researched questions, wrote and edited answer explanations, and incorporated revisions into the text.

W. Rhett Lawton, CFI, CFII, MEI, ATP, Type Rating DA-50, B.S., Brigham Young University, M.B.A., Henderson State University, is one of our aviation editors. Mr. Lawton researched questions, wrote and edited answer explanations, and incorporated revisions into the text.

Erik T. Vrooman, Commercial Pilot, A&P Mechanic, is a graduate of the maintenance program at Embry-Riddle Aeronautical University. In addition to working with Gleim, he is on staff with the College of Missionary Aviation. Mr. Vrooman researched material and incorporated revisions into the text.

The CFIs who have worked with us throughout the years to develop and improve our pilot training materials.

The many FAA employees who helped, in person or by telephone, primarily in Gainesville, Orlando, Oklahoma City, and Washington, DC.

The many pilots who have provided comments and suggestions about *Private Pilot and Recreational Pilot FAA Knowledge Test* during the past several decades.

A PERSONAL THANKS

This manual would not have been possible without the extraordinary effort and dedication of Julie Cutlip, Blaine Hatton, Kelsey Olson, Breanna Rodriguez, Teresa Soard, Justin Stephenson, Joanne Strong, and Elmer Tucker, who typed the entire manuscript and all revisions and drafted and laid out the diagrams, illustrations, and cover for this book.

The authors also appreciate the production and editorial assistance of Jacob Bennett, Melody Dalton, Jessica Felkins, Jim Harvin, Kristen Hennen, Katie Larson, Diana León, Jake Pettifor, Shane Rapp, and Drew Sheppard.

Finally, we appreciate the encouragement, support, and tolerance of our families throughout this project.

ACKNOWLEDGMENT

Image on the cover of a Cirrus SR22-G3 aircraft reproduced with the permission of Cirrus, Copyright 2016 Cirrus Aircraft or its Affiliates. All rights reserved. Inclusion of Cirrus Aircraft copyrighted material in the Publications does not imply any endorsement by Cirrus or its Affiliates of the Publications.

TABLE OF CONTENTS

NOTE: The FAA no longer releases the complete database of test questions to the public. Instead, sample questions are released on the Airmen Testing page of the FAA website on a quarterly basis. These questions are similar to the actual test questions, but they are not exact matches.

Gleim utilizes customer feedback and FAA publications to create additional sample questions that closely represent the topical coverage of each FAA knowledge test. In order to do well on the knowledge test, you must study the Gleim outlines in this book, answer all the questions under exam conditions (i.e., without looking at the answers first), and develop an understanding of the topics addressed. You should not simply memorize questions and answers. This will not prepare you for your FAA knowledge test, and it will not help you develop the knowledge you need to safely operate an aircraft.

Always refer to the Gleim update service (www.gleim.com/updates) to ensure you have the latest information that is available. If you see topics covered on your FAA knowledge test that are not contained in this book, please contact us at www.gleim.com/AviationQuestions to report your experience and help us fine-tune our test preparation materials.

Thank you!

PREFACE

The primary purpose of this book is to provide you with the easiest, fastest, and least expensive means of passing the FAA knowledge tests for the private pilot (airplane) and/or the recreational pilot certificates. The publicly released FAA knowledge test bank does **not** have questions grouped together by topic. We have organized them for you. We have

1. Reproduced all previously released knowledge test questions published by the FAA. We have also included many additional similar test questions, which we believe may appear in some form on your knowledge test.
2. Reordered the questions into 121 logical topics.
3. Organized these topics into 11 study units.
4. Explained the answer immediately to the right of each question.
5. Provided an easy-to-study outline of exactly what you need to know (and no more) at the beginning of each study unit.

Accordingly, you can thoroughly prepare for the FAA pilot knowledge test by

1. Studying the brief outlines at the beginning of each study unit.
2. Answering the question on the left side of each page while covering up the answer explanations on the right side of each page.
3. Reading the answer explanation for each question that you answer incorrectly or have difficulty answering.
4. Facilitating this Gleim process with our **FAA Test Prep Online**. Our software allows you to emulate the FAA test (CATS or PSI). By practicing answering questions on a computer, you will become at ease with the computer testing process and have the confidence to PASS. See pages 17 and 18.
5. Using our **Online Ground School**, which provides you with our outlines, practice problems, and sample tests. This course is easily accessible through the Internet. Also, we give you a money-back guarantee with our **Online Ground School**. If you are unsuccessful, you get your money back!

Additionally, this book will introduce our entire series of pilot training texts, which use the same presentation method: outlines, illustrations, questions, and answer explanations. For example, ***Pilot Handbook*** is a textbook of aeronautical knowledge presented in easy-to-use outline format, with many charts, diagrams, figures, etc., included. While this book contains only the material needed to pass the FAA pilot knowledge test, ***Pilot Handbook*** contains the textbook knowledge required to be a safe and proficient pilot.

Many books create additional work for the user. In contrast, this book and its companion, ***Private Pilot Flight Maneuvers and Practical Test Prep***, facilitate your effort. They are easy to use. The outline/illustration format, type styles, and spacing are designed to improve readability. Concepts are often presented as phrases rather than as complete sentences – similar to notes that you would take in a class lecture.

Also, recognize that this study manual is concerned with **airplane** flight training, not balloon, glider, or helicopter training. We are confident this book, **FAA Test Prep Online**, and/or **Online Ground School** will facilitate speedy completion of your knowledge test. We also wish you the very best as you complete your private pilot and/or recreational pilot certification, in related flying, and in obtaining additional ratings and certificates.

Enjoy Flying Safely!

Irvin N. Gleim
Garrett W. Gleim

August 2016

INTRODUCTION: THE FAA PILOT KNOWLEDGE TEST

The beginning of this introduction explains how to obtain a private pilot certificate, and it explains the content and procedures of the Federal Aviation Administration (FAA) knowledge test, including how to take the test at a computer testing center. The remainder of this introduction discusses and illustrates the Gleim **Online Ground School** and **FAA Test Prep Online**. Achieving a private pilot certificate is fun. Begin today!

Private Pilot and Recreational Pilot FAA Knowledge Test is one of five books contained in the Gleim Private Pilot Kit. The other four books are

1. ***Private Pilot Flight Maneuvers and Practical Test Prep***
2. ***Private Pilot Syllabus***
3. ***Pilot Handbook***
4. ***FAR/AIM***

Private Pilot Flight Maneuvers and Practical Test Prep presents each flight maneuver you will perform in outline/illustration format so you will know what to expect and what to do before each flight lesson. This book will thoroughly prepare you to complete your FAA practical (flight) test confidently and successfully.

Private Pilot Syllabus is a step-by-step syllabus of ground and flight training lesson plans for your private pilot training.

Pilot Handbook is a complete pilot reference book that combines over 100 FAA books and documents, including *AIM*, FARs, ACs, and much more. Aerodynamics, airplane systems, airspace, and navigation are among the topics explained in ***Pilot Handbook***. This book, more than any other, will help make you a better and more proficient pilot.

FAR/AIM is an essential part of every pilot's library. The Gleim ***FAR/AIM*** is an easy-to-read reference book containing all of the Federal Aviation Regulations ("FARs" or "14 CFRs") applicable to general aviation flying, plus the full text of the FAA's *Aeronautical Information Manual (AIM)*.

The Gleim ***Aviation Weather and Weather Services*** is not included in the Private Pilot Kit, but you may want to purchase it if you do not already have it. This book combines all of the information from the FAA's *Aviation Weather* (AC 00-6), *Aviation Weather Services* (AC 00-45), and numerous FAA publications into one easy-to-understand book. It will help you study all aspects of aviation weather and provide you with a single reference book.

WHAT IS A PRIVATE PILOT CERTIFICATE?

A private pilot certificate is much like a driver's license. A private pilot certificate will allow you to fly an airplane and carry passengers and baggage, although not for compensation or hire. However, operating expenses may be shared with your passengers. The certificate, which is plastic (similar to a driver's license), is sent to you by the FAA upon satisfactory completion of your training program, a pilot knowledge test, and a practical test. A sample private pilot certificate is reproduced below. The recreational pilot certificate is the same except it says "recreational."

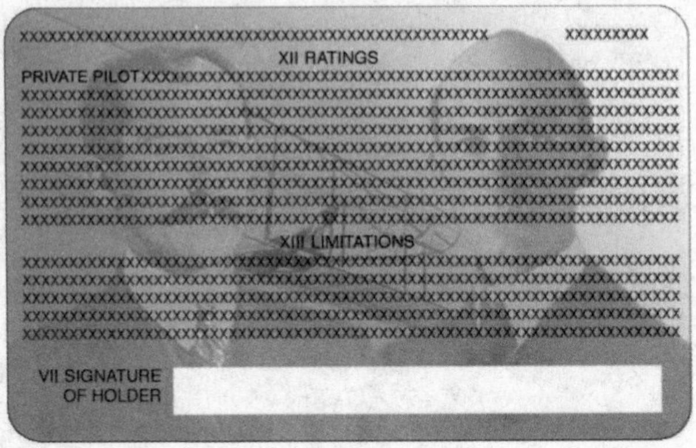

WHAT IS A RECREATIONAL PILOT CERTIFICATE?

The FAA added a recreational pilot certificate in 1989 for those who want to fly locally for fun, i.e., recreation. The objective is to provide only the flight training required for those **NOT** aspiring to fly on trips, at night, with more than one passenger, or to airports with an operating control tower or other airspace requiring air traffic control (ATC) communication. A recreational pilot certificate will take you less time and money to obtain, but your flying privileges will be restricted. The recreational pilot certificate is, however, upgradable to a private pilot certificate.

The recreational pilot knowledge test has 50 questions and includes most of the topics on the private pilot knowledge test. There are 27 questions specific to recreational pilots in Study Unit 4. For the recreational pilot knowledge test, we suggest you study the entire book except the following:

Subunit	Subunit Name
3.3	Beacons and Taxiway Lights
3.7	Collision Avoidance (Qs on night visual scanning)
3.8	ATIS and Ground Control
3.11	Terminal Radar Programs

Subunit	Subunit Name
3.14	ATC Traffic Advisories
3.15	ATC Light Signals
Study Unit 4 FARs	61.31, 61.113, 91.123, 91.130, 91.131, 91.135, 91.157

REQUIREMENTS TO OBTAIN A PRIVATE PILOT CERTIFICATE

1. Be at least 17 years of age.
2. Be able to read, write, and understand English (certificates with operating limitations may be available for medically related deficiencies).
3. Obtain at least a third-class FAA medical certificate (see the sample on the next page).
   a. You must undergo a routine medical examination, which may be administered only by FAA-designated doctors called aviation medical examiners (AME).
      1) For operations requiring a private, recreational, or student pilot certificate, a first-, second-, or third-class medical certificate expires at the end of the last day of the month either
         a) 5 years after the date of examination shown on the certificate, if you have not reached your 40th birthday on or before the date of examination, or
         b) 2 years after the date of examination shown on the certificate, if you have reached your 40th birthday on or before the date of examination.

b. Even if you have a physical handicap, medical certificates can be issued in many cases. Operating limitations may be imposed depending upon the nature of the disability.

c. Your certificated flight instructor (CFI) or fixed-base operator (FBO) will be able to recommend an AME.

   1) An FBO is an airport business that gives flight lessons, sells aviation fuel, repairs airplanes, etc.
   2) Also, the FAA publishes a directory that lists all authorized AMEs by name and address. Copies of this directory are kept at most FAA offices, ATC facilities, and Flight Service Stations (FSSs). Alternatively, go to the Gleim website at www.gleim.com/aviation/amesearch.php.

UNITED STATES OF AMERICA
Department of Transportation
Federal Aviation Administration
BB-5342031
MEDICAL CERTIFICATE 3rd **CLASS**

This certifies that *(Full name and address)*:
Richmond, Kane Everett
7771 Coral Way
N. Ft. Myers, Fl. 33903

Date of Birth	Ht.	Wt.	Hair	Eyes	Sex
1/30/85	5'9"	140	Brn.	Brn.	M

has met the medical standards prescribed in Part 67 Federal Aviation Regulations for this class of Medical Certificate, and the standards prescribed on Part 61 for a Student Pilot Certificate.

Limitations: None

Date of Examination: 4/15/15
Examiner's Serial No.: 11967-1

Examiner
Signature: *E.W. Williams, II, D.O.*
Typed Name: E.W. Williams II, D.O.

AIRMAN'S SIGNATURE *Kane Everett Richmond*

FAA Form 8420-2 (7-92) **Supersedes Previous Edition**

4. Obtain a student pilot certificate.

   a. You must be at least 16 years of age and be able to read, speak, and understand English to receive a student pilot certificate.
   b. To apply, you will meet in person with a flight instructor, FAA inspector at a local Flight Standards District Office, designated pilot evaluator, or airman certificate representative from an approved Part 141 flight school. An application will be processed and sent to the FAA and TSA for review.
   c. Upon approval, your student pilot certificate will be mailed to you.

      1) This process may take 10-21 days.

5. Receive and log ground training from an authorized instructor or complete a home-study course (such as studying this book, ***Private Pilot Flight Maneuvers and Practical Test Prep***, and ***Pilot Handbook*** or using the Gleim **Online Ground School**) to learn
   a. *Applicable Federal Aviation Regulations ... that relate to private pilot privileges, limitations, and flight operations*
   b. *Accident reporting requirements of the National Transportation Safety Board*
   c. *Use of the applicable portions of the Aeronautical Information Manual and FAA ACs (advisory circulars)*
   d. *Use of aeronautical charts for VFR navigation using pilotage, dead reckoning, and navigation systems*
   e. *Radio communication procedures*
   f. *Recognition of critical weather situations from the ground and in flight, windshear avoidance, and the procurement and use of aeronautical weather reports and forecasts*
   g. *Safe and efficient operation of aircraft, including collision avoidance, and recognition and avoidance of wake turbulence*
   h. *Effects of density altitude on takeoff and climb performance*
   i. *Weight and balance computations*
   j. *Principles of aerodynamics, powerplants, and aircraft systems*
   k. *Stall awareness, spin entry, spins, and spin recovery techniques for the airplane...category ratings*
   l. *Aeronautical decision making and judgment*
   m. *Preflight action that includes*
      1) *How to obtain information on runway lengths at airports of intended use, data on takeoff and landing distances, weather reports and forecasts, and fuel requirements*
      2) *How to plan for alternatives if the flight cannot be completed or delays are encountered*
6. Pass a knowledge test with a score of 70% or better. All FAA tests are administered at FAA-designated computer testing centers. The private pilot knowledge test consists of 60 multiple-choice questions selected from the airplane-related questions in the FAA's private pilot test bank; the remaining questions are for balloons, helicopters, etc. The FAA's published airplane-related questions, along with our own similar questions, are reproduced in this book with complete explanations.
7. Accumulate flight experience (FAR 61.109). Receive a total of 40 hr. of flight instruction and solo flight time, including
   a. 20 hr. of flight training from an authorized flight instructor, including at least
      1) 3 hr. of cross-country, i.e., to other airports
      2) 3 hr. at night, including
         a) One cross-country flight of over 100 NM total distance
         b) 10 takeoffs and 10 landings to a full stop at an airport
      3) 3 hr. of instrument flight training in an airplane
      4) 3 hr. in airplanes in preparation for the private pilot practical test within 2 calendar months prior to that test

      NOTE: A maximum of 2.5 hr. of instruction may be accomplished in an FAA-approved flight simulator or flight training device representing an airplane.
   b. 10 hr. of solo flight time in an airplane, including at least
      1) 5 hr. of cross-country flights

2) One solo cross-country flight of at least 150 NM total distance, with full-stop landings at a minimum of three points and with one segment of the flight consisting of a straight-line distance of more than 50 NM between the takeoff and landing locations

3) Three solo takeoffs and landings to a full stop at an airport with an operating control tower

8. Receive flight instruction and demonstrate skill (FAR 61.107).

   a. Obtain a logbook sign-off by your CFI on the following areas of operations:

      1) *Preflight preparation*
      2) *Preflight procedures*
      3) *Airport and seaplane base operations*
      4) *Takeoffs, landings, and go-arounds*
      5) *Performance maneuvers*
      6) *Ground reference maneuvers*
      7) *Navigation*
      8) *Slow flight and stalls*
      9) *Basic instrument maneuvers*
      10) *Emergency operations*
      11) *Night operations*
      12) *Postflight procedures*
      13) *Multi-engine operations (for only multi-engine airplanes)*

   b. Alternatively, enroll in an FAA-certificated pilot school that has an approved private pilot certification course (airplane).

      1) These are known as Part 141 schools or Part 142 training centers because they are authorized by Part 141 or Part 142 of the FARs.

         a) All other regulations concerning the certification of pilots are found in Part 61 of the FARs.

9. Successfully complete a practical (flight) test, which will be given as a final exam by an FAA inspector or designated pilot evaluator and conducted as specified in the FAA's Private Pilot Airman Certification Standards (FAA-S-ACS-6).

   a. FAA inspectors are FAA employees and do not charge for their services.

   b. FAA-designated pilot evaluators are proficient, experienced flight instructors and pilots who are authorized by the FAA to conduct practical tests. They do charge a fee.

> GLEIM SUCCESS TIPS
>
> The FAA's Private Pilot Airman Certification Standards are outlined and reprinted in the Gleim ***Private Pilot Flight Maneuvers and Practical Test Prep*** book.

FAA PILOT KNOWLEDGE TEST AND TESTING SUPPLEMENT

1. This book is designed to help you prepare for and pass the following FAA knowledge tests:

   a. Private Pilot-Airplane (PAR) consists of 60 questions. Time limit is 2.5 hours.

   b. Recreational Pilot-Airplane (RPA) consists of 50 questions. Time limit is 2 hours.

   c. Private Pilot-Airplane Transition (PAT) consists of 30 questions (to upgrade from recreational to private). Time limit is 1.5 hours.

2. The FAA legends and figures are contained in a book titled *Airman Knowledge Testing Supplement for Sport Pilot, Recreational Pilot, and Private Pilot*, which you will be given to use at the time of your test.

   a. For the purpose of test preparation, the appropriate legends and figures are reproduced in color in this book.

b. Following is a list of legends and figures that are **not** included because they pertain to military topics, helicopters, gyroplanes, gliders, and/or topics the FAA removed from the test in 2015 and 2016:

Legend 10	Figure 10	Figure 39	Figure 45	Figure 56
Legend 11	Figure 11	Figure 41	Figure 46	Figure 57
Legend 12	Figure 13	Figure 42	Figure 53	Figure 73
Legend 18	Figure 29	Figure 43	Figure 54	
Legend 19	Figure 30	Figure 44	Figure 55	

GLEIM SUCCESS TIPS

As you practice answering questions, keep in mind that, on test day, you may need to refer to the legends in Appendix 1 of the testing supplement.

3. In an effort to develop better questions, the FAA frequently **pretests** questions on knowledge tests by adding up to five "pretest" questions. The pretest questions will not be graded.
   a. You will NOT know which questions are real and which are pretest, so you must attempt to answer all questions correctly.
   b. When you notice a question NOT covered by Gleim, it might be a pretest question.
      1) We want to know about each pretest question you see.
      2) Please call 800-874-5346 or contact us at www.gleim.com/AviationQuestions with your recollection of any possible pretest questions so we may improve our efforts to prepare future pilots.

FAA'S KNOWLEDGE TESTS: CHEATING OR UNAUTHORIZED CONDUCT POLICY

The following is taken verbatim from an FAA knowledge test. It is reproduced here to remind all test takers about the FAA's policy against cheating and unauthorized conduct, a policy that Gleim consistently supports and upholds. Test takers must click "Yes" to proceed from this page into the actual knowledge test.

14 CFR part 61, section 61.37 Knowledge tests: Cheating or other unauthorized conduct

(a) An applicant for a knowledge test may not:

(1) Copy or intentionally remove any knowledge test;

(2) Give to another applicant or receive from another applicant any part or copy of a knowledge test;

(3) Give assistance on, or receive assistance on, a knowledge test during the period that test is being given;

(4) Take any part of a knowledge test on behalf of another person;

(5) Be represented by, or represent, another person for a knowledge test;

(6) Use any material or aid during the period that the test is being given, unless specifically authorized to do so by the Administrator; and

(7) Intentionally cause, assist, or participate in any act prohibited by this paragraph.

(b) An applicant who the Administrator finds has committed an act prohibited by paragraph (a) of this section is prohibited, for 1 year after the date of committing that act, from:

(1) Applying for any certificate, rating, or authorization issued under this chapter; and

(2) Applying for and taking any test under this chapter.

(c) Any certificate or rating held by an applicant may be suspended or revoked if the Administrator finds that person has committed an act prohibited by paragraph (a) of this section.

FAA PILOT KNOWLEDGE TEST QUESTION BANK

In an effort to keep applicants from simply memorizing test questions, the FAA does not currently disclose all the questions you might see on your FAA knowledge test. We encourage you to take the time to fully learn and understand the concepts explained in the knowledge transfer outlines contained in this book. **Using this book or other Gleim test preparation material to merely memorize the questions and answers is unwise and unproductive, and it will not ensure your success on your FAA knowledge test.** Memorization also greatly reduces the amount of information you will actually learn during your study.

The questions and answers provided in this book include all previously released FAA questions in addition to questions developed from current FAA reference materials that closely approximate the types of questions you should see on your knowledge test. We are confident that by studying our knowledge transfer outlines, answering our questions under exam conditions, and not relying on rote memorization, you will be able to successfully pass your FAA knowledge test and begin learning to become a safe and competent pilot.

FAA QUESTIONS WITH TYPOGRAPHICAL ERRORS

Occasionally, FAA test questions contain typographical errors such that there is no correct answer. The FAA test development process involves many steps and people and, as you would expect, glitches occur in the system that are beyond the control of any one person. We indicate "best" rather than correct answers for some questions. Use these best answers for the indicated questions.

Note that the FAA corrects (rewrites) defective questions as they are discovered; these changes are explained in our updates (see page ii). However, problems due to faulty or out-of-date figures printed in the FAA Computer Testing Supplements are expensive to correct. Thus, it is important to carefully study questions that are noted to have a best answer in this book. Even though the best answer may not be completely correct, you should select it when taking your test.

REORGANIZATION OF FAA QUESTIONS

1. In the public FAA knowledge test question bank releases, the questions are **not** grouped together by topic; i.e., they appear to be presented randomly.
   a. We have reorganized and renumbered the questions into study units and subunits.
2. Pages 457 through 464 contain a list of all the questions in FAA learning statement code order, with cross-references to the study units and question numbers in this book.
   a. For example, question 1-35 is assigned the code PLT003, which means it is found in Study Unit 1 as question 35 in this book and is covered under the FAA learning statement, "Calculate aircraft performance - center of gravity."
   b. Questions relating to helicopters, gliders, balloons, etc., are excluded.

HOW TO PREPARE FOR THE FAA PILOT KNOWLEDGE TEST

1. Begin by carefully reading the rest of this introduction. You need to have a complete understanding of the examination process prior to initiating your study. This knowledge will make your studying more efficient.
2. After you have spent an hour analyzing this introduction, set up a study schedule, including a target date for taking your knowledge test.
   a. Do not let the study process drag on and become discouraging; i.e., the quicker, the better.
   b. Consider enrolling in an organized ground school course, like the Gleim **Online Ground School**, or one held at your local FBO, community college, etc.
   c. Determine where and when you are going to take your knowledge test.

3. Work through Study Units 1 through 11.

   a. All previously released questions in the FAA's private pilot knowledge test question bank that are applicable to airplanes have been grouped into the following 11 categories, which are the titles of Study Units 1 through 11:

      Study Unit 1: Airplanes and Aerodynamics
      Study Unit 2: Airplane Instruments, Engines, and Systems
      Study Unit 3: Airports, Air Traffic Control, and Airspace
      Study Unit 4: Federal Aviation Regulations
      Study Unit 5: Airplane Performance and Weight and Balance
      Study Unit 6: Aeromedical Factors and Aeronautical Decision Making (ADM)
      Study Unit 7: Aviation Weather
      Study Unit 8: Aviation Weather Services
      Study Unit 9: Navigation: Charts and Publications
      Study Unit 10: Navigation Systems
      Study Unit 11: Cross-Country Flight Planning

   b. Within each of the study units listed, questions relating to the same subtopic (e.g., thunderstorms, airplane stability, sectional charts, etc.) are grouped together to facilitate your study program. Each subtopic is called a subunit.

   c. To the right of each question, we present

      1) The correct answer.
      2) The appropriate source document for the answer explanation. These publications can be obtained from the FAA (www.faa.gov) and aviation bookstores.

AAH	*Advanced Avionics Handbook*		Chart Supplement
AC	Advisory Circular	FAR/14 CFR	Federal Aviation Regulations
ACL	Aeronautical Chart Legend	FI Comp	Flight Computer
AFH	*Airplane Flying Handbook*	*IFH*	*Instrument Flying Handbook*
AIM	*Aeronautical Information Manual*	NTSB	National Transportation Safety Board regulations
AvW	*Aviation Weather*	*PHAK*	*Pilot's Handbook of Aeronautical Knowledge*
AWBH	*Aircraft Weight and Balance Handbook*		
AWS	*Aviation Weather Services*		

         a) The codes may refer to an entire document, such as an advisory circular, or to a particular chapter or subsection of a larger document.

            i) See page 467 for a complete list of abbreviations and acronyms used in this book.

      3) A comprehensive answer explanation, including

         a) A discussion of the correct answer or concept
         b) An explanation of why the other two answer choices are incorrect

4. Each study unit begins with a list of its subunit titles. The number after each title is the number of questions that cover the information in that subunit. The two numbers following the number of questions are the page numbers on which the outline and the questions for that particular subunit begin, respectively.

5. Begin by studying the outlines slowly and carefully. The outlines in this part of the book are very brief and have only one purpose: to help you pass the FAA knowledge test.

   a. **CAUTION:** The **sole purpose** of this book is to expedite your passing the FAA knowledge test for the recreational pilot and/or private pilot certificate. Accordingly, all extraneous material (i.e., topics or regulations not directly tested on the FAA knowledge test) is omitted, even though much more knowledge is necessary to fly safely. This additional material is presented in ***Private Pilot Flight Maneuvers and Practical Test Prep*** and ***Pilot Handbook***.

6. Next, answer the questions under exam conditions. Cover the answer explanations on the right side of each page with a piece of paper while you answer the questions.

> GLEIM SUCCESS TIPS
>
> Remember, it is very important to the learning (and understanding) process that you honestly commit yourself to an answer. If you are wrong, your memory will be reinforced by having discovered your error. Therefore, it is crucial to cover up the answer and make an honest attempt to answer the question before reading the answer.

   a. Study the answer explanation for each question that you answer incorrectly, do not understand, or have difficulty with.
   b. Use our **Online Ground School** or **FAA Test Prep Online** to ensure that you do not refer to answers before committing to one AND to simulate actual computer testing center exam conditions.

7. Note that this test book contains questions grouped by topic. Thus, some questions may appear repetitive, while others may be duplicates or near-duplicates. Accordingly, do not work question after question (i.e., waste time and effort) if you are already conversant with a topic and the type of questions asked.
8. As you move through study units, you may need further explanation or clarification of certain topics. You may wish to obtain and use the following Gleim books described on page 1:
   a. ***Private Pilot Flight Maneuvers and Practical Test Prep***
   b. ***Pilot Handbook***
   c. ***Aviation Weather and Weather Services***
9. Keep track of your work. As you complete a subunit, grade yourself with an A, B, C, or ? (use a ? if you need help on the subject) next to the subunit title at the front of the respective study unit.
   a. The A, B, C, or ? is your self-evaluation of your comprehension of the material in that subunit and your ability to answer the questions.

      A means a good understanding.
      B means a fair understanding.
      C means a shaky understanding.
      ? means to ask your CFI or others about the material and/or questions, and read the pertinent sections in ***Private Pilot Flight Maneuvers and Practical Test Prep*** and/or ***Pilot Handbook***.

   b. This procedure will provide you with the ability to quickly see (by looking at the first page of each study unit) how much studying you have done (and how much remains) and how well you have done.
   c. This procedure will also facilitate review. You can spend more time on the subunits that were more difficult for you.
   d. **FAA Test Prep Online** provides you with your historical performance data.

Follow the suggestions given throughout this introduction and you will have no trouble passing the FAA knowledge test the first time you take it.

With this overview of exam requirements, you are ready to begin the easy-to-study outlines and rearranged questions with answers to build your knowledge and confidence and PASS THE FAA's RECREATIONAL PILOT OR PRIVATE PILOT KNOWLEDGE TEST.

The feedback we receive from users indicates that our materials reduce anxiety, improve FAA test scores, and build knowledge. Studying for each test becomes a useful step toward advanced certificates and ratings.

MULTIPLE-CHOICE QUESTION-ANSWERING TECHNIQUE

Because the private pilot knowledge test has a set number of questions (60) and a set time limit (2.5 hours), you can plan your test-taking session to ensure that you leave yourself enough time to answer each question with relative certainty. The following steps will help you move through the knowledge test efficiently and produce better test results.

1. **Budget your time.** We make this point with emphasis. Just as you would fill up your gas tank prior to reaching empty, so too should you finish your exam before time expires.
   a. If you utilize the entire time limit for the test, you will have about 2.5 minutes per question.
   b. If you are adequately prepared for the test, you should finish it well within the time limit.
      1) Use any extra time you have to review questions that you are not sure about, cross-country planning questions with multiple steps and calculations, and similar questions in your exam that may help you answer other questions.
   c. Time yourself when completing study sessions in this book and/or review your time investment reports from the Gleim **FAA Test Prep Online** to track your progress and adherence to the time limit and your own personal time allocation budget.
2. **Answer the questions in consecutive order.**
   a. Do **not** agonize over any one item. Stay within your time budget.
      1) We suggest that you skip cross-country planning questions and other similarly involved computational questions on your first pass through the exam. Come back to them after you have been through the entire test once.
   b. Mark any questions you are unsure of and return to them later as time allows.
      1) Once you initiate test grading, you will no longer be able to review/change any answers.
   c. Never leave a multiple-choice question unanswered. Make your best educated guess in the time allowed. Remember, your score is based on the number of correct responses. You will not be penalized for guessing incorrectly.
3. **For each multiple-choice question,**
   a. **Try to ignore the answer choices.** Do not allow the answer choices to affect your reading of the question.
      1) If three answer choices are presented, two of them are incorrect. These choices are called **distractors** for good reason. Often, distractors are written to appear correct at first glance until further analysis.
      2) In computational items, the distractors are carefully calculated such that they are the result of making common mistakes. Be careful, and double-check your computations if time permits.
   b. **Read the question carefully** to determine the precise requirement.
      1) Focusing on what is required enables you to ignore extraneous information, to focus on the relevant facts, and to proceed directly to determining the correct answer.
         a) Be especially careful to note when the requirement is an **exception**; e.g., "Which of the following is **not** a type of hypoxia?"
   c. **Determine the correct answer** before looking at the answer choices.

d. **Read the answer choices carefully.**

1) Even if the first answer appears to be the correct choice, do **not** skip the remaining answer choices. Questions often require the "best" answer of the choices provided. Thus, each choice requires your consideration.

2) Treat each answer choice as a true/false question as you analyze it.

e. **Click on the best answer.**

1) You have a 33% chance of answering the question correctly by blindly guessing; improve your odds with educated guessing.

2) For many multiple-choice questions, at least one answer choice can be eliminated with minimal effort, thereby increasing your educated guess to a 50-50 proposition.

4. After you have been through all the questions in the test, consult the question status list to determine which questions are unanswered and which are marked for review.

a. Go back to the marked questions and finalize your answer choices.

b. Verify that all questions have been answered.

EDUCATED GUESSING

> The FAA knowledge test sometimes includes questions that are poorly worded or confusing. Expect the unexpected and move forward. Do not let confusing questions affect your concentration or take up too much time; make your best guess and move on.

1. If you don't know the answer, make an educated guess as follows:

a. Rule out answers that you think are incorrect.

b. Speculate on what the FAA is looking for and/or the rationale behind the question.

c. Select the best answer or guess between equally appealing answers. Your first guess is usually the most intuitive. If you cannot make an educated guess, re-read the stem and each answer choice and pick the most intuitive answer. It's just a guess!

2. Avoid lingering on any question for too long. Remember your time budget and the overall test time limit.

SIMULATED FAA PRACTICE TEST

Appendix A, "Private Pilot Practice Test," beginning on page 443, allows you to practice taking the FAA knowledge test without the answers next to the questions. This test has 60 questions randomly selected from the airplane-related questions in our private pilot knowledge test bank. Topical coverage in the practice test is similar to that of the FAA knowledge test.

It is very important that you answer all 60 questions in one sitting. You should not consult the answers, especially when being referred to figures (charts, tables, etc.) throughout this book where the questions are answered and explained. Analyze your performance based on the answer key that follows the practice test.

It is even better to practice with Test Sessions in the Gleim **FAA Test Prep Online**. These simulate actual computer testing conditions, including the screen layouts, instructions, etc., for CATS and PSI.

For more information on the Gleim **FAA Test Prep Online**, see pages 17 and 18.

PART 141 SCHOOLS WITH FAA PILOT KNOWLEDGE TEST EXAMINING AUTHORITY

The FAA permits some FAR Part 141 schools to develop, administer, and grade their own knowledge tests as long as they use questions from the FAA test bank, similar to the questions in this book. The FAA does not provide the correct answers to the Part 141 schools, and the FAA only reviews the Part 141 school test question selection sheets. Thus, some of the answers used by Part 141 test evaluators may not agree with the FAA or with those in this book. The latter is not a problem but may explain why you may miss a question on a Part 141 pilot knowledge test using an answer presented in this book.

AUTHORIZATION TO TAKE THE FAA PILOT KNOWLEDGE TEST

Before taking the private pilot knowledge test, you must receive an endorsement from an authorized instructor who conducted the ground training or reviewed your home-study in the areas listed in item 5. on page 4, certifying that you are prepared to pass the knowledge test.

Recreational pilots have a similarly worded requirement. For your convenience, standard authorization forms for both the private and recreational pilot knowledge tests are reproduced on page 465, which can be easily completed, signed by a flight or ground instructor, torn out, and taken to the test site.

Note that if you use the Gleim **FAA Test Prep Online** or **Online Ground School**, the program will generate an authorization signed in facsimile by Dr. Gleim that is accepted at all CATS and PSI locations.

WHEN TO TAKE THE FAA PILOT KNOWLEDGE TEST

1. You must be at least 15 years of age to take the private pilot knowledge test.
2. You must prepare for the test by successfully completing a ground instruction course or by using this book as your self-developed home study course.
    a. See "Authorization to Take the FAA Pilot Knowledge Test" above.
3. Take the FAA knowledge test within 30 days of beginning your study.
    a. Get the knowledge test behind you.
4. Your practical test must follow within 24 months.
    a. Otherwise, you will have to retake your knowledge test.

WHAT TO TAKE TO THE FAA PILOT KNOWLEDGE TEST

1. An approved flight computer (ideally the one that you use to solve the test questions in this book, i.e., one you are familiar with and have used before)
2. Navigational plotter
3. A pocket calculator you are familiar with and have used before (no instructional material for the calculator is allowed)
4. Authorization to take the knowledge test (see above and page 465)
5. Proper identification that contains your photograph, signature, date of birth, and actual residential address, if different from your mailing address.

NOTE: Paper and pencils are supplied at the examination site.

GLEIM SUCCESS TIPS®

It is essential for each student to own an approved E6B flight computer (manual or electronic) and a navigation plotter. These tools are necessary to answer some questions on the knowledge test and to use during your check ride. Go to www.gleim.com/E6B to access complete instructions on the use of the Gleim E6B flight computer.

COMPUTER TESTING CENTERS

The FAA has contracted with two computer testing services to administer FAA knowledge tests. Both of these computer testing services have testing centers throughout the country. To register for the knowledge test, call one of the computer testing services listed below. More information can be found at www.gleim.com/testing_centers.

CATS (800) 947-4228 PSI (800) 211-2754

COMPUTER TESTING PROCEDURES

When you arrive at the testing center, you will be required to provide positive proof of identification and documentary evidence of your age. The identification must include your photograph, signature, and actual residential address if different from the mailing address. This information may be presented in more than one form of identification. Next, you will sign in on the testing center's daily log. Your signature on the logsheet certifies that, if this is a retest, you meet the applicable requirements (see "Failure on the FAA Pilot Knowledge Test" on page 15) and that you have not passed this test in the past 2 years. Finally, you will present your logbook endorsement or authorization form from your instructor, which authorizes you to take the test. A standard authorization form is provided on page 465 for your use. Both **FAA Test Prep Online** and **Online Ground School** generate an authorization signed in facsimile by Dr. Gleim that is accepted at all CATS and PSI locations.

Next, you will be taken into the testing room and seated at a computer terminal. A person from the testing center will assist you in logging onto the system, and you will be asked to confirm your personal data (e.g., name, Social Security number, etc.). Then you will be given an online introduction to the computer testing system, and you will take a sample test. If you have used our **FAA Test Prep Online**, you will be conversant with the computer testing methodology and environment and will breeze through the sample test. When you have completed your test, an Airman Computer Test Report will be printed out, validated (usually with an embossed seal), and given to you by a person from the testing center. Before you leave, you will be required to sign out on the testing center's daily log.

Each testing service has certain idiosyncrasies in its paperwork, scheduling, and telephone procedures as well as in its software. It is for this reason that our **FAA Test Prep Online** emulates both of the FAA-approved computer testing companies.

YOUR FAA PILOT KNOWLEDGE TEST REPORT

1. You will receive your FAA Pilot Knowledge Test Report upon completion of the test. An example test report is reproduced below.
   a. Note that you will receive only one grade as illustrated.
   b. The expiration date is the date by which you must take your FAA practical test.
   c. The report lists the FAA learning statement codes of the questions you missed so you can review the topics you missed prior to your practical test.

Computer Test Report

U.S. DEPARTMENT OF TRANSPORTATION
Federal Aviation Administration

Airman Knowledge Test Report

NAME:

APPLICANT ID: EXAM ID:

EXAM: Private Pilot Airplane

EXAM DATE: 10/08/2016 EXAM SITE:

SCORE: 96 GRADE: PASS TAKE: 1

Learning statement codes listed below represent incorrectly answered questions. Learning statement codes and their associated statements can be found at **www.faa.gov/training_testing/testing/airmen**.

Reference material associated with the learning statement codes can be found in the appropriate knowledge test guide at **www.faa.gov/training_testing/testing/airmen/test_guides**.

A single code may represent more than one incorrect response.

PLT229 PLT306

EXPIRATION DATE: 10/31/2018 CTD's Embossed Seal

DO NOT LOSE THIS REPORT

AUTHORIZED INSTRUCTOR'S STATEMENT: (If applicable)

On ____________ (date) I gave the above named applicant ____ hours of additional instruction, covering each subject area shown to be deficient, and consider the applicant competent to pass the test.

Name ____________________ Initial____ Cert. No.__________ Type______
(Print clearly)

Signature ______________________________________

FRAUDULENT ALTERATION OF THIS FORM BY ANY PERSON IS A BASIS FOR SUSPENSION OR REVOCATION OF ANY CERTIFICATES OR RATINGS HELD BY THAT PERSON.
THIS INFORMATION IS PROTECTED BY THE PRIVACY ACT. FOR OFFICIAL USE ONLY.

2. Use the FAA Listing of Learning Statement Codes on pages 451 through 456 to determine which topics you had difficulty with.
   a. Look them over and review them with your CFI so (s)he can certify that (s)he reviewed the deficient areas and found you competent in them when you take your practical test. Have your CFI sign off your deficiencies on the FAA Pilot Knowledge Test Report.
3. Keep your FAA Pilot Knowledge Test Report in a safe place because you must submit it to the FAA inspector/evaluator when you take your practical test.

FAILURE ON THE FAA PILOT KNOWLEDGE TEST

1. If you fail (score less than 70%) the knowledge test (which is virtually impossible if you follow the Gleim system), you may retake it after your instructor endorses the bottom of your FAA Pilot Knowledge Test Report certifying that you have received the necessary ground training to retake the test.
2. Upon retaking the test, you will find that the procedure is the same except that you must also submit your FAA Pilot Knowledge Test Report indicating the previous failure to the computer testing center.
3. Note that the pass rate on the private pilot knowledge test is about 89%; only about 1 out of 10 fail the test initially. Reasons for failure include
   a. Failure to study the material tested and mere memorization of correct answers. (Relevant study material is contained in the outlines at the beginning of Study Units 1 through 11 of this book.)
   b. Failure to practice working through the questions under test conditions. (All of the previously released FAA questions on airplanes appear in Study Units 1 through 11 of this book.)
   c. Poor examination technique, such as misreading questions and not understanding the requirements.

GLEIM ONLINE GROUND SCHOOL

1. Gleim **Online Ground School (OGS)** course content is based on the Gleim Knowledge Test books, **FAA Test Prep Online**, FAA publications, and Gleim reference books. The delivery system is modeled on the Gleim FAA-approved online **Flight Instructor Refresher Course**.
   a. Online Ground School courses are available for
      1) Private Pilot
      2) Sport Pilot
      3) CFI/CGI
      4) FOI
      5) Instrument Pilot
      6) Commercial Pilot
      7) ATP
      8) Flight Engineer
      9) Canadian Certificate Conversion
   b. OGS courses are airplane-only and have lessons that correspond to the study units in the Gleim FAA Knowledge Test books.
   c. Each course contains study outlines that automatically reference current FAA publications, the appropriate knowledge test questions, FAA figures, and Gleim answer explanations.
   d. OGS is always up to date.
   e. Users achieve very high knowledge test scores and a near-100% pass rate.
   f. **Gleim Online Ground School is the most flexible course available!** Access your OGS personal classroom from any computer with Internet access 24 hours a day, 7 days a week. Your virtual classroom is never closed!
   g. **Save time and study only the material you need to know!** Gleim **Online Ground School** Certificate Selection will provide you with a customized study plan. You save time because unnecessary questions will be automatically eliminated.
   h. **We are truly interactive. We help you focus on any weaker areas.** Answer explanations for wrong choices help you learn from your mistakes.

GLEIM FAA TEST PREP ONLINE

Computer testing is consistent with aviation's use of computers (e.g., DUATS, flight simulators, computerized cockpits, etc.). All FAA knowledge tests are administered by computer.

Computer testing is natural after computer study and computer-assisted instruction is a very efficient and effective method of study. The Gleim **FAA Test Prep Online** is designed to prepare you for computer testing because our software can simulate both CATS and PSI. We make you comfortable with computer testing!

FAA Test Prep Online contains all of the questions in this book, context-sensitive outline material, and on-screen charts and figures. It allows you to choose either Study Mode or Test Mode.

In Study Mode, the software provides you with an explanation of each answer you choose (correct or incorrect). You design each Study Session:

Topic(s) and/or FAA learning statement codes you wish to cover
Number of questions
Order of questions -- FAA, Gleim, or random
Order of answers to each question -- Gleim or random
Questions marked and/or missed from last session -- test, study, or both
Questions marked and/or missed from all sessions -- test, study, or both
Questions never seen, answered, or answered correctly

In Test Mode, you decide the format: CATS or PSI. When you finish your test, you can and should study the questions missed and access answer explanations. The software emulates the operation of FAA-approved computer testing companies. Thus, you have a complete understanding of how to take an FAA knowledge test and know exactly what to expect before you go to a computer testing center.

The Gleim **FAA Test Prep Online** is an all-in-one program designed to help anyone with a computer, Internet access, and an interest in flying pass the FAA knowledge tests.

Study Sessions and Test Sessions

Study Sessions give you immediate feedback on why your answer selection for a particular question is correct or incorrect and allow you to access the context-sensitive outline material that helps to explain concepts related to the question. Choose from several different question sources: all questions available for that library; questions from a certain topic (Gleim study units and subunits); questions that you missed or marked in the last sessions you created; questions that you have never seen, answered, or answered correctly; questions from certain FAA learning statement codes; etc. You can mix up the questions by selecting to randomize the question and/or answer order so that you do not memorize answer letters.

You may then grade your study sessions and track your study progress using the performance analysis charts and graphs. The Performance Analysis information helps you to focus on areas where you need the most improvement, saving you time in the overall study process. You may then want to go back and study questions that you missed in a previous session, or you may want to create a Study Session of questions that you marked in the previous session. All of these options are made easy with **FAA Test Prep Online**'s Study Sessions.

After studying the outlines and questions in a Study Session, you can further test your skills with a Test Session. These sessions allow you to answer questions under actual testing conditions using one of the simulations of the major testing services. In a Test Session, you will not know which questions you have answered correctly until the session is graded.

Recommended Study Program

1. Start with Study Unit 1 and proceed through study units in chronological order. Follow the three-step process below.
   a. First, carefully study the Gleim Outline.
   b. Second, create a Study Session of all questions in the study unit. Answer and study all questions in the Study Session.
   c. Third, create a Test Session of all questions in the study unit. Answer all questions in the Test Session.
2. After each Study Session and Test Session, create a new Study Session from questions answered incorrectly. This is of critical importance to allow you to learn from your mistakes.

Practice Test

Take an exam in the actual testing environment of either of the major testing centers: CATS or PSI. **FAA Test Prep Online** simulates the testing formats of these testing centers, making it easy for you to study questions under actual exam conditions. After studying with **FAA Test Prep Online**, you will know exactly what to expect when you go in to take your pilot knowledge test.

On-Screen Charts and Figures

One of the most convenient features of **FAA Test Prep Online** is the easily accessible on-screen charts and figures. Many of the questions refer to drawings, maps, charts, and other pictures that provide information to help answer the question. In **FAA Test Prep Online**, you can pull up any of these figures with the click of a button. You can increase or decrease the size of the images, and you may also use our drawing feature to calculate the true course between two given points (required only on the private pilot knowledge test).

Instructor Sign-Off Sheets

FAA Test Prep Online is capable of generating an instructor sign-off for FAA knowledge tests that require one. This sign-off has been approved by the FAA and can be presented at the computer testing center as authorization to take your test--you do NOT need an additional endorsement from your instructor.

In order to obtain the instructor sign-off sheet for your test, you must first answer all relevant questions in **FAA Test Prep Online** correctly. Then, select "Sign-Off Sheets" under the "Additional Features" area on the Main page. If you have answered all of the required questions, the instructor sign-off sheet will appear for you to print. If you have not yet answered all required questions, a list of the unanswered questions, along with their location, will appear.

Free Updates and Technical Support

Gleim offers FREE technical support to all users of the current versions. Call (800) 874-5346, send an email to support@gleim.com, or fill out the technical support request form online (www.gleim.com/support/form.php). Additionally, Gleim **FAA Test Prep Online** is always up to date. The program is automatically updated when any changes are made, so you can be confident that Gleim will prepare you for your knowledge test. For more information on our email update service for books, turn to page ii.

STUDY UNIT ONE
AIRPLANES AND AERODYNAMICS

(6 pages of outline)

This study unit contains outlines of major concepts tested, sample test questions and answers regarding airplanes and aerodynamics, and an explanation of each answer. The table of contents above lists each subunit within this study unit, the number of questions pertaining to that particular subunit, and the pages on which the outline and questions begin, respectively.

GLEIM SUCCESS TIPS®

Recall that the **sole purpose** of this book is to expedite your passing of the FAA pilot knowledge test for the private pilot certificate. Accordingly, all extraneous material (i.e., topics or regulations not directly tested on the FAA pilot knowledge test) is omitted, even though much more knowledge is necessary to fly safely. This additional material is presented in *Pilot Handbook* and *Private Pilot Flight Maneuvers and Practical Test Prep*, available from Gleim Publications, Inc. Order online at www.GleimAviation.com.

1.1 FLIGHT CONTROLS

1. The three primary flight controls of an airplane are the ailerons, the elevator (or stabilator), and the rudder.
   a. Movement of any of these primary flight control surfaces changes the airflow and pressure distribution over and around the airfoil.
      1) These changes affect the lift and drag produced and allow a pilot to control the aircraft about its three axes of rotation.
   b. **Ailerons** are control surfaces attached to each wing that move in the opposite direction from one another to control roll about the longitudinal axis.
      1) EXAMPLE: Moving the yoke or stick to the right causes the right aileron to deflect upward, resulting in decreased lift on the right wing. The left aileron moves in the opposite direction and increases the lift on the left wing. Thus, the increased lift on the left wing and and the decreased lift on the right wing cause the airplane to roll to the right.
   c. The **elevator** is the primary control device for changing the pitch attitude of an airplane, changing the pitch about the lateral axis. It is usually located on the fixed horizontal stabilizer on the tail of the airplane.
      1) EXAMPLE: Pulling back on the yoke or stick deflects the trailing edge of the elevator up. This position creates a downward aerodynamic force, causing the tail of the aircraft to move down and the nose to pitch up.
      2) A **stabilator** is a one-piece horizontal stabilizer and elevator that pivots from a central hinge point.

3) A **canard** is similar to the horizontal stabilizer but is located in front of the main wings. An elevator is attached to the trailing edge of the canard to control pitch.

a) The canard, however, actually creates lift and holds the nose up rather than the aft-tail design that prevents the nose from rotating downward.

d. The **rudder** controls movement of the aircraft about its vertical axis.

1) When deflecting the rudder into the airflow, a horizontal force is exerted in the opposite direction; this motion is called yaw.

2) Rudder effectiveness increases with speed because there is more airflow over the surface of the control device.

2. Secondary flight controls may consist of wing flaps, leading edge devices, spoilers, and trim systems.

a. **Flaps** are attached to the trailing edge of the wing and are used during approach and landing to increase wing lift. This allows an increase in the angle of descent without increasing airspeed.

1) The most common flap used on general aviation aircraft today is the slotted flap.

2) When the slotted flap is lowered, high-pressure air from the lower surface of the wing is ducted to the upper surface of the flap, delaying airflow separation.

b. **Spoilers** are high-drag devices deployed from the wings to reduce lift and increase drag. They are found on gliders and some high-speed aircraft.

c. **Trim systems** are used to relieve the pilot of the need to maintain constant back pressure on the flight controls. They include trim tabs, antiservo tabs, and ground adjustable tabs.

1) Trim tabs are attached to the trailing edge of the elevator.

a) EXAMPLE: If the trim tab is set to the full nose-up position, the tab moves full down. This causes the tail of the airplane to pitch down and the nose to pitch up.

1.2 AERODYNAMIC FORCES

1. The four aerodynamic forces acting on an airplane during flight are

a. Lift: the upward-acting force
b. Weight: the downward-acting force
c. Thrust: the forward-acting force
d. Drag: the rearward-acting force

2. These forces are at equilibrium when the airplane is in unaccelerated flight:

Lift = Weight
Thrust = Drag

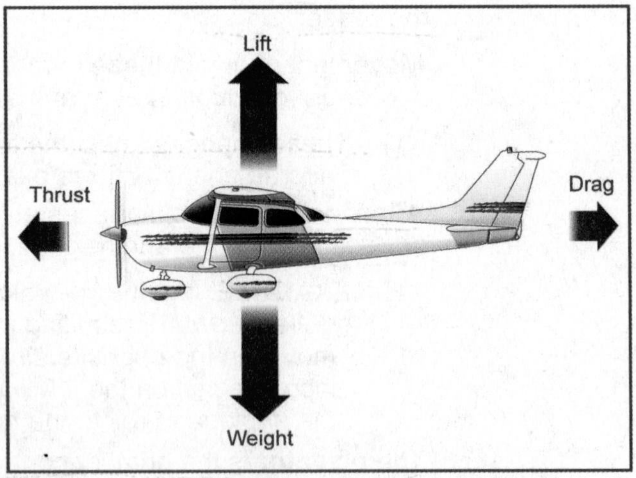

3. **Bernoulli's Principle** states in part that "the internal pressure of a fluid (liquid or gas) decreases at points where the speed of the fluid increases." In other words, high speed flow is associated with low pressure, and low speed flow is associated with high pressure.

a. This principle is applicable to an airplane wing because it is designed and constructed with a curve or camber. When air flows along the upper wing surface, it travels a greater distance in the same period of time (i.e., faster) than the airflow along the lower wing surface.

b. Therefore, the pressure above the wing is less than it is below the wing. This generates a lift force over the upper curved surface of the wing.

1.3 ANGLE OF ATTACK

1. The angle of attack is the angle between the wing chord line and the direction of the relative wind.
   a. The wing chord line is an imaginary straight line from the leading edge to the trailing edge of the wing.
   b. The relative wind is the direction of airflow relative to the wing when the wing is moving through the air.
2. The angle of attack at which a wing stalls remains constant regardless of weight, airplane loading, etc.

1.4 STALLS AND SPINS

1. An airplane can be stalled at any airspeed in any flight attitude. A stall results whenever the critical angle of attack is exceeded.
2. An airplane in a given configuration will stall at the same indicated airspeed regardless of altitude because the airspeed indicator is directly related to air density.
3. An airplane spins when one wing is less stalled than the other wing.
   a. To enter a spin, an airplane must always be stalled first.

1.5 FROST

1. Frost forms when the temperature of the collecting surface is at or below the dew point of the adjacent air and the dew point is below freezing.
   a. The water vapor changes its physical state through deposition and immediately forms as ice crystals on the wing surface.
2. Frost on wings disrupts the smooth airflow over the airfoil by causing early airflow separation from the wing. This
   a. Decreases lift and
   b. Causes friction and increases drag.
3. Frost may make it difficult or impossible for an airplane to take off.
4. Frost should be removed before attempting to take off.

1.6 GROUND EFFECT

1. Ground effect is the result of the interference of the ground (or water) surface with the airflow patterns about an airplane.
2. The vertical component of the airflow around the wing is restricted, which alters the wing's upwash, downwash, and wingtip vortices.
3. The reduction of the wingtip vortices alters the spanwise lift distribution and reduces the induced angle of attack and induced drag.
   a. Thus, the wing will require a lower angle of attack in ground effect to produce the same lift coefficient, or, if a constant angle of attack is maintained, an increase in the lift coefficient will result.
4. An airplane is affected by ground effect when it is within the length of the airplane's wingspan above the ground. The ground effect is most often recognized when the airplane is less than one-half the wingspan's length above the ground.

5. Ground effect may cause an airplane to float on landings or permit it to become airborne with insufficient airspeed to stay in flight above the area of ground effect.
   a. An airplane may settle back to the surface abruptly after flying through the ground effect if the pilot has not attained recommended takeoff airspeed.
6. Ground effect must be considered during takeoffs and landings.
   a. If a pilot fails to understand the relationship between the aircraft and ground effect during takeoff, a hazardous situation is possible because the recommended takeoff speed may not be achieved.
   b. Due to the reduced drag in ground effect, the aircraft may seem capable of takeoff well below the recommended speed. As the aircraft rises out of ground effect with a deficiency of speed, the greater induced drag may result in marginal initial ground performance.
   c. In extreme conditions, the aircraft may be airborne initially with a deficiency of speed and then settle back to the runway.

1.7 AIRPLANE TURN

1. The horizontal component of lift makes an airplane turn.
   a. To attain this horizontal component of lift, the pilot coordinates rudder, aileron, and elevator.
2. The rudder on an airplane controls the yaw, i.e., rotation about the vertical axis, but does not cause the airplane to turn.

1.8 AIRPLANE STABILITY

1. An inherently stable airplane returns to its original condition (position or attitude) after being disturbed. It requires less effort to control.
2. The location of the center of gravity (CG) with respect to the center of lift (or center of pressure) determines the longitudinal stability of an airplane.
   a. Changes in the center of pressure in a wing affects the aircraft's aerodynamic balance and control.
3. Airplanes (except a T-tail) normally pitch down when power is reduced (and the controls are not adjusted) because the downwash on the elevators from the propeller slipstream is reduced and elevator effectiveness is reduced. This allows the nose to drop.
4. When the CG in an airplane is located at or rear of the aft CG limit, the airplane
   a. Develops an inability to recover from stall conditions and
   b. Becomes less stable at all airspeeds.

1.9 TORQUE AND P-FACTOR

1. The torque effect (left-turning tendency) is greatest at low airspeed, high angles of attack, and high power, e.g., on takeoff.
2. P-factor (asymmetric propeller loading) causes the airplane to yaw to the left when at high angles of attack because the descending right side of the propeller (as seen from the rear) has a higher angle of attack (than the upward-moving blade on the left side) and provides more thrust.

1.10 LOAD FACTOR

1. Load factor refers to the additional weight carried by the wings due to the airplane's weight plus the centrifugal force.
   a. The amount of excess load that can be imposed on an airplane's wings varies directly with the airplane's speed and the excess lift available.
      1) At low speeds, very little excess lift is available, so very little excess load can be imposed.
      2) At high speeds, the wings' lifting capacity is so great that the load factor can quickly exceed safety limits.
   b. An increased load factor will result in an airplane stalling at a higher airspeed.
   c. As bank angle increases, the load factor increases. The wings have to carry not only the airplane's weight but the centrifugal force as well.
2. On the exam, a load factor chart like the one below is given with the amount of bank on the horizontal axis (along the bottom of the graph), and the load factor on the vertical axis (up the left side of the graph). Additionally, a table that provides the load factor corresponding to specific bank angles is found on the left side of the chart. Use this table to answer load factor questions.
   a. Compute the load factor by multiplying the airplane's weight by the load factor that corresponds to the given angle of bank. For example, the wings of a 2,000-lb. airplane in a 60° bank must support 4,000 lb. (2,000 lb. × 2.000).
   b. Example load factor chart:

Angle of bank Φ	Load factor n
0°	1.0
10°	1.015
30°	1.154
45°	1.414
60°	2.000
70°	2.923
80°	5.747
85°	11.473
90°	∞

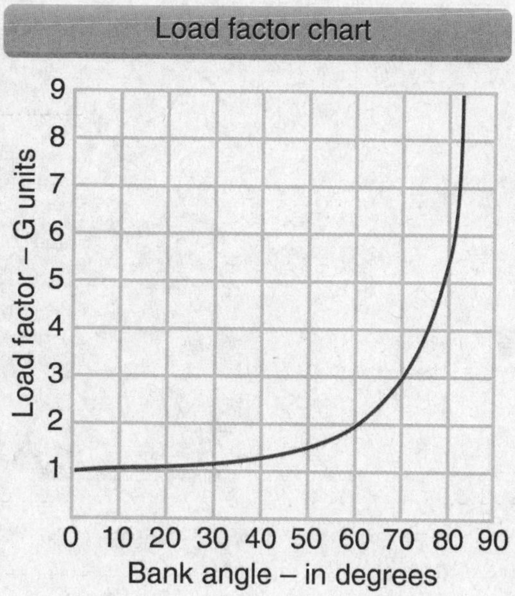

Figure 2. – Load Factor Chart.

3. Load factor (or G units) is a multiple of the regular weight or, alternatively, a multiple of the force of gravity.
   a. Straight-and-level flight has a load factor at 1.0. (Verify on the chart above.)
   b. A 60° level bank has a load factor of 2.0. Due to centrifugal force, the wings must hold up twice the amount of weight.
   c. A 50° level bank has a load factor of about 1.5.

1.11 VELOCITY VS. G-LOADS

1. To determine the load acting on an airplane, multiply the load factor by the airplane's weight.
   a. A level 60° bank imposes a load factor of approximately 2.0.
2. When an airplane is forced into an accelerated stall at twice its normal stalling speed, the load factor is approximately 4 Gs.
3. Velocity/load factor charts have the indicated airspeed on the horizontal axis and the load factor on the vertical axis.
   a. For various operations, one can plot the load factor and the possible impact on the airplane. See the Velocity vs. G-Loads chart below.
   b. One can also plot gusts of various strengths against airspeed to find the resultant load factor.
   c. Point A to J is the stalling speed (V_S).
   d. Point C to H is the maneuvering speed (V_A).
   e. Point D to G is the maximum structural cruising speed (V_{NO}).
   f. Point E to F is the never-exceed speed (V_{NE}).
   g. The line from point C to point E represents the positive limit load factor. The lines from point I to point G and from point G to point F represent the negative limit load factor. The line from point E to point F represents the never-exceed speed (V_{NE}).
      1) Exceeding the positive limit load factor, the negative limit load factor, or V_{NE} would subject an airplane to structural damage or failure.

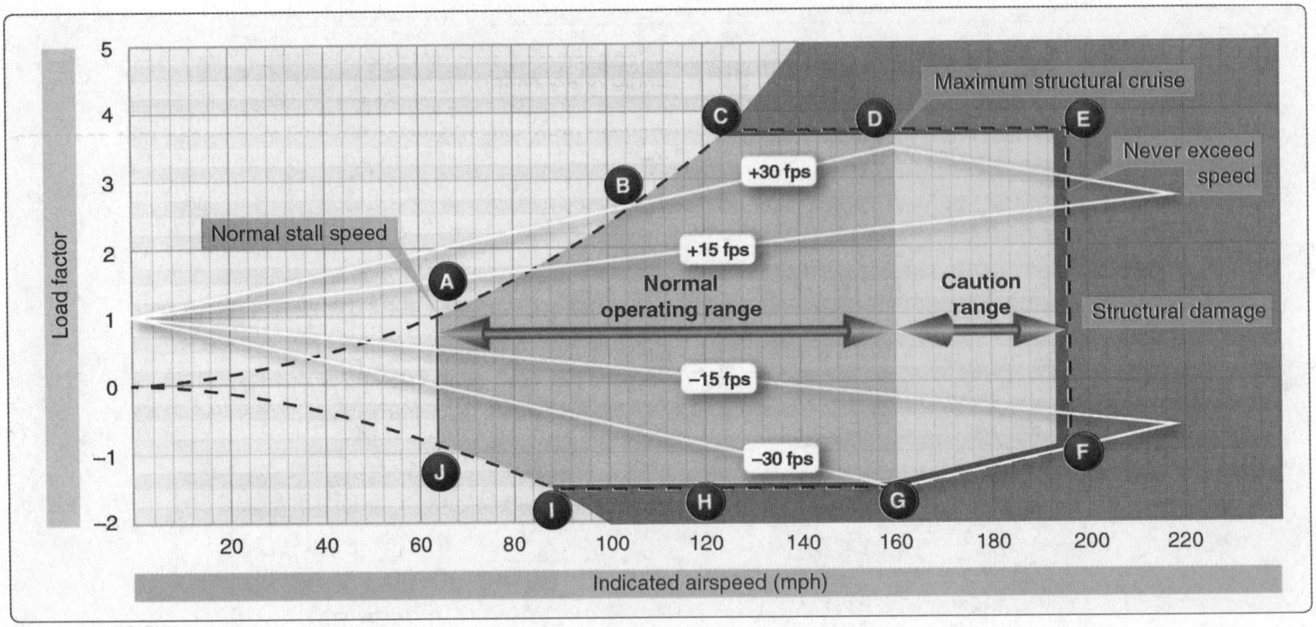

Figure 72. – Velocity vs. G-Loads.

QUESTIONS AND ANSWER EXPLANATIONS: All of the private pilot knowledge test questions chosen by the FAA for release as well as additional questions selected by Gleim relating to the material in the previous outlines are reproduced on the following pages. These questions have been organized into the same subunits as the outlines. To the immediate right of each question are the correct answer and answer explanation. You should cover these answers and answer explanations while responding to the questions. Refer to the general discussion in the Introduction on how to take the FAA knowledge test.

Remember that the questions from the FAA knowledge test bank have been reordered by topic and organized into a meaningful sequence. Also, the first line of the answer explanation gives the citation of the authoritative source for the answer.

QUESTIONS

1.1 Flight Controls

1. What is one purpose of wing flaps?

A. To enable the pilot to make steeper approaches to a landing without increasing the airspeed.

B. To relieve the pilot of maintaining continuous pressure on the controls.

C. To decrease wing area to vary the lift.

Answer (A) is correct. *(PHAK Chap 6)*
DISCUSSION: Extending the flaps increases the wing camber and the angle of attack of the wing. This increases wing lift and induced drag, which enables the pilot to make steeper approaches to a landing without an increase in airspeed.
Answer (B) is incorrect. Trim tabs (not wing flaps) help relieve control pressures. Answer (C) is incorrect. Wing area usually remains the same, except for certain specialized flaps that increase (not decrease) the wing area.

2. One of the main functions of flaps during approach and landing is to

A. decrease the angle of descent without increasing the airspeed.

B. permit a touchdown at a higher indicated airspeed.

C. increase the angle of descent without increasing the airspeed.

Answer (C) is correct. *(PHAK Chap 6)*
DISCUSSION: Extending the flaps increases the wing camber and the angle of attack of the wing. This increases wing lift and induced drag, which enables the pilot to increase the angle of descent without increasing the airspeed.
Answer (A) is incorrect. Extending the flaps increases lift and induced drag, which enables the pilot to increase (not decrease) the angle of descent without increasing the airspeed. Answer (B) is incorrect. Flaps increase lift at slow airspeed, which permits touchdown at a lower (not higher) indicated airspeed.

3. What is the purpose of the rudder on an airplane?

A. To control yaw.

B. To control overbanking tendency.

C. To control roll.

Answer (A) is correct. *(PHAK Chap 6)*
DISCUSSION: The rudder is used to control yaw, which is rotation about the airplane's vertical axis.
Answer (B) is incorrect. The ailerons (not the rudder) control overbanking. Overbanking tendency refers to the outside wing traveling significantly faster than the inside wing in a steep turn and generating incremental lift to raise the outside wing higher unless corrected by aileron pressure. Answer (C) is incorrect. Roll is movement about the longitudinal axis and is controlled by ailerons.

4. Which is not a primary flight control surface?

A. Flaps.

B. Stabilator.

C. Ailerons.

Answer (A) is correct. *(PHAK Chap 6)*
DISCUSSION: The three primary flight controls of an airplane are the ailerons, the elevator (or stabilator), and the rudder.
Answer (B) is incorrect. The stabilator, or elevator, is a primary flight control surface. Answer (C) is incorrect. Ailerons are a primary flight control surface.

5. The elevator controls movement around which axis?

A. Longitudinal.

B. Lateral.

C. Vertical.

Answer (B) is correct. *(PHAK Chap 6)*
DISCUSSION: The elevator is the primary control device for changing the pitch attitude of an airplane about the lateral axis.
Answer (A) is incorrect. Ailerons are control surfaces attached to each wing that move in the opposite direction from one another to control roll about the longitudinal axis. Answer (C) is incorrect. The rudder controls movement of the aircraft about its vertical axis.

6. Which statement is true concerning primary flight controls?

A. The effectiveness of each control surface increases with speed because there is more airflow over them.

B. Only when all three primary flight controls move in sequence do the airflow and pressure distribution change over and around the airfoil.

C. Primary flight controls include ailerons, rudder, elevator, and trim systems.

Answer (A) is correct. *(PHAK Chap 6)*

DISCUSSION: Rudder, aileron, and elevator effectiveness increase with speed because there is more airflow over the surface of the control device.

Answer (B) is incorrect. Movement of any primary flight control surface changes the airflow and pressure distribution over and around the airfoil. Answer (C) is incorrect. The primary flight controls do not include trim systems; these are considered secondary flight controls.

7. Which of the following is true concerning flaps?

A. Flaps are attached to the leading edge of the wing and are used to increase wing lift.

B. Flaps allow an increase in the angle of descent without increasing airspeed.

C. Flaps are high drag devices deployed from the wings to reduce lift.

Answer (B) is correct. *(PHAK Chap 6)*

DISCUSSION: Flaps are attached to the trailing edge of the wing and are used during approach and landing to increase wing lift. This allows an increase in the angle of descent without increasing airspeed.

Answer (A) is incorrect. Flaps are attached to the trailing edge, not the leading edge, of the wing. Answer (C) is incorrect. Spoilers, not flaps, are high-drag devices deployed from the wings to reduce lift and increase drag.

8. Which device is a secondary flight control?

A. Spoilers.

B. Ailerons.

C. Stabilators.

Answer (A) is correct. *(PHAK Chap 6)*

DISCUSSION: Spoilers are high-drag devices that assist an aircraft in slowing down and losing altitude without gaining extra speed. They are common on gliders and some high-speed aircraft.

Answer (B) is incorrect. Ailerons control the roll of the aircraft and are a primary flight control surface. Answer (C) is incorrect. Stabilators function as both a horizontal stabilizer and an elevator, which makes them a primary control surface.

9. Trim systems are designed to do what?

A. They relieve the pilot of the need to maintain constant back pressure on the flight controls.

B. They are used during approach and landing to increase wing lift.

C. They move in the opposite direction from one another to control roll.

Answer (A) is correct. *(PHAK Chap 6)*

DISCUSSION: Trim systems are used to relieve the pilot of the need to maintain constant back pressure on the flight controls. They include trim tabs, anti-servo tabs, and ground adjustable tabs.

Answer (B) is incorrect. Flaps, not trim systems, are used during approach and landing to increase lift. This allows an increase in the angle of descent without increasing airspeed. Answer (C) is incorrect. Ailerons are control surfaces attached to each wing that move in the opposite direction from one another to control roll about the longitudinal axis.

1.2 Aerodynamic Forces

10. The four forces acting on an airplane in flight are

A. lift, weight, thrust, and drag.

B. lift, weight, gravity, and thrust.

C. lift, gravity, power, and friction.

Answer (A) is correct. *(PHAK Chap 5)*

DISCUSSION: Lift is produced by the wings and opposes weight, which is the result of gravity. Thrust is produced by the engine/propeller and opposes drag, which is the resistance of the air as the airplane moves through it.

Answer (B) is incorrect. Gravity reacts with the airplane's mass, thus producing weight, which opposes lift. Answer (C) is incorrect. Gravity results in weight, power produces thrust, and friction is a cause of drag. Power, gravity, velocity, and friction are not aerodynamic forces in themselves.

11. When are the four forces that act on an airplane in equilibrium?

A. During unaccelerated level flight.

B. When the aircraft is accelerating.

C. When the aircraft is at rest on the ground.

Answer (A) is correct. *(PHAK Chap 5)*

DISCUSSION: The four forces (lift, weight, thrust, and drag) that act on an airplane are in equilibrium during unaccelerated level flight.

Answer (B) is incorrect. Thrust must exceed drag in order for the airplane to accelerate. Answer (C) is incorrect. When the airplane is at rest on the ground, there are no aerodynamic forces acting on it other than weight (gravity).

12. What is the relationship of lift, drag, thrust, and weight when the airplane is in straight-and-level flight?

A. Lift equals weight and thrust equals drag.

B. Lift, drag, and weight equal thrust.

C. Lift and weight equal thrust and drag.

Answer (A) is correct. *(PHAK Chap 5)*

DISCUSSION: When the airplane is in straight-and-level flight (assuming no change of airspeed), it is not accelerating, and therefore lift equals weight and thrust equals drag.

Answer (B) is incorrect. Lift equals weight and drag equals thrust. Answer (C) is incorrect. Lift and weight are equal and thrust and drag are equal, but the four are not equal to each other.

13. Which statement relates to Bernoulli's principle?

A. For every action, there is an equal and opposite reaction.

B. An additional upward force is generated as the lower surface of the wing deflects air downward.

C. Air traveling faster over the curved upper surface of an airfoil causes lower pressure on the top surface.

Answer (C) is correct. *(PHAK Chap 4)*

DISCUSSION: Bernoulli's principle states in part that the internal pressure of a fluid (liquid or gas) decreases at points where the speed of the fluid increases. This same principle applies to air flowing over the curved upper surface of a wing.

Answer (A) is incorrect. Newton's Third Law of Motion states that, for every action, there is an equal and opposite reaction. Answer (B) is incorrect. The additional upward force that is generated as the lower surface of the wing deflects air downward is related to Newton's Third Law of Motion.

1.3 Angle of Attack

14. The term "angle of attack" is defined as the angle between the

A. chord line of the wing and the relative wind.

B. airplane's longitudinal axis and that of the air striking the airfoil.

C. airplane's center line and the relative wind.

Answer (A) is correct. *(PHAK Chap 4)*

DISCUSSION: The angle of attack is the angle between the wing chord line and the direction of the relative wind. The wing chord line is a straight line from the leading edge to the trailing edge of the wing. The relative wind is the direction of the airflow relative to the wing when the wing is moving through the air.

Answer (B) is incorrect. Angle of attack is the angle between the wing chord line and the relative wind, not the airplane's longitudinal axis. Answer (C) is incorrect. The centerline of the airplane and its relationship to the relative wind is not a factor in defining angle of attack. Angle of attack is the relationship between the wing chord line and the relative wind.

15. The term "angle of attack" is defined as the angle

A. between the wing chord line and the relative wind.

B. between the airplane's climb angle and the horizon.

C. formed by the longitudinal axis of the airplane and the chord line of the wing.

Answer (A) is correct. *(PHAK Chap 4)*

DISCUSSION: The angle of attack is the angle between the wing chord line and the direction of the relative wind. The wing chord line is a straight line from the leading edge to the trailing edge of the wing. The relative wind is the direction of airflow relative to the wing when the wing is moving through the air.

Answer (B) is incorrect. The angle between the airplane's climb angle and the horizon does not describe any term. Answer (C) is incorrect. The angle formed by the longitudinal axis of the airplane and the chord line of the wing is the angle of incidence (not attack).

16. Angle of attack is defined as the angle between the chord line of an airfoil and the

A. direction of the relative wind.

B. pitch angle of an airfoil.

C. rotor plane of rotation.

Answer (A) is correct. *(PHAK Chap 4)*

DISCUSSION: The angle of attack is the angle between the wing chord line and the direction of the relative wind. The wing chord line is a straight line from the leading edge to the trailing edge of the wing. The relative wind is the direction of airflow relative to the wing when the wing is moving through the air.

Answer (B) is incorrect. Pitch is used in conjunction with the aircraft or longitudinal axis, not the chord line of the airfoil. Answer (C) is incorrect. Rotor plane of rotation deals with helicopters, not fixed-wing aircraft.

17. (Refer to Figure 1 below.) The acute angle A is the angle of

A. incidence.

B. attack.

C. dihedral.

Answer (B) is correct. *(PHAK Chap 4)*

DISCUSSION: The angle between the relative wind and the wing chord line is the angle of attack. The wing chord line is a straight line from the leading edge to the trailing edge of the wing.

Answer (A) is incorrect. The angle of incidence is the acute angle formed by the chord line of the wing and the longitudinal axis of the airplane. Answer (C) is incorrect. The dihedral is the angle at which the wings are slanted upward from the wing root to the wingtip.

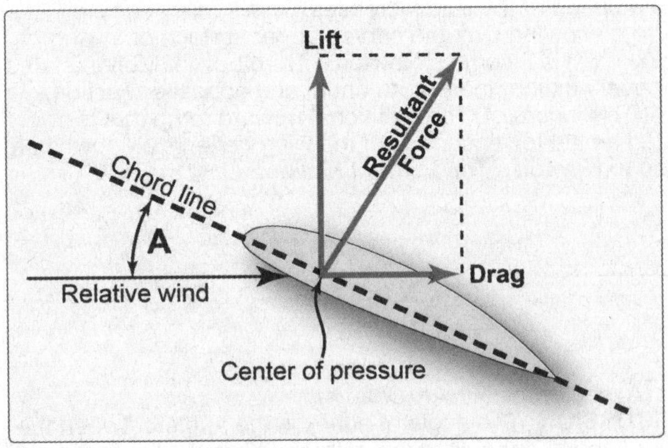

Figure 1. – Lift Vector.

18. The angle between the chord line of an airfoil and the relative wind is known as the angle of

A. lift.

B. attack.

C. incidence.

Answer (B) is correct. *(PHAK Chap 4)*

DISCUSSION: The angle of attack is the acute angle between the chord line of the wing and the direction of the relative wind.

Answer (A) is incorrect. The angle of lift is a nonsense term. Answer (C) is incorrect. The angle of incidence is the acute angle formed by the chord line of the wing and the longitudinal axis of the airplane.

19. The angle of attack at which an airplane wing stalls will

A. increase if the CG is moved forward.

B. change with an increase in gross weight.

C. remain the same regardless of gross weight.

Answer (C) is correct. *(PHAK Chap 5)*

DISCUSSION: A given airplane wing will always stall at the same angle of attack regardless of airspeed, weight, load factor, or density altitude. Each wing has a particular angle of attack (the critical angle of attack) at which the airflow separates from the upper surface of the wing and the stall occurs.

Answer (A) is incorrect. A change in CG will not change the wing's critical angle of attack. Answer (B) is incorrect. The critical angle of attack does not change when gross weight changes.

1.4 Stalls and Spins

20. As altitude increases, the indicated airspeed at which a given airplane stalls in a particular configuration will

A. decrease as the true airspeed decreases.

B. decrease as the true airspeed increases.

C. remain the same regardless of altitude.

Answer (C) is correct. *(AC 61-67C)*

DISCUSSION: All the performance factors of an airplane are dependent upon air density. As air density decreases, the airplane stalls at a higher true airspeed. However, you cannot detect the effect of high density altitude on your airspeed indicator. Accordingly, an airplane will stall in a particular configuration at the same indicated airspeed regardless of altitude.

Answer (A) is incorrect. True airspeed increases, not decreases, with increased altitude, and indicated airspeed at which an airplane stalls remains the same (does not decrease). Answer (B) is incorrect. The indicated airspeed of the stall does not change with increased altitude.

21. In what flight condition must an aircraft be placed in order to spin?

A. Partially stalled with one wing low.

B. In a steep diving spiral.

C. Stalled.

Answer (C) is correct. *(AC 61-67C)*

DISCUSSION: In order to enter a spin, an airplane must always first be stalled. Thereafter, the spin is caused when one wing becomes less stalled than the other wing.

Answer (A) is incorrect. The aircraft must first be fully stalled. Answer (B) is incorrect. A steep diving spiral has a relatively low angle of attack and thus does not produce a stall.

22. During a spin to the left, which wing(s) is/are stalled?

A. Both wings are stalled.

B. Neither wing is stalled.

C. Only the left wing is stalled.

Answer (A) is correct. *(AC 61-67C)*

DISCUSSION: In order to enter a spin, an airplane must always first be stalled. Thereafter, the spin is caused when one wing is less stalled than the other wing. In a spin to the left, the right wing is less stalled than the left wing.

Answer (B) is incorrect. Both wings must be at least partially stalled through the spin. Answer (C) is incorrect. Both wings are stalled; the right wing is simply less stalled than the left.

1.5 Frost

23. How will frost on the wings of an airplane affect takeoff performance?

A. Frost will disrupt the smooth flow of air over the wing, adversely affecting its lifting capability.

B. Frost will change the camber of the wing, increasing its lifting capability.

C. Frost will cause the airplane to become airborne with a higher angle of attack, decreasing the stall speed.

Answer (A) is correct. *(PHAK Chap 12)*

DISCUSSION: Frost does not change the basic aerodynamic shape of the wing, but the roughness of its surface spoils the smooth flow of air, thus causing an increase in drag and an early airflow separation over the wing, resulting in a loss of lift.

Answer (B) is incorrect. Frost will decrease (not increase) lift during takeoff and has no effect on the wing camber. Answer (C) is incorrect. A layer of frost on an airplane will increase drag, which increases (not decreases) the stall speed.

24. Why is frost considered hazardous to flight?

A. Frost changes the basic aerodynamic shape of the airfoils, thereby increasing lift.

B. Frost slows the airflow over the airfoils, thereby increasing control effectiveness.

C. Frost spoils the smooth flow of air over the wings, thereby decreasing lifting capability.

Answer (C) is correct. *(AvW Chap 10)*

DISCUSSION: Frost does not change the basic aerodynamic shape of the wing, but the roughness of its surface spoils the smooth flow of air, thus causing an increase in drag and an early airflow separation over the wing, resulting in a loss of lift.

Answer (A) is incorrect. Frost is thin and does not change the basic aerodynamic shape of the airfoil. Frost causes a decrease in lift. Answer (B) is incorrect. The smooth flow of air over the airfoil is affected, not control effectiveness.

25. How does frost affect the lifting surfaces of an airplane on takeoff?

A. Frost may prevent the airplane from becoming airborne at normal takeoff speed.

B. Frost will change the camber of the wing, increasing lift during takeoff.

C. Frost may cause the airplane to become airborne with a lower angle of attack at a lower indicated airspeed.

Answer (A) is correct. *(AvW Chap 10)*

DISCUSSION: Frost that is not removed from the surface of an airplane prior to takeoff may make it difficult to get the airplane airborne at normal takeoff speed. The frost disrupts the airflow over the wing, which increases drag.

Answer (B) is incorrect. The smoothness of the wing, not its curvature, is affected and lift is decreased (not increased). Answer (C) is incorrect. Ground effect (not frost) may cause an airplane to become airborne with a lower angle of attack at a lower indicated airspeed.

1.6 Ground Effect

26. What is ground effect?

A. The result of the interference of the surface of the Earth with the airflow patterns about an airplane.

B. The result of an alteration in airflow patterns increasing induced drag about the wings of an airplane.

C. The result of the disruption of the airflow patterns about the wings of an airplane to the point where the wings will no longer support the airplane in flight.

Answer (A) is correct. *(PHAK Chap 5)*

DISCUSSION: Ground effect is due to the interference of the ground (or water) surface with the airflow patterns about the airplane in flight. As the wing encounters ground effect, there is a reduction in the upwash, downwash, and the wingtip vortices. The result is a reduction in induced drag. Thus, for a given angle of attack, the wing will produce more lift in ground effect than it does out of ground effect.

Answer (B) is incorrect. The result of the alteration in airflow patterns about the wing decreases, not increases, the induced drag. Answer (C) is incorrect. The disruption of the airflow patterns about the wing decreases induced drag, which causes an increase, not decrease, in lift at a given angle of attack.

27. Floating caused by the phenomenon of ground effect will be most realized during an approach to land when at

A. less than the length of the wingspan above the surface.

B. twice the length of the wingspan above the surface.

C. a higher-than-normal angle of attack.

Answer (A) is correct. *(PHAK Chap 5)*

DISCUSSION: Ground effect is most usually recognized when the airplane is within one-half of the length of its wingspan above the surface. It may extend as high as a full wingspan length above the surface. Due to an alteration of the airflow about the wings, induced drag decreases, which reduces the thrust required at low airspeeds. Thus, any excess speed during the landing flare may result in considerable floating.

Answer (B) is incorrect. Ground effect generally extends up to only one wingspan length, not two. Answer (C) is incorrect. Floating will occur with excess airspeed, which results in a lower-than-normal, not higher-than-normal, angle of attack.

28. What must a pilot be aware of as a result of ground effect?

A. Wingtip vortices increase creating wake turbulence problems for arriving and departing aircraft.

B. Induced drag decreases; therefore, any excess speed at the point of flare may cause considerable floating.

C. A full stall landing will require less up elevator deflection than would a full stall when done free of ground effect.

Answer (B) is correct. *(PHAK Chap 5)*

DISCUSSION: Ground effect reduces the upwash, downwash, and vortices caused by the wings, resulting in a decrease in induced drag. Thus, thrust required at low airspeeds will be reduced, and any excess speed at the point of flare may cause considerable floating.

Answer (A) is incorrect. Wingtip vortices are decreased, not increased. Answer (C) is incorrect. A full stall landing will require more, not less, up elevator deflection since the wing will require a lower angle of attack in ground effect to produce the same amount of lift.

29. An aircraft leaving ground effect during takeoff will

A. experience a reduction in ground friction and require a slight power reduction.

B. experience an increase in induced drag and a decrease in performance.

C. require a lower angle of attack to maintain the same lift coefficient.

Answer (B) is correct. *(PHAK Chap 5)*

DISCUSSION: During the takeoff phase of flight, ground effect produces some important relationships. The airplane leaving ground effect after takeoff encounters just the reverse of the airplane entering ground effect during landing; i.e., the airplane leaving ground effect will (1) require an increase in angle of attack to maintain the same lift coefficient, (2) experience an increase in induced drag and thrust required, (3) experience a decrease in stability and a nose-up change in moment, (4) produce a reduction in static source pressure and an increase in indicated airspeed.

Answer (A) is incorrect. While the aerodynamic characteristics of the tail surfaces and the fuselage are altered by ground effects, the principal effects due to proximity of the ground are the changes in the aerodynamic characteristics of the wing, not a reduction in ground friction. As the wing encounters ground effect and is maintained at a constant lift coefficient, there is consequent reduction in the upwash, downwash, and the wingtip vortices. Answer (C) is incorrect. The aircraft will require a higher angle of attack to maintain the same lift coefficient as when it was in ground effect.

30. Ground effect is most likely to result in which problem?

A. Settling to the surface abruptly during landing.

B. Becoming airborne before reaching recommended takeoff speed.

C. Inability to get airborne even though airspeed is sufficient for normal takeoff needs.

Answer (B) is correct. *(PHAK Chap 5)*

DISCUSSION: Due to the reduction of induced drag in ground effect, the airplane may seem capable of becoming airborne well below the recommended takeoff speed. However, as the airplane rises out of ground effect (a height greater than the wingspan) with a deficiency of speed, the increase in induced drag may result in very marginal initial climb performance. In extreme cases, the airplane may become airborne initially, with a deficiency of airspeed, only to settle back on the runway when attempting to fly out of the ground effect area.

Answer (A) is incorrect. The airplane will experience a little extra lift on landing due to the reduction in induced drag, causing it to float rather than settle abruptly. Answer (C) is incorrect. Ground effect would not hamper the airplane from becoming airborne if the airspeed were sufficient for normal takeoff. Ground effect may allow the airplane to become airborne before reaching the recommended takeoff speed.

1.7 Airplane Turn

31. What force makes an airplane turn?

A. The horizontal component of lift.

B. The vertical component of lift.

C. Centrifugal force.

Answer (A) is correct. *(AFH Chap 3)*

DISCUSSION: When the wings of an airplane are not level, the lift is not entirely vertical and tends to pull the airplane toward the direction of the lower wing. An airplane is turned when the pilot coordinates rudder, aileron, and elevator to bank in order to attain a horizontal component of lift.

Answer (B) is incorrect. The vertical component of lift opposes weight and controls vertical, not horizontal, movement. Answer (C) is incorrect. The horizontal component of lift opposes centrifugal force, which acts toward the outside of the turn.

1.8 Airplane Stability

32. An airplane said to be inherently stable will

A. be difficult to stall.

B. require less effort to control.

C. not spin.

Answer (B) is correct. *(PHAK Chap 5)*

DISCUSSION: An inherently stable airplane will usually return to the original condition of flight (except when in a bank) if disturbed by a force such as air turbulence. Thus, an inherently stable airplane will require less effort to control than an inherently unstable one.

Answer (A) is incorrect. Stability of an airplane has an effect on stall characteristic, not on the difficulty level of entering a stall. Answer (C) is incorrect. An inherently stable aircraft will spin.

33. What determines the longitudinal stability of an airplane?

A. The location of the CG with respect to the center of lift.

B. The effectiveness of the horizontal stabilizer, rudder, and rudder trim tab.

C. The relationship of thrust and lift to weight and drag.

Answer (A) is correct. *(PHAK Chap 5)*

DISCUSSION: The location of the center of gravity with respect to the center of lift determines, to a great extent, the longitudinal stability of the airplane. Positive stability is attained by having the center of lift behind the center of gravity. Then the tail provides negative lift, creating a downward tail force, which counteracts the nose's tendency to pitch down.

Answer (B) is incorrect. The rudder and rudder trim tab control the yaw, not the pitch. Answer (C) is incorrect. The relationship of thrust and lift to weight and drag affects speed and altitude, not longitudinal stability.

34. Changes in the center of pressure of a wing affect the aircraft's

A. lift/drag ratio.

B. lifting capacity.

C. aerodynamic balance and controllability.

Answer (C) is correct. *(PHAK Chap 4)*

DISCUSSION: Center of pressure (CP) is the imaginary but determinable point at which all of the upward lift forces on the wing are concentrated. In general, at high angles of attack the CP moves forward, while at low angles of attack the CP moves aft. The relationship of the CP to center of gravity (CG) affects both aerodynamic balance and controllability.

Answer (A) is incorrect. The lift/drag ratio is determined by angle of attack. Answer (B) is incorrect. Lifting capacity is affected by angle of attack, airspeed, and wing planform.

35. An airplane has been loaded in such a manner that the CG is located aft of the aft CG limit. One undesirable flight characteristic a pilot might experience with this airplane would be

A. a longer takeoff run.

B. difficulty in recovering from a stalled condition.

C. stalling at higher-than-normal airspeed.

Answer (B) is correct. *(PHAK Chap 10)*

DISCUSSION: The recovery from a stall in any airplane becomes progressively more difficult as its center of gravity moves backward. Generally, airplanes become less controllable, especially at slow flight speeds, as the center of gravity is moved backward.

Answer (A) is incorrect. An airplane with an aft CG has less drag, resulting in a shorter, not longer, takeoff run. Answer (C) is incorrect. An airplane with an aft CG flies at a lower angle of attack, resulting in a lower, not higher, stall speed.

36. What causes an airplane (except a T-tail) to pitch nosedown when power is reduced and controls are not adjusted?

A. The CG shifts forward when thrust and drag are reduced.

B. The downwash on the elevators from the propeller slipstream is reduced and elevator effectiveness is reduced.

C. When thrust is reduced to less than weight, lift is also reduced and the wings can no longer support the weight.

Answer (B) is correct. *(PHAK Chap 6)*

DISCUSSION: The relative wind on the tail is the result of the airplane's movement through the air and the propeller slipstream. When that slipstream is reduced, the horizontal stabilizer (except a T-tail) will produce less negative lift and the nose will pitch down.

Answer (A) is incorrect. The CG is not affected by changes in thrust or drag. Answer (C) is incorrect. Thrust and weight have no relationship to each other.

37. Loading an airplane to the most aft CG will cause the airplane to be

A. less stable at all speeds.

B. less stable at slow speeds, but more stable at high speeds.

C. less stable at high speeds, but more stable at low speeds.

Answer (A) is correct. *(PHAK Chap 10)*

DISCUSSION: Airplanes become less stable at all speeds as the center of gravity is moved backward. The rearward center of gravity limit is determined largely by considerations of stability.

Answer (B) is incorrect. An aft CG will cause the airplane to be less stable at all speeds. Answer (C) is incorrect. An aft CG will cause the airplane to be less stable at all speeds.

38. What is the effect of advancing the throttle in flight?

A. Both aircraft groundspeed and angle of attack will increase.

B. Airspeed will remain relatively constant but the aircraft will climb.

C. The aircraft will accelerate, which will cause a turn to the right.

Answer (A) is correct. *(PHAK Chap 5)*

DISCUSSION: When advancing the throttle, the airspeed will increase; therefore, groundspeed will also increase. The aircraft will climb due to an increase in downwash over the horizontal stabilizer as power is applied and the lift created by the airspeed increase.

Answer (B) is incorrect. When advancing the throttle, the airspeed and groundspeed increase. Answer (C) is incorrect. When power is applied to a single-engine aircraft, it will tend to turn to the left due to the left-turning tendency created by the engine and propeller.

1.9 Torque and P-Factor

39. In what flight condition are torque effects more pronounced in a single-engine airplane?

A. Low airspeed, high power, high angle of attack.

B. Low airspeed, low power, low angle of attack.

C. High airspeed, high power, high angle of attack.

Answer (A) is correct. *(PHAK Chap 5)*

DISCUSSION: The effect of torque increases in direct proportion to engine power and inversely to airspeed. Thus, at low airspeeds, high angles of attack, and high power settings, torque is the greatest.

Answer (B) is incorrect. Torque effect is the greatest at high (not low) power settings, and high (not low) angle of attack. Answer (C) is incorrect. Torque effect is the greatest at low (not high) airspeeds.

40. The left turning tendency of an airplane caused by P-factor is the result of the

A. clockwise rotation of the engine and the propeller turning the airplane counterclockwise.

B. propeller blade descending on the right, producing more thrust than the ascending blade on the left.

C. gyroscopic forces applied to the rotating propeller blades acting 90° in advance of the point the force was applied.

Answer (B) is correct. *(PHAK Chap 5)*

DISCUSSION: Asymmetric propeller loading (P-factor) occurs when the airplane is flown at a high angle of attack. The downward-moving blade on the right side of the propeller (as seen from the rear) has a higher angle of attack, which creates higher thrust than the upward-moving blade on the left. Thus, the airplane yaws around the vertical axis to the left.

Answer (A) is incorrect. Torque reaction (not P-factor) is a result of the clockwise rotation of the engine and the propeller turning the airplane counterclockwise. Answer (C) is incorrect. Gyroscopic precession (not P-factor) is a result of the gyroscopic forces applied to the rotating propeller blades acting 90° in advance of the point the force was applied.

41. When does P-factor cause the airplane to yaw to the left?

A. When at low angles of attack.

B. When at high angles of attack.

C. When at high airspeeds.

Answer (B) is correct. *(PHAK Chap 5)*

DISCUSSION: P-factor or asymmetric propeller loading occurs when an airplane is flown at a high angle of attack because the downward-moving blade on the right side of the propeller (as seen from the rear) has a higher angle of attack, which creates higher thrust than the upward-moving blade on the left. Thus, the airplane yaws around the vertical axis to the left.

Answer (A) is incorrect. At low angles of attack, both sides of the propeller have similar angles of attack and “pull” the airplane straight ahead. Answer (C) is incorrect. At high speeds, an airplane is not at a high angle of attack.

1.10 Load Factor

42. The amount of excess load that can be imposed on the wing of an airplane depends upon the

A. position of the CG.

B. speed of the airplane.

C. abruptness at which the load is applied.

Answer (B) is correct. *(PHAK Chap 5)*

DISCUSSION: The amount of excess load that can be imposed on the wing depends upon how fast the airplane is flying. At low speeds, the maximum available lifting force of the wing is only slightly greater than the amount necessary to support the weight of the airplane. Thus, any excess load would simply cause the airplane to stall. At high speeds, the lifting capacity of the wing is so great (as a result of the greater flow of air over the wings) that a sudden movement of the elevator controls (strong gust of wind) may increase the load factor beyond safe limits. This is why maximum speeds are established by airplane manufacturers.

Answer (A) is incorrect. The position of the CG affects the stability of the airplane but not the total load the wings can support. Answer (C) is incorrect. It is the amount of load, not the abruptness of the load, that is limited. However, the abruptness of the maneuver can affect the amount of the load.

43. Which basic flight maneuver increases the load factor on an airplane as compared to straight-and-level flight?

A. Climbs.

B. Turns.

C. Stalls.

Answer (B) is correct. *(PHAK Chap 5)*

DISCUSSION: Turns increase the load factor because the lift from the wings is used to pull the airplane around a corner as well as to offset the force of gravity. The wings must carry the airplane's weight plus offset centrifugal force during the turn. For example, a 60° bank results in a load factor of 2; i.e., the wings must support twice the weight they do in level flight.

Answer (A) is incorrect. The wings only have to carry the weight of the airplane once the airplane is established in a climb. Answer (C) is incorrect. In a stall, the wings are not producing lift.

44. During an approach to a stall, an increased load factor will cause the aircraft to

A. stall at a higher airspeed.

B. have a tendency to spin.

C. be more difficult to control.

Answer (A) is correct. *(PHAK Chap 5)*

DISCUSSION: The greater the load (whether from gross weight or from centrifugal force), the more lift is required. Therefore, an aircraft will stall at higher airspeeds when the load and/or load factor is increased.

Answer (B) is incorrect. An aircraft's tendency to spin is not related to an increase in load factors. Answer (C) is incorrect. An aircraft's stability (not load factor) determines its controllability.

45. (Refer to Figure 2 on page 35.) If an airplane weighs 2,300 pounds, what approximate weight would the airplane structure be required to support during a 60° banked turn while maintaining altitude?

A. 2,300 pounds.

B. 3,400 pounds.

C. 4,600 pounds.

Answer (C) is correct. *(PHAK Chap 5)*

DISCUSSION: Note on Fig. 2 that, at a 60° bank angle, the load factor is 2. Thus, a 2,300-lb. airplane in a 60° bank would require its wings to support 4,600 lb. (2,300 lb. × 2).

Answer (A) is incorrect. An airplane supporting a load of 2,300 lb. in a 60° banked turn would weigh 1,150 lb., not 2,300 lb. Note on Fig. 2 that, at a 60° bank angle, the load factor is 2. Answer (B) is incorrect. An airplane supporting a load of 3,400 lb. in a 60° banked turn would weigh 1,700 lb., not 2,300 lb. Note on Fig. 2 that, at a 60° bank angle, the load factor is 2.

46. (Refer to Figure 2 below.) If an airplane weighs 3,300 pounds, what approximate weight would the airplane structure be required to support during a 30° banked turn while maintaining altitude?

A. 1,200 pounds.

B. 3,100 pounds.

C. 3,960 pounds.

Answer (C) is correct. *(PHAK Chap 5)*

DISCUSSION: Look on the left side of the chart in Fig. 2 to see that, at a 30° bank angle, the load factor is 1.154. Thus, a 3,300-lb. airplane in a 30° bank would require its wings to support 3,808.2 lb. (3,300 lb. × 1.154). The closest answer choice to this value is 3,960 lb.

Answer (A) is incorrect. An airplane supporting a load of 1,200 lb. in a 30° banked turn would weigh 1,000 lb., not 3,300 lb. Look on the left side of the chart in Fig. 2 to see that, at a 30° bank angle, the load factor is 1.154. Answer (B) is incorrect. An airplane supporting a load of 3,100 lb. in a 30° banked turn would weigh 2,583 lb., not 3,300 lb. Look on the left side of the chart in Fig. 2 to see that, at a 30° bank angle, the load factor is 1.154.

47. (Refer to Figure 2 below.) If an airplane weighs 4,500 pounds, what approximate weight would the airplane structure be required to support during a 45° banked turn while maintaining altitude?

A. 4,500 pounds.

B. 6,750 pounds.

C. 7,200 pounds.

Answer (B) is correct. *(PHAK Chap 5)*

DISCUSSION: Look on the left side of the chart in Fig. 2 under 45° and note that the load factor curve is 1.414. Thus, a 4,500-lb. airplane in a 45° bank would require its wings to support 6,363 lb. (4,500 lb. × 1.414). The closest answer choice to this value is 6,750 lb.

Answer (A) is incorrect. An airplane supporting a load of 4,500 lb. in a 45° banked turn would weigh 3,000 lb., not 4,500 lb. Look on the left side of the chart under 45° and note that the load factor curve is 1.414. Answer (C) is incorrect. An airplane supporting a load of 7,200 lb. in a 45° banked turn would weigh 4,800 lb., not 4,500 lb. Look on the left side of the chart under 45° and note that the load factor curve is 1.414.

Angle of bank ϕ	Load factor n
0°	1.0
10°	1.015
30°	1.154
45°	1.414
60°	2.000
70°	2.923
80°	5.747
85°	11.473
90°	∞

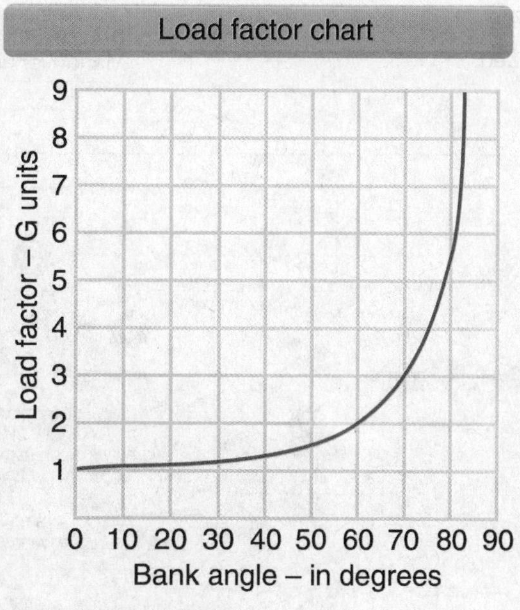

Figure 2. – Load Factor Chart.

1.11 Velocity Vs. G-Loads

48. (Refer to Figure 72 below.) A positive load factor of 2 at 80 mph would cause the airplane to

A. stall.

B. break apart.

C. operate normally, as it is within the normal operating range.

Answer (A) is correct. *(PHAK Chap 5)*

DISCUSSION: The Velocity vs. G-loads chart (Fig. 72) has indicated airspeed on the horizontal axis and load factor on the vertical axis. Locate the intersection of 2 on the vertical axis and 80 on the horizontal axis. Notice that operating where these coordinates intersect, which is the blue shaded area, would be indicative of a stalled condition.

Answer (B) is incorrect. The airspeed causing the airplane to break apart is not measured or documented. Answer (C) is incorrect. The chart has indicated that the airplane would be in a stalled condition and not measured or documented within the red area. The red area is where the airplane is subjected to structural damage.

49. (Refer to Figure 72 below.) What load factor would be created if positive 15 feet per second gusts were encountered at 120 mph?

A. 2.8

B. 3.0

C. 2.0

Answer (C) is correct. *(PHAK Chap 5)*

DISCUSSION: Begin at the bottom of Fig. 72 by locating 120 mph and then move up vertically to the positive 15-feet-per-second (+15 fps) diagonal white line. Next, move left horizontally to determine the load factor of 2.0.

Answer (A) is incorrect. A load factor of 2.8 would be created if gusts of 30 fps were encountered at 120 mph. Answer (B) is incorrect. A load factor of 3.0 would be created if gusts in excess of 30 fps were encountered at 120 mph.

50. (Refer to Figure 72 below.) The airspeed indicated by points A and J is

A. maximum structural cruising speed.

B. normal stall speed.

C. maneuvering speed.

Answer (B) is correct. *(PHAK Chap 5)*

DISCUSSION: Points A and J are the normal stall speed (V_{S1}). At this speed in the clean configuration, the airplane will stall. The normal stall speed is shown on the airspeed indicator at the low-speed end of the green arc.

Answer (A) is incorrect. Maximum structural cruising speed (V_{NO}) is indicated by points D and G. Answer (C) is incorrect. Maneuvering speed (V_A) is indicated by points C and H.

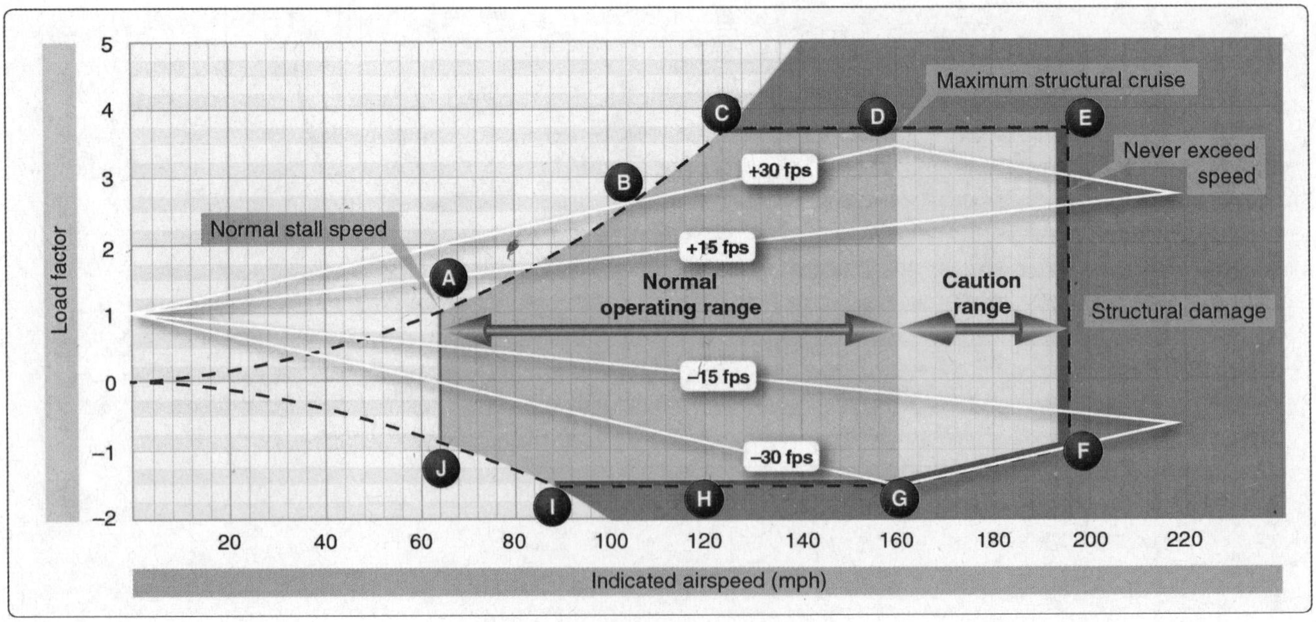

Figure 72. – Velocity vs. G-Loads.

END OF STUDY UNIT

STUDY UNIT TWO
AIRPLANE INSTRUMENTS, ENGINES, AND SYSTEMS

(9 pages of outline)

This study unit contains outlines of major concepts tested, sample test questions and answers regarding the major mechanical and instrument systems in an airplane, and an explanation of each answer. The table of contents above lists each subunit within this study unit, the number of questions pertaining to that particular subunit, and the pages on which the outlines and questions begin, respectively.

Recall that the **sole purpose** of this book is to expedite your passing of the FAA pilot knowledge test for the private pilot certificate. Accordingly, all extraneous material (i.e., topics or regulations not directly tested on the FAA pilot knowledge test) is omitted, even though much more knowledge is necessary to fly safely. This additional material is presented in *Pilot Handbook* and *Private Pilot Flight Maneuvers and Practical Test Prep*, available from Gleim Publications, Inc. Order online at www.GleimAviation.com.

2.1 COMPASS TURNING ERROR

1. During flight, magnetic compasses can be considered accurate only during straight-and-level flight at constant airspeed.
2. The difference between direction indicated by a magnetic compass not installed in an airplane and one installed in an airplane is called deviation.
    a. Magnetic fields produced by metals and electrical accessories in an airplane disturb the compass needles.
3. In the Northern Hemisphere, acceleration/deceleration error occurs when on an east or west heading. Remember ANDS: Accelerate North, Decelerate South.
    a. A magnetic compass will indicate a turn toward the north during acceleration when on an east or west heading.
    b. A magnetic compass will indicate a turn toward the south during deceleration when on an east or west heading.
    c. Acceleration/deceleration error does not occur when on a north or south heading.

4. In the Northern Hemisphere, compass turning error occurs when turning from a north or south heading.
   a. A magnetic compass will lag (and, at the start of a turn, indicate a turn in the opposite direction) when turning from a north heading.
      1) If turning to the east (right), the compass will initially indicate a turn to the west and then lag behind the actual heading until your airplane is headed east (at which point there is no error).
      2) If turning to the west (left), the compass will initially indicate a turn to the east and then lag behind the actual heading until your airplane is headed west (at which point there is no error).
   b. A magnetic compass will lead or precede the turn when turning from a south heading.
   c. Turning errors do not occur when turning from an east or west heading.
   d. These errors diminish as the acceleration/deceleration or turns are completed.
5. The magnets in a compass align with any magnetic field.
   a. Local magnetic fields in an aircraft caused by electrical current flowing in the structure, nearby wiring, certain metals, or any magnetized part of the structure conflict with the earth's magnetic field and cause compass deviation error.
   b. Deviation, unlike variation, changes with heading rather than with geographic location.

2.2 PITOT-STATIC SYSTEM

1. The pitot-static system is a source of pressure for the
   a. Altimeter
   b. Vertical-speed indicator
   c. Airspeed indicator
2. The pitot tube provides impact (or ram) pressure for the airspeed indicator only.
3. When the pitot tube and the outside static vents or just the static vents are clogged, all three instruments mentioned above will provide inaccurate readings.
   a. If only the pitot tube is clogged, only the airspeed indicator will be inoperative.

2.3 AIRSPEED INDICATOR

1. Airspeed indicators have several color-coded markings (shown in Figure 4 at the end of this subunit).
   a. The white arc is the full flap operating range.
      1) The lower limit is the power-off stalling speed with wing flaps and landing gear in the landing position (V_{S0}).
      2) The upper limit is the maximum full flaps-extended speed (V_{FE}).
   b. The green arc is the normal operating range.
      1) The lower limit is the power-off stalling speed in a specified configuration (V_{S1}). This is normally wing flaps up and landing gear retracted.
      2) The upper limit is the maximum structural cruising speed (V_{NO}) for normal operation.
   c. The yellow arc is airspeed that is safe in smooth air only.
      1) It is known as the caution range.
   d. The red radial line is the speed that should never be exceeded (V_{NE}).
      1) This is the maximum speed at which the airplane may be operated in smooth air (or under any circumstances).

2. The most important airspeed limitation that is **not** color-coded is the **design maneuvering speed (V_A)**.
    a. Design maneuvering speed is the speed below which you can move a flight control one time in smooth air to its full deflection, for one axis of airplane rotation only (pitch, roll, or yaw), without risk of damage to the airplane.
    b. It is usually the maximum speed for flight in turbulent air.
    c. It is the maximum speed at which an airplane may be stalled safely.

Figure 4. – Airspeed Indicator.

2.4 ALTIMETER

1. Altimeters have three hands (e.g., as a clock has the hour, minute, and second hands as shown in Figure 3 below and Figure 82 at the end of this subunit).
2. The three hands on the altimeter are the
    a. 10,000-ft. interval (short needle)
    b. 1,000-ft. interval (medium needle)
    c. 100-ft. interval (long needle)
3. Altimeters are numbered 0-9.
4. To read an altimeter,
    a. First, determine whether the short needle points between 0 and 1 (1-10,000), 1 and 2 (10,000-20,000), or 2 and 3 (20,000-30,000). This needle may be a long, thin tip with a triangular end.
    b. Second, determine whether the medium needle is between 0 and 1 (0-1,000), 1 and 2 (1,000-2,000), etc. This may be a short, wide needle in conjunction with the needle with a long, thin tip and triangular end.
    c. Third, determine at which number the long needle is pointing, e.g., 1 for 100 ft., 2 for 200 ft., etc.

Figure 3. – Altimeter.

Figure 82. – Altimeter.

2.5 TYPES OF ALTITUDE

1. Absolute altitude is the altitude above the surface, i.e., AGL.
2. True altitude is the actual distance above mean sea level, i.e., MSL. It is not susceptible to variation with atmospheric conditions.
3. Density altitude is pressure altitude corrected for nonstandard temperatures.
4. Pressure altitude is the height above the standard datum plane of 29.92 in. of mercury. Thus, it is the indicated altitude when the altimeter setting is adjusted to 29.92 in. of mercury (also written 29.92" Hg).
5. Pressure altitude and density altitude are the same at standard temperature.
6. Indicated altitude is the same as true altitude when standard conditions exist and the altimeter is calibrated properly.
7. Pressure altitude and true altitude are the same when standard atmospheric conditions (29.92" Hg and 15°C at sea level) exist.
8. When the altimeter is adjusted on the ground so that indicated altitude equals true altitude at airport elevation, the altimeter setting is that for your location, i.e., approximately the setting you would get from the control tower.

2.6 SETTING THE ALTIMETER

1. The indicated altitude on the altimeter increases when you change the altimeter setting to a higher pressure and decreases when you change the setting to a lower pressure.
   a. This is opposite to the altimeter's reaction due to changes in air pressure.
2. The indicated altitude will change at a rate of approximately 1,000 ft. for 1 in. of pressure change in the altimeter setting.
   a. EXAMPLE: When changing the altimeter setting from 29.15 to 29.85, there is a 0.70 in. change in pressure (29.85 – 29.15). The indicated altitude would increase (due to a higher altimeter setting) by 700 ft. (0.70 × 1,000).

2.7 ALTIMETER ERRORS

1. Since altimeter readings are adjusted for changes in barometric pressure but not for temperature changes, an airplane will be at lower than indicated altitude when flying in colder than standard temperature air when maintaining a constant indicated altitude.
   a. On warm days, the altimeter indicates lower than actual altitude.
2. Likewise, when pressure lowers en route at a constant indicated altitude, your altimeter will indicate higher than actual altitude until you adjust it.
3. Remember, when flying from high to low (temperature or pressure), look out below.
   a. Low to high, clear the sky.

2.8 GYROSCOPIC INSTRUMENTS

1. The attitude indicator, with its miniature aircraft and horizon bar, displays a picture of the attitude of the airplane (Figure 7 below).
   a. The relationship of the miniature airplane (labeled "C" on Figure 7) to the horizon bar (labeled "B" on Figure 7) is the same as the relationship of the real aircraft to the actual horizon.
      1) The banking scale (labeled "A" on Figure 7) shows degrees of bank from level flight.
   b. The relationship of the miniature airplane to the horizon bar should be used for an indication of pitch and bank attitude, i.e., nose high, nose low, left bank, right bank.
   c. The gyro in the attitude indicator rotates in a horizontal plane and depends upon rigidity in space for its operation.
   d. An adjustment knob is provided with which the pilot may move the miniature airplane up or down to align the miniature airplane with the horizon bar to suit the pilot's line of vision.
2. The turn coordinator shows the roll and yaw movement of the airplane (shown in Figure 5 below).
   a. It displays a miniature airplane, which moves proportionally to the roll rate of the airplane. When the bank is held constant, the turn coordinator indicates the rate of turn.
   b. The ball indicates whether the angle of bank is coordinated with the rate of turn.
3. The heading indicator is a gyro instrument that depends on the principle of rigidity in space for its operation (illustrated in Figure 6 below).
   a. Due to gyro precession, it must be periodically realigned with a magnetic compass.
   b. In most light aircraft, the heading indicator may tumble or "spill" when a certain bank or attitude is exceeded. After "spilling," the heading indicator may be reset with the caging knob.

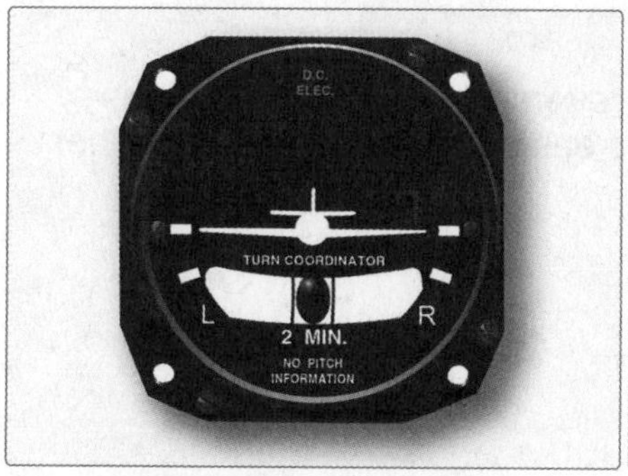

Figure 5. – Turn Coordinator.

Figure 6. – Heading Indicator.

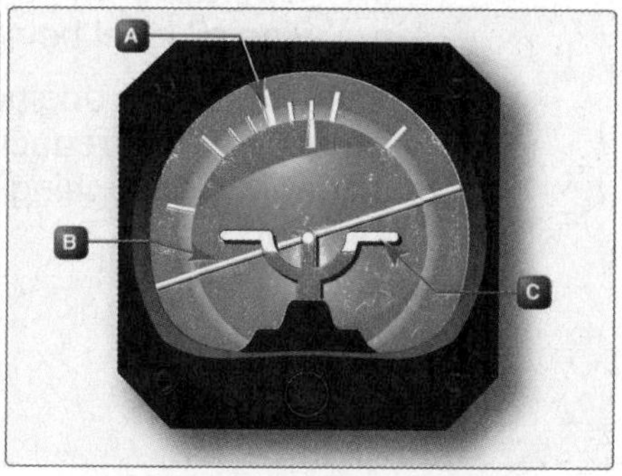

Figure 7. – Attitude Indicator.

2.9 GLASS COCKPITS

1. Glass cockpits, or systems of advanced avionics, are replacing the older round-dial gauges common in many training aircraft.
   a. These systems vary widely but generally provide flight information such as flight progress, engine monitoring, navigation, terrain, traffic, and weather.
   b. These systems are designed to decrease pilot workload, enhance situational awareness, and increase the safety margin.
   c. These systems are displayed in an electronic flight display (EFD).
2. A **primary flight display** (PFD) integrates all flight instruments critical to safe flight on one screen. It is a type of EFD.
   a. Some PFDs incorporate or overlay navigation instruments on top of primary flight instruments.
      1) EXAMPLE: An ILS or VOR may be integrated with the heading indicator.
3. A **multi-function display** (MFD) not only shows primary instrumentation but can combine information from multiple systems on one page or screen. It is another type of EFD.
   a. Moving maps provide a pictorial view of the aircraft's location, route, airspace, and geographical features.

   NOTE: A moving map should not be used as the primary navigation instrument; it should be a supplement, not a substitute, in the navigational process.

   b. Onboard weather systems, including radar, may provide real-time weather.
   c. Other information that could be included on MFDs include terrain and traffic avoidance, checklists, and fuel management systems.
4. Care should be taken that reliance on glass cockpits does not negate safety. A regular scan, both visually outside and inside on backup gauges, should be combined with other means of navigation and checklists to ensure safe flight.

2.10 ENGINE TEMPERATURE

1. Excessively high engine temperature either in the air or on the ground will cause loss of power, excessive oil consumption, and excessive wear on the internal engine.
2. An engine is cooled, in part, by circulating oil through the system to reduce friction and absorb heat from internal engine parts.
3. Engine oil and cylinder head temperatures can exceed their normal operating range because of (among other causes)
   a. Operating with too much power
   b. Climbing too steeply (i.e., at too low an airspeed) in hot weather
   c. Using fuel that has a lower-than-specified octane rating
   d. Operating with too lean a mixture
   e. The oil level being too low
4. Excessively high engine temperatures can be reduced by reversing any of the previous situations, e.g., reducing power, climbing less steeply (increasing airspeed), using higher octane fuel, enriching the mixture, etc.

2.11 CONSTANT-SPEED PROPELLER

1. The advantage of a constant-speed propeller (also known as controllable-pitch) is that it permits the pilot to select the blade angle for the most efficient performance.
2. Constant-speed propeller airplanes have both throttle and propeller controls.
   a. The throttle controls power output, which is registered on the manifold pressure gauge.
   b. The propeller control regulates engine revolutions per minute (RPM), which are registered on the tachometer.
3. To avoid overstressing cylinders, excessively high manifold pressure should not be used with low RPM settings.

2.12 ENGINE IGNITION SYSTEMS

1. One purpose of the dual-ignition system is to provide for improved engine performance.
   a. The other is increased safety.
2. Loose or broken wires in the ignition system can cause problems.
   a. EXAMPLE: If the ignition switch is OFF, the magneto may continue to fire if the ignition switch ground wire is disconnected.
   b. If this occurs, the only way to stop the engine is to move the mixture lever to the idle cut-off position, then have the system checked by a qualified aviation maintenance technician.

2.13 CARBURETOR ICING

1. Carburetor-equipped engines are more susceptible to icing than fuel-injected engines.
   a. The operating principle of float-type carburetors is the difference in air pressure between the venturi throat and the air inlet.
   b. Fuel-injected engines do not have a carburetor.
2. The first indication of carburetor ice on airplanes with fixed-pitch propellers and float-type carburetors is a loss of RPM.
3. Carburetor ice is likely to form when outside air temperature is between 20°F and 70°F and there is visible moisture or high humidity.
4. When carburetor heat is applied to eliminate carburetor ice in an airplane equipped with a fixed-pitch propeller, there will be a further decrease in RPM (due to the less dense hot air entering the engine) followed by a gradual increase in RPM as the ice melts.

2.14 CARBURETOR HEAT

1. Carburetor heat enriches the fuel/air mixture,
   a. Because warm air is less dense than cold air.
   b. When the air density decreases (because the air is warm), the fuel/air mixture (ratio) becomes richer since there is less air for the same amount of fuel.
2. Applying carburetor heat decreases engine output and increases operating temperature.

2.15 FUEL/AIR MIXTURE

1. At higher altitudes, the fuel/air mixture must be leaned to decrease the fuel flow in order to compensate for the decreased air density, i.e., to keep the fuel/air mixture constant.
   a. If you descend from high altitudes to lower altitudes without enriching the mixture, the mixture will become leaner because the air is denser at lower altitudes.

2. If you are running up your engine at a high-altitude airport, you may eliminate engine roughness by leaning the mixture,
   a. Particularly if the engine runs even worse with carburetor heat, since warm air further enriches the mixture.
3. The definition of "fuel/air ratio" is the ratio between the weight of fuel and weight of air entering the cylinder.

2.16 ABNORMAL COMBUSTION

1. Detonation occurs when the fuel/air mixture explodes instead of burning evenly.
2. Detonation is usually caused by using a lower-than-specified grade (octane) of aviation fuel or by excessive engine temperature.
   a. This causes many engine problems including excessive wear and higher than normal operating temperatures.
3. Lower the nose slightly if you suspect that an engine (with a fixed-pitch propeller) is detonating during climbout after takeoff. This will increase cooling and decrease the engine's workload.
4. Pre-ignition is the uncontrolled firing of the fuel/air charge in advance of the normal spark ignition.

2.17 AVIATION FUEL PRACTICES

1. Use of the next-higher-than-specified (octane) grade of fuel is better than using the next-lower-than-specified grade of fuel. This will prevent the possibility of detonation, or running the engine too hot.
2. Filling the fuel tanks at the end of the day prevents moisture condensation by eliminating the airspace in the tanks.
3. All fuel strainer drains and fuel tank sumps should be drained before each flight to make sure there is no water in the fuel system.
4. In an airplane equipped with fuel pumps, the auxiliary electric fuel pump is used in the event the engine-driven fuel pump fails.

2.18 STARTING THE ENGINE

1. After the engine starts, the throttle should be adjusted for proper RPM and the engine gauges, especially the oil pressure, checked.
2. When starting an airplane engine by hand, it is extremely important that a competent pilot be at the controls in the cockpit.

2.19 COLD WEATHER – ATTENTION

1. During cold weather conditions, special attention is required when performing a preflight inspection.
   a. The crankcase breather lines may become clogged with ice. When the crankcase vapor cools, it may condense in the breather lines and subsequently freeze, causing a clogged condition.

2.20 ELECTRICAL SYSTEM

1. Most aircraft have either a 14- or 28-volt direct current electrical system.
2. Engine-driven alternators (or generators) supply electrical current to the electrical system and maintain an electrical charge on the battery.
   a. The alternator voltage output should be slightly higher than the battery voltage to keep the battery charged.
      1) EXAMPLE: A 14-volt alternator system would keep a positive charge on a 12-volt battery.
3. The electrical system is turned on by the master switch, providing electrical current to all electrical systems except the ignition system.
   a. Lights, radios, and electric fuel pumps are examples of equipment that commonly use the electrical system.
4. An ammeter shows if the alternator is producing an adequate supply of electrical power and indicates whether the battery is receiving an electrical charge.
   a. A positive indication on the ammeter shows the rate of charge on the battery, while a negative indication means more current is being drawn from the battery than is being replaced.
5. Alternators provide more electrical power at lower engine RPM than generators do.
6. Electrical system failure (battery and alternator) usually results in avionics system failure.

QUESTIONS AND ANSWER EXPLANATIONS: All of the private pilot knowledge test questions chosen by the FAA for release as well as additional questions selected by Gleim relating to the material in the previous outlines are reproduced on the following pages. These questions have been organized into the same subunits as the outlines. To the immediate right of each question are the correct answer and answer explanation. You should cover these answers and answer explanations while responding to the questions. Refer to the general discussion in the Introduction on how to take the FAA knowledge test.

Remember that the questions from the FAA knowledge test bank have been reordered by topic and organized into a meaningful sequence. Also, the first line of the answer explanation gives the citation of the authoritative source for the answer.

QUESTIONS

2.1 Compass Turning Error

1. In the Northern Hemisphere, a magnetic compass will normally indicate a turn toward the north if

A. an aircraft is decelerated while on an east or west heading.

B. a left turn is entered from a west heading.

C. an aircraft is accelerated while on an east or west heading.

Answer (C) is correct. *(PHAK Chap 8)*

DISCUSSION: In the Northern Hemisphere, a magnetic compass will normally indicate a turn toward the north if an airplane is accelerated while on an east or west heading.

Answer (A) is incorrect. In the Northern Hemisphere, a magnetic compass will normally indicate a turn toward the north if an airplane is accelerated, not decelerated, while on an east or west heading. Answer (B) is incorrect. There is no compass turning error on turns from a west heading.

2. During flight, when are the indications of a magnetic compass accurate?

A. Only in straight-and-level unaccelerated flight.

B. As long as the airspeed is constant.

C. During turns if the bank does not exceed 18°.

Answer (A) is correct. *(PHAK Chap 8)*

DISCUSSION: During flight, the magnetic compass indications can be considered accurate only when in straight-and-level, unaccelerated flight. During acceleration, deceleration, or turns, the compass card will dip and cause false readings.

Answer (B) is incorrect. Even with a constant airspeed, the magnetic compass may not be accurate during a turn. Answer (C) is incorrect. Due to the compass card dip, the compass may not be accurate even during shallow turns.

3. Deviation in a magnetic compass is caused by the

A. presence of flaws in the permanent magnets of the compass.

B. difference in the location between true north and magnetic north.

C. magnetic fields within the aircraft distorting the lines of magnetic force.

Answer (C) is correct. *(PHAK Chap 8)*

DISCUSSION: Magnetic fields produced by metals and electrical accessories in the airplane disturb the compass needle and produce errors. These errors are referred to as compass deviation.

Answer (A) is incorrect. A properly functioning magnetic compass is still subject to deviation. Answer (B) is incorrect. The difference in the location between true and magnetic north refers to magnetic variation, not deviation.

4. Deviation error of the magnetic compass is caused by

A. northerly turning error.

B. certain metals and electrical systems within the aircraft.

C. the difference in location of true north and magnetic north.

Answer (B) is correct. *(PHAK Chap 8)*

DISCUSSION: The compass in an airplane will align with any magnetic field. Magnetic fields created by metals and the electrical system of the aircraft will hinder the ability of the compass to align with the Earth's magnetic field. This phenomenon is known as deviation. Since deviation error varies by heading, a compass correction card is fitted, providing the pilot with the deviation for a given heading.

Answer (A) is incorrect. Northerly turning error is a product of the pulling-vertical component of the Earth's magnetic field. Answer (C) is incorrect. Variation is the error associated with the difference in the location of true and magnetic north.

5. In the Northern Hemisphere, if an aircraft is accelerated or decelerated, the magnetic compass will normally indicate

A. a turn momentarily.

B. correctly when on a north or south heading.

C. a turn toward the south.

Answer (B) is correct. *(PHAK Chap 8)*

DISCUSSION: Acceleration and deceleration errors on magnetic compasses do not occur when on a north or south heading in the Northern Hemisphere. They occur on east and west headings.

Answer (A) is incorrect. Acceleration and deceleration errors occur only on easterly and westerly headings. Answer (C) is incorrect. A turn to the north is indicated upon acceleration and a turn to the south is indicated on deceleration when on east or west headings.

6. In the Northern Hemisphere, a magnetic compass will normally indicate initially a turn toward the west if

A. a left turn is entered from a north heading.

B. a right turn is entered from a north heading.

C. an aircraft is accelerated while on a north heading.

Answer (B) is correct. *(PHAK Chap 8)*

DISCUSSION: Due to the northerly turn error in the Northern Hemisphere, a magnetic compass will initially indicate a turn toward the west if a right (east) turn is entered from a north heading.

Answer (A) is incorrect. If a left (west) turn were made from a north heading, the compass would initially indicate a turn toward the east. Answer (C) is incorrect. Acceleration/deceleration error does not occur on a north heading.

7. In the Northern Hemisphere, the magnetic compass will normally indicate a turn toward the south when

A. a left turn is entered from an east heading.

B. a right turn is entered from a west heading.

C. the aircraft is decelerated while on a west heading.

Answer (C) is correct. *(PHAK Chap 8)*

DISCUSSION: In the Northern Hemisphere, a magnetic compass will normally indicate a turn toward the south if an airplane is decelerated while on an east or west heading.

Answer (A) is incorrect. Turning errors do not occur from an east heading. Answer (B) is incorrect. Turning errors do not occur from a west heading.

8. In the Northern Hemisphere, a magnetic compass will normally indicate initially a turn toward the east if

A. an aircraft is decelerated while on a south heading.

B. an aircraft is accelerated while on a north heading.

C. a left turn is entered from a north heading.

Answer (C) is correct. *(PHAK Chap 8)*

DISCUSSION: In the Northern Hemisphere, a magnetic compass normally initially indicates a turn toward the east if a left (west) turn is entered from a north heading.

Answer (A) is incorrect. Acceleration/deceleration errors do not occur while on a south heading, only on an east or west heading. Answer (B) is incorrect. Acceleration/deceleration errors do not occur while on a north heading, only on an east or west heading.

9. What should be the indication on the magnetic compass as you roll into a standard rate turn to the right from a south heading in the Northern Hemisphere?

A. The compass will initially indicate a turn to the left.

B. The compass will indicate a turn to the right, but at a faster rate than is actually occurring.

C. The compass will remain on south for a short time, then gradually catch up to the magnetic heading of the airplane.

Answer (B) is correct. *(PHAK Chap 8)*

DISCUSSION: When on a southerly heading in the Northern Hemisphere and you roll into a standard rate turn to the right, the magnetic compass indication precedes the turn, showing a greater amount of turn than is actually occurring.

Answer (A) is incorrect. The magnetic compass will initially indicate a turn to the left when you roll into a standard rate turn from a north, not south, heading in the Northern Hemisphere. Answer (C) is incorrect. The magnetic compass indication will precede the turn, not remain constant, when you roll into a standard rate turn from a south heading in the Northern Hemisphere.

2.2 Pitot-Static System

10. The pitot system provides impact pressure for which instrument?

A. Altimeter.

B. Vertical-speed indicator.

C. Airspeed indicator.

Answer (C) is correct. *(PHAK Chap 8)*

DISCUSSION: The pitot system provides impact pressure, or ram pressure, for only the airspeed indicator.

Answer (A) is incorrect. The altimeter operates off the static (not pitot) system. Answer (B) is incorrect. The vertical-speed indicator operates off the static (not pitot) system.

11. Which instrument will become inoperative if the pitot tube becomes clogged?

A. Altimeter.

B. Vertical speed indicator.

C. Airspeed indicator.

Answer (C) is correct. *(PHAK Chap 8)*

DISCUSSION: The pitot-static system is a source of pressure for the altimeter, vertical-speed indicator, and airspeed indicator. The pitot tube is connected directly to the airspeed indicator and provides impact pressure for it alone. Thus, if the pitot tube becomes clogged, only the airspeed indicator will become inoperative.

Answer (A) is incorrect. The altimeter operates off the static system and is not affected by a clogged pitot tube. Answer (B) is incorrect. The vertical speed indicator operates off the static system and is not affected by a clogged pitot tube.

12. If the pitot tube and outside static vents become clogged, which instruments would be affected?

A. The altimeter, airspeed indicator, and turn-and-slip indicator.

B. The altimeter, airspeed indicator, and vertical speed indicator.

C. The altimeter, attitude indicator, and turn-and-slip indicator.

Answer (B) is correct. *(PHAK Chap 8)*

DISCUSSION: The pitot-static system is a source of air pressure for the operation of the altimeter, airspeed indicator, and vertical speed indicator. Thus, if the pitot and outside static vents become clogged, all of these instruments will be affected.

Answer (A) is incorrect. The turn-and-slip indicator is a gyroscopic instrument and does not operate on the pitot-static system. Answer (C) is incorrect. The attitude indicator and turn-and-slip indicator are both gyroscopic instruments and do not operate on the pitot-static system.

13. Which instrument(s) will become inoperative if the static vents become clogged?

A. Airspeed indicator only.

B. Altimeter only.

C. Airspeed indicator, altimeter, and vertical speed indicator.

Answer (C) is correct. *(PHAK Chap 8)*

DISCUSSION: The pitot-static system is a source of air pressure for the operation of the airspeed indicator, altimeter, and vertical speed indicator. Thus, if the static vents become clogged, all three instruments will become inoperative.

Answer (A) is incorrect. Not only the airspeed indicator but also the altimeter and vertical speed indicator will become inoperative. Answer (B) is incorrect. Not only the altimeter but also the airspeed and vertical speed indicators will become inoperative.

2.3 Airspeed Indicator

14. (Refer to Figure 4 below.) What is the caution range of the airplane?

A. 0 to 60 kts.

B. 100 to 165 kts.

C. 165 to 208 kts.

Answer (C) is correct. *(PHAK Chap 8)*

DISCUSSION: The caution range is indicated by the yellow arc on the airspeed indicator. Operation within this range is safe only in smooth air. The airspeed indicator in Fig. 4 indicates the caution range from 165 to 208 kts.

Answer (A) is incorrect. The range of 0-60 kts. is less than stall speed. Answer (B) is incorrect. The range of 100-165 kts. is within the normal operating airspeed range, which extends from minimum flap extension speed to maximum structural cruising speed.

15. (Refer to Figure 4 below.) The maximum speed at which the airplane can be operated in smooth air is

A. 100 kts.

B. 165 kts.

C. 208 kts.

Answer (C) is correct. *(PHAK Chap 8)*

DISCUSSION: The maximum speed at which the airplane can be operated in smooth air is indicated by the red radial line. The airspeed indicator in Fig. 4 indicates the red line is at 208 kts.

Answer (A) is incorrect. The maximum flaps-extended speed is 100 kts., the upper limit of the white arc. Answer (B) is incorrect. The maximum structural cruising speed is 165 kts., the upper limit of the green arc.

16. (Refer to Figure 4 below.) What is the full flap operating range for the airplane?

A. 55 to 100 kts.

B. 55 to 208 kts.

C. 55 to 165 kts.

Answer (A) is correct. *(PHAK Chap 8)*

DISCUSSION: The full flap operating range is indicated by the white arc on the airspeed indicator. The airspeed indicator in Fig. 4 indicates the full flap operating range is from 55 to 100 kts.

Answer (B) is incorrect. The entire operating range of this airplane is 55 to 208 kts. Answer (C) is incorrect. The normal operating range for this airplane (green arc) is 55 to 165 kts.

Figure 4. – Airspeed Indicator.

17. (Refer to Figure 4 above.) Which marking identifies the never-exceed speed?

A. Upper limit of the green arc.

B. Upper limit of the white arc.

C. The red radial line.

Answer (C) is correct. *(PHAK Chap 8)*

DISCUSSION: The red radial line represents the never-exceed speed (V_{NE}). Operating an aircraft beyond V_{NE} may result in severe structural damage.

Answer (A) is incorrect. The upper limit of the green arc represents normal operating speed (V_{NO}). Answer (B) is incorrect. The upper limit of the white arc is the maximum flaps-extended speed (V_{FE}).

18. (Refer to Figure 4 on page 48.) Which color identifies the power-off stalling speed in a specified configuration?

A. Upper limit of the green arc.

B. Upper limit of the white arc.

C. Lower limit of the green arc.

Answer (C) is correct. *(PHAK Chap 8)*

DISCUSSION: The lower airspeed limit of the green arc indicates the power-off stalling speed in a specified configuration. "Specified configuration" refers to flaps up and landing gear retracted.

Answer (A) is incorrect. The upper limit of the green arc is the maximum structural cruising speed. Answer (B) is incorrect. The upper airspeed limit of the white arc is the maximum flaps-extended speed. Structural damage to the flaps could occur if the flaps are extended above this airspeed.

19. (Refer to Figure 4 on page 48.) What is the maximum flaps-extended speed?

A. 65 kts.

B. 100 kts.

C. 165 kts.

Answer (B) is correct. *(PHAK Chap 8)*

DISCUSSION: The maximum flaps-extended speed is indicated by the upper limit of the white arc. This is the highest airspeed at which a pilot should extend full flaps. At higher airspeeds, severe strain or structural failure could result. The upper limit of the white arc on the airspeed indicator shown in Fig. 4 indicates 100 kts.

Answer (A) is incorrect. The lower limit of the green arc is 65 kts., which is the power-off stall speed in a specified configuration. Answer (C) is incorrect. The upper limit of the green arc is 165 kts., which is the maximum structural cruising speed.

20. (Refer to Figure 4 on page 48.) Which color identifies the normal flap operating range?

A. The yellow arc.

B. The green arc.

C. The white arc.

Answer (C) is correct. *(PHAK Chap 8)*

DISCUSSION: The normal flap operating range is indicated by the white arc. The power-off stall speed with flaps extended is at the lower limit of the arc, and the maximum speed at which flaps can be extended without damage to them is the upper limit of the arc.

Answer (A) is incorrect. The yellow arc well exceeds the upper limit of the white arc, which is the maximum flap extended speed. Answer (B) is incorrect. The green arc represents the normal operating range.

21. (Refer to Figure 4 on page 48.) Which color identifies the power-off stalling speed with wing flaps and landing gear in the landing configuration?

A. Upper limit of the green arc.

B. Upper limit of the white arc.

C. Lower limit of the white arc.

Answer (C) is correct. *(PHAK Chap 8)*

DISCUSSION: The lower limit of the white arc indicates the power-off stalling speed with wing flaps and landing gear in the landing position.

Answer (A) is incorrect. The upper limit of the green arc is the maximum structural cruising speed. Answer (B) is incorrect. The upper limit of the white arc is the maximum flaps-extended speed.

22. (Refer to Figure 4 on page 48.) What is the maximum structural cruising speed?

A. 100 kts.

B. 165 kts.

C. 208 kts.

Answer (B) is correct. *(PHAK Chap 8)*

DISCUSSION: The maximum structural cruising speed is the maximum speed for normal operation and is indicated as the upper limit of the green arc on an airspeed indicator. The upper limit of the green arc on the airspeed indicator shown in Fig. 4 indicates 165 kts.

Answer (A) is incorrect. This is the upper limit of the white arc and is the maximum speed at which the flaps can be extended. Answer (C) is incorrect. This is the speed that should never be exceeded. Beyond this speed, structural damage to the airplane may occur.

23. What does the red line on an airspeed indicator represent?

A. Maneuvering speed.

B. Turbulent or rough-air speed.

C. Never-exceed speed.

Answer (C) is correct. *(PHAK Chap 8)*

DISCUSSION: The red line on an airspeed indicator indicates the maximum speed at which the airplane can be operated in smooth air, which should never be exceeded intentionally. This speed is known as the never-exceed speed.

Answer (A) is incorrect. Maneuvering speed is not indicated on the airspeed indicator. Answer (B) is incorrect. Turbulent or rough-air speed is not indicated on the airspeed indicator.

24. What is an important airspeed limitation that is not color coded on airspeed indicators?

A. Never-exceed speed.

B. Maximum structural cruising speed.

C. Maneuvering speed.

Answer (C) is correct. *(PHAK Chap 8)*

DISCUSSION: The maneuvering speed of an airplane is an important airspeed limitation not color-coded on the airspeed indicator. It is found in the airplane manual (Pilot's Operating Handbook) or placarded in the cockpit. Maneuvering speed is the maximum speed at which full deflection of the airplane controls can be made without incurring structural damage. Maneuvering speed or less should be held in turbulent air to prevent structural damage due to excessive loads.

Answer (A) is incorrect. The never-exceed speed is indicated on the airspeed indicator by a red radial line. Answer (B) is incorrect. The maximum structural cruising speed is indicated by the upper limit of the green arc on the airspeed indicator.

2.4 Altimeter

25. (Refer to Figure 3 on page 51.) Altimeter 1 indicates

A. 500 feet.

B. 1,500 feet.

C. 10,500 feet.

Answer (C) is correct. *(PHAK Chap 8)*

DISCUSSION: The altimeter has three needles. The short needle indicates 10,000-ft. intervals, the middle-length needle indicates 1,000-ft. intervals, and the long needle indicates 100-ft. intervals. In altimeter 1, the shortest needle is on 1, which indicates about 10,000 feet. The middle-length needle indicates half-way between zero and 1, which is 500 feet. This is confirmed by the longest needle on 5, indicating 500 ft., i.e., 10,500 feet.

Answer (A) is incorrect. If it were indicating just 500 ft., the short and medium needles would have to be on or near zero. Answer (B) is incorrect. If it were 1,500 ft., the shortest needle would be near zero and the middle needle would be between the 1 and the 2.

26. (Refer to Figure 3 on page 51.) Altimeter 3 indicates

A. 9,500 feet.

B. 10,950 feet.

C. 15,940 feet.

Answer (A) is correct. *(PHAK Chap 8)*

DISCUSSION: Altimeter 3 indicates 9,500 ft. because the shortest needle is near 1 (i.e., about 10,000 ft.), the middle needle is between 9 and the 0, indicating between 9,000 and 10,000 ft., and the long needle is on 5, indicating 500 feet.

Answer (B) is incorrect. For 10,950 ft., the middle needle would have to be near the 1 and the long needle would have to be between the 9 and 0. Answer (C) is incorrect. For 15,940 ft., the short needle would have to be between 1 and 2, the middle needle near the 6, and the large needle between the 9 and 0.

27. (Refer to Figure 3 on page 51.) Which altimeter(s) indicate(s) more than 10,000 feet?

A. 1, 2, and 3.

B. 1 and 2 only.

C. 1 only.

Answer (B) is correct. *(PHAK Chap 8)*

DISCUSSION: Altimeters 1 and 2 indicate over 10,000 ft. because 1 indicates 10,500 ft. and 2 indicates 14,500 feet. The short needle on 3 points just below 1, i.e., below 10,000 feet.

Answer (A) is incorrect. Altimeter 3 is indicating 9,500 ft., which is less than 10,000 feet. Answer (C) is incorrect. Altimeter 2 is indicating 14,500 ft., which is also more than 10,000 feet.

28. (Refer to Figure 3 on page 51.) Altimeter 2 indicates

A. 1,500 feet.

B. 4,500 feet.

C. 14,500 feet.

Answer (C) is correct. *(PHAK Chap 8)*

DISCUSSION: Altimeter 2 indicates 14,500 ft. because the shortest needle is between the 1 and the 2, indicating about 15,000 ft.; the middle needle is between 4 and 5, indicating 4,500 ft.; and the long needle is on 5, indicating 500 ft., i.e., 14,500 feet.

Answer (A) is incorrect. For 1,500 ft., the middle needle would have to be between 1 and 2, and the shortest needle between 0 and 1. Answer (B) is incorrect. For 4,500 ft., the shortest needle would have to be between 0 and 1.

Figure 3. – Altimeter.

29. (Refer to Figure 82 below.) Altimeter 3 indicates

A. 9,500 feet.

B. 10,500 feet.

C. 4,500 feet.

Answer (A) is correct. *(PHAK Chap 8)*

DISCUSSION: The long, thin needle is past the fourth tick mark and just before the 1 (<10,000); the short needle is between the 9 and 0 (representing more than 9 thousands of feet); and the long, wide needle is on the 5 (representing 5 hundreds of feet). Therefore, the altimeter indicates 9,500 feet.

Answer (B) is incorrect. The altimeter would indicate 10,500 feet if the long, thin needle was slightly past the 1 (>10,000); the short needle was between the 0 and 1 (representing less than 11 thousands of feet); and the long, wide needle was on the 5 (representing 5 hundreds of feet).

Answer (C) is incorrect. The altimeter would indicate 4,500 feet if the long, thin needle was between the second and third tick marks to the right of 0 (>2,000); the short needle was halfway between the 4 and 5 (representing 4.5 thousands of feet); and the long, wide needle was on 5 (representing 5 hundreds of feet).

Figure 82. – Altimeter.

30. (Refer to Figure 82 below.) Altimeter 1 indicates

A. 4,500 feet.

B. 1,500 feet.

C. 500 feet.

Answer (C) is correct. *(PHAK Chap 8)*

DISCUSSION: The long, thin needle is between 0 and 1 (<10,000); the short needle is between 0 and 1 (<1,000); and the long, wide needle is on 5 (500). Therefore, the altimeter indicates 500 feet.

Answer (A) is incorrect. The altimeter would indicate 4,500 feet if the long, thin needle was between the second and third tick marks to the right of 0 (appropriately representing <10,000); the short needle was halfway between the 4 and 5 (representing 4.5 thousands of feet); and the long, wide needle was on the 5 (representing 5 hundreds of feet). Answer (B) is incorrect. The altimeter would indicate 1,500 feet if the long, thin needle was just to the right of 0 prior to the second tick mark (appropriately representing <10,000 feet); the short needle was between the 0 and 2 (representing 1.5 thousands of feet); and the long, wide needle was on the 5 (indicating 5 hundreds of feet).

Figure 82. – Altimeter.

31. (Refer to Figure 82 above.) Altimeter 2 indicates

A. 500 feet.

B. 1,500 feet.

C. 4,500 feet.

Answer (B) is correct. *(PHAK Chap 8)*

DISCUSSION: The long, thin needle is to the right of 0, just before the first tick mark (<2,000); the short needle is halfway between the 1 and 2 (representing 1.5 thousands of feet); and the long, wide needle is on the 5 (representing 5 hundreds of feet). Therefore, the altimeter indicates 1,500 feet.

Answer (A) is incorrect. The altimeter would indicate 500 feet if the long, thin needle was just to the right of 0 prior to the first tick mark (<10,000); the short needle was between the 0 and 1, pointing between the second and third tick marks (representing less than 1 thousand feet); and the long, wide needle was on the 5 (representing 5 hundreds of feet). Answer (C) is incorrect. The altimeter would indicate 4,500 feet if the long, thin needle was between the second and third tick marks to the right of 0; the short needle was halfway between the 4 and 5 (representing 4.5 thousands of feet); and the wide needle was on 5 (representing 5 hundreds of feet).

32. (Refer to Figure 82 above.) Which altimeter(s) indicate(s) more than 9,000 feet?

A. 1, 2, and 3.

B. 1 and 2 only.

C. 3 only.

Answer (C) is correct. *(PHAK Chap 8)*

DISCUSSION: Altimeter 3 indicates 9,500 feet. Altimeters 1 and 2 both indicate under 9,000 feet.

Answer (A) is incorrect. Altimeters 1 and 2 indicate under 9,000 feet. Answer (B) is incorrect. Altimeter 1 indicates 500 feet, and altimeter 2 indicates 1,500 feet. Both are less than 9,000 feet.

2.5 Types of Altitude

33. What is absolute altitude?

A. The altitude read directly from the altimeter.

B. The vertical distance of the aircraft above the surface.

C. The height above the standard datum plane.

Answer (B) is correct. *(PHAK Chap 8)*

DISCUSSION: Absolute altitude is altitude above the surface, i.e., AGL.

Answer (A) is incorrect. It is indicated altitude. Answer (C) is incorrect. It is pressure altitude.

34. What is true altitude?

A. The vertical distance of the aircraft above sea level.

B. The vertical distance of the aircraft above the surface.

C. The height above the standard datum plane.

Answer (A) is correct. *(PHAK Chap 8)*

DISCUSSION: True altitude is the actual altitude above mean sea level, i.e., MSL.

Answer (B) is incorrect. It represents absolute altitude. Answer (C) is incorrect. It is pressure altitude.

35. What is density altitude?

A. The height above the standard datum plane.

B. The pressure altitude corrected for nonstandard temperature.

C. The altitude read directly from the altimeter.

Answer (B) is correct. *(PHAK Chap 8)*

DISCUSSION: Density altitude is the pressure altitude corrected for nonstandard temperature.

Answer (A) is incorrect. It defines pressure altitude. Answer (C) is incorrect. It is indicated altitude.

36. What is pressure altitude?

A. The indicated altitude corrected for position and installation error.

B. The altitude indicated when the barometric pressure scale is set to 29.92.

C. The indicated altitude corrected for nonstandard temperature and pressure.

Answer (B) is correct. *(PHAK Chap 8)*

DISCUSSION: Pressure altitude is the airplane's height above the standard datum plane of 29.92" Hg. If the altimeter is set to 29.92" Hg, the indicated altitude is the pressure altitude.

Answer (A) is incorrect. "Corrected for position and installation error" is used to define calibrated airspeed, not a type of altitude. Answer (C) is incorrect. It describes density altitude.

37. Altimeter setting is the value to which the barometric pressure scale of the altimeter is set so the altimeter indicates

A. calibrated altitude at field elevation.

B. absolute altitude at field elevation.

C. true altitude at field elevation.

Answer (C) is correct. *(PHAK Chap 8)*

DISCUSSION: Altimeter setting is the value to which the scale of the pressure altimeter is set so that the altimeter indicates true altitude at field elevation.

Answer (A) is incorrect. "Calibrated" refers to airspeed and airspeed indicators, not altitude and altimeters. Answer (B) is incorrect. Absolute altitude is the altitude above the surface, not above MSL.

38. Under what condition is indicated altitude the same as true altitude?

A. If the altimeter has no mechanical error.

B. When at sea level under standard conditions.

C. When at 18,000 feet MSL with the altimeter set at 29.92.

Answer (B) is correct. *(PHAK Chap 8)*

DISCUSSION: Indicated altitude (what you read on your altimeter) approximates the true altitude (distance above mean sea level) when standard conditions exist and your altimeter is properly calibrated.

Answer (A) is incorrect. The indicated altitude must be adjusted for nonstandard temperature for true altitude. Answer (C) is incorrect. The altimeter reads pressure altitude when set to 29.92, and that is only true altitude under standard conditions.

39. Under what condition is pressure altitude and density altitude the same value?

A. At sea level, when the temperature is 0°F.

B. When the altimeter has no installation error.

C. At standard temperature.

Answer (C) is correct. *(PHAK Chap 8)*

DISCUSSION: Pressure altitude and density altitude are the same when temperature is standard.

Answer (A) is incorrect. Standard temperature at sea level is 59°F, not 0°F. Answer (B) is incorrect. Installation error refers to pitot tubes and airspeed, not altimeter and altitude.

40. Under which condition will pressure altitude be equal to true altitude?

A. When the atmospheric pressure is 29.92" Hg.

B. When standard atmospheric conditions exist.

C. When indicated altitude is equal to the pressure altitude.

Answer (B) is correct. *(AvW Chap 3)*

DISCUSSION: Pressure altitude equals true altitude when standard atmospheric conditions (29.92" Hg and 15°C at sea level) exist.

Answer (A) is incorrect. Standard temperature must also exist. Answer (C) is incorrect. Indicated altitude does not necessarily relate to true or pressure altitudes.

2.6 Setting the Altimeter

41. If it is necessary to set the altimeter from 29.15 to 29.85, what change occurs?

A. 70-foot increase in indicated altitude.

B. 70-foot increase in density altitude.

C. 700-foot increase in indicated altitude.

Answer (C) is correct. *(PHAK Chap 8)*

DISCUSSION: When increasing the altimeter setting from 29.15 to 29.85, the indicated altitude increases by 700 feet. The altimeter-indicated altitude moves in the same direction as the altimeter setting and changes about 1,000 ft. for every change of 1" Hg in the altimeter setting.

Answer (A) is incorrect. A change in pressure of .7" Hg is equal to 700 ft., not 70 ft., of altitude. Answer (B) is incorrect. Density altitude is not affected by changing the altimeter setting.

42. If a pilot changes the altimeter setting from 30.11 to 29.96, what is the approximate change in indication?

A. Altimeter will indicate .15" Hg higher.

B. Altimeter will indicate 150 feet higher.

C. Altimeter will indicate 150 feet lower.

Answer (C) is correct. *(PHAK Chap 8)*

DISCUSSION: Atmospheric pressure decreases approximately 1" of Hg (mercury) for every 1,000 ft. of altitude gained. As an altimeter setting is changed, the change in altitude indication changes the same way (i.e., approximately 1,000 ft. for every 1" change in altimeter setting) and in the same direction (i.e., lowering the altimeter setting lowers the altitude reading). Thus, changing from 30.11 to 29.96 is a decrease of .15 in., or 150 ft. (.15 × 1,000 ft.) lower.

Answer (A) is incorrect. The altimeter indicates feet, not inches, of mercury. Answer (B) is incorrect. The altimeter will show 150 ft. lower, not higher.

2.7 Altimeter Errors

43. If a flight is made from an area of low pressure into an area of high pressure without the altimeter setting being adjusted, the altimeter will indicate

A. the actual altitude above sea level.

B. higher than the actual altitude above sea level.

C. lower than the actual altitude above sea level.

Answer (C) is correct. *(AvW Chap 3)*

DISCUSSION: When an altimeter setting is at a lower value than the correct setting, the altimeter is indicating less than it should and thus would be showing lower than the actual altitude above sea level.

Answer (A) is incorrect. The altimeter will show actual altitude only when it is set correctly. Answer (B) is incorrect. The increase in pressure causes the altimeter to read lower, not higher, than actual altitude.

44. If a flight is made from an area of high pressure into an area of lower pressure without the altimeter setting being adjusted, the altimeter will indicate

A. lower than the actual altitude above sea level.

B. higher than the actual altitude above sea level.

C. the actual altitude above sea level.

Answer (B) is correct. *(AvW Chap 3)*

DISCUSSION: When flying from higher pressure to lower pressure without adjusting your altimeter, the altimeter will indicate a higher than actual altitude. As you adjust an altimeter barometric setting lower, the altimeter indicates lower.

Answer (A) is incorrect. The decrease in pressure causes the altimeter to read higher, not lower, than actual altitude. Answer (C) is incorrect. The altimeter will show actual altitude only when it is set correctly.

45. Which condition would cause the altimeter to indicate a lower altitude than true altitude?

A. Air temperature lower than standard.

B. Atmospheric pressure lower than standard.

C. Air temperature warmer than standard.

Answer (C) is correct. *(AvW Chap 3)*

DISCUSSION: In air that is warmer than standard temperature, the airplane will be higher than the altimeter indicates. Said another way, the altimeter will indicate a lower altitude than actually flown.

Answer (A) is incorrect. When flying in air that is colder than standard temperature, the airplane will be lower than the altimeter indicates ("high to low, look out below"). Answer (B) is incorrect. The altimeter setting corrects the altimeter for nonstandard pressure.

46. Under what condition will true altitude be lower than indicated altitude?

A. In colder than standard air temperature.

B. In warmer than standard air temperature.

C. When density altitude is higher than indicated altitude.

Answer (A) is correct. *(AvW Chap 3)*

DISCUSSION: The airplane will be lower than the altimeter indicates when flying in air that is colder than standard temperature. Remember that altimeter readings are adjusted for changes in barometric pressure but not for changes in temperature. When one flies from warmer to cold air and keeps a constant indicated altitude at a constant altimeter setting, the plane has actually descended.

Answer (B) is incorrect. The altimeter indicates lower than actual altitude in warmer than standard temperature. Answer (C) is incorrect. A higher density altitude is usually the result of warmer, not colder, than standard temperature.

47. How do variations in temperature affect the altimeter?

A. Pressure levels are raised on warm days and the indicated altitude is lower than true altitude.

B. Higher temperatures expand the pressure levels and the indicated altitude is higher than true altitude.

C. Lower temperatures lower the pressure levels and the indicated altitude is lower than true altitude.

Answer (A) is correct. *(PHAK Chap 8)*

DISCUSSION: On warm days, the atmospheric pressure levels are higher than on cold days. Your altimeter will indicate a lower than true altitude. Remember, "low to high, clear the sky."

Answer (B) is incorrect. Expanding (or raising) the pressure levels will cause indicated altitude to be lower (not higher) than true altitude. Answer (C) is incorrect. Lower pressure levels will cause indicated altitude to be higher (not lower) than true altitude.

2.8 Gyroscopic Instruments

48. (Refer to Figure 5 below.) A turn coordinator provides an indication of the

A. movement of the aircraft about the yaw and roll axes.

B. angle of bank up to but not exceeding 30°.

C. attitude of the aircraft with reference to the longitudinal axis.

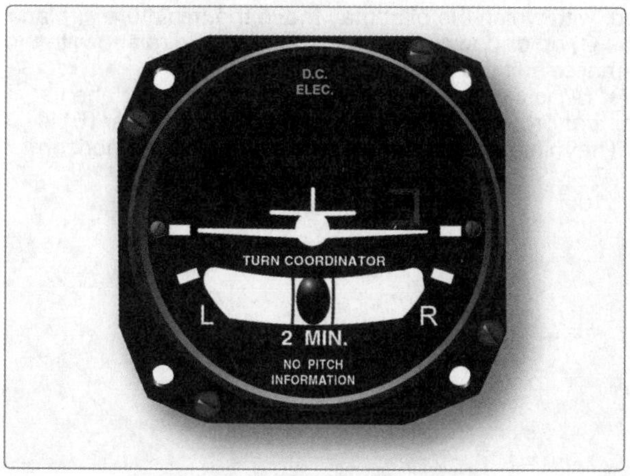

Figure 5. – Turn Coordinator.

Answer (A) is correct. *(PHAK Chap 8)*

DISCUSSION: There really are no yaw and roll axes; i.e., an airplane yaws about its vertical axis and rolls about its longitudinal axis. However, this is the best answer since the turn coordinator does indicate the roll and yaw movement of the airplane. The movement of the miniature airplane is proportional to the roll rate of the airplane. When the roll rate is reduced to zero (i.e., when the bank is held constant), the instrument provides an indication of the rate of turn.

Answer (B) is incorrect. The turn coordinator shows the rate of turn rather than angle of bank. Answer (C) is incorrect. The turn coordinator does not show the attitude of the airplane (as does the attitude indicator); it shows the rate of the roll and turn.

49. (Refer to Figure 6 below.) To receive accurate indications during flight from a heading indicator, the instrument must be

A. set prior to flight on a known heading.

B. calibrated on a compass rose at regular intervals.

C. periodically realigned with the magnetic compass as the gyro precesses.

Answer (C) is correct. *(PHAK Chap 8)*

DISCUSSION: Due to gyroscopic precession, directional gyros must be periodically realigned with a magnetic compass. Friction is the major cause of its drifting from the correct heading.

Answer (A) is incorrect. The instrument must be periodically reset, not just set initially. Answer (B) is incorrect. There is no calibration of the heading indicator; rather, it is reset.

50. (Refer to Figure 6 below.) After practicing unusual attitudes, you notice the heading indicator is off by 110°. The heading indicator can be reset by

A. pushing the cage knob.

B. pulling the cage knob.

C. leaving it alone, because it will be the exact same as the compass heading.

Answer (A) is correct. *(PHAK Chap 8)*

DISCUSSION: The heading indicator referred to in Fig. 6 has indications on the knob in the lower left corner of the instrument. It has to be pushed in to cage the instrument.

Answer (B) is incorrect. Normal operation for this particular instrument is with the knob in the out position. Answer (C) is incorrect. After doing aggressive maneuvers in excess of 55° in most light aircraft, the heading indicator will have to be reset and adjusted to the correct compass heading.

Figure 6. – Heading Indicator.

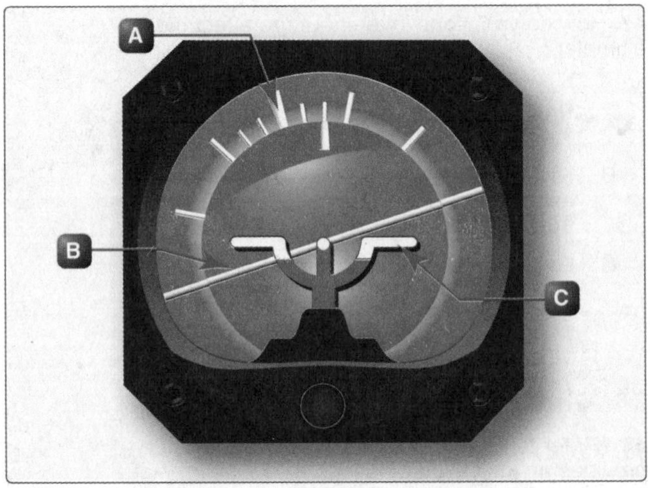

Figure 7. – Attitude Indicator.

51. (Refer to Figure 7 above.) The proper adjustment to make on the attitude indicator during level flight is to align the

A. horizon bar to the level-flight indication.

B. horizon bar to the miniature airplane.

C. miniature airplane to the horizon bar.

Answer (C) is correct. *(PHAK Chap 8)*

DISCUSSION: The horizon bar (marked as B) on Fig. 7 represents the true horizon. This bar is fixed to the gyro and remains on a horizontal plane as the airplane is pitched or banked about its lateral or longitudinal axis, indicating the attitude of the airplane relative to the true horizon. An adjustment knob is provided, with which the pilot may move the miniature airplane (marked as C) up or down to align the miniature airplane with the horizontal bar to suit the pilot's line of vision.

Answer (A) is incorrect. Aligning the miniature airplane to the horizon bar provides a level-flight indication. Answer (B) is incorrect. The miniature airplane is adjustable, not the horizon bar.

52. (Refer to Figure 7 on page 56.) How should a pilot determine the direction of bank from an attitude indicator such as the one illustrated?

A. By the direction of deflection of the banking scale (A).

B. By the direction of deflection of the horizon bar (B).

C. By the relationship of the miniature airplane (C) to the deflected horizon bar (B).

Answer (C) is correct. *(PHAK Chap 8)*

DISCUSSION: The direction of bank on the attitude indicator (AI) is indicated by the relationship of the miniature airplane to the deflecting horizon bar. The miniature airplane's relative position to the horizon indicates its attitude: nose high, nose low, left bank, right bank.

Answer (A) is incorrect. The banking scale (marked as A) may move in the opposite direction, which is confusing. Answer (B) is incorrect. The horizon bar (marked as B) moves in the direction opposite the turn.

2.9 Glass Cockpits

53. What is a benefit of flying with a glass cockpit?

A. There is no longer a need to carry paper charts in flight.

B. Situational awareness is increased.

C. Terrain avoidance is guaranteed.

Answer (B) is correct. *(AAH Chap 5)*

DISCUSSION: Glass cockpits are designed to decrease pilot workload, enhance situational awareness, and increase the safety margin.

Answer (A) is incorrect. Pilots should still have current information and backup electronic navigation to enhance safety. Answer (C) is incorrect. Terrain avoidance is not guaranteed solely by means of relying on advanced avionics.

54. What steps must be taken when flying with glass cockpits to ensure safe flight?

A. Use the moving map for primary means of navigation, use the MFD to check engine systems and weather, back up with supplementary forms of information.

B. Regularly scan each item on the PFD, confirm on the MFD.

C. Regularly scan both inside and outside, use all appropriate checklists, and cross-check with other forms of information.

Answer (C) is correct. *(AAH Chap 5)*

DISCUSSION: A regular scan, both visually outside and inside on backup gauges, should be combined with other means of navigation and checklists to ensure safe flight.

Answer (A) is incorrect. The moving map should not be the sole means of navigation. Moving maps should be used as a supplement, not as a replacement. Answer (B) is incorrect. While you should scan both the PFD and MFD, more is needed to ensure a safe flight, such as visually scanning outside and confirming indications from other sources.

55. An aircraft which is equipped with an Electronic Flight Display (EFD) can

A. compensate for an airman's lack of skill or knowledge.

B. offer new capabilities and simplify the basic flying task.

C. improve flight awareness by allowing the pilot to simply watch for alerts.

Answer (B) is correct. *(PHAK Chap 2)*

DISCUSSION: EFDs offer new capabilities, such as enhanced situational awareness, and simplify basic flying tasks, such as traditional cross-country flight planning and fuel management.

Answer (A) is incorrect. It is important to remember that EFDs do not replace basic flight knowledge and skills. An EFD is a tool for improving flight safety. Risk increases when the pilot believes gadgets will compensate for lack of skill and knowledge. It is especially important to recognize there are limits to what the electronic systems in any light GA aircraft can do. Being PIC requires sound ADM, which sometimes means saying "no" to a flight. Answer (C) is incorrect. An advanced avionics aircraft offers increased safety with enhanced situational awareness. Tools like the moving map, topography, terrain awareness, traffic, and weather datalink displays give the pilot unprecedented information for enhanced situational awareness, but, without a well-planned information management strategy, these tools also make it easy for an unwary pilot to slide into the complacent role of passenger in command.

2.10 Engine Temperature

56. An abnormally high engine oil temperature indication may be caused by

A. the oil level being too low.

B. operating with a too high viscosity oil.

C. operating with an excessively rich mixture.

Answer (A) is correct. *(PHAK Chap 7)*

DISCUSSION: Operating with an excessively low oil level prevents the oil from being cooled adequately; i.e., an inadequate supply of oil will not be able to transfer engine heat to the engine's oil cooler (similar to a car engine's water radiator). Insufficient oil may also damage an engine from excessive friction within the cylinders and on other metal-to-metal contact parts.

Answer (B) is incorrect. The higher the viscosity, the better the lubricating and cooling capability of the oil. Answer (C) is incorrect. A rich fuel/air mixture usually decreases (not increases) engine temperature.

57. Excessively high engine temperatures will

A. cause damage to heat-conducting hoses and warping of the cylinder cooling fins.

B. cause loss of power, excessive oil consumption, and possible permanent internal engine damage.

C. not appreciably affect an aircraft engine.

Answer (B) is correct. *(PHAK Chap 7)*

DISCUSSION: Excessively high engine temperatures will result in loss of power, excessive oil consumption, and possible permanent internal engine damage.

Answer (A) is incorrect. Excessively high engine temperatures may cause internal engine damage, but external damage is less likely. Answer (C) is incorrect. An excessively high engine temperature can cause a loss of performance and possibly internal engine damage.

58. Excessively high engine temperatures, either in the air or on the ground, will

A. increase fuel consumption and may increase power due to the increased heat.

B. result in damage to heat-conducting hoses and warping of cylinder cooling fans.

C. cause loss of power, excessive oil consumption, and possible permanent internal engine damage.

Answer (C) is correct. *(PHAK Chap 7)*

DISCUSSION: Operating the engine at excessively high temperatures will cause loss of power and excessive oil consumption, and can permanently damage engines.

Answer (A) is incorrect. Overheating can cause excessive oil, not fuel, consumption and a loss, not increase, of power. Answer (B) is incorrect. Hoses are not used to transfer heat in airplane engines. Also, it is extremely unlikely one could overheat an engine to an extent to warp the cylinder cooling fans.

59. For internal cooling, air cooled engines are especially dependent on

A. a properly functioning thermostat.

B. air flowing over the exhaust manifold.

C. the circulation of lubricating oil.

Answer (C) is correct. *(PHAK Chap 7)*

DISCUSSION: An engine accomplishes much of its cooling by the flow of oil through the lubrication system. The lubrication system aids in cooling by reducing friction and absorbing heat from internal engine parts. Many airplane engines use an oil cooler, a small radiator device that will cool the oil before it is recirculated through the engine.

Answer (A) is incorrect. Airplanes with air-cooled engines do not use thermostats. Answer (B) is incorrect. Air flowing over the exhaust manifold would have little effect on internal engine parts cooling.

60. If the engine oil temperature and cylinder head temperature gauges have exceeded their normal operating range, the pilot may have been operating with

A. the mixture set too rich.

B. higher-than-normal oil pressure.

C. too much power and with the mixture set too lean.

Answer (C) is correct. *(PHAK Chap 7)*

DISCUSSION: If the engine oil temperature and cylinder head temperature gauges exceed their normal operating range, it is possible that the power setting is too high and the fuel/air mixture is set excessively lean. These conditions may cause engine overheating.

Answer (A) is incorrect. A rich mixture setting normally causes lower (not higher-than-normal) engine temperature. Answer (B) is incorrect. A higher-than-normal oil pressure does not normally increase the engine temperature.

61. What action can a pilot take to aid in cooling an engine that is overheating during a climb?

A. Reduce rate of climb and increase airspeed.
B. Reduce climb speed and increase RPM.
C. Increase climb speed and increase RPM.

Answer (A) is correct. *(PHAK Chap 7)*
DISCUSSION: If an airplane is overheating during a climb, the engine temperature will be decreased if the airspeed is increased. Airspeed will increase if the rate of climb is reduced.
Answer (B) is incorrect. Reducing airspeed hinders cooling and increasing RPM will further increase engine temperature. Answer (C) is incorrect. Increasing RPM will increase (not decrease) engine temperature.

62. What is one procedure to aid in cooling an engine that is overheating?

A. Enrich the fuel mixture.
B. Increase the RPM.
C. Reduce the airspeed.

Answer (A) is correct. *(PHAK Chap 7)*
DISCUSSION: Enriched fuel mixtures have a cooling effect on an engine.
Answer (B) is incorrect. Increasing the RPM increases the engine's internal heat. Answer (C) is incorrect. Reducing the airspeed decreases the airflow needed for cooling, thus increasing the engine's temperature.

2.11 Constant-Speed Propeller

63. How is engine operation controlled on an engine equipped with a constant-speed propeller?

A. The throttle controls power output as registered on the manifold pressure gauge and the propeller control regulates engine RPM.
B. The throttle controls power output as registered on the manifold pressure gauge and the propeller control regulates a constant blade angle.
C. The throttle controls engine RPM as registered on the tachometer and the mixture control regulates the power output.

Answer (A) is correct. *(PHAK Chap 7)*
DISCUSSION: Airplanes equipped with controllable-pitch propellers have both a throttle control and a propeller control. The throttle controls the power output of the engine, which is registered on the manifold pressure gauge. This is a simple barometer that measures the air pressure in the engine intake manifold in inches of mercury. The propeller control regulates the engine RPM, which is registered on a tachometer.
Answer (B) is incorrect. The propeller blade angle changes to control the RPM. Answer (C) is incorrect. The throttle controls power output (not RPM), and the mixture controls the fuel to air ratio (not power output).

64. A precaution for the operation of an engine equipped with a constant-speed propeller is to

A. avoid high RPM settings with high manifold pressure.
B. avoid high manifold pressure settings with low RPM.
C. always use a rich mixture with high RPM settings.

Answer (B) is correct. *(PHAK Chap 7)*
DISCUSSION: For any given RPM, there is a manifold pressure that should not be exceeded. Manifold pressure is excessive for a given RPM when the cylinder design pressure is exceeded, placing undue stress on them. If repeated or extended, the stress would weaken the cylinder components and eventually cause engine failure.
Answer (A) is incorrect. It is the relationship of high manifold pressure with low RPM that is dangerous (not high RPM with high manifold pressure). Answer (C) is incorrect. The mixture control is related to engine cylinder temperature, not to RPM.

65. What is an advantage of a constant-speed propeller?

A. Permits the pilot to select and maintain a desired cruising speed.
B. Permits the pilot to select the blade angle for the most efficient performance.
C. Provides a smoother operation with stable RPM and eliminates vibrations.

Answer (B) is correct. *(PHAK Chap 7)*
DISCUSSION: A controllable-pitch propeller (constant-speed) permits the pilot to select the blade angle that will result in the most efficient performance given the flight conditions. A low blade angle and a decreased pitch reduces the propeller drag and allows more engine RPM (power) for takeoffs. After airspeed is attained during cruising flight, the propeller blade is changed to a higher angle to increase pitch. The blade takes a larger bite of air at a lower RPM and consequently increases the efficiency of the flight. This process is similar to shifting gears in an automobile from low to high gear.
Answer (A) is incorrect. A desired cruising speed is possible with any airplane. Answer (C) is incorrect. Vibrations are eliminated through propeller balancing, not a constant-speed propeller.

2.12 Engine Ignition Systems

66. One purpose of the dual ignition system on an aircraft engine is to provide for

A. improved engine performance.

B. uniform heat distribution.

C. balanced cylinder head pressure.

Answer (A) is correct. *(PHAK Chap 7)*

DISCUSSION: Most airplane engines are equipped with dual ignition systems, which have two magnetos to supply the electrical current to two spark plugs for each combustion chamber. The main advantages of the dual system are increased safety and improved burning and combustion of the mixture, which results in improved performance.

Answer (B) is incorrect. The heat distribution within a cylinder is usually not uniform, even with dual ignition. Answer (C) is incorrect. Balanced cylinder-head pressure is a nonsense phrase.

67. If the ignition switch ground wire becomes disconnected, the magneto

A. will not operate because the battery is disconnected from the circuit.

B. may continue to fire.

C. will not operate.

Answer (B) is correct. *(PHAK Chap 7)*

DISCUSSION: Loose or broken wires in the ignition system can cause problems. For example, if the ignition switch is OFF, the magneto may continue to fire if the ignition switch ground wire is disconnected. If this occurs, the only way to stop the engine is to move the mixture lever to the idle cut-off position, then have the system checked by a qualified aviation maintenance technician.

Answer (A) is incorrect. The magneto may continue to fire if the ignition switch ground wire is disconnected. Answer (C) is incorrect. The magneto may continue to fire if the ignition switch ground wire is disconnected.

2.13 Carburetor Icing

68. With regard to carburetor ice, float-type carburetor systems in comparison to fuel injection systems are generally considered to be

A. more susceptible to icing.

B. equally susceptible to icing.

C. less susceptible to icing.

Answer (A) is correct. *(PHAK Chap 7)*

DISCUSSION: Float-type carburetor systems are generally more susceptible to icing than fuel-injected engines due to the cooling effect resulting from fuel vaporization and a decrease in air pressure at the venturi in a carburetor. When there is high humidity and the temperature is between 20°F and 70°F, there is a high potential for carburetor icing, particularly at low power settings.

Answer (B) is incorrect. Fuel injection systems are less susceptible to internal icing than carburetor systems, although air intake icing is equally possible in both systems. Answer (C) is incorrect. Carburetor icing may occur in high humidity with no visible moisture, causing it to be more susceptible to carburetor icing.

69. Which condition is most favorable to the development of carburetor icing?

A. Any temperature below freezing and a relative humidity of less than 50 percent.

B. Temperature between 32°F and 50°F and low humidity.

C. Temperature between 20°F and 70°F and high humidity.

Answer (C) is correct. *(PHAK Chap 7)*

DISCUSSION: The most favorable condition for carburetor icing is when the temperature is between 20°F and 70°F. Due to the sudden cooling that takes place in the carburetor, icing can occur even with temperatures as high as 100°F and humidity as low as 50%. During low or closed throttle settings, an engine is particularly susceptible to carburetor icing.

Answer (A) is incorrect. The development of carburetor icing is possible at temperatures up to 100°F and high humidity. It is most favorable between 20°F and 70°F. Answer (B) is incorrect. Low humidity will generally preclude icing, and the correct temperature range is 20°F to 70°F for the most favorable conditions.

70. The possibility of carburetor icing exists even when the ambient air temperature is as

A. high as 70°F and the relative humidity is high.

B. high as 95°F and there is visible moisture.

C. low as 0°F and the relative humidity is high.

Answer (A) is correct. *(PHAK Chap 7)*

DISCUSSION: The most favorable condition for carburetor icing is when the temperature is between 20°F and 70°F. Due to the sudden cooling that takes place in the carburetor, icing can occur even with temperatures as high as 100°F and humidity as low as 50%. During low or closed throttle settings, an engine is particularly susceptible to carburetor icing.

Answer (B) is incorrect. Icing is usually not a problem above 70°F. Temperature and relative humidity, not visible moisture, are the variables that affect the possibility of carburetor icing. Answer (C) is incorrect. Icing is usually not a problem below 20°F.

71. If an aircraft is equipped with a fixed-pitch propeller and a float-type carburetor, the first indication of carburetor ice would most likely be

A. increase of RPM.

B. engine roughness.

C. decrease of RPM.

Answer (C) is correct. *(PHAK Chap 7)*

DISCUSSION: In an airplane equipped with a fixed-pitch propeller and float-type carburetor, the first indication of carburetor ice would be a decrease in RPM.

Answer (A) is incorrect. A carburetor icing condition causes a drop in RPM, not an increase. Answer (B) is incorrect. A decrease in engine RPM should be evident before engine roughness became noticeable.

72. If an aircraft is equipped with a fixed-pitch propeller and a float-type carburetor, the first indication of carburetor ice would most likely be

A. a drop in oil temperature and cylinder head temperature.

B. engine roughness.

C. loss of RPM.

Answer (C) is correct. *(PHAK Chap 7)*

DISCUSSION: In an airplane equipped with a fixed-pitch propeller and float-type carburetor, the first indication of carburetor ice would be a loss in RPM.

Answer (A) is incorrect. A carburetor icing condition does not cause a drop in oil temperature or cylinder head temperature. Answer (B) is incorrect. A loss in engine RPM should be evident before engine roughness became noticeable.

73. The operating principle of float-type carburetors is based on the

A. automatic metering of air at the venturi as the aircraft gains altitude.

B. difference in air pressure at the venturi throat and the air inlet.

C. increase in air velocity in the throat of a venturi causing an increase in air pressure.

Answer (B) is correct. *(PHAK Chap 7)*

DISCUSSION: In a float-type carburetor, air flows into the carburetor and through a venturi tube (a narrow throat in the carburetor). As the air flows more rapidly through the venturi, a low pressure area is created that draws the fuel from a main fuel jet located at the throat of the carburetor and into the airstream, where it is mixed with flowing air. It is called a float-type carburetor in that a ready supply of gasoline is kept in the float bowl by a float, which activates a fuel inlet valve.

Answer (A) is incorrect. The metering at the venturi is fuel, not air, and this is done manually with a mixture control. Answer (C) is incorrect. The increase in air velocity in the throat of a venturi causes a decrease (not increase) in air pressure (which draws the gas from the main fuel jet into the low-pressure air).

74. The presence of carburetor ice in an aircraft equipped with a fixed-pitch propeller can be verified by applying carburetor heat and noting

A. an increase in RPM and then a gradual decrease in RPM.

B. a decrease in RPM and then a constant RPM indication.

C. a decrease in RPM and then a gradual increase in RPM.

Answer (C) is correct. *(PHAK Chap 7)*

DISCUSSION: The presence of carburetor ice in an airplane equipped with a fixed-pitch propeller can be verified by applying carburetor heat and noting a decrease in RPM and then a gradual increase. The decrease in RPM as heat is applied is caused by less dense hot air entering the engine and reducing power output. Also, if ice is present, melting water entering the engine may also cause a loss in performance. As the carburetor ice melts, however, the RPM gradually increases until it stabilizes when the ice is completely removed.

Answer (A) is incorrect. The warm air decreases engine power output and RPM. Ice melting further decreases RPM and then RPM increases slightly after the ice melts. Answer (B) is incorrect. After the ice melts, the RPM will increase gradually (not remain constant).

2.14 Carburetor Heat

75. Generally speaking, the use of carburetor heat tends to

A. decrease engine performance.

B. increase engine performance.

C. have no effect on engine performance.

Answer (A) is correct. *(PHAK Chap 7)*

DISCUSSION: Use of carburetor heat tends to decrease the engine performance and also to increase the operating temperature. Warmer air is less dense, and engine performance decreases with density. Thus, carburetor heat should not be used when full power is required (as during takeoff) or during normal engine operation except as a check for the presence or removal of carburetor ice.

Answer (B) is incorrect. Carburetor heat decreases (not increases) engine performance. Answer (C) is incorrect. Carburetor heat does have an effect on performance.

76. Applying carburetor heat will

A. result in more air going through the carburetor.

B. enrich the fuel/air mixture.

C. not affect the fuel/air mixture.

Answer (B) is correct. *(PHAK Chap 7)*

DISCUSSION: Applying carburetor heat will enrich the fuel/air mixture. Warm air is less dense than cold air, hence the application of heat increases the fuel-to-air ratio.

Answer (A) is incorrect. Applying carburetor heat will not result in more air going into the carburetor. Answer (C) is incorrect. Applying carburetor heat will enrich the fuel/air mixture.

77. What change occurs in the fuel/air mixture when carburetor heat is applied?

A. A decrease in RPM results from the lean mixture.

B. The fuel/air mixture becomes richer.

C. The fuel/air mixture becomes leaner.

Answer (B) is correct. *(PHAK Chap 7)*

DISCUSSION: When carburetor heat is applied, hot air is introduced into the carburetor. Hot air is less dense than cold air; therefore, the decrease in air density with a constant amount of fuel makes a richer mixture.

Answer (A) is incorrect. A drop in RPM as carburetor heat is applied is due to the less dense air and melting ice, not a lean mixture. Answer (C) is incorrect. When carburetor heat is applied, the fuel/air mixture becomes richer, not leaner.

2.15 Fuel/Air Mixture

78. During the run-up at a high-elevation airport, a pilot notes a slight engine roughness that is not affected by the magneto check but grows worse during the carburetor heat check. Under these circumstances, what would be the most logical initial action?

A. Check the results obtained with a leaner setting of the mixture.

B. Taxi back to the flight line for a maintenance check.

C. Reduce manifold pressure to control detonation.

Answer (A) is correct. *(PHAK Chap 7)*

DISCUSSION: If, during a run-up at a high-elevation airport, you notice a slight roughness that is not affected by a magneto check but grows worse during the carburetor heat check, you should check the results obtained with a leaner setting of the mixture control. At a high-elevation field, the air is less dense and the application of carburetor heat increases the already too rich fuel-to-air mixture. By leaning the mixture during the run-up, the condition should improve.

Answer (B) is incorrect. This mixture condition is normal at a high-elevation field. However, if after leaning the mixture a satisfactory run-up cannot be obtained, the pilot should taxi back to the flight line for a maintenance check. Answer (C) is incorrect. The question describes a symptom of an excessively rich mixture, not detonation.

79. The basic purpose of adjusting the fuel/air mixture at altitude is to

A. decrease the amount of fuel in the mixture in order to compensate for increased air density.

B. decrease the fuel flow in order to compensate for decreased air density.

C. increase the amount of fuel in the mixture to compensate for the decrease in pressure and density of the air.

Answer (B) is correct. *(PHAK Chap 7)*

DISCUSSION: At higher altitudes, the air density is decreased. Thus, the mixture control must be adjusted to decrease the fuel flow in order to maintain a constant fuel/air ratio.

Answer (A) is incorrect. Air density decreases (not increases) at altitude. Answer (C) is incorrect. The mixture is decreased (not increased) in order to compensate for decreased air density.

80. While cruising at 9,500 feet MSL, the fuel/air mixture is properly adjusted. What will occur if a descent to 4,500 feet MSL is made without readjusting the mixture?

A. The fuel/air mixture may become excessively lean.

B. There will be more fuel in the cylinders than is needed for normal combustion, and the excess fuel will absorb heat and cool the engine.

C. The excessively rich mixture will create higher cylinder head temperatures and may cause detonation.

Answer (A) is correct. *(PHAK Chap 7)*

DISCUSSION: At 9,500 ft., the mixture control is adjusted to provide the proper fuel/air ratio. As the airplane descends, the density of the air increases and there will be less fuel to air in the ratio, causing a leaner running engine. This excessively lean mixture will create higher cylinder temperature and may cause detonation.

Answer (B) is incorrect. As air becomes more dense during the descent, there will be less (not more) fuel in the cylinders than is needed. Answer (C) is incorrect. The mixture will be excessively lean (not rich). Also, a rich mixture would create lower (not higher) cylinder head temperatures.

81. Fuel/air ratio is the ratio between the

A. volume of fuel and volume of air entering the cylinder.

B. weight of fuel and weight of air entering the cylinder.

C. weight of fuel and weight of air entering the carburetor.

Answer (B) is correct. *(PHAK Chap 7)*

DISCUSSION: The fuel/air ratio, i.e., mixture, is the ratio between the weight of fuel and the weight of air entering the cylinder.

Answer (A) is incorrect. As altitude increases, the amount of air in a fixed volume (i.e., air density) decreases. Thus, the ratio is between weights, not volume. Answer (C) is incorrect. The carburetor is where the fuel/air ratio is established prior to entering the cylinders.

2.16 Abnormal Combustion

82. Detonation occurs in a reciprocating aircraft engine when

A. the spark plugs are fouled or shorted out or the wiring is defective.

B. hot spots in the combustion chamber ignite the fuel/air mixture in advance of normal ignition.

C. the unburned charge in the cylinders explodes instead of burning normally.

Answer (C) is correct. *(PHAK Chap 7)*

DISCUSSION: Detonation occurs when the fuel/air mixture in the cylinders explodes instead of burning normally. This more rapid force slams the piston down instead of pushing it.

Answer (A) is incorrect. If the spark plugs are "fouled" or the wiring is defective, the cylinders would not be firing; i.e., there would be no combustion. Answer (B) is incorrect. Hot spots in the combustion chamber igniting the fuel/air mixture in advance of normal ignition is pre-ignition.

83. Detonation may occur at high-power settings when

A. the fuel mixture ignites instantaneously instead of burning progressively and evenly.

B. an excessively rich fuel mixture causes an explosive gain in power.

C. the fuel mixture is ignited too early by hot carbon deposits in the cylinder.

Answer (A) is correct. *(PHAK Chap 7)*

DISCUSSION: Detonation occurs when the fuel/air mixture in the cylinders explodes instead of burning progressively and evenly. This more rapid force slams the piston down instead of pushing it.

Answer (B) is incorrect. An excessively rich fuel mixture lowers the temperature inside the cylinder, thus inhibiting the complete combustion of the fuel and producing an appreciable lack of power. Answer (C) is incorrect. Hot carbon deposits in the combustion chamber igniting the fuel/air mixture too early, or in advance of normal ignition, is termed pre-ignition.

84. If a pilot suspects that the engine (with a fixed-pitch propeller) is detonating during climb-out after takeoff, the initial corrective action to take would be to

A. lean the mixture.

B. lower the nose slightly to increase airspeed.

C. apply carburetor heat.

Answer (B) is correct. *(PHAK Chap 7)*

DISCUSSION: If you suspect engine detonation during climb-out after takeoff, you would normally decrease the pitch to increase airspeed (more cooling) and decrease the load on the engine. Detonation is usually caused by a poor grade of fuel or an excessive engine temperature.

Answer (A) is incorrect. Leaning the mixture will increase engine temperature and increase detonation. Answer (C) is incorrect. While carburetor heat will increase the fuel-to-air ratio, hot air flowing into the carburetor will not lower engine temperature. Also, the less dense air will decrease the engine power for climb-out.

85. If the grade of fuel used in an aircraft engine is lower than specified for the engine, it will most likely cause

A. a mixture of fuel and air that is not uniform in all cylinders.

B. lower cylinder head temperatures.

C. detonation.

Answer (C) is correct. *(PHAK Chap 7)*

DISCUSSION: If the grade of fuel used in an airplane engine is lower than specified for the engine, it will probably cause detonation. Lower grades of fuel ignite at lower temperatures. A higher temperature engine (which should use a higher grade of fuel) may cause lower grade fuel to explode (detonate) rather than burn evenly.

Answer (A) is incorrect. The carburetor meters the lower-grade fuel quantity in the same manner as a higher grade of fuel. Answer (B) is incorrect. A lower grade of fuel will cause higher (not lower) cylinder head temperatures.

86. The uncontrolled firing of the fuel/air charge in advance of normal spark ignition is known as

A. combustion.

B. pre-ignition.

C. detonation.

Answer (B) is correct. *(PHAK Chap 7)*

DISCUSSION: Pre-ignition is the ignition of the fuel prior to normal ignition or ignition before the electrical arcing occurs at the spark plug. Pre-ignition may be caused by excessively hot exhaust valves, carbon particles, or spark plugs and electrodes heated to an incandescent, or glowing, state. These hot spots are usually caused by high temperatures encountered during detonation. A significant difference between pre-ignition and detonation is that, if the conditions for detonation exist in one cylinder, they usually exist in all cylinders, but pre-ignition often takes place in only one or two cylinders.

Answer (A) is incorrect. Combustion is the normal process that takes place inside the cylinders. Answer (C) is incorrect. Detonation is an uncontrolled, explosive ignition of the fuel/air mixture within the cylinder's combustion chamber caused by a combination of excessively high temperature and pressure in the cylinder.

2.17 Aviation Fuel Practices

87. What type fuel can be substituted for an aircraft if the recommended octane is not available?

A. The next higher octane aviation gas.

B. The next lower octane aviation gas.

C. Unleaded automotive gas of the same octane rating.

Answer (A) is correct. *(PHAK Chap 7)*

DISCUSSION: If the recommended octane is not available for an airplane, the next higher octane aviation gas should be used.

Answer (B) is incorrect. If the grade of fuel used in an airplane engine is lower than specified for the engine, it will probably cause detonation. Answer (C) is incorrect. Except for very special situations, only aviation gas should be used.

88. Filling the fuel tanks after the last flight of the day is considered a good operating procedure because this will

A. force any existing water to the top of the tank away from the fuel lines to the engine.

B. prevent expansion of the fuel by eliminating airspace in the tanks.

C. prevent moisture condensation by eliminating airspace in the tanks.

Answer (C) is correct. *(PHAK Chap 7)*

DISCUSSION: Filling the fuel tanks after the last flight of the day is considered good operating practice because it prevents moisture condensation by eliminating airspace in the tanks. Humid air may result in condensation at night when the airplane cools.

Answer (A) is incorrect. Water is heavier than fuel and will always settle to the bottom of the tank. Answer (B) is incorrect. Filling the fuel tank will not prevent expansion of the fuel.

89. To properly purge water from the fuel system of an aircraft equipped with fuel tank sumps and a fuel strainer quick drain, it is necessary to drain fuel from the

A. fuel strainer drain.

B. lowest point in the fuel system.

C. fuel strainer drain and the fuel tank sumps.

Answer (C) is correct. *(PHAK Chap 7)*

DISCUSSION: One should purge water from both the fuel strainer drain and all the fuel tank sumps on an airplane. This is the purpose of such drains. They are placed at low areas of the fuel system and should be drained prior to each flight.

Answer (A) is incorrect. All drains, not just the fuel strainer, should be checked for water. Answer (B) is incorrect. All fuel drains and sumps, not just the lowest point in the system, should be checked for water.

90. On aircraft equipped with fuel pumps, when is the auxiliary electric driven pump used?

A. All the time to aid the engine-driven fuel pump.

B. In the event engine-driven fuel pump fails.

C. Constantly except in starting the engine.

Answer (B) is correct. *(PHAK Chap 7)*

DISCUSSION: In a fuel pump system, two fuel pumps are used on most airplanes. The main fuel pump is engine-driven, and an auxiliary electric-driven pump is provided for use in the event the engine pump fails.

Answer (A) is incorrect. An auxiliary fuel pump is a backup system to the engine-driven fuel pump; it is not intended to aid the engine-driven fuel pump. Answer (C) is incorrect. The auxiliary electric fuel pump is normally used in starting the engine.

91. Which would most likely cause the cylinder head temperature and engine oil temperature gauges to exceed their normal operating ranges?

A. Using fuel that has a lower-than-specified fuel rating.

B. Using fuel that has a higher-than-specified fuel rating.

C. Operating with higher-than-normal oil pressure.

Answer (A) is correct. *(PHAK Chap 7)*

DISCUSSION: Use of fuel with lower-than-specified fuel ratings, e.g., 80 octane instead of 100, can cause many problems, including higher operating temperatures, detonation, etc.

Answer (B) is incorrect. Higher octane fuels usually result in lower cylinder head temperatures. Answer (C) is incorrect. Higher-than-normal oil pressure provides better lubrication and cooling (although too high an oil pressure can break parts, lines, etc.).

2.18 Starting the Engine

92. What should be the first action after starting an aircraft engine?

A. Adjust for proper RPM and check for desired indications on the engine gauges.

B. Place the magneto or ignition switch momentarily in the OFF position to check for proper grounding.

C. Test each brake and the parking brake.

Answer (A) is correct. *(PHAK Chap 7)*

DISCUSSION: After the engine starts, the engine speed should be adjusted to the proper RPM. Then the engine gauges should be reviewed, with the oil pressure being the most important gauge initially.

Answer (B) is incorrect. This check is normally done just prior to engine shutdown. Answer (C) is incorrect. This check is done during taxi.

93. Should it become necessary to handprop an airplane engine, it is extremely important that a competent pilot

A. call "contact" before touching the propeller.

B. be at the controls in the cockpit.

C. be in the cockpit and call out all commands.

Answer (B) is correct. *(PHAK Chap 7)*

DISCUSSION: Because of the hazards involved in handstarting airplane engines, every precaution should be exercised. It is extremely important that a competent pilot be at the controls in the cockpit. Also, the person turning the propeller should be thoroughly familiar with the technique.

Answer (A) is incorrect. The person handpropping the airplane yells "gas off, switch off, throttle closed, brakes set" before touching the propeller initially. Contact means the magnetos are on, i.e., "hot." This is not done until starting is attempted. Answer (C) is incorrect. The person handpropping the airplane (not the person in the cockpit) calls out the commands.

2.19 Cold Weather – Attention

94. During preflight in cold weather, crankcase breather lines should receive special attention because they are susceptible to being clogged by

A. congealed oil from the crankcase.

B. moisture from the outside air which has frozen.

C. ice from crankcase vapors that have condensed and subsequently frozen.

Answer (C) is correct. *(AC 91-13C)*

DISCUSSION: Frozen crankcase breather lines prevent oil from circulating adequately in the engine and may even result in broken oil lines or oil being pumped out of the crankcase. Accordingly, you must always visually inspect to make sure that the crankcase breather lines are free of ice. The ice may have formed as a result of the crankcase vapors freezing in the lines after the engine has been turned off.

Answer (A) is incorrect. Oil in the crankcase virtually never gets into the breather lines but rather remains in the bottom of the crankcase. Answer (B) is incorrect. Very cold outside air has a low moisture content.

2.20 Electrical System

95. An electrical system failure (battery and alternator) occurs during flight. In this situation, you would

A. experience avionics equipment failure.

B. probably experience failure of the engine ignition system, fuel gauges, aircraft lighting system, and avionics equipment.

C. probably experience engine failure due to the loss of the engine-driven fuel pump and also experience failure of the radio equipment, lights, and all instruments that require alternating current.

Answer (A) is correct. *(PHAK Chap 7)*

DISCUSSION: A battery and alternator failure during flight inevitably results in avionics equipment failure due to the lack of electricity.

Answer (B) is incorrect. The engine ignition systems are based on magnetos, which generate their own electricity to operate the spark plugs. Answer (C) is incorrect. Engine-driven fuel pumps are mechanical and not dependent upon electricity.

96. A positive indication on an ammeter

A. indicates the aircraft's battery will soon lose its charge.

B. shows the rate of charge on the battery.

C. means more current is being drawn from the battery than is being replaced.

Answer (B) is correct. *(PHAK Chap 7)*

DISCUSSION: A positive indication on the ammeter shows the rate of charge on the battery.

Answer (A) is incorrect. A battery will not lose its charge while being charged, which is what a positive indication on an ammeter indicates. Answer (C) is incorrect. A negative indication on an ammeter means more current is being drawn from the battery than is being replaced.

97. To keep a battery charged, the alternator voltage output should be

A. less than the battery voltage.

B. equal to the battery voltage.

C. higher than the battery voltage.

Answer (C) is correct. *(PHAK Chap 7)*

DISCUSSION: The alternator voltage output should be slightly higher than the battery voltage to keep the battery charged. For example, a 14-volt alternator system would keep a positive charge on a 12-volt battery.

Answer (A) is incorrect. If the alternator voltage output were less than the battery voltage, the battery would quickly lose its charge. Answer (B) is incorrect. If there were no difference in voltage, the battery would not have or keep a full charge.

98. Which of the following is a true statement concerning electrical systems?

A. The master switch provides current to the electrical system.

B. The airspeed indicator is driven by the electrical system.

C. Lights and radios use the electrical system for power.

Answer (C) is correct. *(PHAK Chap 7)*

DISCUSSION: Lights, radios, and electrical fuel pumps are examples of equipment that commonly use the electrical system.

Answer (A) is incorrect. The master switch permits electrical current to flow from its source independent of the ignition system. It does not generate or provide electricity in the same way an alternator, generator, or battery does. Answer (B) is incorrect. The airspeed indicator operates on the pitot-static system, not the electrical system.

END OF STUDY UNIT

STUDY UNIT THREE
AIRPORTS, AIR TRAFFIC CONTROL, AND AIRSPACE

(13 pages of outline)

This study unit contains outlines of major concepts tested; sample test questions and answers regarding airports, Air Traffic Control, and airspace; and an explanation of each answer. The table of contents above lists each subunit within this study unit, the number of questions pertaining to that particular subunit, and the pages on which the outlines and questions begin, respectively.

Recall that the **sole purpose** of this book is to expedite your passing of the FAA pilot knowledge test for the private pilot certificate. Accordingly, all extraneous material (i.e., topics or regulations not directly tested on the FAA pilot knowledge test) is omitted, even though much more knowledge is necessary to fly safely. This additional material is presented in *Pilot Handbook* and *Private Pilot Flight Maneuvers and Practical Test Prep*, available from Gleim Publications, Inc. Order online at www.GleimAviation.com.

3.1 RUNWAY MARKINGS

1. The number at the start of each runway indicates its magnetic alignment divided by 10°; e.g., Runway 26 indicates 260° magnetic; Runway 9 indicates 090° magnetic.
    a. Runways are numbered by the direction in which they point.
2. A displaced threshold is a threshold (marked as a broad solid line across the runway) that is not at the beginning of the full strength runway pavement. The remainder of the runway, following the displaced threshold, is the landing portion of the runway (shown in Figure A below).
    a. The paved area before the displaced threshold (marked by arrows) is available for taxiing, the landing rollout, and takeoff of aircraft.

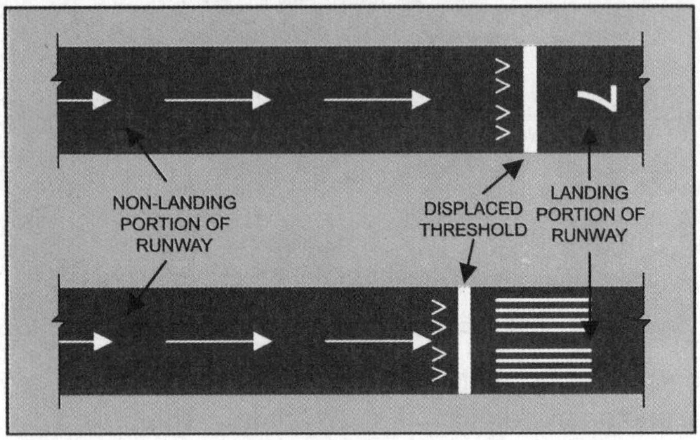

Figure A

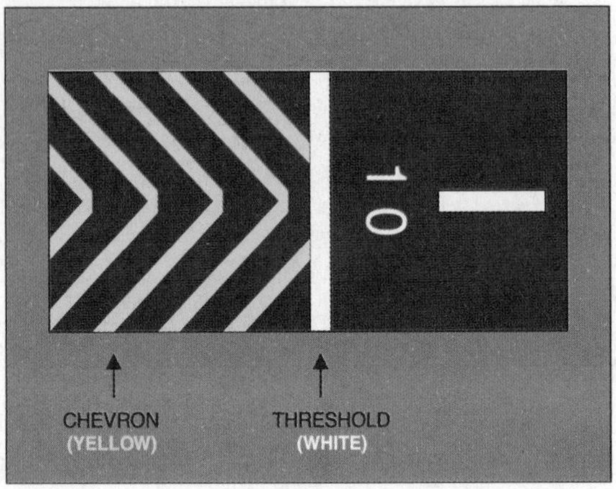

Figure B

3. Chevrons (illustrated in Figure B above) mark any surface or area extending beyond the usable runway that appears usable but that, due to the nature of its structure, is unusable runway.
    a. This area is not available for any use, not even taxiing.
4. Closed runways are marked by an “X” on each runway end that is closed.
5. Runway holding position markings indicate where an aircraft is supposed to stop. They consist of four yellow lines, two continuous and two dashed, extending across the width of the taxiway or runway. The solid (continuous) lines are always on the side where the aircraft is to hold.

3.2 TAXIWAY AND DESTINATION SIGNS

1. Destination signs have black characters on a yellow background with an arrow showing the direction of the taxiing route to the destination listed. Outbound destinations commonly show directions to the take-off runways.
    a. Examples of destination signs are shown in Figure 65 on the next page.
        1) They are signs I, J, and K.
        2) In that figure, Sign K designates the direction of taxiway bravo.
2. Taxiway location signs identify the taxiway on which an aircraft is currently located.
    a. Location signs feature a black background with yellow lettering and do not have directional arrows.
3. Taxiway directional signs indicate the designation and direction of a taxiway.
    a. When turning from one taxiway to another, a taxiway directional sign indicates the designation and direction of a taxiway leading out of the intersection.

b. Taxiway directional signs feature a yellow background with black lettering and directional arrows.

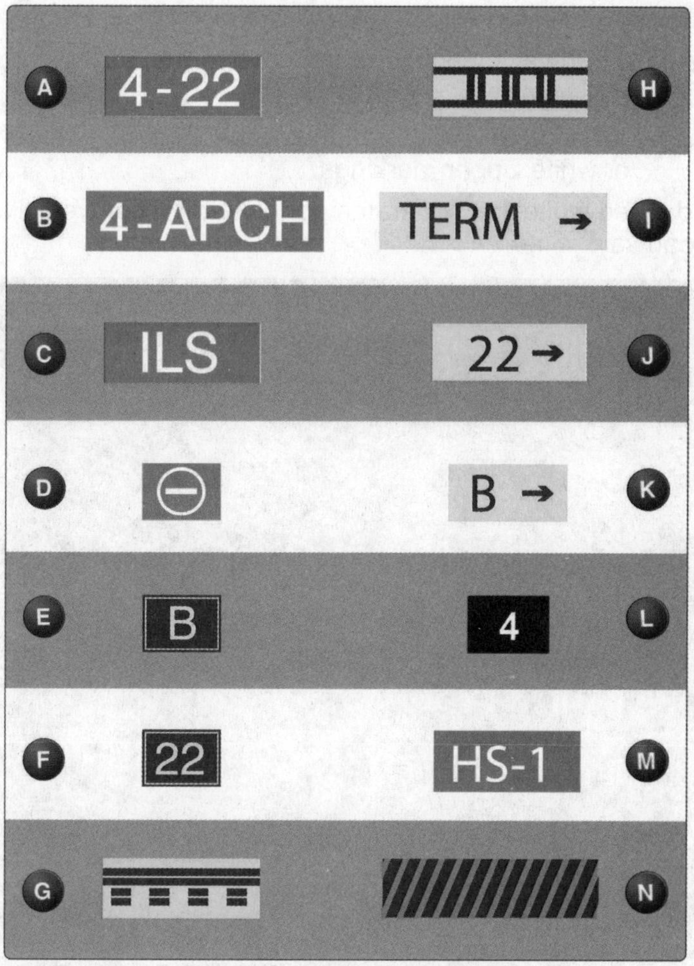

Figure 65. – U.S. Airport Signs.

4. When approaching taxiway holding lines from the side with continuous lines, the pilot should not cross the lines without an ATC clearance.
   a. Taxiway holding lines are painted across the width of the taxiway and are yellow.
5. A runway holding position sign is a mandatory instruction sign with white characters on a red background. It is located at the holding position on taxiways that intersect a runway or on runways that intersect other runways.
6. Each of the letters below corresponds to the type of sign or marking in Figure 65.

   A. Runway Holding Position Sign
   B. Holding Position Sign for a Runway Approach Area
   C. Holding Position Sign for ILS Critical Area
   D. Sign Prohibiting Aircraft Entry into an Area
   E. Taxiway Location Sign
   F. Runway Location Sign
   G. Runway Boundary Sign
   H. ILS Critical Area Boundary Sign
   I. Direction Sign for Terminal
   J. Direction Sign for Common Taxiing Route to Runway
   K. Direction Sign for Runway Exit
   L. Runway Distance Remaining Sign
   M. Hold Short-1
   N. Taxiway Ending Sign

7. Vehicle Roadway Markings
   a. Vehicle roadway markings define pathways for vehicles to cross areas of the airport used by aircraft.
      1) Vehicle roadway markings exist in two forms, as indicated by letter C in Figure 64 below.
         a) The edge of vehicle roadway markings may be defined by a solid white line or white zipper markings.
      2) A dashed white line separates opposite-direction vehicle traffic inside the roadway.

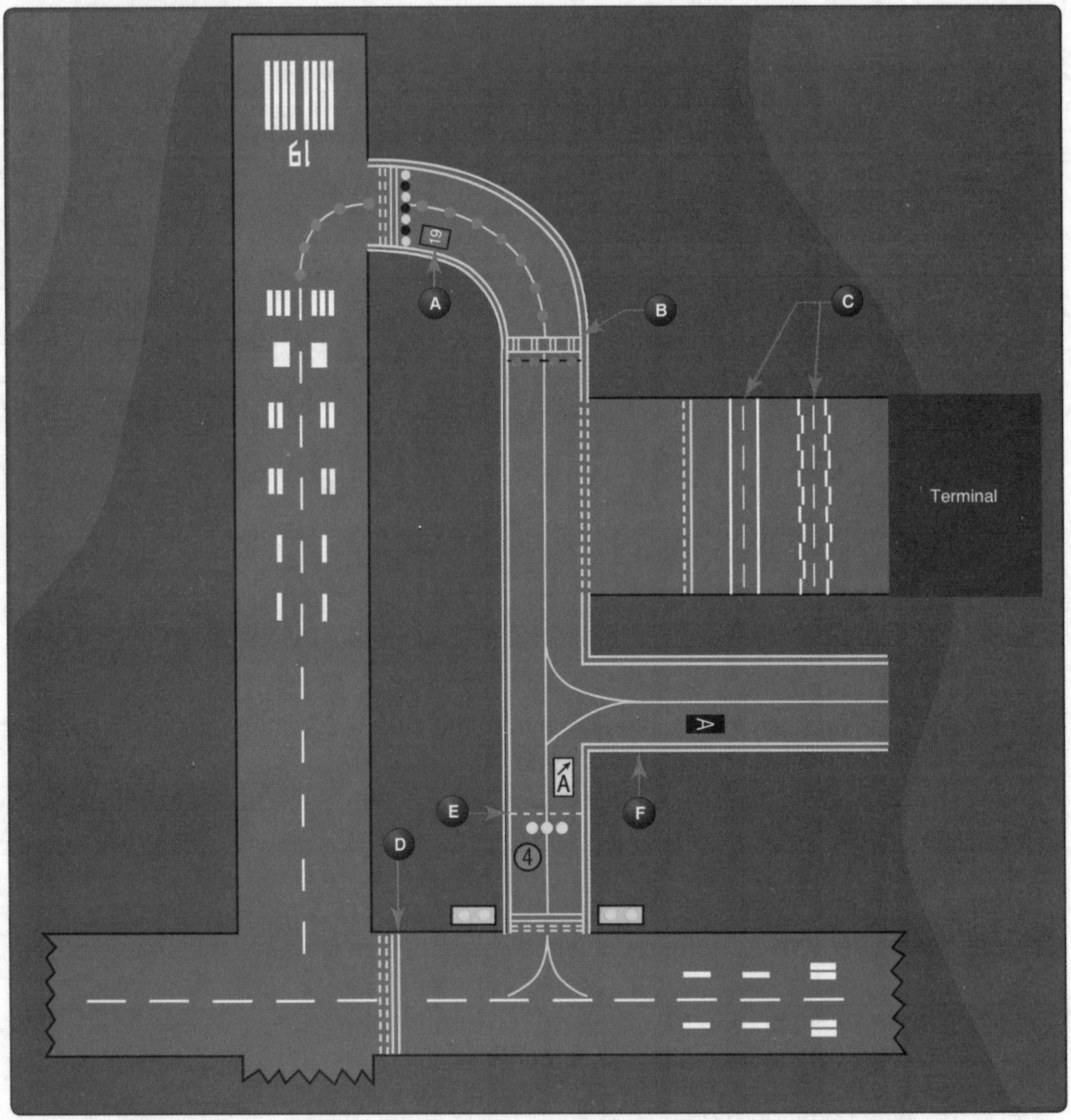

Figure 64. – Airport Markings.

8. Each of the letters below corresponds to the type of airport markings in Figure 64.
   A. Holding Position Markings at Beginning of Takeoff Runway 19
   B. ILS Critical Area Boundary Marking
   C. Roadway Edge Stripes
   D. Runway Holding Position Marking
   E. Taxiway Holding Position Marker
   F. Taxiway Boundary

9. Yellow Demarcation Bar

   a. The yellow demarcation bar is a 3-ft.-wide, painted yellow bar that separates a displaced threshold from a blast pad, stopway, or taxiway that precedes the runway.

Yellow Demarcation Bar

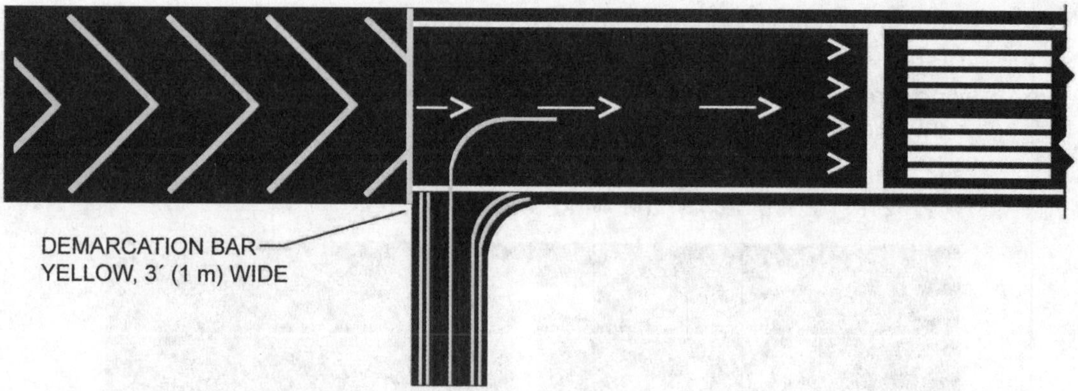

3.3 BEACONS AND TAXIWAY LIGHTS

1. Operation of the green and white rotating beacon at an airport located in Class D airspace during the day indicates that the weather is not VFR; i.e.,

   a. The visibility is less than 3 SM or
   b. The ceiling is less than 1,000 feet.

2. A lighted heliport may be identified by a green, yellow, and white rotating beacon.
3. Military airports are indicated by beacons with two white flashes between each green flash.
4. Airport taxiways are lighted with blue edge lights.
5. To operate pilot-controlled lighting (PCL), you should first click the mic seven times, which turns everything on. For high-intensity lights, leave it alone. For medium-intensity lights, click it five times. For low-intensity lights, click it three times.

3.4 AIRPORT TRAFFIC PATTERNS

1. If you are approaching an airport without an operating control tower,
   a. Left turns are standard, unless otherwise specified.
   b. You must comply with any FAA traffic pattern for that airport when departing.
2. The recommended entry to an airport traffic pattern is 45° to the downwind leg, at the approximate midpoint, at traffic pattern altitude (1,000 ft. AGL).
3. Remember, you land

   a. In the same direction as the tip of the tetrahedron is pointing,
   b. As if you were flying out of the large (open) end of the wind cone, or
   c. Toward the cross-bar end of a wind "T" (visualize the "T" as an airplane with no nose, with the top of the "T" being the wings).
4. If there is no segmented circle installed at the airport, traffic pattern indicators may be installed on or near the end of the runway.

5. The segmented circle system provides traffic pattern information at airports without operating control towers. It consists of the
   a. Segmented circle – located in a position affording maximum visibility to pilots in the air and on the ground, and providing a centralized point for the other elements of the system
   b. Landing strip indicators – showing the alignment of landing runways (legs sticking out of the segmented circle)
   c. Wind direction indicator – a wind cone, wind sock, or wind tee installed near the runways to indicate wind direction
      1) The large end of the wind cone/wind sock points into the wind as does the large end (cross bar) of the wind tee.

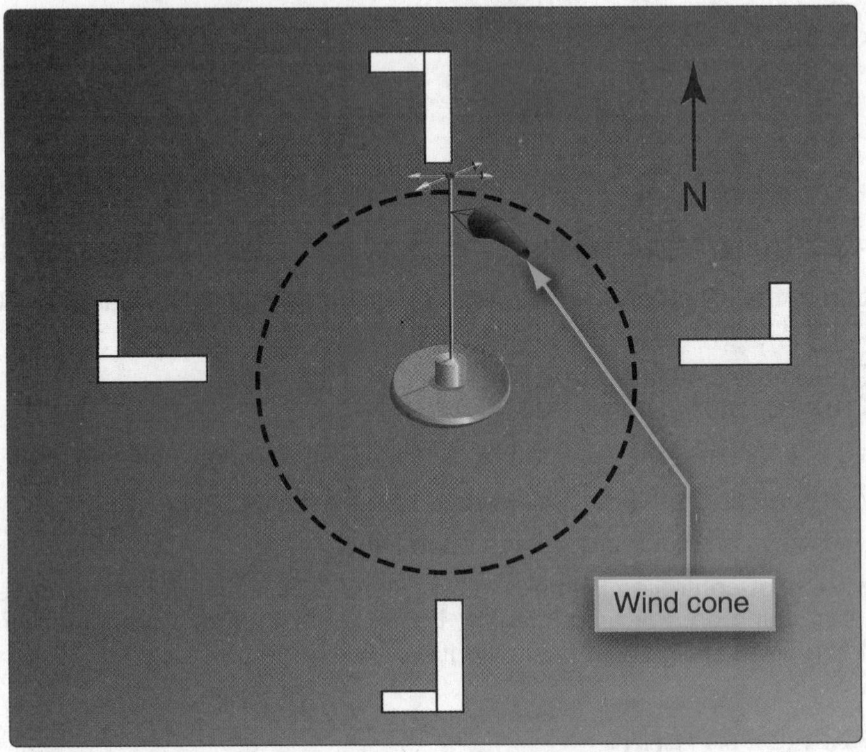

Figure 49. – Airport Diagram.

   d. Landing direction indicator – a tetrahedron on a swivel installed when conditions at the airport warrant its use. It is used to indicate the direction of takeoffs and landings. It should be located at the center of a segmented circle and may be lighted for night operations.
      1) The small end points toward the direction in which a takeoff or landing should be made; i.e., the small end points into the wind.
   e. Traffic pattern indicators – indicators at right angles to the landing strip indicator showing the direction of turn from base to final and upwind to crosswind
      1) In Figure 49 above, Runways 22 and 36 use left traffic, while Runways 4 and 18 use right traffic.
      2) The "X" indicates that Runways 4 and 22 are closed.
      3) The area behind the displaced thresholds of Runways 18 and 36 (marked by arrows) can be used for taxiing and takeoff but not for landing.

3.5 VISUAL APPROACH SLOPE INDICATORS (VASI)

1. Visual approach slope indicators (VASI) are a system of lights to provide visual descent information during an approach to landing.
2. The standard VASI consists of a two-barred tier of lights. You are
   a. Below the glide path if both light bars are red; i.e., "red means dead."
   b. On the glide path if the far (on top visually) lights are red and the near (on bottom visually) lights are white.
   c. Above the glide path if both light bars are white.
3. Remember, red over white (i.e., R before W alphabetically) is the desired sequence.
   a. White over red is impossible.
4. VASI only projects a glide path. It has no bearing on runway alignment.
5. On a precision approach path indicator (PAPI),
   a. Low is four red lights (less than 2.5°).
   b. Slightly low is one white and three reds (2.8°).
   c. On glide path is two whites and two reds (3.0°).
   d. Slightly high is three whites and one red (3.2°).
   e. High is four whites (more than 3.5°).
6. On a pulsating approach slope indicator (a VASI with flashing/pulsating signals),
   a. Low is a pulsating red.
   b. On glide path is a steady white or alternating red/white (depending on model).
   c. High is a pulsating white.
7. Each pilot of an airplane approaching to land on a runway served by a visual approach slope indicator shall maintain an altitude at or above the glide slope until a lower altitude is necessary for landing (FAR 91.129).

3.6 WAKE TURBULENCE

1. Wingtip vortices (wake turbulence) are only created when airplanes develop lift.
2. The greatest vortex strength occurs when the generating aircraft is heavy, clean, and slow.
3. The circulation of the vortex is outward, upward, and around each wingtip.
4. Wingtip vortex turbulence tends to sink into the flight path of airplanes operating below the airplane generating the turbulence.
   a. Thus, you should fly above the flight path of a large jet rather than below.
   b. You should also fly upwind rather than downwind of the flight path, since the vortices will drift with the wind.
5. The most dangerous wind, when taking off or landing behind a heavy aircraft, is the light quartering tailwind. It will push the vortices into your touchdown zone, even if you are executing proper procedures.

3.7 COLLISION AVOIDANCE

1. Navigation lights on the aircraft consist of a red light on the left wing, a green light on the right wing, and a white light on the tail. In night flight,
   a. When an airplane is crossing in front of you from your right to left, you will observe a red light.
   b. When an airplane is crossing in front of you from your left to right, you will observe a green light.
   c. When an airplane is flying away from you, you will observe a steady white light(s).
   d. When an airplane is approaching you head-on, you will observe a red and green light but no white light.
   e. Note that the navigation lights on the wings cannot be seen from the rear.
2. A flashing red light on an aircraft is a rotating beacon and may be seen from any angle.
3. In daylight, the most effective way to scan for other aircraft is to use a series of short, regularly spaced eye movements that bring successive areas of the sky into your central visual field.
   a. Each movement should not exceed 10°, and each area should be observed for at least 1 second to enable detection.
   b. Only a very small center area of the eye has the ability to send clear, sharply focused messages to the brain.
4. At night, collision avoidance scanning must use the off-center portions of the eyes. These portions are most effective at seeing objects at night.
   a. Accordingly, peripheral vision should be used, scanning small sectors and using off-center viewing.
5. Any aircraft that appears to have no relative motion with respect to your aircraft and stays in one scan quadrant is likely to be on a collision course.
   a. If it increases in size, you should take immediate evasive action.
6. Prior to each maneuver, a pilot should visually scan the entire area for collision avoidance.
   a. When climbing or descending VFR on an airway, you should execute gentle banks left and right to facilitate scanning for other aircraft.
7. All pilots are responsible for collision avoidance when operating in an alert area.
8. Most midair collision accidents occur during clear days.
   a. A near midair collision is defined as an incident associated with
      1) The operation of an aircraft in which a possibility of collision occurs as a result of proximity of less than 500 ft. to another aircraft or
      2) A report that is received from a pilot or a flight crew member stating that a collision hazard existed between two or more aircraft.
   b. Reporting responsibility: It is the responsibility of the pilot and/or flight crew to determine whether a near midiar collision actually occurred and, if so, to initiate a near midair collision report.
9. Pilots are encouraged to turn on their landing lights when operating below 10,000 feet, day or night, especially when operating in conditions of reduced visibility.
10. ADS-B (Automatic Dependent Surveillance-Broadcast) is technology that allows air traffic controllers (and ADS-B equipped aircraft) to see traffic with more precision. Instead of relying on old radar technology, ADS-B uses highly accurate GPS signals. Because of this, ADS-B works where radar often will not.
    a. This system
       1) Works in remote areas such as mountainous terrain

2) Functions at low altitudes and even on the ground
3) Can be used to monitor traffic on the taxiways and runways
4) Allows air traffic controllers as well as aircraft with certain equipment to receive ADS-B traffic
5) Provides subscription-free weather information to all aircraft flying over the U.S.

b. ADS-B will be required in 2020. This system helps make our skies safer. For more information, visit www.garmin.com/us/intheair/ads-b.

3.8 ATIS AND GROUND CONTROL

1. Automatic Terminal Information Service (ATIS) is a continuous broadcast of recorded noncontrol information in selected high activity terminal areas (i.e., busy airports).
   a. The information is essential but routine.
2. The information included is the latest weather sequence, active runways, and other pertinent remarks.
   a. Ceilings are usually not broadcast if they are above 5,000 ft., and visibility is usually not mentioned if it is more than 5 statute miles.
3. After landing, you should contact ground control only when so instructed by the tower.
4. A clearance to taxi to the active runway is a clearance to taxi via taxiways to the active runway. You may not cross any runway along your taxi route unless specifically cleared by ATC to do so.
   a. When cleared to a runway, you are cleared to that runway's runup area, but not onto the active runway itself.
   b. "Line up and wait" is the instruction to taxi onto the active runway and prepare for takeoff, but not to take off.

3.9 CLASS D AIRSPACE AND AIRPORT ADVISORY AREA

1. Class D airspace is an area of controlled airspace surrounding an airport with an operating control tower, not associated with Class B or Class C airspace areas.
   a. Airspace at an airport with a part-time control tower is classified as Class D airspace only when the control tower is operating.
   b. When the control tower ceases operation for the day, the airspace reverts to Class E, or a combination of Class E and G airspace during the hours the tower is not in operation.
2. Class D airspace is depicted by a blue segmented (dashed) circle on a sectional chart.
3. When departing a non-tower satellite airport within Class D airspace, you must establish and maintain two-way radio communication with the primary airport's control tower.
   a. The primary airport is the airport for which the Class D airspace is designated.
   b. A satellite airport is any other airport within the Class D airspace area.
4. Class D airspace is normally the airspace up to 2,500 ft. above the surface of the airport.
   a. The actual lateral dimensions of Class D airspace are based on the instrument procedures for which the controlled airspace is established.
5. Two-way radio communication with the control tower is required for landings and takeoffs at all tower-controlled airports, regardless of weather conditions.
6. Airport Advisory Areas exist at noncontrolled airports that have a Flight Service Station (FSS) physically located on that airport. The FSS provides advisory (not control) information on traffic, weather, etc., to requesting aircraft.

3.10 CLASS C AIRSPACE

1. Class C airspace consists of a surface area (formerly called the inner circle) and a shelf area (formerly called the outer circle).
   a. The surface area has a 5-NM radius from the primary airport extending from the surface to 4,000 ft. above the airport elevation.
   b. The shelf area is an area from 5 to 10 NM from the primary airport extending from 1,200 ft. to 4,000 ft. above the airport elevation.
2. Surrounding the Class C airspace is the outer area. The outer area is not classified as Class C airspace.
   a. ATC provides the same radar services as provided in Class C airspace.
   b. The normal radius of the outer area of Class C airspace is 20 NM from the primary airport.
3. The minimum equipment needed to operate in Class C airspace
   a. 4096 code transponder,
   b. Mode C (altitude encoding) capability, and
   c. Two-way radio communication capability.
4. You must establish and maintain two-way radio communication with ATC prior to entering Class C airspace. A clearance is not required because a clearance relates to IFR operations.
5. When departing from a satellite airport without an operating control tower, you must contact ATC as soon as practicable after takeoff.

3.11 TERMINAL RADAR PROGRAMS

1. Terminal radar programs for VFR aircraft are classified as basic, TRSA, Class C, and Class B service.
   a. Basic radar service provides safety alerts, traffic advisories, and limited vectoring on a workload-permitting basis.
   b. TRSA service provides sequencing and separation for all participating VFR aircraft operating within a Terminal Radar Service Area (TRSA).
2. Terminal radar program participation is voluntary for VFR traffic.
   a. Contact approach control when inbound.
   b. When departing, you should request radar traffic information from ground control on initial contact, along with your direction of flight.

3.12 TRANSPONDERS AND TRANSPONDER CODES

1. There are three kinds of civilian transponders used in U.S. airspace:
   a. Mode A
      1) A Mode A transponder, when requested by the air traffic control radar beacon system (ATCRBS), transmits a four-digit squawk code to ATC.
   b. Mode C (Automatic Altitude Reporting)
      1) This type of transponder converts your airplane's altitude in 100-ft. increments to coded digital information, which is transmitted in the reply to the interrogating radar facility. A Mode C transponder provides this information in addition to transmitting the four-digit squawk code.
      2) If your airplane is Mode C-equipped, you must set your transponder to reply Mode C (i.e., set function switch to ALT) unless ATC requests otherwise.

3) Mode C is required when flying
   a) At or above 10,000 ft. MSL, except in that airspace below 2,500 ft. AGL
   b) Within 30 NM of a Class B airspace primary airport
   c) Within and above a Class C airspace area
   d) Into, within, or across the U.S. ADIZ (Air Defense Identification Zone)

c. Mode S (Selective)

1) Mode S (Selective) transponders are designed to help air traffic control in busy areas and allow automatic collision avoidance.
   a) Mode S transponders allow TCAS (Traffic Alert and Collision Avoidance System) and TIS (Traffic Information System) to function.
2) Mode S transponders broadcast information about the equipped aircraft to the Secondary Surveillance Radar (SSR) system, TCAS receivers on board aircraft, and to the ADS-B system.
   a) This information includes the call sign of the aircraft and/or the transponder's permanent unit code (i.e., not the four-digit user-entered squawk code).
   b) These transponders also receive ground-based radar information through a datalink and can display that information to pilots to aid in collision avoidance.

2. The military has multiple kinds of transponders, and the military type that corresponds to civilian Mode A and civilian Mode C is referred to as military Mode 3. You may see FAA questions that refer to Mode A/3 or Mode C/3. The "3" is referring to military transponders, so just think "Mode A" or "Mode C."
3. Code 1200 is the standard VFR transponder code.
4. The ident feature should not be engaged unless instructed by ATC.
5. Certain special codes should never be engaged (except in an emergency), as they may cause problems at ATC centers:
   a. 7500 is the hijacking code.
   b. 7600 is the lost radio communication code.
   c. 7700 is the general emergency code.
   d. 7777 is the military interceptor code.

3.13 RADIO PHRASEOLOGY

1. When contacting a Flight Service Station to open, close, or file a flight plan, the proper call sign is the name of the FSS followed by "radio" (e.g., McAlester Radio).
2. Civilian aircraft should state their aircraft call sign with the make or model aircraft (e.g., Cessna 44WH or Baron 2DF).
   a. When a make or model is used, the initial November is dropped from the call sign.
3. Pilots should state each digit of the call sign individually (e.g., 6449U = six, four, four, niner, uniform).
4. When calling out altitudes up to but not including 18,000 ft., state the separate digits of the thousands, plus the hundreds, if appropriate (e.g., 4,500 ft. = four thousand five hundred).
   a. Unless otherwise noted, the altitudes are MSL.

3.14 ATC TRAFFIC ADVISORIES

1. Radar traffic information services provide pilots with traffic advisories of nearby aircraft.
2. Traffic advisories provide information based on the position of other aircraft from your airplane in terms of clock direction in a no-wind condition (i.e., it is based on your ground track, not heading).
   a. 12 o'clock is straight ahead.
   b. 3 o'clock is directly off your right wing.
   c. 6 o'clock is directly behind you.
   d. 9 o'clock is directly off your left wing.
   e. Other positions are described accordingly, e.g., 2 o'clock, 10 o'clock.
3. Traffic advisories usually also include
   a. Distance away in miles
   b. Direction of flight of other aircraft
   c. Altitude of other aircraft

3.15 ATC LIGHT SIGNALS

1. In the absence of radio communications, the tower can communicate with you by light signals.
2. Light signal meanings depend on whether you are on the ground or in the air.
3. Acknowledge light signals in the air by rocking wings in daylight and blinking lights at night.
4. If your radio fails and you wish to land at a tower-controlled airport, remain outside or above the airport's traffic pattern until the direction and flow of traffic has been determined, then join the traffic pattern and maintain visual contact with the tower to receive light signals.

Light Signal	On the Ground	In the Air
Steady Green	Cleared for takeoff	Cleared to land
Flashing Green	Cleared to taxi	Return for landing *(to be followed by steady green at proper time)*
Steady Red	Stop	Give way to other aircraft and continue circling
Flashing Red	Taxi clear of landing area (runway) in use	Airport unsafe -- Do not land
Flashing White	Return to starting point on airport	Not applicable
Alternating Red and Green	General warning signal -- Exercise extreme caution	General warning signal -- Exercise extreme caution

3.16 ELTs AND VHF/DF

1. ELTs transmit simultaneously on 121.5 and 243.0 megahertz.
   a. You can monitor either frequency during flight and before shutdown (after landing) to ensure your ELT has not been activated.
2. The VHF/Direction Finder facility is a ground operation that displays the magnetic direction of the airplane from the station each time the airplane transmits a signal to it.
3. In order to take advantage of VHF/DF radio reception for assistance in locating a position, an airplane must have both a VHF transmitter and a receiver. The transmitter and receiver are necessary to converse with a ground station having VHF/DF facilities.
   a. The transmitter is also needed to send the signal that the Direction Finder identifies in terms of magnetic heading from the facility.

3.17 EMERGENCY RADIO FREQUENCY

1. Whenever a pilot encounters an emergency condition in an aircraft, (s)he can obtain assistance simply by contacting the air traffic control facility or other agency in whose area of responsibility the aircraft is operating, stating the nature of the emergency, the pilot's intentions, and the assistance desired.
   a. If the pilot is not in contact with ATC, (s)he should broadcast on radio frequency 121.5 MHz. If the pilot must make an emergency landing, (s)he should set the transponder on 7700 (emergency squawk code).
   b. The distress or urgency message should consist of the following:
      1) If *distress*, begin with "MAYDAY, MAYDAY, MAYDAY"
         a) If *urgency*, begin with "PAN-PAN, PAN-PAN, PAN-PAN"
      2) Station name or "any station"
      3) Aircraft identification and type
      4) Present position and heading (if lost, last known position, time, and heading since that position)
      5) Nature of the emergency
      6) Pilot's intentions and any requests
   c. Other information that may be broadcast with the previous items (depending on the situation) include the following:
      1) Weather conditions (if applicable)
      2) Altitude or flight level
      3) Fuel remaining in minutes
      4) Number of people on board
      5) Any other useful information

3.18 LAND AND HOLD SHORT OPERATIONS (LAHSO)

1. Land and hold short operations (LAHSO) take place at some airports with an operating control tower in order to increase airport capacity and improve the flow of traffic.
   a. LAHSO requires that you land and hold short of an intersecting runway, an intersecting taxiway, or some other designated point on a runway.
2. Before accepting a clearance to land and hold short, you must determine that you can safely land and stop within the available landing distance (ALD).
   a. ALD data are published in the special notices section of the Chart Supplement.
   b. ATC will provide ALD data upon your request.
3. Student pilots should not participate in the LAHSO program.
4. The pilot in command has the final authority to accept or decline any LAHSO clearance.
   a. Decline a LAHSO clearance if you determine it will compromise safety.
5. You should receive a LAHSO clearance only when there is a minimum ceiling of 1,000 ft. and visibility of 3 statute miles.
   a. The intent of having basic VFR weather conditions is to allow pilots to maintain visual contact with other aircraft and ground vehicle operations.

QUESTIONS AND ANSWER EXPLANATIONS: All of the private pilot knowledge test questions chosen by the FAA for release as well as additional questions selected by Gleim relating to the material in the previous outlines are reproduced on the following pages. These questions have been organized into the same subunits as the outlines. To the immediate right of each question are the correct answer and answer explanation. You should cover these answers and answer explanations while responding to the questions. Refer to the general discussion in the Introduction on how to take the FAA knowledge test.

Remember that the questions from the FAA knowledge test bank have been reordered by topic and organized into a meaningful sequence. Also, the first line of the answer explanation gives the citation of the authoritative source for the answer.

QUESTIONS

3.1 Runway Markings

1. (Refer to Figure 48 on page 81 and Legend 3 on page 82.) According to the airport diagram, which statement is true?

A. Runway 30 is equipped at position E with emergency arresting gear to provide a means of stopping military aircraft.

B. Takeoffs may be started at position A on Runway 12, and the landing portion of this runway begins at position B.

C. The takeoff and landing portion of Runway 12 begins at position B.

Answer (B) is correct. *(AIM Para 2-3-3)*

DISCUSSION: In Fig. 48, RWY 12 takeoffs may be started at position A, and the landing portion of this runway begins at position B. In this example, a displaced threshold exists at the beginning of RWY 12. The threshold is depicted on the airport diagram as three oblong circles (8) going across and near the end of the runway, designating the beginning portion of a runway usable for landing. The paved area behind the displaced runway threshold is available for taxiing, the landing rollout, and takeoff.

Answer (A) is incorrect. Arresting cables are depicted as a black zig-zag line across the runway. On an active runway, they are indicated by black lines extending out from the sides of the runway. Unidirectional (single) or bidirectional (two) arrows along the side of the runway point in the direction of the arresting gear operation painted across the runway at positions of the arresting cables. Position E is grey, indicating an overrun area. Answer (C) is incorrect. Only the landing portion of RWY 12 begins at position B. The takeoff may be started in the paved area behind the displaced runway threshold (i.e., position A).

2. (Refer to Figure 48 on page 81.) That portion of the runway identified by the letter A may be used for

A. landing.

B. taxiing and takeoff.

C. taxiing and landing.

Answer (B) is correct. *(AIM Para 2-3-3)*

DISCUSSION: The portion of the runway identified by the letter B is a displaced threshold. A displaced threshold can be determined by the 8 on the diagram, which the letter B points to. At the airport, a displaced runway can be distinguished from a regular runway by the arrow heads that run across the width of the displaced runway (just before the white threshold bar). A displaced threshold means the runway may be used for taxiing or takeoffs but not for landings.

Answer (A) is incorrect. Area A may be used for the landing rollout or taxi but not the actual landing. Answer (C) is incorrect. Area C identifies a closed runway indicated by the "x" at the end of the runway.

3. (Refer to Figure 48 on page 81.) What is the difference between area A and area E on the airport depicted?

A. "A" may be used for taxi and takeoff; "E" may be used only as an overrun.

B. "A" may be used for all operations except heavy aircraft landings; "E" may be used only as an overrun.

C. "A" may be used only for taxiing; "E" may be used for all operations except landings.

Answer (A) is correct. *(AIM Para 2-3-3)*

DISCUSSION: Area A in Fig. 48 is the paved area behind a displaced runway threshold, as identified by the 8 symbol pointed to by B. This area may be used for taxiing, the landing rollout, and the takeoff of aircraft. Area E is a stopway area, as identified by the lighter shade. This area, due to the nature of its structure, is unusable except as an overrun.

Answer (B) is incorrect. Area A cannot be used by any aircraft for landing. Answer (C) is incorrect. Area A can also be used for takeoff and landing rollout. Area E cannot be used for any type of operation, except as an overrun.

4. (Refer to Figure 48 below.) Area C on the airport depicted is classified as a

A. stabilized area.

B. multiple heliport.

C. closed runway.

Answer (C) is correct. *(AIM Para 2-3-6)*

DISCUSSION: The runway marked by the arrow C in Fig. 48 has Xs on the runway, indicating it is closed.

Answer (A) is incorrect. Stabilized areas are designed to be load bearing but may be limited to emergency use only. Area E on the airport indicates a stabilized area. Answer (B) is incorrect. Heliports are marked by Hs, not Xs.

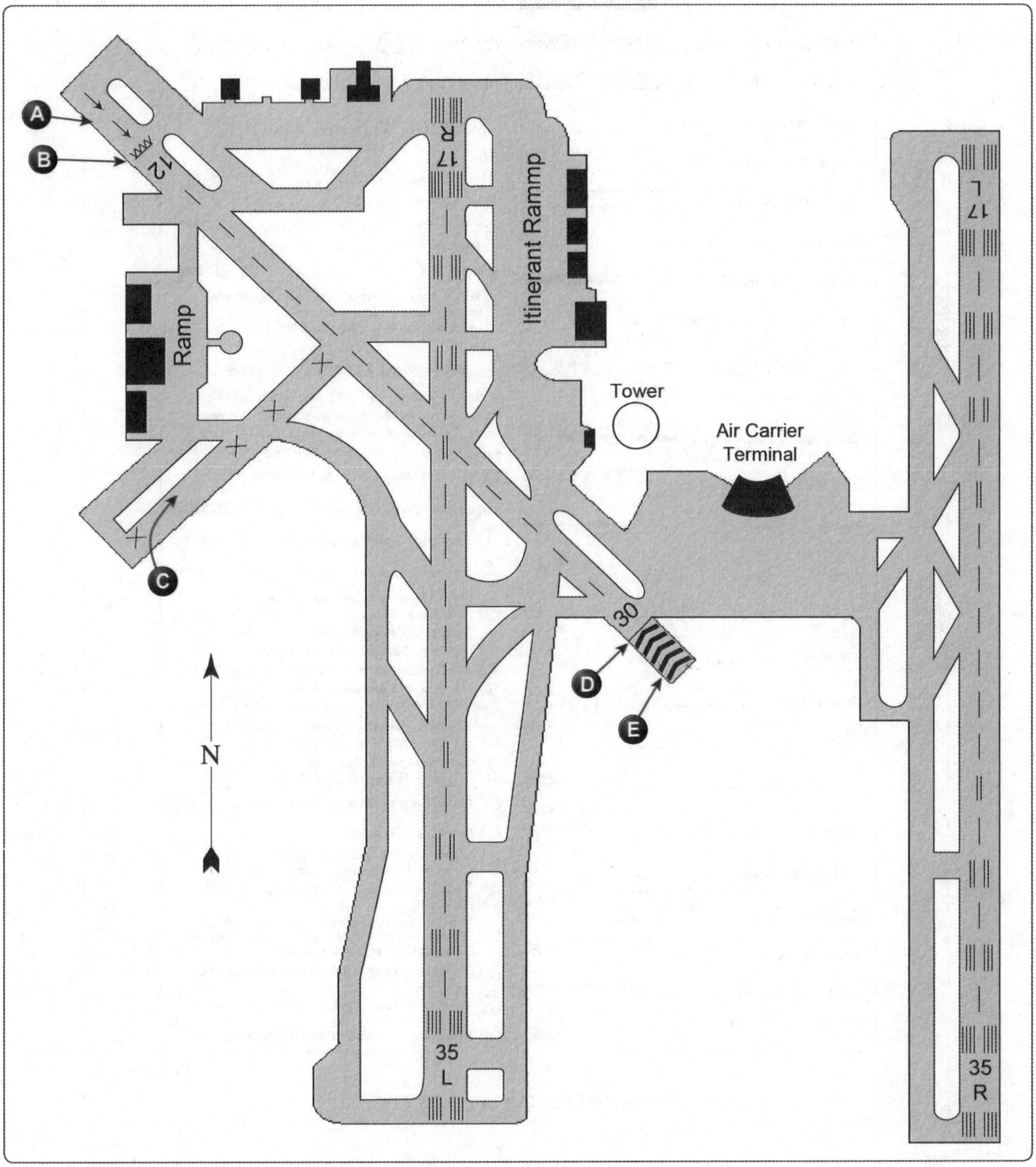

Figure 48. – Airport Diagram.

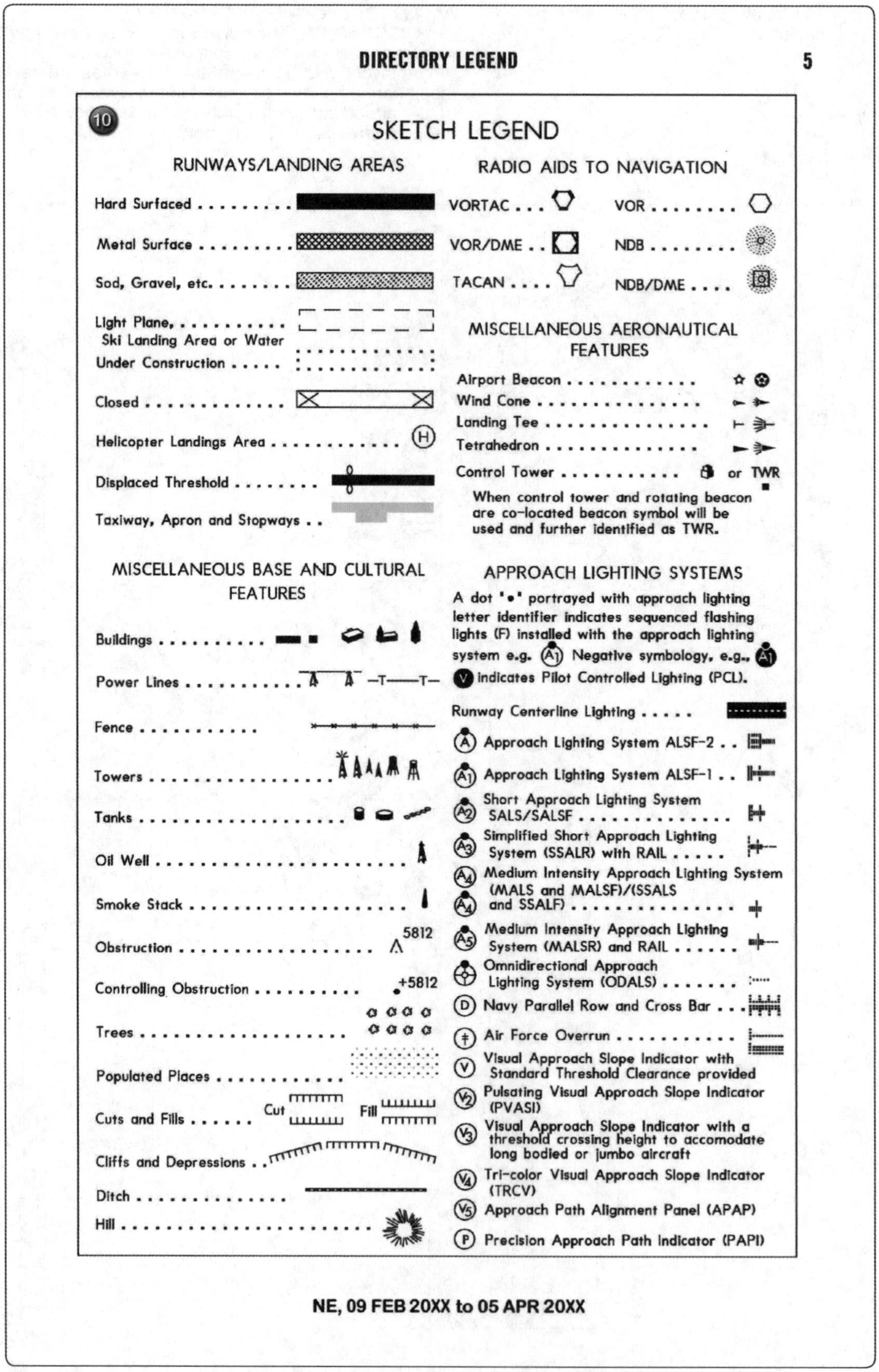

Legend 3. – Chart Supplements U.S. (formerly Airport/Facility Directory).

5. The numbers 8 and 26 on the approach ends of the runway indicate that the runway is orientated approximately

A. 008° and 026° true.

B. 080° and 260° true.

C. 080° and 260° magnetic.

Answer (C) is correct. *(AIM Para 2-3-3)*

DISCUSSION: Runway numbers are determined from the approach direction. The runway number is the whole number nearest one-tenth the magnetic direction of the centerline. Thus, the numbers 8 and 26 on a runway indicate that the runway is oriented approximately 080° and 260° magnetic.

Answer (A) is incorrect. The ending digit, not a leading zero, is dropped. Answer (B) is incorrect. Runways are numbered based on magnetic, not true, direction.

6. The numbers 9 and 27 on a runway indicate that the runway is oriented approximately

A. 009° and 027° true.

B. 090° and 270° true.

C. 090° and 270° magnetic.

Answer (C) is correct. *(AIM Para 2-3-3)*

DISCUSSION: Runway numbers are determined from the approach direction. The runway number is the whole number nearest one-tenth the magnetic direction of the centerline. Thus, the numbers 9 and 27 on a runway indicate that the runway is oriented approximately 090° and 270° magnetic.

Answer (A) is incorrect. The ending digit, not a leading zero, is dropped. Answer (B) is incorrect. Runways are numbered based on magnetic (not true) direction.

3.2 Taxiway and Destination Signs

7. When approaching taxiway holding lines from the side with the continuous lines, the pilot

A. may continue taxiing.

B. should not cross the lines without ATC clearance.

C. should continue taxiing until all parts of the aircraft have crossed the lines.

Answer (B) is correct. *(AIM Para 2-3-5)*

DISCUSSION: When approaching taxiway holding lines, the solid (continuous) lines are always on the side where the aircraft is to hold. Therefore, do not cross the hold line without ATC clearance.

Answer (A) is incorrect. You cannot cross the hold line without ATC clearance. Answer (C) is incorrect. No part of the aircraft can cross the hold line without ATC clearance.

8. What is the purpose of the runway/runway hold position sign?

A. Denotes entrance to runway from a taxiway.

B. Denotes area protected for an aircraft approaching or departing a runway.

C. Denotes intersecting runways.

Answer (C) is correct. *(AIM Para 2-3-8)*

DISCUSSION: Runway/runway hold position signs are a type of mandatory instruction sign used to denote intersecting runways. These are runways that intersect and are being used for “Land, Hold Short” operations or are normally used for taxiing. These signs have a red background with white lettering. Runway/runway hold position signs are identical to the signs used for taxiway/runway intersections.

Answer (A) is incorrect. A runway/runway hold position sign is located on a runway and denotes an intersecting runway, not the entrance to a runway from a taxiway. Answer (B) is incorrect. A runway approach area holding position sign protects an area from approaching or departing aircraft.

9. What does the outbound destination sign identify?

A. Identifies entrance to the runway from a taxiway.

B. Identifies runway on which an aircraft is located.

C. Identifies direction to take-off runways.

Answer (C) is correct. *(AIM Para 2-3-11)*

DISCUSSION: Outbound destination signs define taxiing directions to takeoff runways. Destination signs have a yellow background with a black inscription. Outbound destination signs always have an arrow showing the direction of the taxiing route to the takeoff runway.

Answer (A) is incorrect. A runway holding position sign, not an outbound destination sign, identifies the entrance to a runway from a taxiway. Runway holding position signs consist of a red background with white inscription. Answer (B) is incorrect. A runway location sign, not an outbound destination sign, identifies the runway on which the aircraft is currently located. Runway location signs consist of a black background with a yellow inscription and a yellow border.

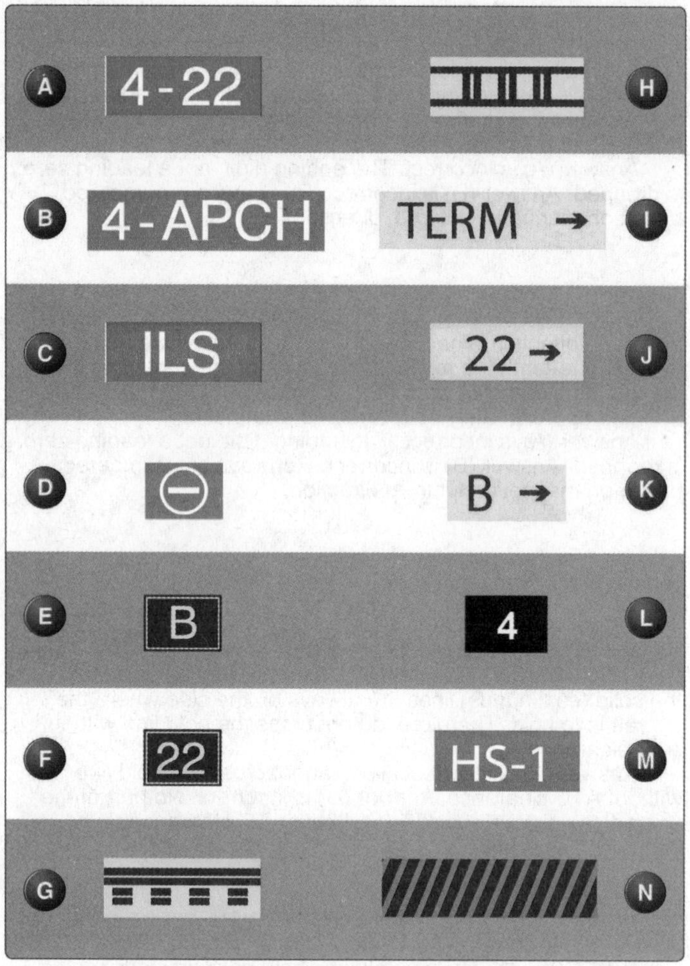

Figure 65. – U.S. Airport Signs.

10. (Refer to Figure 65 above.) Which sign is a designation and direction of an exit taxiway from a runway?

A. J.

B. F.

C. K.

Answer (C) is correct. *(AIM Para 2-3-11)*

DISCUSSION: Sign K designates the direction of taxiway B; while both J and K are destination signs, only K designates the route to a taxiway.

Answer (A) is incorrect. Though a destination sign, Sign J designates the direction of Runway 22, not the direction of a taxiway. Answer (B) is incorrect. Sign F is a location sign indicating that the aircraft is located on Runway 22.

11. (Refer to Figure 65 above.) Which sign identifies your position on a runway?

A. E.

B. F.

C. L.

Answer (C) is correct. *(AIM Para 2-3-13)*

DISCUSSION: The sign depicted by “L” is a runway distance remaining sign. It shows you the remaining runway distance in thousands of feet.

Answer (A) is incorrect. The sign depicted by “E” is a taxiway location sign. It does not provide any information regarding your position on the runway. Answer (B) is incorrect. The sign depicted by “F” is a runway location sign. While it does indicate the runway you are on, it does not specifically indicate your position on that runway.

12. (Refer to Figure 65 above.) Which sign identifies where aircraft are prohibited from entering?

A. D.

B. G.

C. B.

Answer (A) is correct. *(AIM Para 2-3-8)*

DISCUSSION: Mandatory instruction signs have a red background with a white inscription and are used to denote an entrance to a runway or critical area and areas where an aircraft is prohibited from entering.

Answer (B) is incorrect. “G” is a runway boundary sign. Answer (C) is incorrect. “B” is a holding position sign for a runway approach area.

13. (Refer to Figure 65 on page 84.) (Refer to E.) This sign is a visual clue that

A. confirms the aircraft's location to be on taxiway "B."

B. warns the pilot of approaching taxiway "B."

C. indicates "B" holding area is ahead.

Answer (A) is correct. *(AIM Chap 3)*

DISCUSSION: The taxiway location sign consists of a yellow letter on a black background with a yellow border. This sign confirms the pilot is on taxiway "B."

Answer (B) is incorrect. A direction sign with a yellow background, a black letter, and an arrow pointing to taxiway "B" would be required to warn a pilot that (s)he is approaching taxiway "B." Answer (C) is incorrect. A taxiway location sign defines a position on a taxiway, not a holding area.

14. (Refer to Figure 65 on page 84.) (Refer to F.) This sign confirms your position on

A. runway 22.

B. routing to runway 22.

C. taxiway 22.

Answer (A) is correct. *(AIM Chap 2)*

DISCUSSION: A runway location sign has a black background with a yellow inscription and a yellow border. The inscription on the sign informs the pilot (s)he is located on Runway 22.

Answer (B) is incorrect. A direction sign with a yellow background and black inscription would be required to inform a pilot (s)he is routing to Runway 22. Answer (C) is incorrect. Only runways are numbered. Taxiways are always identified by a letter.

15. (Refer to Figure 65 on page 84.) (Refer to G.) From the cockpit, this marking confirms the aircraft to be

A. on a taxiway, about to enter runway zone.

B. on a runway, about to clear.

C. near an instrument approach clearance zone.

Answer (B) is correct. *(AIM Chap 2)*

DISCUSSION: When the runway holding position line is viewed from the runway side, the pilot is presented with two dashed bars. The PIC must ensure the entire aircraft has cleared the runway holding position line prior to coming to a stop.

Answer (A) is incorrect. A pilot entering a runway from a taxiway is presented with the two solid bars on the runway holding position marking, not the dashed lines. Answer (C) is incorrect. The marking depicted is a runway holding position marking and is not related to any form of clearance zone.

16. (Refer to Figure 65 on page 84.) Which of the signs in the figure is a mandatory instruction sign?

A. D.

B. G.

C. H.

Answer (A) is correct. *(AIM Para 2-3-8)*

DISCUSSION: Mandatory signs have a red background with a white inscription and are used to denote an entrance to a runway or critical area and areas where an aircraft is prohibited from entering. "D" is a "No Entry" sign.

Answer (B) is incorrect. "G" is a runway boundary sign. It is located on taxiways on the back side of certain runway/taxiway holding position signs or runway approach area signs. Answer (C) is incorrect. The ILS critical area sign has a yellow background and black lines drawn that looks like a sideways ladder. This sign identifies the ILS critical area exit boundary. If an aircraft is on this line and instrument approaches are in progress, the ILS signal may be blocked. Do not cross or block this during IMC unless clearance is given.

17. When turning onto a taxiway from another taxiway, what is the purpose of the taxiway directional sign?

A. Indicates direction to take-off runway.

B. Indicates designation and direction of exit taxiway from runway.

C. Indicates designation and direction of taxiway leading out of an intersection.

Answer (C) is correct. *(AIM Para 2-3-10)*

DISCUSSION: Direction signs consist of black lettering on a yellow background. These signs identify the designations of taxiways leading out of an intersection. An arrow next to each taxiway designation indicates the direction that an aircraft must turn in order to taxi onto that taxiway.

Answer (A) is incorrect. Outbound destination signs, not direction signs, indicate the direction that must be taken out of an intersection in order to follow the preferred taxi route to a runway. Answer (B) is incorrect. The question specifies that you are turning onto a taxiway from another taxiway, not from a runway.

18. (Refer to Figure 64 below.) Which marking indicates a vehicle lane?

A. A.

B. C.

C. E.

Answer (B) is correct. *(AIM Para 2-3-6)*

DISCUSSION: Vehicle roadway markings define a route of travel for vehicles to cross areas intended for use by aircraft. The roadway is defined by solid white lines, with a dashed line in the middle to separate traffic traveling in opposite directions. White zipper markings may be used instead of solid white lines to define the edge of the roadway at some airports.

Answer (A) is incorrect. This marking represents a surface painted holding position sign, not a vehicle lane. In this instance, the marking indicates the aircraft is holding short of Runway 19. Answer (C) is incorrect. This marking represents a standard taxiway holding position and is used by ATC to hold aircraft short of an intersecting taxiway.

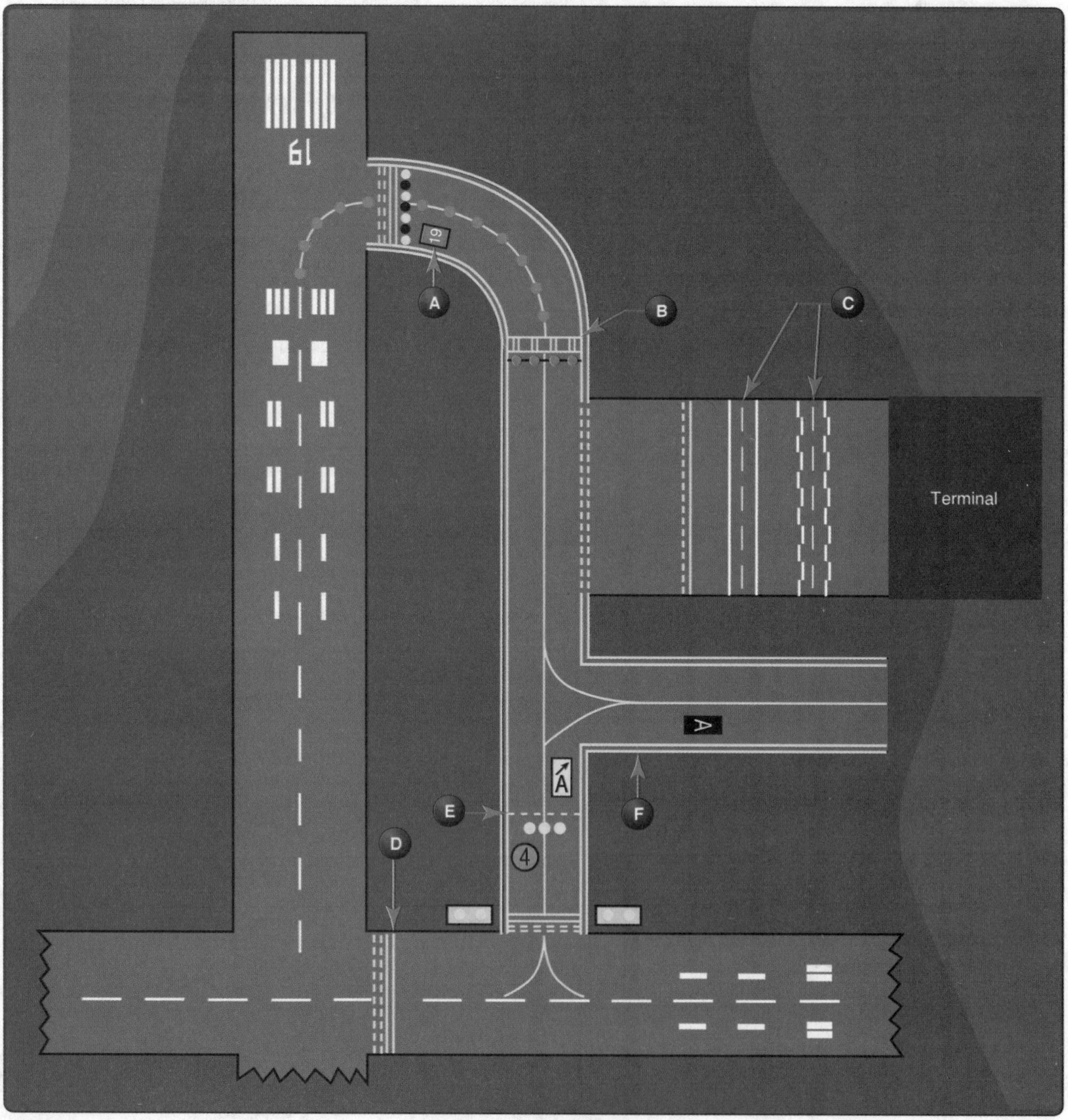

Figure 64. – Airport Markings.

19. What purpose does the taxiway location sign serve?

A. Provides general taxiing direction to named runway.

B. Denotes entrance to runway from a taxiway.

C. Identifies taxiway on which an aircraft is located.

Answer (C) is correct. *(AIM Para 2-3-9)*

DISCUSSION: Taxiway location signs are used to identify a taxiway on which the aircraft is currently located. Taxiway location signs consist of a black background with a yellow inscription and yellow border.

Answer (A) is incorrect. A runway destination sign, not a taxiway location sign, provides general taxiing information to a named runway. Answer (B) is incorrect. A runway holding position sign, not a taxiway location sign, identifies the entrance to a runway from a taxiway. Runway holding position signs consist of a red background with white inscription.

20. The 'yellow demarcation bar' marking indicates

A. runway with a displaced threshold that precedes the runway.

B. a hold line from a taxiway to a runway.

C. the beginning of available runway for landing on the approach side.

Answer (A) is correct. *(AIM Para 2-3-3, AIM Fig 2-3-6)*

DISCUSSION: A demarcation bar is a 3-ft.-wide yellow stripe that separates a runway with a displaced threshold from a blast pad, stopway, or taxiway that precedes the runway.

Answer (B) is incorrect. A set of solid yellow and dashed yellow lines represents the hold lines between a taxiway and runway. Answer (C) is incorrect. The yellow demarcation bar delineates the beginning of the displaced threshold, which is not a landing surface.

3.3 Beacons and Taxiway Lights

21. A lighted heliport may be identified by a

A. green, yellow, and white rotating beacon.

B. flashing yellow light.

C. blue lighted square landing area.

Answer (A) is correct. *(AIM Para 2-1-10)*

DISCUSSION: A lighted heliport may be identified by a green, yellow, and white rotating beacon.

Answer (B) is incorrect. A flashing yellow light is sometimes used to help a pilot locate a lighted water airport. It is used in conjunction with the lighted water airport's white and yellow rotating beacon. Answer (C) is incorrect. A lighted heliport may be identified by a green, yellow, and white rotating beacon, not a blue lighted square landing area.

22. A military air station can be identified by a rotating beacon that emits

A. white and green alternating flashes.

B. two quick, white flashes between green flashes.

C. green, yellow, and white flashes.

Answer (B) is correct. *(AIM Para 2-1-8)*

DISCUSSION: Lighted land airports are distinguished by white and green airport beacons. To further distinguish it as a military airport, there are two quick white flashes between each green.

Answer (A) is incorrect. White and green alternating flashes designate a lighted civilian land airport. Answer (C) is incorrect. Green, yellow, and white flashes designate a lighted heliport.

23. An airport's rotating beacon operated during daylight hours indicates

A. there are obstructions on the airport.

B. that weather at the airport located in Class D airspace is below basic VFR weather minimums.

C. the Air Traffic Control tower is not in operation.

Answer (B) is correct. *(AIM Para 2-1-8)*

DISCUSSION: Operation of the airport beacon during daylight hours often indicates that weather at the airport located in controlled airspace (e.g., Class D airspace) is below basic VFR weather minimums, i.e., less than 1,000 ft. ceiling or 3 SM visibility. Note that there is no regulatory requirement for daylight operation of an airport's rotating beacon.

Answer (A) is incorrect. The obstructions near or on airports are usually listed in NOTAMs or the Chart Supplement as appropriate to their hazard. Answer (C) is incorrect. There is no visual signal of tower operation/non-operation.

24. How can a military airport be identified at night?

A. Alternate white and green light flashes.

B. Dual peaked (two quick) white flashes between green flashes.

C. White flashing lights with steady green at the same location.

Answer (B) is correct. *(AIM Para 2-1-8)*

DISCUSSION: Military airport beacons flash alternately white and green but are differentiated from civil beacons by two quick white flashes between the green flashes.

Answer (A) is incorrect. Alternating white and green beacon light flashes indicate lighted civil land airports. Answer (C) is incorrect. There is no such airport signal.

25. Airport taxiway edge lights are identified at night by

A. white directional lights.

B. blue omnidirectional lights.

C. alternate red and green lights.

Answer (B) is correct. *(AIM Para 2-1-9)*

DISCUSSION: Taxiway edge lights are used to outline the edges of taxiways during periods of darkness or restricted visibility conditions. These lights are identified at night by blue omnidirectional lights.

Answer (A) is incorrect. White lights are standard runway edge lights. Answer (C) is incorrect. Alternate red and green lights are a light gun signal, which means exercise extreme caution to all aircraft.

26. To set the high intensity runway lights on medium intensity, the pilot should click the microphone seven times, and then click it

A. one time within 4 seconds.

B. three times within 3 seconds.

C. five times within 5 seconds.

Answer (C) is correct. *(AIM Para 2-1-7)*

DISCUSSION: To turn on and set the runway lights on medium intensity, the recommended procedure is to key the mic seven times; this ensures that all the lights are on and at high intensity. Next, key the mic five times to get the medium-intensity setting. Lighting systems are activated by keying the mic within a 5-second interval.

Answer (A) is incorrect. Keying only one time will not adjust or turn the lights on at all. Answer (B) is incorrect. Three additional microphone clicks will give the low-intensity setting.

3.4 Airport Traffic Patterns

27. Which is the correct traffic pattern departure procedure to use at a noncontrolled airport?

A. Depart in any direction consistent with safety, after crossing the airport boundary.

B. Make all turns to the left.

C. Comply with any FAA traffic pattern established for the airport.

Answer (C) is correct. *(14 CFR 91.127)*

DISCUSSION: Each person operating an airplane to or from an airport without an operating control tower shall (1) in the case of an airplane approaching to land, make all turns of that airplane to the left unless the airport displays approved light signals or visual markings indicating that turns should be made to the right, in which case the pilot shall make all turns to the right, and (2) in the case of an airplane departing the airport, comply with any FAA traffic pattern for that airport.

Answer (A) is incorrect. The correct traffic pattern departure procedure at a noncontrolled airport is to comply with any FAA established traffic pattern, not to depart in any direction after crossing the airport boundary. Answer (B) is incorrect. The FAA may establish right- or left-hand traffic patterns, not only left-hand traffic.

28. The recommended entry position to an airport traffic pattern is

A. 45° to the base leg just below traffic pattern altitude.

B. to enter 45° at the midpoint of the downwind leg at traffic pattern altitude.

C. to cross directly over the airport at traffic pattern altitude and join the downwind leg.

Answer (B) is correct. *(AIM Para 4-3-3)*

DISCUSSION: The recommended entry position to an airport traffic pattern is to enter 45° at the midpoint of the downwind leg at traffic pattern altitude.

Answer (A) is incorrect. The recommended entry to an airport traffic pattern is to enter 45° at the midpoint of the downwind, not base, leg and at traffic pattern altitude, not below. Answer (C) is incorrect. The recommended entry to an airport traffic pattern is to enter 45° at the midpoint of the downwind, not to cross directly over the airport and join the downwind leg. Also, flying at traffic pattern altitude directly over an airport is an example of poor judgment in collision avoidance precautions.

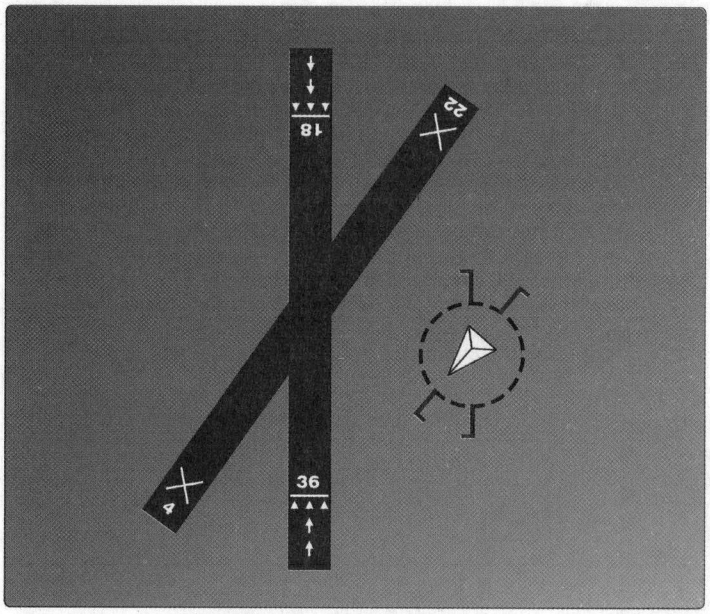

Figure 49. – Airport Diagram.

29. (Refer to Figure 49 above.) If the wind is as shown by the landing direction indicator, the pilot should land on

A. Runway 18 and expect a crosswind from the right.

B. Runway 22 directly into the wind.

C. Runway 36 and expect a crosswind from the right.

Answer (A) is correct. *(AIM Para 4-3-4)*

DISCUSSION: Given a wind as shown by the landing direction indicator in Fig. 49, the pilot should land to the south on Runway 18 and expect a crosswind from the right. The tetrahedron points to the wind that is from the southwest.

Answer (B) is incorrect. Runways 4 and 22 are closed, as indicated by the X at each end of the runway. Answer (C) is incorrect. The wind is from the southwest (not the northeast). The landing should be into the wind.

30. (Refer to Figure 49 above.) The arrows that appear on the end of the north/south runway indicate that the area

A. may be used only for taxiing.

B. is usable for taxiing, takeoff, and landing.

C. cannot be used for landing, but may be used for taxiing and takeoff.

Answer (C) is correct. *(AIM Para 2-3-3)*

DISCUSSION: The arrows that appear on the end of the north/south runway (displaced thresholds) as shown in Fig. 49 indicate that the area cannot be used for landing but may be used for taxiing, takeoff, and the landing rollout.

Answer (A) is incorrect. Takeoffs as well as taxiing are permitted. Answer (B) is incorrect. Landings are not permitted on the area before the displaced threshold.

31. (Refer to Figure 49 above.) Select the proper traffic pattern and runway for landing.

A. Left-hand traffic and Runway 18.

B. Right-hand traffic and Runway 18.

C. Left-hand traffic and Runway 22.

Answer (B) is correct. *(AIM Para 4-3-4)*

DISCUSSION: The tetrahedron indicates wind direction by pointing into the wind. On Fig. 49, Runways 4 and 22 are closed, as indicated by the X at each end of the runway. Accordingly, with the wind from the southwest, the landing should be made on Runway 18. Runway 18 has right-hand traffic, as indicated by the traffic pattern indicator at a 90° angle to the landing runway indicator in the segmented circle.

Answer (A) is incorrect. Runway 18 uses a right-hand (not left-hand) pattern. Answer (C) is incorrect. The X markings indicate that Runways 4 and 22 are closed.

32. (Refer to Figure 50 below.) The segmented circle indicates that the airport traffic is

A. left-hand for Runway 36 and right-hand for Runway 18.

B. left-hand for Runway 18 and right-hand for Runway 36.

C. right-hand for Runway 9 and left-hand for Runway 27.

Answer (A) is correct. *(AIM Para 4-3-4)*

DISCUSSION: A segmented circle (Fig. 50) is installed at uncontrolled airports to provide traffic pattern information. The landing runway indicators are shown coming out of the segmented circle to show the alignment of landing runways. In Fig. 50 (given the answer choices), the available runways are 18-36 and 9-27.

The traffic pattern indicators are at the end of the landing runway indicators and are angled out at 90°. These indicate the direction of turn from base to final. Thus, the airport traffic is left-hand for Runway 36 and right-hand for Runway 18. It is also left-hand for Runway 9 and right-hand for Runway 27.

Answer (B) is incorrect. Runway 18 is right, not left, and Runway 36 is left, not right. Answer (C) is incorrect. Runway 9 is left, not right, and Runway 27 is right, not left.

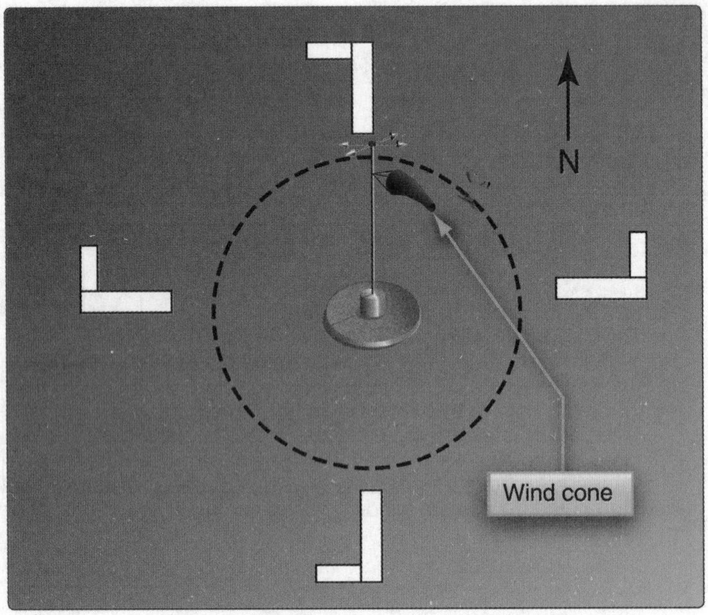

Figure 50. – Wind Cone to Wind Sock.

33. (Refer to Figure 50 above.) The traffic patterns indicated in the segmented circle have been arranged to avoid flights over an area to the

A. south of the airport.

B. north of the airport.

C. southeast of the airport.

Answer (C) is correct. *(AIM Para 4-3-4)*

DISCUSSION: The traffic patterns indicated in the segmented circle depicted in Fig. 50 have been arranged to avoid flights over an area to the southeast of the airport. All departures from the runways are to the north or west. All approaches to the airport indicate a pattern of arrival from 180° clockwise to 90°, leaving the southeastern quadrant free of flight.

Answer (A) is incorrect. Arrivals on Runway 36 and departures on Runway 18 result in traffic to the south. Answer (B) is incorrect. Runway 9-27 produces traffic to the north in addition to Runway 36 departures and Runway 18 arrivals.

34. (Refer to Figure 50 above.) Which runway and traffic pattern should be used as indicated by the wind cone in the segmented circle?

A. Right-hand traffic on Runway 9.

B. Right-hand traffic on Runway 18.

C. Left-hand traffic on Runway 36.

Answer (C) is correct. *(AIM Para 4-3-4)*

DISCUSSION: The appropriate traffic pattern and runway, given a wind from the northwest (Fig. 50), is left-hand traffic on Runway 36, which would have a quartering headwind.

Answer (A) is incorrect. Runway 9 uses a left-hand pattern. Also, this would be a tailwind landing. Answer (B) is incorrect. Even though there is right traffic on Runway 18, this would be a tailwind landing.

35. (Refer to Figure 50 on page 90.) The segmented circle indicates that a landing on Runway 26 will be with a

A. right-quartering headwind.
B. left-quartering headwind.
C. right-quartering tailwind.

Answer (A) is correct. *(AIM Para 4-3-4)*
DISCUSSION: The wind cone at the center of the segmented circle depicted in Fig. 50 indicates that a landing on Runway 26 will be with a right-quartering headwind. The large end of the wind cone is pointing to the direction from which the wind is coming, i.e., a northwest headwind on the right quarter of an airplane landing from the east to the west.
Answer (B) is incorrect. A left-quartering headwind would be encountered landing on Runway 35. Answer (C) is incorrect. A right-quartering tailwind would be encountered landing on Runway 17.

3.5 Visual Approach Slope Indicators (VASI)

36. A below glide slope indication from a pulsating approach slope indicator is a

A. pulsating white light.
B. steady white light.
C. pulsating red light.

Answer (C) is correct. *(AIM Para 2-1-2)*
DISCUSSION: A pulsating VASI indicator normally consists of a single light unit projecting a two-color visual approach path into the final approach area of the runway upon which the indicator is installed. The below glide slope indication is a pulsating red, the above glide slope is pulsating white, and the on glide slope is a steady white light. The useful range of this system is about 4 mi. during the day and up to 10 mi. at night.
Answer (A) is incorrect. A pulsating white light is an above glide slope indication. Answer (B) is incorrect. Steady white is the on glide slope indication.

37. When approaching to land on a runway served by a visual approach slope indicator (VASI), the pilot shall

A. maintain an altitude that captures the glide slope at least 2 miles downwind from the runway threshold.
B. maintain an altitude at or above the glide slope.
C. remain on the glide slope and land between the two-light bar.

Answer (B) is correct. *(14 CFR 91.129)*
DISCUSSION: An airplane approaching to land on a runway served by a VASI shall maintain an altitude at or above the glide slope until a lower altitude is necessary for a safe landing.
Answer (A) is incorrect. A VASI should not be used for descent until the airplane is visually lined up with the runway. Answer (C) is incorrect. It is unsafe to concentrate on the VASI after nearing the approach end of the runway; i.e., turn your attention to landing the airplane.

38. While operating in class D airspace, each pilot of an aircraft approaching to land on a runway served by a visual approach slope indicator (VASI) shall

A. maintain a 3° glide until approximately 1/2 mile to the runway before going below the VASI.
B. maintain an altitude at or above the glide slope until a lower altitude is necessary for a safe landing.
C. stay high until the runway can be reached in a power-off landing.

Answer (B) is correct. *(14 CFR 91.129)*
DISCUSSION: When approaching to land on a runway served by a VASI, each pilot of an airplane must fly at or above the VASI glide path until a lower altitude is necessary for a safe landing.
Answer (A) is incorrect. A VASI may be adjusted to provide a glide slope more or less than 3°. Answer (C) is incorrect. Higher than the VASI glide path is not required.

39. A slightly high glide slope indication from a precision approach path indicator is

A. four white lights.
B. three white lights and one red light.
C. two white lights and two red lights.

Answer (B) is correct. *(AIM Para 2-1-2)*
DISCUSSION: A precision approach path indicator (PAPI) has a row of four lights, each of which is similar to a VASI in that they emit a red or white light. Above the glide slope (more than 3.5°) is indicated by four white lights, a slightly above glide slope (3.2°) is indicated by three white lights and one red light, on glide slope (3°) is indicated by two white and two red lights, slightly below glide slope (2.8°) is indicated by one white and three red lights, and below (too low) the glide slope (less than 2.5°) is indicated by four red lights.
Answer (A) is incorrect. Four white lights is a high or more than 3.5° glide slope. Answer (C) is incorrect. Two white and two red lights is an on glide slope (3°).

40. (Refer to Figure 47 below.) VASI lights as shown by illustration C indicate that the airplane is

A. off course to the left.

B. above the glide slope.

C. below the glide slope.

Answer (B) is correct. *(AIM Para 2-1-2)*

DISCUSSION: In illustration C of Fig. 47, both rows of lights are white, which means the airplane is above the glide path.

Answer (A) is incorrect. The VASI does not alert a pilot as to runway alignment, but a pilot who is excessively to the left or right may not be able to see the VASI lights at all. Answer (C) is incorrect. If the airplane is below the glide path, both rows of lights would show red, as indicated by illustration D.

41. (Refer to Figure 47 below.) Illustration A indicates that the aircraft is

A. below the glide slope.

B. on the glide slope.

C. above the glide slope.

Answer (B) is correct. *(AIM Para 2-1-2)*

DISCUSSION: Illustration A indicates that the airplane is on the glide path (glide slope). The basic principle of the VASI is that of color differentiation between red and white. Each light unit projects a beam of light having a white segment in the upper part and a red segment in the lower part of the beam. Thus, to be on the glide slope you need to be on the lower part of the far light (red) and on the upper part of the near light (white).

Answer (A) is incorrect. If the airplane is below the glide path, both rows of lights will be red, as indicated in D. Answer (C) is incorrect. If the aircraft is above the glide path, both lights will be white, as indicated in C.

42. (Refer to Figure 47 below.) While on final approach to a runway equipped with a standard 2-bar VASI, the lights appear as shown by illustration D. This means that the aircraft is

A. above the glide slope.

B. below the glide slope.

C. on the glide slope.

Answer (B) is correct. *(AIM Para 2-1-2)*

DISCUSSION: In illustration D of Fig. 47, both rows of lights are red. Thus, the aircraft is below the glide path. Remember, "red means dead."

Answer (A) is incorrect. If the airplane is above the glide path, the lights would both show white, as indicated by illustration C. Answer (C) is incorrect. If the airplane is on the glide path, the lights would be red over white, as indicated by illustration A.

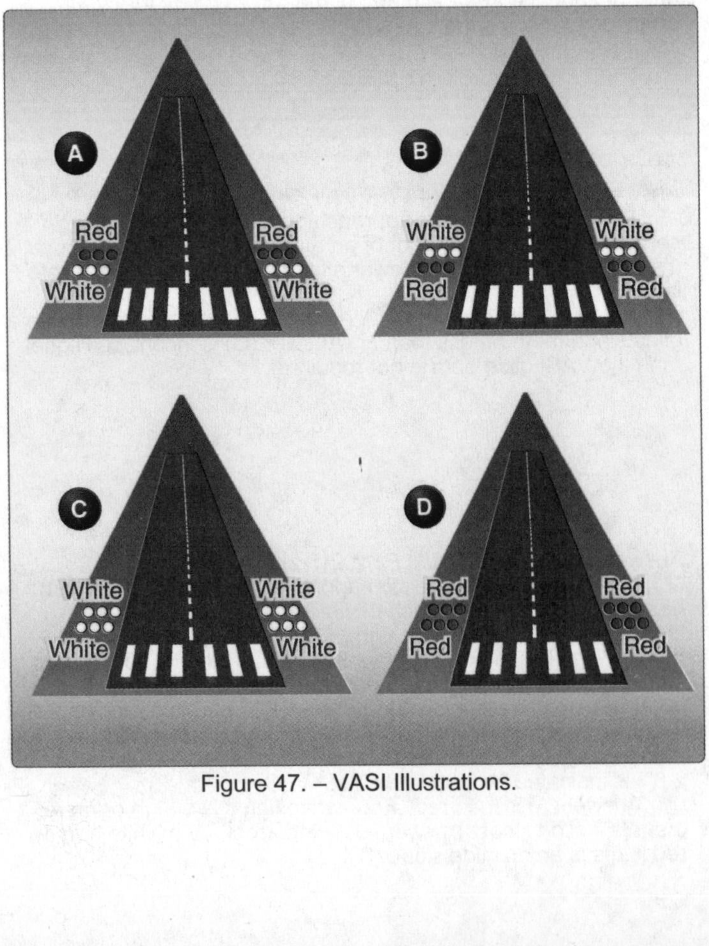

Figure 47. – VASI Illustrations.

43. Each pilot of an aircraft approaching to land on a runway served by a visual approach slope indicator (VASI) shall

A. maintain a 3° glide to the runway.

B. maintain an altitude at or above the glide slope.

C. stay high until the runway can be reached in a power-off landing.

Answer (B) is correct. *(14 CFR 91.129)*

DISCUSSION: When approaching to land on a runway served by a VASI, each pilot of an airplane must fly at or above the VASI glide path until a lower altitude is necessary for a safe landing.

Answer (A) is incorrect. A VASI may be adjusted to provide a glide slope more or less than 3°. Answer (C) is incorrect. Higher than the VASI glide path is not required.

44. Which approach and landing objective is assured when the pilot remains on the proper glidepath of the VASI?

A. Continuation of course guidance after transition to VFR.

B. Safe obstruction clearance in the approach area.

C. Course guidance from the visual descent point to touchdown.

Answer (B) is correct. *(AIM Para 2-1-2)*

DISCUSSION: The visual approach slope indicator (VASI) provides safe obstruction clearance within ± 10° of the extended runway centerline out to 4 NM. Pilots are advised to remain on the VASI-directed glide path throughout the entire approach to ensure obstruction clearance.

Answer (A) is incorrect. The VASI provides visual descent guidance, not course guidance. Course guidance implies lateral as well as vertical guidance. Answer (C) is incorrect. The VASI provides visual descent guidance, not course guidance. Course guidance implies lateral as well as vertical guidance.

45. Which approach and landing objective is assured when the pilot remains on the proper glidepath of the VASI?

A. Runway identification and course guidance.

B. Safe obstruction clearance in the approach area.

C. Lateral course guidance to the runway.

Answer (B) is correct. *(AIM Para 2-1-2)*

DISCUSSION: The visual approach slope indicator (VASI) provides safe obstruction clearance within ±10° of the extended runway centerline out to 4 NM. Pilots are advised to remain on the VASI-directed glide path throughout the entire approach to ensure obstruction clearance.

Answer (A) is incorrect. The VASI provides visual descent guidance, not course guidance and runway identification. Course guidance implies lateral as well as vertical guidance. Answer (C) is incorrect. The VASI provides visual descent guidance, not lateral course guidance.

3.6 Wake Turbulence

46. Wingtip vortices are created only when an aircraft is

A. operating at high airspeeds.

B. heavily loaded.

C. developing lift.

Answer (C) is correct. *(AIM Para 7-3-4)*

DISCUSSION: Wingtip vortices are the result of the pressure differential over and under a wing when that wing is producing lift. Wingtip vortices do not develop when an airplane is taxiing, although prop blast or jet thrust turbulence can be experienced near the rear of a large airplane that is taxiing.

Answer (A) is incorrect. The greatest turbulence is produced from an airplane operating at a slow airspeed. Answer (B) is incorrect. Even though a heavily loaded airplane may produce greater turbulence, an airplane does not have to be heavily loaded in order to produce wingtip vortices. Wingtip vortices are produced only when an airplane is developing lift.

47. When taking off or landing at an airport where heavy aircraft are operating, one should be particularly alert to the hazards of wingtip vortices because this turbulence tends to

A. rise from a crossing runway into the takeoff or landing path.

B. rise into the traffic pattern area surrounding the airport.

C. sink into the flightpath of aircraft operating below the aircraft generating the turbulence.

Answer (C) is correct. *(AIM Para 7-3-4)*

DISCUSSION: When taking off or landing at a busy airport where large, heavy airplanes are operating, you should be particularly alert to the hazards of wingtip vortices because this turbulence tends to sink into the flight paths of airplanes operating below the airplane generating the turbulence. Wingtip vortices are caused by a differential in high and low pressure at the wingtip of an airplane, creating a spiraling effect trailing behind the wingtip, similar to a horizontal tornado.

Answer (A) is incorrect. Wingtip vortices always trail behind an airplane and descend toward the ground. However, they do drift with the wind and will not stay directly behind an airplane if there is a crosswind. Answer (B) is incorrect. Wingtip vortices sink, not rise.

48. Wingtip vortices created by large aircraft tend to

A. sink below the aircraft generating turbulence.

B. rise into the traffic pattern.

C. rise into the takeoff or landing path of a crossing runway.

Answer (A) is correct. *(AIM Para 7-3-4)*

DISCUSSION: Wingtip vortices created by large airplanes tend to sink below the airplane generating the turbulence.

Answer (B) is incorrect. Wingtip vortices sink, not rise. Answer (C) is incorrect. Wingtip vortices do not rise or gain altitude, but sink toward the ground. However, they may move horizontally left or right depending on crosswind conditions.

49. How does the wake turbulence vortex circulate around each wingtip?

A. Inward, upward, and around each tip.

B. Inward, upward, and counterclockwise.

C. Outward, upward, and around each tip.

Answer (C) is correct. *(AIM Para 7-3-4)*

DISCUSSION: Since the pressure differential is caused by a lower pressure above the wing and a higher pressure below the wing, the air from the bottom moves out, up, and around each wingtip.

Answer (A) is incorrect. The air moves out around the edge of the wing, not in underneath the wing. Answer (B) is incorrect. The air moves out around the edge of the wing. From behind, the left wingtip vortex is clockwise and the right wingtip vortex is counterclockwise.

50. The greatest vortex strength occurs when the generating aircraft is

A. light, dirty, and fast.

B. heavy, dirty, and fast.

C. heavy, clean, and slow.

Answer (C) is correct. *(AIM Para 7-3-3)*

DISCUSSION: Vortices are the greatest when the wingtips are at high angles of attack. This occurs at high gross weight, flaps up, and low airspeed (heavy, clean, and slow).

Answer (A) is incorrect. Light aircraft produce less vortex turbulence than heavy aircraft. The use of flaps, spoilers, etc., (i.e., dirty) diminishes vortex turbulence. Answer (B) is incorrect. Being dirty and/or fast causes the wingtip to be at a lower angle of attack, presenting less of a danger than when clean and/or slow.

51. The wind condition that requires maximum caution when avoiding wake turbulence on landing is a

A. light, quartering headwind.

B. light, quartering tailwind.

C. strong headwind.

Answer (B) is correct. *(AIM Para 7-3-4)*

DISCUSSION: The most dangerous wind condition when avoiding wake turbulence on landing is a light, quartering tailwind. The tailwind can push the vortices forward, which could put it in the touchdown zone of your aircraft even if you used proper procedures and landed beyond the touchdown point of the preceding aircraft. Also, the quartering wind may push the upwind vortices to the middle of the runway.

Answer (A) is incorrect. Headwinds push the vortices out of your touchdown zone if you land beyond the touchdown point of the preceding aircraft. Answer (C) is incorrect. Strong winds help diffuse wake turbulence vortices.

52. When departing behind a heavy aircraft, the pilot should avoid wake turbulence by maneuvering the aircraft

A. below and downwind from the heavy aircraft.

B. above and upwind from the heavy aircraft.

C. below and upwind from the heavy aircraft.

Answer (B) is correct. *(AIM Para 7-3-6)*

DISCUSSION: The proper procedure for departing behind a large aircraft is to rotate prior to the large aircraft's rotation point, then fly above and upwind of the large aircraft. Since vortices sink and drift downwind, this should keep you clear.

Answer (A) is incorrect. You should remain above and upwind from the heavy aircraft. Answer (C) is incorrect. You should fly above the flight path of the large aircraft to avoid the sinking vortices.

53. When landing behind a large aircraft, the pilot should avoid wake turbulence by staying

A. above the large aircraft's final approach path and landing beyond the large aircraft's touchdown point.

B. below the large aircraft's final approach path and landing before the large aircraft's touchdown point.

C. above the large aircraft's final approach path and landing before the large aircraft's touchdown point.

Answer (A) is correct. *(AIM Para 7-3-6)*

DISCUSSION: When landing behind a large aircraft, your flight path should be above the other aircraft's flight path since the vortices sink. When the aircraft touches down, the vortices will stop, so you should thus touch down beyond where the large aircraft did.

Answer (B) is incorrect. Below the flight path, you will fly through the sinking vortices generated by the large aircraft. Answer (C) is incorrect. By landing before the large aircraft's touchdown point, you will have to fly below the preceding aircraft's flight path.

54. (Refer to Figure 48 below.) With winds reported as from 300° at 4 knots, you are given instructions to taxi to runway 30 for departure and to expect to take off after an airliner, which is departing from runway 35L. What effect would you expect from the airliner's vortices?

A. The winds will push the vortices into your takeoff path.

B. The crosswind will prevent lateral movement of the vortices.

C. The downwind vortex will rapidly dissipate.

Answer (A) is correct. *(AIM Para 7-3-4)*

DISCUSSION: A light wind between 1 to 5 knots could result in the upwind vortex remaining over the runway and hasten the drift of the downwind vortex toward your runway of intended departure.

Answer (B) is incorrect. A crosswind will decrease the lateral movement of the upwind vortex and increase the movement of the downwind vortex. Thus, with a light crosswind of 4 knots for Runway 35L, you can expect the airliner's upwind vortex to remain over runway 35L and the downwind vortex to hasten in drift toward your runway of intended departure. Answer (C) is incorrect. With a light crosswind of 4 knots, the wind will not rapidly dissipate the downwind vortex and, in this instance, the downwind vortex will move toward your runway of intended departure.

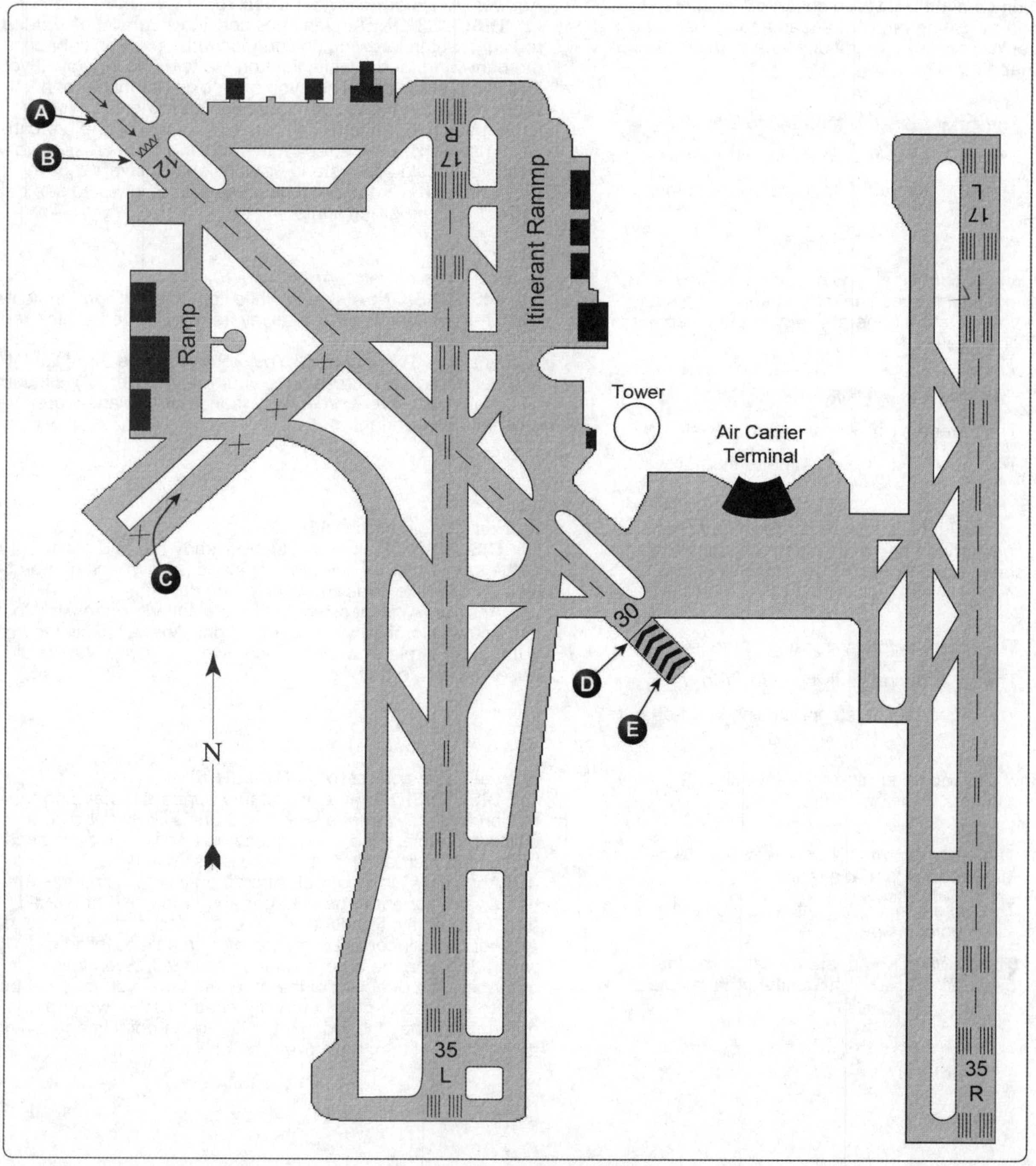

Figure 48. – Airport Diagram.

55. When landing behind a large aircraft, which procedure should be followed for vortex avoidance?

A. Stay above its final approach flightpath all the way to touchdown.

B. Stay below and to one side of its final approach flightpath.

C. Stay well below its final approach flightpath and land at least 2,000 feet behind.

Answer (A) is correct. *(AIM Para 7-3-6)*

DISCUSSION: When landing behind a large aircraft, stay above its final approach flight path all the way to touchdown; i.e., touch down beyond the touchdown point of the large aircraft.

Answer (B) is incorrect. You should stay at or above, not below, its flight path. Answer (C) is incorrect. You should stay at or above, not below, its flight path, and land beyond, not behind, its touchdown point.

3.7 Collision Avoidance

56. During a night flight, you observe a steady red light and a flashing red light ahead and at the same altitude. What is the general direction of movement of the other aircraft?

A. The other aircraft is crossing to the left.

B. The other aircraft is crossing to the right.

C. The other aircraft is approaching head-on.

Answer (A) is correct. *(AFH Chap 10)*

DISCUSSION: Airplane position lights consist of a steady red light on the left wing (looking forward), a green light on the right wing, and a white light on the tail. Accordingly, if you observe a steady red light, you are looking at the tip of a left wing, which means the other plane is traveling from your right to left (crossing to the left). The red flashing light is the beacon.

Answer (B) is incorrect. If the airplane were crossing to the right, you would see a steady green light. Answer (C) is incorrect. If the airplane were approaching head-on, you would see both the red and the green lights.

57. During a night flight, you observe a steady white light and a flashing red light ahead and at the same altitude. What is the general direction of movement of the other aircraft?

A. The other aircraft is flying away from you.

B. The other aircraft is crossing to the left.

C. The other aircraft is crossing to the right.

Answer (A) is correct. *(AFH Chap 10)*

DISCUSSION: A steady white light (the tail light) indicates the other airplane is moving away from you. The flashing red light is the beacon light.

Answer (B) is incorrect. You would observe a red light if another plane were crossing to your left. Answer (C) is incorrect. You would observe a green light if another airplane were crossing to your right.

58. During a night flight, you observe steady red and green lights ahead and at the same altitude. What is the general direction of movement of the other aircraft?

A. The other aircraft is crossing to the left.

B. The other aircraft is flying away from you.

C. The other aircraft is approaching head-on.

Answer (C) is correct. *(AFH Chap 10)*

DISCUSSION: If you observe steady red and green lights at the same altitude, the other airplane is approaching head-on. You should take evasive action to the right.

Answer (A) is incorrect. If the airplane were crossing to the left, you would observe only a red light. Answer (B) is incorrect. If the other airplane were headed away from you, you would observe a white (tail) light.

59. How can you determine if another aircraft is on a collision course with your aircraft?

A. The other aircraft will always appear to get larger and closer at a rapid rate.

B. The nose of each aircraft is pointed at the same point in space.

C. There will be no apparent relative motion between your aircraft and the other aircraft.

Answer (C) is correct. *(AIM Para 8-1-8)*

DISCUSSION: Any aircraft that appears to have no relative motion and stays in one scan quadrant is likely to be on a collision course. Also, if a target shows no lateral or vertical motion but increases in size, take evasive action.

Answer (A) is incorrect. Aircraft on collision courses may not always appear to grow larger and/or to close at a rapid rate. Frequently, the degree of proximity cannot be detected. Answer (B) is incorrect. You may not be able to tell in exactly which direction the other airplane is pointed. Even if you could determine the direction of the other airplane, you may not be able to accurately project the flight paths of the two airplanes to determine if they indeed point to the same point in space and will arrive there at the same time (i.e., collide).

60. The most effective method of scanning for other aircraft for collision avoidance during daylight hours is to use

A. regularly spaced concentration on the 3-, 9-, and 12-o'clock positions.

B. a series of short, regularly spaced eye movements to search each 10-degree sector.

C. peripheral vision by scanning small sectors and utilizing offcenter viewing.

Answer (B) is correct. *(AC 90-48D)*

DISCUSSION: The most effective way to scan for other aircraft during daylight hours is to use a series of short, regularly spaced eye movements that bring successive areas of the sky into your central visual field. Each movement should not exceed 10°, and each area should be observed for at least one second to enable detection. Only a very small center area of the eye has the ability to send clear, sharply focused messages to the brain. All other areas provide less detail.

Answer (A) is incorrect. The spacing between the positions should be 10°, not 90°. Answer (C) is incorrect. This is the recommended nighttime scanning procedure.

61. The most effective method of scanning for other aircraft for collision avoidance during nighttime hours is to use

A. regularly spaced concentration on the 3-, 9-, and 12-o'clock positions.

B. a series of short, regularly spaced eye movements to search each 30-degree sector.

C. peripheral vision by scanning small sectors and utilizing offcenter viewing.

Answer (C) is correct. *(AC 90-48D)*

DISCUSSION: At night, collision avoidance scanning must use the off-center portions of the eyes; these portions are most effective at seeing objects at night. Accordingly, in order to perceive a very dim lighted object in a certain direction (i.e., another aircraft), you should use peripheral vision and scan small sectors adjacent to the object; short stops of a few seconds in each scan area will help to detect the light and its movement. This is in contrast to daytime searching for air traffic, when center viewing should be used.

Answer (A) is incorrect. All areas (up, below, and on all sides) should be scanned for other air traffic. Do not concentrate only on the 3-, 9-, and 12-o'clock positions. Answer (B) is incorrect. Smaller than 30° sectors should be scanned.

62. Prior to starting each maneuver, pilots should

A. check altitude, airspeed, and heading indications.

B. visually scan the entire area for collision avoidance.

C. announce their intentions on the nearest CTAF.

Answer (B) is correct. *(AIM Para 4-4-14)*

DISCUSSION: Prior to each maneuver, a pilot should visually scan the entire area for collision avoidance. Many maneuvers require a clearing turn, which should be used for this purpose.

Answer (A) is incorrect. Altitude, speed, and heading may not all be critical to every maneuver. Collision avoidance is! Answer (C) is incorrect. CTAF is used for operations at an uncontrolled airport, not for pilots doing maneuvers away from an airport.

63. What procedure is recommended when climbing or descending VFR on an airway?

A. Execute gentle banks left and right for continuous visual scanning of the airspace.

B. Advise the nearest FSS of the altitude changes.

C. Fly away from the centerline of the airway before changing altitude.

Answer (A) is correct. *(AC 90-48D)*

DISCUSSION: When climbing (descending) VFR on an airway, you should execute gentle banks left and right to facilitate scanning for other aircraft. Collision avoidance is a constant priority and especially pertinent to climbs and descents on airways where other traffic is expected.

Answer (B) is incorrect. An FSS provides no en route traffic service. Answer (C) is incorrect. It is not necessary to leave the center of the airway, only to scan for other aircraft.

64. Most midair collision accidents occur during

A. hazy days.

B. clear days.

C. cloudy nights.

Answer (B) is correct. *(AC 90-48D)*

DISCUSSION: Most midair collision accidents and reported near midair collision incidents occur during good VFR weather conditions (i.e., clear days) and during the hours of daylight. This is when more aircraft are likely to be flying.

Answer (A) is incorrect. During hazy days, fewer pilots will be flying, and those who are will be more vigilant in their scanning for other traffic. Answer (C) is incorrect. During cloudy nights, fewer pilots will be flying, and those who are will be more vigilant in their scanning for other traffic.

65. Responsibility for collision avoidance in an alert area rests with

A. the controlling agency.

B. all pilots.

C. Air Traffic Control.

Answer (B) is correct. *(AIM Para 3-4-6)*

DISCUSSION: Alert areas may contain a high volume of pilot training or other unusual activity. Pilots using the area as well as pilots crossing the area are equally responsible for collision avoidance.

Answer (A) is incorrect. Pilots are responsible for collision avoidance, not controlling agencies. Answer (C) is incorrect. Pilots are responsible for collision avoidance, not ATC.

66. Eye movements during daytime collision avoidance scanning should

A. not exceed 10 degrees and view each sector at least 1 second.

B. be 30 degrees and view each sector at least 3 seconds.

C. use peripheral vision by scanning small sectors and utilizing off-center viewing.

Answer (A) is correct. *(AC 90-48C)*

DISCUSSION: The most effective way to scan for other aircraft during daylight hours is to use a series of short, regularly spaced eye movements that bring successive areas of the sky into your central visual field. Each movement should not exceed 10°, and each area should be observed for at least 1 second to enable detection. Only a very small center area of the eye has the ability to send clear, sharply focused messages to the brain.

Answer (B) is incorrect. The spacing for the scan between positions should be 10°, not 30°. Answer (C) is incorrect. At night, collision avoidance scanning must use the off-center portions of the eyes. These portions are most effective at seeing objects at night. Accordingly, peripheral vision should be used, scanning small sectors and using off-screen viewing. This is in contrast to daytime searching for air traffic when center viewing should be used.

67. The Aeronautical Information Manual (AIM) specifically encourages pilots to turn on their landing lights when operating below 10,000 feet, day or night, and especially when operating

A. in Class B airspace.

B. in conditions of reduced visibility.

C. within 15 miles of a towered airport.

Answer (B) is correct. *(AIM Para 4-3-23)*

DISCUSSION: The FAA has a voluntary pilot safety program known as "Operation Lights On" to enhance the see-and-avoid concept. Pilots are encouraged to turn on their landing lights when operating below 10,000 feet, day or night, especially when operating within 10 miles of any airport or in conditions of reduced visibility.

Answer (A) is incorrect. The *AIM* does not indicate any specific airspace. Pilots should turn on their landing lights in conditions of reduced visibility, regardless of the airspace in which they are operating. Answer (C) is incorrect. Lights should be used within 10 miles of any airport, towered or not.

68. It is the responsibility of the pilot and crew to report a near midair collision as a result of proximity of at least

A. 50 feet or less to another aircraft.

B. 500 feet or less to another aircraft.

C. 1,000 feet or less to another aircraft.

Answer (B) is correct. *(AIM Para 7-6-3)*

DISCUSSION: A near midair collision is defined as an incident associated with the operation of an airplane in which a possibility of collision occurs as a result of proximity of less than 500 ft. to another airplane. It is the responsibility of the pilot and/or flight crew to determine whether a near midair collision did actually occur and to initiate a near midair collision report.

Answer (A) is incorrect. A near midair collision is reported if the possibility of a collision occurs as a result of proximity of less than 500 ft., not 50 ft., to another airplane. Answer (C) is incorrect. Proximity of greater than 500 ft. is not considered a near midair collision and would not be reported as such.

3.8 ATIS and Ground Control

69. After landing at a tower-controlled airport, when should the pilot contact ground control?

A. When advised by the tower to do so.

B. Prior to turning off the runway.

C. After reaching a taxiway that leads directly to the parking area.

Answer (A) is correct. *(AIM Para 4-3-20)*

DISCUSSION: After landing at a tower-controlled airport, you should contact ground control on the appropriate frequency only when instructed by the tower.

Answer (B) is incorrect. A pilot should not change frequencies unless instructed to do so by the tower. Sometimes the tower controller will be handling both tower and ground frequencies. Switching without permission may be confusing to ATC. Answer (C) is incorrect. A pilot should not change frequencies unless instructed to do so by the tower. Sometimes the tower controller will be handling both tower and ground frequencies. Switching without permission may be confusing to ATC.

70. If instructed by ground control to taxi to Runway 9, the pilot may proceed

A. via taxiways and across runways to, but not onto, Runway 9.

B. to the next intersecting runway where further clearance is required.

C. via taxiways and across runways to Runway 9, where an immediate takeoff may be made.

Answer (B) is correct. *(AIM Para 4-3-18)*

DISCUSSION: A taxi clearance from ATC authorizes the pilot to utilize taxiways along the taxi route, but a specific crossing clearance must be issued for all runways along the route.

Answer (A) is incorrect. A clearance to taxi to the active runway means a pilot has been given permission to taxi via taxiways to, but not onto, the active runway. ATC must issue a specific clearance to cross any runway along the taxi route. Answer (C) is incorrect. The clearance to taxi to a runway does not permit taxiing onto the active runway.

71. Automatic Terminal Information Service (ATIS) is the continuous broadcast of recorded information concerning

A. pilots of radar-identified aircraft whose aircraft is in dangerous proximity to terrain or to an obstruction.

B. nonessential information to reduce frequency congestion.

C. noncontrol information in selected high-activity terminal areas.

Answer (C) is correct. *(AIM Para 4-1-13)*

DISCUSSION: The continuous broadcast of recorded noncontrol information is known as the Automatic Terminal Information Service (ATIS). ATIS includes weather, active runway, and other information that arriving and departing pilots need to know.

Answer (A) is incorrect. A controller who has a radar-identified aircraft under his or her control will issue a terrain or obstruction alert to an aircraft that is in dangerous proximity to terrain or to an obstruction. Answer (B) is incorrect. ATIS is considered essential (not nonessential) information, but routine, i.e., noncontrol.

72. Absence of the sky condition and visibility on an ATIS broadcast indicates that

A. weather conditions are at or above VFR minimums.

B. the sky condition is clear and visibility is unrestricted.

C. the ceiling is at least 5,000 feet and visibility is 5 miles or more.

Answer (C) is correct. *(AIM Para 4-1-13)*

DISCUSSION: The ceiling/sky condition, visibility, and obstructions to vision may be omitted from the ATIS broadcast if the ceiling is above 5,000 ft. with visibility more than 5 statute miles.

Answer (A) is incorrect. The absence of the sky condition and visibility on an ATIS broadcast implies that the ceiling is above 5,000 ft. and the visibility is more than 5 statute miles. Answer (B) is incorrect. The absence of the sky condition and visibility on an ATIS broadcast implies that the ceiling is above 5,000 ft., not clear, and the visibility is more than 5 SM, not unrestricted.

3.9 Class D Airspace and Airport Advisory Area

73. A blue segmented circle on a Sectional Chart depicts which class airspace?

A. Class B.

B. Class C.

C. Class D.

Answer (C) is correct. *(AIM Para 3-2-5)*

DISCUSSION: A blue segmented circle on a sectional chart depicts Class D airspace.

Answer (A) is incorrect. Class B airspace is depicted on a sectional chart by a solid, not segmented, blue circle. Answer (B) is incorrect. Class C airspace is depicted on a sectional chart by a solid magenta, not a blue segmented, circle.

74. Airspace at an airport with a part-time control tower is classified as Class D airspace only

A. when the weather minimums are below basic VFR.

B. when the associated control tower is in operation.

C. when the associated Flight Service Station is in operation.

Answer (B) is correct. *(AIM Para 3-2-5)*

DISCUSSION: A Class D airspace area is automatically in effect when and only when the associated part-time control tower is in operation regardless of weather conditions, availability of radar services, or time of day. Airports with part-time operating towers only have a part-time Class D airspace area.

Answer (A) is incorrect. A Class D airspace area is automatically in effect when the tower is in operation, regardless of the weather conditions. Answer (C) is incorrect. A Class D airspace area is in effect when the associated control tower, not FSS, is in operation.

75. When a control tower located on an airport within Class D airspace ceases operation for the day, what happens to the airspace designation?

A. The airspace designation normally will not change.

B. The airspace remains Class D airspace as long as a weather observer or automated weather system is available.

C. The airspace reverts to Class E or a combination of Class E and G airspace during the hours the tower is not in operation.

Answer (C) is correct. *(AIM Para 3-2-5)*

DISCUSSION: When a tower ceases operation, the Class D airspace reverts to Class E or a combination of Class G and Class E.

Answer (A) is incorrect. Class D airspace is designated when there is an operating control tower. When the tower ceases operation for the day, the airspace reverts to Class E or a combination of Class G and Class E airspace. Answer (B) is incorrect. The airspace reverts to Class E, not Class D, when the tower ceases operation for the day and an approved weather observer or automated weather system is available.

76. A non-tower satellite airport, within the same Class D airspace as that designated for the primary airport, requires radio communications be established and maintained with the

A. satellite airport's UNICOM.

B. associated Flight Service Station.

C. primary airport's control tower.

Answer (C) is correct. *(AIM Para 3-2-5)*

DISCUSSION: Each pilot departing a non-tower satellite airport, within Class D airspace, must establish and maintain two-way radio communications with the primary airport's control tower as soon as practicable after departing.

Answer (A) is incorrect. When departing a satellite airport without an operating control tower in Class D airspace, you must establish and maintain two-way radio communications with the primary airport's control tower, not the satellite airport's UNICOM. Answer (B) is incorrect. When departing a satellite airport without an operating control tower in Class D airspace, you must establish and maintain two-way radio communications with the primary airport's control tower, not the associated FSS.

77. Unless otherwise authorized, two-way radio communications with Air Traffic Control are required for landings or takeoffs at all towered airports

A. regardless of weather conditions.

B. only when weather conditions are less than VFR.

C. within Class D airspace only when weather conditions are less than VFR.

Answer (A) is correct. *(14 CFR 91.129)*

DISCUSSION: Two-way radio communications with air traffic control (ATC) are required for landing and taking off at all tower controlled airports, regardless of weather conditions. However, light signals from the tower may be used during radio failure.

Answer (B) is incorrect. Radio communication is also required in VFR weather as well as IFR weather at all tower-controlled airports. Answer (C) is incorrect. Radio communication is required in both VFR and IFR weather when landing at or taking off at all tower-controlled airports within Class D airspace.

78. The lateral dimensions of Class D airspace are based on

A. the number of airports that lie within the Class D airspace.

B. 5 statute miles from the geographical center of the primary airport.

C. the instrument procedures for which the controlled airspace is established.

Answer (C) is correct. *(AIM Para 3-2-5)*

DISCUSSION: The lateral dimensions of Class D airspace are based upon the instrument procedures for which the controlled airspace is established.

Answer (A) is incorrect. While the FAA will attempt to exclude satellite airports as much as possible from Class D airspace, the major criteria for the lateral dimension will be based on the instrument procedures for which the controlled airspace is established. Answer (B) is incorrect. The lateral dimensions of Class D airspace are based on the instrument procedures for which the Class D airspace is established, not a specified radius from the primary airport.

79. Prior to entering an Airport Advisory Area, a pilot should

A. monitor ATIS for weather and traffic advisories.

B. contact approach control for vectors to the traffic pattern.

C. contact the local FSS for airport and traffic advisories.

Answer (C) is correct. *(AIM Para 4-1-9)*

DISCUSSION: Airport Advisory Areas exist at noncontrolled airports that have a Flight Service Station (FSS) located on that airport. The FSS provides advisory (not control) information on traffic, weather, etc., to requesting aircraft. Accordingly, pilots should (not must) contact FSSs for advisory services.

Answer (A) is incorrect. ATIS (automatic terminal information service) provides prerecorded weather and airport data but not traffic advisories. Answer (B) is incorrect. Approach control may provide vectors to the airport, but the controller will instruct you to switch to the advisory frequency for airport and traffic advisories.

80. When should pilots state their position on the airport when calling the tower for takeoff?

A. When visibility is less than 1 mile.

B. When parallel runways are in use.

C. When departing from a runway intersection.

Answer (C) is correct. *(AIM Para 4-3-10)*

DISCUSSION: Intersection departures are often performed at busy, tower-controlled airports. When notifying the tower that you are ready for departure, you must inform the controller of your location so that (s)he can positively identify you before clearing you for takeoff.

Answer (A) is incorrect. When visibility is less than 1 mile, the field will be operating under instrument flight rules. As a private pilot without an instrument rating, you will not be operating in these conditions. Answer (B) is incorrect. Controllers only require that you notify them of your position when departing from a runway intersection.

3.10 Class C Airspace

81. The radius of the procedural outer area of Class C airspace is normally

A. 10 NM.

B. 20 NM.

C. 30 NM.

Answer (B) is correct. *(AIM Para 3-2-4)*

DISCUSSION: A 20-NM radius procedural outer area surrounds the primary airport in Class C airspace. This area is not charted and generally does not require action from the pilot.

Answer (A) is incorrect. Each Class C airspace is individually tailored to the specific area; however, most Class C airspace consists of a charted 5-NM radius core area that extends from the surface to 4,000 ft. AGL and a charted 10-NM radius shelf that extends from 1,200 ft. AGL to 4,000 ft. AGL. Answer (C) is incorrect. A 30-NM outer area does not surround Class C airspace; however, a 30-NM Mode C veil does surround Class B airspace.

82. All operations within Class C airspace must be

A. on a flight plan filed prior to arrival or departure.

B. in communications with the responsible ATC facility.

C. in an aircraft equipped with a transponder with automatic altitude reporting capability.

Answer (B) is correct. *(AIM Para 3-2-4)*

DISCUSSION: All aircraft operating in Class C airspace are required to contact and establish communications with approach control on the appropriate frequency.

Answer (A) is incorrect. Flight plans are not required in Class C airspace. Answer (C) is incorrect. ATC may allow an aircraft without a functioning transponder to enter Class C airspace.

83. Under what condition may an aircraft operate from a satellite airport within Class C airspace?

A. The pilot must file a flight plan prior to departure.

B. The pilot must monitor ATC until clear of the Class C airspace.

C. The pilot must contact ATC as soon as practicable after takeoff.

Answer (C) is correct. *(AIM Para 3-2-4)*

DISCUSSION: Aircraft departing from a satellite airport within Class C airspace with an operating control tower must establish and maintain two-way radio communication with the control tower and thereafter as instructed by ATC. When departing a satellite airport without an operating control tower, the pilot must contact and maintain two-way radio communication with ATC as soon as practicable after takeoff.

Answer (A) is incorrect. Flight plans are not required in Class C airspace. Answer (B) is incorrect. The pilot must maintain communication with ATC, not just monitor ATC, in Class C airspace.

84. Which initial action should a pilot take prior to entering Class C airspace?

A. Contact approach control on the appropriate frequency.

B. Contact the tower and request permission to enter.

C. Contact the FSS for traffic advisories.

Answer (A) is correct. *(AIM Para 3-2-4)*

DISCUSSION: Prior to entering Class C airspace, a pilot must contact and establish communication with approach control on the appropriate frequency.

Answer (B) is incorrect. The tower normally controls the air traffic in the traffic pattern, not the aircraft entering the Class C airspace area. Answer (C) is incorrect. The pilot should contact approach control, not FSS, prior to entering Class C airspace.

85. The vertical limit of Class C airspace above the primary airport is normally

A. 1,200 feet AGL.

B. 3,000 feet AGL.

C. 4,000 feet AGL.

Answer (C) is correct. *(AIM Para 3-2-4)*

DISCUSSION: The vertical limit (ceiling) of Class C airspace is normally 4,000 ft. above the primary airport elevation.

Answer (A) is incorrect. This is the floor, not the vertical limit, of the Class C airspace shelf area (5 to 10 NM from primary airport). Answer (B) is incorrect. The vertical limit of Class C airspace is normally 4,000 ft. AGL, not 3,000 ft. AGL, above the elevation of the primary airport.

3.11 Terminal Radar Programs

86. TRSA Service in the terminal radar program provides

A. IFR separation (1,000 feet vertical and 3 miles lateral) between all aircraft.

B. warning to pilots when their aircraft are in unsafe proximity to terrain, obstructions, or other aircraft.

C. sequencing and separation for participating VFR aircraft.

Answer (C) is correct. *(AIM Para 4-1-17)*

DISCUSSION: TRSA service in the terminal radar program provides sequencing and separation for all participating VFR aircraft within the airspace defined as a Terminal Radar Service Area (TRSA). Pilot participation is urged but is not mandatory.

Answer (A) is incorrect. TRSA service provides VFR aircraft with a 500-ft., not 1,000-ft., vertical clearance from other aircraft. Answer (B) is incorrect. TRSA service is for traffic advisories, separation between aircraft, and vectoring, not for obstruction clearance.

87. From whom should a departing VFR aircraft request radar traffic information during ground operations?

A. Clearance delivery.

B. Tower, just before takeoff.

C. Ground control, on initial contact.

Answer (C) is correct. *(AIM Para 4-1-17)*

DISCUSSION: Pilots of departing VFR aircraft are encouraged to request radar traffic information by notifying ground control on initial contact with their request and proposed direction of flight.

Answer (A) is incorrect. Clearance delivery is usually used at busier airports where radar traffic information may be provided without request. Answer (B) is incorrect. Ground control rather than tower control is the appropriate place to make the request (giving ATC more time to coordinate your request).

88. Basic radar service in the terminal radar program is best described as

A. safety alerts, traffic advisories, and limited vectoring to VFR aircraft.

B. mandatory radar service provided by the Automated Radar Terminal System (ARTS) program.

C. wind-shear warning at participating airports.

Answer (A) is correct. *(AIM Para 4-1-17)*

DISCUSSION: Basic radar service in the terminal radar program provides safety alerts, traffic advisories, and limited vectoring (on a workload-permitting basis) to VFR aircraft.

Answer (B) is incorrect. Mandatory radar service is required only in Class B and Class C airspace. Answer (C) is incorrect. The Low-Level Wind Shear Alert System (LLWAS) is based on information gathered from various wind (speed and direction) sensors on and around the airport, not on radar.

3.12 Transponders and Transponder Codes

89. If Air Traffic Control advises that radar service is terminated when the pilot is departing Class C airspace, the transponder should be set to code

A. 0000

B. 1200

C. 4096

Answer (B) is correct. *(AIM Para 4-1-19)*

DISCUSSION: The code 1200 designates VFR operations when another number is not assigned by ATC.

Answer (A) is incorrect. This is not a transponder code. Answer (C) is incorrect. The numbers only go up to 7, so a 9 is not possible.

90. When making routine transponder code changes, pilots should avoid inadvertent selection of which codes?

A. 7200

B. 7000

C. 7500

Answer (C) is correct. *(AIM Para 4-1-19)*

DISCUSSION: Some special codes set aside for emergencies should be avoided during routine VFR flights. They are 7500 for hijacking, 7600 for lost radio communications, and 7700 for a general emergency. Additionally, you should know that code 7777 is reserved for military interceptors.

Answer (A) is incorrect. Code 7200 may be assigned by ATC. Answer (B) is incorrect. Code 7000 may be assigned by ATC.

91. When making routine transponder code changes, pilots should avoid inadvertent selection of which code?

A. 1200.

B. 7600.

C. 4096.

Answer (B) is correct. *(AIM Para 4-1-19)*

DISCUSSION: Some special codes set aside for emergencies should be avoided during routine VFR flights. They are 7500 for hijacking, 7600 for lost radio communications, and 7700 for a general emergency. Additionally, you should know that code 7777 is reserved for military interceptors.

Answer (A) is incorrect. This is the standard VFR code. Answer (C) is incorrect. This is the number of possible codes, not an actual code itself. Additionally, the transponder digits only go up to 7, so a 9 is not possible.

92. When operating under VFR below 18,000 feet MSL, unless otherwise authorized, what transponder code should be selected?

A. 1200.

B. 7600.

C. 7700.

Answer (A) is correct. *(AIM Para 4-1-19)*

DISCUSSION: The standard VFR transponder code is 1200. Since all flight operations above 18,000 ft. MSL are to be IFR, code 1200 is not used above that height.

Answer (B) is incorrect. This is the lost radio communications code. Answer (C) is incorrect. This is the general emergency code.

93. At an altitude below 18,000 feet MSL, which transponder code should be selected?

A. Mode A/3, Code 1200.

B. Mode F, Code 1200.

C. Mode C, Code 4096.

Answer (A) is correct. *(AIM Para 4-1-20)*

DISCUSSION: The standard VFR transponder code is 1200. Since all flight operations above 18,000 ft. MSL are to be IFR, code 1200 is not used above that height.

Answer (B) is incorrect. The standard VFR transponder code is 1200, but Mode F is not a valid transponder type. Answer (C) is incorrect. Mode C is a valid transponder type, but 4096 is the number of possible codes, not an actual code itself. Additionally, the transponder digits only go up to 7, so a 9 is not possible.

94. Which of the following codes should be set for VFR flight in Class E airspace?

A. 1200, Mode A/3.

B. 1200, Mode F.

C. 4600, Mode S.

Answer (A) is correct. *(AIM Para 4-1-19)*

DISCUSSION: The standard VFR transponder code is 1200. Since all flight operations above 18,000 ft. MSL are to be IFR, code 1200 is not used above that height.

Answer (B) is incorrect. The standard VFR transponder code is 1200, but Mode F is not a valid transponder type. Answer (C) is incorrect. Mode S is a valid transponder type, but 4600 is not the correct standard VFR transponder code.

95. Unless otherwise authorized, if flying a transponder equipped aircraft, a pilot should squawk which VFR code?

A. 1200

B. 7600

C. 7700

Answer (A) is correct. *(AIM Para 4-1-20)*

DISCUSSION: A pilot flying a transponder-equipped aircraft should set that transponder on code (squawk) 1200, which is the VFR code.

Answer (B) is incorrect. Code 7600 is the lost communication code. Answer (C) is incorrect. Code 7700 is the general emergency code.

3.13 Radio Phraseology

96. When flying HAWK N666CB, the proper phraseology for initial contact with McAlester FSS is

A. "MC ALESTER RADIO, HAWK SIX SIX SIX CHARLIE BRAVO, RECEIVING ARDMORE VORTAC, OVER."

B. "MC ALESTER STATION, HAWK SIX SIX SIX CEE BEE, RECEIVING ARDMORE VORTAC, OVER."

C. "MC ALESTER FLIGHT SERVICE STATION, HAWK NOVEMBER SIX CHARLIE BRAVO, RECEIVING ARDMORE VORTAC, OVER."

Answer (A) is correct. *(AIM Para 4-2-3)*

DISCUSSION: When calling a ground station, pilots should begin with the name of the facility and the type of facility. Any FSS is referred to as "Radio." When the aircraft manufacturer's name or model is stated, the prefix "N" is dropped. When transmitting and receiving on different frequencies, indicate the name of the VOR or frequency on which a reply is expected. Thus, the proper phraseology on initial contact with McAlester FSS is McAlester Radio, Hawk Six Six Six Charlie Bravo, Receiving Ardmore VORTAC, Over. (NOTE: The word "over" has been dropped from common usage.)

Answer (B) is incorrect. It is McAlester radio, not station, and CB is Charlie Bravo, not cee bee. Answer (C) is incorrect. It is radio, not flight service station. November is dropped in favor of Hawk; also, it is six, six, six Charlie Bravo (not six Charlie Bravo).

97. The correct method of stating 4,500 feet MSL to ATC is

A. "FOUR THOUSAND FIVE HUNDRED."

B. "FOUR POINT FIVE."

C. "FORTY-FIVE HUNDRED FEET MSL."

Answer (A) is correct. *(AIM Para 4-2-9)*

DISCUSSION: The proper phraseology for altitudes up to but not including 18,000 ft. MSL is to state the separate digits of the thousands, plus the hundreds, if appropriate. It would be "four thousand, five hundred."

Answer (B) is incorrect. Four point five is slang (not correct) phraseology. Answer (C) is incorrect. The thousand is spoken separately from the hundreds and not together. A stated altitude is understood to be MSL, unless otherwise stated.

98. The correct method of stating 10,500 feet MSL to ATC is

A. "TEN THOUSAND, FIVE HUNDRED FEET."

B. "TEN POINT FIVE."

C. "ONE ZERO THOUSAND, FIVE HUNDRED."

Answer (C) is correct. *(AIM Para 4-2-9)*

DISCUSSION: The proper phraseology for altitudes up to but not including 18,000 ft. MSL is to state the separate digits of the thousands, plus the hundreds, if appropriate. It would be one zero thousand, five hundred.

Answer (A) is incorrect. It is one zero, not ten. Answer (B) is incorrect. Ten point five is slang (not correct) phraseology.

3.14 ATC Traffic Advisories

99. ATC advises, "traffic 12 o'clock," this advisory is relative to your

A. true course.

B. ground track.

C. magnetic heading.

Answer (B) is correct. *(AIM Para 4-1-15)*

DISCUSSION: When issuing radar traffic information, the controller will provide the direction of the traffic from your airplane in relation to the 12-hr. clock based on your ground track or magnetic course.

Answer (A) is incorrect. The controller will issue radar traffic information in relation to the 12-hr. clock based on your airplane's magnetic, not true, course. Answer (C) is incorrect. The controller will issue radar traffic information in relation to the 12-hr. clock based on your airplane's ground track, not magnetic heading.

100. An ATC radar facility issues the following advisory to a pilot flying on a heading of 090°:

"TRAFFIC 3 O'CLOCK, 2 MILES, WESTBOUND..."

Where should the pilot look for this traffic?

A. East.

B. South.

C. West.

Answer (B) is correct. *(AIM Para 4-1-14)*

DISCUSSION: If you receive traffic information service from radar and are told you have traffic at the 3 o'clock position, traffic is in the direction of the right wingtip, or to the south.

Answer (A) is incorrect. East is the 12 o'clock position. Answer (C) is incorrect. West is the 6 o'clock position.

101. An ATC radar facility issues the following advisory to a pilot flying on a heading of 360°:

"TRAFFIC 10 O'CLOCK, 2 MILES, SOUTHBOUND..."

Where should the pilot look for this traffic?

A. Northwest.

B. Northeast.

C. Southwest.

Answer (A) is correct. *(AIM Para 4-1-14)*

DISCUSSION: The controller is telling you that traffic is at 10 o'clock and 2 mi. 9 o'clock is the left wingtip, and 10 o'clock is 2/3 of the way from the nose of the airplane (12 o'clock) to the left wingtip. Thus, you are looking northwest.

Answer (B) is incorrect. Northeast would be in the 1 to 2 o'clock position. Answer (C) is incorrect. Southwest would be in the 7 to 8 o'clock position.

102. An ATC radar facility issues the following advisory to a pilot during a local flight:

"TRAFFIC 2 O'CLOCK, 5 MILES, NORTHBOUND..."

Where should the pilot look for this traffic?

A. Between directly ahead and 90° to the left.

B. Between directly behind and 90° to the right.

C. Between directly ahead and 90° to the right.

Answer (C) is correct. *(AIM Para 4-1-14)*

DISCUSSION: The right wingtip is 3 o'clock, and the nose is 12 o'clock. A controller report of traffic 2 o'clock, 5 mi., northbound indicates that the traffic is to the right of the airplane's nose, just ahead of the right wingtip.

Answer (A) is incorrect. The area directly ahead to 90° left is the area from 12 o'clock to 9 o'clock. Answer (B) is incorrect. The area directly behind to 90° right is the area from 6 o'clock to 3 o'clock.

103. An ATC radar facility issues the following advisory to a pilot flying north in a calm wind:

"TRAFFIC 9 O'CLOCK, 2 MILES, SOUTHBOUND..."

Where should the pilot look for this traffic?

A. South.

B. North.

C. West.

Answer (C) is correct. *(AIM Para 4-1-14)*

DISCUSSION: Traffic at 9 o'clock is off the left wingtip. The nose of the airplane is 12 o'clock, the left wingtip is 9 o'clock, the tail is 6 o'clock, and the right wingtip is 3 o'clock. With a north heading, the aircraft at 9 o'clock would be west of you.

Answer (A) is incorrect. South would be the 6 o'clock position. Answer (B) is incorrect. North would be the 12 o'clock position.

3.15 ATC Light Signals

104. While on final approach for landing, an alternating green and red light followed by a flashing red light is received from the control tower. Under these circumstances, the pilot should

A. discontinue the approach, fly the same traffic pattern and approach again, and land.

B. exercise extreme caution and abandon the approach, realizing the airport is unsafe for landing.

C. abandon the approach, circle the airport to the right, and expect a flashing white light when the airport is safe for landing.

Answer (B) is correct. *(14 CFR 91.125)*

DISCUSSION: An alternating red and green light signaled from a control tower means "exercise extreme caution" whether to an airplane on the ground or in the air. The flashing red light received while in the air indicates the airport is not safe, and the pilot should not land.

Answer (A) is incorrect. A flashing green (not red) light means to return for a landing. Answer (C) is incorrect. A flashing green (not red) light means to return for a landing, and a flashing white light does not have a meaning to aircraft in flight.

105. A steady green light signal directed from the control tower to an aircraft in flight is a signal that the pilot

A. is cleared to land.

B. should give way to other aircraft and continue circling.

C. should return for landing.

Answer (A) is correct. *(14 CFR 91.125)*

DISCUSSION: A steady green light signal from the tower to an airplane in flight means cleared to land.

Answer (B) is incorrect. Give way to other aircraft and continue circling is signaled by a steady red light to an airplane in the air. Answer (C) is incorrect. Return for landing is signaled by a flashing green light to an airplane in the air.

106. A flashing white light signal from the control tower to a taxiing aircraft is an indication to

A. taxi at a faster speed.

B. taxi only on taxiways and not cross runways.

C. return to the starting point on the airport.

Answer (C) is correct. *(14 CFR 91.125)*

DISCUSSION: A flashing white light given to an aircraft taxiing along the ground means to return to the aircraft's starting point.

Answer (A) is incorrect. There is no light signal that means to taxi at a faster speed. Answer (B) is incorrect. There is no light signal (by itself) that means to taxi only on taxiways and not cross runways.

107. If the control tower uses a light signal to direct a pilot to give way to other aircraft and continue circling, the light will be

A. flashing red.

B. steady red.

C. alternating red and green.

Answer (B) is correct. *(14 CFR 91.125)*

DISCUSSION: A steady red light signal given to an aircraft in the air means to give way to other aircraft and continue circling.

Answer (A) is incorrect. When in the air, a flashing red light means airport unsafe, do not land. Answer (C) is incorrect. Alternating red and green light always means exercise extreme caution.

108. Which light signal from the control tower clears a pilot to taxi?

A. Flashing green.

B. Steady green.

C. Flashing white.

Answer (A) is correct. *(14 CFR 91.125)*

DISCUSSION: A flashing green gives the pilot permission to taxi.

Answer (B) is incorrect. A steady green light means cleared to take off if on the ground or to land if in the air. Answer (C) is incorrect. A flashing white light means to return to the starting point on the airport for aircraft only on the ground.

109. An alternating red and green light signal directed from the control tower to an aircraft in flight is a signal to

A. hold position.

B. exercise extreme caution.

C. not land; the airport is unsafe.

Answer (B) is correct. *(14 CFR 91.125)*

DISCUSSION: A flashing red and green light given anytime means exercise extreme caution.

Answer (A) is incorrect. A steady red when taxiing means hold your position. There is no light signal to tell you to hold your position when in flight, only to give way to other aircraft and continue circling. Answer (C) is incorrect. A flashing red light means do not land; airport unsafe.

110. If the aircraft's radio fails, what is the recommended procedure when landing at a controlled airport?

A. Observe the traffic flow, enter the pattern, and look for a light signal from the tower.

B. Enter a crosswind leg and rock the wings.

C. Flash the landing lights and cycle the landing gear while circling the airport.

Answer (A) is correct. *(AIM Para 4-2-13)*

DISCUSSION: If your radio fails and you wish to land at a tower controlled airport, remain outside or above the airport's traffic pattern until the direction and flow of traffic has been determined, then join the airport traffic pattern and maintain visual contact with the tower to receive light signals.

Answer (B) is incorrect. Crosswind entry is not required; also, you rock the wings to acknowledge light signals during daylight hours. Answer (C) is incorrect. Flashing the landing light is a method of acknowledging light signals at night, and cycling the landing gear is not an option available to fixed-gear aircraft.

3.16 ELTs and VHF/DF

111. When activated, an emergency locator transmitter (ELT) transmits on

A. 118.0 and 118.8 MHz.

B. 121.5 and 243.0 MHz.

C. 123.0 and 119.0 MHz.

Answer (B) is correct. *(AIM Para 6-2-5)*

DISCUSSION: When activated, an ELT transmits simultaneously on the international distress frequencies of 121.5 and 243.0 megahertz.

Answer (A) is incorrect. These are not emergency frequencies. Answer (C) is incorrect. These are not emergency frequencies.

112. Which procedure is recommended to ensure that the emergency locator transmitter (ELT) has not been activated?

A. Turn off the aircraft ELT after landing.

B. Ask the airport tower if they are receiving an ELT signal.

C. Monitor 121.5 before engine shutdown.

Answer (C) is correct. *(AIM Para 6-2-5)*

DISCUSSION: To ensure that your ELT has not been activated, you can monitor 121.5 MHz or 243.0 MHz in flight when a receiver is available and prior to engine shutdown at the end of each flight.

Answer (A) is incorrect. If you turn off the ELT, there is no way of telling whether it has been activated. Answer (B) is incorrect. The tower or ATC should not be bothered by questions about your ELT transmissions. If, however, you do receive signals on 121.5, IMMEDIATELY report it to ATC and/or FSS.

113. The letters VHF/DF appearing in the Chart Supplement for a certain airport indicate that

A. this airport is designated as an airport of entry.

B. the Flight Service Station has equipment with which to determine your direction from the station.

C. this airport has a direct-line phone to the Flight Service Station.

Answer (B) is correct. *(AIM Para 1-1-16)*

DISCUSSION: The VHF/Direction Finder (DF) facility is a ground operation that displays the magnetic direction of the airplane from the station each time the airplane communication radio transmits a signal to it. It is used by ATC and FSS to assist lost pilots by telling them which direction they are from the receiving station.

Answer (A) is incorrect. An airport of entry is indicated by the letters AOE. Answer (C) is incorrect. A direct phone line to FSS is indicated by the letters DL following the FSS identifier.

3.17 Emergency Radio Frequency

114. While on a VFR cross country and not in contact with ATC, what frequency would you use in the event of an emergency?

A. 121.5 MHz.

B. 122.5 MHz.

C. 128.75 MHz.

Answer (A) is correct. *(AIM Para 6-3-1)*

DISCUSSION: Whenever a pilot encounters an emergency condition (s)he can obtain assistance simply by contacting the air traffic facility or other agency in whose area of responsibility the aircraft is operating. If not in contact with ATC, the pilot can broadcast on the emergency frequency 121.5 MHz for possible assistance.

Answer (B) is incorrect. Radio frequency 122.5 MHz is one of two frequencies used for Flight Service Stations (FSSs), while 121.5 MHz is used for emergencies. Answer (C) is incorrect. The frequency 128.75 is used for various control towers. If you have an emergency while talking to a control tower, you should advise them of your emergency. If you are not in contact with ATC, use the emergency frequency 121.5 MHz to obtain assistance.

3.18 Land and Hold Short Operations (LAHSO)

115. Who should not participate in the Land and Hold Short Operations (LAHSO) program?

A. Recreational pilots only.

B. Military pilots.

C. Student pilots.

Answer (C) is correct. *(AIM Para 4-3-11)*

DISCUSSION: LAHSO take place at some airports with an operating control tower in order to increase the total capacity and improve the flow of traffic. LAHSO requires that a pilot not use the full length of the runway, but rather that (s)he stop and hold short before reaching an intersecting runway, taxiway, or other specified point on the landing runway. Student pilots or pilots who are not familiar with LAHSO should not participate in the program.

Answer (A) is incorrect. A recreational pilot cannot operate at an airport with an operating control tower (unless working on obtaining his or her private pilot certificate under the supervision of a CFI) and would not have a choice as to whether or not to participate. Answer (B) is incorrect. Student pilots or pilots unfamiliar with LAHSO, not military pilots, should not participate in the program.

116. Who has final authority to accept or decline any land and hold short (LAHSO) clearance?

A. Pilot in command.

B. Owner/operator.

C. Second-in-command.

Answer (A) is correct. *(AIM Para 4-3-11)*

DISCUSSION: Land and hold short operations (LAHSO) take place at some airports with an operating control tower in order to increase the total capacity and improve the flow of traffic. LAHSO requires that a pilot not use the full length of the runway, but rather that (s)he stop and hold short before reaching an intersecting runway, taxiway, or other specified point on the landing runway. LAHSO requires familiarity with the available landing distance (ALD) for given LAHSO combinations and with the landing performance of the aircraft. The pilot in command has the final authority to accept or decline any land and hold short clearance.

Answer (B) is incorrect. The pilot in command, regardless of whether or not (s)he is the owner, has the final authority to accept or decline a LAHSO clearance. Answer (C) is incorrect. The pilot in command, not the second in command, has final authority to accept or decline a LAHSO clearance.

117. Who has final authority to accept or decline any land and hold short (LAHSO) clearance?

A. Pilot in command.

B. Air Traffic Controller.

C. Second in command.

Answer (A) is correct. *(AIM Para 4-3-11)*

DISCUSSION: Land and hold short operations (LAHSO) take place at some airports with an operating control tower in order to increase and improve the flow of traffic. LAHSO requires that a pilot not use the length of the runway, but rather that (s)he stop and hold short before reaching an intersecting runway, taxiway, or other specified point on the landing runway. LAHSO requires familiarity with the available landing distance (ALD) for given LAHSO combinations and with the landing performance of the aircraft. The pilot in command has the final authority to accept or decline any land and hold short clearance.

Answer (B) is incorrect. An air traffic controller cannot accept, nor can (s)he force a pilot in command to accept, a LAHSO clearance. Answer (C) is incorrect. The pilot in command, not the second in command, has the final authority to accept or decline a LAHSO clearance.

118. When should pilots decline a land and hold short (LAHSO) clearance?

A. When it will compromise safety.

B. Only when the tower operator concurs.

C. Pilots cannot decline clearance.

Answer (A) is correct. *(AIM Para 4-3-11)*

DISCUSSION: Land and hold short operations (LAHSO) take place at some airports with an operating control tower in order to increase the total capacity and improve the flow of traffic. LAHSO requires that a pilot not use the full length of the runway, but rather that (s)he stop and hold short before reaching an intersecting runway, taxiway, or other specified point on the landing runway. LAHSO requires familiarity with the available landing distance (ALD) for given LAHSO combinations and with the landing performance of the aircraft. Pilots are expected to decline a land and hold short clearance if they determine that it will compromise safety.

Answer (B) is incorrect. The pilot in command has the final authority to accept or decline a land and hold short clearance; agreement from the tower operator is not required. Answer (C) is incorrect. The pilot in command has the authority to decline a land and hold short clearance.

119. Where is the "Available Landing Distance" (ALD) data published for an airport that utilizes Land and Hold Short Operations (LAHSO)?

A. Special Notices section of the Chart Supplement.

B. *Aeronautical Information Manual (AIM)*.

C. 14 CFR Part 91, *General Operating and Flight Rules*.

Answer (A) is correct. *(AIM Para 4-3-11)*

DISCUSSION: LAHSO take place at some airports with an operating control tower in order to increase the total capacity and improve the flow of traffic. LAHSO requires that a pilot not use the full length of the runway, but rather that (s)he stop and hold short before reaching an intersecting runway, taxiway, or other specified point on the landing runway. LAHSO requires familiarity with the ALD for given LAHSO combinations and with the landing performance of the aircraft. ALD data are published in the special notices section of the Chart Supplement.

Answer (B) is incorrect. The ALD data are published in the Chart Supplement, not in the *AIM*, which contains information on how LAHSO are to be conducted. Answer (C) is incorrect. ALD data are published in the Chart Supplement, not in 14 CFR Part 91.

120. What is the minimum visibility for a pilot to receive a land and hold short (LAHSO) clearance?

A. 3 nautical miles.

B. 3 statute miles.

C. 1 statute mile.

Answer (B) is correct. *(AIM Para 4-3-11)*

DISCUSSION: You should receive a land and hold short (LAHSO) clearance only when there is a minimum ceiling of 1,000 ft. and visibility of 3 statute miles. The intent of having basic VFR weather conditions is to allow pilots to maintain visual contact with other aircraft and ground vehicle operations.

Answer (A) is incorrect. The minimum visibility for a pilot to receive a land and hold short (LAHSO) clearance is 3 SM, not 3 nautical miles. Remember, visibility is reported in statute miles, not nautical miles. Answer (C) is incorrect. The minimum visibility for a pilot to receive a special VFR clearance, not a land and hold short clearance, is 1 statute mile.

END OF STUDY UNIT

STUDY UNIT FOUR
FEDERAL AVIATION REGULATIONS

(16 pages of outline)

This study unit contains outlines of major concepts tested, sample test questions and answers regarding Federal Aviation Regulations (FARs), and an explanation of each answer. The table of contents above and on the previous page lists each subunit within this study unit, the number of questions pertaining to that particular subunit, and the pages on which the outlines and questions begin, respectively.

Recall that the **sole purpose** of this book is to expedite your passing of the FAA pilot knowledge test for the private pilot certificate. Accordingly, all extraneous material (i.e., topics or regulations not directly tested on the FAA pilot knowledge test) is omitted, even though much more knowledge is necessary to fly safely. This additional material is presented in *Pilot Handbook* and *Private Pilot Flight Maneuvers and Practical Test Prep*, available from Gleim Publications, Inc. Order online at www.GleimAviation.com.

NOTE: The FAA refers to the Federal Aviation Regulations as "14 CFRs" rather than "FARs." CFR stands for Code of Federal Regulations, and the Federal Aviation Regulations are in Title 14. For example, FAR Part 1 and FAR 61.109 are now referred to as 14 CFR Part 1 and 14 CFR Sec. 61.109, respectively. Due to CFIs' and pilots' widespread use of the acronym FAR, we use FAR and 14 CFR interchangeably to familiarize you with both.

The 27 questions beginning on page 138 specifically refer to recreational pilots. Recreational pilots are responsible for all applicable FARs. Subpart D of FAR Part 61, "Recreational Pilots," specifically applies. It is numbered 61.96 through 61.101.

61.96	Applicability and Eligibility Requirements: General
61.97	Aeronautical Knowledge
61.98	Flight Proficiency
61.99	Aeronautical Experience
61.100	Pilots Based on Small Islands
61.101	Recreational Pilot Privileges and Limitations

All of the 27 recreational pilot questions test FAR 61.101.

4.1 FAR PART 1

1.1 General Definitions

1. **Night** means the time between the end of evening civil twilight and the beginning of morning civil twilight, as published in the American Air Almanac, converted to local time.
   a. Note that for "recency of experience" (FAR 61.57), night is defined as from 1 hr. after sunset to 1 hr. before sunrise.
   b. Be careful; there are questions on both definitions.
2. **Aircraft categories** (for certification of airmen); broad classifications of aircraft
   a. Airplane
   b. Rotorcraft
   c. Glider
   d. Lighter-than-air
3. **Airplane classes** (for certification of airmen)
   a. Single-engine land
   b. Multi-engine land
   c. Single-engine sea
   d. Multi-engine sea
4. **Rotorcraft classes** (for certification of airmen)
   a. Helicopter
   b. Gyrocopter
5. **Lighter-than-air classes** (for certification of airmen)
   a. Airship
   b. Free balloon
   c. Hot air balloon
   d. Gas balloon
6. Note the previous category and class definitions are for certification of airmen purposes. For certification of aircraft there are different definitions:
   a. **Category** (for certification of aircraft purposes) is based on intended use or operating limitations.
      1) Transport
      2) Normal
      3) Utility
      4) Limited
      5) Restricted
      6) Acrobatic
      7) Provisional

b. **Classes** as used for certification of aircraft are the same as, or very similar to, categories for certification of airmen, e.g., airplane, rotorcraft, glider, lighter-than-air.

7. **Air traffic control (ATC) clearance** means an authorization to proceed under specific traffic conditions in controlled airspace.

1.2 Abbreviations and Symbols

1. V_{FE} means maximum flap extended speed.
2. V_{LE} means maximum landing gear extended speed.
3. V_{NO} means maximum structural cruising speed.
4. V_A means design maneuvering speed.
5. V_{S0} means the stalling speed or the minimum steady flight speed in the landing configuration.
6. V_X means speed for best angle of climb.
7. V_Y means speed for best rate of climb.

4.2 FAR PART 21

21.181 Duration of Airworthiness Certificates

1. Airworthiness certificates remain in force as long as maintenance and alteration of the aircraft are performed per FARs.

4.3 FAR PART 39

39.1 Applicability

1. Airworthiness Directives (ADs) are issued under FAR Part 39 by the FAA to require correction of unsafe conditions found in an airplane, an airplane engine, a propeller, or an appliance when such conditions exist and are likely to exist or develop in other products of the same design.
   a. Since ADs are issued under FAR Part 39, they are regulatory and must be complied with, unless a specific exemption is granted.

39.3 General

1. No person may operate a product to which an AD applies except in accordance with the requirements of that AD.
   a. Thus, you may operate an airplane that is not in compliance with an AD, if such operation is allowed by the AD.

4.4 FAR PART 43

43.3 Persons Authorized to Perform Maintenance, Preventive Maintenance, Rebuilding, and Alterations

1. A person who holds a pilot certificate (e.g., private pilot) may perform preventive maintenance on any airplane owned or operated by that pilot that is not used in air carrier services.

43.7 Persons Authorized to Approve Aircraft, Airframes, Aircraft Engines, Propellers, Appliances, or Component Parts for Return to Service after Maintenance, Preventive Maintenance, Rebuilding, or Alteration

1. To approve the airplane for return to service, after preventive maintenance was done by a pilot, the pilot must hold at least a private pilot certificate.

43.9 Maintenance Records

1. After preventive maintenance has been performed, the signature, certificate number, and kind of certificate held by the person approving the work, the date, and a description of the work must be entered in the aircraft maintenance records.

43 Appendix A. Major Alterations and Repairs and Preventive Maintenance

1. Preventive maintenance means simple or minor preservation operations and the replacement of small standard parts not involving complex assembly operations. Examples include replenishing hydraulic fluid and servicing landing gear wheel bearings.

4.5 FAR PART 47

1. A Dealer's Aircraft Registration Certificate is another form of aircraft registration.
   a. It is valid only for flights within the United States by the manufacturer or a dealer for flight testing or demonstration for sale.
2. Effective March 31, 2008, 14 CFR 47.41(b) requires the removal of the original aircraft registration certificate once the aircraft is sold.
   a. The back side of that registration must be filled out with the appropriate information from the sale as well as the new owner's name. The certificate must then be mailed back to the FAA Registry in Oklahoma City.

4.6 FAR PART 61

61.3 Requirements for Certificates, Ratings, and Authorizations

1. When acting as a pilot in command or as a required pilot flight crewmember, you must have a valid pilot certificate and a current and appropriate medical certificate in your personal possession or readily accessible in the airplane.
2. You must present your pilot certificate or medical certificate upon the request of the Administrator of the FAA or his or her representative; the NTSB; or any federal, state, or local law enforcement officer.

61.15 Offenses Involving Alcohol or Drugs

1. Each person holding a certificate under Part 61 shall provide a written report of each motor vehicle action involving alcohol or drugs to the FAA, Civil Aviation Security Division, no later than 60 days after the motor vehicle action.

61.23 Medical Certificates: Requirement and Duration

1. For operations requiring a private, recreational, or student pilot certificate, a first-, second-, or third-class medical certificate
   a. At the end of the 60th month after the date of examination shown on the certificate, if you have not reached your 40th birthday on or before the date of examination or
   b. At the end of the 24th month after the date of examination shown on the certificate, if you have reached your 40th birthday on or before the date of examination.

61.31 Type Rating Requirements, Additional Training, and Authorization Requirements

1. To act as pilot in command of a complex airplane, you must receive and log ground and flight training and receive a logbook endorsement.
   a. A complex airplane is defined as an airplane with retractable landing gear, flaps, and a controllable pitch propeller.

2. To act as pilot in command of a high-performance airplane, you must receive and log ground and flight training and receive a logbook endorsement.
   a. A high-performance airplane is defined as an airplane with an engine of more than 200 horsepower.
3. A person may not act as pilot in command of any of the following aircraft unless (s)he holds a type rating for that aircraft:
   a. A large aircraft (i.e., over 12,500 lb. gross weight)
   b. A turbojet-powered airplane
   c. Other aircraft specified by the FAA through aircraft type certification procedures

61.51 Pilot Logbooks

1. A recreational pilot must carry his or her logbook with the required authorized instructor endorsements on all solo flights
   a. That exceed 50 NM from the airport at which training was received,
   b. Within airspace that requires communication with air traffic control,
   c. Conducted between sunset and sunrise, or
   d. In an aircraft for which the pilot does not hold an appropriate category or class rating.

61.56 Flight Review

1. A flight review must have been satisfactorily completed within the previous 24 calendar months to act as pilot in command of an aircraft for which that pilot is rated. A flight review consists of a minimum of 1 hour of flight training by an authorized instructor and 1 hour of ground training.
2. The expiration of the 24-month period for the flight review falls on the last day of the 24th month after the month of the examination date (i.e., 24 calendar months).

61.57 Recent Flight Experience: Pilot in Command

1. To carry passengers, you must have made three landings and three takeoffs within the preceding 90 days.
   a. All three landings must be made in aircraft of the same category, class, and, if a type rating is required, type as the one in which passengers are to be carried.
      1) The categories are airplane, rotorcraft, glider, and lighter-than-air.
      2) The classes are single-engine land, single-engine sea, multi-engine land, and multi-engine sea.
   b. The landings must be to a full stop if the airplane is tailwheel (conventional) rather than nosewheel.
2. To carry passengers at night, you must, within the last 90 days, have made three takeoffs and three landings to a full stop at night in an aircraft of the same category, class, and type, if required.
   a. Night in this case is defined as the period beginning 1 hr. after sunset and ending 1 hr. before sunrise.

61.60 Change of Address

1. You must notify the FAA Airmen Certification Branch in writing of any change in your permanent mailing address.
2. You may not exercise the privileges of your pilot certificate after 30 days from moving unless you make this notification.

61.69 Glider Towing: Experience and Training Requirements

1. Any person may tow a glider if that person has
   a. At least a private pilot certificate
   b. 100 hr. of pilot in command time in the aircraft category, class, and type, if required, that the pilot is using to tow a glider
   c. A logbook endorsement from an authorized instructor certifying that the person has received ground and flight training in gliders
   d. Within the preceding 24 months
      1) Made at least three actual or simulated glider tows while accompanied by a qualified pilot or
      2) Made at least three flights as pilot in command of a glider towed by an aircraft

61.113 Private Pilot Privileges and Limitations: Pilot in Command

1. Private pilots may not pay less than an equal (pro rata) share of the operating expenses of a flight with the passengers.
   a. These operating expenses may involve only fuel, oil, airport expenditures, or rental fees.
2. Private pilots may operate an aircraft carrying passengers on business only if the flight is incidental to that business or employment and the pilot is not paid as a pilot.
   a. For example, a CPA who is a private pilot might fly an aircraft carrying CPAs to a client. Such flight is incidental to the CPA's professional duties or business.
3. A pilot may act as a pilot in command of an aircraft used in a passenger-carrying airlift sponsored by a charitable organization for which passengers make donations to the organization if
   a. The local FSDO (FAA Flight Standards District Office) is notified at least 7 days before the flight;
   b. The flight is conducted from an adequate public airport;
   c. The pilot has logged at least 500 hours;
   d. No acrobatic or formation flights are performed;
   e. The aircraft holds a standard airworthiness certificate and is airworthy;
   f. The flight is day-VFR; and
   g. The flight is non-stop, begins and ends at the same airport, and is conducted within a 25-NM radius of that airport.

4.7 RECREATIONAL PILOT RELATED FARS

61.101 Recreational Pilot Privileges and Limitations

NOTE: This section is not tested on the Private Pilot Airplane (PAR) or Private Pilot-Airplane Transition (PAT) knowledge test.

1. A recreational pilot may carry only one passenger.
   a. A recreational pilot may not pay less than the pro rata (equal) share of the operating expenses of a flight with a passenger, provided the expenses involve only fuel, oil, airport expenses, or aircraft rental fees.
2. A recreational pilot may act as pilot in command of an airplane
   a. Only when the flight is within 50 NM of an airport at which the pilot has received ground and flight training from an authorized flight instructor. The pilot must have in his or her possession a logbook endorsement that permits flight within 50 NM from the departure airport.

b. When the flight exceeds 50 NM if (s)he receives ground and flight training on the cross-country training requirements for a private pilot and has his or her logbook endorsed certifying proficiency in cross-country flight by an authorized instructor

3. A recreational pilot may not act as pilot in command of an aircraft
   a. Certificated for more than four occupants, with more than one engine, with an engine of more than 180 horsepower, or with retractable landing gear
   b. Classified as a multi-engine airplane, powered-lift, glider, airship, or balloon
   c. Carrying a passenger or property for compensation or hire
   d. In furtherance of a business
   e. Between sunset and sunrise (e.g., night time)
   f. In airspace in which communication with ATC is required
   g. At an altitude of more than 10,000 ft. MSL or 2,000 ft. AGL, whichever is higher
   h. With flight or surface visibility of less than 3 SM
      1) In Class G airspace, the cloud clearance requirements are clear of clouds when 1,200 ft. AGL or less and 1,000 ft. above, 500 ft. below, and 2,000 ft. horizontally from clouds when more than 1,200 ft. AGL, but less than 10,000 ft. MSL.
   i. Without visual reference to the surface
   j. On a flight outside the U.S. unless authorized by the country in which the flight is conducted
   k. For demonstration of that aircraft in flight to a prospective buyer
   l. Used in a passenger-carrying airlift and sponsored by a charitable organization
   m. Towing any object
4. A recreational pilot may not act as a required pilot flight crewmember on any aircraft for which more than one pilot is required.
5. A recreational pilot who has logged fewer than 400 flight hr. and who has not logged pilot in command time in an aircraft within the preceding 180 days may not act as pilot in command of an aircraft until the pilot has received flight training from an authorized flight instructor who certifies in the pilot's logbook that the pilot is competent to act as pilot in command.
6. The recreational pilot certificate states, "Holder does not meet ICAO requirements."
7. For the purpose of obtaining additional certificates or ratings, while under the supervision of an authorized flight instructor, a recreational pilot may fly as sole occupant of an aircraft
   a. For which the pilot does not hold an appropriate category or class rating
   b. Within airspace that requires communication with air traffic control
   c. Between sunset and sunrise, provided the flight or surface visibility is at least 5 SM
   d. In excess of 50 NM from an airport at which flight instruction is received

   NOTE: For any of these situations, the recreational pilot shall carry the logbook that has been properly endorsed for each flight by an authorized flight instructor.
8. When flying a transponder-equipped aircraft, a recreational pilot should set that transponder on code (squawk) 1200, which is the VFR code.

4.8 FAR PART 71

71.71 Extent of Federal Airways

1. Federal airways include that Class E airspace
   a. Extending upward from 1,200 ft. AGL to and including 17,999 ft. MSL
   b. Within parallel boundary lines 4 NM each side of the airway's centerline

4.9 FAR PART 91: 91.3 – 91.151

91.3 Responsibility and Authority of the Pilot in Command

1. In emergencies, a pilot may deviate from the FARs to the extent needed to maintain the safety of the airplane and passengers.
2. The pilot in command of an aircraft is directly responsible for, and is the final authority as to, the operation of that aircraft.
3. A written report of any deviations from FARs should be filed with the FAA upon request.

91.7 Civil Aircraft Airworthiness

1. The pilot in command is responsible for determining that the airplane is airworthy prior to every flight.
   a. The pilot in command shall discontinue the flight when unairworthy conditions (whether electrical, mechanical, or structural) occur.

91.9 Civil Aircraft Flight Manual, Marking, and Placard Requirements

1. The airworthiness certificate, the FAA registration certificate, and the aircraft flight manual or operating limitations must be aboard.
2. The acronym ARROW can be used as a memory aid. The FCC (Federal Communications Commission), not the FAA, requires the radio station license. As of January 1, 1997, the radio station license is required only for international flights.

   A irworthiness certificate
   R egistration certificate
   R adio station license (FCC requirement for international flight)
   O perating limitations, including
   W eight and balance data

3. The operating limitations of an airplane may be found in the current FAA-approved flight manual, approved manual material, markings, and placards, or any combination thereof.
   a. An exception exists in the case of aircraft issued an experimental airworthiness certificate or a special light-sport airworthiness certificate.
      1) The operating limitations for these aircraft are attached to the airworthiness certificate, which is carried on board the aircraft.

91.15 Dropping Objects

1. No pilot in command of a civil aircraft may allow any object to be dropped from that aircraft in flight that creates a hazard to persons or property.
   a. However, this section does not prohibit the dropping of any object if reasonable precautions are taken to avoid injury or damage to persons or property.

91.17 Alcohol or Drugs

1. No person may act as a crewmember of a civil airplane while having .04 percent by weight or more alcohol in the blood or if any alcoholic beverages have been consumed within the preceding 8 hours.
2. No person may act as a crewmember of a civil airplane if using any drug that affects the person's faculties in any way contrary to safety.
3. Operating or attempting to operate an aircraft as a crewmember while under the influence of drugs or alcohol is grounds for the denial of an application for a certificate, rating, or authorization issued under 14 CFR Part 91.

91.103 Preflight Action

1. Pilots are required to familiarize themselves with all available information concerning the flight prior to every flight, and specifically to determine,
   a. For any flight, runway lengths at airports of intended use and the airplane's takeoff and landing requirements, and
   b. For IFR flights or those not in the vicinity of an airport,
      1) Weather reports and forecasts,
      2) Fuel requirements,
      3) Alternatives available if the planned flight cannot be completed, and
      4) Any known traffic delays.

91.105 Flight Crewmembers at Stations

1. During takeoff and landing, and while en route, each required flight crewmember shall keep his or her safety belt fastened while at his or her station.
   a. If shoulder harnesses are available, they must be used for takeoff and landing.

91.107 Use of Safety Belts, Shoulder Harnesses, and Child Restraint Systems

1. Pilots must ensure that each occupant is briefed on how to use the safety belts and, if installed, shoulder harnesses.
2. Pilots must notify all occupants to fasten their safety belts before taxiing, taking off, or landing.
3. All passengers of airplanes must wear their safety belts during taxi, takeoffs, and landings.
   a. A passenger who has not reached his or her second birthday may be held by an adult.
   b. Sport parachutists may use the floor of the aircraft as a seat (but still must use safety belts).

91.111 Operating near Other Aircraft

1. No person may operate an aircraft in formation flight except by prior arrangement with the pilot in command of each aircraft in the formation.

91.113 Right-of-Way Rules: Except Water Operations

1. Aircraft in distress have the right-of-way over all other aircraft.
2. When two aircraft are approaching head on or nearly so, the pilot of each aircraft should turn to his or her right, regardless of category.
3. When two aircraft of different categories are converging, the right-of-way depends upon who has the least maneuverability. Thus, the right-of-way belongs to
   a. Balloons over
   b. Gliders over
   c. Airships over
   d. Airplanes or rotorcraft
4. When aircraft of the same category are converging at approximately the same altitude, except head on or nearly so, the aircraft to the other's right has the right-of-way.
   a. If an airplane of the same category as yours is approaching from your right side, it has the right-of-way.

5. When two or more aircraft are approaching an airport for the purpose of landing, the aircraft at the lower altitude has the right-of-way.
   a. This rule shall not be abused by cutting in front of or overtaking another aircraft.
6. An aircraft towing or refueling another aircraft has the right-of-way over all engine-driven aircraft.

91.115 Right-of-Way Rules: Water Operations

1. When aircraft, or an aircraft and a vessel, are on crossing courses, the aircraft or vessel to the other's right has the right-of-way.

91.117 Aircraft Speed

1. The speed limit is 250 kt. (288 MPH) when flying below 10,000 ft. MSL and in Class B airspace.
2. When flying under Class B airspace or in VFR corridors through Class B airspace, the speed limit is 200 kt. (230 MPH).
3. When at or below 2,500 ft. AGL and within 4 NM of the primary airport of Class C or Class D airspace, the speed limit is 200 kt. (230 MPH).

91.119 Minimum Safe Altitudes: General

1. Over congested areas (cities, towns, settlements, or open-air assemblies), a pilot must maintain an altitude of 1,000 ft. above the highest obstacle within a horizontal radius of 2,000 ft. of the airplane.
2. The minimum altitude over other than congested areas is 500 ft. AGL.
   a. Over open water or sparsely populated areas, an airplane may not be operated closer than 500 ft. to any person, vessel, vehicle, or structure.
3. Altitude in all areas must be sufficient to permit an emergency landing without undue hazard to persons or property on the surface if a power unit fails.

91.121 Altimeter Settings

1. Prior to takeoff, the altimeter should be set to the current local altimeter setting. If the current local altimeter setting is not available, use the departure airport elevation.
2. The altimeter of an airplane is required to be set to 29.92 at or above 18,000 ft. MSL to guarantee vertical separation of airplanes above 18,000 ft. MSL.

91.123 Compliance with ATC Clearances and Instructions

1. When an ATC clearance is obtained, no pilot may deviate from that clearance, except in an emergency, unless an amended clearance is obtained or the deviation is in response to a traffic alert and collision avoidance system resolution advisory. If you feel a rule deviation will occur, you should immediately advise ATC.
2. If you receive priority from ATC in an emergency, you must, upon request, file a detailed report within 48 hr. to the chief of that ATC facility even if no rule has been violated.
3. During an in-flight emergency, the pilot in command may deviate from the FARs to the extent necessary to handle the emergency.
   a. The pilot should notify ATC about the deviation as soon as possible.
   b. If priority is given, a written report (if requested) must be submitted in 48 hours.

91.130 Operations in Class C Airspace

1. Class C airspace is controlled airspace that requires radio communication with ATC.
   a. A pilot must establish two-way radio communication prior to entering Class C airspace and maintain it while within Class C airspace, regardless of weather conditions.

91.131 Operations in Class B Airspace

1. Class B airspace is controlled airspace found at larger airports with high volumes of traffic.
2. Requirements for operating within Class B airspace:
   a. A pilot must hold at least a private pilot certificate or a student pilot certificate with the appropriate logbook endorsements.
   b. Authorization must be received from ATC, regardless of weather conditions.
   c. The airplane must have a two-way communications radio and a transponder equipped with Mode C that permits ATC to obtain an altitude readout on its radar screen.
      1) A VOR receiver is required only when operating IFR.
3. Student pilot operations in Class B airspace are only permitted with appropriate logbook endorsements.
   a. For flight through Class B airspace, the student pilot must
      1) Receive ground and flight instructions pertaining to that specific Class B airspace area
      2) Have a CFI logbook endorsement within 90 days for solo flight in that specific Class B airspace area
   b. For takeoffs and landings at an airport within Class B airspace, the student pilot must
      1) Receive ground and flight instructions pertaining to that specific Class B airspace area
      2) Have a CFI logbook endorsement within 90 days for solo flight at that specific airport
   c. No student pilot may take off or land at the following airports:

Andrews AFB	Miami International
Atlanta Hartsfield	Newark International
Boston Logan	New York Kennedy
Chicago O'Hare International	New York La Guardia
Dallas/Fort Worth International	San Francisco International
Los Angeles International	Washington National

4. With certain exceptions, all aircraft within a 30-NM radius of a Class B primary airport and from the surface up to 10,000 ft. MSL must have an operable transponder with Mode C.

91.133 Restricted and Prohibited Areas

1. Restricted areas are a type of special use airspace within which your right to fly is limited.
   a. Restricted areas have unusual and often invisible hazards to aircraft (e.g., balloons, military operations, etc.).
   b. Although restricted areas are not always in use during the times posted in the legend of sectional charts, permission to fly in that airspace must be obtained from the controlling agency. The controlling agency is listed for each restricted area at the bottom of sectional charts.

91.135 Operations in Class A Airspace

1. Since Class A airspace requires operation under IFR at specific flight levels assigned by ATC, VFR flights are prohibited.

91.151 Fuel Requirements for Flight in VFR Conditions

1. During the day, FARs require fuel sufficient to fly to the first point of intended landing and then for an additional 30 min., assuming normal cruise speed.
2. At night, sufficient fuel to fly an additional 45 min. is required.

4.10 FAR PART 91: 91.155 – 91.519

91.155 Basic VFR Weather Minimums

Airspace	Flight Visibility	Distance from Clouds
Class A	Not Applicable	Not applicable
Class B	3 SM	Clear of clouds
Class C	3 SM	500 ft. below 1,000 ft. above 2,000 ft. horiz.
Class D	3 SM	500 ft. below 1,000 ft. above 2,000 ft. horiz.
Class E		
Less than 10,000 ft. MSL	3 SM	500 ft. below 1,000 ft. above 2,000 ft. horiz.
At or above 10,000 ft. MSL	5 SM	1,000 ft. below 1,000 ft. above 1 SM horiz.

Airspace	Flight Visibility	Distance from Clouds
Class G:		
1,200 ft. or less above the surface (regardless of MSL altitude)		
Day	1 SM	Clear of clouds
Night, except as provided in 1. below	3 SM	500 ft. below 1,000 ft. above 2,000 ft. horiz.
More than 1,200 ft. above the surface but less than 10,000 ft. MSL		
Day	1 SM	500 ft. below 1,000 ft. above 2,000 ft. horiz.
Night	3 SM	500 ft. below 1,000 ft. above 2,000 ft. horiz.
More than 1,200 ft. above the surface and at or above 10,000 ft. MSL	5 SM	1,000 ft. below 1,000 ft. above 1 SM horiz.

1. An airplane may be operated clear of clouds in Class G airspace at night below 1,200 ft. AGL when the visibility is less than 3 SM but more than 1 SM in an airport traffic pattern and within 1/2 NM of the runway.
2. Except when operating under a special VFR clearance,
   a. You may not operate your airplane beneath the ceiling under VFR within the lateral boundaries of the surface areas of Class B, Class C, Class D, or Class E airspace designated for an airport when the ceiling is less than 1,000 feet.
   b. You may not take off, land, or enter the traffic pattern of an airport in Class B, Class C, Class D, or Class E airspace unless the ground visibility is at least 3 SM. If ground visibility is not reported, flight visibility must be at least 3 statute miles.

91.157 Special VFR Weather Minimums

1. With some exceptions, special VFR clearances can be requested in Class B, Class C, Class D, or Class E airspace areas. You must remain clear of clouds and have visibility of at least 1 statute mile.
2. Flight under special VFR clearance at night is only permitted if the pilot has an instrument rating and the aircraft is IFR equipped.
3. Special VFR is an ATC clearance obtained from the control tower. If there is no control tower, obtain the clearance from the appropriate air traffic control facility.

91.159 VFR Cruising Altitude or Flight Level

1. Specified altitudes are required for VFR cruising flight at more than 3,000 ft. AGL and below 18,000 ft. MSL.
   a. The altitude prescribed is based upon the magnetic course (not magnetic heading).
   b. The altitude is prescribed in ft. above mean sea level (MSL).
   c. Use an odd thousand-foot MSL altitude plus 500 ft. for magnetic courses of 0° to 179°, e.g., 3,500, 5,500, 7,500 feet.
   d. Use an even thousand-foot MSL altitude plus 500 ft. for magnetic courses of 180° to 359°, e.g., 4,500, 6,500, or 8,500 feet.
   e. As a memory aid, "East is odd; west is even odder."

91.203 Civil Aircraft: Certifications Required

1. No person may operate a civil aircraft unless the aircraft has a U.S. airworthiness certificate displayed in a manner that makes it legible to passengers and crew.
2. To operate a civil aircraft, a valid U.S. registration issued to the owner of the aircraft must be on board.

91.207 Emergency Locator Transmitters

1. ELT batteries must be replaced (or recharged, if rechargeable) after 1 cumulative hr. of use or after 50% of their useful life expires.
2. ELTs may only be tested on the ground during the first 5 min. after the hour. No airborne checks are allowed.

91.209 Aircraft Lights

1. Airplanes operating (on the ground or in the air) between sunset and sunrise must display lighted position (navigation) lights, except in Alaska.

91.211 Supplemental Oxygen

1. All occupants must be provided with oxygen in an airplane operated at cabin pressure altitudes above 15,000 ft. MSL.
   a. Pilots and crewmembers may not operate an airplane at cabin pressure altitudes above 12,500 ft. MSL up to and including 14,000 ft. MSL for more than 30 min. without supplemental oxygen.
   b. Pilots and crewmembers must use supplemental oxygen at cabin pressure altitudes above 14,000 ft. MSL.

91.215 ATC Transponder and Altitude Reporting Equipment and Use

1. All aircraft must have and use an altitude-encoding transponder when operating
   a. Within Class A airspace
   b. Within Class B airspace
   c. Within 30 NM of the Class B airspace primary airport
   d. Within and above Class C airspace
   e. Above 10,000 ft. MSL except at and below 2,500 ft. AGL

91.303 Aerobatic Flight

1. Aerobatic flight includes all intentional maneuvers that
   a. Are not necessary for normal flight and
   b. Involve an abrupt change in the airplane's attitude.
2. Aerobatic flight is prohibited
   a. When flight visibility is less than 3 SM;
   b. When altitude is less than 1,500 ft. above the ground;
   c. Within the lateral boundaries of the surface areas of Class B, Class C, Class D, or Class E airspace designated for an airport;
   d. Within 4 NM of the centerline of any federal airway; or
   e. Over any congested area or over an open-air assembly of people.

91.307 Parachutes and Parachuting

1. With certain exceptions, each occupant of an aircraft must wear an approved parachute during any intentional maneuver exceeding
   a. 60° bank or
   b. A nose-up or nose-down attitude of 30°.
2. Parachutes that are available for emergency use must be packed within a specific time period, based on the materials from which they are constructed.
   a. Parachutes that include a canopy, shrouds, and harness that are composed exclusively of nylon, rayon, or other similar synthetic fibers must have been repacked by a certificated and appropriately rated parachute rigger within the preceding 180 days.
   b. Parachutes that include any part that is composed of silk, pongee, or other natural fiber or materials must be repacked by a certificated and appropriately rated parachute rigger within the preceding 60 days.

91.313 Restricted Category Civil Aircraft: Operating Limitations

1. Restricted category civil aircraft may not normally be operated
   a. Over densely populated areas,
   b. In congested airways, or
   c. Near a busy airport where passenger transport is conducted.

91.319 Aircraft Having Experimental Certificates: Operating Limitations

1. No person may operate an aircraft that has an experimental or restricted certificate over a densely populated area or in a congested airway unless authorized by the FAA.

91.403 General

1. The owner or operator of an aircraft is primarily responsible for maintaining that aircraft in an airworthy condition and for complying with all Airworthiness Directives (ADs).
2. An operator is a person who uses, or causes to use or authorizes to use, an aircraft for the purpose of air navigation, including the piloting of an aircraft, with or without the right of legal control (i.e., owner, lessee, or otherwise).
   a. Thus, the pilot in command is also responsible for ensuring that the aircraft is maintained in an airworthy condition and that there is compliance with all ADs.

91.405 Maintenance Required

1. Each owner or operator of an aircraft shall ensure that maintenance personnel make the appropriate entries in the aircraft maintenance records indicating the aircraft has been approved for return to service.

91.407 Operation after Maintenance, Preventive Maintenance, Rebuilding, or Alteration

1. When aircraft alterations or repairs change the flight characteristics, the aircraft must be test flown and approved for return to service prior to carrying passengers.
   a. The pilot test flying the aircraft must be at least a private pilot and rated for the type of aircraft being tested.

91.409 Inspections

1. Annual inspections expire on the last day of the 12th calendar month after the previous annual inspection.
2. All aircraft that are used for compensation or hire, including flight instruction, must be inspected on a 100-hr. basis in addition to the annual inspection.
   a. 100-hr. inspections are due every 100 hr. from the prior due time, regardless of when the inspection was actually performed.

91.413 ATC Transponder Tests and Inspections

1. No person may use an ATC transponder unless it has been tested and inspected within the preceding 24 calendar months.

91.417 Maintenance Records

1. An airplane may not be flown unless it has been given an annual inspection within the preceding 12 calendar months.
   a. The annual inspection expires after 1 year, on the last day of the month of issuance.
2. The completion of the annual inspection and the airplane's return to service should be appropriately documented in the airplane maintenance records.
   a. The documentation should include the current status of airworthiness directives and the method of compliance.
3. The airworthiness of an airplane can be determined by a preflight inspection and a review of the maintenance records.

91.519 Passenger Briefings

1. The pilot in command is responsible for ensuring that all passengers have been orally briefed prior to takeoff. The areas that should constitute this briefing are
   a. Smoking,
   b. Use of safety belts and shoulder harnesses,
   c. Location and means of opening the passenger entry door and emergency exits,
   d. Location of survival equipment,
   e. Ditching procedures and the use of flotation equipment, and
   f. Normal and emergency use of oxygen equipment if installed in the airplane.

4.11 NTSB PART 830

830.5 Immediate Notification

1. Even when no injuries occur to occupants, an airplane accident resulting in substantial damage must be reported to the nearest National Transportation Safety Board (NTSB) field office immediately.
2. The following incidents must also be reported immediately to the NTSB:
   a. Inability of any required crewmember to perform normal flight duties because of in-flight injury or illness
   b. In-flight fire
   c. Flight control system malfunction or failure
   d. An overdue airplane that is believed to be involved in an accident
   e. An airplane collision in flight
   f. Turbine (jet) engine failures

830.10 Preservation of Aircraft Wreckage, Mail, Cargo, and Records

1. Prior to the time the Board or its authorized representative takes custody of aircraft wreckage, mail, or cargo, such wreckage, mail, or cargo may not be disturbed or moved except to
   a. Remove persons injured or trapped,
   b. Protect the wreckage from further damage, or
   c. Protect the public from injury.

830.15 Reports and Statements to Be Filed

1. The operator of an aircraft shall file a report on Board Form 6120.1/2 within 10 days after an accident.
   a. A report must be filed within 7 days if an overdue aircraft is still missing.
2. A report on an incident for which immediate notification is required (830.5) shall be filed only when requested by an authorized representative of the Board.

QUESTIONS AND ANSWER EXPLANATIONS: All of the private pilot knowledge test questions chosen by the FAA for release as well as additional questions selected by Gleim relating to the material in the previous outlines are reproduced on the following pages. These questions have been organized into the same subunits as the outlines. To the immediate right of each question are the correct answer and answer explanation. You should cover these answers and answer explanations while responding to the questions. Refer to the general discussion in the Introduction on how to take the FAA knowledge test.

Remember that the questions from the FAA knowledge test bank have been reordered by topic and organized into a meaningful sequence. Also, the first line of the answer explanation gives the citation of the authoritative source for the answer.

QUESTIONS

4.1 FAR Part 1

1.1 General Definitions

1. With respect to the certification of airmen, which are categories of aircraft?

A. Gyroplane, helicopter, airship, free balloon.

B. Airplane, rotorcraft, glider, lighter-than-air.

C. Single-engine land and sea, multiengine land and sea.

Answer (B) is correct. *(14 CFR 1.1)*

DISCUSSION: Category of aircraft, as used with respect to the certification, ratings, privileges, and limitations of airmen, means a broad classification of aircraft. Examples include airplane, rotorcraft, glider, and lighter-than-air.

Answer (A) is incorrect. Gyroplane, helicopter, airship, and free balloon are classes (not categories) used with respect to the certification of airmen. Answer (C) is incorrect. Single-engine land and sea and multiengine land and sea are classes (not categories) used with respect to the certification of airmen.

2. With respect to the certification of airmen, which is a class of aircraft?

A. Airplane, rotorcraft, glider, lighter-than-air.

B. Single-engine land and sea, multiengine land and sea.

C. Lighter-than-air, airship, hot air balloon, gas balloon.

Answer (B) is correct. *(14 CFR 1.1)*

DISCUSSION: Class of aircraft, as used with respect to the certification, ratings, privileges, and limitations of airmen, means a classification of aircraft within a category having similar operating characteristics. Examples include single engine, multiengine, land, water, gyroplane, helicopter, airship, and free balloon.

Answer (A) is incorrect. Airplane, rotorcraft, glider, and lighter-than-air are categories, not classes, used with respect to the certification of airmen. Answer (C) is incorrect. Lighter-than-air is a category, not class, of aircraft used with respect to the certification of airmen.

3. The definition of nighttime is

A. sunset to sunrise.

B. 1 hour after sunset to 1 hour before sunrise.

C. the time between the end of evening civil twilight and the beginning of morning civil twilight.

Answer (C) is correct. *(14 CFR 1.1)*

DISCUSSION: "Night" means the time between the end of evening civil twilight and the beginning of morning civil twilight (as published in the *American Air Almanac*) converted to local time.

Answer (A) is incorrect. "Sunset to sunrise" is the time during which navigation lights must be used. Answer (B) is incorrect. The definition for nighttime recency of experience requirements is 1 hr. after sunset to 1 hr. before sunrise.

4. With respect to the certification of aircraft, which is a category of aircraft?

A. Normal, utility, acrobatic.

B. Airplane, rotorcraft, glider.

C. Landplane, seaplane.

Answer (A) is correct. *(14 CFR 1.1)*

DISCUSSION: Category of aircraft, as used with respect to the certification of aircraft, means a grouping of aircraft based upon intended use or operating limitations. Examples include transport, normal, utility, acrobatic, limited, restricted, and provisional.

Answer (B) is incorrect. Airplane, rotorcraft, and glider are categories of aircraft used with respect to the certification of airmen, not aircraft. Answer (C) is incorrect. Landplane and seaplane are classes, not categories, of aircraft used with respect to the certification of aircraft.

5. With respect to the certification of aircraft, which is a class of aircraft?

A. Airplane, rotorcraft, glider, balloon.

B. Normal, utility, acrobatic, limited.

C. Transport, restricted, provisional.

Answer (A) is correct. *(14 CFR 1.1)*

DISCUSSION: Class of aircraft, as used with respect to the certification of aircraft, means a broad grouping of aircraft having similar characteristics of propulsion, flight, or landing. Examples include airplane, rotorcraft, glider, balloon, landplane, and seaplane.

Answer (B) is incorrect. Normal, utility, acrobatic, and limited are categories, not classes, of aircraft used with respect to the certification of aircraft. Answer (C) is incorrect. Transport, restricted, and provisional are categories, not classes, of aircraft used with respect to the certification of aircraft.

6. An ATC clearance provides

A. priority over all other traffic.

B. adequate separation from all traffic.

C. authorization to proceed under specified traffic conditions in controlled airspace.

Answer (C) is correct. *(14 CFR 1.1)*

DISCUSSION: A clearance issued by ATC is predicated on known traffic and known physical airport conditions. An ATC clearance means an authorization by ATC, for the purpose of preventing collision between known airplanes, for an airplane to proceed under specified conditions within controlled airspace.

Answer (A) is incorrect. An ATC clearance does not necessarily give priority over other traffic (although it might in some instances). Answer (B) is incorrect. An ATC clearance only provides separation from other participating traffic.

1.2 Abbreviations and Symbols

7. Which V-speed represents maximum flap extended speed?

A. V_{FE}.

B. V_{LOF}.

C. V_{FC}.

Answer (A) is correct. *(14 CFR 1.2)*

DISCUSSION: V_{FE} means the maximum flap extended speed.

Answer (B) is incorrect. V_{LOF} means liftoff (not maximum flap extended) speed. Answer (C) is incorrect. V_{FC} means maximum speed for stability characteristics, not maximum flap extended speed.

8. Which V-speed represents maximum landing gear extended speed?

A. V_{LE}.

B. V_{LO}.

C. V_{FE}.

Answer (A) is correct. *(14 CFR 1.2)*

DISCUSSION: V_{LE} means the maximum landing gear extended speed.

Answer (B) is incorrect. V_{LO} is the maximum landing gear operating (not extended) speed. Answer (C) is incorrect. V_{FE} is the maximum flap (not landing gear) extended speed.

9. V_{NO} is defined as the

A. normal operating range.

B. never-exceed speed.

C. maximum structural cruising speed.

Answer (C) is correct. *(14 CFR 1.2)*

DISCUSSION: V_{NO} is defined as the maximum structural cruising speed.

Answer (A) is incorrect. The normal airspeed operating range is indicated by the green arc on the airspeed indicator. There is no V-speed for this range. Answer (B) is incorrect. V_{NE} (not V_{NO}) is the never-exceed speed.

10. Which V-speed represents maneuvering speed?

A. V_A.

B. V_{LO}.

C. V_{NE}.

Answer (A) is correct. *(14 CFR 1.2)*

DISCUSSION: V_A means design maneuvering speed.

Answer (B) is incorrect. V_{LO} is the maximum landing gear operating, not the maneuvering, speed. Answer (C) is incorrect. V_{NE} is the never-exceed, not the maneuvering, speed.

11. V_{SO} is defined as the

A. stalling speed or minimum steady flight speed in the landing configuration.

B. stalling speed or minimum steady flight speed in a specified configuration.

C. stalling speed or minimum takeoff safety speed.

Answer (A) is correct. *(14 CFR 1.2)*

DISCUSSION: V_{SO} is defined as the stalling speed or minimum steady flight speed in the landing configuration.

Answer (B) is incorrect. V_{S1} (not V_{SO}) is the stalling speed or minimum steady flight speed in a specified configuration. Answer (C) is incorrect. V_S (not V_{SO}) is the stalling speed, and V_2 min. (not V_{SO}) is the minimum takeoff safety speed.

12. Which would provide the greatest gain in altitude in the shortest distance during climb after takeoff?

A. V_Y.

B. V_A.

C. V_X.

Answer (C) is correct. *(14 CFR 1.2 and AFH Chap 3)*

DISCUSSION: V_X means the best angle of climb airspeed (i.e., the airspeed which will provide the greatest gain in altitude in the shortest distance).

Answer (A) is incorrect. V_Y is the airspeed for the best rate (not angle) of climb. Answer (B) is incorrect. V_A is the design maneuvering airspeed, not the best angle of climb airspeed.

13. After takeoff, which airspeed would the pilot use to gain the most altitude in a given period of time?

A. V_Y.

B. V_X.

C. V_A.

Answer (A) is correct. *(14 CFR 1.2 and AFH Chap 3)*

DISCUSSION: V_Y means the airspeed for the best rate of climb (i.e., the airspeed that you use to gain the most altitude in a given period of time).

Answer (B) is incorrect. V_X is the airspeed for the best angle (not rate) of climb. Answer (C) is incorrect. V_A is the design maneuvering airspeed, not the best rate of climb airspeed.

4.2 FAR Part 21

21.181 Duration of Airworthiness Certificates

14. How long does the Airworthiness Certificate of an aircraft remain valid?

A. As long as the aircraft has a current Registration Certificate.

B. Indefinitely, unless the aircraft suffers major damage.

C. As long as the aircraft is maintained and operated as required by Federal Aviation Regulations.

Answer (C) is correct. *(14 CFR Part 21)*

DISCUSSION: The airworthiness certificate of an airplane remains valid as long as the airplane is in an airworthy condition, i.e., operated and maintained as required by the FARs.

Answer (A) is incorrect. The registration certificate is the document evidencing ownership. A changed registration has no effect on the airworthiness certificate. Answer (B) is incorrect. The airplane must be maintained and operated according to the FARs, not indefinitely. Even if the aircraft suffers major damage, as long as all required repairs are made, the Airworthiness Certificate remains valid.

4.3 FAR Part 39

39.1 Applicability

15. What should an owner or operator know about Airworthiness Directives (ADs)?

A. For informational purposes only.

B. They are mandatory.

C. They are voluntary.

Answer (B) is correct. *(14 CFR Part 39)*

DISCUSSION: ADs are issued under FAR Part 39 by the FAA to require correction of unsafe conditions found in an airplane, an airplane engine, a propeller, or an appliance when such conditions exist and are likely to exist or develop in other products of the same design. Since ADs are issued under FAR Part 39, they are regulatory and must be complied with, unless a specific exemption is granted.

Answer (A) is incorrect. ADs outline required maintenance; they are not for informational purposes only. Answer (C) is incorrect. ADs are mandatory, not voluntary.

39.3 General

16. May a pilot operate an aircraft that is not in compliance with an Airworthiness Directive (AD)?

A. Yes, under VFR conditions only.

B. Yes, ADs are only voluntary.

C. Yes, if allowed by the AD.

Answer (C) is correct. *(14 CFR Part 39)*

DISCUSSION: An AD is used to notify aircraft owners and other interested persons of unsafe conditions and prescribe the conditions under which the product (e.g., an aircraft) may continue to be operated. An AD may be one of an emergency nature requiring immediate compliance upon receipt or one of a less urgent nature requiring compliance within a relatively longer period of time. You may operate an airplane that is not in compliance with an AD, if such operation is allowed by the AD.

Answer (A) is incorrect. An AD, not the operating conditions, may allow an aircraft to be operated before compliance with the AD. Answer (B) is incorrect. ADs are mandatory, not voluntary.

4.4 FAR Part 43

43.3 Persons Authorized to Perform Maintenance, Preventive Maintenance, Rebuilding, and Alterations

17. What regulation allows a private pilot to perform preventive maintenance?

A. 14 CFR Part 91.403.

B. 14 CFR Part 43.3.

C. 14 CFR Part 61.113.

Answer (B) is correct. *(14 CFR 43.3)*

DISCUSSION: Preventive maintenance means simple or minor preservation operations and the replacement of small standard parts not involving complex assembly operations. Appendix A to Part 43 provides a list of work that is considered preventive maintenance. Part 43 allows a person who holds a pilot certificate to perform preventive maintenance on any aircraft owned or operated by that pilot that is not used in air carrier service.

Answer (A) is incorrect. FAR 91.403 provides the general operating rules relating to maintenance, not those relating to who can perform preventive maintenance. Answer (C) is incorrect. FAR 61.113 provides the limitations and privileges of a private pilot as pilot in command.

43.7 Persons Authorized to Approve Aircraft, Airframes, Aircraft Engines, Propellers, Appliances, or Component Parts for Return to Service after Maintenance, Preventive Maintenance, Rebuilding, or Alteration

18. Who may perform preventive maintenance on an aircraft and approve it for return to service?

A. Student or Recreational pilot.

B. Private or Commercial pilot.

C. None of the answers are correct.

Answer (B) is correct. *(14 CFR 43.7)*

DISCUSSION: A person who holds a pilot certificate issued under Part 61 may perform preventive maintenance on any airplane owned or operated by that pilot that is not used in air carrier service. To approve the airplane for return to service after preventive maintenance is performed by a pilot, the pilot must hold at least a private pilot certificate.

Answer (A) is incorrect. While a student or recreational pilot may perform preventive maintenance on any airplane owned or operated by that pilot, the pilot must hold at least a private pilot certificate to approve the airplane's return to service. Answer (C) is incorrect. Any pilot may perform preventive maintenance on an airplane owned or operated by that pilot, but the pilot must hold at least a private pilot certificate to approve the airplane's return to service.

43.9 Maintenance Records

19. Preventive maintenance has been performed on an aircraft. What paperwork is required?

A. A full, detailed description of the work done must be entered in the airframe logbook.

B. The date the work was completed, and the name of the person who did the work must be entered in the airframe and engine logbook.

C. The signature, certificate number, and kind of certificate held by the person approving the work and a description of the work must be entered in the aircraft maintenance records.

Answer (C) is correct. *(14 CFR 43.9)*

DISCUSSION: After preventive maintenance has been performed, the signature, certificate number, and kind of certificate held by the person approving the work and a description of the work must be entered in the aircraft maintenance records.

Answer (A) is incorrect. The signature, certificate number, and kind of certificate, in addition to the description of work performed, must be entered into the maintenance records. Answer (B) is incorrect. A description of work completed, signature, certificate number, and kind of certificate held by the person approving the work (if different than the person who did the work), in addition to the date the work was completed, must be entered into the maintenance records.

43 Appendix A. Major Alterations and Repairs and Preventive Maintenance

20. Which operation would be described as preventive maintenance?

A. Servicing landing gear wheel bearings.

B. Alteration of main seat support brackets.

C. Engine adjustments to allow automotive gas to be used.

Answer (A) is correct. *(14 CFR Part 43)*

DISCUSSION: Appendix A to Part 43 provides a list of work that is considered preventive maintenance. Preventive maintenance means simple or minor preservation operations and the replacement of small standard parts not involving complex assembly operations. Servicing landing gear wheel bearings, such as cleaning and greasing, is considered preventive maintenance.

Answer (B) is incorrect. The alteration of main seat support brackets is considered an airframe major repair, not preventive maintenance. Answer (C) is incorrect. Engine adjustments to allow automotive gas to be used is considered a powerplant major alteration, not preventive maintenance.

21. Which operation would be described as preventive maintenance?

A. Repair of landing gear brace struts.

B. Replenishing hydraulic fluid.

C. Repair of portions of skin sheets by making additional seams.

Answer (B) is correct. *(14 CFR Part 43)*

DISCUSSION: Appendix A to Part 43 provides a list of work that is considered preventive maintenance. Preventive maintenance means simple or minor preservation operations and the replacement of small standard parts not involving complex assembly operations. An example of preventive maintenance is replenishing hydraulic fluid.

Answer (A) is incorrect. The repair of landing gear brace struts is considered an airframe major repair, not preventive maintenance. Answer (C) is incorrect. The repair of portions of skin sheets by making additional seams is considered an airframe major repair, not preventive maintenance.

4.5 FAR Part 47

22. Is it legal to fly on the dealer's registration after a buyer purchased an airplane from that dealer?

A. Yes, the airplane can be flown by the buyer for 30 days.

B. No, the airplane cannot be flown by the buyer and has to be registered.

C. Yes, the airplane can be flown by the buyer for 120 days.

Answer (B) is correct. *(14 CFR Part 47)*

DISCUSSION: A Dealer's Aircraft Registration Certificate is another form of registration. It is valid only for flights within the United States by the manufacturer or a dealer for flight testing or demonstration for sale and must be removed by the dealer when the aircraft is sold. The back side of the registration is filled out with the appropriate information from the sale as well as the new owner's name. The certificate must then be mailed back to the FAA registry in Oklahoma City. Doing so protects the buyer and seller. This requirement is law under FAR 47.41(b), which became effective March 31, 2008.

Answer (A) is incorrect. Once the airplane changes ownership, the seller's aircraft registration certificate is removed. Answer (C) is incorrect. Once the airplane changes ownership, the aircraft's registration is removed, the form on the back is filled out, and the certificate is then sent to the FAA.

4.6 FAR Part 61

61.3 Requirements for Certificates, Ratings, and Authorizations

23. When must a current pilot certificate be in the pilot's personal possession or readily accessible in the aircraft?

A. When acting as a crew chief during launch and recovery.

B. Only when passengers are carried.

C. Anytime when acting as pilot in command or as a required crewmember.

Answer (C) is correct. *(14 CFR 61.3)*

DISCUSSION: Current and appropriate pilot and medical certificates must be in your personal possession or readily accessible in the aircraft when you act as pilot in command (PIC) or as a required pilot flight crewmember.

Answer (A) is incorrect. A current pilot certificate must be in your personal possession when acting as a PIC or as a required crewmember of an aircraft, not when acting as a crew chief during launch and recovery of an airship. Answer (B) is incorrect. Anytime you fly as PIC or as a required crewmember, you must have a current pilot certificate in your personal possession regardless of whether passengers are carried or not.

24. A recreational or private pilot acting as pilot in command, or in any other capacity as a required pilot flight crewmember, must have in his or her personal possession or readily accessible in the aircraft a current

A. logbook endorsement to show that a flight review has been satisfactorily accomplished.

B. medical certificate if required and an appropriate pilot certificate.

C. endorsement on the pilot certificate to show that a flight review has been satisfactorily accomplished.

Answer (B) is correct. *(14 CFR 61.3)*

DISCUSSION: Current and appropriate pilot and medical certificates must be in your personal possession or readily accessible in the aircraft when you act as pilot in command (PIC) or as a required pilot flight crewmember.

Answer (A) is incorrect. As a private pilot, you need not have your logbook in your possession or readily accessible aboard the airplane. A recreational pilot must carry a logbook to show evidence of an endorsement that permits certain flights, not to show completion of a flight review. Answer (C) is incorrect. The endorsement after satisfactorily completing a flight review is made in your pilot logbook, not on your pilot certificate.

25. What document(s) must be in your personal possession or readily accessible in the aircraft while operating as pilot in command of an aircraft?

A. Certificates showing accomplishment of a checkout in the aircraft and a current biennial flight review.

B. A pilot certificate with an endorsement showing accomplishment of an annual flight review and a pilot logbook showing recency of experience.

C. An appropriate pilot certificate and an appropriate current medical certificate if required.

Answer (C) is correct. *(14 CFR 61.3)*

DISCUSSION: Current and appropriate pilot and medical certificates must be in your personal possession or readily accessible in the aircraft when you act as pilot in command (PIC) or as a required pilot flight crewmember.

Answer (A) is incorrect. Flight reviews and checkouts in aircraft are documented in your logbook rather than on separate certificates and need not be in your personal possession. Answer (B) is incorrect. The endorsement after satisfactorily completing a flight review is made in your logbook, not on your pilot certificate. You are not required to have your pilot logbook in your personal possession while acting as pilot in command.

26. Each person who holds a pilot certificate or a medical certificate shall present it for inspection upon the request of the Administrator, the National Transportation Safety Board, or any

A. authorized representative of the Department of Transportation.

B. person in a position of authority.

C. federal, state, or local law enforcement officer.

Answer (C) is correct. *(14 CFR 61.3)*

DISCUSSION: Each person who holds a pilot certificate, flight instructor certificate, medical certificate, authorization, or license required by the FARs shall present it for inspection upon the request of the Administrator (of the FAA), an authorized representative of the National Transportation Safety Board, or any federal, state, or local law enforcement officer.

Answer (A) is incorrect. An authorized representative of the Department of Transportation is just one example of those who can ask to inspect pilot and medical certificates. Answer (B) is incorrect. Not just any person with any kind of authority, such as a foreman, can inspect your pilot certificate or medical certificate.

<u>61.15 Offenses Involving Alcohol or Drugs</u>

27. How soon after the conviction for driving while intoxicated by alcohol or drugs shall it be reported to the FAA, Civil Aviation Security Division?

A. No later than 60 days after the motor vehicle action.

B. No later than 30 working days after the motor vehicle action.

C. Required to be reported upon renewal of medical certificate.

Answer (A) is correct. *(14 CFR 61.15)*

DISCUSSION: Each person holding a certificate under Part 61 shall provide a written report of each motor vehicle action involving alcohol or drugs to the FAA, Civil Aviation Security Division, no later than 60 days after the motor vehicle action.

Answer (B) is incorrect. FAR 61.15 allows a person 60 days after the motor vehicle action, not 30 days. Answer (C) is incorrect. A person must notify the Civil Aviation Security Division no later than 60 days after a motor vehicle action involving drugs or alcohol.

28. How soon after the conviction for driving while intoxicated by alcohol or drugs shall it be reported to the FAA, and which division should this be reported to?

A. Within 60 days to the Airmen Records Division.

B. Within 60 days to the Civil Aviation Security Division.

C. Within 60 days to the Regulatory Support Division.

Answer (B) is correct. *(14 CFR 61.15)*

DISCUSSION: Each person holding a certificate under Part 61 shall provide a written report of each motor vehicle action involving alcohol or drugs to the FAA, Civil Aviation Security Division, no later than 60 days after the motor vehicle action.

Answer (A) is incorrect. The Airmen Records Division handles the certification of airmen, not alcohol and/or drug convictions. Answer (C) is incorrect. The Regulatory Support Division is involved in airmen testing, designee standardization, and the management of aviation data systems.

61.23 Medical Certificates: Requirement and Duration

29. A Third-Class Medical Certificate is issued to a 36-year-old pilot on August 10, this year. To exercise the privileges of a Private Pilot Certificate, the medical certificate will be valid until midnight on

A. August 10, 3 years later.

B. August 31, 5 years later.

C. August 31, 3 years later.

Answer (B) is correct. *(14 CFR 61.23)*

DISCUSSION: A pilot may exercise the privileges of a private pilot certificate under a third-class medical certificate until it expires at the end of the last day of the month 5 years after it was issued, for pilots less than 40 years old on the date of the medical examination. A third-class medical certificate issued to a 36-year-old pilot on Aug. 10 will be valid until midnight on Aug. 31, 5 years later.

Answer (A) is incorrect. Medical certificates expire at the last day of the month. Thus, a medical certificate issued on Aug. 10 will expire on Aug. 31, not Aug. 10. Additionally, since the pilot is less than 40 years old, the third-class medical certificate is valid for 5 years, not 3 years. Answer (C) is incorrect. A pilot may exercise the privileges of a private pilot certificate under a third-class medical certificate until it expires at the end of the last day of the month 5 years later if the pilot was less than 40 years old on the date of the medical examination.

30. A Third-Class Medical Certificate is issued to a 51-year-old pilot on May 3, this year. To exercise the privileges of a Private Pilot Certificate, the medical certificate will be valid until midnight on

A. May 3, 1 year later.

B. May 31, 1 year later.

C. May 31, 2 years later.

Answer (C) is correct. *(14 CFR 61.23)*

DISCUSSION: A pilot may exercise the privileges of a private pilot certificate under a third-class medical certificate until it expires at the end of the last day of the month 2 years after it was issued, for pilots 40 years old or older on the date of the medical examination. A third-class medical certificate issued to a 51-year-old pilot on May 3 will be valid until midnight on May 31, 2 years later.

Answer (A) is incorrect. Medical certificates expire on the last day of the month. Thus, a medical certificate issued on May 3 will expire on May 31, not May 3. Additionally, a third-class medical certificate is valid for 2 years, not 1 year, if the pilot is over 40 years old. Answer (B) is incorrect. A pilot may exercise the privileges of a private pilot certificate under a third-class medical certificate until it expires at the end of the last day of the month, 2 years, not 1 year, later if the pilot was 40 years old or older on the date of the examination.

31. For private pilot operations, a Second-Class Medical Certificate issued to a 42-year-old pilot on July 15, this year, will expire at midnight on

A. July 15, 2 years later.

B. July 31, 1 year later.

C. July 31, 2 years later.

Answer (C) is correct. *(14 CFR 61.23)*

DISCUSSION: For private pilot operations, a second-class medical certificate will expire at the end of the last day of the month, 2 years after it was issued, for pilots 40 years old or older on the date of the medical examination. For private pilot operations, a second-class medical certificate issued to a 42-year-old pilot on July 15 will be valid until midnight on July 31, 2 years later.

Answer (A) is incorrect. A medical certificate expires on the last day of the month. Thus, a medical certificate issued on July 15 will expire on July 31, not July 15. Answer (B) is incorrect. A second-class medical certificate is valid for 1 year for operations requiring a commercial pilot certificate.

32. A Third-Class Medical Certificate was issued to a 19-year-old pilot on August 10, this year. To exercise the privileges of a recreational or private pilot certificate, the medical certificate will expire at midnight on

A. August 10, 2 years later.

B. August 31, 5 years later.

C. August 31, 2 years later.

Answer (B) is correct. *(14 CFR 61.23)*

DISCUSSION: A pilot may exercise the privileges of a recreational or private pilot certificate under a third-class medical certificate until it expires at the end of the last day of the month 5 years after it was issued, for pilots less than 40 years old at the time of the medical examination. A third-class medical certificate issued to a 19-year-old pilot on Aug. 10 will be valid until midnight on Aug. 31, 5 years later.

Answer (A) is incorrect. Medical certificates expire at the end of the month. A medical certificate issued on Aug. 10 will expire at midnight on Aug. 31, not Aug. 10. Additionally, since the pilot is less than 40 years old, the third-class medical certificate is valid for 5 years, not 3 years. Answer (C) is incorrect. A pilot may exercise the privileges of a recreational or private pilot certificate under a third-class medical certificate until it expires at the end of the last day of the month 2 years later if the pilot was 40 years old or older, not less than 40 years old, on the date of the medical examination.

33. For private pilot operations, a First-Class Medical Certificate issued to a 23-year-old pilot on October 21, this year, will expire at midnight on

A. October 21, 2 years later.

B. October 31, next year.

C. October 31, 5 years later.

Answer (C) is correct. *(14 CFR 61.23)*

DISCUSSION: For private pilot operations, a first-class medical certificate will expire at the end of the last day of the 60th calendar month (5 years) after the month of the date of examination shown on the medical certificate for pilots less than 40 years old on the date of the medical examination. Thus, a first-class medical certificate issued to a 23-year-old pilot on October 21 will be valid until midnight on October 31, 60 calendar months (5 years) after the month of the date of examination.

Answer (A) is incorrect. Medical certificates expire on the last day of the calendar month, meaning a medical certificate issued on October 21 will expire on October 31. Additionally, for private pilot operations, a first-class medical certificate will expire at the end of the last day of the 60th calendar month after the month of the date of examination shown on the medical certificate. Thus, the medical certificate is valid for 5 years, not 2 years, for a pilot less than 40 years old on the date of the medical examination. Answer (B) is incorrect. A first-class medical certificate is valid for 1 year for operations requiring a commercial pilot certificate.

61.31 Type Rating Requirements, Additional Training, and Authorization Requirements

34. Before a person holding a private pilot certificate may act as pilot in command of a high-performance airplane, that person must have

A. passed a flight test in that airplane from an FAA inspector.

B. an endorsement in that person's logbook that he or she is competent to act as pilot in command.

C. received ground and flight instruction from an authorized flight instructor who then endorses that person's logbook.

Answer (C) is correct. *(14 CFR 61.31)*

DISCUSSION: A private pilot may not act as pilot in command of a high-performance airplane (an airplane with an engine of more than 200 horsepower) unless (s)he has received and logged ground and flight training from an authorized instructor who has certified in his or her logbook that (s)he is proficient to operate a high-performance airplane.

Answer (A) is incorrect. No FAA flight test is required, only ground and flight training and an endorsement from an authorized flight instructor. Answer (B) is incorrect. The ground and flight training and endorsement must be by an authorized flight instructor.

35. What is the definition of a high-performance airplane?

A. An airplane with 180 horsepower, or retractable landing gear, flaps, and a fixed-pitch propeller.

B. An airplane with a normal cruise speed in excess of 200 knots.

C. An airplane with an engine of more than 200 horsepower.

Answer (C) is correct. *(14 CFR 61.31)*

DISCUSSION: A high-performance airplane is defined as an airplane with an engine of more than 200 horsepower.

Answer (A) is incorrect. A high-performance airplane is an airplane with an engine of more than 200 horsepower, not an airplane with 180 horsepower, or retractable landing gear, flaps, and a fixed-pitch propeller. Answer (B) is incorrect. A high-performance airplane is an airplane with an engine of more than 200 horsepower, not an airplane with a normal cruise speed in excess of 200 knots.

36. The pilot in command is required to hold a type rating in which aircraft?

A. Aircraft operated under an authorization issued by the Administrator.

B. Aircraft having a gross weight of more than 12,500 pounds.

C. Aircraft involved in ferry flights, training flights, or test flights.

Answer (B) is correct. *(14 CFR 61.31)*

DISCUSSION: A person may not act as pilot in command of any of the following aircraft unless (s)he holds a type rating for that aircraft:

(1) A large aircraft (except lighter-than-air), i.e., over 12,500 lb. gross weight
(2) A turbojet-powered airplane
(3) Other aircraft specified by the FAA through aircraft type certificate procedures

Answer (A) is incorrect. All aircraft, not only those requiring type ratings, are operated under an authorization issued by the Administrator of the FAA. Answer (C) is incorrect. Any type of aircraft can be involved in ferry flights, training flights, or test flights and may not require a type rating (e.g., your single-engine trainer airplane on a training flight).

37. In order to act as pilot in command of a high-performance airplane, a pilot must have

A. made and logged three solo takeoffs and landings in a high-performance airplane.

B. received and logged ground and flight instruction in an airplane that has more than 200 horsepower.

C. passed a flight test in a high-performance airplane.

Answer (B) is correct. *(14 CFR 61.31)*

DISCUSSION: Prior to acting as pilot in command of an airplane with an engine of more than 200 horsepower, a person is required to receive and log ground and flight training in such an airplane from an authorized flight instructor who has certified in the pilot's logbook that the individual is proficient to operate a high-performance airplane.

Answer (A) is incorrect. In order to act as pilot in command of a high-performance airplane, you must have received and logged ground and flight training from an authorized flight instructor, not have made three solo takeoffs and landings. Answer (C) is incorrect. You must have received and logged ground and flight training, and a logbook endorsement from an authorized flight instructor, not a flight test, is required prior to acting as a pilot in command of a high-performance airplane.

61.51 Pilot Logbooks

38. As pilot in command with a recreational certificate, you must have in your personal possession while exercising the privileges of that certificate

A. a current logbook endorsement for an accomplished flight review.

B. a current pilot and medical certificate.

C. a pilot logbook documenting recent experience requirements.

Answer (B) is correct. *(14 CFR 61.3, 61.51)*

DISCUSSION: When acting as a pilot in command or as a required pilot flight crew member, you must have a valid pilot certificate and a current and appropriate medical certificate (or driver's license, if appropriate) in your personal possession or readily accessible in the airplane.

Answer (A) is incorrect. A recreational pilot must carry a logbook to show evidence of an endorsement that permits certain flights, not to show completion of a flight review. (S)he must carry his or her logbook with the required authorized instructor endorsements on all solo flights (1) that exceed 50 NM from the airport at which training was received, (2) within airspace that requires communication with air traffic control, (3) conducted between sunset and sunrise, or (4) in an aircraft for which the pilot does not hold an appropriate category or class rating. Answer (C) is incorrect. A recreational pilot must carry his or her logbook with the required authorized instructor endorsements when on solo flights that exceed 50 nautical miles.

61.56 Flight Review

39. If a recreational or private pilot had a flight review on October 30, this year, when is the next flight review required?

A. October 30, 2 years later.

B. October 31, next year.

C. October 31, 2 years later.

Answer (C) is correct. *(14 CFR 61.56)*

DISCUSSION: A pilot is required to have a flight review within the preceding 24 calendar months before the month in which the pilot acts as pilot in command. Thus, a pilot who had a flight review on October 30 of this year must have a flight review completed by October 31, 2 years later.

Answer (A) is incorrect. Flight reviews expire at the end of the month. Thus, a flight review on October 30 will expire on October 31. Answer (B) is incorrect. A flight review is valid for 2 years, not 1 year.

40. Each recreational or private pilot is required to have

A. a biennial flight review.

B. an annual flight review.

C. a semiannual flight review.

Answer (A) is correct. *(14 CFR 61.56)*

DISCUSSION: Each recreational or private pilot is required to have a biennial (every 2 years) flight review.

Answer (B) is incorrect. Each pilot is required to have a biennial, not annual, flight review. Answer (C) is incorrect. Each pilot is required to have a biennial, not semiannual, flight review.

41. If a recreational or private pilot had a flight review on August 8, this year, when is the next flight review required?

A. August 8, next year.

B. August 31, 1 year later.

C. August 31, 2 years later.

Answer (C) is correct. *(14 CFR 61.56)*

DISCUSSION: A pilot is required to have a flight review within the preceding 24 calendar months before the month in which the pilot acts as pilot in command. Thus, a recreational or private pilot who had a flight review on Aug. 8 of this year must have a flight review completed by Aug. 31, 2 years later.

Answer (A) is incorrect. Flight reviews expire at the end of the month. Thus, a flight review on Aug. 8 will expire on Aug. 31, not Aug. 8. Answer (B) is incorrect. A flight review is valid for 2 years, not 1 year.

42. To act as pilot in command of an aircraft carrying passengers, a pilot must show by logbook endorsement the satisfactory completion of a flight review or completion of a pilot proficiency check within the preceding

A. 6 calendar months.

B. 12 calendar months.

C. 24 calendar months.

Answer (C) is correct. *(14 CFR Part 61)*

DISCUSSION: To act as pilot in command of an aircraft (whether carrying passengers or not), a pilot must show by logbook endorsement the satisfactory completion of a flight review or completion of a pilot proficiency check within the preceding 24 calendar months.

Answer (A) is incorrect. A pilot must have satisfactorily completed a flight review or completion of a pilot proficiency check within the preceding 24 (not 6) calendar months. Answer (B) is incorrect. A pilot must have satisfactorily completed a flight review or completion of a pilot proficiency check within the preceding 24 (not 12) calendar months.

61.57 Recent Flight Experience: Pilot in Command

43. To act as pilot in command of an aircraft carrying passengers, the pilot must have made at least three takeoffs and three landings in an aircraft of the same category, class, and if a type rating is required, of the same type, within the preceding

A. 90 days.

B. 12 calendar months.

C. 24 calendar months.

Answer (A) is correct. *(14 CFR Part 61)*

DISCUSSION: To act as pilot in command of an airplane with passengers aboard, you must have made at least three takeoffs and three landings (to a full stop if in a tailwheel airplane) in an airplane of the same category, class, and, if a type rating is required, of the same type within the preceding 90 days. Category refers to airplane, rotorcraft, etc.; class refers to single- or multi-engine, land or sea.

Answer (B) is incorrect. A flight review, not recency experience, is required every 24, not 12, calendar months. Answer (C) is incorrect. A flight review, not recency experience, is normally required of all pilots every 24 months.

44. If recency of experience requirements for night flight are not met and official sunset is 1830, the latest time passengers may be carried is

A. 1829.

B. 1859.

C. 1929.

Answer (C) is correct. *(14 CFR 61.57)*

DISCUSSION: For the purpose of night recency experience flight time, night is defined as the period beginning 1 hr. after sunset and ending 1 hr. before sunrise. If you have not met the night experience requirements and official sunset is 1830, a landing must be accomplished at or before 1929 if passengers are carried.

Answer (A) is incorrect. This is the time that night begins for the purpose of turning on aircraft position (navigation) lights. Answer (B) is incorrect. There is no regulation concerning the time 30 min. after official sunset.

45. To act as pilot in command of an aircraft carrying passengers, the pilot must have made three takeoffs and three landings within the preceding 90 days in an aircraft of the same

A. make and model.

B. category and class, but not type.

C. category, class, and type, if a type rating is required.

Answer (C) is correct. *(14 CFR Part 61)*

DISCUSSION: No one may act as pilot in command of an airplane carrying passengers unless within the preceding 90 days (s)he has made three takeoffs and three landings as sole manipulator of the controls in an aircraft of the same category and class and, if a type rating is required, the same type. If the aircraft is a tailwheel airplane, the landings must have been to a full stop.

Answer (A) is incorrect. It must be the same category and class (not make and model) and, if a type rating is required, the same type. Answer (B) is incorrect. It must be the same type aircraft if a type rating is required for that aircraft.

46. The three takeoffs and landings that are required to act as pilot in command at night must be done during the time period from

A. sunset to sunrise.

B. 1 hour after sunset to 1 hour before sunrise.

C. the end of evening civil twilight to the beginning of morning civil twilight.

Answer (B) is correct. *(14 CFR 61.57)*

DISCUSSION: No one may act as pilot in command of an aircraft carrying passengers at night (i.e., the period from 1 hr. after sunset to 1 hr. before sunrise as published in the American Air Almanac) unless (s)he has made three takeoffs and three landings to a full stop within the preceding 90 days, at night, in the category and class of aircraft to be used.

Answer (A) is incorrect. The period from sunset to sunrise is the time that aircraft lights are required to be on, not the time period for night recency experience. Answer (C) is incorrect. The end of evening civil twilight to the beginning of morning civil twilight is the definition of night, not the time period for night recency experience.

47. To meet the recency of experience requirements to act as pilot in command carrying passengers at night, a pilot must have made at least three takeoffs and three landings to a full stop within the preceding 90 days in

A. the same category and class of aircraft to be used.

B. the same type of aircraft to be used.

C. any aircraft.

Answer (A) is correct. *(14 CFR 61.57)*

DISCUSSION: No one may act as pilot in command of an aircraft carrying passengers at night (i.e., the period from 1 hr. after sunset to 1 hr. before sunrise) unless (s)he has made three takeoffs and three landings to a full stop within the preceding 90 days, at night, in the category and class of aircraft to be used.

Answer (B) is incorrect. Unless a type-rating is required, it does not have to be the same type of aircraft. ("Type" refers to a specific make and general model, e.g., Cessna 152/172.) Answer (C) is incorrect. It must be the same category and class (not any) of aircraft to be used.

48. The takeoffs and landings required to meet the recency of experience requirements for carrying passengers in a tailwheel airplane

A. may be touch and go or full stop.

B. must be touch and go.

C. must be to a full stop.

Answer (C) is correct. *(14 CFR Part 61)*

DISCUSSION: To comply with recency requirements for carrying passengers in a tailwheel airplane, one must have made three takeoffs and landings to a full stop within the past 90 days.

Answer (A) is incorrect. In a tailwheel airplane, the takeoffs and landings must be to a full stop only, not touch and go. Answer (B) is incorrect. In a tailwheel airplane, the takeoffs and landings must be to a full stop, not touch and go.

49. Your cousin wants you to take him flying. You must have made at least three takeoffs and three landings in your aircraft within the preceding

A. 90 days.

B. 60 days.

C. 30 days.

Answer (A) is correct. *(14 CFR 61.57)*

DISCUSSION: To carry passengers, you must have made three landings and three takeoffs within the preceding 90 days. All three landings must be made in aircraft of the same category, class, and, if a type rating is required, type as the one in which passengers are to be carried.

Answer (B) is incorrect. To carry passengers, a pilot is required to have made at least three landings and three takeoffs within the preceding 90 days, not 60 days. Answer (C) is incorrect. According to 14 CFR Sec. 61.57, to carry passengers, a pilot must have made at least three landings and three takeoffs within the preceding 90 days, not 30 days.

61.60 Change of Address

50. If a certificated pilot changes permanent mailing address and fails to notify the FAA Airmen Certification Branch of the new address, the pilot is entitled to exercise the privileges of the pilot certificate for a period of only

A. 30 days after the date of the move.

B. 60 days after the date of the move.

C. 90 days after the date of the move.

Answer (A) is correct. *(14 CFR Part 61)*

DISCUSSION: If you have changed your permanent mailing address, you may not exercise the privileges of your pilot certificate after 30 days from the date of the address change unless you have notified the FAA in writing of the change. You are required to notify the Airmen Certification Branch at P.O. Box 25082, Oklahoma City, OK 73125. You may also use the airmen services system on the FAA website.

NOTE: While you must notify the FAA if your address changes, you are not required to carry a certificate that shows your current address. The FAA will not issue a new certificate upon receipt of your new address unless you send a written request and $2 to the address shown above.

Answer (B) is incorrect. If you change your permanent mailing address, you may exercise the privileges of your pilot certificate for a period of only 30 (not 60) days after the date you move unless you notify the FAA in writing of the change. Answer (C) is incorrect. If you change your permanent mailing address, you may exercise the privileges of your pilot certificate for a period of only 30 (not 90) days after the date you move unless you notify the FAA in writing of the change.

61.69 Glider Towing: Experience and Training Requirements

51. A certificated private pilot may not act as pilot in command of an aircraft towing a glider unless there is entered in the pilot's logbook a minimum of

A. 100 hours of pilot flight time in any aircraft the pilot is using to tow a glider.

B. 100 hours of pilot-in-command time in the aircraft category, class, and type, if required, that the pilot is using to tow a glider.

C. 200 hours of pilot-in-command time in the aircraft category, class, and type, if required, that the pilot is using to tow a glider.

Answer (B) is correct. *(14 CFR 61.69[a][2])*

DISCUSSION: As a private pilot, you may not act as pilot in command of an aircraft towing a glider unless you have had, and entered in your logbook, at least 100 hr. of pilot-in-command time in the aircraft category, class, and type, if required, that you are using to tow a glider.

Answer (A) is incorrect. You must have logged at least 100 hr. as pilot in command in the aircraft category, class, and type, if required, that you are using to tow a glider, not just any aircraft. Answer (C) is incorrect. You must have logged at least 100 hr., not 200 hr., as pilot in command.

52. To act as pilot in command of an aircraft towing a glider, a pilot is required to have made within the preceding 24 months

A. at least three flights as observer in a glider being towed by an aircraft.

B. at least three flights in a powered glider.

C. at least three actual or simulated glider tows while accompanied by a qualified pilot.

Answer (C) is correct. *(14 CFR 61.69)*

DISCUSSION: To act as pilot in command of an aircraft towing a glider, you are required to have made, in the preceding 24 months,

(1) At least three actual or simulated glider tows while accompanied by a qualified pilot or

(2) At least three flights as pilot in command of a glider towed by an aircraft.

Answer (A) is incorrect. You are required to have made within the preceding 24 months at least three flights as pilot in command, not as an observer, of a glider being towed by an aircraft. Answer (B) is incorrect. You are required to have made within the preceding 24 months at least three flights as pilot in command of a glider towed by an aircraft, not three flights in a powered glider.

61.113 Private Pilot Privileges and Limitations: Pilot in Command

53. In regard to privileges and limitations, a private pilot may

A. act as pilot in command of an aircraft carrying a passenger for compensation if the flight is in connection with a business or employment.

B. not pay less than the pro rata share of the operating expenses of a flight with passengers provided the expenses involve only fuel, oil, airport expenditures, or rental fees.

C. not be paid in any manner for the operating expenses of a flight.

Answer (B) is correct. *(14 CFR 61.113)*

DISCUSSION: A private pilot may not pay less than an equal (pro rata) share of the operating expenses of a flight with passengers. These expenses may involve only fuel, oil, airport expenditures (e.g., landing fees, tie-down fees, etc.), or rental fees.

Answer (A) is incorrect. A private pilot cannot act as pilot in command of an aircraft carrying a passenger for compensation. Answer (C) is incorrect. A private pilot may equally share the operating expenses of a flight with his or her passengers.

54. According to regulations pertaining to privileges and limitations, a private pilot may

A. be paid for the operating expenses of a flight if at least three takeoffs and three landings were made by the pilot within the preceding 90 days.

B. not pay less than the pro rata share of the operating expenses of a flight with passengers provided the expenses involve only fuel, oil, airport expenditures, or rental fees.

C. not be paid in any manner for the operating expenses of a flight.

Answer (B) is correct. *(14 CFR 61.113)*

DISCUSSION: A private pilot may not pay less than an equal (pro rata) share of the operating expenses of a flight with passengers. These expenses may involve only fuel, oil, airport expenditures (e.g., landing fees, tie-down fees, etc.), or rental fees.

Answer (A) is incorrect. A private pilot may be paid for the operating expenses of a flight in connection with any business or employment if the flight is only incidental to that business or employment and no passengers or property are carried for compensation or hire, not if the pilot has made three takeoffs and landings in the preceding 90 days. Answer (C) is incorrect. A private pilot may equally share the operating expenses of a flight with his or her passengers.

55. What exception, if any, permits a private pilot to act as pilot in command of an aircraft carrying passengers who pay for the flight?

A. If the passengers pay all the operating expenses.

B. If a donation is made to a charitable organization for the flight.

C. There is no exception.

Answer (B) is correct. *(14 CFR 61.113)*

DISCUSSION: A private pilot may act as pilot in command of an airplane used in a passenger-carrying airlift sponsored by a charitable organization for which passengers make donations to the organization, provided the following requirements are met: the local FSDO is notified at least 7 days before the flight, the flight is conducted from an adequate public airport, the pilot has logged at least 500 hr., no acrobatic or formation flights are performed, the 100-hr. inspection of the airplane requirement is complied with, and the flight is day-VFR.

Answer (A) is incorrect. A private pilot may only share the operating costs, not have the passengers pay for all the operating costs. Answer (C) is incorrect. The exception is a passenger-carrying airlift sponsored by a charitable organization.

4.7 Recreational Pilot Related FARs

61.101 Recreational Pilot Privileges and Limitations

NOTE: Questions 56 through 82 are not included on the private pilot knowledge test.

56. A recreational pilot acting as pilot in command must have in his or her personal possession while aboard the aircraft

A. a current logbook endorsement to show that a flight review has been satisfactorily accomplished.

B. the pilot logbook to show recent experience requirements to serve as pilot in command have been met.

C. a current logbook endorsement that permits flight within 50 nautical miles from the departure airport.

Answer (C) is correct. *(14 CFR 61.101)*

DISCUSSION: A recreational pilot acting as pilot in command must have in his or her personal possession while aboard the airplane a current logbook endorsement that permits flight within 50 NM from the departure airport.

Answer (A) is incorrect. To act as pilot in command, a recreational pilot must have in his or her personal possession while aboard the aircraft a current logbook endorsement that permits flight within 50 NM from the departure airport, not an endorsement to show that a flight review has been satisfactorily completed. Answer (B) is incorrect. To act as pilot in command, a recreational pilot must have in his or her personal possession while aboard the aircraft a current logbook endorsement that permits flight within 50 NM from the departure airport, not a logbook showing that the recent experience requirements have been met.

57. How many passengers is a recreational pilot allowed to carry on board?

A. One.

B. Two.

C. Three.

Answer (A) is correct. *(14 CFR 61.101)*

DISCUSSION: Recreational pilots may carry no more than one passenger.

Answer (B) is incorrect. A recreational pilot is allowed to carry only one passenger (not two). Answer (C) is incorrect. A recreational pilot is allowed to carry only one passenger (not three).

58. When may a recreational pilot act as pilot in command of an aircraft at night?

A. When obtaining an additional certificate or rating under the supervision of an authorized instructor, provided the surface or flight visibility is at least 1 statute mile.

B. When obtaining an additional certificate or rating under the supervision of an authorized instructor, provided the surface or flight visibility is at least 3 statute miles.

C. When obtaining an additional certificate or rating under the supervision of an authorized instructor, provided the surface or flight visibility is at least 5 statute miles.

Answer (C) is correct. *(14 CFR 61.101)*

DISCUSSION: A recreational pilot obtaining an additional certificate or rating under the supervision of an authorized instructor is treated as a student pilot with respect to flight at night, since recreational pilots do not have night-flying privilege. Therefore, a recreational pilot may act as pilot in command of an aircraft at night when obtaining an additional certificate or rating under the supervision of an authorized instructor, provided the surface or flight visibility is at least 5 statute miles.

Answer (A) is incorrect. A recreational pilot may act as pilot in command of an aircraft at night when obtaining an additional certificate or rating under the supervision of an authorized instructor, provided the surface or flight visibility is at least 5 statute miles, not 1 statute mile. Answer (B) is incorrect. A recreational pilot may act as pilot in command of an aircraft at night when obtaining an additional certificate or rating under the supervision of an authorized instructor, provided the surface or flight visibility is at least 5 statute miles, not 3 statute miles.

59. According to regulations pertaining to privileges and limitations, a recreational pilot may

A. be paid for the operating expenses of a flight.

B. not pay less than the pro rata share of the operating expenses of a flight with a passenger.

C. not be paid in any manner for the operating expenses of a flight.

Answer (B) is correct. *(14 CFR 61.101)*

DISCUSSION: A recreational pilot may not pay less than an equal (pro rata) share of the operating expenses of the flight with a passenger. These expenses may involve only fuel, oil, airport expenditures (e.g., landing fees, tie-down fees, etc.), or rental fees.

Answer (A) is incorrect. Operating expenses can only be shared by a passenger, not paid for by a passenger; i.e., a recreational pilot cannot carry a passenger or property for compensation or hire. Answer (C) is incorrect. A recreational pilot may equally share operating expenses of the flight with the passenger.

60. When may a recreational pilot act as pilot in command on a cross-country flight that exceeds 50 nautical miles from the departure airport?

A. After receiving ground and flight instructions on cross-country training and a logbook endorsement.

B. After attaining 100 hours of pilot-in-command time and a logbook endorsement.

C. 12 calendar months after receiving his or her recreational pilot certificate and a logbook endorsement.

Answer (A) is correct. *(14 CFR 61.101)*

DISCUSSION: A recreational pilot may act as pilot in command on a cross-country flight that exceeds 50 NM from the departure airport, provided that person has received ground and flight training from an authorized instructor on the cross-country training requirements for a private pilot certificate and has received a logbook endorsement, which is in the person's possession in the aircraft, certifying the person is proficient in cross-country flying.

Answer (B) is incorrect. A recreational pilot may act as pilot in command on a cross-country flight that exceeds 50 NM from the departure airport after receiving ground and flight training from an authorized instructor on the cross-country training requirements for a private pilot certificate and after receiving a logbook endorsement, not after attaining 100 hr. as pilot-in-command time and a logbook endorsement. Answer (C) is incorrect. A recreational pilot may act as pilot in command on a cross-country flight after receiving ground and flight training from an authorized instructor on the cross-country training requirements for a private pilot certificate and after receiving a logbook endorsement, not 12 months after receiving his or her recreational pilot certificate and a logbook endorsement.

61. In regard to privileges and limitations, a recreational pilot may

A. fly for compensation or hire within 50 nautical miles from the departure airport with a logbook endorsement.

B. not pay less than the pro rata share of the operating expenses of a flight with a passenger.

C. not be paid in any manner for the operating expenses of a flight from a passenger.

Answer (B) is correct. *(14 CFR 61.101)*

DISCUSSION: A recreational pilot may not pay less than an equal (pro rata) share of the operating expenses of the flight with a passenger. These expenses may involve only fuel, oil, airport expenditures (e.g., landing fees, tie-down fees, etc.), or rental fees.

Answer (A) is incorrect. Recreational pilots may not fly for compensation or hire. Answer (C) is incorrect. A recreational pilot may equally share operating expenses of the flight with a passenger.

62. A recreational pilot may act as pilot in command of an aircraft that is certificated for a maximum of how many occupants?

A. Two.

B. Three.

C. Four.

Answer (C) is correct. *(14 CFR 61.101)*

DISCUSSION: Recreational pilots may not act as pilot in command of an aircraft that is certificated for more than four occupants. Note, however, that only two occupants are permitted, the recreational pilot and a passenger.

Answer (A) is incorrect. A recreational pilot can act as pilot in command of an aircraft that is certificated for up to four (not two) occupants. Answer (B) is incorrect. Recreational pilots can act as pilot in command of an aircraft certificated for up to four (not three) occupants.

63. A recreational pilot may act as pilot in command of an aircraft with a maximum engine horsepower of

A. 160.

B. 180.

C. 200.

Answer (B) is correct. *(14 CFR 61.101)*

DISCUSSION: A recreational pilot may act as pilot in command of an aircraft with a maximum engine horsepower of 180.

Answer (A) is incorrect. A recreational pilot may act as pilot in command of an aircraft with a maximum horsepower of 180 (not 160). Answer (C) is incorrect. A recreational pilot may act as pilot in command of an aircraft with a maximum horsepower of 180 (not 200).

64. With respect to daylight hours, what is the earliest time a recreational pilot may take off?

A. One hour before sunrise.

B. At sunrise.

C. At the beginning of morning civil twilight.

Answer (B) is correct. *(14 CFR 61.101)*

DISCUSSION: A recreational pilot may not act as pilot in command of an airplane between sunset and sunrise. Thus, the earliest time a recreational pilot may take off is at sunrise.

Answer (A) is incorrect. The earliest time a recreational pilot may take off is at sunrise, not 1 hr. before sunrise. Answer (C) is incorrect. The earliest time a recreational pilot may take off is at sunrise, not at the beginning of morning civil twilight.

65. What exception, if any, permits a recreational pilot to act as pilot in command of an aircraft carrying a passenger for hire?

A. If the passenger pays no more than the operating expenses.

B. If a donation is made to a charitable organization for the flight.

C. There is no exception.

Answer (C) is correct. *(14 CFR 61.101)*

DISCUSSION: Recreational pilots may not act as pilot in command of an aircraft for compensation or hire. There is no exception.

Answer (A) is incorrect. A passenger may share expenses, but not pay for the flight. Answer (B) is incorrect. Acting as pilot in command of an aircraft used in a passenger carrying airlift and sponsored by a charitable organization is specifically prohibited by FAR 61.101.

66. When may a recreational pilot operate to or from an airport that lies within Class C airspace?

A. Anytime the control tower is in operation.

B. When the ceiling is at least 1,000 feet and the surface visibility is at least 2 miles.

C. After receiving training and a logbook endorsement from an authorized instructor.

Answer (C) is correct. *(14 CFR 61.101)*

DISCUSSION: For the purpose of obtaining an additional certificate or rating while under the supervision of an authorized flight instructor, a recreational pilot may fly as sole occupant of an airplane within airspace that requires communication with ATC, such as Class C airspace. [Note that in this situation, (s)he is active as a student pilot, not a recreational pilot.]

Answer (A) is incorrect. A recreational pilot may only fly within airspace that requires communication with ATC (e.g., Class C airspace) when under the supervision of an authorized flight instructor for the purpose of obtaining an additional certificate or rating, regardless of whether the control tower is operating. Answer (B) is incorrect. A recreational pilot may only fly within airspace that requires communication with ATC (e.g., Class C airspace) when under the supervision of an authorized flight instructor for the purpose of obtaining an additional certificate or rating, not simply when the ceiling is at least 1,000 ft. and the surface visibility is at least 3 statute miles.

67. (Refer to Figure 22 on page 141.) (Refer to area 1.) The visibility and cloud clearance requirements to operate over Sandpoint Airport at less than 700 feet AGL are

A. 3 miles and clear of clouds.

B. 3 miles and 1,000 feet above, 500 feet below, and 2,000 feet horizontally from each cloud.

C. 1 mile and 1,000 feet above, 500 feet below, and 2,000 feet horizontally from each cloud.

Answer (A) is correct. *(14 CFR 61.101, 91.155)*

DISCUSSION: Sandpoint Airport is about 1 in. above the number 1 in Fig. 22. The airspace around Sandpoint Airport is Class G from the surface to 2,827 ft. MSL (700 ft. AGL). For a recreational pilot to operate over Sandpoint Airport at less than 700 ft. AGL, the visibility and cloud clearance requirements are 3 SM and clear of clouds.

Answer (B) is incorrect. The cloud clearance of 1,000 ft. above, 500 ft. below, and 2,000 ft. horizontally is the requirement in Class G airspace above 1,200 ft. AGL, not less than 700 ft. AGL. Answer (C) is incorrect. A recreational pilot must have a visibility of, at minimum, 3 SM, not 1 SM, and the cloud clearance of 1,000 ft. above, 500 ft. below, and 2,000 ft. horizontally is the requirement in Class G airspace above 1,200 ft. AGL, not less than 700 ft. AGL.

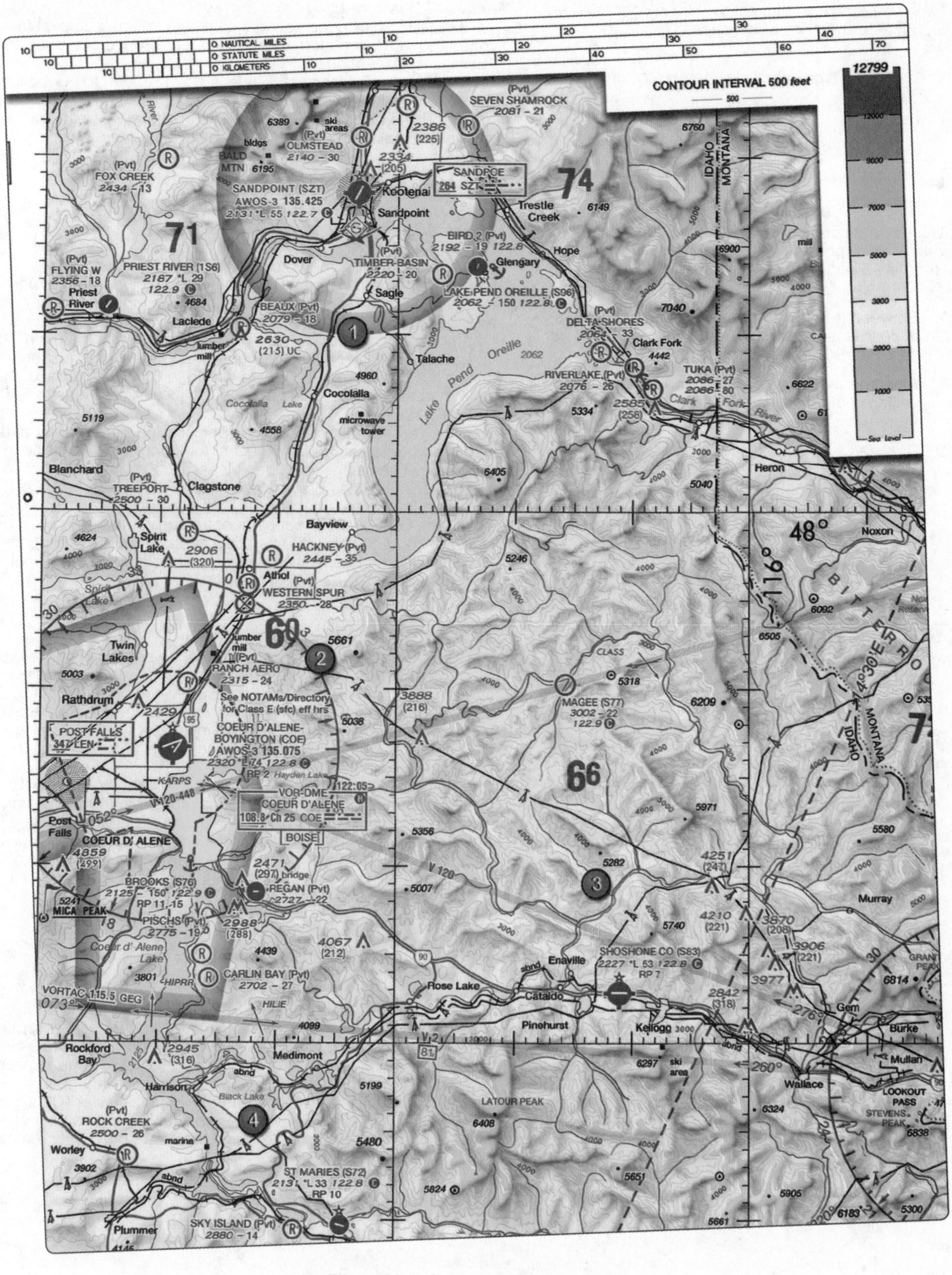

Figure 22. – Sectional Chart Excerpt.
NOTE: Chart is not to scale and should not be used for navigation. Use associated scale.

68. May a recreational pilot act as pilot in command of an aircraft in furtherance of a business?

A. Yes, if the flight is only incidental to that business.

B. Yes, providing the aircraft does not carry a person or property for compensation or hire.

C. No, it is not allowed.

Answer (C) is correct. *(14 CFR 61.101)*

DISCUSSION: Recreational pilots may not act as pilot in command of an aircraft that is used in furtherance of a business. There is no exception.

Answer (A) is incorrect. There is no exception to permit recreational pilots to use aircraft in furtherance of a business. Answer (B) is incorrect. There is no exception to permit recreational pilots to use aircraft in furtherance of a business.

69. Under what conditions may a recreational pilot operate at an airport that lies within Class D airspace and that has a part-time control tower in operation?

A. Between sunrise and sunset when the tower is in operation, the ceiling is at least 2,500 feet, and the visibility is at least 3 miles.

B. Any time when the tower is in operation, the ceiling is at least 3,000 feet, and the visibility is more than 1 mile.

C. Between sunrise and sunset when the tower is closed, the ceiling is at least 1,000 feet, and the visibility is at least 3 miles.

Answer (C) is correct. *(14 CFR 61.101)*

DISCUSSION: A recreational pilot may not operate in airspace in which communication with ATC is required, e.g., Class D airspace. When a part-time control tower at an airport in Class D airspace is closed, the Class D airspace is classified as either Class E or Class G airspace, which does not require communication with ATC. A recreational pilot must maintain flight or surface visibility of 3 SM or greater, and the flight must be during the day. To operate at an airport in Class E airspace, the ceiling must be at least 1,000 ft. and the visibility at least 3 SM (FAR 91.155).

Answer (A) is incorrect. The condition to operate at an airport with a part-time control tower is that the control tower not be in operation. The ceiling must be at least 1,000 ft., not 2,500 ft., at an airport in Class E airspace. Answer (B) is incorrect. The condition to operate at an airport with a part-time control tower is that the control tower not be in operation. The ceiling must be at least 1,000 ft., not 3,000 ft., at an airport in Class E airspace, and visibility for a recreational pilot must be at least 3 SM, not 1 statute mile.

70. When must a recreational pilot have a pilot-in-command flight check?

A. Every 400 hours.

B. Every 180 days.

C. If the pilot has less than 400 total flight hours and has not flown as pilot in command in an aircraft within the preceding 180 days.

Answer (C) is correct. *(14 CFR 61.101)*

DISCUSSION: The recreational pilot who has logged fewer than 400 flight hr. and has not logged pilot in command time in an aircraft within the preceding 180 days may not act as pilot in command of an aircraft until the pilot has received flight instruction from an authorized flight instructor who certifies in the pilot's logbook that the pilot is competent to act as pilot in command of the aircraft.

Answer (A) is incorrect. A recreational pilot must have a pilot-in-command check if the pilot has less than 400 total flight hr. and has not flown as pilot in command in an aircraft within the preceding 180 days, not every 400 hours. Answer (B) is incorrect. The 180 days refers to the time interval from the most recent time the recreational pilot (with less than 400 flight hr.) acted as pilot in command.

71. What minimum visibility and clearance from clouds are required for a recreational pilot in Class G airspace at 1,200 feet AGL or below during daylight hours?

A. 1 mile visibility and clear of clouds.

B. 3 miles visibility and clear of clouds.

C. 3 miles visibility, 500 feet below the clouds.

Answer (B) is correct. *(14 CFR 61.101 and 91.155)*

DISCUSSION: Recreational pilots may not act as pilot in command of an aircraft when the visibility is less than 3 statute miles. Additionally, FAR 91.155 specifies basic VFR weather minimums which permit pilots to fly in Class G airspace 1,200 ft. AGL or below at 1 SM clear of clouds. Thus, the 3-SM recreational pilot limitation and the clear of clouds situation apply.

Answer (A) is incorrect. Recreational pilots may never fly when visibility is less than 3 statute miles. Answer (C) is incorrect. At 1,200 ft. AGL or below in Class G airspace, there is no separation from cloud requirement. One must only remain clear of clouds.

72. A recreational pilot may fly as sole occupant of an aircraft at night while under the supervision of a flight instructor provided the flight or surface visibility is at least

A. 3 miles.

B. 4 miles.

C. 5 miles.

Answer (C) is correct. *(14 CFR 61.101)*

DISCUSSION: For the purposes of obtaining additional certificates or ratings, a recreational pilot may fly as sole occupant in the aircraft between sunset and sunrise while under the supervision of an authorized flight instructor, providing the flight or surface visibility is at least 5 statute miles.

Answer (A) is incorrect. A recreational pilot may fly as sole occupant of an airplane at night while under the supervision of a flight instructor provided the flight or surface visibility is at least 5 SM, not 3 statute miles. Answer (B) is incorrect. A recreational pilot may fly as sole occupant of an airplane at night while under the supervision of a flight instructor provided the flight or surface visibility is at least 5 SM, not 4 statute miles.

73. Outside controlled airspace, the minimum flight visibility requirement for a recreational pilot flying VFR above 1,200 feet AGL and below 10,000 feet MSL during daylight hours is

A. 1 mile.

B. 3 miles.

C. 5 miles.

Answer (B) is correct. *(14 CFR 61.101 and 91.155)*

DISCUSSION: Recreational pilots may not act as pilot in command of an aircraft when the visibility is less than 3 statute miles.

Answer (A) is incorrect. The minimum flight visibility requirement for a recreational pilot is 3 SM, not 1 statute mile. Answer (C) is incorrect. The minimum flight visibility requirement for a recreational pilot is 3 SM, not 5 statute miles.

74. If sunset is 2021 and the end of evening civil twilight is 2043, when must a recreational pilot terminate the flight?

A. 2021.

B. 2043.

C. 2121.

Answer (A) is correct. *(14 CFR 61.101)*

DISCUSSION: A recreational pilot may not act as pilot in command of an airplane between sunset and sunrise. Thus, if sunset is 2021, the recreational pilot must terminate the flight at 2021.

Answer (B) is incorrect. The requirements regarding recreational pilots are in terms of sunset and sunrise, not evening civil twilight. Answer (C) is incorrect. A recreational pilot must stop flying at sunset, not 1 hr. after sunset.

75. Under what conditions, if any, may a recreational pilot demonstrate an aircraft in flight to a prospective buyer?

A. The buyer pays all the operating expenses.

B. The flight is not outside the United States.

C. None.

Answer (C) is correct. *(14 CFR 61.101)*

DISCUSSION: Recreational pilots may not act as pilot in command of an aircraft to demonstrate that aircraft in flight to a prospective buyer.

Answer (A) is incorrect. It is prohibited. A passenger may only share, not pay all of, the operating expenses. Answer (B) is incorrect. Recreational pilots may not act as pilot in command to demonstrate an aircraft to a prospective buyer.

76. When, if ever, may a recreational pilot act as pilot in command in an aircraft towing a banner?

A. If the pilot has logged 100 hours of flight time in powered aircraft.

B. If the pilot has an endorsement in his or her pilot logbook from an authorized flight instructor.

C. It is not allowed.

Answer (C) is correct. *(14 CFR 61.101)*

DISCUSSION: Recreational pilots may not act as pilot in command of an aircraft that is towing any object.

Answer (A) is incorrect. A recreational pilot may not act as pilot in command of an airplane that is towing a banner regardless of the amount of flight time. Answer (B) is incorrect. A recreational pilot may not act as pilot in command of an airplane that is towing a banner.

77. Unless otherwise authorized, if flying a transponder equipped aircraft, a recreational pilot should squawk which VFR code?

A. 1200

B. 7600

C. 7700

Answer (A) is correct. *(AIM Para 4-1-20)*

DISCUSSION: A pilot flying a transponder-equipped aircraft should set that transponder on code (squawk) 1200, which is the VFR code.

Answer (B) is incorrect. Code 7600 is the lost communication code. Answer (C) is incorrect. Code 7700 is the general emergency code.

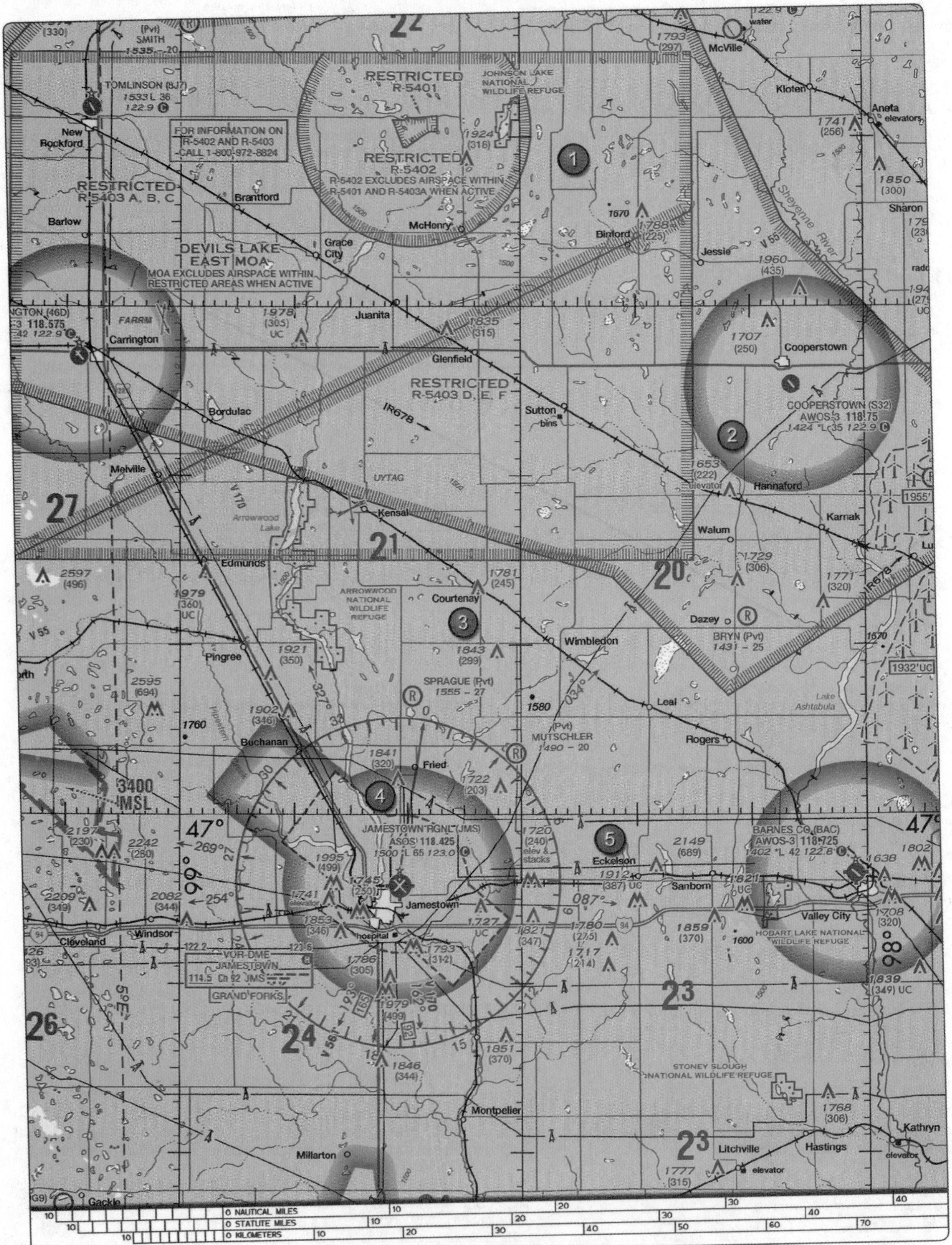

Figure 26. – Sectional Chart Excerpt.
NOTE: Chart is not to scale and should not be used for navigation. Use associated scale.

78. When may a recreational pilot fly above 10,000 feet MSL?

A. When 2,000 feet AGL or below.

B. When 2,500 feet AGL or below.

C. When outside of controlled airspace.

Answer (A) is correct. *(14 CFR 61.101)*

DISCUSSION: Recreational pilots may not act as pilot in command of an aircraft at an altitude of more than 10,000 ft. MSL or 2,000 ft. AGL, whichever is higher. Thus, an airplane may fly above 10,000 ft. MSL only if below 2,000 ft. AGL.

Answer (B) is incorrect. A recreational pilot may fly above 10,000 ft. MSL when 2,000 (not 2,500) ft. AGL or below. Answer (C) is incorrect. The higher of 10,000 ft. MSL or 2,000 ft. AGL limitation on recreational pilots is both in and out of controlled airspace.

79. During daytime, what is the minimum flight or surface visibility required for recreational pilots in Class G airspace below 10,000 feet MSL?

A. 1 mile.

B. 3 miles.

C. 5 miles.

Answer (B) is correct. *(14 CFR 61.101)*

DISCUSSION: The minimum flight or surface visibility required for recreational pilots in Class G airspace below 10,000 ft. MSL during the day is 3 statute miles.

Answer (A) is incorrect. The minimum daytime flight or surface visibility for recreational pilots in Class G airspace below 10,000 ft. MSL is 3, not 1, statute miles. Answer (C) is incorrect. The minimum daytime flight or surface visibility for recreational pilots in Class G airspace below 10,000 ft. MSL is 3, not 5, statute miles.

80. During daytime, what is the minimum flight visibility required for recreational pilots in controlled airspace below 10,000 feet MSL?

A. 1 mile.

B. 3 miles.

C. 5 miles.

Answer (B) is correct. *(14 CFR 61.101)*

DISCUSSION: The minimum flight visibility for recreational pilots in Class E airspace below 10,000 ft. MSL during the day is 3 statute miles.

Answer (A) is incorrect. The minimum daytime flight or surface visibility for recreational pilots in Class E airspace below 10,000 ft. MSL is 3 SM, not 1 statute mile. Answer (C) is incorrect. The minimum daytime flight or surface visibility for recreational pilots in Class E airspace below 10,000 ft. MSL is 3 SM, not 5 statute miles.

81. (Refer to Figure 26 on page 144.) (Refer to area 2.) The visibility and cloud clearance requirements to operate over the town of Cooperstown below 700 feet AGL are

A. 1 mile and 1,000 feet above, 500 feet below, and 2,000 feet horizontally from clouds.

B. 3 miles and clear of clouds.

C. 1 mile and clear of clouds.

Answer (B) is correct. *(14 CFR 61.101 and 91.155)*

DISCUSSION: The town of Cooperstown is about 3/4 in. above and to the right of the number 2 in Fig. 26. The airspace over the town of Cooperstown (yellow color) is Class G from the surface to 2,124 ft. MSL (700 ft. AGL) since the town lies inside the magenta shaded area. For a recreational pilot to operate over the town of Cooperstown below 700 ft. AGL, the minimum visibility is 3 SM and the cloud clearance requirement is to remain clear of clouds.

Answer (A) is incorrect. The minimum visibility requirement for a recreational pilot is 3 SM, not 1 statute mile. Additionally, the cloud clearance requirement in Class G airspace below 1,200 ft. AGL is to remain clear of clouds, not to remain 1,000 ft. above, 500 ft. below, and 2,000 ft. horizontally. Answer (C) is incorrect. The minimum visibility requirement for a recreational pilot is 3 SM, not 1 statute mile.

82. (Refer to Figure 26 on page 144.) (Refer to area 2.) The day VFR visibility and cloud clearance requirements to operate over the town of Cooperstown, after departing and climbing out of the Cooperstown Airport at or below 700 feet AGL are

A. 1 mile and clear of clouds.

B. 1 mile and 1,000 feet above, 500 feet below, and 2,000 feet horizontally from clouds.

C. 3 miles and clear of clouds.

Answer (C) is correct. *(14 CFR 61.101 and 91.155)*

DISCUSSION: The magenta ring around the Cooperstown Airport indicates that Class E airspace in the area begins 700 ft. above the surface. The airspace underlying this ring is Class G airspace; normally, the day VFR visibility and cloud clearance requirements for operating in Class G airspace are 1 mile and clear of clouds. However, a recreational pilot must maintain 3 SM visibility and remain clear of clouds.

Answer (A) is incorrect. The minimum visibility requirement for a recreational pilot is 3 SM, not 1 statute mile. Answer (B) is incorrect. These are the minimums for Class C airspace, Class D airspace, and Class E airspace below 10,000 ft. MSL, while the question asks about the Class G airspace minimums. Additionally, a recreational pilot must maintain 3 SM visibility, not 1 SM.

4.8 FAR Part 71

71.71 Extent of Federal Airways

83. The width of a federal airway from either side of the centerline is

A. 4 nautical miles.

B. 6 nautical miles.

C. 8 nautical miles.

Answer (A) is correct. *(14 CFR Part 71)*

DISCUSSION: The width of a Federal Airway from either side of the centerline is 4 nautical miles.

Answer (B) is incorrect. The width of a Federal Airway from either side of the centerline is 4 NM, not 6 nautical miles. Answer (C) is incorrect. The width of a Federal Airway from either side of the centerline is 4 NM, not 8 nautical miles.

84. Unless otherwise specified, Federal Airways include that Class E airspace extending upward from

A. 700 feet above the surface, up to and including 17,999 feet MSL.

B. 1,200 feet above the surface, up to and including 17,999 feet MSL.

C. the surface, up to and including 18,000 feet MSL.

Answer (B) is correct. *(14 CFR Part 71)*

DISCUSSION: Unless otherwise specified, Federal Airways include that Class E airspace extending from 1,200 ft. above the surface, up to and including 17,999 ft.

Answer (A) is incorrect. Federal Airways extend from 1,200 (not 700) ft. above the surface, up to and including 17,999 ft. MSL. Answer (C) is incorrect. Federal Airways extend from 1,200 ft. above the surface, up to and including 17,999 ft. MSL, not 18,000 ft. MSL. The airspace that extends upward from 18,000 ft. MSL is Class A airspace.

4.9 FAR Part 91: 91.3 – 91.151

91.3 Responsibility and Authority of the Pilot in Command

85. The final authority as to the operation of an aircraft is the

A. Federal Aviation Administration.

B. pilot in command.

C. aircraft manufacturer.

Answer (B) is correct. *(14 CFR 91.3)*

DISCUSSION: The final authority as to the operation of an aircraft is the pilot in command.

Answer (A) is incorrect. The final authority as to the operation of an aircraft is the pilot in command, not the FAA. Answer (C) is incorrect. The final authority as to the operation of an aircraft is the pilot in command, not the aircraft manufacturer.

91.7 Civil Aircraft Airworthiness

86. Who is responsible for determining if an aircraft is in condition for safe flight?

A. A certificated aircraft mechanic.

B. The pilot in command.

C. The owner or operator.

Answer (B) is correct. *(14 CFR 91.7)*

DISCUSSION: The pilot in command of an aircraft is directly responsible for, and is the final authority for, determining whether the airplane is in condition for safe flight.

Answer (A) is incorrect. The pilot in command (not a certificated aircraft mechanic) is responsible for determining if an aircraft is in condition for safe flight. Answer (C) is incorrect. The pilot in command (not the owner or operator) is responsible for determining if an aircraft is in condition for safe flight.

91.9 Civil Aircraft Flight Manual, Marking, and Placard Requirements

87. Where may an aircraft's operating limitations be found?

A. On the Airworthiness Certificate.

B. In the current, FAA-approved flight manual, approved manual material, markings, and placards, or any combination thereof.

C. In the aircraft airframe and engine logbooks.

Answer (B) is correct. *(14 CFR 91.9)*

DISCUSSION: An aircraft's operating limitations may be found in the current, FAA-approved flight manual, approved manual material, markings, and placards, or any combination thereof.

Answer (A) is incorrect. The airworthiness certificate only indicates the airplane was in an airworthy condition when delivered from the factory, not its operating limitations. Answer (C) is incorrect. The airframe and engine logbooks contain the airplane's maintenance record, not its operating limitations.

88. Where may an aircraft's operating limitations be found if the aircraft has an Experimental or Special light-sport airworthiness certificate?

A. Attached to the Airworthiness Certificate.

B. In the current, FAA-approved flight manual.

C. In the aircraft airframe and engine logbooks.

Answer (A) is correct. *(14 CFR 91.9)*

DISCUSSION: The operating limitations for experimental aircraft and aircraft issued a special light-sport airworthiness certificate are attached to the airworthiness certificate itself.

Answer (B) is incorrect. Aircraft that are issued standard airworthiness certificates contain operating limitations in their FAA-approved flight manuals, but the operating limitations for experimental aircraft and aircraft issued a special light-sport airworthiness certificate are attached to the airworthiness certificate itself. Answer (C) is incorrect. The operating limitations for experimental aircraft and aircraft issued a special light-sport airworthiness certificate are attached to the airworthiness certificate itself. They are not found in the aircraft's airframe and engine logbooks.

91.15 Dropping Objects

89. Under what conditions may objects be dropped from an aircraft?

A. Only in an emergency.

B. If precautions are taken to avoid injury or damage to persons or property on the surface.

C. If prior permission is received from the Federal Aviation Administration.

Answer (B) is correct. *(14 CFR 91.15)*

DISCUSSION: No pilot in command of a civil aircraft may allow any object to be dropped from that aircraft in flight that creates a hazard to persons or property. However, this section does not prohibit the dropping of any object if reasonable precautions are taken to avoid injury or damage to persons or property.

Answer (A) is incorrect. Objects may be dropped from an aircraft if precautions are taken to avoid injury or damage to persons or property on the surface, not only in an emergency. Answer (C) is incorrect. Objects may be dropped from an aircraft if precautions are taken to avoid injury or damage to persons or property on the surface. Prior permission from the FAA is not required.

91.17 Alcohol or Drugs

90. No person may attempt to act as a crewmember of a civil aircraft with

A. .008 percent by weight or more alcohol in the blood.

B. .004 percent by weight or more alcohol in the blood.

C. .04 percent by weight or more alcohol in the blood.

Answer (C) is correct. *(14 CFR 91.17)*

DISCUSSION: No person may act or attempt to act as a crewmember of a civil aircraft while having a .04% by weight or more alcohol in the blood.

Answer (A) is incorrect. No person may attempt to act as a crewmember of a civil aircraft with .04% (not .008%) by weight or more alcohol in the blood. Answer (B) is incorrect. No person may attempt to act as a crewmember of a civil aircraft with .04% (not .004%) by weight or more alcohol in the blood.

91. Under what condition, if any, may a pilot allow a person who is obviously under the influence of drugs to be carried aboard an aircraft?

A. In an emergency or if the person is a medical patient under proper care.

B. Only if the person does not have access to the cockpit or pilot's compartment.

C. Under no condition.

Answer (A) is correct. *(14 CFR 91.17)*

DISCUSSION: No pilot of a civil aircraft may allow a person who demonstrates by manner or physical indications that the individual is under the influence of drugs to be carried in that aircraft, except in an emergency or if the person is a medical patient under proper care.

Answer (B) is incorrect. No pilot may allow a person who is obviously under the influence of drugs to be carried aboard an aircraft except in an emergency or if the person is a medical patient under proper care, not if that person does not have access to the cockpit or pilot's compartment. Answer (C) is incorrect. A pilot may allow a person who is obviously under the influence of drugs to be carried aboard an aircraft in an emergency or if the person is a medical patient under proper care.

92. A person may not act as a crewmember of a civil aircraft if alcoholic beverages have been consumed by that person within the preceding

A. 8 hours.

B. 12 hours.

C. 24 hours.

Answer (A) is correct. *(14 CFR 91.17)*

DISCUSSION: No person may act as a crewmember of a civil aircraft if alcoholic beverages have been consumed by that person within the preceding 8 hours.

Answer (B) is incorrect. No person may act as a crewmember of a civil aircraft within 8 hr. (not 12 hr.) after the consumption of any alcoholic beverage. Answer (C) is incorrect. No person may act as a crewmember of a civil aircraft within 8 hr. (not 24 hr.) after the consumption of any alcoholic beverage.

91.103 Preflight Action

93. Preflight action, as required for all flights away from the vicinity of an airport, shall include

A. the designation of an alternate airport.

B. a study of arrival procedures at airports/heliports of intended use.

C. an alternate course of action if the flight cannot be completed as planned.

Answer (C) is correct. *(14 CFR 91.103)*

DISCUSSION: Preflight actions for flights not in the vicinity of an airport include checking weather reports and forecasts, fuel requirements, alternatives available if the planned flight cannot be completed, and any known traffic delays.

Answer (A) is incorrect. Preflight action, as required for all flights away from the vicinity of an airport, shall include an alternate course of action if the flight cannot be completed as planned, not just the designation of an alternate airport. Answer (B) is incorrect. Preflight action, as required for all flights away from the vicinity of an airport, shall include an alternate course of action if the flight cannot be completed as planned, not simply a study of arrival procedures at airports of intended use.

94. In addition to other preflight actions for a VFR flight away from the vicinity of the departure airport, regulations specifically require the pilot in command to

A. review traffic control light signal procedures.

B. check the accuracy of the navigation equipment and the emergency locator transmitter (ELT).

C. determine runway lengths at airports of intended use and the aircraft's takeoff and landing distance data.

Answer (C) is correct. *(14 CFR 91.103)*

DISCUSSION: Preflight actions for a VFR flight away from the vicinity of the departure airport specifically require the pilot in command to determine runway lengths at airports of intended use and the aircraft's takeoff and landing distance data.

Answer (A) is incorrect. Preflight actions for a VFR flight away from the vicinity of an airport require the pilot in command to determine runway lengths at airports of intended use and takeoff and landing distance data, not to review traffic control light signal procedures. Answer (B) is incorrect. Preflight actions for a VFR flight away from the vicinity of an airport require the pilot in command to determine runway lengths at airports of intended use and takeoff and landing distance data, not to check navigation equipment accuracy and the ELT.

95. Which preflight action is specifically required of the pilot prior to each flight?

A. Check the aircraft logbooks for appropriate entries.

B. Become familiar with all available information concerning the flight.

C. Review wake turbulence avoidance procedures.

Answer (B) is correct. *(14 CFR 91.103)*

DISCUSSION: Each pilot in command will, before beginning a flight, become familiar with all available information concerning that flight.

Answer (A) is incorrect. During preflight action, the pilot is required to become familiar with all available information concerning the flight, not just to check the aircraft logbook for appropriate entries. Answer (C) is incorrect. During preflight action, the pilot is required to become familiar with all available information concerning the flight, not simply review wake turbulence avoidance procedures.

91.105 Flight Crewmembers at Stations

96. Flight crewmembers are required to keep their safety belts and shoulder harnesses fastened during

A. takeoffs and landings.

B. all flight conditions.

C. flight in turbulent air.

Answer (A) is correct. *(14 CFR 91.105)*

DISCUSSION: During takeoff and landing and while en route, each required flight crewmember shall keep his or her safety belt fastened while at the crewmember station. If shoulder harnesses are available, they must be used by crewmembers during takeoff and landing.

Answer (B) is incorrect. Flight crewmembers are required to keep their shoulder harnesses fastened only during takeoffs and landings, not during all flight conditions. Answer (C) is incorrect. Flight crewmembers are required to keep their shoulder harnesses fastened only during takeoffs and landings, not during flight in turbulent air.

97. Which best describes the flight conditions under which flight crewmembers are specifically required to keep their safety belts and shoulder harnesses fastened?

A. Safety belts during takeoff and landing; shoulder harnesses during takeoff and landing.

B. Safety belts during takeoff and landing; shoulder harnesses during takeoff and landing and while en route.

C. Safety belts during takeoff and landing and while en route; shoulder harnesses during takeoff and landing.

Answer (C) is correct. *(14 CFR 91.105)*

DISCUSSION: During takeoff and landing and while en route, each required flight crewmember shall keep his or her safety belt fastened while at the crewmember station. If shoulder harnesses are available, they must be used by crewmembers during takeoff and landing.

Answer (A) is incorrect. Safety belts must be worn while en route. Answer (B) is incorrect. Safety belts (not shoulder harnesses) are required to be fastened while en route.

91.107 Use of Safety Belts, Shoulder Harnesses, and Child Restraint Systems

98. With respect to passengers, what obligation, if any, does a pilot in command have concerning the use of safety belts?

A. The pilot in command must instruct the passengers to keep their safety belts fastened for the entire flight.

B. The pilot in command must brief the passengers on the use of safety belts and notify them to fasten their safety belts during taxi, takeoff, and landing.

C. The pilot in command has no obligation in regard to passengers' use of safety belts.

Answer (B) is correct. *(14 CFR 91.107)*

DISCUSSION: The pilot in command is required to brief the passengers on the use of safety belts and notify them to fasten their safety belts during taxi, takeoff, and landing.

Answer (A) is incorrect. The pilot in command is only required to notify the passengers to fasten their safety belts during taxi, takeoff, and landing, not during the entire flight. Answer (C) is incorrect. The pilot in command has the obligation both to instruct passengers on the use of safety belts and to require their use during taxi, takeoffs, and landings.

99. Safety belts are required to be properly secured about which persons in an aircraft and when?

A. Pilots only, during takeoffs and landings.

B. Passengers, during taxi, takeoffs, and landings only.

C. Each person on board the aircraft during the entire flight.

Answer (B) is correct. *(14 CFR 91.107)*

DISCUSSION: Regulations require that safety belts in an airplane be properly secured about all passengers during taxi, takeoffs, and landings.

Answer (A) is incorrect. Regulations require passengers as well as crewmembers to wear safety belts during takeoffs and landings. Answer (C) is incorrect. Although it is a good procedure, safety belts are required only for passengers during taxi, takeoffs, and landings.

100. With certain exceptions, safety belts are required to be secured about passengers during

A. taxi, takeoffs, and landings.

B. all flight conditions.

C. flight in turbulent air.

Answer (A) is correct. *(14 CFR 91.107)*

DISCUSSION: During the taxi, takeoff, and landing of U.S.-registered civil aircraft, each person on board that aircraft must occupy a seat or berth with a safety belt and shoulder harness, if installed, properly secured about him or her. However, a person who has not reached his or her second birthday may be held by an adult who is occupying a seat or berth, and a person on board for the purpose of engaging in sport parachuting may use the floor of the aircraft as a seat (but is still required to use approved safety belts for takeoff).

Answer (B) is incorrect. Safety belts are required to be secured about passengers only during taxi, takeoffs, and landings, not during all flight conditions. Answer (C) is incorrect. Safety belts are required to be secured about passengers during taxi, takeoffs, and landings, not during flight in turbulent air.

91.111 Operating near Other Aircraft

101. No person may operate an aircraft in formation flight

A. over a densely populated area.

B. in Class D airspace under special VFR.

C. except by prior arrangement with the pilot in command of each aircraft.

Answer (C) is correct. *(14 CFR 91.111)*

DISCUSSION: No person may operate in formation flight except by arrangement with the pilot in command of each aircraft in formation.

Answer (A) is incorrect. No person may operate an aircraft in formation flight except by prior arrangement with the pilot in command of each aircraft. There are no restrictions about formation flights over a densely populated area. Answer (B) is incorrect. No person may operate an aircraft in formation flight except by prior arrangement with the pilot in command of each aircraft. There are no restrictions about formation flight in Class D airspace under special VFR.

91.113 Right-of-Way Rules: Except Water Operations

102. An airplane and an airship are converging. If the airship is left of the airplane's position, which aircraft has the right-of-way?

A. The airship.

B. The airplane.

C. Each pilot should alter course to the right.

Answer (A) is correct. *(14 CFR 91.113)*

DISCUSSION: When aircraft of different categories are converging, the less maneuverable aircraft has the right-of-way. Thus, the airship has the right-of-way in this question.

Answer (B) is incorrect. When converging, the airship has the right-of-way over an airplane or rotorcraft. Answer (C) is incorrect. Each pilot would alter course to the right if the airship and airplane were approaching head-on, or nearly so, not converging.

103. When two or more aircraft are approaching an airport for the purpose of landing, the right-of-way belongs to the aircraft

A. that has the other to its right.

B. that is the least maneuverable.

C. at the lower altitude, but it shall not take advantage of this rule to cut in front of or to overtake another.

Answer (C) is correct. *(14 CFR 91.113)*

DISCUSSION: When two or more aircraft are approaching an airport for the purpose of landing, the aircraft at the lower altitude has the right-of-way, but it shall not take advantage of this rule to cut in front of or overtake another aircraft.

Answer (A) is incorrect. When two or more aircraft are approaching an airport for the purpose of landing, the right-of-way belongs to the aircraft at the lower altitude, not the aircraft that has the other to the right. Answer (B) is incorrect. When two or more aircraft are approaching an airport for the purpose of landing, the right-of-way belongs to the aircraft at the lower altitude, not the aircraft that is the least maneuverable.

104. Which aircraft has the right-of-way over the other aircraft listed?

A. Glider.

B. Airship.

C. Aircraft refueling other aircraft.

Answer (A) is correct. *(14 CFR 91.113)*

DISCUSSION: If aircraft of different categories are converging, the right-of-way depends upon who has the least maneuverability. A glider has right-of-way over an airship, airplane, or rotorcraft.

Answer (B) is incorrect. An airship has the right-of-way over an airplane or rotorcraft but not a glider. Answer (C) is incorrect. Aircraft refueling other aircraft have right-of-way over all engine-driven aircraft. A glider has no engine.

105. What action should the pilots of a glider and an airplane take if on a head-on collision course?

A. The airplane pilot should give way to the left.

B. The glider pilot should give way to the right.

C. Both pilots should give way to the right.

Answer (C) is correct. *(14 CFR 91.113)*

DISCUSSION: When aircraft are approaching head-on, or nearly so (regardless of category), each aircraft shall alter course to the right.

Answer (A) is incorrect. The glider has the right-of-way unless the two aircraft are approaching head-on, in which case both pilots should give way by turning to the right. Answer (B) is incorrect. Both pilots of a glider and an airplane should give way to the right, not only the glider pilot.

106. What action is required when two aircraft of the same category converge, but not head-on?

A. The faster aircraft shall give way.

B. The aircraft on the left shall give way.

C. Each aircraft shall give way to the right.

Answer (B) is correct. *(14 CFR 91.113)*

DISCUSSION: When two aircraft of the same category converge (but not head-on), the aircraft to the other's right has the right-of-way. Thus, an airplane on the left gives way to the airplane on the right.

Answer (A) is incorrect. When two aircraft of the same category converge (but not head-on), the aircraft on the left (not the faster aircraft) shall give way. Answer (C) is incorrect. The required action when two aircraft are approaching head-on or nearly so is for each aircraft to give way to the right.

107. Which aircraft has the right-of-way over the other aircraft listed?

A. Airship.

B. Aircraft towing other aircraft.

C. Gyroplane.

Answer (B) is correct. *(14 CFR 91.113)*

DISCUSSION: An aircraft towing or refueling another aircraft has the right-of-way over all engine-driven aircraft. An airship is an engine-driven, lighter-than-air aircraft that can be steered.

Answer (A) is incorrect. An airship has the right-of-way over an airplane or rotorcraft, but not an aircraft towing other aircraft. Answer (C) is incorrect. A gyroplane (which is a rotorcraft) must give way to both an airship and aircraft towing other aircraft.

108. Which aircraft has the right-of-way over all other air traffic?

A. A balloon.

B. An aircraft in distress.

C. An aircraft on final approach to land.

Answer (B) is correct. *(14 CFR 91.113)*

DISCUSSION: An aircraft in distress has the right-of-way over all other aircraft.

Answer (A) is incorrect. An aircraft in distress (not a balloon) has the right-of-way over all other air traffic. Answer (C) is incorrect. An aircraft in distress (not an aircraft on final approach to land) has the right-of-way over all other air traffic.

91.115 Right-of-Way Rules: Water Operations

109. A seaplane and a motorboat are on crossing courses. If the motorboat is to the left of the seaplane, which has the right-of-way?

A. The motorboat.

B. The seaplane.

C. Both should alter course to the right.

Answer (B) is correct. *(14 CFR 91.115)*

DISCUSSION: When aircraft, or an aircraft and a vessel (e.g., a motorboat), are on crossing courses, the aircraft or vessel to the other's right has the right-of-way. Since the seaplane is to the motorboat's right, the seaplane has the right-of-way.

Answer (A) is incorrect. On crossing courses, the aircraft or vessel to the other's right has the right-of-way. Since the seaplane is to the right of the motorboat, the seaplane (not the motorboat) has the right-of-way. Answer (C) is incorrect. Both would alter course to the right only if they were approaching head-on, or nearly so.

91.117 Aircraft Speed

110. When flying in a VFR corridor designated through Class B airspace, the maximum speed authorized is

A. 180 knots.

B. 200 knots.

C. 250 knots.

Answer (B) is correct. *(14 CFR 91.117)*

DISCUSSION: No person may operate an airplane in a VFR corridor designated through Class B airspace at an indicated airspeed of more than 200 kt. (230 MPH).

Answer (A) is incorrect. When flying in a VFR corridor designated through Class B airspace, the maximum speed authorized is 200 (not 180) knots. Answer (C) is incorrect. This is the maximum speed authorized below 10,000 ft. MSL, not when flying in a VFR corridor through Class B airspace.

111. Unless otherwise authorized, what is the maximum indicated airspeed at which a person may operate an aircraft below 10,000 feet MSL?

A. 200 knots.

B. 250 knots.

C. 288 knots.

Answer (B) is correct. *(14 CFR 91.117)*

DISCUSSION: Unless otherwise authorized by ATC, no person may operate an aircraft below 10,000 ft. MSL at an indicated airspeed of more than 250 kt. (288 MPH).

Answer (A) is incorrect. This is the maximum indicated airspeed when at or below 2,500 ft. above the surface and within 4 NM of the primary airport of a Class C or Class D airspace area, not the maximum indicated airspeed for operations below 10,000 ft. MSL. Answer (C) is incorrect. The maximum indicated airspeed below 10,000 ft. MSL is 288 MPH, not 288 knots.

112. When flying in the airspace underlying Class B airspace, the maximum speed authorized is

A. 200 knots.

B. 230 knots.

C. 250 knots.

Answer (A) is correct. *(14 CFR 91.117)*

DISCUSSION: No person may operate an airplane in the airspace underlying Class B airspace at an indicated airspeed of more than 200 kt. (230 MPH).

Answer (B) is incorrect. The maximum indicated airspeed authorized in the airspace underlying Class B airspace is 230 MPH, not 230 knots. Answer (C) is incorrect. This is the maximum indicated airspeed when operating an airplane below 10,000 ft. MSL, not in the airspace underlying Class B airspace.

113. Unless otherwise authorized, the maximum indicated airspeed at which aircraft may be flown when at or below 2,500 feet AGL and within 4 nautical miles of the primary airport of Class C airspace is

A. 200 knots.

B. 230 knots.

C. 250 knots.

Answer (A) is correct. *(14 CFR 91.117)*

DISCUSSION: Unless otherwise authorized, the maximum indicated airspeed at which an airplane may be flown when at or below 2,500 ft. AGL and within 4 NM of the primary airport of Class C airspace is 200 kt. (230 MPH).

Answer (B) is incorrect. The figure of 230 MPH, not 230 kt., is the maximum indicated airspeed at which an airplane may be flown when at or below 2,500 ft. AGL and within 4 NM of the primary airport of a Class C airspace area. Answer (C) is incorrect. The figure of 250 kt. is the maximum indicated airspeed at which an airplane may be flown below 10,000 ft. MSL or in Class B airspace, not when at or below 2,500 ft. AGL and within 4 NM of the primary airport of a Class C airspace area.

91.119 Minimum Safe Altitudes: General

114. Except when necessary for takeoff or landing, what is the minimum safe altitude for a pilot to operate an aircraft anywhere?

A. An altitude allowing, if a power unit fails, an emergency landing without undue hazard to persons or property on the surface.

B. An altitude of 500 feet above the surface and no closer than 500 feet to any person, vessel, vehicle, or structure.

C. An altitude of 500 feet above the highest obstacle within a horizontal radius of 1,000 feet.

Answer (A) is correct. *(14 CFR 91.119)*

DISCUSSION: Except when necessary for takeoff or landing, no person may operate an aircraft anywhere below an altitude allowing, if a power unit fails, an emergency landing without undue hazard to persons or property on the surface.

Answer (B) is incorrect. An altitude of 500 ft. above the surface is the minimum safe altitude over other than congested areas and no closer than 500 ft. to any person, vessel, vehicle, or structure is the minimum safe altitude over open water or sparsely populated areas. Answer (C) is incorrect. The minimum safe altitude anywhere is an altitude that allows an emergency landing to be made without undue hazards to persons or property on the surface, not 500 ft. above the highest obstacle within a horizontal radius of 1,000 feet.

115. Except when necessary for takeoff or landing, what is the minimum safe altitude required for a pilot to operate an aircraft over congested areas?

A. An altitude of 1,000 feet above any person, vessel, vehicle, or structure.

B. An altitude of 500 feet above the highest obstacle within a horizontal radius of 1,000 feet of the aircraft.

C. An altitude of 1,000 feet above the highest obstacle within a horizontal radius of 2,000 feet of the aircraft.

Answer (C) is correct. *(14 CFR 91.119)*

DISCUSSION: When operating an aircraft over any congested area of a city, town, or settlement, or over an open-air assembly of persons, a pilot must remain at an altitude of 1,000 ft. above the highest obstacle within a horizontal radius of 2,000 ft. of the aircraft.

Answer (A) is incorrect. The minimum safe altitude to operate an aircraft over a congested area is an altitude of 1,000 ft. above the highest obstacle (not above any person, vessel, vehicle, or structure) within a horizontal distance of 2,000 feet. Answer (B) is incorrect. The minimum safe altitude to operate an aircraft over a congested area is an altitude of 1,000 (not 500) ft. above the highest obstacle within a horizontal radius of 2,000 (not 1,000) ft. of the aircraft.

116. Except when necessary for takeoff or landing, what is the minimum safe altitude required for a pilot to operate an aircraft over other than a congested area?

A. An altitude allowing, if a power unit fails, an emergency landing without undue hazard to persons or property on the surface.

B. An altitude of 500 feet AGL, except over open water or a sparsely populated area, which requires 500 feet from any person, vessel, vehicle, or structure.

C. An altitude of 500 feet above the highest obstacle within a horizontal radius of 1,000 feet.

Answer (B) is correct. *(14 CFR 91.119)*

DISCUSSION: Over other than congested areas, an altitude of 500 ft. above the surface is required. Over open water and sparsely populated areas, a distance of 500 ft. from any person, vessel, vehicle, or structure must be maintained.

Answer (A) is incorrect. An altitude allowing, if a power unit fails, an emergency landing without undue hazard to persons or property on the surface is the general minimum safe altitude for anywhere, not specifically for operation over other than a congested area. Answer (C) is incorrect. The minimum safe altitude over other than a congested area is an altitude of 500 ft. AGL (not above the highest obstacle within a horizontal radius of 1,000 ft.), except over open water or a sparsely populated area, which requires 500 ft. from any person, vessel, vehicle, or structure.

117. Except when necessary for takeoff or landing, an aircraft may not be operated closer than what distance from any person, vessel, vehicle, or structure?

A. 500 feet.

B. 700 feet.

C. 1,000 feet.

Answer (A) is correct. *(14 CFR 91.119)*

DISCUSSION: Over other than congested areas, an altitude of 500 ft. above the surface is required. Over open water and sparsely populated areas, a distance of 500 ft. from any person, vessel, vehicle, or structure must be maintained.

Answer (B) is incorrect. An aircraft may not be operated closer than 500 (not 700) ft. from any person, vessel, vehicle, or structure. Answer (C) is incorrect. An aircraft may not be operated closer than 500 (not 1,000) ft. from any person, vessel, vehicle, or structure.

91.121 Altimeter Settings

118. Prior to takeoff, the altimeter should be set to which altitude or altimeter setting?

A. The current local altimeter setting, if available, or the departure airport elevation.

B. The corrected density altitude of the departure airport.

C. The corrected pressure altitude for the departure airport.

Answer (A) is correct. *(14 CFR 91.121)*

DISCUSSION: Prior to takeoff, the altimeter should be set to either the local altimeter setting or to the departure airport elevation.

Answer (B) is incorrect. Density altitude is pressure altitude corrected for nonstandard temperature variations and is determined from flight computers or graphs, not an altimeter. Answer (C) is incorrect. Pressure altitude is only used at or above 18,000 ft. MSL.

119. If an altimeter setting is not available before flight, to which altitude should the pilot adjust the altimeter?

A. The elevation of the nearest airport corrected to mean sea level.

B. The elevation of the departure area.

C. Pressure altitude corrected for nonstandard temperature.

Answer (B) is correct. *(14 CFR 91.121)*

DISCUSSION: When the local altimeter setting is not available at takeoff, the pilot should adjust the altimeter to the elevation of the departure area.

Answer (A) is incorrect. Airport elevation is always expressed in true altitude, or feet above MSL. Answer (C) is incorrect. Pressure altitude adjusted for nonstandard temperature is density altitude, not true altitude.

120. At what altitude shall the altimeter be set to 29.92 when climbing to cruising flight level?

A. 14,500 feet MSL.

B. 18,000 feet MSL.

C. 24,000 feet MSL.

Answer (B) is correct. *(14 CFR 91.121)*

DISCUSSION: Pressure altitude is the altitude used for all flights at and above 18,000 ft. MSL, i.e., in Class A airspace. When climbing to or above 18,000 ft. MSL, one does not use local altimeter settings, but rather 29.92" Hg after reaching 18,000 ft. MSL.

Answer (A) is incorrect. The figure of 14,500 feet MSL is the base of Class E airspace unless otherwise indicated. Answer (C) is incorrect. The figure of 24,000 feet MSL is the altitude above which DME is required aboard the airplane.

91.123 Compliance with ATC Clearances and Instructions

121. When must a pilot who deviates from a regulation during an emergency send a written report of that deviation to the Administrator?

A. Within 7 days.

B. Within 10 days.

C. Upon request.

Answer (C) is correct. *(14 CFR 91.123)*

DISCUSSION: A pilot who deviates from a regulation during an emergency must send a written report of that deviation to the Administrator of the FAA only upon request.

Answer (A) is incorrect. A written report of a deviation from a regulation during an emergency must be sent to the Administrator upon request, not within 7 days. Answer (B) is incorrect. A written report of a deviation from a regulation during an emergency must be sent to the Administrator upon request, not within 10 days.

122. When would a pilot be required to submit a detailed report of an emergency which caused the pilot to deviate from an ATC clearance?

A. Within 48 hours if requested by ATC.

B. Immediately.

C. Within 7 days.

Answer (A) is correct. *(14 CFR 91.123)*

DISCUSSION: Each pilot in command who is given priority by ATC in an emergency shall, if requested by ATC, submit a detailed report within 48 hrs. to the manager of that ATC facility.

Answer (B) is incorrect. A pilot would be required to submit a detailed report of an emergency when requested by ATC (not immediately). Answer (C) is incorrect. A pilot would be required to submit a detailed report of an emergency when requested by ATC (not within 7 days).

123. If an in-flight emergency requires immediate action, the pilot in command may

A. deviate from any rule of 14 CFR part 91 to the extent required to meet the emergency, but must submit a written report to the Administrator within 24 hours.

B. deviate from any rule of 14 CFR part 91 to the extent required to meet that emergency.

C. not deviate from any rule of 14 CFR part 91 unless prior to the deviation approval is granted by the Administrator.

Answer (B) is correct. *(14 CFR 91.123)*

DISCUSSION: In an in-flight emergency requiring immediate action, the pilot in command may deviate from any rule of 14 CFR part 91 to the extent required to meet that emergency. A written report of the deviation must be sent to the Administrator of the FAA only if requested.

Answer (A) is incorrect. A written report must be sent to the Administrator of the FAA only upon request. Answer (C) is incorrect. The pilot in command may deviate from any rule of 14 CFR part 91 to the extent required to meet that emergency without the approval of the Administrator of the FAA.

124. As Pilot in Command of an aircraft, under which situation can you deviate from an ATC clearance?

A. When operating in Class A airspace at night.

B. If an ATC clearance is not understood and in VFR conditions.

C. In response to a traffic alert and collision avoidance system resolution advisory.

Answer (C) is correct. *(14 CFR 91.123)*

DISCUSSION: No pilot may deviate from an ATC clearance unless an amended clearance is obtained, an emergency exists, or the deviation is in response to a traffic alert and collision avoidance system resolution advisory. A written report of the deviation must be sent to the Administrator of the FAA only if requested.

Answer (A) is incorrect. A pilot cannot deviate from an ATC clearance in any airspace unless it is an emergency or in response to a traffic alert and collision avoidance resolution advisory. Answer (B) is incorrect. When a pilot is uncertain of an ATC clearance, that pilot shall immediately request clarification from ATC.

125. When an ATC clearance has been obtained, no pilot in command may deviate from that clearance unless that pilot obtains an amended clearance. The one exception to this regulation is

A. when the clearance states, "at pilot's discretion."

B. an emergency.

C. if the clearance contains a restriction.

Answer (B) is correct. *(14 CFR 91.123)*

DISCUSSION: When an ATC clearance has been obtained, no pilot in command may deviate from that clearance, except in an emergency, unless an amended clearance is obtained.

Answer (A) is incorrect. The words "at the pilot's discretion" are part of an ATC clearance, so this is not an exception. Answer (C) is incorrect. Any restriction is still part of the clearance, so this is not an exception.

126. What action, if any, is appropriate if the pilot deviates from an ATC instruction during an emergency and is given priority?

A. Take no special action since you are pilot in command.

B. File a detailed report within 48 hours to the chief of the appropriate ATC facility, if requested.

C. File a report to the FAA Administrator, as soon as possible.

Answer (B) is correct. *(14 CFR 91.123)*

DISCUSSION: Each pilot in command who is given priority by ATC in an emergency shall, if requested by ATC, submit a detailed report within 48 hr. to the manager of that ATC facility.

Answer (A) is incorrect. As pilot in command, you must file a detailed report within 48 hr. to the chief of the appropriate ATC facility, if requested. Answer (C) is incorrect. A detailed report must be filed to the chief of the appropriate ATC facility (not the FAA Administrator) if requested (not as soon as possible).

91.130 Operations in Class C Airspace

127. Two-way radio communication must be established with the Air Traffic Control facility having jurisdiction over the area prior to entering which class airspace?

A. Class C.

B. Class E.

C. Class G.

Answer (A) is correct. *(14 CFR 91.130)*

DISCUSSION: No person may operate an aircraft in Class C airspace unless two-way radio communication is established with the ATC facility having jurisdiction over the airspace prior to entering that area.

Answer (B) is incorrect. While a Class E airspace area is controlled airspace, two-way radio communication is not required to be established with ATC prior to entering VFR weather conditions. Answer (C) is incorrect. Two-way radio communication with ATC is not required for any operations in Class G airspace.

91.131 Operations in Class B Airspace

128. With certain exceptions, all aircraft within 30 miles of a Class B primary airport from the surface upward to 10,000 feet MSL must be equipped with

A. an operable VOR or TACAN receiver.

B. instruments and equipment required for IFR operations.

C. an operable transponder having either Mode S or 4096-code capability with Mode C automatic altitude reporting capability.

Answer (C) is correct. *(14 CFR 91.131)*

DISCUSSION: All aircraft within 30 NM of a Class B primary airport must be equipped with an operable transponder having either Mode S or 4096-code capability with Mode C automatic altitude reporting capability. The exception is any aircraft that was not originally certificated with an engine-driven electrical system or that has not subsequently been certified with such a system installed, balloon, or glider may conduct operations in the airspace within 30 NM of a Class B airspace primary airport provided such operations are conducted (1) outside any Class A, Class B, or Class C airspace area; and (2) below the altitude of the ceiling of a Class B or Class C airspace area or 10,000 ft. MSL, whichever is lower.

Answer (A) is incorrect. An operable VOR or TACAN receiver is not required within 30 NM of a Class B primary airport, only an operable transponder having either Mode S or 4096-code capability with Mode C automatic altitude reporting capability. Answer (B) is incorrect. An operable transponder having either Mode S or 4096-code capability with Mode C automatic altitude reporting capability is required within 30 NM of a Class B primary airport, not instruments and equipment required for IFR operations.

129. What minimum pilot certification is required for operation within Class B airspace?

A. Recreational Pilot Certificate.

B. Private Pilot Certificate or Student Pilot Certificate with appropriate logbook endorsements.

C. Private Pilot Certificate with an instrument rating.

Answer (B) is correct. *(14 CFR 91.131)*

DISCUSSION: No person may take off or land aircraft at an airport within Class B airspace or operate an aircraft within Class B airspace unless (s)he is at least a private pilot or, if a student pilot, (s)he has the appropriate logbook endorsement required by FAR 61.95.

Answer (A) is incorrect. A recreational pilot is restricted from operating in airspace (e.g., Class B airspace) that requires communication with ATC. Answer (C) is incorrect. An instrument rating is not required to operate in Class B airspace.

130. What minimum pilot certification is required for operation within Class B airspace?

A. Private Pilot Certificate or Student Pilot Certificate with appropriate logbook endorsements.

B. Commercial Pilot Certificate.

C. Private Pilot Certificate with an instrument rating.

Answer (A) is correct. *(14 CFR 91.131)*

DISCUSSION: No person may take off or land aircraft at an airport within Class B airspace or operate an aircraft within Class B airspace unless (s)he is at least a private pilot or, if a student pilot, (s)he has the appropriate logbook endorsement required by FAR 61.95.

Answer (B) is incorrect. The minimum pilot certification to operate in Class B airspace is a private pilot certificate or student pilot certificate with appropriate logbook endorsements, not a commercial pilot certificate. Answer (C) is incorrect. An instrument rating is not required to operate in Class B airspace.

91.133 Restricted and Prohibited Areas

131. Under what condition, if any, may pilots fly through a restricted area?

A. When flying on airways with an ATC clearance.

B. With the controlling agency's authorization.

C. Regulations do not allow this.

Answer (B) is correct. *(14 CFR 91.133)*

DISCUSSION: An aircraft may not be operated within a restricted area unless permission has been obtained from the controlling agency. Frequently, the ATC within the area acts as the controlling agent's authorization; e.g., an approach control in a military restricted area can permit aircraft to enter it when the restricted area is not active.

Answer (A) is incorrect. Airways do not penetrate restricted areas. Answer (C) is incorrect. Restricted areas may be entered with proper authorization.

91.135 Operations in Class A Airspace

132. In which type of airspace are VFR flights prohibited?

A. Class A.

B. Class B.

C. Class C.

Answer (A) is correct. *(14 CFR 91.135)*

DISCUSSION: Class A airspace (from 18,000 ft. MSL up to and including FL 600) requires operation under IFR at specific flight levels assigned by ATC. Accordingly, VFR flights are prohibited.

Answer (B) is incorrect. VFR flights are prohibited in Class A, not Class B, airspace. Answer (C) is incorrect. VFR flights are prohibited in Class A, not Class C, airspace.

91.151 Fuel Requirements for Flight in VFR Conditions

133. What is the specific fuel requirement for flight under VFR at night in an airplane?

A. Enough to complete the flight at normal cruising speed with adverse wind conditions.

B. Enough to fly to the first point of intended landing and to fly after that for 30 minutes at normal cruising speed.

C. Enough to fly to the first point of intended landing and to fly after that for 45 minutes at normal cruising speed.

Answer (C) is correct. *(14 CFR 91.151)*

DISCUSSION: The night VFR requirement is enough fuel to fly to the first point of intended landing and to fly thereafter for 45 min. at normal cruising speed given forecast conditions.

Answer (A) is incorrect. The fuel requirements are based upon the wind conditions existing that day plus the 45-min. reserve. Answer (B) is incorrect. A 30-min. reserve is the requirement for day flight.

134. What is the specific fuel requirement for flight under VFR during daylight hours in an airplane?

A. Enough to complete the flight at normal cruising speed with adverse wind conditions.

B. Enough to fly to the first point of intended landing and to fly after that for 30 minutes at normal cruising speed.

C. Enough to fly to the first point of intended landing and to fly after that for 45 minutes at normal cruising speed.

Answer (B) is correct. *(14 CFR 91.151)*

DISCUSSION: The day-VFR requirement is enough fuel to fly to the first point of intended landing and thereafter for 30 min. at normal cruising speed.

Answer (A) is incorrect. The fuel requirements are based upon the wind conditions existing that day plus the 30-min. reserve. Answer (C) is incorrect. A 45-min. reserve is the requirement for night flight.

4.10 FAR Part 91: 91.155 – 91.519

91.155 Basic VFR Weather Minimums

135. The basic VFR weather minimums for operating an aircraft within Class D airspace are

A. 500-foot ceiling and 1 mile visibility.

B. 1,000-foot ceiling and 3 miles visibility.

C. clear of clouds and 2 miles visibility.

Answer (B) is correct. *(14 CFR 91.155)*

DISCUSSION: The basic VFR weather minimums for operating an aircraft within Class D airspace are a 1,000-ft. ceiling and 3 SM visibility.

Answer (A) is incorrect. The basic VFR weather minimums for operating an aircraft in Class D airspace are a 1,000-ft., not 500-ft., ceiling and 3 (not 1) SM visibility. Answer (C) is incorrect. The basic VFR weather minimums for operating an aircraft in Class D airspace are a 1,000-ft. ceiling, not clear of clouds, and 3 (not 2) SM visibility.

136. The minimum flight visibility required for VFR flights above 10,000 feet MSL and more than 1,200 feet AGL in controlled airspace is

A. 1 mile.

B. 3 miles.

C. 5 miles.

Answer (C) is correct. *(14 CFR 91.155)*

DISCUSSION: Controlled airspace is the generic term for Class A, B, C, D, or E airspace. Of these, only in Class E airspace is the minimum flight visibility 5 SM for VFR flights at or above 10,000 ft. MSL.

Note: AGL altitudes are not used in controlled airspace. In Class E airspace, the visibility and distance from clouds are given for (1) below 10,000 ft. MSL and (2) at or above 10,000 ft. MSL.

Answer (A) is incorrect. This is the visibility in Class G, not Class E, airspace when more than 1,200 ft. AGL but less, not more, than 10,000 ft. MSL. Answer (B) is incorrect. This is the minimum visibility in Class E airspace when below, not at or above, 10,000 ft. MSL.

137. VFR flight in controlled airspace above 1,200 feet AGL and below 10,000 feet MSL requires a minimum visibility and vertical cloud clearance of

A. 3 miles, and 500 feet below or 1,000 feet above the clouds in controlled airspace.

B. 5 miles, and 1,000 feet below or 1,000 feet above the clouds at all altitudes.

C. 5 miles, and 1,000 feet below or 1,000 feet above the clouds only in Class A airspace.

Answer (A) is correct. *(14 CFR 91.155)*

DISCUSSION: Controlled airspace is the generic term for Class A, B, C, D, or E airspace. Only in Class C, D, or below 10,000 ft. MSL in Class E airspace are the minimum flight visibility and vertical distance from cloud for VFR flight required to be 3 SM, and 500 ft. below or 1,000 ft. above the clouds.

NOTE: AGL altitudes are not used in controlled airspace. In Class E airspace, the visibility and distance from clouds are given for (1) below 10,000 ft. MSL and (2) at or above 10,000 ft. MSL.

Answer (B) is incorrect. Five SM and 1,000 ft. above and below the clouds is the minimum visibility and vertical cloud clearance in Class E airspace at altitudes at or above, not below, 10,000 ft. MSL. Answer (C) is incorrect. VFR flight in Class A airspace is prohibited.

138. For VFR flight operations above 10,000 feet MSL and more than 1,200 feet AGL, the minimum horizontal distance from clouds required is

A. 1,000 feet.

B. 2,000 feet.

C. 1 mile.

Answer (C) is correct. *(14 CFR 91.155)*

DISCUSSION: For VFR flight operations in Class G airspace at altitudes more than 1,200 ft. AGL and at or above 10,000 ft. MSL, the minimum horizontal distance from clouds required is 1 statute mile.

Note: The FAA question fails to specify what type of airspace. Since AGL altitudes are not used in controlled airspace (Class A, B, C, D, or E), that implies Class G airspace.

Answer (A) is incorrect. The figure of 1,000 feet is the minimum vertical, not horizontal, distance from the clouds. Answer (B) is incorrect. The figure of 2,000 feet is the minimum horizontal distance from clouds in Class G airspace at night below, not above, 10,000 ft. MSL and when at altitudes more than 1,200 ft. AGL but less, not more, than 10,000 ft. MSL.

139. What minimum flight visibility is required for VFR flight operations on an airway below 10,000 feet MSL?

A. 1 mile.

B. 3 miles.

C. 4 miles.

Answer (B) is correct. *(14 CFR 91.155)*

DISCUSSION: An airway includes that Class E airspace extending upward from 1,200 ft. AGL to, but not including, 18,000 ft. MSL. The minimum flight visibility for VFR flight operations in Class E airspace less than 10,000 ft. MSL is 3 statute miles.

Answer (A) is incorrect. One SM is the minimum daytime visibility for a VFR flight below 10,000 ft. MSL in Class G, not Class E, airspace. Answer (C) is incorrect. The minimum flight visibility for VFR flight operations in Class E airspace below 10,000 ft. MSL is 3 SM, not 4 statute miles.

140. The minimum distance from clouds required for VFR operations on an airway below 10,000 feet MSL is

A. remain clear of clouds.

B. 500 feet below, 1,000 feet above, and 2,000 feet horizontally.

C. 500 feet above, 1,000 feet below, and 2,000 feet horizontally.

Answer (B) is correct. *(14 CFR 91.155)*

DISCUSSION: An airway includes that Class E airspace extending upward from 1,200 ft. AGL to, but not including, 18,000 ft. MSL. The minimum distance from clouds below 10,000 ft. MSL in Class E airspace is 500 ft. below, 1,000 ft. above, and 2,000 ft. horizontally.

Answer (A) is incorrect. Clear of clouds is the minimum distance from clouds required in Class B, not Class E, airspace. Answer (C) is incorrect. The minimum distance from clouds required for VFR operations in Class E airspace below 10,000 ft. MSL is 500 ft. below, not above; 1,000 ft. above, not below; and 2,000 ft. horizontally.

141. What minimum visibility and clearance from clouds are required for VFR operations in Class G airspace at 700 feet AGL or below during daylight hours?

A. 1 mile visibility and clear of clouds.

B. 1 mile visibility, 500 feet below, 1,000 feet above, and 2,000 feet horizontal clearance from clouds.

C. 3 miles visibility and clear of clouds.

Answer (A) is correct. *(14 CFR 91.155)*

DISCUSSION: Below 1,200 ft. AGL in Class G airspace during daylight hours, the VFR weather minimum is 1 SM visibility and clear of clouds.

Answer (B) is incorrect. One SM visibility, 500 ft. below, 1,000 ft. above, and 2,000 ft. horizontal clearance from clouds is the minimum visibility and clearance from clouds in Class G airspace at more than 1,200 ft. AGL but less than 10,000 ft. MSL, not at 700 ft. AGL. At night the requirement is 3 SM and 500 ft. below, 1,000 ft. above, and 2,000 ft. horizontal from clouds. Answer (C) is incorrect. Three SM visibility and clear of clouds are the visibility and clearance from clouds requirements in Class B, not Class G, airspace.

142. During operations outside controlled airspace at altitudes of more than 1,200 feet AGL, but less than 10,000 feet MSL, the minimum flight visibility for VFR flight at night is

A. 1 mile.

B. 3 miles.

C. 5 miles.

Answer (B) is correct. *(14 CFR 91.155)*

DISCUSSION: When operating outside controlled airspace (i.e., Class G airspace) at night at altitudes of more than 1,200 ft. AGL, but less than 10,000 ft. MSL, the minimum flight visibility is 3 statute miles.

Answer (A) is incorrect. One SM is the minimum day, not night, flight visibility in Class G airspace at altitudes of more than 1,200 ft. AGL, but less than 10,000 ft. MSL. Answer (C) is incorrect. Five SM is for operations more than 1,200 ft. AGL and at or above, not below, 10,000 ft. MSL in Class G airspace.

143. During operations outside controlled airspace at altitudes of more than 1,200 feet AGL, but less than 10,000 feet MSL, the minimum flight visibility for day VFR is

A. 1 mile.

B. 3 miles.

C. 5 miles.

Answer (A) is correct. *(14 CFR 91.155)*

DISCUSSION: One SM is the minimum day flight visibility in Class G airspace at altitudes of more than 1,200 ft. AGL, but less than 10,000 ft. MSL.

Answer (B) is incorrect. The minimum flight visibility is 3 statute miles when operating outside controlled airspace (i.e., Class G airspace) at night at altitudes of more than 1,200 ft. AGL, but less than 10,000 ft. MSL. Answer (C) is incorrect. Five SM is for operations more than 1,200 ft. AGL and at or above, not below, 10,000 ft. MSL in Class G airspace.

144. (Refer to Figure 78 on page 159.) What are the basic VFR weather minima required to takeoff from the Onawa, IA (K36) airport during the day?

A. 3 statute miles visibility, 500 feet below the clouds, 1,000 feet above the clouds and 2,000 feet horizontally from the clouds.

B. 0 statute miles, clear of clouds.

C. 1 statute mile, clear of clouds.

Answer (C) is correct. *(AIM Para 3-1-4)*

DISCUSSION: Onawa, IA, (K36) airport is surrounded by Class G airspace. The VFR weather minima in Class G airspace below 1,200 feet AGL (regardless of MSL altitude) is 1 statute mile of visibility and clear of clouds.

Answer (A) is incorrect. Class C (day and night), D (day and night), and E (day VFR only and less than 10,000 feet MSL) are all 3 statute miles of visibility, 500 feet below the clouds, 1,000 feet above the clouds, and 2,000 feet horizontally from the clouds. Answer (B) is incorrect. There is no VFR weather minima with visibility of 0 statute miles.

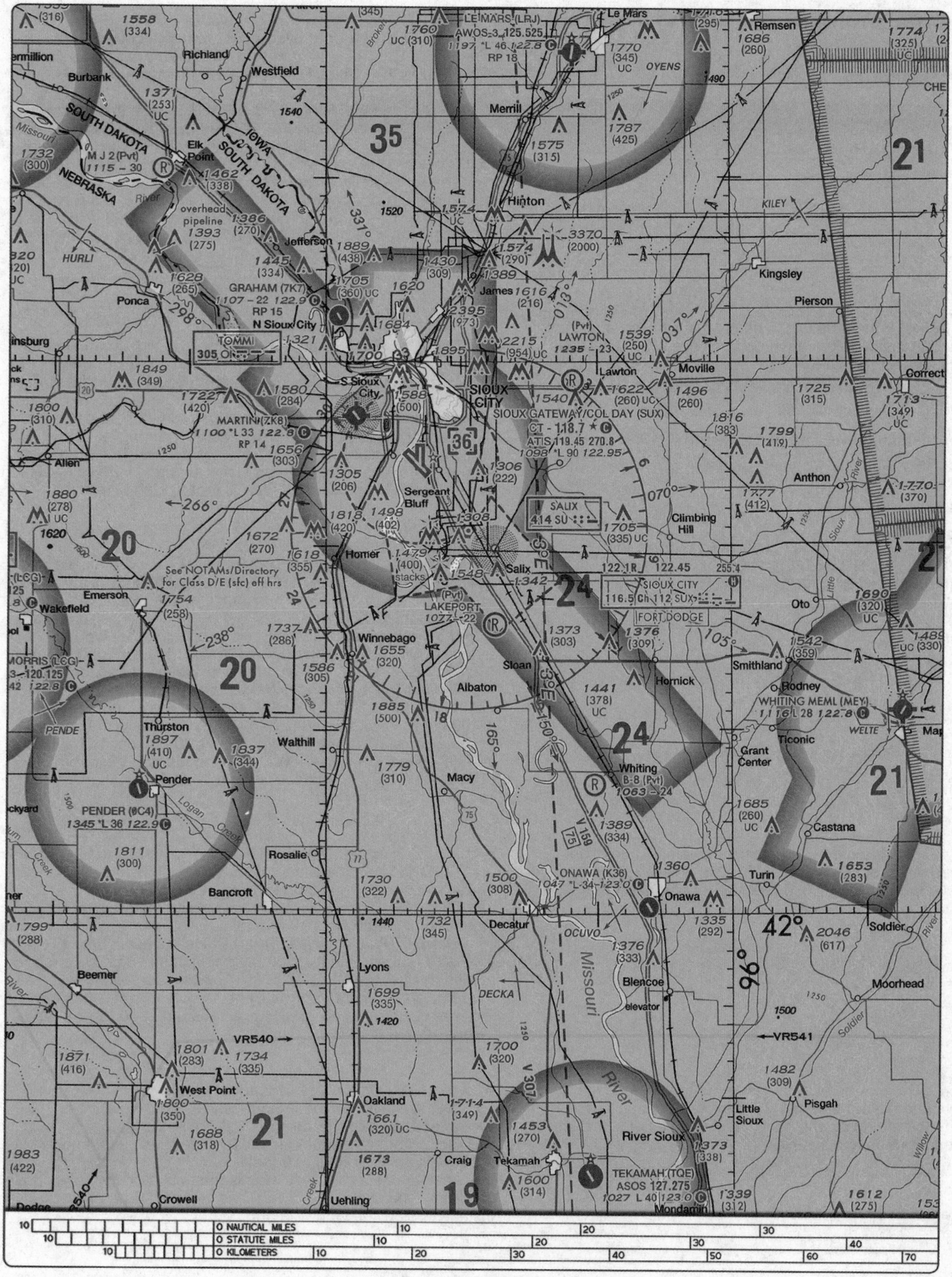

Figure 78. – Sectional Chart Excerpt.
NOTE: Chart is not to scale and should not be used for navigation. Use associated scale.

145. During operations within controlled airspace at altitudes of more than 1,200 feet AGL, but less than 10,000 feet MSL, the minimum distance above clouds requirement for VFR flight is

A. 500 feet.

B. 1,000 feet.

C. 1,500 feet.

Answer (B) is correct. *(14 CFR 91.155)*

DISCUSSION: Controlled airspace is the generic term for Class A, B, C, D, or E airspace. Only in Class C, D, or below 10,000 ft. MSL in Class E airspace are the minimum flight visibility and vertical distance from clouds for VFR flight required to be 3 SM, and 500 ft. below or 1,000 ft. above the clouds.

NOTE: AGL altitudes are not used in controlled airspace. In Class E airspace, the visibility and distance from clouds are given for (1) below 10,000 ft. MSL and (2) at or above 10,000 ft. MSL.

Answer (A) is incorrect. This is the minimum distance below, not above, clouds requirement for VFR flight in Class E airspace at altitudes of less than 10,000 ft. MSL. Answer (C) is incorrect. The minimum distance above clouds requirement for VFR flight in Class E airspace at altitudes of less than 10,000 ft. MSL is 1,000 ft., not 1,500 feet.

146. No person may take off or land an aircraft under basic VFR at an airport that lies within Class D airspace unless the

A. flight visibility at that airport is at least 1 mile.

B. ground visibility at that airport is at least 1 mile.

C. ground visibility at that airport is at least 3 miles.

Answer (C) is correct. *(14 CFR 91.155)*

DISCUSSION: No person may take off or land an aircraft at any airport that lies within Class D airspace under basic VFR unless the ground visibility is 3 statute miles. If ground visibility is not reported, flight visibility during landing or takeoff, or while operating in the traffic pattern, must be at least 3 statute miles.

Answer (A) is incorrect. Flight visibility during landing or takeoff under basic VFR must be at least 3, not 1, statute miles. Answer (B) is incorrect. Ground visibility during landing or takeoff under basic VFR must be at least 3, not 1, statute miles.

147. During operations at altitudes of more than 1,200 feet AGL and at or above 10,000 feet MSL, the minimum distance above clouds requirement for VFR flight is

A. 500 feet.

B. 1,000 feet.

C. 1,500 feet.

Answer (B) is correct. *(14 CFR 91.155)*

DISCUSSION: During operations in Class G airspace at altitudes of more than 1,200 ft. AGL and at or above 10,000 ft. MSL, the minimum distance above clouds requirement for VFR flight is 1,000 feet.

NOTE: The FAA question fails to specify what type of airspace. Since AGL altitudes are not used in controlled airspace (Class A, B, C, D, and E), that implies Class G airspace.

Answer (A) is incorrect. This is the vertical distance below, not above, the clouds for VFR operations below, not at or above, 10,000 ft. MSL and above 1,200 ft. AGL in Class G airspace. Answer (C) is incorrect. The figure of 1,000 ft., not 1,500 ft., is the vertical distance required above the clouds for VFR operations above 1,200 ft. AGL and at or above 10,000 ft. MSL in Class G airspace.

148. Outside controlled airspace, the minimum flight visibility requirement for VFR flight above 1,200 feet AGL and below 10,000 feet MSL during daylight hours is

A. 1 mile.

B. 3 miles.

C. 5 miles.

Answer (A) is correct. *(14 CFR 91.155)*

DISCUSSION: Outside controlled airspace (i.e., Class G airspace) at altitudes above 1,200 ft. AGL and below 10,000 ft. MSL, the minimum flight visibility requirement for VFR flight during the day is 1 statute mile.

Answer (B) is incorrect. Three SM is the minimum VFR flight visibility required at night, not day, for flights in Class G airspace at altitudes below 10,000 ft. MSL. Answer (C) is incorrect. Five SM is the minimum VFR flight visibility required for flights in Class G airspace above 1,200 ft. AGL and at or above, not below, 10,000 ft. MSL.

149. During operations outside controlled airspace at altitudes of more than 1,200 feet AGL, but less than 10,000 feet MSL, the minimum distance below clouds requirement for VFR flight at night is

A. 500 feet.

B. 1,000 feet.

C. 1,500 feet.

Answer (A) is correct. *(14 CFR 91.155)*

DISCUSSION: Outside controlled airspace (i.e., Class G airspace) at altitudes above 1,200 ft. AGL and less than 10,000 ft. MSL, the minimum distance below clouds requirement for VFR flight at night is 500 feet.

Answer (B) is incorrect. This is the minimum distance above, not below, the clouds. Answer (C) is incorrect. The minimum distance below the clouds is 500 ft., not 1,500 feet.

150. During operations within controlled airspace at altitudes of less than 1,200 feet AGL, the minimum horizontal distance from clouds requirement for VFR flight is

A. 1,000 feet.

B. 1,500 feet.

C. 2,000 feet.

Answer (C) is correct. *(14 CFR 91.155)*

DISCUSSION: Controlled airspace is the generic term for Class A, B, C, D, or E airspace. Only in Class C, D, or below 10,000 ft. MSL in Class E airspace is the minimum horizontal distance from clouds for VFR flight required to be 2,000 feet.

NOTE: AGL altitudes are not used in controlled airspace. In Class E airspace, the visibility and distance from clouds are given for (1) below 10,000 ft. MSL and (2) at or above 10,000 ft. MSL.

Answer (A) is incorrect. This is the minimum vertical, not horizontal, distance above the clouds in Class E airspace below 10,000 ft. MSL. Answer (B) is incorrect. The minimum horizontal distance is 2,000 ft., not 1,500 feet.

151. Normal VFR operations in Class D airspace with an operating control tower require the visibility and ceiling to be at least

A. 1,000 feet and 1 mile.

B. 1,000 feet and 3 miles.

C. 2,500 feet and 3 miles.

Answer (B) is correct. *(14 CFR 91.155)*

DISCUSSION: The basic VFR weather minimums for operating an aircraft within Class D airspace are a 1,000-ft. ceiling and 3 SM visibility.

Answer (A) is incorrect. The basic VFR weather minimums for operating an aircraft in Class D airspace are a 1,000-ft. ceiling and 3 SM, not 1 SM, visibility. Answer (C) is incorrect. The basic VFR weather minimums for operating an aircraft in Class D airspace are a 1,000-ft., not 2,500-ft., ceiling and 3 SM visibility.

91.157 Special VFR Weather Minimums

152. What ATC facility should the pilot contact to receive a special VFR departure clearance in Class D airspace?

A. Automated Flight Service Station.

B. Air Traffic Control Tower.

C. Air Route Traffic Control Center.

Answer (B) is correct. *(14 CFR 91.157)*

DISCUSSION: When special VFR is needed, the pilot should contact the Air Traffic Control Tower to receive a departure clearance in Class D airspace.

Answer (A) is incorrect. A pilot may request a clearance through an FSS for a special VFR clearance in Class E, not Class D, airspace. The FSS would only act as a relay point between the pilot and the ATC facility responsible for the Class E airspace (i.e., FSS personnel cannot issue a clearance). Answer (C) is incorrect. An Air Route Traffic Control Center can issue a clearance for a special VFR for an airport in Class E, not Class D, airspace.

153. A special VFR clearance authorizes the pilot of an aircraft to operate VFR while within Class D airspace when the visibility is

A. less than 1 mile and the ceiling is less than 1,000 feet.

B. at least 1 mile and the aircraft can remain clear of clouds.

C. at least 3 miles and the aircraft can remain clear of clouds.

Answer (B) is correct. *(14 CFR 91.157)*

DISCUSSION: To operate within Class D airspace under special VFR clearance, visibility must be at least 1 statute mile. There is no ceiling requirement, but the aircraft must remain clear of clouds.

Answer (A) is incorrect. A special VFR clearance authorizes the pilot to operate VFR within Class D airspace if the visibility is at least, not below, 1 statute mile. Answer (C) is incorrect. A special VFR clearance requires the pilot to maintain at least 1 SM, not 3 SM, visibility and remain clear of clouds.

154. No person may operate an airplane within Class D airspace at night under special VFR unless the

A. flight can be conducted 500 feet below the clouds.

B. airplane is equipped for instrument flight.

C. flight visibility is at least 3 miles.

Answer (B) is correct. *(14 CFR 91.157)*

DISCUSSION: To operate under special VFR within Class D airspace at night, the pilot must be instrument rated and the airplane equipped for instrument flight.

Answer (A) is incorrect. The only additional requirement at night for special VFR in Class D airspace is that the airplane be IFR equipped and the pilot be instrument rated, not that the flight be conducted 500 ft. below the clouds. Answer (C) is incorrect. For special VFR at night in Class D airspace, the flight visibility must be at least 1 SM, not 3 statute miles.

155. What are the minimum requirements for airplane operations under special VFR in Class D airspace at night?

A. The airplane must be under radar surveillance at all times while in Class D airspace.

B. The airplane must be equipped for IFR with an altitude reporting transponder.

C. The pilot must be instrument rated, and the airplane must be IFR equipped.

Answer (C) is correct. *(14 CFR 91.157)*

DISCUSSION: To operate under special VFR within Class D airspace at night, the pilot must be instrument rated and the airplane must be IFR equipped.

Answer (A) is incorrect. To operate an airplane under special VFR at night in Class D airspace, there is no requirement that the airplane be under radar surveillance. Answer (B) is incorrect. There is no requirement for an altitude reporting transponder for special VFR at night in Class D airspace, but the pilot must be instrument rated.

156. What is the minimum weather condition required for airplanes operating under special VFR in Class D airspace?

A. 1 mile flight visibility.

B. 1 mile flight visibility and 1,000-foot ceiling.

C. 3 miles flight visibility and 1,000-foot ceiling.

Answer (A) is correct. *(14 CFR 91.157)*

DISCUSSION: To operate within Class D airspace under special VFR clearance, visibility must be at least 1 statute mile. There is no ceiling requirement, but the aircraft must remain clear of clouds.

Answer (B) is incorrect. To operate within Class D airspace under a special VFR clearance, there is no (not 1,000-ft.) ceiling requirement other than to remain clear of clouds. Answer (C) is incorrect. Three SM flight visibility and 1,000-ft. ceiling are basic (not special) VFR weather minimums to operate an airplane in Class D airspace.

91.159 VFR Cruising Altitude or Flight Level

157. Which VFR cruising altitude is acceptable for a flight on a Victor Airway with a magnetic course of 175°? The terrain is less than 1,000 feet.

A. 4,500 feet.

B. 5,000 feet.

C. 5,500 feet.

Answer (C) is correct. *(14 CFR 91.159)*

DISCUSSION: When operating a VFR flight above 3,000 ft. AGL on a magnetic course of 0° through 179°, fly any odd thousand-ft. MSL altitude plus 500 feet. Thus, on a magnetic course of 175°, an appropriate VFR cruising altitude is 5,500 feet.

Answer (A) is incorrect. An acceptable VFR cruising altitude would be 4,500 ft. if you were on a magnetic course of 180° to 359°, not 175°. Answer (B) is incorrect. On a magnetic course of 175°, the acceptable VFR cruising altitude is an odd thousand plus 500 ft. (5,500 ft., not 5,000 feet).

158. Which cruising altitude is appropriate for a VFR flight on a magnetic course of 135°?

A. Even thousand.

B. Even thousand plus 500 feet.

C. Odd thousand plus 500 feet.

Answer (C) is correct. *(14 CFR 91.159)*

DISCUSSION: When operating a VFR flight above 3,000 ft. AGL on a magnetic course of 0° through 179°, fly any odd thousand-ft. MSL altitude plus 500 feet. Thus, on a magnetic course of 135°, an appropriate VFR cruising altitude is an odd thousand plus 500 feet.

Answer (A) is incorrect. A VFR flight on a magnetic course of 135° will use an odd (not even) thousand, plus 500 ft. altitude. Answer (B) is incorrect. A VFR flight on a magnetic course of 135° will use an odd (not even) thousand plus 500 ft. altitude.

159. Which VFR cruising altitude is appropriate when flying above 3,000 feet AGL on a magnetic course of 185°?

A. 4,000 feet.

B. 4,500 feet.

C. 5,000 feet.

Answer (B) is correct. *(14 CFR 91.159)*

DISCUSSION: When operating a VFR flight above 3,000 ft. AGL on a magnetic course of 180° through 359°, fly any even thousand-ft. MSL altitude, plus 500 ft. Thus, on a magnetic course of 185°, an appropriate VFR cruising altitude is 4,500 feet.

Answer (A) is incorrect. On a magnetic course of 185° the appropriate VFR cruising altitude is an even thousand-ft. plus 500 ft. altitude (4,500 ft., not 4,000 ft.). Answer (C) is incorrect. On a magnetic course of 185° the appropriate VFR cruising altitude is an even (not odd) thousand-ft., plus 500 ft. (4,500 ft., not 5,000 ft.).

160. Each person operating an aircraft at a VFR cruising altitude shall maintain an odd-thousand plus 500-foot altitude while on a

A. magnetic heading of 0° through 179°.

B. magnetic course of 0° through 179°.

C. true course of 0° through 179°.

Answer (B) is correct. *(14 CFR 91.159)*

DISCUSSION: When operating above 3,000 ft. AGL but less than 18,000 ft. MSL on a magnetic course of 0° to 179°, fly at an odd thousand-ft. MSL altitude plus 500 feet.

Answer (A) is incorrect. A magnetic heading includes wind correction, and VFR cruising altitudes are based on magnetic course, i.e., without wind correction. Answer (C) is incorrect. True course does not include an adjustment for magnetic variation.

91.203 Civil Aircraft: Certifications Required

161. In addition to a valid Airworthiness Certificate, what documents or records must be aboard an aircraft during flight?

A. Aircraft engine and airframe logbooks, and owner's manual.

B. Radio operator's permit, and repair and alteration forms.

C. Operating limitations and Registration Certificate.

Answer (C) is correct. *(14 CFR 91.203, 91.9)*

DISCUSSION: FAR 91.203 requires both an Airworthiness Certificate and a Registration Certificate to be aboard aircraft during flight. FAR 91.9 requires that operating limitations be available in the aircraft in an approved Airplane Flight Manual, approved manual material, markings, and placards, or any combination thereof.

Answer (A) is incorrect. The airframe and engine logbooks are usually maintained and stored on the ground. Answer (B) is incorrect. Repair and alteration forms are handled in the maintenance shop. Also, the Radio Operator's permit, although carried by the pilot, is an FCC requirement. A pilot may still fly without it as long as (s)he does not use any radio equipment that transmits a signal (e.g., communication, DME, or transponder).

91.207 Emergency Locator Transmitters

162. When must batteries in an emergency locator transmitter (ELT) be replaced or recharged, if rechargeable?

A. After any inadvertent activation of the ELT.

B. When the ELT has been in use for more than 1 cumulative hour.

C. When the ELT can no longer be heard over the airplane's communication radio receiver.

Answer (B) is correct. *(14 CFR 91.207)*

DISCUSSION: ELT batteries must be replaced or recharged (if rechargeable) when the transmitter has been in use for more than 1 cumulative hr. or when 50% of their useful life (or useful life of charge) has expired.

Answer (A) is incorrect. The batteries in an ELT must be replaced (or recharged, if rechargeable) only after the transmitter has been used for more than 1 cumulative hr., not after any inadvertent activation of the transmitter. Answer (C) is incorrect. ELT batteries are replaced (or recharged, if rechargeable) based on use or useful life, not when an ELT can no longer be heard over the airplane's communication radio receiver.

163. When may an emergency locator transmitter (ELT) be tested?

A. Anytime.

B. At 15 and 45 minutes past the hour.

C. During the first 5 minutes after the hour.

Answer (C) is correct. *(AIM Para 6-2-5)*

DISCUSSION: ELTs may only be tested on the ground during the first 5 min. after the hour. Other times it is only allowed with prior arrangement with the nearest FAA Control Tower or FSS. No airborne checks are allowed.

Answer (A) is incorrect. An ELT should only be tested during the first 5 min. after the hour, not anytime. Answer (B) is incorrect. An ELT should only be tested during the first 5 min. after the hour, not at 15 and 45 min. past the hour.

164. When are non-rechargeable batteries of an emergency locator transmitter (ELT) required to be replaced?

A. Every 24 months.

B. When 50 percent of their useful life expires.

C. At the time of each 100-hour or annual inspection.

Answer (B) is correct. *(14 CFR 91.207)*

DISCUSSION: Non-rechargeable batteries of an ELT must be replaced when 50% of their useful life expires or after the transmitter has been in use for more than 1 cumulative hour.

Answer (A) is incorrect. Every 24 months is the requirement for the transponder to be tested and inspected, not when non-rechargeable ELT batteries are to be replaced. Answer (C) is incorrect. Non-rechargeable ELT batteries are replaced when 50% of their useful life expires or after 1 cumulative hr. of use, not necessarily at the time of each 100-hr. or annual inspection.

165. When must the battery in an emergency locator transmitter (ELT) be replaced (or recharged if the battery is rechargeable)?

A. After one-half the battery's useful life.

B. During each annual and 100-hour inspection.

C. Every 24 calendar months.

Answer (A) is correct. *(14 CFR 91.207)*

DISCUSSION: ELT batteries must be replaced or recharged after 50% of their useful life has expired or when the transmitter has been in use for more than 1 cumulative hour.

Answer (B) is incorrect. ELT batteries must be replaced (or recharged) after one-half the battery's useful life has expired, not during each annual and 100-hr. inspection. Answer (C) is incorrect. A transponder (not an ELT battery) must be tested and inspected every 24 calendar months.

91.209 Aircraft Lights

166. Except in Alaska, during what time period should lighted position lights be displayed on an aircraft?

A. End of evening civil twilight to the beginning of morning civil twilight.

B. 1 hour after sunset to 1 hour before sunrise.

C. Sunset to sunrise.

Answer (C) is correct. *(14 CFR 91.209)*

DISCUSSION: Except in Alaska, no person may operate an aircraft during the period from sunset to sunrise unless the aircraft's lighted position lights are on.

Answer (A) is incorrect. End of evening civil twilight to the beginning of morning civil twilight is the definition of night, not the time period in which lighted position lights be displayed on an aircraft. Answer (B) is incorrect. The period from 1 hr. after sunset to 1 hr. before sunrise is the time used to meet night recency requirements, not when the aircraft position lights should be on.

91.211 Supplemental Oxygen

167. Unless each occupant is provided with supplemental oxygen, no person may operate a civil aircraft of U.S. registry above a maximum cabin pressure altitude of

A. 12,500 feet MSL.

B. 14,000 feet MSL.

C. 15,000 feet MSL.

Answer (C) is correct. *(14 CFR 91.211)*

DISCUSSION: No person may operate a civil aircraft of U.S. registry at cabin pressure altitudes above 15,000 ft. MSL unless each occupant is provided with supplemental oxygen.

Answer (A) is incorrect. At cabin pressure altitudes above 12,500 ft. MSL, up to and including 14,000 ft. MSL, only the minimum required flight crew, not each occupant, must be provided with and use supplemental oxygen after 30 min. at those altitudes. Answer (B) is incorrect. At cabin pressure altitudes above 14,000 ft. MSL, only the minimum required flight crew, not each occupant, must be provided with and continuously use supplemental oxygen at those altitudes.

168. When operating an aircraft at cabin pressure altitudes above 12,500 feet MSL up to and including 14,000 feet MSL, supplemental oxygen shall be used during

A. the entire flight time at those altitudes.

B. that flight time in excess of 10 minutes at those altitudes.

C. that flight time in excess of 30 minutes at those altitudes.

Answer (C) is correct. *(14 CFR 91.211)*

DISCUSSION: At cabin pressure altitudes above 12,500 ft. MSL, up to and including 14,000 ft. MSL, the required minimum flight crew must use supplemental oxygen only after 30 min. at those altitudes.

Answer (A) is incorrect. At cabin pressure altitudes above 12,500 ft. MSL up to and including 14,000 ft. MSL, supplemental oxygen shall be used during that time in excess of 30 min. (not the entire flight time) at those altitudes. Answer (B) is incorrect. At cabin pressure altitudes above 12,500 ft. MSL up to and including 14,000 ft. MSL, supplemental oxygen shall be used during that time in excess of 30 (not 10) min. at those altitudes.

91.215 ATC Transponder and Altitude Reporting Equipment and Use

169. An operable 4096-code transponder with an encoding altimeter is required in which airspace?

A. Class A, Class B (and within 30 miles of the Class B primary airport), and Class C.

B. Class D and Class E (below 10,000 feet MSL).

C. Class D and Class G (below 10,000 feet MSL).

Answer (A) is correct. *(14 CFR 91.215)*

DISCUSSION: An operable transponder with an encoding altimeter (Mode C) is required in Class A, Class B (and within 30 NM of the Class B primary airport), and Class C airspace, and at or above 10,000 ft. MSL excluding that airspace below 2,500 ft. AGL.

Answer (B) is incorrect. An operable 4096-code transponder with an encoding altimeter is not required to operate in Class D or Class E (below 10,000 ft. MSL) airspace. Answer (C) is incorrect. An operable 4096-code transponder with an encoding altimeter is not required to operate in Class D or Class G (below 10,000 ft. MSL) airspace.

170. An operable 4096-code transponder and Mode C encoding altimeter are required in

A. Class B airspace and within 30 miles of the Class B primary airport.

B. Class D airspace.

C. Class E airspace below 10,000 feet MSL.

Answer (A) is correct. *(14 CFR 91.215)*

DISCUSSION: An operable 4096-code transponder and Mode C encoding altimeter are required in Class B airspace and within 30 NM of the Class B primary airport.

Answer (B) is incorrect. An operable 4096-code transponder and Mode C encoding altimeter are required in Class B airspace and within 30 NM of the Class B primary airport, not Class D airspace. Answer (C) is incorrect. An operable 4096-code transponder and Mode C encoding altimeter are required in Class B airspace and within 30 NM of the Class B primary airport, not Class E airspace below 10,000 ft. MSL.

91.303 Aerobatic Flight

171. In which class of airspace is aerobatic flight prohibited?

A. Class E airspace not designated for federal airways above 1,500 feet AGL.

B. Class E airspace below 1,500 feet AGL.

C. Class G airspace above 1,500 feet AGL.

Answer (B) is correct. *(14 CFR 91.303)*

DISCUSSION: No person may operate an aircraft in aerobatic flight below an altitude of 1,500 ft. AGL.

Answer (A) is incorrect. Aerobatic flight is prohibited in Class E airspace within 4 NM of the centerline of a federal airway, not in all Class E airspace. Answer (C) is incorrect. Aerobatic flight is only prohibited below 1,500 ft. AGL.

172. No person may operate an aircraft in acrobatic flight when the flight visibility is less than

A. 3 miles.

B. 5 miles.

C. 7 miles.

Answer (A) is correct. *(14 CFR 91.303)*

DISCUSSION: No person may operate an aircraft in acrobatic flight when the flight visibility is less than 3 statute miles.

Answer (B) is incorrect. The minimum flight visibility for acrobatic flight is 3 SM, not 5 statute miles. Answer (C) is incorrect. The minimum flight visibility for acrobatic flight is 3 SM, not 7 statute miles.

173. What is the lowest altitude permitted for acrobatic flight?

A. 1,000 feet AGL.

B. 1,500 feet AGL.

C. 2,000 feet AGL.

Answer (B) is correct. *(14 CFR 91.303)*

DISCUSSION: No person may operate an aircraft in acrobatic flight below 1,500 ft. AGL.

Answer (A) is incorrect. The lowest altitude permitted for acrobatic flight is 1,500 ft. AGL, not 1,000 ft. AGL. Answer (C) is incorrect. The lowest altitude permitted for acrobatic flight is 1,500 ft. AGL, not 2,000 ft. AGL.

174. No person may operate an aircraft in acrobatic flight when

A. flight visibility is less than 5 miles.

B. over any congested area of a city, town, or settlement.

C. less than 2,500 feet AGL.

Answer (B) is correct. *(14 CFR 91.303)*

DISCUSSION: No person may operate an aircraft in acrobatic flight over any congested area of a city, town, or settlement.

Answer (A) is incorrect. The flight visibility limitation for acrobatic flight is 3 SM, not 5 statute miles. Answer (C) is incorrect. The minimum altitude for acrobatic flight is 1,500 ft. AGL, not 2,500 ft. AGL.

91.307 Parachutes and Parachuting

175. With certain exceptions, when must each occupant of an aircraft wear an approved parachute?

A. When a door is removed from the aircraft to facilitate parachute jumpers.

B. When intentionally pitching the nose of the aircraft up or down 30° or more.

C. When intentionally banking in excess of 30°.

Answer (B) is correct. *(14 CFR 91.307)*

DISCUSSION: Unless each occupant of an airplane is wearing an approved parachute, no pilot carrying any other person (other than a crewmember) may execute any intentional maneuver that exceeds a bank of 60° or a nose-up or nose-down attitude of 30° relative to the horizon.

Answer (A) is incorrect. Pilots of airplanes that are carrying parachute jumpers are not required to use a parachute. Answer (C) is incorrect. A parachute is required when an intentional bank that exceeds 60°, not 30°, is to be made.

176. A parachute composed of nylon, rayon, or other synthetic fibers must have been packed by a certificated and appropriately rated parachute rigger within the preceding

A. 60 days.

B. 90 days.

C. 180 days.

Answer (C) is correct. *(14 CFR 91.307)*

DISCUSSION: No pilot of a civil aircraft may allow a parachute that is available for emergency use to be carried in that aircraft unless it is an approved type and, if a chair type, it has been packed by a certificated and appropriately rated parachute rigger within the preceding 180 days, if synthetic fibers are used in its design.

Answer (A) is incorrect. A parachute constructed with natural fibers, not synthetic fibers, must be repacked within the preceding 60 days. Answer (B) is incorrect. A parachute composed of synthetic fibers must have been repacked within the preceding 180 days, not 90 days.

177. An approved parachute constructed of natural fibers may be carried in an aircraft for emergency use if it has been packed by an appropriately rated parachute rigger within the preceding

A. 60 days.

B. 120 days.

C. 180 days.

Answer (A) is correct. *(14 CFR 91.307)*

DISCUSSION: No pilot of a civil aircraft may allow a parachute that is available for emergency use to be carried in that aircraft unless it is an approved type and has been packed by a certificated and appropriately rated parachute rigger within the preceding 60 days, if natural fibers are used in its design.

Answer (B) is incorrect. A parachute constructed of natural fibers must have been repacked within the preceding 60 days, not 120 days. Answer (C) is incorrect. A parachute constructed from synthetic fibers, not natural fibers, must be repacked every 180 days.

91.313 Restricted Category Civil Aircraft: Operating Limitations

178. Which is normally prohibited when operating a restricted category civil aircraft?

A. Flight under instrument flight rules.

B. Flight over a densely populated area.

C. Flight within Class D airspace.

Answer (B) is correct. *(14 CFR 91.313)*

DISCUSSION: Normally, no person may operate a restricted category civil aircraft over a densely populated area.

Answer (A) is incorrect. Flight over a densely populated area, not IFR flight, is normally prohibited when operating a restricted category civil aircraft. Answer (C) is incorrect. Flight over a densely populated area, not within Class D airspace, is normally prohibited when operating a restricted category civil aircraft.

91.319 Aircraft Having Experimental Certificates: Operating Limitations

179. Unless otherwise specifically authorized, no person may operate an aircraft that has an experimental certificate .

A. beneath the floor of Class B airspace.

B. over a densely populated area or in a congested airway.

C. from the primary airport within Class D airspace.

Answer (B) is correct. *(14 CFR 91.319)*

DISCUSSION: Unless otherwise specifically authorized, no person may operate an aircraft that has an experimental certificate over a densely populated area or along a congested airway.

Answer (A) is incorrect. Normally no person may operate an aircraft that has an experimental certificate along a congested airway, not beneath the floor of Class B airspace. Answer (C) is incorrect. A person can operate an aircraft that has an experimental certificate from the primary airport within Class D airspace as long as ATC is notified of the experimental nature of the aircraft.

91.403 General

180. The responsibility for ensuring that an aircraft is maintained in an airworthy condition is primarily that of the

A. pilot in command.

B. owner or operator.

C. mechanic who performs the work.

Answer (B) is correct. *(14 CFR 91.403)*

DISCUSSION: The owner or operator of an aircraft is primarily responsible for maintaining that aircraft in an airworthy condition. The term "operator" includes the pilot in command.

Answer (A) is incorrect. The owner or operator, not only the pilot in command, of an aircraft is responsible for ensuring the airworthiness of the aircraft. Answer (C) is incorrect. Although a mechanic will perform inspections and maintenance, the primary responsibility for an aircraft's airworthiness lies with its owner or operator.

181. Who is responsible for ensuring Airworthiness Directives (ADs) are complied with?

A. Owner or operator.

B. Repair station.

C. Mechanic with inspection authorization (IA).

Answer (A) is correct. *(14 CFR 91.403)*

DISCUSSION: ADs are regulatory and must be complied with, unless a specific exemption is granted. It is the responsibility of the owner or operator to ensure compliance with all pertinent ADs, including those ADs that require recurrent or continuing action.

Answer (B) is incorrect. The owner or operator, not a repair station, is responsible for ensuring ADs are complied with. Answer (C) is incorrect. The owner or operator, not a mechanic with inspection authorization, is responsible for ensuring ADs are complied with.

91.405 Maintenance Required

182. The responsibility for ensuring that maintenance personnel make the appropriate entries in the aircraft maintenance records indicating the aircraft has been approved for return to service lies with the

A. owner or operator.

B. pilot in command.

C. mechanic who performed the work.

Answer (A) is correct. *(14 CFR 91.405)*

DISCUSSION: Each owner or operator of an aircraft shall ensure that maintenance personnel make the appropriate entries in the aircraft maintenance records indicating the aircraft has been approved for return to service.

Answer (B) is incorrect. The owner or operator, not only the pilot in command, is responsible for ensuring that maintenance personnel make the proper entries in the aircraft's maintenance records. Answer (C) is incorrect. The owner or operator, not the mechanic who performed the work, is responsible for ensuring that proper entries are made in the aircraft's maintenance records.

183. Who is responsible for ensuring appropriate entries are made in maintenance records indicating the aircraft has been approved for return to service?

A. Owner or operator.

B. Certified mechanic.

C. Repair station.

Answer (A) is correct. *(14 CFR 91.405)*

DISCUSSION: It is the responsibility of the owner or operator of an aircraft to ensure that appropriate entries are made in maintenance records by maintenance personnel indicating the aircraft has been approved for return to service.

Answer (B) is incorrect. The certified mechanic performing the work must make the entries, but it is the responsibility of the owner or operator to ensure that the entries have been made. Answer (C) is incorrect. It is the responsibility of the owner or operator, not a repair station, to ensure appropriate entries have been made.

91.407 Operation after Maintenance, Preventive Maintenance, Rebuilding, or Alteration

184. If an alteration or repair substantially affects an aircraft's operation in flight, that aircraft must be test flown by an appropriately-rated pilot and approved for return to service prior to being operated

A. by any private pilot.

B. with passengers aboard.

C. for compensation or hire.

Answer (B) is correct. *(14 CFR 91.407)*

DISCUSSION: If an alteration or repair has been made that substantially affects the airplane's flight characteristics, the airplane must be test flown and approved for return to service by an appropriately rated pilot prior to being operated with passengers aboard. The test pilot must be at least a private pilot and appropriately rated for the airplane being tested, must make an operational check of the alteration or repair made, and must log the flight in the aircraft records.

Answer (A) is incorrect. If an alteration or repair substantially affects an aircraft's operation in flight, a private pilot may only test fly that airplane if (s)he is appropriately rated to fly that airplane. Answer (C) is incorrect. After any alteration or repair that substantially affects an aircraft's operation in flight, that aircraft must be test flown and approved for return to service prior to being operated with any passengers aboard, not for compensation or hire.

185. Before passengers can be carried in an aircraft that has been altered in a manner that may have appreciably changed its flight characteristics, it must be flight tested by an appropriately-rated pilot who holds at least a

A. Commercial Pilot Certificate with an instrument rating.

B. Private Pilot Certificate.

C. Commercial Pilot Certificate and a mechanic's certificate.

Answer (B) is correct. *(14 CFR 91.407)*

DISCUSSION: If an alteration or repair has been made that may have changed an airplane's flight characteristics, the airplane must be test flown and approved for return to service by an appropriately rated pilot prior to being operated with passengers aboard. The test pilot must be at least a private pilot and appropriately rated for the airplane being tested.

Answer (A) is incorrect. The test flight must be made by an appropriately rated pilot who holds at least a private (not commercial) pilot certificate. An instrument rating is not required. Answer (C) is incorrect. The test flight must be made by an appropriately rated pilot who holds at least a private (not commercial) pilot certificate. A mechanic's certificate is not required for the test pilot.

91.409 Inspections

186. A 100-hour inspection was due at 3302.5 hours. The 100-hour inspection was actually done at 3309.5 hours. When is the next 100-hour inspection due?

A. 3312.5 hours.

B. 3402.5 hours.

C. 3395.5 hours.

Answer (B) is correct. *(14 CFR 91.409)*

DISCUSSION: Since the last 100-hr. inspection was due at 3302.5 hr., the next 100-hr. inspection is due at 3402.5 hr. (3302.5 + 100). The 100-hr. limitation may be exceeded by not more than 10 hr. while en route to reach a place where the inspection can be done; this excess time must be included in computing the next 100 hr. of time in service.

Answer (A) is incorrect. This is the latest time on the tachometer the last 100-hr. inspection could have been completed, not when the next 100-hr. inspection is due. Answer (C) is incorrect. Adding the remaining 93 hr. to when the last 100-hr. inspection was due at 3302.5 hr. (3302.5 + 93 = 3395.5) is incorrect. The next 100-hr. inspection is due at 3402.5 hr. (3302.5 + 100 = 3402.5).

187. An aircraft's annual condition inspection was performed on July 12, this year. The next annual inspection will be due no later than

A. July 1, next year.

B. July 13, next year.

C. July 31, next year.

Answer (C) is correct. *(14 CFR 91.409)*

DISCUSSION: Annual condition inspections expire on the last day of the 12th calendar month after the previous annual condition inspection. If an annual condition inspection is performed on July 12 of this year, it will expire at midnight on July 31 next year.

Answer (A) is incorrect. Annual condition inspections are due on the last day of the month. Thus, if an annual condition inspection is performed July 12, this year the next annual condition inspection is due July 31 (not July 1), next year. Answer (B) is incorrect. Annual condition inspections are due on the last day of the month. Thus, if an annual condition inspection is performed July 12, this year the next annual condition inspection is due July 31 (not July 13), next year.

188. What aircraft inspections are required for rental aircraft that are also used for flight instruction?

A. Annual condition and 100-hour inspections.

B. Biannual condition and 100-hour inspections.

C. Annual condition and 50-hour inspections.

Answer (A) is correct. *(14 CFR 91.409)*

DISCUSSION: All aircraft that are used for hire (e.g., rental) and flight instruction must be inspected on a 100-hr. basis. Also, an annual condition inspection must be completed.

Answer (B) is incorrect. An annual, not biannual, condition inspection is required for all aircraft. A 100-hr. inspection is also required for aircraft rented for flight instruction. Answer (C) is incorrect. Besides an annual condition inspection, aircraft rented for flight instruction purposes are also required to have a 100- (not 50-) hr. inspection.

189. An aircraft had a 100-hour inspection when the tachometer read 1259.6. When is the next 100-hour inspection due?

A. 1349.6 hours.

B. 1359.6 hours.

C. 1369.6 hours.

Answer (B) is correct. *(14 CFR 91.409)*

DISCUSSION: The next 100-hr. inspection is due within 100 hr. of time in service. The 100-hr. may be exceeded by 10 hr. in order to get to a place where the work can be done. However, this additional time is included in computing the next 100 hr. period. Therefore, in this question, add 100 hr. to 1259.6 to get the next inspection, due at 1359.6 hours.

Answer (A) is incorrect. The 100-hr. inspection is due when the tachometer indicates 1359.6 hr. (1259.6 + 100), not 1349.6 hours. Answer (C) is incorrect. This is 10 hr. over the 100-hr. limitation that is allowed if the aircraft is en route to reach a place where the inspection can be done. The 100-hr. inspection is due at 1359.6 hr. (1259.6 + 100), not 1369.6 hours.

91.413 ATC Transponder Tests and Inspections

190. No person may use an ATC transponder unless it has been tested and inspected within at least the preceding

A. 6 calendar months.

B. 12 calendar months.

C. 24 calendar months.

Answer (C) is correct. *(14 CFR 91.413)*

DISCUSSION: No person may use an ATC transponder that is specified in the regulations unless within the preceding 24 calendar months it has been tested and found to comply with its operating specifications.

Answer (A) is incorrect. An ATC transponder must be tested and inspected every 24 (not 6) calendar months. Answer (B) is incorrect. An ATC transponder must be tested and inspected every 24 (not 12) calendar months.

191. Maintenance records show the last transponder inspection was performed on September 1, 2014. The next inspection will be due no later than

A. September 30, 2015.

B. September 1, 2016.

C. September 30, 2016.

Answer (C) is correct. *(14 CFR 91.413)*

DISCUSSION: No person may use an ATC transponder that is specified in the regulations unless within the preceding 24 calendar months it has been tested and found to comply with its operating specifications. Thus, if the last inspection was performed on September 1, 2014, the next inspection will be due no later than September 30, 2016.

Answer (A) is incorrect. The requirement states that the transponder must be inspected every 24 calendar months, not every 12. Answer (B) is incorrect. The "calendar month" requirement means that the inspection may be done on any date from the first to the last day of the month. Therefore, the transponder must be inspected no later than the end of the month of September, not the beginning.

91.417 Maintenance Records

192. Completion of an annual condition inspection and the return of the aircraft to service should always be indicated by

A. the relicensing date on the Registration Certificate.

B. an appropriate notation in the aircraft maintenance records.

C. an inspection sticker placed on the instrument panel that lists the annual inspection completion date.

Answer (B) is correct. *(14 CFR 91.417)*

DISCUSSION: Completion of an annual condition inspection and the return of the aircraft to service should always be indicated by an appropriate notation in the aircraft's maintenance records.

Answer (A) is incorrect. The registration certificate shows ownership, not completion of an annual inspection. Answer (C) is incorrect. Maintenance information is found in the airplane logbooks, not on inspection stickers.

193. To determine the expiration date of the last annual aircraft inspection, a person should refer to the

A. Airworthiness Certificate.

B. Registration Certificate.

C. aircraft maintenance records.

Answer (C) is correct. *(14 CFR 91.417)*

DISCUSSION: After maintenance inspections have been completed, maintenance personnel should make the appropriate entries in the aircraft maintenance records or logbooks. This is where the date of the last annual inspection can be found.

Answer (A) is incorrect. To determine the expiration date of the last annual inspection, a person should refer to the aircraft maintenance records, not the Airworthiness Certificate. Answer (B) is incorrect. To determine the expiration date of the last annual inspection, a person should refer to the aircraft maintenance records, not the Registration Certificate.

194. Which records or documents shall the owner or operator of an aircraft keep to show compliance with an applicable Airworthiness Directive?

A. Aircraft maintenance records.

B. Airworthiness Certificate and Pilot's Operating Handbook.

C. Airworthiness and Registration Certificates.

Answer (A) is correct. *(14 CFR 91.417)*

DISCUSSION: Aircraft maintenance records must show the current status of applicable airworthiness directives (ADs) including, for each, the method of compliance, the AD number, and revision date. If the AD involves recurring action, the records must show the time and date when the next action is required.

Answer (B) is incorrect. Compliance with an AD is found in aircraft maintenance records, not the Airworthiness Certificate and Pilot's Operating Handbook. Answer (C) is incorrect. Compliance with an AD is found in aircraft maintenance records, not in the Airworthiness and Registration Certificates.

195. The airworthiness of an aircraft can be determined by a preflight inspection and a

A. statement from the owner or operator that the aircraft is airworthy.

B. log book endorsement from a flight instructor.

C. review of the maintenance records.

Answer (C) is correct. *(14 CFR 91.417)*

DISCUSSION: As pilot in command, you are responsible for determining whether your aircraft is in condition for safe flight. Only by conducting a preflight inspection and a review of the maintenance records can you determine whether all required maintenance has been performed and, thus, whether the aircraft is airworthy.

Answer (A) is incorrect. A statement from the owner or operator that the aircraft is airworthy does not ensure that all required maintenance has been performed. Answer (B) is incorrect. A log book endorsement from a flight instructor does not give any assurance that the aircraft has received required maintenance, and it is not required for determining airworthiness.

91.519 Passenger Briefings

196. The party directly responsible for the pre-takeoff briefing of passengers is the

A. pilot in command.

B. safety officer.

C. ground crew.

Answer (A) is correct. *(14 CFR 91.519)*

DISCUSSION: Before each takeoff, the pilot in command of an airplane carrying passengers shall ensure that all passengers have been orally briefed on smoking, the use of safety belts and shoulder harnesses, location and means of opening a passenger door as a means of emergency exit, location of survival equipment, ditching procedures and the use of the flotation equipment, and the normal and emergency use of oxygen equipment if installed in the airplane.

Answer (B) is incorrect. Passenger briefings are the responsibility of the pilot in command, not a safety officer. Answer (C) is incorrect. Passenger briefings are the responsibility of the pilot in command, not the ground crew.

197. Pre-takeoff briefing of passengers for a flight is the responsibility of

A. all passengers.

B. the pilot.

C. a crewmember.

Answer (B) is correct. *(14 CFR 91.519)*

DISCUSSION: Before each takeoff, the pilot in command of an airplane carrying passengers shall ensure that all passengers have been orally briefed on smoking, the use of safety belts and shoulder harnesses, location and means of opening a passenger door as a means of emergency exit, location of survival equipment, ditching procedures and the use of the flotation equipment, and the normal and emergency use of oxygen equipment if installed in the airplane.

Answer (A) is incorrect. It is the responsibility of the pilot in command to brief the passengers; passengers cannot self-brief. Answer (C) is incorrect. A pilot in command can delegate the role of the pre-takeoff briefing to a crew member, but (s)he is ultimately the one responsible for ensuring the briefing has been completed.

198. Pre-takeoff briefing of passengers about the use of seat belts is the responsibility of

A. all passengers.

B. the pilot.

C. a crewmember.

Answer (B) is correct. *(14 CFR 91.519)*

DISCUSSION: Before each takeoff, the pilot in command of an airplane carrying passengers shall ensure that all passengers have been orally briefed on smoking, the use of safety belts and shoulder harnesses, location and means of opening a passenger door as a means of emergency exit, location of survival equipment, ditching procedures and the use of the flotation equipment, and the normal and emergency use of oxygen equipment if installed in the airplane.

Answer (A) is incorrect. It is the responsibility of the pilot in command to brief the passengers; passengers cannot self-brief. Answer (C) is incorrect. A pilot in command can delegate the role of the pre-takeoff briefing to a crew member, but (s)he is ultimately the one responsible for ensuring the briefing has been completed.

4.11 NTSB Part 830

830.5 Immediate Notification

199. If an aircraft is involved in an accident which results in substantial damage to the aircraft, the nearest NTSB field office should be notified

A. immediately.

B. within 48 hours.

C. within 7 days.

Answer (A) is correct. *(NTSB 830.5)*

DISCUSSION: The NTSB must be notified immediately and by the most expeditious means possible when an aircraft accident or any of various listed incidents occurs or when an aircraft is overdue and is believed to have been in an accident.

Answer (B) is incorrect. An aircraft involved in an accident must be reported immediately (not within 48 hr.) to the NTSB office. Answer (C) is incorrect. An aircraft accident must be reported immediately (not within 7 days) to the nearest NTSB office.

200. Which incident would necessitate an immediate notification to the nearest NTSB field office?

A. An in-flight generator/alternator failure.

B. An in-flight fire.

C. An in-flight loss of VOR receiver capability.

Answer (B) is correct. *(NTSB 830.5)*

DISCUSSION: The NTSB must be notified immediately and by the most expeditious means possible when an aircraft accident or any of various listed incidents occurs or when an aircraft is overdue and believed to have been in an accident. The following are considered incidents:

1. Flight control system malfunction or failure;
2. Inability of any required flight crewmember to perform normal flight duties as a result of injury or illness;
3. Failure of structural components of a turbine engine, excluding compressor and turbine blades and vanes;
4. In-flight fire; or
5. Aircraft collision in flight.

Answer (A) is incorrect. An in-flight generator/alternator failure does not require immediate notification. Answer (C) is incorrect. An in-flight loss of VOR receiver capability does not require any type of notification to the NTSB.

201. Which incident requires an immediate notification be made to the nearest NTSB field office?

A. An overdue aircraft that is believed to be involved in an accident.

B. An in-flight radio communications failure.

C. An in-flight generator or alternator failure.

Answer (A) is correct. *(NTSB 830.5)*

DISCUSSION: The NTSB must be notified immediately and by the most expeditious means possible when an aircraft is overdue and is believed to have been involved in an accident.

Answer (B) is incorrect. An in-flight radio communications failure does not require notification to the NTSB at any time. Answer (C) is incorrect. An in-flight generator or alternator failure does not require notification to the NTSB at any time.

202. Which incident requires an immediate notification to the nearest NTSB field office?

A. A forced landing due to engine failure.

B. Landing gear damage, due to a hard landing.

C. Flight control system malfunction or failure.

Answer (C) is correct. *(NTSB 830.5)*

DISCUSSION: The NTSB must be notified immediately and by the most expeditious means possible when an aircraft accident or any of various listed incidents occurs or when an aircraft is overdue and believed to have been in an accident. The following are considered incidents:

1. Flight control system malfunction or failure;
2. Inability of any required flight crewmember to perform normal flight duties as a result of injury or illness;
3. Failure of structural components of a turbine engine, excluding compressor and turbine blades and vanes;
4. In-flight fire; or
5. Aircraft collision in flight.

Answer (A) is incorrect. Only failure of structural components of a turbine engine (not a forced landing due to engine failure) must be reported immediately to the nearest NTSB office. Answer (B) is incorrect. Landing gear damage due to a hard landing is not considered an incident that requires immediate notification to the NTSB.

830.10 Preservation of Aircraft Wreckage, Mail, Cargo, and Records

203. May aircraft wreckage be moved prior to the time the NTSB takes custody?

A. Yes, but only if moved by a federal, state, or local law enforcement officer.

B. Yes, but only to protect the wreckage from further damage.

C. No, it may not be moved under any circumstances.

Answer (B) is correct. *(NTSB 830.10)*

DISCUSSION: Prior to the time the Board or its authorized representative takes custody of aircraft wreckage, mail, or cargo, such wreckage, mail, or cargo may not be disturbed or moved except to the extent necessary to

1. Remove persons injured or trapped,
2. Protect the wreckage from further damage, or
3. Protect the public from injury.

Answer (A) is incorrect. Aircraft wreckage can only be moved to protect the wreckage from further damage, protect the public from injury, or remove persons injured or trapped, not by any federal, state, or local law enforcement officer. Answer (C) is incorrect. Aircraft wreckage may be moved in certain circumstances, such as to remove persons injured or trapped, to protect the wreckage from further damage, or to protect the public from injury.

830.15 Reports and Statements to Be Filed

204. The operator of an aircraft that has been involved in an accident is required to file an NTSB accident report within how many days?

A. 5

B. 7

C. 10

Answer (C) is correct. *(NTSB 830.15)*

DISCUSSION: The operator of an aircraft shall file a report on NTSB Form 6120.1/2 within 10 days after an accident, or after 7 days if an overdue aircraft is still missing. A report on an incident for which notification is required shall be filed only as required.

Answer (A) is incorrect. NTSB Form 6120.1/2 is required within 10 (not 5) days after an accident. Answer (B) is incorrect. NTSB Form 6120.1/2 is required within 10 (not 7) days after an accident.

205. The operator of an aircraft that has been involved in an incident is required to submit a report to the nearest field office of the NTSB

A. within 7 days.

B. within 10 days.

C. when requested.

Answer (C) is correct. *(NTSB 830.15)*

DISCUSSION: The operator of an aircraft shall file a report on NTSB Form 6120.1/2 only when requested. A report is required within 10 days of an accident or after 7 days if an overdue aircraft is still missing.

Answer (A) is incorrect. The time allowed to file a written report on an overdue aircraft that is still missing is 7 days; an incident requires a report only when requested. Answer (B) is incorrect. A report must be filed within 10 days of an accident; an incident requires a report only when requested.

END OF STUDY UNIT

STUDY UNIT FIVE
AIRPLANE PERFORMANCE AND WEIGHT AND BALANCE

(15 pages of outline)

This study unit contains outlines of major concepts tested, sample test questions and answers regarding airplane performance and weight and balance, and an explanation of each answer. The table of contents above lists each subunit within this study unit, the number of questions pertaining to that particular subunit, and the pages on which the outlines and questions begin, respectively.

Recall that the **sole purpose** of this book is to expedite your passing of the FAA pilot knowledge test for the private pilot certificate. Accordingly, all extraneous material (i.e., topics or regulations not directly tested on the FAA pilot knowledge test) is omitted, even though much more knowledge is necessary to fly safely. This additional material is presented in *Pilot Handbook* and *Private Pilot Flight Maneuvers and Practical Test Prep*, available from Gleim Publications, Inc. Order online at www.GleimAviation.com.

Many of the topics in this study unit require interpretation of graphs and charts. Graphs and charts pictorially describe the relationship between two or more variables. Thus, they are a substitute for solving one or more equations. Each time you must interpret (i.e., get an answer from) a graph or chart, you should do the following:

1. Understand clearly what is required, e.g., landing roll distance, weight, etc.
2. Analyze the chart or graph to determine the variables involved, including
   a. Labeled sides (axes) of the graph or chart and
   b. Labeled lines within the graph or chart.
3. Plug the data given in the question into the graph or chart.
4. Finally, determine the value of the item required in the question.

5.1 DENSITY ALTITUDE

1. Density altitude is a measurement of the density of the air expressed in terms of altitude.
   a. Air density varies inversely with altitude; i.e., air is very dense at low altitudes and less dense at high altitudes.
   b. Temperature, humidity, and barometric pressure also affect air density.
      1) A scale of air density to altitude has been established using a standard temperature and pressure for each altitude. At sea level, standard is 15°C and 29.92" Hg.
      2) When temperature and pressure are not at standard (which is extremely common), density altitude will not be the same as true altitude.

2. You are required to know how barometric pressure, temperature, and humidity affect density altitude. Visualize the following:
   a. As barometric pressure increases, the air becomes more compressed and compact. This is an increase in density. Air density is higher if the pressure is high, so the density altitude is said to be lower.
      1) Density altitude is increased by a decrease in pressure.
      2) Density altitude is decreased by an increase in pressure.
   b. As temperature increases, the air expands and therefore becomes less dense. This decrease in density means a higher density altitude. Remember, air is normally less dense at higher altitudes.
      1) Density altitude is increased by an increase in temperature.
      2) Density altitude is decreased by a decrease in temperature.
   c. As relative humidity increases, the air becomes less dense. A given volume of moist air weighs less than the same volume of dry air. This decrease in density means a higher density altitude.
      1) Density altitude is increased by an increase in humidity.
      2) Density altitude is decreased by a decrease in humidity.
3. Said another way, density altitude varies directly with temperature and humidity, and inversely with barometric pressure:
   a. Cold, dry air and higher barometric pressure = low density altitude.
   b. Hot, humid air and lower barometric pressure = high density altitude.
4. Pressure altitude is based on standard temperature. Therefore, density altitude will exceed pressure altitude if the temperature is above standard.
5. The primary reason for computing density altitude is to determine airplane performance.
   a. High density altitude reduces an airplane's overall performance.
      1) For example, climb performance is less and takeoff distance is longer.
      2) Propellers have less efficiency because there is less air for the propeller to get a grip on.
   b. However, the same indicated airspeed is used for takeoffs and landings regardless of altitude or air density because the airspeed indicator is also directly affected by air density.

5.2 DENSITY ALTITUDE COMPUTATIONS

1. Density altitude is determined most easily by finding the pressure altitude (indicated altitude when your altimeter is set to 29.92) and adjusting for the temperature.
   a. The adjustment may be made using your flight computer or a density altitude chart. This part of the FAA test requires you to use a density altitude chart.
2. When using a density altitude chart (see Figure 8 at the end of this subunit),
   a. Adjust the airport elevation to pressure altitude by adding or subtracting the conversion factor for the current altimeter setting.
   b. To adjust the pressure altitude for nonstandard temperature, plot the intersection of the actual air temperature (listed on the horizontal axis of the chart) with the pressure altitude lines that slope diagonally upward. Move left horizontally from the intersection to read density altitude on the vertical axis of the chart.

c. EXAMPLE: Outside air temperature 90°F
Altimeter setting 30.20" Hg
Airport elevation 4,725 ft.

Referring to Figure 8, you determine the density altitude to be approximately 7,400 feet. This is found as follows:

1) The altimeter setting of 30.20 requires a –257 altitude correction factor.
2) Subtract 257 from field elevation of 4,725 ft. to obtain pressure altitude of 4,468 ft.
3) Locate 90°F on the bottom axis of the chart and move up to intersect the diagonal pressure altitude line of 4,468 ft.
4) Move horizontally to the left axis of the chart to obtain the density altitude of about 7,400 ft.
5) Note that while true altitude (i.e., airport elevation) is 4,725 ft., density altitude is about 7,400 ft.
6) Finally, note that you may determine the effects of temperature changes on density altitude simply by following the above chart procedure and substituting different temperatures.

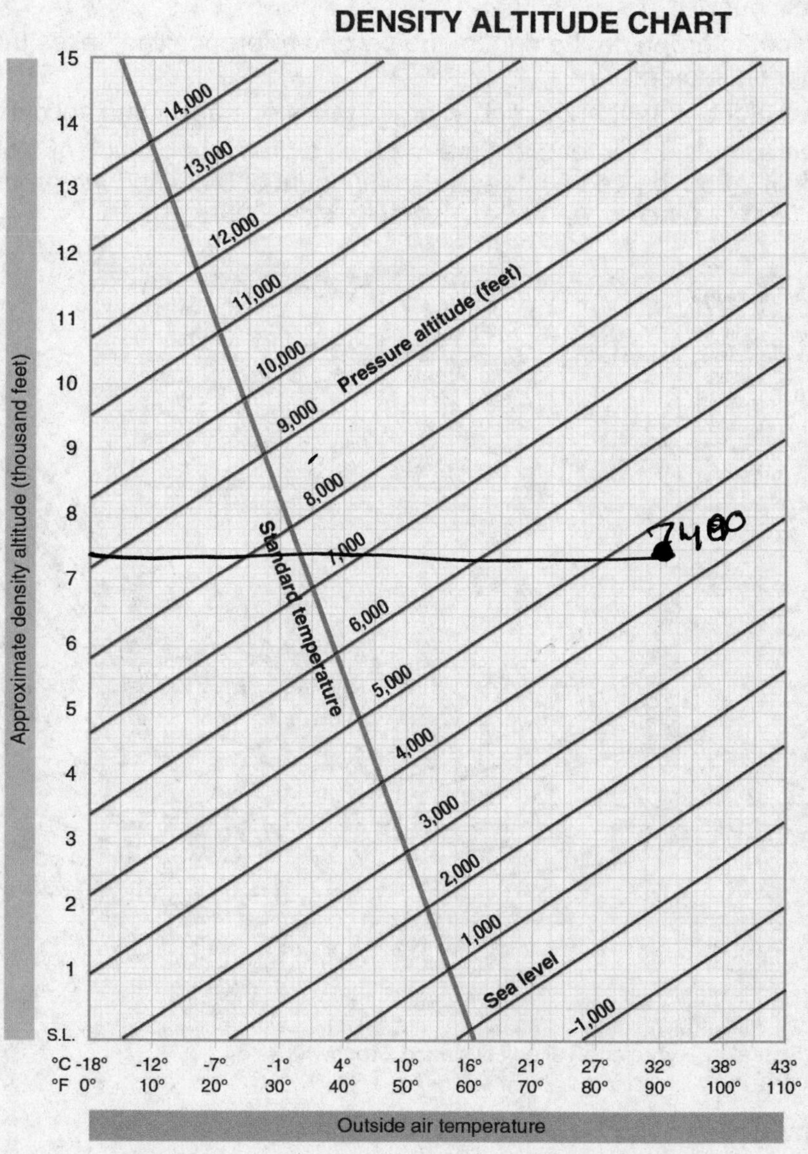

Altimeter setting ("Hg)	Pressure altitude conversion factor
28.0	1,824
28.1	1,727
28.2	1,630
28.3	1,533
28.4	1,436
28.5	1,340
28.6	1,244
28.7	1,148
28.8	1,053
28.9	957
29.0	863
29.1	768
29.2	673
29.3	579
29.4	485
29.5	392
29.6	298
29.7	205
29.8	112
29.9	20
29.92	0
30.0	–73
30.1	–165
30.2	–257
30.3	–348
30.4	–440
30.5	–531
30.6	–622
30.7	–712
30.8	–803
30.9	–893
31.0	–983

Figure 8. – Density Altitude Chart.

5.3 TAKEOFF DISTANCE

1. Conditions that reduce airplane takeoff and climb performance are
   a. High altitude
   b. High temperature
   c. High humidity
2. Takeoff distance performance is displayed in the airplane operating manual either
   a. In chart form or
   b. On a graph
3. If a graph, it is usually presented in terms of density altitude. Thus, one must first adjust the airport elevation for nonstandard pressure and temperature.
   a. In the graph used on this exam (Figure 40 below), the first section on the left uses outside air temperature and pressure altitude to obtain density altitude.
      1) The curved line on the left portion is standard atmosphere, which you use when the question calls for standard temperature.
   b. The second section of the graph, to the right of the first reference line, takes the weight in pounds into account.
   c. The third section of the graph, to the right of the second reference line, takes the headwind or tailwind into account.
   d. The fourth section of the graph, at the right margin, takes obstacles into account.
   e. EXAMPLE: Given an outside air temperature of 15°C, a pressure altitude of 5,650 ft., a takeoff weight of 2,950 lb., and a headwind component of 9 kt., find the ground roll and the total takeoff distance over a 50-ft. obstacle. Use Figure 40.

Example:	
OAT	15 °C (59 °F)
Pressure altitude	5,650 feet
Takeoff weight	2,950 lb
Headwind comp.	9.0 knots
Ground roll	1,375 feet
Total distance over a 50 feet obstacle	2,300 feet
Takeoff speed at	
Lift-off	66 knots (76 mph)
50 feet	72 knots (83 mph)

Associated conditions	
Power	Full throttle 2,600 rpm
Mixture	Lean to appropriate fuel pressure
Flaps	Up
Landing gear	Retract after positive climb established
Cowl flaps	Open

Weight pounds	Takeoff speed			
	Lift-off		50 ft	
	kts	MPH	kts	MPH
2,950	66	76	72	83
2,800	64	74	70	81
2,600	63	72	68	78
2,400	61	70	66	76
2,200	58	67	63	73

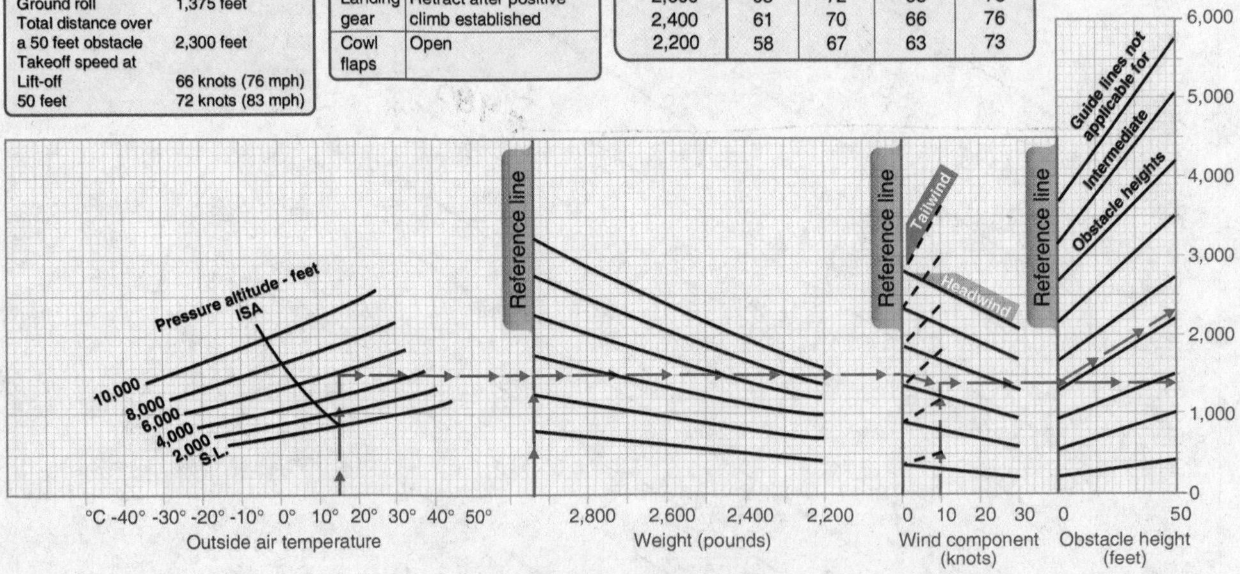

Figure 40. – Airplane Takeoff Distance Graph.

f. The solution to the example problem is marked with the dotted arrows on the graph. Move straight up from 15°C (which is also where the standard temperature line begins) to the pressure altitude of 5,650 ft. and then horizontally to the right to the first reference line. It is not necessary to adjust for weight because the airplane is at maximum weight of 2,950 pounds. Continuing to the next reference line, the headwind component of 9 kt. means an adjustment downward in the wind component section (parallel to the guidelines). Finally, moving straight to the right gives the ground roll of 1,375 feet. The total takeoff distance over a 50-ft. obstacle, following parallel to the guideline up and to the right, is 2,300 feet.

5.4 CRUISE POWER SETTINGS

1. Cruise power settings are found by use of a table (Figure 35 below).
   a. It is based on 65% power.
   b. It consists of three sections to adjust for varying temperatures:
      1) Standard temperature (in middle)
      2) ISA –20°C (on left)
      3) ISA +20°C (on right)
   c. Values found on the table based on various pressure altitudes and temperatures include
      1) Engine RPM
      2) Manifold pressure (in. Hg)
      3) Fuel flow in gal. per hr. (with the expected fuel pressure gauge indication in pounds per square inch)
      4) True airspeed (kt. and MPH)
2. The FAA test questions gauge your ability to find values on the chart and interpolate between lines (Figure 35).
   a. EXAMPLE: A value for 9,500 ft. would be 75% of the distance between the number for 8,000 ft. and the number for 10,000 feet.
   b. EXAMPLE: At a pressure altitude of 6,000 ft. and a temperature of 26°C and with no wind, a 1,000-NM trip would take 71.42 gal. of fuel (1,000 ÷ 161 kt. = 6.21 hr.) (6.21 hr. × 11.5 gph = 71.42 gallons).

Cruise power settings
65% Maximum continuous power (or full throttle 2,800 pounds)

Press ALT.	ISA –20 °C (–36 °F)								Standard day (ISA)								ISA +20 °C (+36 °F)							
	IOAT		Engine speed	MAN. press	Fuel flow per engine		TAS		IOAT		Engine speed	MAN. press	Fuel flow per engine		TAS		IOAT		Engine speed	MAN. press	Fuel flow per engine		TAS	
Feet	°F	°C	RPM	IN HG	PSI	GPH	KTS	MPH	°F	°C	RPM	IN HG	PSI	GPH	KTS	MPH	°F	°C	RPM	IN HG	PSI	GPH	KTS	MPH
SL	27	–3	2,450	20.7	6.6	11.5	147	169	63	17	2,450	21.2	6.6	11.5	150	173	99	37	2,450	21.8	6.6	11.5	153	176
2,000	19	–7	2,450	20.4	6.6	11.5	149	171	55	13	2,450	21.0	6.6	11.5	153	176	91	33	2,450	21.5	6.6	11.5	156	180
4,000	12	–11	2,450	20.1	6.6	11.5	152	175	48	9	2,450	20.7	6.6	11.5	156	180	84	29	2,450	21.3	6.6	11.5	159	183
6,000	5	–15	2,450	19.8	6.6	11.5	155	178	41	5	2,450	20.4	6.6	11.5	158	182	79	26	2,450	21.0	6.6	11.5	161	185
8,000	–2	–19	2,450	19.5	6.6	11.5	157	181	36	2	2,450	20.2	6.6	11.5	161	185	72	22	2,450	20.8	6.6	11.5	164	189
10,000	–8	–22	2,450	19.2	6.6	11.5	160	184	28	–2	2,450	19.9	6.6	11.5	163	188	64	18	2,450	20.3	6.5	11.4	166	191
12,000	–15	–26	2,450	18.8	6.4	11.5	162	186	21	–6	2,450	18.8	6.1	10.9	163	188	57	14	2,450	18.8	5.9	10.6	163	188
14,000	–22	–30	2,450	17.4	5.8	10.5	159	183	14	–10	2,450	17.4	5.6	10.1	160	184	50	10	2,450	17.4	5.4	9.8	160	184
16,000	–29	–34	2,450	16.1	5.3	9.7	156	180	7	–14	2,450	16.1	5.1	9.4	156	180	43	6	2,450	16.1	4.9	9.1	155	178

Note: 1. Full throttle manifold pressure settings are approximate.
2. Shaded area represents operation with full throttle.

Figure 35. – Airplane Power Setting Table.

5.5 CROSSWIND COMPONENTS

1. Airplanes have a limit to the amount of direct crosswind in which they can land. When the wind is not directly across the runway (i.e., quartering), a crosswind component chart may be used to determine the amount of direct crosswind. Variables on the crosswind component charts are
   a. Angle between wind and runway
   b. Wind velocity

   NOTE: The coordinates on the vertical and horizontal axes of the graph will indicate the headwind and crosswind components of a quartering wind.
2. Refer to the crosswind component graph, which is Figure 36 below.
   a. Note the example on the chart of a 40-kt. wind at a 30° angle.
   b. Find the 30° wind angle line. This is the angle between the wind direction and runway direction, e.g., runway 18 and wind from 210°.
   c. Find the 40-kt. wind velocity arc. Note the intersection of the wind arc and the 30° angle line.
      1) Drop straight down to determine the crosswind component of 20 kt.; i.e., landing in this situation would be like having a direct crosswind of 20 knots.

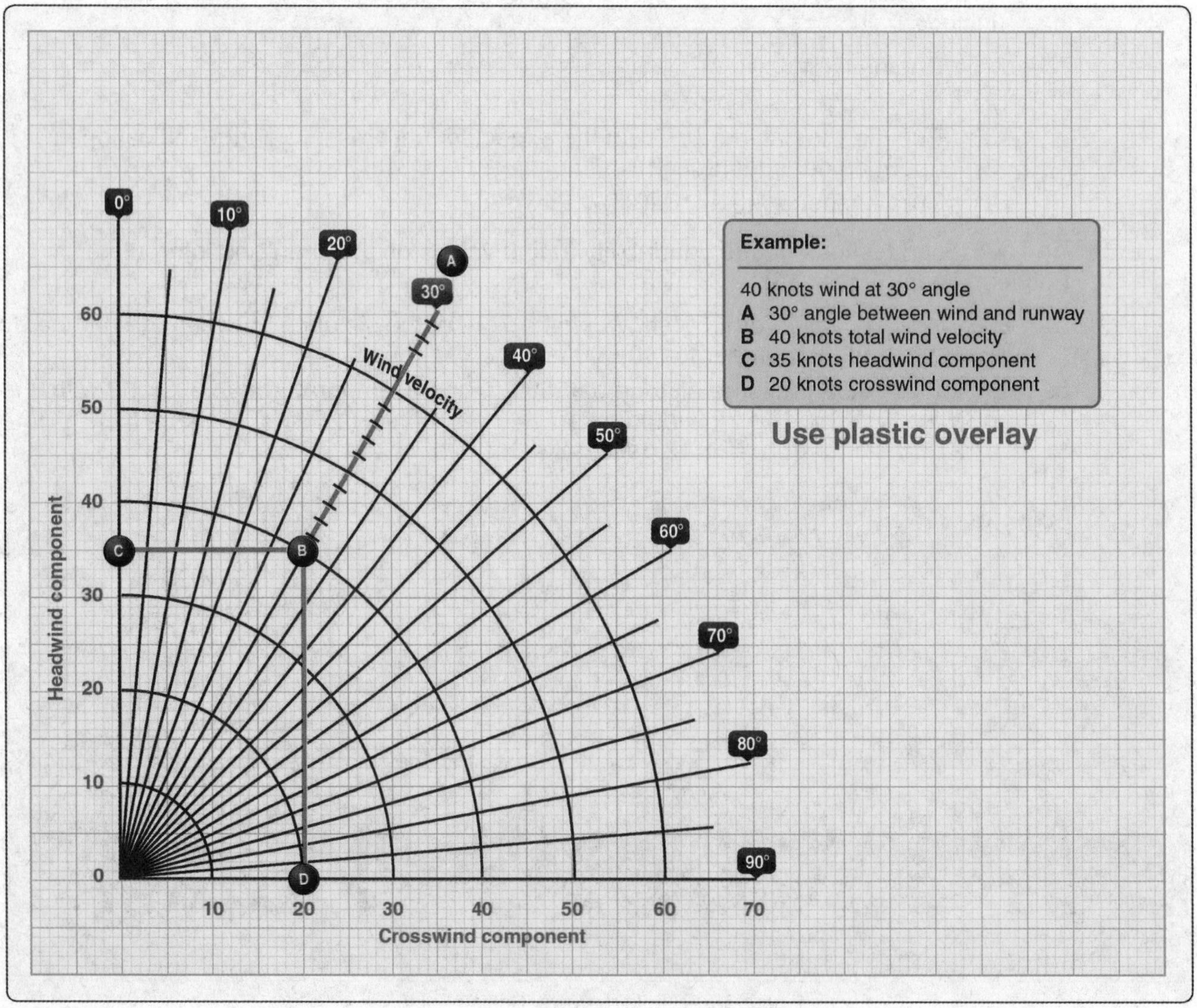

Figure 36. – Crosswind Component Graph.

2) Move horizontally to the left to determine the headwind component of 35 kt.; i.e., landing in this situation would be like having a headwind of 35 knots.

3) EXAMPLE: You have been given 20 kt. as the maximum crosswind component for the airplane, and the angle between the runway and the wind is 30°. What is the maximum wind velocity without exceeding the 20-kt. crosswind component? Find where the 20-kt. crosswind line from the bottom of the chart crosses the 30° angle line, and note that it intersects the 40-kt. wind velocity line. This means you can land an airplane with a 20-kt. maximum crosswind component in a 40-kt. wind from a 30° angle to the runway.

5.6 LANDING DISTANCE

1. Required landing distances differ at various altitudes and temperatures due to changes in air density.
   a. However, indicated airspeed for landing is the same at all altitudes.
2. Landing distance information is given in airplane operating manuals in chart or graph form to adjust for headwind, temperature, and dry grass runways.
3. If an emergency situation requires a downwind landing, pilots should expect a higher groundspeed at touchdown, a longer ground roll, and the likelihood of overshooting the desired touchdown point.
4. It is imperative that you distinguish between distances for clearing a 50-ft. obstacle and distances without a 50-ft. obstacle at the beginning of the runway (the latter is described as the ground roll).
5. See Figure 37 below for an example landing distance graph. It is used in the same manner as the takeoff distance graph (Figure 40) discussed and displayed beginning on page 176.

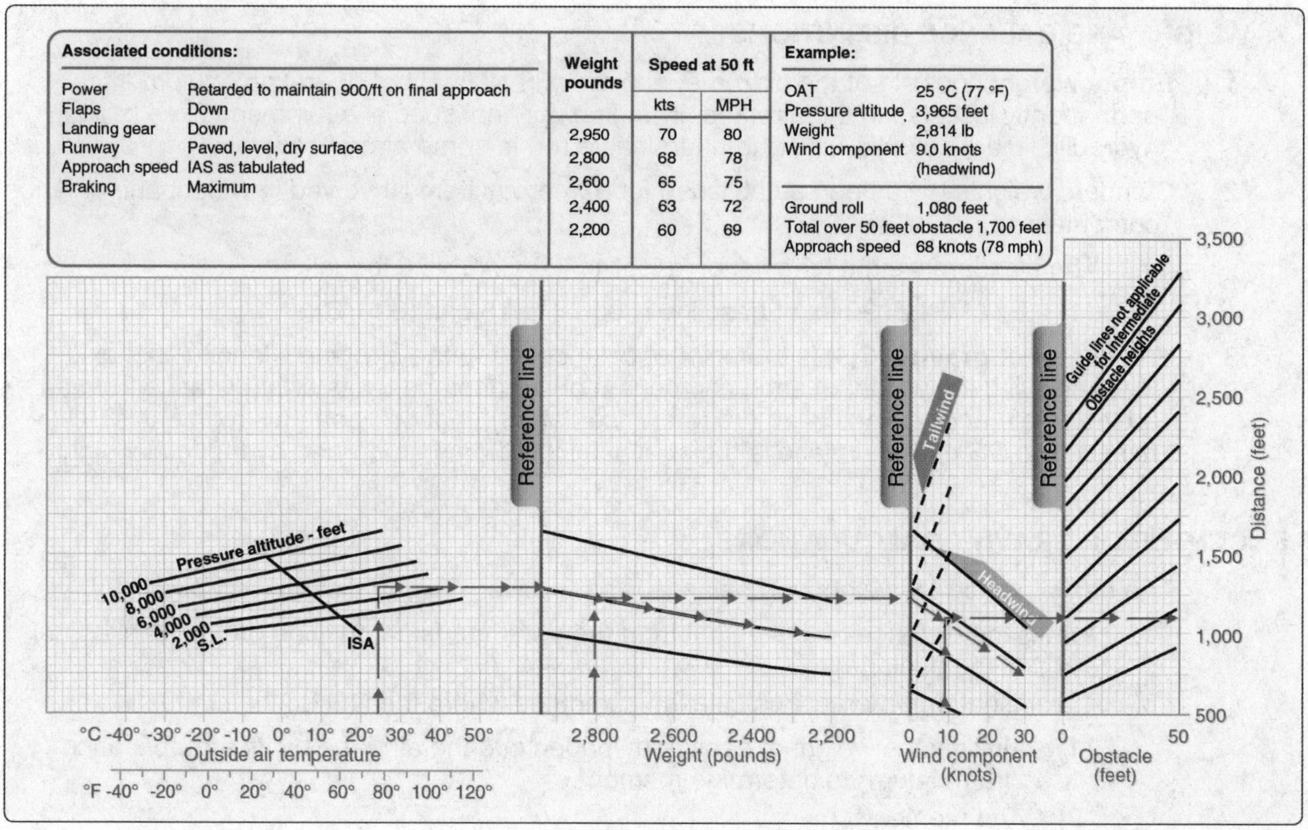

Figure 37. – Airplane Landing Distance Graph.

6. Refer to Figure 38 below, which is a landing distance table.
   a. It has been computed for landing with no wind, at standard temperature, and at pressure altitude.
   b. The bottom "notes" tell you how to adjust for wind, nonstandard temperature, and a grass runway.
      1) Note 1 says to decrease the distance for a headwind. Note that tailwind hurts much more than headwind helps, so you cannot use the headwind formula in reverse.
   c. EXAMPLE: Given standard air temperature, 8-kt. headwind, and pressure altitude of 2,500 ft., find both the ground roll and the landing distance to clear a 50-ft. obstacle.
      1) On the table (Figure 38) for 2,500 ft., at standard temperature with no wind, the ground roll is 470 ft., and the distance to clear a 50-ft. obstacle is 1,135 feet. These amounts must be decreased by 20% because of the headwind (8 kt. ÷ 4 × 10% = 20%). Therefore, the ground roll is 376 ft. (470 × 80%) and the distance to clear a 50-ft. obstacle is 908 ft. (1,135 × 80%).

Landing distance									Flaps lowered to 40° – Power off Hard surface runway – Zero wind
Gross weight lb	Approach speed, IAS, MPH	At sea level & 59 °F		At 2,500 feet & 50 °F		At 5,000 feet & 41 °F		At 7,500 feet & 32 °F	
		Ground roll	Total to clear 50 feet OBS	Ground roll	Total to clear 50 feet OBS	Ground roll	Total to clear 50 feet OBS	Ground roll	Total to clear 50 feet OBS
1,600	60	445	1,075	470	1,135	495	1,195	520	1,255

NOTE:
1. Decrease the distances shown by 10% for each 4 knots of headwind.
2. Increase the distance by 10% for each 60 °F temperature increase above standard.
3. For operation on a dry, grass runway, increase distance (both "ground roll" and "total to clear 50 feet obstacle") by 20% of the "total to clear 50 feet obstacle" figure.

Figure 38. – Airplane Landing Distance Table.

5.7 WEIGHT AND BALANCE DEFINITIONS

1. **Empty weight** consists of the airframe, engine, and all items of operating equipment permanently installed in the airplane, including optional special equipment, fixed ballast, hydraulic fluid, unusable fuel, and undrainable (or, in some aircraft, all) oil.
2. Standard weights have been established for numerous items involved in weight and balance computations.
   a. The standard weight for aviation gasoline (AVGAS) is 6 lb./gallon.
      1) EXAMPLE: 90 lb. of gasoline is equal to 15 gal. (90 ÷ 6).
3. The **center of gravity** (CG) is the point of balance along the airplane's longitudinal axis. By multiplying the weight of each component of the airplane by its arm (distance from an arbitrary reference point, called the reference datum), that component's moment is determined. The CG of the airplane is the sum of all the moments divided by the total weight.

5.8 CENTER OF GRAVITY CALCULATIONS

1. The basic formula for weight and balance is as follows: *Weight* × *Arm* = *Moment*
   a. Arm is the distance of the weight from the datum (a fixed position on the longitudinal axis of the airplane).
   b. The weight/arm/moment calculation computes where the CG is.
      1) Multiply the weight of each item loaded into the airplane by its arm (distance from datum) to determine moment.
      2) Add moments.
      3) Divide total moments by total weight to obtain CG (expressed in distance from the datum).

c. EXAMPLE: You have items A, B, and C in the airplane. Note the airplane's empty weight is given as 1,500 lb. with a 20-in. arm.

	Weight		Arm		Moment
Empty airplane	1,500	×	20	=	30,000
A (pilot and passenger)	300	×	25	=	7,500
B (25 gal. of fuel × 6 lb./gal.)	150	×	30	=	4,500
C (baggage)	100	×	40	=	4,000
	2,050				46,000

The total loaded weight of the airplane is 2,050 pounds. Take the total moments of 46,000 lb.-in. divided by the total weight of 2,050 lb. to obtain the CG of 22.44 inches.

The weight and CG are then checked to see whether they are within allowable limits.

2. The moment of an object is a measure of the force that causes a tendency of the object to rotate about a point or axis. It is usually expressed in pound-inches. In the following figures, assume that a weight of 50 lb. is placed on the board at a point (station) 100 in. from the datum (fulcrum). The downward force of the weight at that spot can be determined by multiplying 50 lb. by 100 in., which produces a moment of 5,000 pound-inches.

   a. To establish a balance, a total moment of 5,000 lb.-in. must be applied to the other end of the board. Any combination of weight and distance that, when multiplied, produces 5,000 lb.-in. moment to the left of the datum will balance the board.

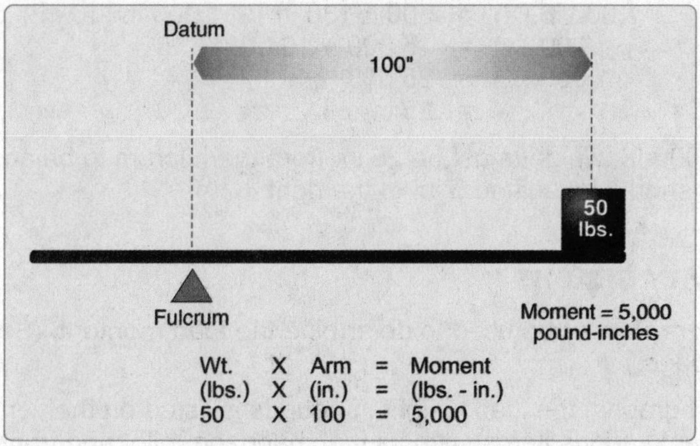

   b. If a 100-lb. weight is placed at a point (station) 25 in. on the other side of the datum, and a second 50-lb. weight is placed at a point (station) 50 in. on the other side of the datum, the sum of the products of these two weights and their distances will total a moment of 5,000 lb.-in., which will balance the board. (See the figure below.)

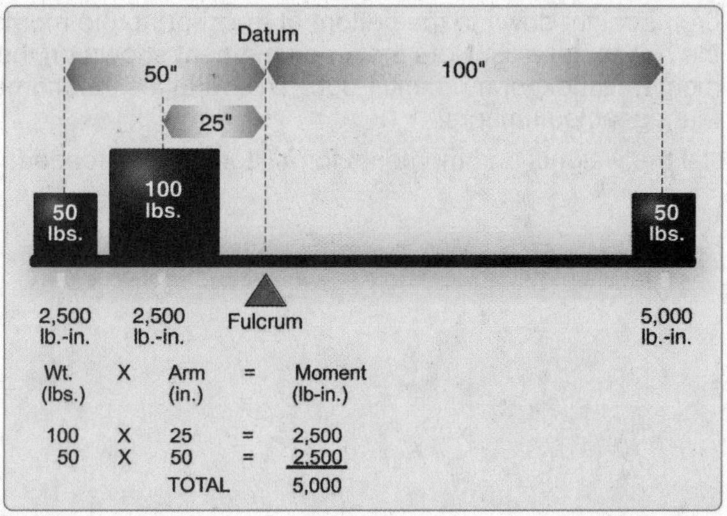

3. When asked to balance the plank on the fulcrum, compute and sum the moments left and right. Then set left and right equal to each other and solve for the desired variable.

   a. EXAMPLE: How should the 1,000-lb. weight in the following diagram be shifted to balance the plank on the fulcrum?

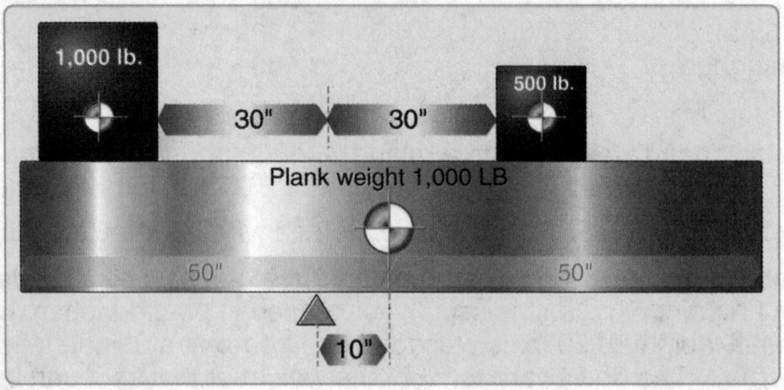

Compute and sum the moments left and right. Note that the plank itself weighs 1,000 lb. and that its CG is 10 in. right of the fulcrum. Set them equal to one another and solve for the desired variable:

$$\begin{aligned} \text{Left} &= \text{Right} \\ 1{,}000\text{ lb.}(X) &= 500\text{ lb.}(30\text{ in.}) + 1{,}000\text{ lb.}(10\text{ in.}) \\ 1{,}000\ (X) &= 15{,}000 + 10{,}000 \\ 1{,}000\ (X) &= 25{,}000 \\ X &= 25\text{ in.} \end{aligned}$$

The 1,000-lb. weight must be 25 in. from the fulcrum to balance the plank. Thus, the weight should be shifted 5 in. to the right.

5.9 CENTER OF GRAVITY GRAPHS

1. The **loading graph** may be used to determine the load moment. (See top graph in Figure 34 on the next page.)

   a. On most graphs, the load weight in pounds is listed on the vertical axis. Diagonal lines represent various items such as fuel, baggage, pilot and front seat passengers, and back seat passengers.

      1) Move horizontally to the right across the chart from the amount of weight to intersect the line that represents the particular item.
      2) From the point of intersection of the weight with the appropriate diagonal line, drop straight down to the bottom of the chart to the moments displayed on the horizontal axis. Note that each moment shown on the graph is actually a moment index, or moment/1,000. This reduces the moments to smaller, more manageable numbers.

   b. Then total the weights and moments for all items being loaded.

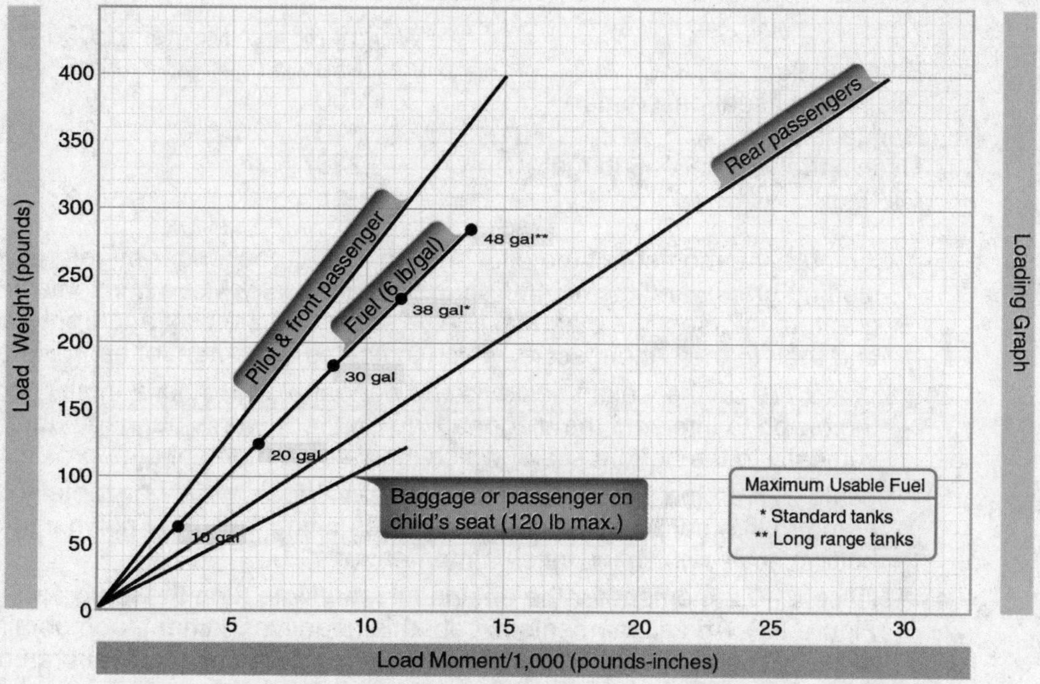

Notes: 1. Lines representing adjustable seats show the pilot or passenger center of gravity on adjustable seats positioned for an average occupant. Refer to the Loading Arrangements diagram for forward and aft limits of occupant CG range.

2. Engine Oil: 8 qt = 15 lb at −0.2 Moment/1,000

Note: The empty weight of this airplane does not include the weight of the oil.

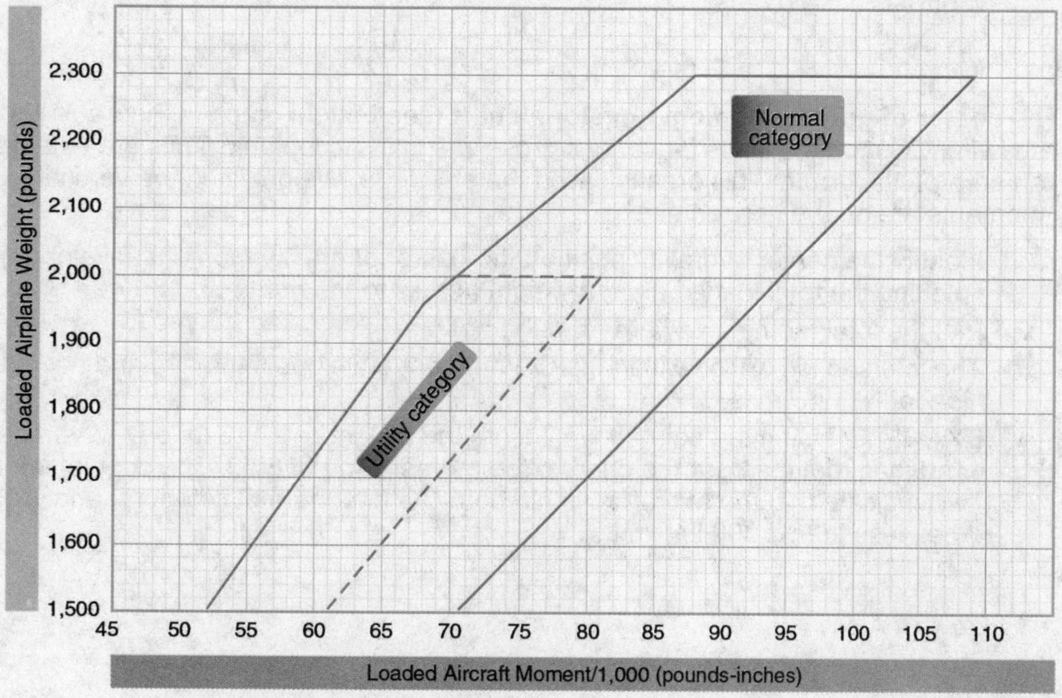

Figure 34. – Airplane Weight and Balance Graphs.

c. EXAMPLE: Determine the load (total) moment/1,000 in the following situation:

	Weight (lb.)	Moment/1,000 (lb.-in.)
Empty weight	1,350	51.5
Pilot & front seat passenger	400	?
Baggage	120	?
Usable fuel (38 gal. × 6 lb./gal.)	228	?
Oil (8 qt.)	15	–0.2

1) Compute the moment of the pilot and front seat passenger by referring to the loading graph, and locate 400 on the weight scale. Move horizontally across the graph to intersect the diagonal line representing the pilot and front passenger, and then to the bottom scale, which indicates a moment of approximately 15.0.
2) Locate 120 on the weight scale for the baggage. Move horizontally across the graph to intersect the diagonal line that represents baggage, then down vertically to the bottom scale, which indicates a moment of approximately 11.5.
3) Locate 228 on the weight scale for the usable fuel. Move horizontally across the graph to intersect the diagonal line representing fuel, then down vertically to the bottom scale, which indicates a moment of 11.0.
4) Notice a –0.2 moment for the engine oil (see Note 2 on the top graph in Figure 34). Add all moments except this negative moment, and obtain a total of 89.0. Then subtract the negative moment to obtain a total aircraft moment of 88.8.

d. Now add all the weights to determine that the airplane's maximum gross weight is not exceeded.

	Weight (lb.)	Moment/1,000 (lb.-in.)
Empty weight	1,350	51.5
Pilot & passengers	400	15.0
Baggage	120	11.5
Fuel	228	11.0
Oil	15	–0.2
	2,113	88.8

2. The **center of gravity moment envelope chart** (see bottom graph in Figure 34) is a graph showing CG moment limits for various gross weights. Acceptable limits are established as an area on the graph. This area is called the envelope. Weight is on the vertical axis, and moments are on the horizontal axis.
   a. Identify the center of gravity point on the center of gravity moment envelope graph by plotting the total loaded aircraft weight across to the right.
   b. Plot the total moment upward from the bottom.
   c. The intersection will be within the CG moment envelope if the airplane has been loaded within limits.
   d. EXAMPLE: Using the data above, locate the weight of 2,113 lb. on the vertical axis, and then move across the chart to the moment line of 88.8. The point of intersection will indicate that the aircraft is within both CG (i.e., normal category) and gross weight (i.e., less than 2,300 lb.) limits.

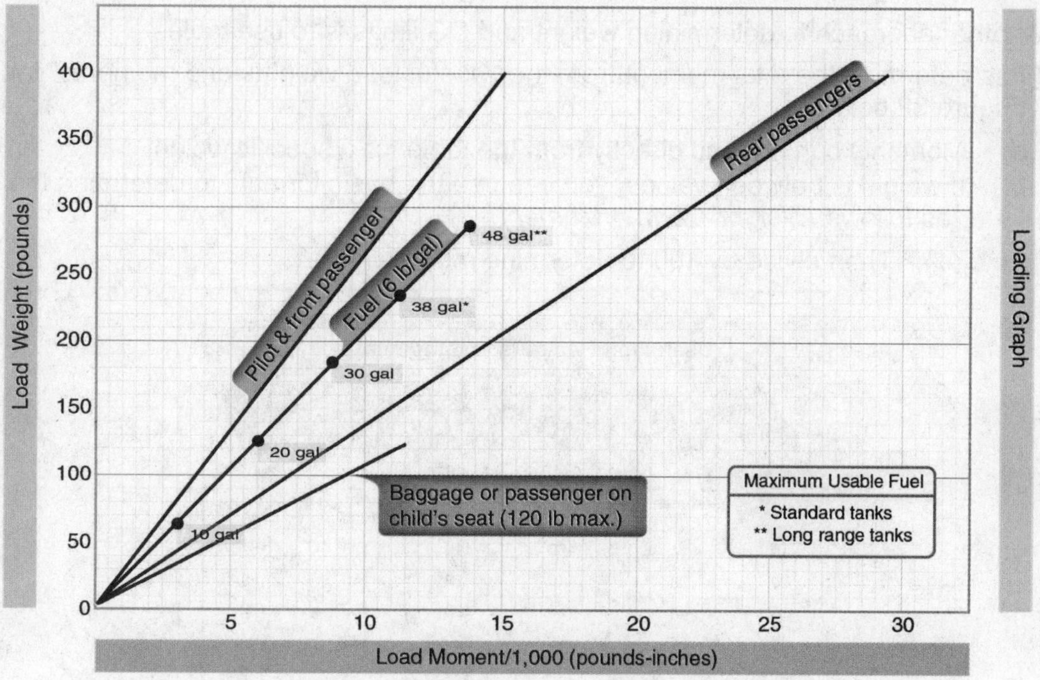

Notes: 1. Lines representing adjustable seats show the pilot or passenger center of gravity on adjustable seats positioned for an average occupant. Refer to the Loading Arrangements diagram for forward and aft limits of occupant CG range.

2. Engine Oil: 8 qt = 15 lb at −0.2 Moment/1,000

Note: The empty weight of this airplane ***does not include*** *the weight of the oil.*

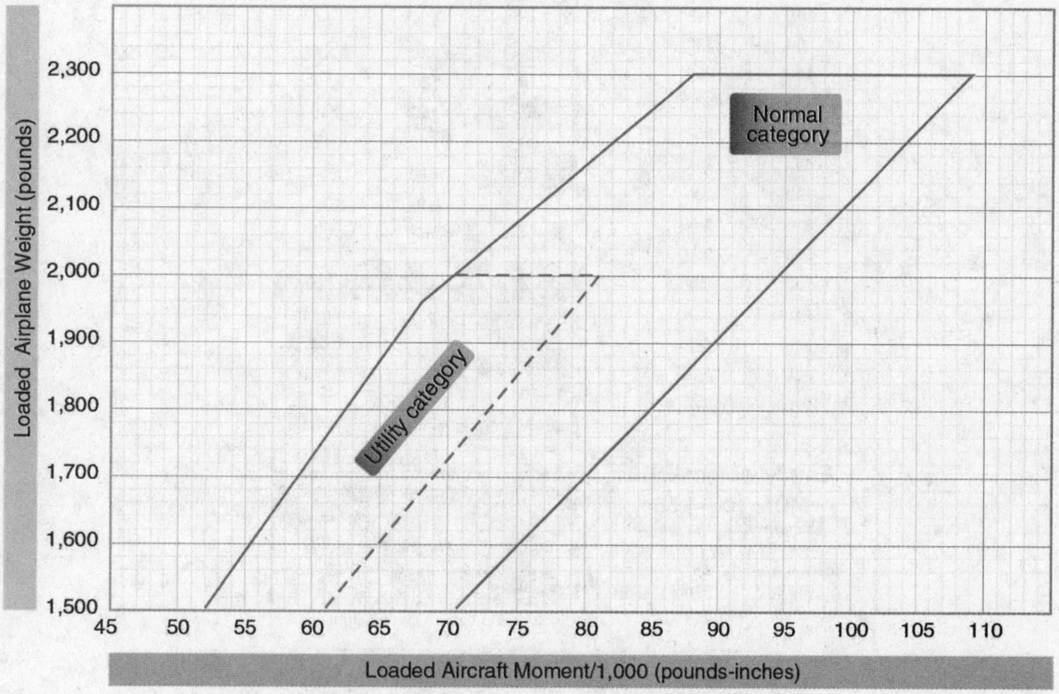

Figure 34. – Airplane Weight and Balance Graphs.

5.10 CENTER OF GRAVITY TABLES

1. Another approach to determining weight and CG limits is to use tables.
2. First, determine the total moment from the "Useful load weights and moments" table (Figure 32 below).
   a. Moments can be read directly from the table for a specific weight.
   b. If weight is between values, you can use the basic formula to determine the moment as follows: *Weight × Arm = Moment*.
      1) Then divide by 100 to determine moment/100.

Useful load weights and moments

Baggage or 5th seat occupant — ARM 140

Weight	Moment/100
10	14
20	28
30	42
40	56
50	70
60	84
70	98
80	112
90	126
100	140
110	154
120	168
130	182
140	196
150	210
160	224
170	238
180	252
190	266
200	280
210	294
220	308
230	322
240	336
250	350
260	364
270	378

Occupants

Front seats ARM 85		Rear seats ARM 121	
Weight	Moment/100	Weight	Moment/100
120	102	120	145
130	110	130	157
140	119	140	169
150	128	150	182
160	136	160	194
170	144	170	206
180	153	180	218
190	162	190	230
200	170	200	242

Usable fuel — Main wing tanks ARM 75

Gallons	Weight	Moment/100
5	30	22
10	60	45
15	90	68
20	120	90
25	150	112
30	180	135
35	210	158
40	240	180
44	264	198

Auxiliary wing tanks ARM 94

Gallons	Weight	Moment/100
5	30	28
10	60	56
15	90	85
19	114	107

*Oil

Quarts	Weight	Moment/100
10	19	5

*Included in basic empty weight.

Empty weight~2,015
MOM/100~1,554

Moment limits vs weight
Moment limits are based on the following weight and center of gravity limit data (landing gear down).

Weight condition	Forward CG limit	AFT CG limit
2,950 lb (takeoff or landing)	82.1	84.7
2,525 lb	77.5	85.7
2,475 lb or less	77.0	85.7

Figure 32. – Airplane Weight and Balance Tables.

3. Then use the "Moment limits vs weight" table (Figure 33 below) to see if the total moment is within maximum and minimum limits for the gross weight.

Moment limits vs weight (continued)

Weight	Minimum Moment/100	Maximum Moment/100	Weight	Minimum Moment/100	Maximum Moment/100
2,100	1,617	1,800	2,500	1,932	2,143
2,110	1,625	1,808	2,510	1,942	2,151
2,120	1,632	1,817	2,520	1,953	2,160
2,130	1,640	1,825	2,530	1,963	2,168
2,140	1,648	1,834	2,540	1,974	2,176
2,150	1,656	1,843	2,550	1,984	2,184
2,160	1,663	1,851	2,560	1,995	2,192
2,170	1,671	1,860	2,570	2,005	2,200
2,180	1,679	1,868	2,580	2,016	2,208
2,190	1,686	1,877	2,590	2,026	2,216
2,200	1,694	1,885	2,600	2,037	2,224
2,210	1,702	1,894	2,610	2,048	2,232
2,220	1,709	1,903	2,620	2,058	2,239
2,230	1,717	1,911	2,630	2,069	2,247
2,240	1,725	1,920	2,640	2,080	2,255
2,250	1,733	1,928	2,650	2,090	2,263
2,260	1,740	1,937	2,660	2,101	2,271
2,270	1,748	1,945	2,670	2,112	2,279
2,280	1,756	1,954	2,680	2,123	2,287
2,290	1,763	1,963	2,690	2,133	2,295
2,300	1,771	1,971	2,700	2,144	2,303
2,310	1,779	1,980	2,710	2,155	2,311
2,320	1,786	1,988	2,720	2,166	2,319
2,330	1,794	1,997	2,730	2,177	2,326
2,340	1,802	2,005	2,740	2,188	2,334
2,350	1,810	2,014	2,750	2,199	2,342
2,360	1,817	2,023	2,760	2,210	2,350
2,370	1,825	2,031	2,770	2,221	2,358
2,380	1,833	2,040	2,780	2,232	2,366
2,390	1,840	2,048	2,790	2,243	2,374
2,400	1,848	2,057	2,800	2,254	2,381
2,410	1,856	2,065	2,810	2,265	2,389
2,420	1,863	2,074	2,820	2,276	2,397
2,430	1,871	2,083	2,830	2,287	2,405
2,440	1,879	2,091	2,840	2,298	2,413
2,450	1,887	2,100	2,850	2,309	2,421
2,460	1,894	2,108	2,860	2,320	2,428
2,470	1,902	2,117	2,870	2,332	2,436
2,480	1,911	2,125	2,880	2,343	2,444
2,490	1,921	2,134	2,890	2,354	2,452
			2,900	2,365	2,460
			2,910	2,377	2,468
			2,920	2,388	2,475
			2,930	2,399	2,483
			2,940	2,411	2,491
			2,950	2,422	2,499

Figure 33. – Airplane Weight and Balance Tables.

QUESTIONS AND ANSWER EXPLANATIONS: All of the private pilot knowledge test questions chosen by the FAA for release as well as additional questions selected by Gleim relating to the material in the previous outlines are reproduced on the following pages. These questions have been organized into the same subunits as the outlines. To the immediate right of each question are the correct answer and answer explanation. You should cover these answers and answer explanations while responding to the questions. Refer to the general discussion in the Introduction on how to take the FAA knowledge test.

Remember that the questions from the FAA knowledge test bank have been reordered by topic and organized into a meaningful sequence. Also, the first line of the answer explanation gives the citation of the authoritative source for the answer.

QUESTIONS

5.1 Density Altitude

1. What are the standard temperature and pressure values for sea level?

A. 15°C and 29.92" Hg.

B. 59°C and 1013.2 millibars.

C. 59°F and 29.92 millibars.

Answer (A) is correct. *(PHAK Chap 12)*

DISCUSSION: The standard temperature and pressure values for sea level are 15°C and 29.92" Hg. This is equivalent to 59°F and 1013.2 millibars of mercury.

Answer (B) is incorrect. Standard temperature is 59°F (not 59°C). Answer (C) is incorrect. Standard pressure is 29.92" Hg (not 29.92 millibars).

2. What effect, if any, does high humidity have on aircraft performance?

A. It increases performance.

B. It decreases performance.

C. It has no effect on performance.

Answer (B) is correct. *(PHAK Chap 11)*

DISCUSSION: As the air becomes more humid, it becomes less dense. This is because a given volume of moist air weighs less than the same volume of dry air. Less dense air reduces aircraft performance.

Answer (A) is incorrect. High humidity reduces (not increases) performance. Answer (C) is incorrect. The three factors that affect aircraft performance are pressure, temperature, and humidity.

3. Which factor would tend to increase the density altitude at a given airport?

A. An increase in barometric pressure.

B. An increase in ambient temperature.

C. A decrease in relative humidity.

Answer (B) is correct. *(AvW Chap 3)*

DISCUSSION: When air temperature increases, density altitude increases because, at a higher temperature, the air is less dense.

Answer (A) is incorrect. Density altitude decreases as barometric pressure increases. Answer (C) is incorrect. Density altitude decreases as relative humidity decreases.

4. What effect does high density altitude, as compared to low density altitude, have on propeller efficiency and why?

A. Efficiency is increased due to less friction on the propeller blades.

B. Efficiency is reduced because the propeller exerts less force at high density altitudes than at low density altitudes.

C. Efficiency is reduced due to the increased force of the propeller in the thinner air.

Answer (B) is correct. *(AvW Chap 3)*

DISCUSSION: The propeller produces thrust in proportion to the mass of air being accelerated through the rotating propeller. If the air is less dense, the propeller efficiency is decreased. Remember, higher density altitude refers to less dense air.

Answer (A) is incorrect. There is decreased, not increased, efficiency. Answer (C) is incorrect. The propeller exerts less (not more) force on the air when the air is thinner, i.e., at higher density altitudes.

5. What effect does high density altitude have on aircraft performance?

A. It increases engine performance.

B. It reduces climb performance.

C. It increases takeoff performance.

Answer (B) is correct. *(PHAK Chap 11)*

DISCUSSION: High density altitude reduces all aspects of an airplane's performance, including takeoff and climb performance.

Answer (A) is incorrect. Engine performance is decreased (not increased). Answer (C) is incorrect. Takeoff runway length is increased, i.e., reduces takeoff performance.

6. Which combination of atmospheric conditions will reduce aircraft takeoff and climb performance?

A. Low temperature, low relative humidity, and low density altitude.

B. High temperature, low relative humidity, and low density altitude.

C. High temperature, high relative humidity, and high density altitude.

Answer (C) is correct. *(PHAK Chap 11)*

DISCUSSION: Takeoff and climb performance are reduced by high density altitude. High density altitude is a result of high temperatures and high relative humidity.

Answer (A) is incorrect. Low temperature, low relative humidity, and low density altitude all improve airplane performance. Answer (B) is incorrect. Low relative humidity and low density altitude both improve airplane performance.

7. If the outside air temperature (OAT) at a given altitude is warmer than standard, the density altitude is

A. equal to pressure altitude.

B. lower than pressure altitude.

C. higher than pressure altitude.

Answer (C) is correct. *(PHAK Chap 11)*

DISCUSSION: When temperature increases, the air expands and therefore becomes less dense. This decrease in density means a higher density altitude. Pressure altitude is based on standard temperature. Thus, density altitude exceeds pressure altitude when the temperature is warmer than standard.

Answer (A) is incorrect. Density altitude equals pressure altitude only when temperature is standard. Answer (B) is incorrect. Density altitude is lower than pressure altitude when the temperature is below standard.

8. You have planned a cross-country flight on a warm spring morning. Your course includes a mountain pass, which is at 11,500 feet MSL. The service ceiling of your airplane is 14,000 feet MSL. After checking the local weather report, you are able to calculate the density altitude of the mountain pass as 14,800 feet MSL. Which of the following is the correct action to take?

A. Replan your journey to avoid the mountain pass.

B. Continue as planned since density altitude is only a factor for takeoff.

C. Continue as planned because mountain thermals will assist your climb.

Answer (A) is correct. *(PHAK Chap 11)*

DISCUSSION: Because the density altitude through the mountain pass is higher than the service ceiling of the aircraft, it will be impossible to fly through the pass given the current conditions. You must replan your journey to avoid the mountain pass.

Answer (B) is incorrect. Density altitude affects all aspects of aircraft performance, not just takeoff performance. Answer (C) is incorrect. Mountain thermals cannot be relied upon to safely carry you through the mountain pass.

9. A pilot and two passengers landed on a 2,100 foot east-west gravel strip with an elevation of 1,800 feet. The temperature is warmer than expected and after computing the density altitude it is determined the takeoff distance over a 50 foot obstacle is 1,980 feet. The airplane is 75 pounds under gross weight. What would be the best choice?

A. Takeoff to the west because the headwind will give the extra climb-out time needed.

B. Try a takeoff without the passengers to make sure the climb is adequate.

C. Wait until the temperature decreases, and recalculate the takeoff performance.

Answer (C) is correct. *(PHAK Chap 11)*

DISCUSSION: The majority of pilot-induced accidents occur during the takeoff and landing phases of flight. In this instance, the pilot in command of this aircraft has an important decision to make. The takeoff distance over a 50-foot obstacle appears on initial inspection to be possible (1,980 feet on a 2,100-foot runway). It is important to remember, however, the performance charts are based on ideal conditions and created by testing brand new aircraft with optimal performance and highly experienced test pilots at the controls. It would be ill-advised for this pilot to attempt to take off. The pilot should wait for the temperature to decrease and recalculate the takeoff performance.

Answer (A) is incorrect. There are no winds provided in this question and no guarantee the takeoff performance to the west would be improved in any way. Answer (B) is incorrect. The decision to attempt a takeoff without the passengers and ensure climb performance is flawed in a few ways. Charts provided in the aircraft information manual should be used to determine climb performance prior to a flight. Coming to the realization the climb performance is not sufficient to clear terrain features and obstacles once airborne is a position no pilot wants to find him/herself in. If the pilot did attempt to take off without the passengers and the climb performance was adequate, there is absolutely no reason to believe the performance would be sufficient when the passengers are added and the weight of the aircraft is increased.

5.2 Density Altitude Computations

10. (Refer to Figure 8 on page 191.) Determine the density altitude for these conditions:

Altimeter setting 30.35
Runway temperature . . . . +25°F
Airport elevation . . . . 3,894 ft. MSL

A. 2,000 feet MSL.

B. 2,900 feet MSL.

C. 3,500 feet MSL.

3,894
− 344
3,550

3894
− 394
3,500

Answer (A) is correct. *(PHAK Chap 11)*

DISCUSSION: With an altimeter setting of 30.35" Hg, 394 ft. must be subtracted from a field elevation of 3,894 to obtain a pressure altitude of 3,500 feet. Note that the higher-than-normal pressure of 30.35 means the pressure altitude will be less than true altitude. The 394 ft. was found by interpolation: 30.3 on the graph is –348, and 30.4 was –440 feet. Adding one-half the –92 ft. difference (–46 ft.) to –348 ft. results in –394 feet. Once you have found the pressure altitude, use the chart to plot 3,500 ft. pressure altitude at 25°F, to reach 2,000 ft. density altitude. Note that since the temperature is lower than standard, the density altitude is lower than the pressure altitude.

Answer (B) is incorrect. This would be the density altitude if you added (not subtracted) 394 ft. to 3,894 feet. Answer (C) is incorrect. This is pressure (not density) altitude.

11. (Refer to Figure 8 on page 191.) What is the effect of a temperature increase from 30 to 50 °F on the density altitude if the pressure altitude remains at 3,000 feet MSL?

A. 1,000-foot increase.

B. 1,100-foot decrease.

C. 1,300-foot increase.

Answer (C) is correct. *(PHAK Chap 11)*

DISCUSSION: Increasing the temperature from 30°F to 50°F, given a constant pressure altitude of 3,000 ft., requires you to find the 3,000-ft. line on the density altitude chart at the 30°F level. At this point, the density altitude is approximately 1,650 feet. Then move up the 3,000-ft. line to 50°F, where the density altitude is approximately 2,950 feet. There is an approximate 1,300-ft. increase (2,950 – 1,650 feet). Note that 50°F is just about standard and pressure altitude is very close to density altitude.

Answer (A) is incorrect. A 1,000-ft. increase would be caused by a temperature increase to 45°F. Answer (B) is incorrect. A decrease in density altitude would be caused by a decrease, not an increase, in temperature.

12. (Refer to Figure 8 on page 191.) What is the effect of a temperature increase from 35 to 50°F on the density altitude if the pressure altitude remains at 3,000 feet MSL?

A. 1,000-foot increase.

B. 1,100-foot decrease.

C. 1,300-foot increase.

Answer (A) is correct. *(PHAK Chap 11)*

DISCUSSION: Increasing the temperature from 35°F to 50°F, given a constant pressure altitude of 3,000 ft., requires you to find the 3,000-ft. line on the density altitude chart at the 35°F level. At this point, the density altitude is approximately 1,950 feet. Then move up the 3,000-ft. line to 50°F, where the density altitude is approximately 2,950 feet. There is an approximate 1,000-ft. increase (2,950 – 1,950 feet). Note that 50°F is just about standard, and pressure altitude is very close to density altitude.

Answer (B) is incorrect. A 1,100-ft. decrease would require a temperature decrease to 54°F. Answer (C) is incorrect. A 1,300-ft. increase would be caused by a temperature increase to 58°F.

13. (Refer to Figure 8 on page 191.) Determine the pressure altitude at an airport that is 3,563 feet MSL with an altimeter setting of 29.96.

3563
− 36
3527

A. 3,527 feet MSL.

B. 3,556 feet MSL.

C. 3,639 feet MSL.

Answer (A) is correct. *(PHAK Chap 11)*

DISCUSSION: Note that the question asks only for pressure altitude, not density altitude. Pressure altitude is determined by adjusting the altimeter setting to 29.92" Hg, i.e., adjusting for nonstandard pressure. This is the true altitude plus or minus the pressure altitude conversion factor (based on current altimeter setting). On the chart, an altimeter setting of 30.0 requires you to subtract 73 ft. to determine pressure altitude (note that at 29.92, nothing is subtracted because that is pressure altitude). Since 29.96 is halfway between 29.92 and 30.0, you need only subtract 36 (–73/2) from 3,563 ft. to obtain a pressure altitude of 3,527 ft. (3,563 – 36). Note that a higher-than-standard barometric pressure means pressure altitude is lower than true altitude.

Answer (B) is incorrect. You must subtract 36 (not 7) from 3,563 ft. to obtain the correct pressure altitude. Answer (C) is incorrect. You must subtract 36 (not add 76) from 3,563 ft. to obtain the correct pressure altitude.

14. (Refer to Figure 8 below.) What is the effect of a temperature decrease and a pressure altitude increase on the density altitude from 90°F and 1,250 feet pressure altitude to 55°F and 1,750 feet pressure altitude?

A. 1,700-foot increase.

B. 1,300-foot decrease.

C. 1,700-foot decrease.

Answer (C) is correct. *(PHAK Chap 11)*

DISCUSSION: The requirement is the effect of a temperature decrease and a pressure altitude increase on density altitude. First, find the density altitude at 90°F and 1,250 ft. (approximately 3,600 feet). Then find the density altitude at 55°F and 1,750 ft. pressure altitude (approximately 1,900 feet). Next, subtract the two numbers. Subtracting 1,900 ft. from 3,600 ft. equals a 1,700-ft. decrease in density altitude.

Answer (A) is incorrect. Such a large decrease in temperature would decrease, not increase, density altitude. Answer (B) is incorrect. Density altitude would decrease 1,300 ft. if the temperature decreased to 60°F, not 55°F.

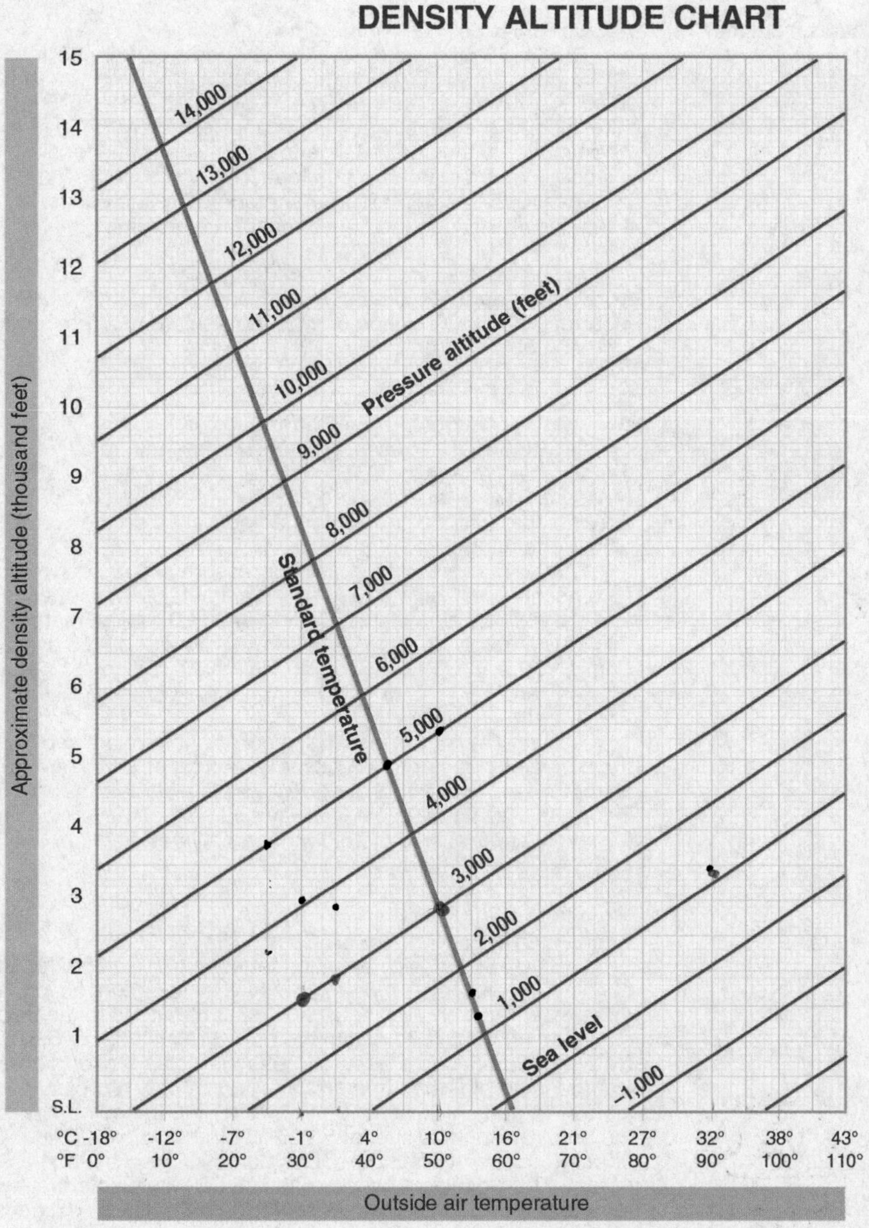

Altimeter setting ("Hg)	Pressure altitude conversion factor
28.0	1,824
28.1	1,727
28.2	1,630
28.3	1,533
28.4	1,436
28.5	1,340
28.6	1,244
28.7	1,148
28.8	1,053
28.9	957
29.0	863
29.1	768
29.2	673
29.3	579
29.4	485
29.5	392
29.6	298
29.7	205
29.8	112
29.9	20
29.92	0
30.0	–73
30.1	–165
30.2	–257
30.3	–348
30.4	–440
30.5	–531
30.6	–622
30.7	–712
30.8	–803
30.9	–893
31.0	–983

Figure 8. – Density Altitude Chart.

15. (Refer to Figure 8 on page 193.) Determine the pressure altitude at an airport that is 1,386 feet MSL with an altimeter setting of 29.97.

A. 1,341 feet MSL.

B. 1,451 feet MSL.

C. 1,562 feet MSL.

Answer (A) is correct. *(PHAK Chap 11)*

DISCUSSION: Pressure altitude is determined by adjusting the altimeter setting to 29.92" Hg. This is the true altitude plus or minus the pressure altitude conversion factor (based on current altimeter setting). Since 29.97 is not a number given on the conversion chart, you must interpolate. Compute 5/8 of –73 (since 29.97 is 5/8 of the way between 29.92 and 30.0), which is 45. Subtract 45 ft. from 1,386 ft. to obtain a pressure altitude of 1,341 feet. Note that if the altimeter setting is greater than standard (e.g., 29.97), the pressure altitude (i.e., altimeter set to 29.92) will be less than true altitude.

Answer (B) is incorrect. You must subtract 45 ft. (not add 65) from 1,386 ft. to obtain the correct pressure altitude. Answer (C) is incorrect. You must subtract 45 ft. (not add 176) from 1,386 ft. to obtain the correct pressure altitude.

16. (Refer to Figure 8 on page 193.) What is the effect of a temperature increase from 25 to 50° F on the density altitude if the pressure altitude remains at 5,000 feet?

A. 1,200-foot increase.

B. 1,400-foot increase.

C. 1,650-foot increase.

Answer (C) is correct. *(PHAK Chap 11)*

DISCUSSION: Increasing the temperature from 25°F to 50°F, given a pressure altitude of 5,000 ft., requires you to find the 5,000-ft. line on the density altitude chart at the 25°F level. At this point, the density altitude is approximately 3,850 feet. Then move up the 5,000-ft. line to 50°F, where the density altitude is approximately 5,500 feet. There is about a 1,650-ft. increase (5,500 – 3,850 feet). As temperature increases, so does density altitude; i.e., the atmosphere becomes thinner (less dense).

Answer (A) is incorrect. An 1,200-ft. increase would result from a temperature increase of 18°F (not 25°F). Answer (B) is incorrect. An 1,400-ft. increase would result from a temperature increase of 20°F (not 25°F).

17. (Refer to Figure 8 on page 193.) Determine the pressure altitude with an indicated altitude of 1,380 feet MSL with an altimeter setting of 28.22 at standard temperature.

A. 3,010 feet MSL.

B. 2,991 feet MSL.

C. 2,913 feet MSL.

Answer (B) is correct. *(PHAK Chap 11)*

DISCUSSION: Pressure altitude is determined by adjusting the altimeter setting to 29.92" Hg, i.e., adjusting for nonstandard pressure. This is the indicated altitude of 1,380 ft. plus or minus the pressure altitude conversion factor (based on the current altimeter setting).

On the right side of Fig. 8 is a pressure altitude conversion factor schedule. Add 1,533 ft. for an altimeter setting of 28.30 and 1,630 ft. for an altimeter setting of 28.20. Using interpolation, you must subtract 20% of the difference between 28.3 and 28.2 from 1,630 ft. (1,630 – 1,533 = 97 × .2 = 19). Since 1,630 – 19 = 1,611, add 1,611 ft. to 1,380 ft. to get the pressure altitude of 2,991 feet.

Answer (A) is incorrect. This figure is obtained by adding the conversion factor for an altimeter setting of 28.20, not an altimeter setting of 28.22, to the indicated altitude. Answer (C) is incorrect. This figure is obtained by adding the conversion factor for an altimeter setting of 28.30, not an altimeter setting of 28.22, to the indicated altitude.

18. (Refer to Figure 8 on page 193.) Determine the density altitude for these conditions:

Altimeter setting	29.25
Runway temperature	+81°F
Airport elevation	5,250 ft MSL

A. 4,600 feet MSL.

B. 5,877 feet MSL.

C. 8,500 feet MSL.

Answer (C) is correct. *(PHAK Chap 11)*

DISCUSSION: With an altimeter setting of 29.25" Hg, about 626 ft. (579 plus 1/2 the 94-ft. pressure altitude conversion factor difference between 29.2 and 29.3) must be added to the field elevation of 5,250 ft. to obtain the pressure altitude, or 5,876 feet. Note that barometric pressure is less than standard and pressure altitude is greater than true altitude. Next, convert pressure altitude to density altitude. On the chart, find the point at which the pressure altitude line for 5,876 ft. crosses the 81°F line. The density altitude at that spot shows somewhere in the mid-8,000s of feet. The closest answer choice is 8,500 feet. Note that, when temperature is higher than standard, density altitude exceeds pressure altitude.

Answer (A) is incorrect. This would be pressure altitude if 650 ft. were subtracted from, not added to, 5,250 ft. MSL. Answer (B) is incorrect. This is pressure altitude, not density altitude.

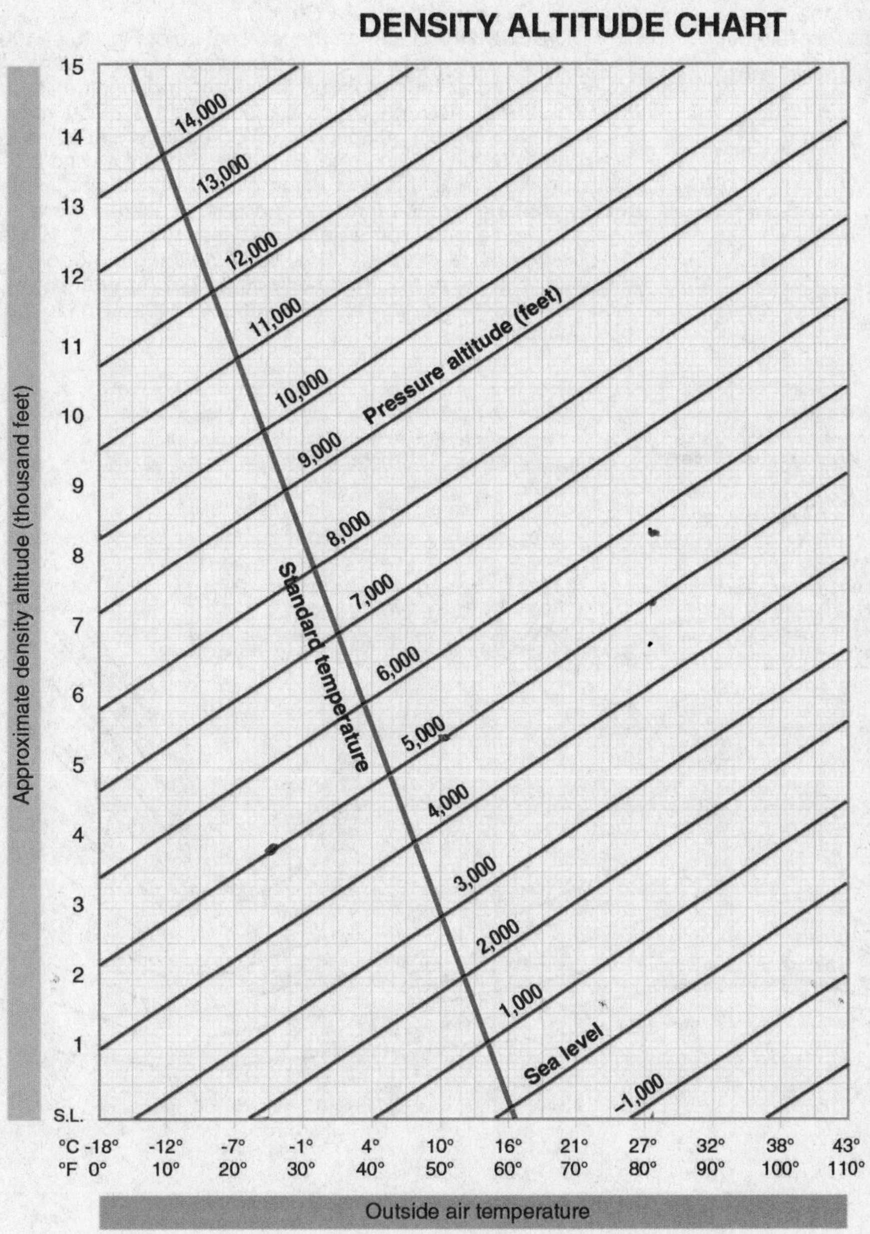

Altimeter setting ("Hg)	Pressure altitude conversion factor
28.0	1,824
28.1	1,727
28.2	1,630
28.3	1,533
28.4	1,436
28.5	1,340
28.6	1,244
28.7	1,148
28.8	1,053
28.9	957
29.0	863
29.1	768
29.2	673
29.3	579
29.4	485
29.5	392
29.6	298
29.7	205
29.8	112
29.9	20
29.92	0
30.0	–73
30.1	–165
30.2	–257
30.3	–348
30.4	–440
30.5	–531
30.6	–622
30.7	–712
30.8	–803
30.9	–893
31.0	–983

Figure 8. – Density Altitude Chart.

5.3 Takeoff Distance

19. (Refer to Figure 40 below.) Determine the approximate ground roll distance required for takeoff.

OAT . . . . 100°F
Pressure altitude . . . . 2,000 ft
Takeoff weight . . . . 2,750 lb
Headwind component . . . . Calm

A. 1,150 feet.

B. 1,300 feet.

C. 1,800 feet.

Answer (A) is correct. *(PHAK Chap 11)*

DISCUSSION: Begin on the left section of Fig. 40 at 100°F (see outside air temperature at the bottom). Move up vertically to the pressure altitude of 2,000 feet. Then proceed horizontally to the first reference line. Since takeoff weight is 2,750, move parallel to the closest guideline to 2,750 pounds. Then proceed horizontally to the second reference line. Since the wind is calm, proceed again horizontally to the right-hand margin of the diagram (ignore the third reference line because there is no obstacle, i.e., ground roll is desired), which will be at 1,150 feet.

Answer (B) is incorrect. This would be the ground roll distance required at maximum takeoff weight. Answer (C) is incorrect. This would be the total distance required to clear a 50-ft. obstacle.

Example:	
OAT	15 °C (59 °F)
Pressure altitude	5,650 feet
Takeoff weight	2,950 lb
Headwind comp.	9.0 knots
Ground roll	1,375 feet
Total distance over a 50 feet obstacle	2,300 feet
Takeoff speed at	
Lift-off	66 knots (76 mph)
50 feet	72 knots (83 mph)

Associated conditions	
Power	Full throttle 2,600 rpm
Mixture	Lean to appropriate fuel pressure
Flaps	Up
Landing gear	Retract after positive climb established
Cowl flaps	Open

Weight pounds	Takeoff speed			
	Lift-off		50 ft	
	kts	MPH	kts	MPH
2,950	66	76	72	83
2,800	64	74	70	81
2,600	63	72	68	78
2,400	61	70	66	76
2,200	58	67	63	73

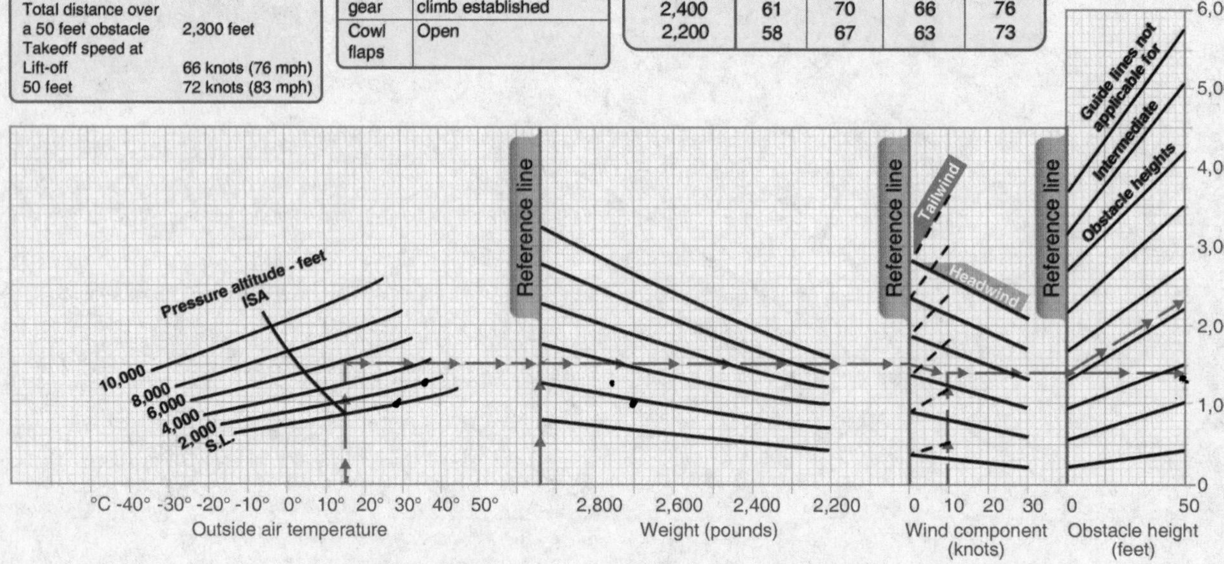

Figure 40. – Airplane Takeoff Distance Graph.

20. (Refer to Figure 40 on page 194.) Determine the total distance required for takeoff to clear a 50-foot obstacle.

OAT	Std
Pressure altitude	Sea level
Takeoff weight	2,700 lb
Headwind component	Calm

A. 1,000 feet.

B. 1,400 feet.

C. 1,700 feet.

Answer (B) is correct. *(PHAK Chap 11)*

DISCUSSION: Begin in the left section of Fig. 40 by finding the intersection of the sea level pressure altitude and standard temperature (59°F) and proceed horizontally to the right to the first reference line. Then proceed parallel to the closest guideline, to 2,700 pounds. From there, proceed horizontally to the right to the third reference line. You skip the second reference line because the wind is calm. Then proceed upward parallel to the closest guideline to the far right side. To clear the 50-ft. obstacle, you need a takeoff distance of about 1,400 feet.

Answer (A) is incorrect. This would be the total distance required at 2,200 lb. takeoff weight. Answer (C) is incorrect. This would be the total distance required at maximum takeoff weight.

21. (Refer to Figure 40 on page 194.) Determine the total distance required for takeoff to clear a 50-foot obstacle.

OAT	Std
Pressure altitude	4,000 ft
Takeoff weight	2,800 lb
Headwind component	Calm

A. 1,500 feet.

B. 1,750 feet.

C. 2,000 feet.

Answer (B) is correct. *(PHAK Chap 11)*

DISCUSSION: The takeoff distance to clear a 50-ft. obstacle is required. Begin on the left side of the graph at standard temperature (as represented by the curved line labeled "ISA"). From the intersection of the standard temperature line and the 4,000-ft. pressure altitude, proceed horizontally to the right to the first reference line, and then move parallel to the closest guideline to 2,800 pounds. From there, proceed horizontally to the right to the third reference line (skip the second reference line because there is no wind), and move upward parallel to the closest guideline all the way to the far right. You are at 1,750 ft., which is the takeoff distance to clear a 50-ft. obstacle.

Answer (A) is incorrect. This would be the total distance required with a 10-kt. headwind. Answer (C) is incorrect. This would be the total distance required at maximum takeoff weight.

22. (Refer to Figure 40 on page 194.) Determine the approximate ground roll distance required for takeoff.

OAT	90°F
Pressure altitude	2,000 ft
Takeoff weight	2,500 lb
Headwind component	20 kts

A. 650 feet.

B. 850 feet.

C. 1,000 feet.

Answer (A) is correct. *(PHAK Chap 11)*

DISCUSSION: Begin with the intersection of the 2,000-ft. pressure altitude curve and 90°F in the left section of Fig. 40. Move horizontally to the right to the first reference line, and then parallel to the closest guideline to 2,500 pounds. Then move horizontally to the right to the second reference line, and then parallel to the closest guideline to the right to 20 knots. Then move horizontally to the right, directly to the right margin because there is no obstacle clearance. You should end up at about 650 ft., which is the required ground roll when there is no obstacle to clear.

Answer (B) is incorrect. This would be the ground roll distance required if the wind were calm. Answer (C) is incorrect. This would be the ground roll distance required at maximum takeoff weight.

5.4 Cruise Power Settings

23. (Refer to Figure 35 below.) What fuel flow should a pilot expect at 11,000 feet on a standard day with 65 percent maximum continuous power?

A. 10.6 gallons per hour.

B. 11.2 gallons per hour.

C. 11.8 gallons per hour.

Answer (B) is correct. *(PHAK Chap 11)*

DISCUSSION: Note that the entire chart applies to 65% maximum continuous power (regardless of the throttle), so use the middle section of the chart, which is labeled a standard day.

The fuel flow at 11,000 ft. on a standard day would be 1/2 of the way between the fuel flow at 10,000 ft. (11.5 GPH) and the fuel flow at 12,000 ft. (10.9 GPH). Thus, the fuel flow at 11,000 ft. would be 11.5 – 0.3, or 11.2 GPH.

Answer (A) is incorrect. You must add (not subtract) 0.3 to 10.9 to obtain the correct fuel flow. Answer (C) is incorrect. You must subtract (not add) 0.3 from 11.5 to obtain the correct fuel flow.

24. (Refer to Figure 35 below.) What is the expected fuel consumption for a 1,000-nautical mile flight under the following conditions?

Pressure altitude . . . . 8,000 ft
Temperature . . . . 22°C
Manifold pressure . . . . 20.8" Hg
Wind . . . . Calm

A. 60.2 gallons.

B. 70.1 gallons.

C. 73.2 gallons.

Answer (B) is correct. *(PHAK Chap 11)*

DISCUSSION: To determine the fuel consumption, you need to know the number of hours the flight will last and the gallons per hour the airplane will use. The chart is divided into three sections. They differ based on air temperature. Use the right section of the chart, as the temperature at 8,000 ft. is 22°C.

At a pressure altitude of 8,000 ft., 20.8" Hg manifold pressure, and 22°C, the fuel flow is 11.5 GPH and the true airspeed is 164 knots. Given a calm wind, the 1,000-NM trip will take 6.09 hr. (1,000 NM ÷ 164 knots).

$$6.09 \text{ hr.} \times 11.5 \text{ GPH} = 70.1 \text{ gal.}$$

Answer (A) is incorrect. This is the expected fuel consumption for a 1,000-NM flight with a true airspeed of 189 (not 164) knots. Answer (C) is incorrect. This is the expected fuel consumption for a 1,000-NM flight with a true airspeed of 157 (not 164) knots.

Cruise power settings
65% Maximum continuous power (or full throttle 2,800 pounds)

Press ALT.	ISA –20 °C (–36 °F)								Standard day (ISA)								ISA +20 °C (+36 °F)							
	IOAT		Engine speed	MAN. press	Fuel flow per engine		TAS		IOAT		Engine speed	MAN. press	Fuel flow per engine		TAS		IOAT		Engine speed	MAN. press	Fuel flow per engine		TAS	
Feet	°F	°C	RPM	IN HG	PSI	GPH	KTS	MPH	°F	°C	RPM	IN HG	PSI	GPH	KTS	MPH	°F	°C	RPM	IN HG	PSI	GPH	KTS	MPH
SL	27	–3	2,450	20.7	6.6	11.5	147	169	63	17	2,450	21.2	6.6	11.5	150	173	99	37	2,450	21.8	6.6	11.5	153	176
2,000	19	–7	2,450	20.4	6.6	11.5	149	171	55	13	2,450	21.0	6.6	11.5	153	176	91	33	2,450	21.5	6.6	11.5	156	180
4,000	12	–11	2,450	20.1	6.6	11.5	152	175	48	9	2,450	20.7	6.6	11.5	156	180	84	29	2,450	21.3	6.6	11.5	159	183
6,000	5	–15	2,450	19.8	6.6	11.5	155	178	41	5	2,450	20.4	6.6	11.5	158	182	79	26	2,450	21.0	6.6	11.5	161	185
8,000	–2	–19	2,450	19.5	6.6	11.5	157	181	36	2	2,450	20.2	6.6	11.5	161	185	72	22	2,450	20.8	6.6	11.5	164	189
10,000	–8	–22	2,450	19.2	6.6	11.5	160	184	28	–2	2,450	19.9	6.6	11.5	163	188	64	18	2,450	20.3	6.5	11.4	166	191
12,000	–15	–26	2,450	18.8	6.4	11.5	162	186	21	–6	2,450	18.8	6.1	10.9	163	188	57	14	2,450	18.8	5.9	10.6	163	188
14,000	–22	–30	2,450	17.4	5.8	10.5	159	183	14	–10	2,450	17.4	5.6	10.1	160	184	50	10	2,450	17.4	5.4	9.8	160	184
16,000	–29	–34	2,450	16.1	5.3	9.7	156	180	7	–14	2,450	16.1	5.1	9.4	156	180	43	6	2,450	16.1	4.9	9.1	155	178

Note: 1. Full throttle manifold pressure settings are approximate.
2. Shaded area represents operation with full throttle.

Figure 35. – Airplane Power Setting Table.

10,000 , 10 500 , 11000 , 11500

25. (Refer to Figure 35 on page 196.) What is the expected fuel consumption for a 500-nautical mile flight under the following conditions?

Pressure altitude	4,000 ft
Temperature	+29°C
Manifold pressure	21.3" Hg
Wind	Calm

A. 31.4 gallons.

B. 36.1 gallons.

C. 40.1 gallons.

Answer (B) is correct. *(PHAK Chap 11)*

DISCUSSION:

1. Reference the ISA +20°C (+36°F) section of the "Cruise Power" settings chart (because indicated temperature is approximately 20° above ISA).
2. Reference the 4,000 feet Pressure Altitude row in the ISA +20°C section of the chart. IOAT is +29°C, manifold pressure is 21.3" Hg, fuel flow per engine is 11.5 GPH, and TAS is 159.
3. Calculate the time it will take to travel 500 NM at 159 kt.:

$$500 \text{ NM} \div 159 \frac{\text{NM}}{\text{hr.}} = 3.14 \text{ hr.}$$

4. Calculate the expected fuel consumption:

$$3.14 \text{ hr.} \times 11.5 \text{ GPH} = 36.1 \text{ gal.}$$

Answer (A) is incorrect. This is the expected fuel consumption for a 500-NM flight with a true airspeed of 183 (not 159) knots. Answer (C) is incorrect. This is the expected fuel consumption for a 500-NM flight with a true airspeed of 143 (not 159) knots.

26. (Refer to Figure 35 on page 196.) Determine the approximate manifold pressure setting with 2,450 RPM to achieve 65 percent maximum continuous power at 6,500 feet with a temperature of 36°F higher than standard.

A. 19.8" Hg.

B. 20.8" Hg.

C. 21.0" Hg.

Answer (C) is correct. *(PHAK Chap 11)*

DISCUSSION: The part of the chart on the right is for temperatures 36°F greater than standard. At 6,500 ft. with a temperature of 36°F higher than standard, the required manifold pressure change is 1/4 of the difference between the 21.0" Hg at 6,000 ft. and the 20.8" Hg at 8,000 ft., or slightly less than 21.0. Thus, 21.0 is the best answer given. The manifold pressure is closer to 21.0 than 20.8.

Answer (A) is incorrect. This setting would achieve 65% power at 36°F below (not above) standard temperature. Answer (B) is incorrect. The manifold pressure at 6,500 ft. is closer to 21.0 than 20.8.

27. (Refer to Figure 35 on page 196.) Approximately what true airspeed should a pilot expect with 65 percent maximum continuous power at 9,500 feet with a temperature of 36°F below standard?

A. 163 KTS.

B. 161 KTS.

C. 158 KTS.

Answer (C) is correct. *(PHAK Chap 11)*

DISCUSSION: The left part of the chart applies to 36°F below standard. At 8,000 ft., TAS is 157 KTS. At 10,000 ft., TAS is 160 KTS. At 9,500 ft., with a temperature 36°F below standard, the expected true airspeed is 75% above the 157 KTS at 8,000 ft. toward the 160 KTS at 10,000 ft., i.e., approximately 158 KTS.

Answer (A) is incorrect. The expected TAS at 6,000 ft. is 163 KTS. Answer (B) is incorrect. The expected TAS at 8,000 ft. is 161 KTS.

28. (Refer to Figure 35 on page 196.) Approximately what true airspeed should a pilot expect with full throttle at 10,500 feet with a temperature of 36°F above standard?

A. 190 KTS.

B. 159 KTS.

C. 165 KTS.

Answer (C) is correct. *(PHAK Chap 11)*

DISCUSSION: The chart on the right side of Fig. 35 applies to 36°F above standard. At 10,000 ft., TAS is 166 kt. At 12,000 ft., TAS is 163 kt. We can then interpolate these results and assume 11,000 ft. is 164.5 kt. We then interpolate 10,000 (166 kt.) and 11,000 (164.5 kt.) and arrive at the answer of 165.25 kt.

Answer (A) is incorrect. A TAS of 190 kt. cannot be found on this chart. The maximum speed for this aircraft is 166 kt., found at 10,000 ft. pressure altitude. Logically, a TAS of 190 kt. is not between 163 kt. and 166 kt., where our TAS at 10,500 ft. will be found. Answer (B) is incorrect. The expected TAS of 159 kt. would be appropriate around 14,000 ft., not at 10,500 ft. with full throttle.

5.5 Crosswind Components

29. (Refer to Figure 36 below.) What is the crosswind component for a landing on Runway 18 if the tower reports the wind as 220° at 30 knots?

A. 19 knots.

B. 23 knots.

C. 30 knots.

Answer (A) is correct. *(PHAK Chap 11)*

DISCUSSION: The requirement is the crosswind component, which is found on the horizontal axis of the graph. You are given a 30-kt. wind speed (the wind speed is shown on the circular lines or arcs). First, calculate the angle between the wind and the runway (220° – 180° = 40°). Next, find the intersection of the 40° line and the 30-kt. wind velocity arc. Then, proceed downward to determine a crosswind component of 19 knots.

Note the crosswind component is on the horizontal axis and the headwind component is on the vertical axis.

Answer (B) is incorrect. This is the headwind (not crosswind) component. Answer (C) is incorrect. This is the total wind (not crosswind component).

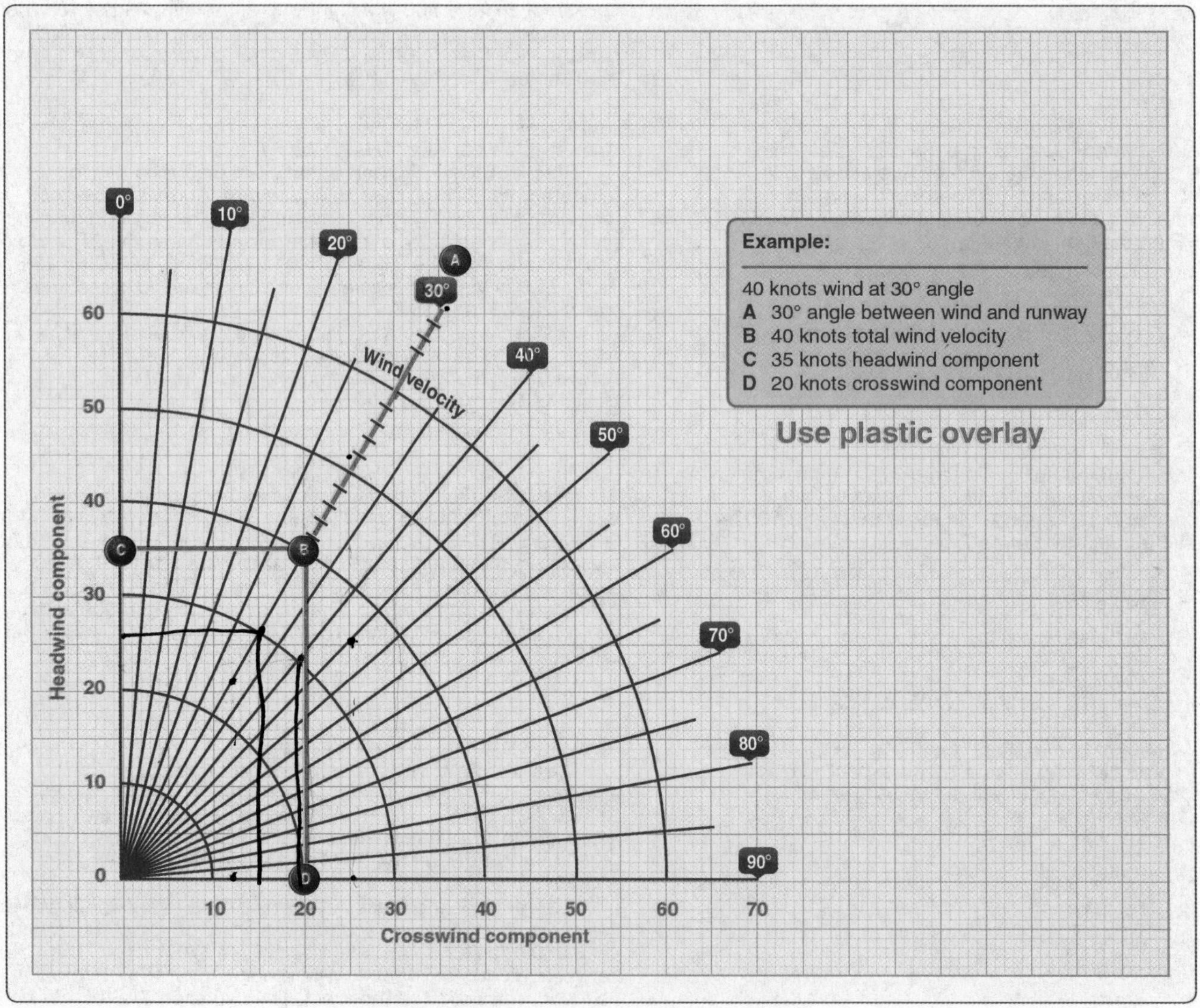

Figure 36. – Crosswind Component Graph.

30. (Refer to Figure 36 on page 198.) What is the headwind component for a landing on Runway 18 if the tower reports the wind as 220° at 30 knots?

A. 19 knots.

B. 23 knots.

C. 26 knots.

Answer (B) is correct. *(PHAK Chap 11)*

DISCUSSION: The headwind component is on the vertical axis (left-hand side of the graph). Find the same intersection as in the preceding question, i.e., the 30-kt. wind speed arc, and the 40° angle between wind direction and flight path (220° – 180°). Then move horizontally to the left and read approximately 23 knots.

Answer (A) is incorrect. This is the crosswind (not headwind) component. Answer (C) is incorrect. This would be the headwind component if the wind were 30° (not 40°) off the runway.

31. (Refer to Figure 36 on page 198.) Determine the maximum wind velocity for a 45° crosswind if the maximum crosswind component for the airplane is 25 knots.

A. 25 knots.

B. 29 knots.

C. 35 knots.

Answer (C) is correct. *(PHAK Chap 11)*

DISCUSSION: Start on the bottom of the graph's horizontal axis at 25 kt. and move straight upward to the 45° angle between wind direction and flight path line (halfway between the 40° and 50° lines). Note that you are halfway between the 30 and 40 arc-shaped wind speed lines, which means that the maximum wind velocity for a 45° crosswind is 35 kt. if the airplane is limited to a 25-kt. crosswind component.

Answer (A) is incorrect. This would be the maximum wind velocity for a 90° (not 45°) crosswind. Answer (B) is incorrect. This would be the maximum wind velocity for a 60° (not 45°) crosswind.

32. (Refer to Figure 36 on page 198.) With a reported wind of north at 20 knots, which runway is acceptable for use for an airplane with a 13-knot maximum crosswind component?

A. Runway 6.

B. Runway 29.

C. Runway 32.

Answer (C) is correct. *(PHAK Chap 11)*

DISCUSSION: If the wind is from the north (i.e., either 360° or 0°) at 20 kt., runway 32, i.e., 320°, would provide a 40° crosswind component (360° – 320°). Given a 20-kt. wind, find the intersection between the 20-kt. arc and the angle between wind direction and the flight path of 40°. Dropping straight downward to the horizontal axis gives 13 kt., which is the maximum crosswind component of the example airplane.

Answer (A) is incorrect. Runway 6 would have a crosswind component of approximately 17 knots. Answer (B) is incorrect. Runway 29 would have a crosswind component of 19 knots.

33. (Refer to Figure 36 on page 198.) What is the maximum wind velocity for a 30° crosswind if the maximum crosswind component for the airplane is 12 knots?

A. 16 knots.

B. 20 knots.

C. 24 knots.

Answer (C) is correct. *(PHAK Chap 11)*

DISCUSSION: Start on the graph's horizontal axis at 12 kt. and move upward to the 30° angle between wind direction and flight path line. Note that you are almost halfway between the 20 and 30 arc-shaped wind speed lines, which means that the maximum wind velocity for a 30° crosswind is approximately 24 kt. if the airplane is limited to a 12-kt. crosswind component.

Answer (A) is incorrect. This would be the maximum wind velocity for a 50° (not 30°) crosswind. Answer (B) is incorrect. This would be the maximum wind velocity for a 40° (not 30°) crosswind.

34. (Refer to Figure 36 on page 198.) With a reported wind of south at 20 knots, which runway is appropriate for an airplane with a 13-knot maximum crosswind component?

A. Runway 10.

B. Runway 14.

C. Runway 24.

Answer (B) is correct. *(PHAK Chap 11)*

DISCUSSION: If the wind is from the south at 20 kt., runway 14, i.e., 140°, would provide a 40° crosswind component (180° – 140°). Given a 20-kt. wind, find the intersection between the 20-kt. arc and the angle between wind direction and the flight path of 40°. Dropping straight downward to the horizontal axis gives 13 kt., which is the maximum crosswind component of the example airplane.

Answer (A) is incorrect. Runway 10 would have a crosswind component of 20 knots. Answer (C) is incorrect. Runway 24 would have a crosswind component of approximately 17 knots.

5.6 Landing Distance

35. (Refer to Figure 37 below.) Determine the total distance required to land.

OAT	Std
Pressure altitude	10,000 ft
Weight	2,400 lb
Wind component	Calm
Obstacle	50 ft

A. 750 feet.

B. 1,925 feet.

C. 1,450 feet.

Answer (B) is correct. *(PHAK Chap 11)*

DISCUSSION: The landing distance graphs are very similar to the takeoff distance graphs. Begin with the pressure altitude line of 10,000 ft. and the intersection with the standard temperature line, which begins at 15°C and slopes up and to the left; i.e., standard temperature decreases as pressure altitude increases. Then move horizontally to the right to the first reference line. Proceed parallel to the closest guideline to 2,400 pounds. Proceed horizontally to the right to the second reference line. Since the wind is calm, proceed horizontally to the third reference line. Given a 50-ft. obstacle, proceed parallel to the closest guideline to the right margin to determine a distance of approximately 1,925 feet.

Answer (A) is incorrect. This is the total distance required to land with a 30-kt. headwind, not a calm wind, and without an obstacle, not with a 50-ft. obstacle. Answer (C) is incorrect. This is the approximate total distance required to land at a pressure altitude of 2,000 ft., not 10,000 ft., and a weight of 2,300 lb., not 2,400 pounds.

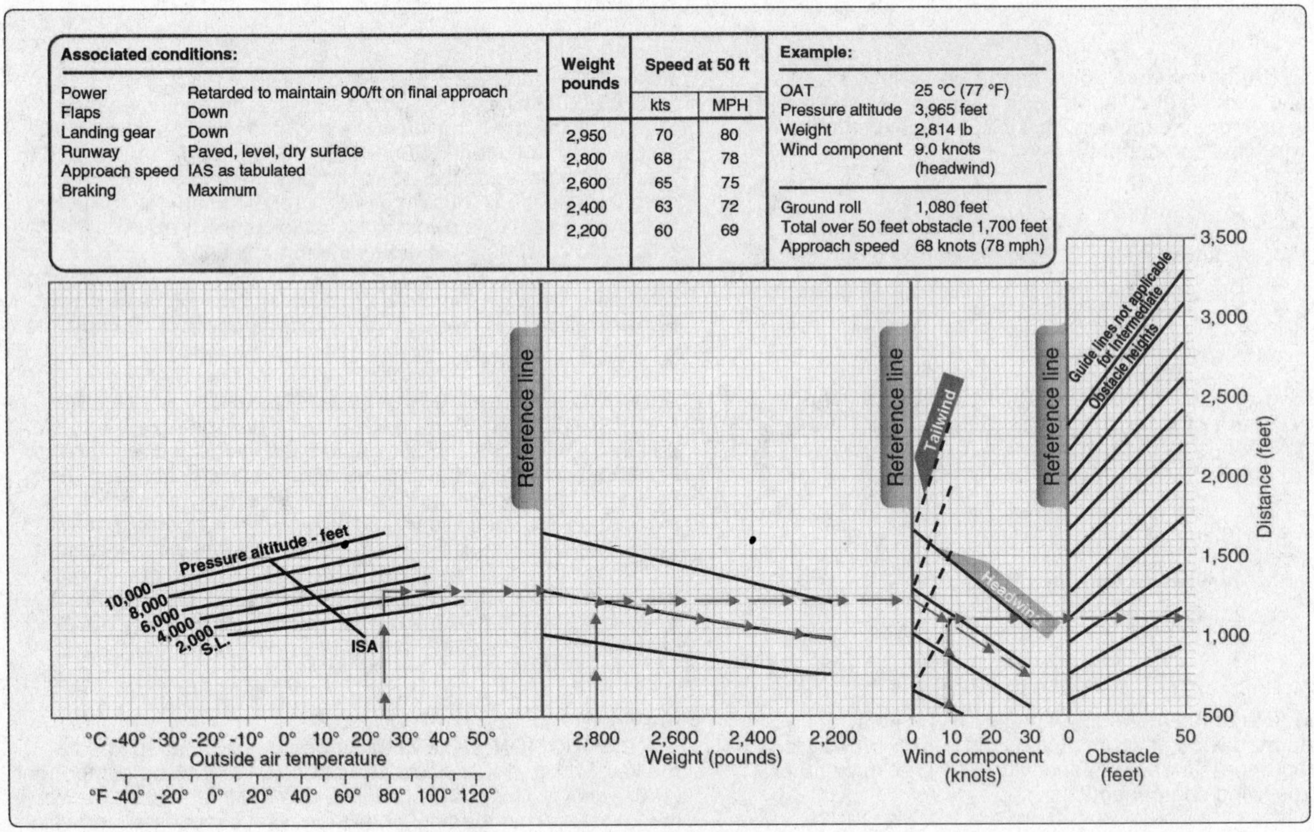

Figure 37. – Airplane Landing Distance Graph.

36. (Refer to Figure 37 on page 200.) Determine the approximate total distance required to land over a 50-ft. obstacle.

OAT	90°F
Pressure altitude	4,000 ft
Weight	2,800 lb
Headwind component	10 kts

A. 1,525 feet.

B. 1,775 feet.

C. 1,950 feet.

Answer (B) is correct. *(PHAK Chap 11)*

DISCUSSION: To determine the total landing distance, begin at the left side of Fig. 37 on the 4,000-ft. pressure altitude line at the intersection of 90°F. Proceed horizontally to the right to the first reference line. Proceed parallel to the closest guideline to 2,800 lb., and then straight across to the second reference line. Since the headwind component is 10 kt., proceed parallel to the closest headwind guideline to the 10-kt. line. Then move directly to the right, to the third reference line. Given a 50-ft. obstacle, proceed parallel to the closest guideline for obstacles to find the total distance of approximately 1,775 feet.

Answer (A) is incorrect. A distance of 1,525 ft. would be the total distance required with an 18-kt. headwind, not a 10-kt. headwind. Answer (C) is incorrect. A distance of 1,950 ft. would be the total distance required with calm wind conditions, not with a 10-kt. headwind.

37. (Refer to Figure 37 on page 200.) Determine the total distance required to land.

OAT	90°F
Pressure altitude	3,000 ft
Weight	2,900 lb
Headwind component	10 kts
Obstacle	50 ft

A. 1,450 feet.

B. 1,550 feet.

C. 1,725 feet.

Answer (C) is correct. *(PHAK Chap 11)*

DISCUSSION: To determine the total landing distance, begin with pressure altitude of 3,000 ft. (between the 2,000- and 4,000-ft. lines) at its intersection with 90°F. Proceed horizontally to the right to the first reference line, and then parallel to the closest guideline to 2,900 pounds. From that point, proceed horizontally to the second reference line. Since there is a headwind component of 10 kt., proceed parallel to the closest headwind guideline down to 10 kt. and then horizontally to the right to the third reference line. Given a 50-ft. obstacle, proceed parallel to the closest guideline for obstacles to find the landing distance of approximately 1,725 feet.

Answer (A) is incorrect. This would be the total distance required with a 20-kt., not 10-kt., headwind. Answer (B) is incorrect. This would be the total distance required at a pressure altitude of 2,000 ft., not 3,000 feet.

38. (Refer to Figure 37 on page 200.) Determine the total distance required to land.

OAT	32°F
Pressure altitude	8,000 ft
Weight	2,600 lb
Headwind component	20 kts
Obstacle	50 ft

A. 850 feet.

B. 1,400 feet.

C. 1,750 feet.

Answer (B) is correct. *(PHAK Chap 11)*

DISCUSSION: To determine the total landing distance, begin with the pressure altitude of 8,000 ft. at its intersection with 32°F (0°C). Proceed horizontally to the first reference line, and then parallel to the closest guideline to 2,600 pounds. From that point, proceed horizontally to the second reference line. Since there is a headwind component of 20 kt., follow parallel to the closest headwind guideline down to 20 kt., and then horizontally to the right to the third reference line. Given a 50-ft. obstacle, proceed parallel to the closest guideline for obstacles to find the landing distance of approximately 1,400 feet.

Answer (A) is incorrect. This would be the ground roll with no obstacle. Answer (C) is incorrect. This would be the total distance required at maximum landing weight.

39. If an emergency situation requires a downwind landing, pilots should expect a faster

A. airspeed at touchdown, a longer ground roll, and better control throughout the landing roll.

B. groundspeed at touchdown, a longer ground roll, and the likelihood of overshooting the desired touchdown point.

C. groundspeed at touchdown, a shorter ground roll, and the likelihood of undershooting the desired touchdown point.

Answer (B) is correct. *(AFH Chap 8)*

DISCUSSION: A downwind landing, in an emergency or other situation, will result in a faster groundspeed at touchdown, which means a longer ground roll, which in turn increases the likelihood of overshooting the desired touchdown point.

Answer (A) is incorrect. The airspeed will probably be the same even though the groundspeed is greater, and the control during the landing roll will be less due to the high groundspeed. Answer (C) is incorrect. The ground roll is longer, not shorter, and there is a greater likelihood of overshooting, not undershooting, the touchdown point due to the faster groundspeed.

40. (Refer to Figure 38 on page 203.) Determine the approximate landing ground roll distance.

Pressure altitude . . . . Sea level
Headwind . . . . 4 kts
Temperature . . . . Std

A. 356 feet.
B. 401 feet.
C. 490 feet.

Answer (B) is correct. *(PHAK Chap 11)*

DISCUSSION: At sea level, the ground roll is 445 feet. The standard temperature needs no adjustment. According to Note 1 in Fig. 38, the distance should be decreased 10% for each 4 kt. of headwind, so the headwind of 4 kt. means that the landing distance is reduced by 10%. The result is 401 ft. (445 ft. × 90%).

Answer (A) is incorrect. This would be the ground roll with an 8-kt., not a 4-kt., headwind. Answer (C) is incorrect. Ground roll is reduced, not increased, to account for headwind.

41. (Refer to Figure 38 on page 203.) Determine the total distance required to land over a 50-ft. obstacle.

Pressure altitude . . . . 3,750 ft
Headwind . . . . 12 kts
Temperature . . . . Std

A. 794 feet.
B. 836 feet.
C. 816 feet.

Answer (C) is correct. *(PHAK Chap 11)*

DISCUSSION: The total distance to clear a 50-ft. obstacle for a 3,750-ft. pressure altitude is required. Note that this altitude lies halfway between 2,500 ft. and 5,000 feet. Halfway between the total distance at 2,500 ft. of 1,135 ft. and the total distance at 5,000 ft. of 1,195 ft. is 1,165 feet. Since the headwind is 12 kt., the total distance must be reduced by 30% (10% for each 4 kt.).

70% × 1,165 = 816 ft.

Answer (A) is incorrect. This would be the total distance to land at a pressure altitude of 2,500 ft., not 3,750 ft., with a 12-kt. headwind and standard temperature. Answer (B) is incorrect. This would be the total distance to land at a pressure altitude of 5,000 ft., not 3,750 ft., with a 12-kt. headwind and standard temperature.

42. (Refer to Figure 38 on page 203.) Determine the approximate landing ground roll distance.

Pressure altitude . . . . 5,000 ft
Headwind . . . . Calm
Temperature . . . . 101°F

A. 495 feet.
B. 545 feet.
C. 445 feet.

Answer (B) is correct. *(PHAK Chap 11)*

DISCUSSION: The ground roll distance at 5,000 ft. is 495 feet. According to Note 2 in Fig. 38, since the temperature is 60°F above standard, the distance should be increased by 10%.

495 ft. × 110% = 545 ft.

Answer (A) is incorrect. This would be ground roll if the temperature were 41°F, not 101°F. Answer (C) is incorrect. This is obtained by decreasing, not increasing, the distance for a temperature 60°F above standard.

43. (Refer to Figure 38 on page 203.) Determine the approximate landing ground roll distance.

Pressure altitude . . . . 1,250 ft
Headwind . . . . 8 kts
Temperature . . . . Std

A. 275 feet.
B. 366 feet.
C. 470 feet.

Answer (B) is correct. *(PHAK Chap 11)*

DISCUSSION: The landing ground roll at a pressure altitude of 1,250 ft. is required. The difference between landing distance at sea level and 2,500 ft. is 25 ft. (470 – 445). One-half of this distance (12) plus the 445 ft. at sea level is 457 feet. The temperature is standard, requiring no adjustment. The headwind of 8 kt. requires the distance to be decreased by 20%. Thus, the distance required will be 366 ft. (457 × 80%).

Answer (A) is incorrect. The distance should be decreased by 20% (not 40%). Answer (C) is incorrect. This is the distance required at 2,500 ft. in a calm wind.

44. (Refer to Figure 38 on page 203.) Determine the total distance required to land over a 50-foot obstacle.

Pressure altitude . . . . 5,000 ft
Headwind . . . . 8 kts
Temperature . . . . 41°F
Runway . . . . Hard surface

A. 837 feet.
B. 956 feet.
C. 1,076 feet.

Answer (B) is correct. *(PHAK Chap 11)*

DISCUSSION: Under standard conditions, the distance to land over a 50-ft. obstacle at 5,000 ft. is 1,195 feet. The temperature is standard, requiring no adjustment. The headwind of 8 kt., however, requires that the distance be decreased by 20% (10% for each 4 kt. headwind). Thus, the landing ground roll will be 956 ft. (80% of 1,195).

Answer (A) is incorrect. The distance should be decreased by 20% (not 30%). Answer (C) is incorrect. The distance should be decreased by 20% (not 10%).

45. (Refer to Figure 38 below.) Determine the total distance required to land over a 50-foot obstacle.

Pressure altitude . . . . 7,500 ft
Headwind . . . . 8 kts
Temperature . . . . 32°F
Runway . . . . Hard surface

A. 1,004 feet.

B. 1,205 feet.

C. 1,506 feet.

Answer (A) is correct. *(PHAK Chap 11)*

DISCUSSION: Under normal conditions, the total landing distance required to clear a 50-ft. obstacle is 1,255 feet. The temperature is standard (32°F), requiring no adjustment. The headwind of 8 kt. reduces the 1,255 by 20% (10% for each 4 knots). Thus, the total distance required will be 1,004 ft. (1,255 × 80%).

Answer (B) is incorrect. This results from incorrectly assuming that an adjustment for a dry grass runway is necessary and then applying that adjustment (an increase of 20%) to 1,004 ft. than to the total landing distance required to clear a 50-ft. obstacle as stated in Note 3, which is 1,255 feet. Answer (C) is incorrect. This is obtained by increasing, not decreasing, the distance for the headwind.

Landing distance — Flaps lowered to 40° – Power off, Hard surface runway – Zero wind

Gross weight lb	Approach speed, IAS, MPH	At sea level & 59 °F		At 2,500 feet & 50 °F		At 5,000 feet & 41 °F		At 7,500 feet & 32 °F	
		Ground roll	Total to clear 50 feet OBS	Ground roll	Total to clear 50 feet OBS	Ground roll	Total to clear 50 feet OBS	Ground roll	Total to clear 50 feet OBS
1,600	60	445	1,075	470	1,135	495	1,195	520	1,255

NOTE:
1. Decrease the distances shown by 10% for each 4 knots of headwind.
2. Increase the distance by 10% for each 60 °F temperature increase above standard.
3. For operation on a dry, grass runway, increase distance (both "ground roll" and "total to clear 50 feet obstacle") by 20% of the "total to clear 50 feet obstacle" figure.

Figure 38. – Airplane Landing Distance Table.

5.7 Weight and Balance Definitions

46. Which items are included in the empty weight of an aircraft?

A. Unusable fuel and undrainable oil.

B. Only the airframe, powerplant, and optional equipment.

C. Full fuel tanks and engine oil to capacity.

Answer (A) is correct. *(PHAK Chap 10)*

DISCUSSION: The empty weight of an airplane includes airframe, engines, and all items of operating equipment that have fixed locations and are permanently installed. It includes optional and special equipment, fixed ballast, hydraulic fluid, unusable fuel, and undrainable oil.

Answer (B) is incorrect. Unusable and undrainable fuel and oil and permanently installed optional equipment are also included in empty weight. Answer (C) is incorrect. Usable fuel (included in full fuel) and full engine oil are not components of basic empty weight.

47. An aircraft is loaded 110 pounds over maximum certificated gross weight. If fuel (gasoline) is drained to bring the aircraft weight within limits, how much fuel should be drained?

A. 15.7 gallons.

B. 16.2 gallons.

C. 18.4 gallons.

Answer (C) is correct. *(PHAK Chap 10)*

DISCUSSION: Fuel weighs 6 lb./gallon. If an airplane is 110 lb. over maximum gross weight, 18.4 gal. (110 lb. ÷ 6) must be drained to bring the airplane weight within limits.

Answer (A) is incorrect. Fuel weighs 6 (not 7) lb./gallon. Answer (B) is incorrect. Fuel weighs 6 (not 6.8) lb./gallon.

48. If an aircraft is loaded 90 pounds over maximum certificated gross weight and fuel (gasoline) is drained to bring the aircraft weight within limits, how much fuel should be drained?

A. 10 gallons.

B. 12 gallons.

C. 15 gallons.

Answer (C) is correct. *(PHAK Chap 10)*

DISCUSSION: Since fuel weighs 6 lb./gal., draining 15 gal. (90 lb. ÷ 6) will reduce the weight of an airplane that is 90 lb. over maximum gross weight to the acceptable amount.

Answer (A) is incorrect. Fuel weighs 6 (not 9) lb./gallon. Answer (B) is incorrect. Fuel weighs 6 (not 7.5) lb./gallon.

49. GIVEN:

	WEIGHT (LB)	ARM (IN)	MOMENT (LB-IN)
Empty weight	1,495.0	101.4	151,593.0
Pilot and passengers	380.0	64.0	
Fuel (30 gal usable no reserve)		96.0	

The CG is located how far aft of datum?

A. CG 92.44.

B. CG 94.01.

C. CG 119.8.

Answer (B) is correct. *(PHAK Chap 10)*

DISCUSSION: To compute the CG, you must first multiply each weight by the arm to get the moment. Note that the fuel is given as 30 gallons. To get the weight, multiply the 30 by 6 lb. per gal. (30 × 6) = 180 pounds.

	Weight (lb.)	Arm (in.)	Moment (lb.-in.)
Empty weight	1,495.0	101.4	151,593.0
Pilot and passengers	380.0	64.0	24,320.0
Fuel (30 × 6)	180.0	96.0	17,280.0
	2,055.0		193,193.0

Now add the weights and moments. To get CG, you divide total moment by total weight (193,193 ÷ 2,055.0) = a CG of 94.01 inches.

Answer (A) is incorrect. The total moment must be divided by the total weight to obtain the correct CG. Answer (C) is incorrect. The total moment must be divided by the total weight to obtain the correct CG.

50. (Refer to Figure 34 on page 205.) What is the maximum amount of fuel that may be aboard the airplane on takeoff if loaded as follows?

	WEIGHT (LB)	MOM/1000
Empty weight	1,350	51.5
Pilot and front passenger	340	
Rear passengers	310	
Baggage	45	
Oil, 8 qt.		

A. 24 gallons.

B. 32 gallons.

C. 40 gallons.

Answer (C) is correct. *(PHAK Chap 10)*

DISCUSSION: To find the maximum amount of fuel this airplane can carry, add the empty weight (1,350), pilot and front passenger weight (340), rear passengers (310), baggage (45), and oil (15), for a total of 2,060 pounds. (Find the oil weight and moment by consulting Note 2 on Fig. 34. It is 15 lb. and –0.2 moments.) Gross weight maximum on the center of gravity moment envelope chart is 2,300. Thus, 240 lb. of weight (2,300 – 2,060) is available for fuel. Since each gallon of fuel weighs 6 lb., this airplane can carry 40 gal. of fuel (240 ÷ 6 lb. per gal.) if its center of gravity moments do not exceed the limit. Note that long-range tanks were not mentioned; assume they exist.

Compute the moments for each item. The empty weight moment is given as 51.5. Calculate the moment for the pilot and front passenger as 12.5, the rear passengers as 22.5, the fuel as 11.5, the baggage as 4.0, and the oil as –0.2. These total to 101.8, which is within the envelope, so 40 gal. of fuel may be carried.

	Weight	Moment/1000 lb.-in.
Empty weight	1,350	51.5
Pilot and front seat passenger	340	12.5
Rear passengers	310	22.5
Baggage	45	4.0
Fuel (40 gal. × 6 lb./gal.)	240	11.5
Oil	15	–0.2
	2,300	101.8

Answer (A) is incorrect. More than 24 gal. of fuel may be carried. Answer (B) is incorrect. More than 32 gal. of fuel may be carried.

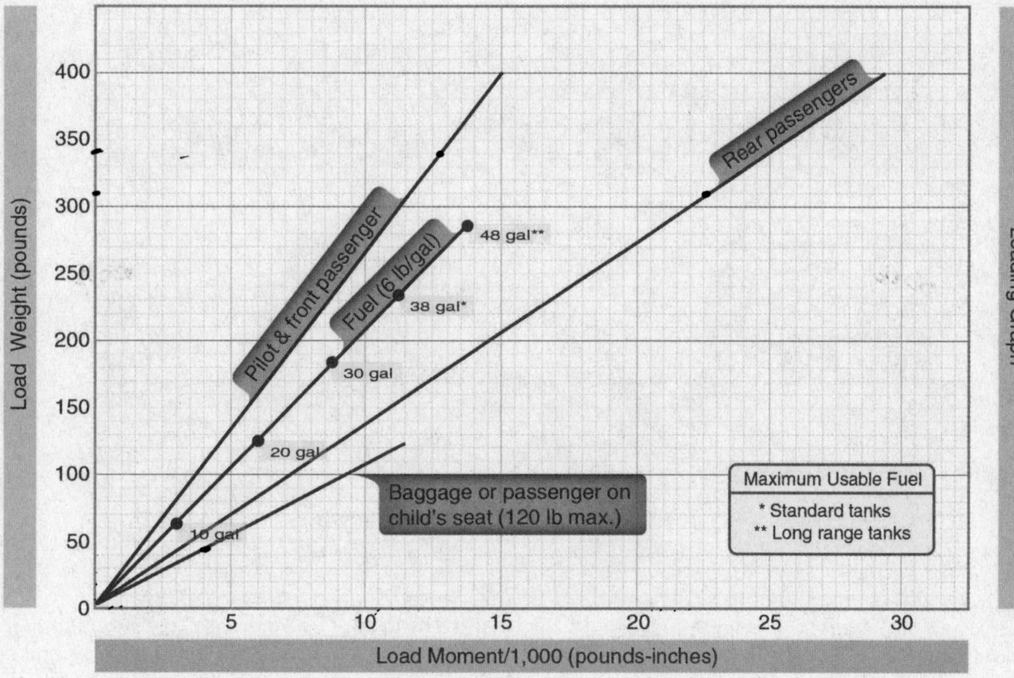

Notes: 1. Lines representing adjustable seats show the pilot or passenger center of gravity on adjustable seats positioned for an average occupant. Refer to the Loading Arrangements diagram for forward and aft limits of occupant CG range.

2. Engine Oil: 8 qt = 15 lb at −0.2 Moment/1,000

Note: The empty weight of this airplane ***does not include*** *the weight of the oil.*

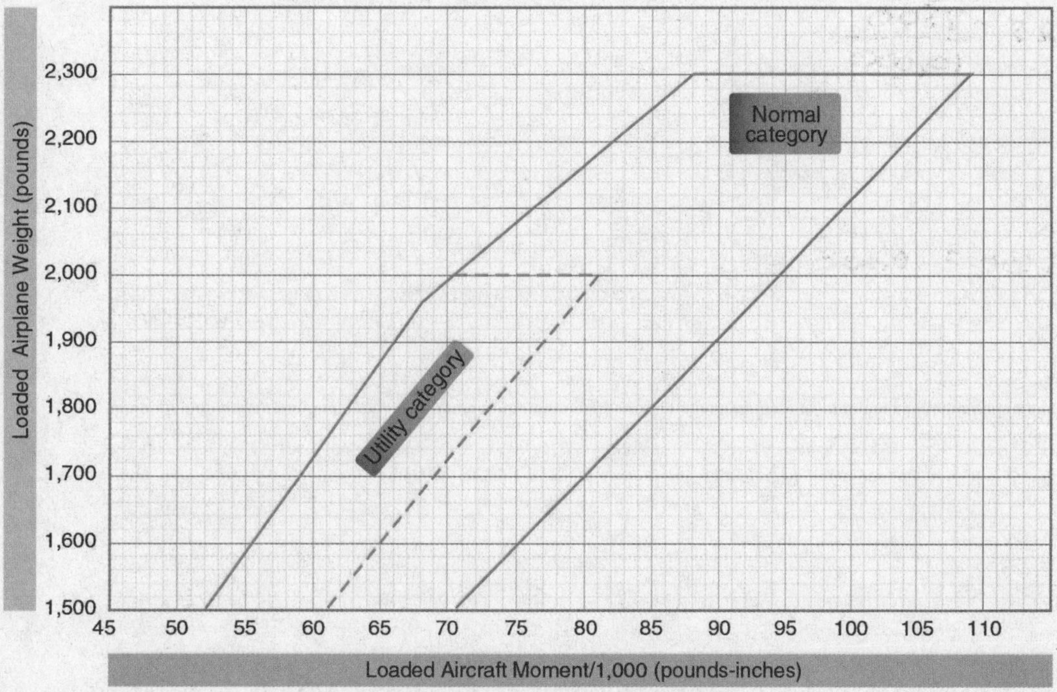

Figure 34. – Airplane Weight and Balance Graphs.

5.8 Center of Gravity Calculations

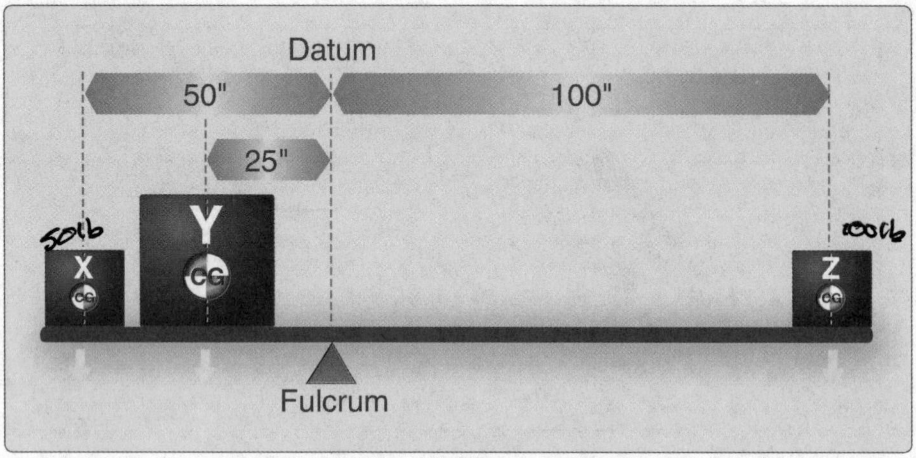

Figure 61. – Weight and Balance Diagram.

51. (Refer to Figure 61 above.) If 50 pounds of weight is located at point X and 100 pounds at point Z, how much weight must be located at point Y to balance the plank?

A. 30 pounds.

B. 50 pounds.

C. 300 pounds.

x = 50x50 = 2500

y = 300x25 = 7500

10,000

z = 100x100 = 10.000

2500 + y = 10,000

Answer (C) is correct. *(PHAK Chap 10)*

DISCUSSION: Compute and sum the moments left and right of the fulcrum. Set them equal to one another and solve for the desired variable:

$$
\begin{aligned}
\text{left} &= \text{right} \\
50 \text{ lb.}(50 \text{ in.}) + Y(25 \text{ in.}) &= 100 \text{ lb.}(100 \text{ in.}) \\
2{,}500 + 25Y &= 10{,}000 \\
25Y &= 7{,}500 \\
Y &= 300 \text{ lb.}
\end{aligned}
$$

Answer (A) is incorrect. This weight in the place of Y would cause the plank to be heavier on the right side. Answer (B) is incorrect. This weight in the place of Y would cause the plank to be heavier on the right side.

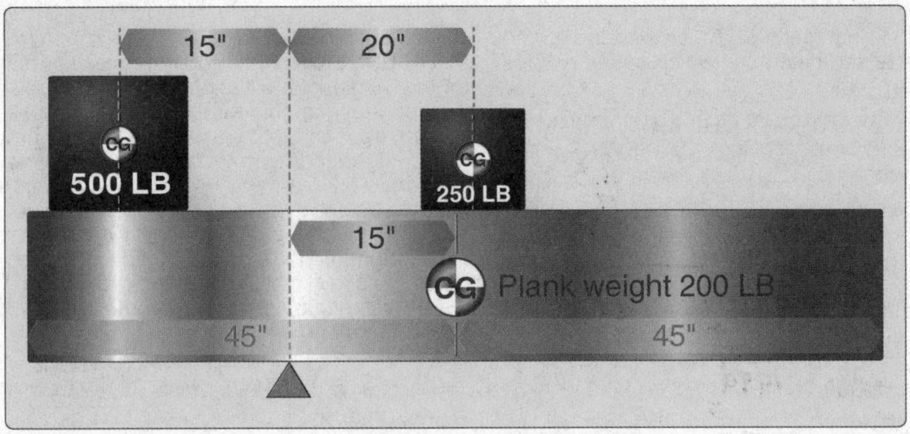

Figure 60. – Weight and Balance Diagram.

52. (Refer to Figure 60 above.) How should the 500-pound weight be shifted to balance the plank on the fulcrum?

A. 1 inch to the left.

B. 1 inch to the right.

C. 4.5 inches to the right.

left = right
500x = 250(20) + 200(15)
500x = 5000 + 3000
500x = 8000
x = 16

Answer (A) is correct. *(PHAK Chap 10)*

DISCUSSION: To find the desired location of the 500-lb. weight, compute and sum the moments left and right of the fulcrum. Set them equal to one another and solve for the desired variable:

$$\begin{aligned} \text{left} &= \text{right} \\ 500 \text{ lb.}(X) &= 250 \text{ lb.}(20 \text{ in.}) + 200 \text{ lb.}(15 \text{ in.}) \\ 500X &= 8{,}000 \\ X &= 16 \text{ in.} \end{aligned}$$

The 500-lb. weight must be 16 in. from the fulcrum to balance the plank. The weight should be shifted 1 in. to the left.

Answer (B) is incorrect. The 500-lb. weight should be 16 in. from the fulcrum; thus, it must be moved 1 in. to the left, not right, to balance the plank. Answer (C) is incorrect. Shifting the 500-lb. weight 4.5 in. to the right would cause the plank to be heavier on the right side.

5.9 Center of Gravity Graphs

53. (Refer to Figure 34 on page 209.) Calculate the moment of the airplane and determine which category is applicable.

	WEIGHT (LB)	MOM/1000
Empty weight	1,350	51.5
Pilot and front passenger	310	
Rear passengers	96	
Fuel, 38 gal.		
Oil, 8 qt.		–0.2

A. 79.2, utility category.

B. 80.8, utility category.

C. 81.2, normal category.

Answer (B) is correct. *(PHAK Chap 10)*

DISCUSSION: First, total the weight and get 1,999 lb. Note that the 38 gal. of fuel weighs 228 lb. (38 gal. × 6 lb./gallon).

Find the moments for the pilot and front seat passenger, rear passengers, and fuel by using the loading graph in Fig. 34. Find the oil weight and moment by consulting Note 2 on Fig. 34. It is 15 lb. and –0.2 moments. Total the moments as shown in the schedule below.

Now refer to the center of gravity moment envelope. Find the gross weight of 1,999 on the vertical scale, and move horizontally across the chart until intersecting the vertical line that represents the 80.8 moment. Note that a moment of 80.8 lb.-in. falls into the utility category envelope.

	Weight lb.	Moment/1000 lb.-in.
Empty weight	1,350	51.5
Pilot and front seat passenger	310	11.5
Rear passengers	96	6.7
Fuel (38 gal. × 6 lb./gal.)	228	11.3
Oil	15	–0.2
	1,999	80.8

Answer (A) is incorrect. A moment of 79.2 is 1.6 less than the correct moment of 80.8 pound-inches. Answer (C) is incorrect. The moment of the oil must be subtracted, not added.

54. (Refer to Figure 34 on page 209.) Determine the moment with the following data:

	WEIGHT (LB)	MOM/1000
Empty weight	1,350	51.5
Pilot and front passenger	340	
Fuel (std tanks)	Capacity	
Oil, 8 qt.		

A. 69.9 pound-inches.

B. 75.4 pound-inches.

C. 77.6 pound-inches.

Answer (B) is correct. *(PHAK Chap 10)*

DISCUSSION: To find the CG moment/1000, find the moments for each item and total the moments as shown in the schedule below. For the fuel, the loading graph shows the maximum as 38 gal. for standard tanks (38 gal. × 6 lb. = 228 pounds). (Find the oil weight and moment by consulting Note 2 on Fig. 34; it is 15 lb. and –0.2 moments.) These total 75.4, so this answer is correct.

	Weight lb.	Moment/1000 lb.-in.
Empty weight	1,350	51.5
Pilot and front seat passenger	340	12.8
Fuel	228	11.3
Oil	15	–0.2
	1,933	75.4

Answer (A) is incorrect. This would be the moment with only 20 gal. (not full capacity) of fuel on board. Answer (C) is incorrect. This would be the moment with full long-range (not standard) tanks on board.

55. (Refer to Figure 34 on page 209.) Determine the aircraft loaded moment and the aircraft category.

	WEIGHT (LB)	MOM/1000
Empty weight	1,350	51.5
Pilot and front passenger	380	
Fuel, 48 gal	288	
Oil, 8 qt.		

A. 78.2, normal category.

B. 79.2, normal category.

C. 80.4, utility category.

Answer (B) is correct. *(PHAK Chap 10)*

DISCUSSION: The moments for the pilot, front passenger, fuel, and oil must be found on the loading graph in Fig. 34. Total all the moments and the weight as shown in the schedule below.

Now refer to the center of gravity moment envelope graph. Find the gross weight of 2,033 on the vertical scale, and move horizontally across the graph until intersecting the vertical line that represents the 79.2 moment. A moment of 79.2 lb.-in. falls into the normal category envelope.

	Weight lb.	Moment/1000 lb.-in.
Empty weight	1,350	51.5
Pilot and front seat passenger	380	14.2
Fuel (capacity)	288	13.7
Oil	15	–0.2
	2,033	79.2

Answer (A) is incorrect. A moment of 78.2 lb.-in. is 1.0 less than the correct moment of 79.2 pound-inches. Answer (C) is incorrect. A moment of 80.4 lb.-in. is 1.2 more than the correct moment of 79.2 pound-inches.

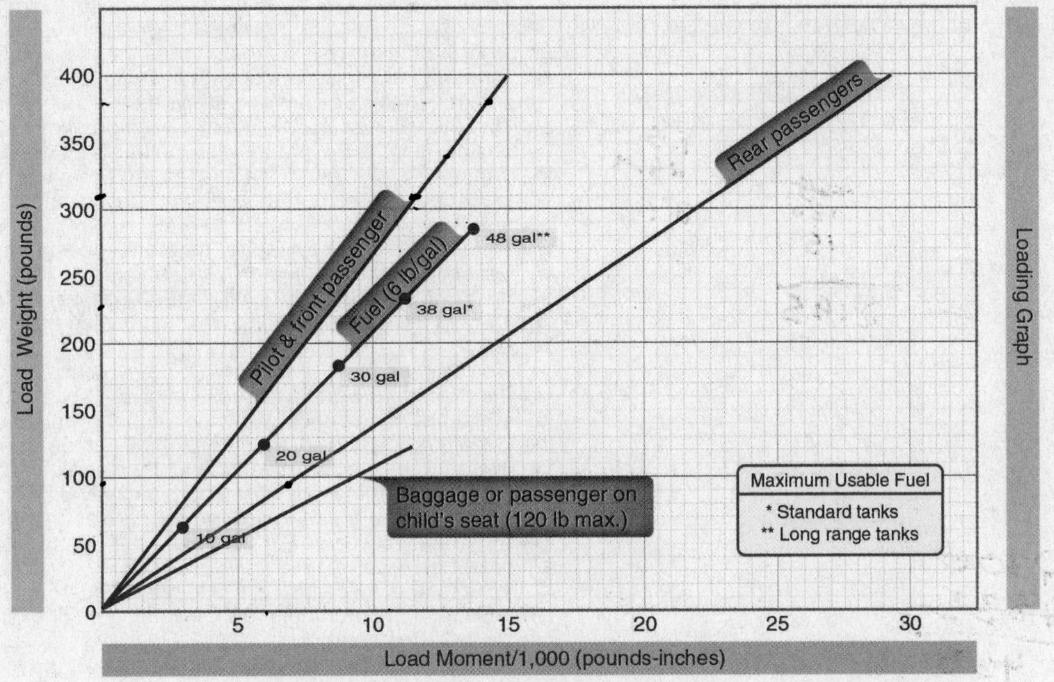

Notes: 1. Lines representing adjustable seats show the pilot or passenger center of gravity on adjustable seats positioned for an average occupant. Refer to the Loading Arrangements diagram for forward and aft limits of occupant CG range.

2. Engine Oil: 8 qt = 15 lb at −0.2 Moment/1,000

Note: The empty weight of this airplane does not include the weight of the oil.

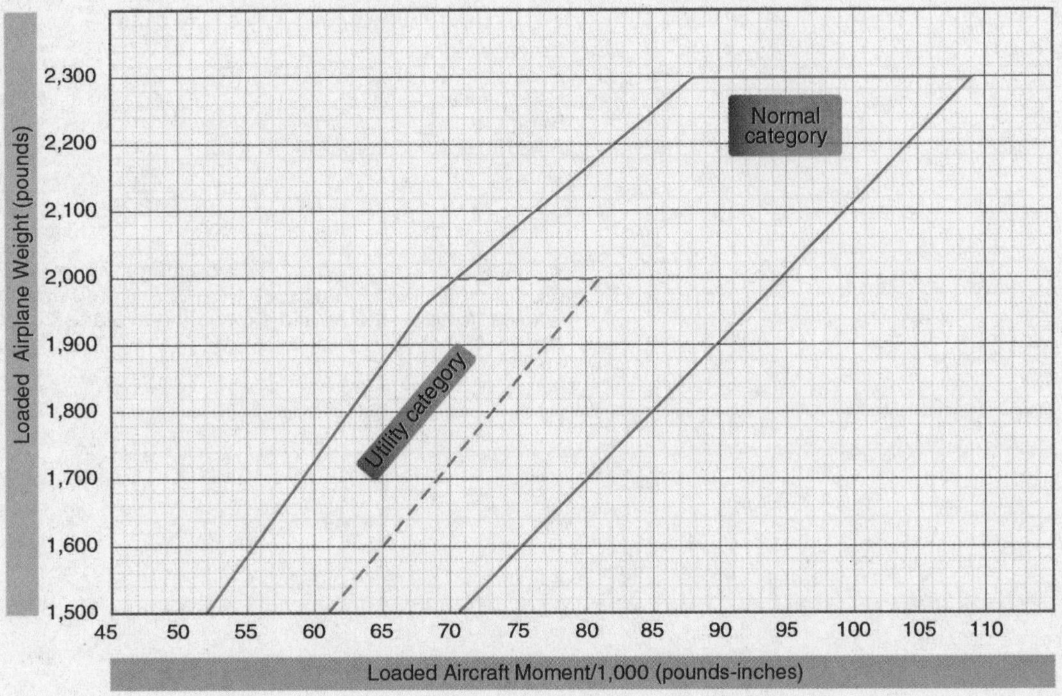

Figure 34. – Airplane Weight and Balance Graphs.

56. (Refer to Figure 34 on page 211.) What is the maximum amount of baggage that may be loaded aboard the airplane for the CG to remain within the moment envelope?

	WEIGHT (LB)	MOM/1000
Empty weight	1,350	51.5
Pilot and front passenger	250	
Rear passengers	400	
Baggage		---
Fuel, 30 gal.		
Oil, 8 qt.		–0.2

A. 105 pounds.

B. 110 pounds.

C. 120 pounds.

Answer (A) is correct. *(PHAK Chap 10)*

DISCUSSION: To compute the amount of weight left for baggage, compute each individual moment by using the loading graph and add them up. First, compute the moment for the pilot and front seat passenger with a weight of 250 pounds. Refer to the loading graph and the vertical scale at the left side and find the value of 250. From this position, move to the right horizontally across the graph until you intersect the diagonal line that represents pilot and front passenger. From this point, move vertically down to the bottom scale, which indicates a moment of about 9.2.

To compute rear passenger moment, measure up the vertical scale of the loading graph to a value of 400, horizontally across to intersect the rear passenger diagonal line, and down vertically to the moment scale, which indicates approximately 29.0.

To compute the moment of the fuel, you must recall that fuel weighs 6 lb. per gallon. The question gives 30 gal., for a total fuel weight of 180 pounds. Now move up the weight scale on the loading graph to 180, then horizontally across to intersect the diagonal line that represents fuel, then vertically down to the moment scale, which indicates approximately 8.7.

To get the weight of the oil, see Note 2 at the bottom of the loading graph section of Fig. 34. It gives 15 lb. as the weight with a moment of –0.2.

Now total the weights (2,195 lb. including 15 lb. of engine oil). Also total the moments (98.2 including engine oil with a negative 0.2 moment).

With this information, refer to the center of gravity moment envelope chart. Note that the maximum weight in the envelope is 2,300 pounds. The amount of 2,300 lb. – 2,195 lb. already totaled leaves a maximum possible 105 lb. for baggage. However, you must be sure 105 lb. of baggage does not exceed the 109 moments allowed at the top of the envelope. On the loading graph, 105 lb. of baggage indicates approximately 10 moments.

Thus, a total of 108.2 moments (98.2 + 10) is within the 109 moments allowed on the envelope for 2,300 lb. of weight. Therefore, baggage of 105 lb. can be loaded.

	Weight	Moment/1000 lb.-in.
Empty weight	1,350	51.5
Pilot and front seat passenger	250	9.2
Rear passengers	400	29.0
Baggage	?	?
Fuel (30 gal. × 6 lb./gal.)	180	8.7
Oil	15	–0.2
	2,195	98.2 (without baggage)

Answer (B) is incorrect. This baggage weight would exceed the airplane's maximum gross weight. Answer (C) is incorrect. This baggage weight would exceed the airplane's maximum gross weight.

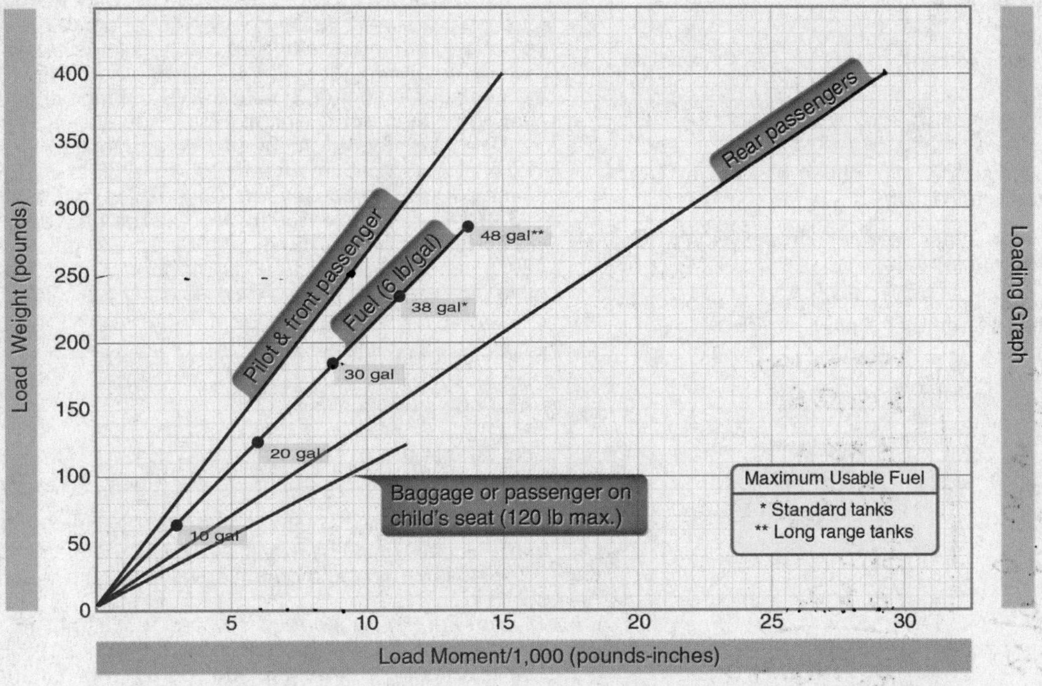

Notes: 1. Lines representing adjustable seats show the pilot or passenger center of gravity on adjustable seats positioned for an average occupant. Refer to the Loading Arrangements diagram for forward and aft limits of occupant CG range.

2. Engine Oil: 8 qt = 15 lb at −0.2 Moment/1,000

Note: The empty weight of this airplane <u>does not include</u> the weight of the oil.

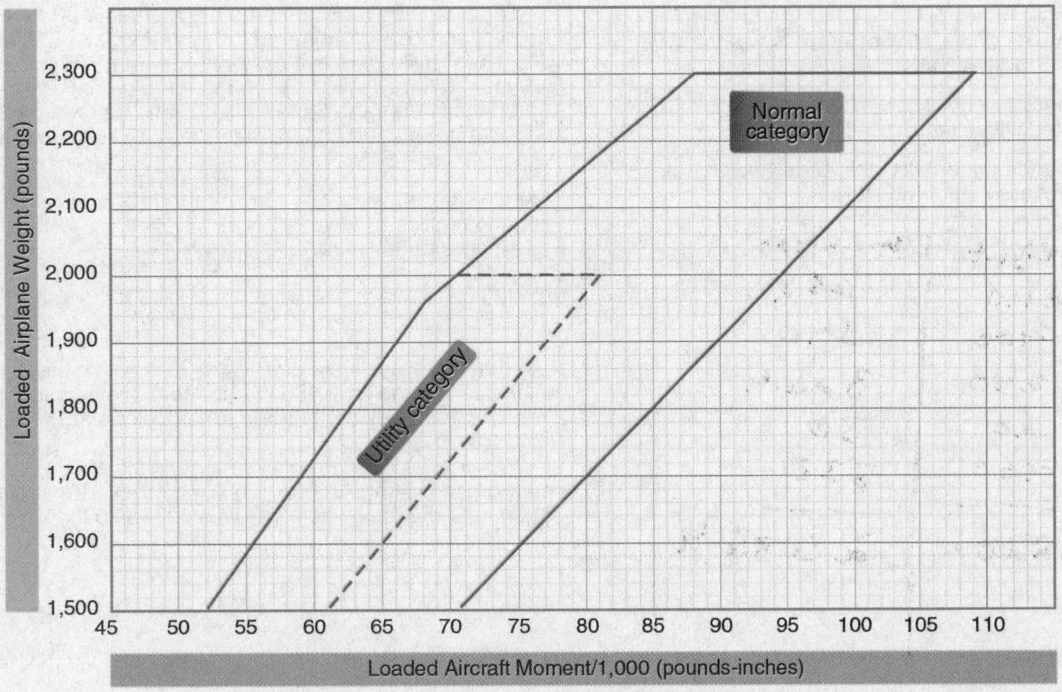

Figure 34. – Airplane Weight and Balance Graphs.

57. (Refer to Figure 67 on page 213.) Determine the condition of the airplane:

Pilot and copilot . . . . 375 lb
Passengers -- aft position. . . . . 245 lb
Baggage . . . . 65 lb
Fuel . . . . 70 gal

A. 185 pounds under allowable gross weight; CG is located within limits.

B. 162 pounds under allowable gross weight; CG is located within limits.

C. 162 pounds under allowable gross weight; CG is located aft of the aft limit.

weight	mom/100
375	318.75
245	333.2
65	97.5
420	315
2110	1652
3215	2,716.45

Answer (A) is correct. *(PHAK Chap 10)*

DISCUSSION: Both the total weight and the total moment must be calculated. As in most weight and balance problems, you should begin by setting up a schedule as below. Note that the empty weight in Fig. 67 is given as 2,110 with a moment/100 in. of 1,652 (note the use of moment/100 on this chart), and that empty weight includes the oil.

The next step is to compute the moment/100 for each item. The pilot and copilot moment/100 is 318.75 lb.-in. (375 lb. × 85 in. ÷ 100). The passengers (aft position) moment/100 is 333.2 lb.-in. (245 lb. × 136 in. ÷ 100). The baggage moment/100 is 97.5 lb.-in.(65 lb. × 150 in. ÷ 100). The 70-gal. fuel weight is 420 lb., and the moment/100 is 315 lb.-in. (read directly from the table).

	Weight	Moment/100
Empty weight w/oil	2,110	1,652.00
Pilot and copilot	375	318.75
Passengers (aft position)	245	333.20
Baggage	65	97.50
Fuel (70 gal.)	420	315.00
	3,215	2,716.45

Note that the gross weight of 3,215 lb. is within the 3,400 lb. maximum allowable by 185 lb., and that the moment/100 of 2,716.45 is within the moment envelope at the intersection with 3,215 lb.

Answer (B) is incorrect. You are 185 lb., not 162 lb., under gross weight. Answer (C) is incorrect. You are 185 lb., not 162 lb., under gross weight, and you are within, not aft of, the allowable CG limits.

58. (Refer to Figure 67 on page 213.) Determine the condition of the airplane:

Pilot and copilot . . . . 400 lb
Passengers -- aft position. . . . . 240 lb
Baggage . . . . 20 lb
Fuel . . . . 75 gal

A. 157 pounds under allowable gross weight; CG is located within limits.

B. 180 pounds under allowable gross weight; CG is located within limits.

C. 180 pounds under allowable gross weight, but CG is located aft of the aft limit.

weight	mom/100
2110	1652
400	340
240	326.4
20	30
450	338
3220	2686.4

Answer (B) is correct. *(PHAK Chap 10)*

DISCUSSION: Both the total weight and the total moment must be calculated. As in most weight and balance problems, you should begin by setting up a schedule as below. Note that the empty weight in Fig. 67 is given as 2,110 with a moment/100 in. of 1,652 (note the use of moment/100 on this chart), and that empty weight includes the oil.

The next step is to compute the moment/100 for each item. The pilot and copilot moment/100 is 340 lb.-in. (400 lb. × 85 in. ÷ 100). The passengers (aft position) moment/100 is 326.4 lb.-in. (240 lb. × 136 in. ÷ 100). The baggage moment/100 is 30 lb.-in. (read directly from the table). The 75-gal. fuel weight is 450 lb., and the moment/100 is 338 lb.-in. (read directly from the table).

	Weight	Moment/100
Empty weight w/oil	2,110	1,652.00
Pilot and copilot	400	340.00
Passengers (aft position)	240	326.40
Baggage	20	30.00
Fuel (75 gal.)	450	338.00
	3,220	2,686.40

Note that the gross weight of 3,220 lb. is within the 3,400 lb. maximum allowable by 180 lb., and that this moment/100 of 2,686.4 lb.-in. is within the moment envelope at the intersection with 3,220 lb.

Answer (A) is incorrect. The airplane is 180 lb., not 157 lb., under gross weight. Answer (C) is incorrect. The airplane is within, not aft of, allowable CG limits at 3,220 lb.

Empty Weight Data

*Oil is included in empty weight	Empty Weight (pountds)	Empty Weight Moment (/100)
Certificated Weight	2,110	1,652

Fuel

ARM 75 inches

Gallons	Weight (pounds)	Moment (in-lb)	Gallons	Weight (pounds)	Moment (in-lb)
5	30	23	45	270	203
10	60	45	49	294	221
15	90	68	55	330	248
20	120	90	60	360	270
25	150	113	65	390	293
30	180	135	70	420	315
35	210	158	75	450	338
40	240	180	80	480	360

Occupants

Front seats		Rear seats		
ARM 85 inches			Fwd Position ARM 111 inches	Alt Position ARM 136 inches
Weight (pounds)	Moment (in-lb)	Weight (pounds)	Moment (in-lb)	Moment (in-lb)
120	102	120	133	163
130	111	130	144	177
140	119	140	155	190
150	128	150	167	204
160	136	160	178	218
170	145	170	189	231
180	153	180	200	245
190	162	190	211	258
200	170	200	222	273

Baggage

ARM 150

Weight (pounds)	Moment (in-lb)
10	15
20	30
30	45
40	60
50	75
60	90
70	105
80	120
90	135
100	150
110	165
120	180
130	195
140	210
150	225
160	240
170	255
180	270
190	285
200	300
210	315
220	330
230	345
240	360
250	375
260	390
270	405

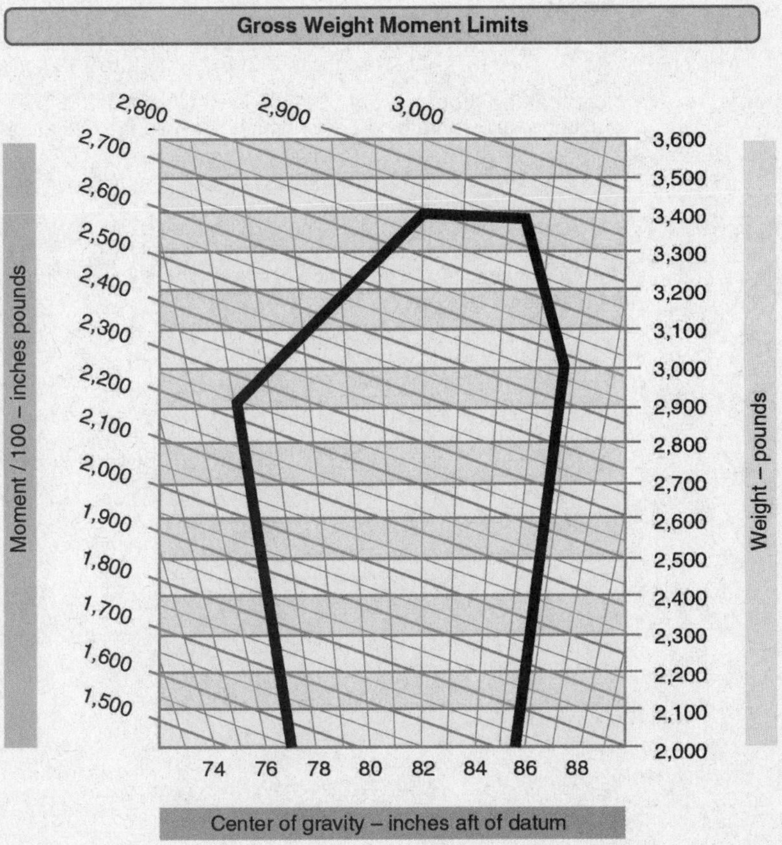

NOTE: All moments are equal to

$$\frac{\text{weight} \times \text{arm}}{100}$$

Figure 67. – Weight and Balance Chart.

59. (Refer to Figure 67 on page 215.) Determine the condition of the airplane:

Pilot and copilot . . . . 316 lb
Passengers
  Fwd position. . . . . 130 lb
  Aft position. . . . . 147 lb
Baggage . . . . 50 lb
Fuel . . . . 75 gal

A. 197 pounds under allowable gross weight; CG 83.6 inches aft of datum.

B. 163 pounds under allowable gross weight; CG 82 inches aft of datum.

C. 197 pounds under allowable gross weight; CG 84.6 inches aft of datum.

Answer (A) is correct. *(PHAK Chap 10)*

DISCUSSION: Both the total weight and the total moment must be calculated. As in most weight and balance problems, you should begin by setting up a schedule as below. Note that the empty weight in Fig. 67 is given as 2,110 with a moment/100 in. of 1,652 (note the use of moment/100 on this chart), and that empty weight includes the oil. Be aware that some table values do not result in an accurate mathematical answer. You should use the table as a guide, but do not neglect to check your math.

The next step is to compute the moment/100 for each item. The pilot and copilot together weigh 316 lb., and their moment/100 is 268.6 lb.-in. (316 lb. × 85 in. ÷ 100). The passengers (forward position) moment/100 is 144.3 lb.-in. (130 lb. × 111 in. ÷ 100). The passengers (aft position) moment/100 is 199.92 lb.-in. (147 lb. × 136 in. ÷ 100). The baggage moment/100 is 75 lb.-in. (read directly from the table). The 75-gal. fuel weight is 450 lb., and the moment/100 is 338 lb.-in. (read directly from the table).

	Weight	Moment/100
Empty weight w/oil	2,110	1,652.00
Pilot and copilot	316	268.60
Passengers		
Fwd position	130	144.30
Aft position	147	199.92
Baggage	50	75.00
Fuel (75 gal.)	450	338.00
	3,203	2,677.82

Note that the gross weight of 3,203 is within the 3,400-lb. maximum allowable by 197 lb., which is within the CG envelope.

$$CG = \frac{2,677.82}{3,203} \times 100 = 83.6 \text{ in. aft of datum}$$

Answer (B) is incorrect. The airplane is 197 lb., not 163 lb., under gross weight and the CG is 83.6 in., not 82.0 in., aft of datum. Answer (C) is incorrect. The airplane's CG is 83.6 in., not 84.6 in., aft of datum.

Empty Weight Data		
*Oil is included in empty weight	Empty Weight (pountds)	Empty Weight Moment (/100)
Certificated Weight	2,110	1,652

Occupants				
Front seats			Rear seats	
ARM 85 inches			Fwd Position ARM 111 inches	Alt Position ARM 136 inches
Weight (pounds)	Moment (in-lb)	Weight (pounds)	Moment (in-lb)	Moment (in-lb)
120	102	120	133	163
130	111	130	144	177
140	119	140	155	190
150	128	150	167	204
160	136	160	178	218
170	145	170	189	231
180	153	180	200	245
190	162	190	211	258
200	170	200	222	273

Fuel					
ARM 75 inches					
Gallons	Weight (pounds)	Moment (in-lb)	Gallons	Weight (pounds)	Moment (in-lb)
5	30	23	45	270	203
10	60	45	49	294	221
15	90	68	55	330	248
20	120	90	60	360	270
25	150	113	65	390	293
30	180	135	70	420	315
35	210	158	75	450	338
40	240	180	80	480	360

Baggage	
ARM 150	
Weight (pounds)	Moment (in-lb)
10	15
20	30
30	45
40	60
50	75
60	90
70	105
80	120
90	135
100	150
110	165
120	180
130	195
140	210
150	225
160	240
170	255
180	270
190	285
200	300
210	315
220	330
230	345
240	360
250	375
260	390
270	405

Gross Weight Moment Limits

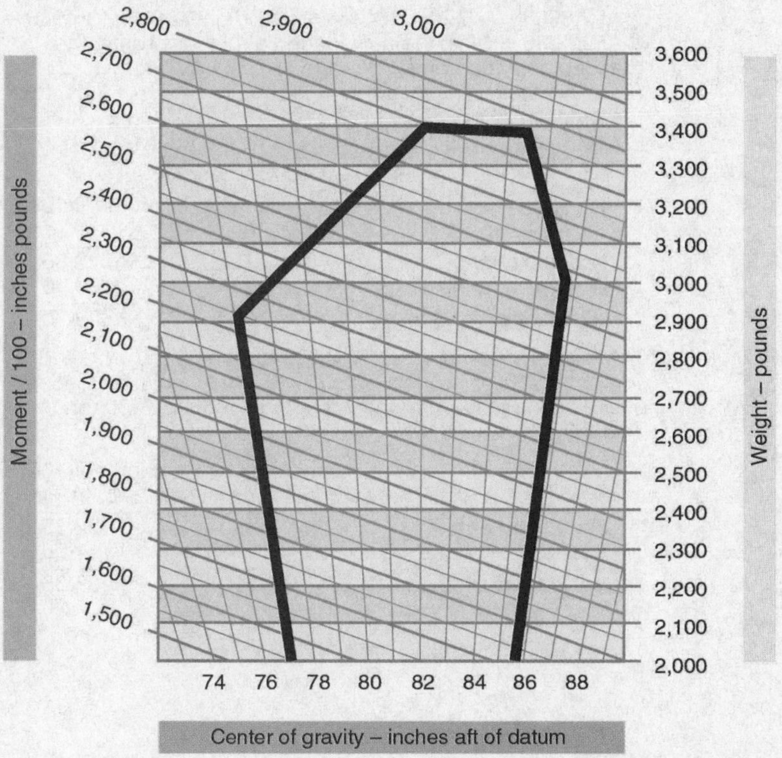

NOTE: All moments are equal to

$$\frac{\text{weight} \times \text{arm}}{100}$$

Figure 67. – Weight and Balance Chart.

5.10 Center of Gravity Tables

60. (Refer to Figure 32 on page 217 and Figure 33 on page 217.) With the airplane loaded as follows, what action can be taken to balance the airplane?

Front seat occupants . . . . 411 lb
Rear seat occupants . . . . 100 lb
Main wing tanks . . . . 44 gal

A. Fill the auxiliary wing tanks.

B. Add a 100-pound weight to the baggage compartment.

C. Transfer 10 gallons of fuel from the main tanks to the auxiliary tanks.

weight	mom(100)
2015	1554
411	349.35
100	121
264	198
2790	2222.35

Answer (B) is correct. *(PHAK Chap 10)*

DISCUSSION: You need to calculate the weight and moment of the loaded airplane. The weight of the empty plane, including oil, is 2,015 lb., and it has a moment of 1,554. The 411 lb. in the front seats has a total moment of 349.35 [411 × 85 (ARM) = 34,935 ÷ 100 = 349.35]. The rear seat occupants have a weight of 100 lb. and a moment of 121.0 [100 × 121 (ARM) = 12,100 ÷ 100 = 121.0]. The fuel weight is given on the chart as 264 lb. with a moment of 198.

	Weight lb.	Moment/100 lb.-in.
Empty weight	2,015	1,554.00
Front seat	411	349.35
Rear seat	100	121.00
Fuel	264	198.00
Loaded airplane	2,790	2,222.35

On the Fig. 33 chart, the acceptable moment/100 range for 2,790 lb. is 2,243 to 2,374. Thus, the CG of 2,222.35 is forward of the acceptable moment/100 range.

	Weight lb.	Moment/100 lb.-in.
Loaded airplane	2,790	2,222.35
Baggage	100	140.00
New loaded airplane	2,890	2,362.35

At 2,890 lb. (2,790 + 100) and a moment/100 of 2,362.35 (2,222.35 + 140), the new loaded airplane is within the acceptable moment/100 range of 2,354 to 2,452.

Answer (A) is incorrect. At 2,904 lb. (2,790 + 114) and a moment/100 of 2,329.35 (2,222.35 + 107), the new loaded airplane is forward of the acceptable moment/100 range of 2,370 to 2,463.

	Weight lb.	Moment/100 lb.-in.
Loaded airplane	2,790	2,222.35
Fill aux wing tanks	114	107.00
New loaded airplane	2,904	2,329.35

Answer (C) is incorrect. At 2,790 lb. (2,790 + 0) and a moment/100 of 2,233.35 (2,222.35 + 11), the new loaded airplane is forward of the acceptable moment/100 range of 2,243 to 2,374.

	Weight lb.	Moment/100 lb.-in.
Loaded airplane	2,790	2,222.35
Transfer 10 gallons	0	11.00
New loaded airplane	2,790	2,233.35

Useful load weights and moments

Baggage or 5th seat occupant

ARM 140

Weight	Moment/100
10	14
20	28
30	42
40	56
50	70
60	84
70	98
80	112
90	126
100	140
110	154
120	168
130	182
140	196
150	210
160	224
170	238
180	252
190	266
200	280
210	294
220	308
230	322
240	336
250	350
260	364
270	378

Occupants

Front seats ARM 85		Rear seats ARM 121	
Weight	Moment/100	Weight	Moment/100
120	102	120	145
130	110	130	157
140	119	140	169
150	128	150	182
160	136	160	194
170	144	170	206
180	153	180	218
190	162	190	230
200	170	200	242

Usable fuel

Main wing tanks ARM 75

Gallons	Weight	Moment/100
5	30	22
10	60	45
15	90	68
20	120	90
25	150	112
30	180	135
35	210	158
40	240	180
44	264	198

Auxiliary wing tanks ARM 94

Gallons	Weight	Moment/100
5	30	28
10	60	56
15	90	85
19	114	107

*Oil

Quarts	Weight	Moment/100
10	19	5

*Included in basic empty weight.

Empty weight~2,015

MOM/100~1,554

Moment limits vs weight

Moment limits are based on the following weight and center of gravity limit data (landing gear down).

Weight condition	Forward CG limit	AFT CG limit
2,950 lb (takeoff or landing)	**82.1**	**84.7**
2,525 lb	**77.5**	**85.7**
2,475 lb or less	**77.0**	**85.7**

Figure 32. – Airplane Weight and Balance Tables.

Moment limits vs weight (continued)

Weight	Minimum Moment/100	Maximum Moment/100
2,100	1,617	1,800
2,110	1,625	1,808
2,120	1,632	1,817
2,130	1,640	1,825
2,140	1,648	1,834
2,150	1,656	1,843
2,160	1,663	1,851
2,170	1,671	1,860
2,180	1,679	1,868
2,190	1,686	1,877
2,200	1,694	1,885
2,210	1,702	1,894
2,220	1,709	1,903
2,230	1,717	1,911
2,240	1,725	1,920
2,250	1,733	1,928
2,260	1,740	1,937
2,270	1,748	1,945
2,280	1,756	1,954
2,290	1,763	1,963
2,300	1,771	1,971
2,310	1,779	1,980
2,320	1,786	1,988
2,330	1,794	1,997
2,340	1,802	2,005
2,350	1,810	2,014
2,360	1,817	2,023
2,370	1,825	2,031
2,380	1,833	2,040
2,390	1,840	2,048
2,400	1,848	2,057
2,410	1,856	2,065
2,420	1,863	2,074
2,430	1,871	2,083
2,440	1,879	2,091
2,450	1,887	2,100
2,460	1,894	2,108
2,470	1,902	2,117
2,480	1,911	2,125
2,490	1,921	2,134

Weight	Minimum Moment/100	Maximum Moment/100
2,500	1,932	2,143
2,510	1,942	2,151
2,520	1,953	2,160
2,530	1,963	2,168
2,540	1,974	2,176
2,550	1,984	2,184
2,560	1,995	2,192
2,570	2,005	2,200
2,580	2,016	2,208
2,590	2,026	2,216
2,600	2,037	2,224
2,610	2,048	2,232
2,620	2,058	2,239
2,630	2,069	2,247
2,640	2,080	2,255
2,650	2,090	2,263
2,660	2,101	2,271
2,670	2,112	2,279
2,680	2,123	2,287
2,690	2,133	2,295
2,700	2,144	2,303
2,710	2,155	2,311
2,720	2,166	2,319
2,730	2,177	2,326
2,740	2,188	2,334
2,750	2,199	2,342
2,760	2,210	2,350
2,770	2,221	2,358
2,780	2,232	2,366
2,790	2,243	2,374
2,800	2,254	2,381
2,810	2,265	2,389
2,820	2,276	2,397
2,830	2,287	2,405
2,840	2,298	2,413
2,850	2,309	2,421
2,860	2,320	2,428
2,870	2,332	2,436
2,880	2,343	2,444
2,890	2,354	2,452
2,900	2,365	2,460
2,910	2,377	2,468
2,920	2,388	2,475
2,930	2,399	2,483
2,940	2,411	2,491
2,950	2,422	2,499

Figure 33. – Airplane Weight and Balance Tables.

61. (Refer to Figure 32 on page 219 and Figure 33 on page 219.) Determine if the airplane weight and balance is within limits.

Front seat occupants . . . . 340 lb
Rear seat occupants . . . . 295 lb
Fuel (main wing tanks) . . . . 44 gal
Baggage . . . . 56 lb

A. 20 pounds overweight, CG aft of aft limits.

B. 20 pounds overweight, CG within limits.

C. 20 pounds overweight, CG forward of forward limits.

Answer (B) is correct. *(PHAK Chap 10)*

DISCUSSION: Both the total weight and the total moment must be calculated. As in most weight and balance problems, you should begin by setting up a schedule as below. Note that the empty weight in Fig. 32 is given as 2,015 with a moment/100 in. of 1,554 (note the change to moment/100 on this chart) and that empty weight includes the oil.

The next step is to compute the moment/100 for each item. The front seat occupants' moment/100 is 289 (340 × 85 ÷ 100). The rear seat occupants' moment/100 is 357 (295 × 121 ÷ 100). The fuel (main tanks) weight of 264 lb. and moment/100 of 198 is read directly from the table. The baggage moment/100 is 78 (56 × 140 ÷ 100).

The last step is to go to the Moment Limits vs. Weight chart (Fig. 33) and note that the maximum weight allowed is 2,950, which means that the plane is 20 lb. over. At a moment/100 of 2,476, the plane is within the CG limits because the moments/100 may be from 2,422 to 2,499 at 2,950 pounds.

	Weight lb.	Moment/100 lb.-in.
Empty weight w/oil	2,015	1,554
Front seat	340	289
Rear seat	295	357
Fuel (44 gal. × 6 lb/gal)	264	198
Baggage	56	78
	2,970	2,476

Answer (A) is incorrect. The total moment of 2,476 lb.-in. is less (not more) than the aft limit of 2,499 lb.-in. at 2,950 pounds. Answer (C) is incorrect. The total moment of 2,476 lb.-in. is more (not less) than the forward limit of 2,422 lb.-in. at 2,900 pounds.

62. (Refer to Figure 32 on page 219 and Figure 33 on page 219.) Calculate the weight and balance and determine if the CG and the weight of the airplane are within limits.

Front seat occupants . . . . 350 lb
Rear seat occupants . . . . 325 lb
Baggage . . . . 27 lb
Fuel . . . . 35 gal

A. CG 81.7, out of limits forward.

B. CG 83.4, within limits.

C. CG 84.1, within limits.

Answer (B) is correct. *(PHAK Chap 10)*

DISCUSSION: Total weight, total moment, and CG must all be calculated. As in most weight and balance problems, you should begin by setting up the schedule as shown below.

Next, go to the Moment Limits vs. Weight chart (Fig. 33), and note that the maximum weight allowed is 2,950, which means that this airplane is 23 lb. under maximum weight. At a total moment of 2,441, it is also within the CG limits (2,399 to 2,483) at that weight.

Finally, compute the CG. Recall that Fig. 32 gives moment per 100 inches. The total moment is therefore 244,100 (2,441 × 100). The CG is 244,100/2,927 = 83.4.

	Weight	Moment/100 lb.-in.
Empty weight w/oil	2,015	1,554
Front seat	350	298
Rear seat	325	393
Fuel, main (35 gal.)	210	158
Baggage	27	38
	2,927	2,441

Answer (A) is incorrect. The correct moment of 2,441 lb.-in./100 is within CG limits. Answer (C) is incorrect. You must divide the total moment by the total weight to arrive at the correct CG of 83.4 inches.

Useful load weights and moments

Baggage or 5th seat occupant

ARM 140

Weight	Moment/100
10	14
20	28
30	42
40	56
50	70
60	84
70	98
80	112
90	126
100	140
110	154
120	168
130	182
140	196
150	210
160	224
170	238
180	252
190	266
200	280
210	294
220	308
230	322
240	336
250	350
260	364
270	378

Occupants

Front seats ARM 85		Rear seats ARM 121	
Weight	Moment/100	Weight	Moment/100
120	102	120	145
130	110	130	157
140	119	140	169
150	128	150	182
160	136	160	194
170	144	170	206
180	153	180	218
190	162	190	230
200	170	200	242

Usable fuel

Main wing tanks ARM 75

Gallons	Weight	Moment/100
5	30	22
10	60	45
15	90	68
20	120	90
25	150	112
30	180	135
35	210	158
40	240	180
44	264	198

Auxiliary wing tanks ARM 94

Gallons	Weight	Moment/100
5	30	28
10	60	56
15	90	85
19	114	107

*Oil

Quarts	Weight	Moment/100
10	19	5

*Included in basic empty weight.

Empty weight~2,015

MOM/100~1,554

Moment limits vs weight

Moment limits are based on the following weight and center of gravity limit data (landing gear down).

Weight condition	Forward CG limit	AFT CG limit
2,950 lb (takeoff or landing)	82.1	84.7
2,525 lb	77.5	85.7
2,475 lb or less	77.0	85.7

Figure 32. – Airplane Weight and Balance Tables.

Moment limits vs weight (continued)

Weight	Minimum Moment/100	Maximum Moment/100
2,100	1,617	1,800
2,110	1,625	1,808
2,120	1,632	1,817
2,130	1,640	1,825
2,140	1,648	1,834
2,150	1,656	1,843
2,160	1,663	1,851
2,170	1,671	1,860
2,180	1,679	1,868
2,190	1,686	1,877
2,200	1,694	1,885
2,210	1,702	1,894
2,220	1,709	1,903
2,230	1,717	1,911
2,240	1,725	1,920
2,250	1,733	1,928
2,260	1,740	1,937
2,270	1,748	1,945
2,280	1,756	1,954
2,290	1,763	1,963
2,300	1,771	1,971
2,310	1,779	1,980
2,320	1,786	1,988
2,330	1,794	1,997
2,340	1,802	2,005
2,350	1,810	2,014
2,360	1,817	2,023
2,370	1,825	2,031
2,380	1,833	2,040
2,390	1,840	2,048
2,400	1,848	2,057
2,410	1,856	2,065
2,420	1,863	2,074
2,430	1,871	2,083
2,440	1,879	2,091
2,450	1,887	2,100
2,460	1,894	2,108
2,470	1,902	2,117
2,480	1,911	2,125
2,490	1,921	2,134

Weight	Minimum Moment/100	Maximum Moment/100
2,500	1,932	2,143
2,510	1,942	2,151
2,520	1,953	2,160
2,530	1,963	2,168
2,540	1,974	2,176
2,550	1,984	2,184
2,560	1,995	2,192
2,570	2,005	2,200
2,580	2,016	2,208
2,590	2,026	2,216
2,600	2,037	2,224
2,610	2,048	2,232
2,620	2,058	2,239
2,630	2,069	2,247
2,640	2,080	2,255
2,650	2,090	2,263
2,660	2,101	2,271
2,670	2,112	2,279
2,680	2,123	2,287
2,690	2,133	2,295
2,700	2,144	2,303
2,710	2,155	2,311
2,720	2,166	2,319
2,730	2,177	2,326
2,740	2,188	2,334
2,750	2,199	2,342
2,760	2,210	2,350
2,770	2,221	2,358
2,780	2,232	2,366
2,790	2,243	2,374
2,800	2,254	2,381
2,810	2,265	2,389
2,820	2,276	2,397
2,830	2,287	2,405
2,840	2,298	2,413
2,850	2,309	2,421
2,860	2,320	2,428
2,870	2,332	2,436
2,880	2,343	2,444
2,890	2,354	2,452
2,900	2,365	2,460
2,910	2,377	2,468
2,920	2,388	2,475
2,930	2,399	2,483
2,940	2,411	2,491
2,950	2,422	2,499

Figure 33. – Airplane Weight and Balance Tables.

63. (Refer to Figure 32 on page 221 and Figure 33 on page 221.) What is the maximum amount of baggage that can be carried when the airplane is loaded as follows?

Front seat occupants	387 lb
Rear seat occupants	293 lb
Fuel	35 gal

A. 45 pounds.

B. 63 pounds.

C. 220 pounds.

Answer (A) is correct. *(PHAK Chap 10)*

DISCUSSION: The maximum allowable weight on the Moment Limits vs. Weight chart (Fig. 33) is 2,950 pounds. The total of the given weights is 2,905 lb. (including the empty weight of the airplane at 2,015 lb. and the fuel at 6 lb./gal.), so baggage cannot weigh more than 45 pounds.

It is still necessary to compute total moments to verify that the position of these weights does not move the CG out of CG limits.

The total moment of 2,459 lies safely between the moment limits of 2,422 and 2,499 on Fig. 33, at the maximum weight, so this airplane can carry as much as 45 lb. of baggage when loaded in this manner.

	Weight	Moment/100 lb.-in.
Empty weight w/oil	2,015	1,554
Front seat	387	329
Rear seat	293	355
Fuel, main (35 gal.)	210	158
Baggage	45	63
	2,950	2,459

Answer (B) is incorrect. This baggage weight would load the airplane above its maximum gross weight. Answer (C) is incorrect. This baggage weight would load the airplane above its maximum gross weight.

64. (Refer to Figure 32 on page 221 and Figure 33 on page 221.) Upon landing, the front passenger (180 pounds) departs the airplane. A rear passenger (204 pounds) moves to the front passenger position. What effect does this have on the CG if the airplane weighed 2,690 pounds and the MOM/100 was 2,260 just prior to the passenger transfer?

A. The CG moves forward approximately 3 inches.

B. The weight changes, but the CG is not affected.

C. The CG moves forward approximately 0.1 inch.

Answer (A) is correct. *(AWBH Chap 2)*

DISCUSSION: The requirement is the effect of a change in loading. Look at Fig. 32 for occupants. Losing the 180-lb. passenger from the front seat reduces the MOM/100 by 153. Moving the 204-lb. passenger from the rear seat to the front reduces the MOM/100 by about 74 (247 – 173). The total moment reduction is thus about 227 (153 + 74). As calculated below, the CG moves forward from 84.01 to 81.00 inches.

$$\text{Old CG} = \frac{226{,}000 \text{ lb.-in.}}{2{,}690 \text{ lb.}} = 84.01 \text{ in.}$$

$$\text{New CG} = \frac{203{,}300 \text{ lb.-in.}}{2{,}510 \text{ lb.}} = 81.00 \text{ in.}$$

Answer (B) is incorrect. Intuitively, one can see that the CG will be affected. Answer (C) is incorrect. Intuitively, one can see that the CG will move forward more than only 0.1 inch.

65. (Refer to Figure 32 on page 221 and Figure 33 on page 221.) What effect does a 35-gallon fuel burn (main tanks) have on the weight and balance if the airplane weighed 2,890 pounds and the MOM/100 was 2,452 at takeoff?

A. Weight is reduced by 210 pounds and the CG is aft of limits.

B. Weight is reduced by 210 pounds and the CG is unaffected.

C. Weight is reduced to 2,680 pounds and the CG moves forward.

Answer (A) is correct. *(AWBH Chap 2)*

DISCUSSION: The effect of a 35-gal. fuel burn on weight balance is required. Burning 35 gal. of fuel will reduce weight by 210 lb. and moment by 158. At 2,680 lb. (2,890 – 210), the 2,294 MOM/100 (2,452 – 158) is above the maximum moment of 2,287; i.e., CG is aft of limits. This is why weight and balance should always be computed for the beginning and end of each flight.

Answer (B) is incorrect. Intuitively, one can see that the CG would be affected. Answer (C) is incorrect. Although the moment has decreased, the CG (moment divided by weight) has moved aft.

Useful load weights and moments

Baggage or 5th seat occupant
ARM 140

Weight	Moment/100
10	14
20	28
30	42
40	56
50	70
60	84
70	98
80	112
90	126
100	140
110	154
120	168
130	182
140	196
150	210
160	224
170	238
180	252
190	266
200	280
210	294
220	308
230	322
240	336
250	350
260	364
270	378

Occupants

Front seats ARM 85		Rear seats ARM 121	
Weight	Moment/100	Weight	Moment/100
120	102	120	145
130	110	130	157
140	119	140	169
150	128	150	182
160	136	160	194
170	144	170	206
180	153	180	218
190	162	190	230
200	170	200	242

Usable fuel
Main wing tanks ARM 75

Gallons	Weight	Moment/100
5	30	22
10	60	45
15	90	68
20	120	90
25	150	112
30	180	135
35	210	158
40	240	180
44	264	198

Auxiliary wing tanks ARM 94

Gallons	Weight	Moment/100
5	30	28
10	60	56
15	90	85
19	114	107

***Oil**

Quarts	Weight	Moment/100
10	19	5

*Included in basic empty weight.

Empty weight~2,015
MOM/100~1,554

Moment limits vs weight
Moment limits are based on the following weight and center of gravity limit data (landing gear down).

Weight condition	Forward CG limit	AFT CG limit
2,950 lb (takeoff or landing)	82.1	84.7
2,525 lb	77.5	85.7
2,475 lb or less	77.0	85.7

Figure 32. – Airplane Weight and Balance Tables.

Moment limits vs weight (continued)

Weight	Minimum Moment/100	Maximum Moment/100
2,100	1,617	1,800
2,110	1,625	1,808
2,120	1,632	1,817
2,130	1,640	1,825
2,140	1,648	1,834
2,150	1,656	1,843
2,160	1,663	1,851
2,170	1,671	1,860
2,180	1,679	1,868
2,190	1,686	1,877
2,200	1,694	1,885
2,210	1,702	1,894
2,220	1,709	1,903
2,230	1,717	1,911
2,240	1,725	1,920
2,250	1,733	1,928
2,260	1,740	1,937
2,270	1,748	1,945
2,280	1,756	1,954
2,290	1,763	1,963
2,300	1,771	1,971
2,310	1,779	1,980
2,320	1,786	1,988
2,330	1,794	1,997
2,340	1,802	2,005
2,350	1,810	2,014
2,360	1,817	2,023
2,370	1,825	2,031
2,380	1,833	2,040
2,390	1,840	2,048
2,400	1,848	2,057
2,410	1,856	2,065
2,420	1,863	2,074
2,430	1,871	2,083
2,440	1,879	2,091
2,450	1,887	2,100
2,460	1,894	2,108
2,470	1,902	2,117
2,480	1,911	2,125
2,490	1,921	2,134

Weight	Minimum Moment/100	Maximum Moment/100
2,500	1,932	2,143
2,510	1,942	2,151
2,520	1,953	2,160
2,530	1,963	2,168
2,540	1,974	2,176
2,550	1,984	2,184
2,560	1,995	2,192
2,570	2,005	2,200
2,580	2,016	2,208
2,590	2,026	2,216
2,600	2,037	2,224
2,610	2,048	2,232
2,620	2,058	2,239
2,630	2,069	2,247
2,640	2,080	2,255
2,650	2,090	2,263
2,660	2,101	2,271
2,670	2,112	2,279
2,680	2,123	2,287
2,690	2,133	2,295
2,700	2,144	2,303
2,710	2,155	2,311
2,720	2,166	2,319
2,730	2,177	2,326
2,740	2,188	2,334
2,750	2,199	2,342
2,760	2,210	2,350
2,770	2,221	2,358
2,780	2,232	2,366
2,790	2,243	2,374
2,800	2,254	2,381
2,810	2,265	2,389
2,820	2,276	2,397
2,830	2,287	2,405
2,840	2,298	2,413
2,850	2,309	2,421
2,860	2,320	2,428
2,870	2,332	2,436
2,880	2,343	2,444
2,890	2,354	2,452
2,900	2,365	2,460
2,910	2,377	2,468
2,920	2,388	2,475
2,930	2,399	2,483
2,940	2,411	2,491
2,950	2,422	2,499

Figure 33. – Airplane Weight and Balance Tables.

66. (Refer to Figure 32 on page 223 and Figure 33 on page 223.) Determine if the airplane weight and balance is within limits.

Front seat occupants	415 lb
Rear seat occupants	110 lb
Fuel, main tanks	44 gal
Fuel, aux. tanks	19 gal
Baggage	32 lb

A. 19 pounds overweight, CG within limits.

B. 19 pounds overweight, CG out of limits forward.

C. Weight within limits, CG out of limits.

Answer (C) is correct. *(PHAK Chap 10)*

DISCUSSION: Both the weight and the total moment must be calculated. Begin by setting up the schedule shown below. The fuel must be separated into main and auxiliary tanks, but weights and moments for both tanks are provided in Fig. 32.

Since 415 lb. is not shown on the front seat table, simply multiply the weight by the arm shown at the top of the table (415 lb. × 85 in. = 35,275 lb.-in.) and divide by 100 for moment/100 of 353 (35,275 ÷ 100 = 352.75). The rear seat moment must also be multiplied (110 lb. × 121 in. = 13,310 pound-inches). Divide by 100 to get 133.1, or 133 lb.-in. ÷ 100. The last step is to go to the Moment Limits vs. Weight chart (Fig. 33). The maximum weight allowed is 2,950, which means that the airplane weight is within the limits. However, the CG is out of limits because the minimum moment/100 for a weight of 2,950 lb. is 2,422.

	Weight	Moment/100 lb.-in.
Empty weight w/oil	2,015	1,554
Front seat	415	353
Rear seat	110	133
Fuel, main	264	198
Fuel, aux.	114	107
Baggage	32	45
	2,950	2,390

Answer (A) is incorrect. The airplane's weight of 2,950 lb. is within limits. Answer (B) is incorrect. The airplane's weight of 2,950 lb. is within limits.

67. (Refer to Figure 32 on page 223 and Figure 33 on page 223.) Which action can adjust the airplane's weight to maximum gross weight and the CG within limits for takeoff?

Front seat occupants	425 lb
Rear seat occupants	300 lb
Fuel, main tanks	44 gal

A. Drain 12 gallons of fuel.

B. Drain 9 gallons of fuel.

C. Transfer 12 gallons of fuel from the main tanks to the auxiliary tanks.

Answer (B) is correct. *(PHAK Chap 10)*

DISCUSSION: First, determine the total weight to see how much must be reduced. As shown below, this original weight is 3,004 pounds. Fig. 33 shows the maximum weight as 2,950 pounds. Thus, you must adjust the total weight by removing 54 lb. (3,004 – 2,950). Since fuel weighs 6 lb./gal., you must drain at least 9 gallons.

To check for CG, recompute the total moment using a new fuel moment of 158 (from the chart) for 210 pounds. The plane now weighs 2,950 lb. with a total moment of 2,437, which falls within the moment limits on Fig. 33.

	Original Weight	Adjusted Weight	Moment/100 lb.-in.
Empty weight with oil	2,015	2,015	1,554
Front seat	425	425	362
Rear seat	300	300	363
Fuel	264	210	158
	3,004	2,950	2,437

Answer (A) is incorrect. It is not necessary to drain 12 gal., only 9 gallons. Answer (C) is incorrect. Transferring fuel to auxiliary tanks will only affect the moment, not the total weight.

Useful load weights and moments

Baggage or 5th seat occupant — ARM 140

Weight	Moment/100
10	14
20	28
30	42
40	56
50	70
60	84
70	98
80	112
90	126
100	140
110	154
120	168
130	182
140	196
150	210
160	224
170	238
180	252
190	266
200	280
210	294
220	308
230	322
240	336
250	350
260	364
270	378

Occupants

Front seats ARM 85		Rear seats ARM 121	
Weight	Moment/100	Weight	Moment/100
120	102	120	145
130	110	130	157
140	119	140	169
150	128	150	182
160	136	160	194
170	144	170	206
180	153	180	218
190	162	190	230
200	170	200	242

Usable fuel

Main wing tanks ARM 75

Gallons	Weight	Moment/100
5	30	22
10	60	45
15	90	68
20	120	90
25	150	112
30	180	135
35	210	158
40	240	180
44	264	198

Auxiliary wing tanks ARM 94

Gallons	Weight	Moment/100
5	30	28
10	60	56
15	90	85
19	114	107

*Oil

Quarts	Weight	Moment/100
10	19	5

*Included in basic empty weight.

Empty weight~2,015

MOM/100~1,554

Moment limits vs weight

Moment limits are based on the following weight and center of gravity limit data (landing gear down).

Weight condition	Forward CG limit	AFT CG limit
2,950 lb (takeoff or landing)	82.1	84.7
2,525 lb	77.5	85.7
2,475 lb or less	77.0	85.7

Figure 32. – Airplane Weight and Balance Tables.

Moment limits vs weight (continued)

Weight	Minimum Moment/100	Maximum Moment/100
2,100	1,617	1,800
2,110	1,625	1,808
2,120	1,632	1,817
2,130	1,640	1,825
2,140	1,648	1,834
2,150	1,656	1,843
2,160	1,663	1,851
2,170	1,671	1,860
2,180	1,679	1,868
2,190	1,686	1,877
2,200	1,694	1,885
2,210	1,702	1,894
2,220	1,709	1,903
2,230	1,717	1,911
2,240	1,725	1,920
2,250	1,733	1,928
2,260	1,740	1,937
2,270	1,748	1,945
2,280	1,756	1,954
2,290	1,763	1,963
2,300	1,771	1,971
2,310	1,779	1,980
2,320	1,786	1,988
2,330	1,794	1,997
2,340	1,802	2,005
2,350	1,810	2,014
2,360	1,817	2,023
2,370	1,825	2,031
2,380	1,833	2,040
2,390	1,840	2,048
2,400	1,848	2,057
2,410	1,856	2,065
2,420	1,863	2,074
2,430	1,871	2,083
2,440	1,879	2,091
2,450	1,887	2,100
2,460	1,894	2,108
2,470	1,902	2,117
2,480	1,911	2,125
2,490	1,921	2,134

Weight	Minimum Moment/100	Maximum Moment/100
2,500	1,932	2,143
2,510	1,942	2,151
2,520	1,953	2,160
2,530	1,963	2,168
2,540	1,974	2,176
2,550	1,984	2,184
2,560	1,995	2,192
2,570	2,005	2,200
2,580	2,016	2,208
2,590	2,026	2,216
2,600	2,037	2,224
2,610	2,048	2,232
2,620	2,058	2,239
2,630	2,069	2,247
2,640	2,080	2,255
2,650	2,090	2,263
2,660	2,101	2,271
2,670	2,112	2,279
2,680	2,123	2,287
2,690	2,133	2,295
2,700	2,144	2,303
2,710	2,155	2,311
2,720	2,166	2,319
2,730	2,177	2,326
2,740	2,188	2,334
2,750	2,199	2,342
2,760	2,210	2,350
2,770	2,221	2,358
2,780	2,232	2,366
2,790	2,243	2,374
2,800	2,254	2,381
2,810	2,265	2,389
2,820	2,276	2,397
2,830	2,287	2,405
2,840	2,298	2,413
2,850	2,309	2,421
2,860	2,320	2,428
2,870	2,332	2,436
2,880	2,343	2,444
2,890	2,354	2,452
2,900	2,365	2,460
2,910	2,377	2,468
2,920	2,388	2,475
2,930	2,399	2,483
2,940	2,411	2,491
2,950	2,422	2,499

Figure 33. – Airplane Weight and Balance Tables.

END OF STUDY UNIT

Update Service

Visit the GLEIM® website for free updates, which are available until the next edition is published.

gleim.com/updates

STUDY UNIT SIX
AEROMEDICAL FACTORS AND AERONAUTICAL DECISION MAKING (ADM)

(3 pages of outline)

This study unit contains outlines of major concepts tested, sample test questions and answers regarding aeromedical factors and aeronautical decision making (ADM), and an explanation of each answer. The table of contents above lists each subunit within this study unit, the number of questions pertaining to that particular subunit, and the pages on which the outlines and questions begin, respectively.

GLEIM SUCCESS TIPS

Recall that the **sole purpose** of this book is to expedite your passing of the FAA pilot knowledge test for the private pilot certificate. Accordingly, all extraneous material (i.e., topics or regulations not directly tested on the FAA pilot knowledge test) is omitted, even though much more knowledge is necessary to fly safely. This additional material is presented in *Pilot Handbook* and *Private Pilot Flight Maneuvers and Practical Test Prep*, available from Gleim Publications, Inc. Order online at www.GleimAviation.com.

6.1 HYPOXIA

1. The following are four types of hypoxia based on their causes:
   a. **Hypoxic hypoxia** is a result of insufficient oxygen available to the body as a whole.
      1) EXAMPLE: Reduction of partial pressure at high altitude, a blocked airway, or drowning
   b. **Hypemic hypoxia** occurs when the blood is not able to take up and transport a sufficient amount of oxygen to the cells in the body. The oxygen deficiency is in the blood, not the result of too little inhaled oxygen.
      1) EXAMPLE: Carbon monoxide poisoning
   c. **Stagnant hypoxia** results when oxygen-rich blood in the lungs is not moving.
      1) EXAMPLE: Shock, reduced circulation due to extreme cold, or pulling excessive Gs in flight
   d. **Histotoxic hypoxia** is the inability of cells to effectively use oxygen.
      1) EXAMPLE: Impairment due to alcohol and drugs
2. Symptoms of hypoxia include an initial feeling of euphoria but lead to more serious concerns such as headache, delayed reaction time, visual impairment, and eventual unconsciousness.
3. The correct response to counteract feelings of hypoxia is to lower altitude or use supplemental oxygen.

6.2 HYPERVENTILATION

1. Hyperventilation occurs when an excessive amount of air is breathed out of the lungs, e.g., when one becomes excited or undergoes stress, tension, fear, or anxiety.
   a. This results in an excessive amount of carbon dioxide passed out of the body and too much oxygen retained.
   b. The symptoms are dizziness, hot and cold sensations, nausea, etc.
2. Overcome hyperventilation symptoms by slowing the breathing rate, breathing into a bag, or talking aloud.

6.3 SPATIAL DISORIENTATION

1. Spatial disorientation, e.g., not knowing whether you are going up, going down, or turning, is a state of temporary confusion resulting from misleading information being sent to the brain by various sensory organs.
2. If you lose outside visual references and become disoriented, you are experiencing spatial disorientation. This occurs when you rely on the sensations of muscles and the inner ear to tell you what the airplane's attitude is.
   a. This might occur during a night flight, in clouds, or in dust.
3. Ways to overcome the effects of spatial disorientation include relying on the airplane instruments, avoiding sudden head movements, and ensuring that outside visual references are fixed points on the surface.

6.4 VISION

1. Pilots should adapt their eyes for night flying by avoiding bright white lights for 30 min. prior to flight.
2. Due to the eye's physiology, off-center eyesight is better than direct at night. Pilots should scan slowly at night to permit off-center viewing.
3. Scanning for traffic is best accomplished by bringing small portions of the sky into the central field of vision slowly and in succession.
4. Haze can create the illusion of traffic or terrain being farther away than they actually are.

6.5 CARBON MONOXIDE

1. Carbon monoxide (CO) is a colorless, odorless gas produced by all combustion engines.
2. CO can enter a cockpit or cabin through heater and defrost vents.
   a. If a leak is detected or a pilot smells gas fumes or exhaust, immediate corrective action should be taken. This could include turning off the heater, opening air vents or windows, if appropriate, and using supplemental oxygen, if available.
3. Blurred (hazy) thinking and vision, uneasiness, dizziness, and tightness across the forehead are early symptoms of carbon monoxide poisoning. They are followed by a headache and, with large accumulations of carbon monoxide, a loss of muscle power.
   a. Tobacco smoke also causes CO poisoning and physiological debilitation, which are medically disqualifying for pilots.
4. Increases in altitude increase susceptibility to carbon monoxide poisoning because of decreased oxygen availability.

6.6 AERONAUTICAL DECISION MAKING (ADM)

1. **Aeronautical decision making (ADM)** is a systematic approach to the mental process used by pilots to consistently determine the best course of action in response to a given set of circumstances.
2. Risk management is the part of the decision-making process that relies on situational awareness, problem recognition, and good judgment to reduce risks associated with each flight.
   a. The four fundamental risk elements in the ADM process that comprise any given aviation situation are the
      1) Pilot
      2) Aircraft
      3) Environment
      4) Mission (type of operation)
3. Most pilots have fallen prey to dangerous tendencies or behavioral problems at some time. Scud running, continuing visual flight into instrument conditions, and neglecting checklists are three examples of these dangerous tendencies or behavioral problems that must be identified and eliminated.
   a. In scud running, a pilot pushes his or her capabilities and the airplane to the limits by trying to maintain visual contact with the terrain while trying to avoid contact with it during low visibility and ceilings.
   b. Continuing visual flight into instrument conditions often leads to spatial disorientation or collision with the ground or obstacles.
   c. Neglect of checklists is an example of a pilot's unjustified reliance on his or her short- and long-term memory for repetitive tasks.
4. ADM addresses five hazardous attitudes that contribute to poor pilot judgment.
   a. Recognition of hazardous attitudes (thoughts) is the first step in neutralizing them in the ADM process.
   b. When you recognize a hazardous attitude, you should label it as hazardous and then correct it by stating the corresponding antidote, as shown below.

Hazardous Attitude	Antidote
Antiauthority: *Don't tell me!*	Follow the rules. They are usually right.
Impulsivity: *Do something quickly!*	Not so fast. Think first.
Invulnerability: *It won't happen to me.*	It could happen to me.
Macho: *I can do it.*	Taking chances is foolish.
Resignation: *What's the use?*	I'm not helpless. I can make a difference.

5. You are responsible for determining whether or not you are fit to fly for a particular flight.
   a. You should ask, "Could I pass my medical examination right now?" If you cannot answer with an absolute yes, you should not fly.
6. Human error is the one common factor of most preventable accidents.
   a. A pilot who is involved in an accident usually knows what went wrong and was aware of the possible hazards when (s)he was making the decision that led to the wrong course of action.

QUESTIONS AND ANSWER EXPLANATIONS: All of the private pilot knowledge test questions chosen by the FAA for release as well as additional questions selected by Gleim relating to the material in the previous outlines are reproduced on the following pages. These questions have been organized into the same subunits as the outlines. To the immediate right of each question are the correct answer and answer explanation. You should cover these answers and answer explanations while responding to the questions. Refer to the general discussion in the Introduction on how to take the FAA knowledge test.

Remember that the questions from the FAA knowledge test bank have been reordered by topic and organized into a meaningful sequence. Also, the first line of the answer explanation gives the citation of the authoritative source for the answer.

QUESTIONS

6.1 Hypoxia

1. Which statement best defines hypoxia?

A. A state of oxygen deficiency in the body.

B. An abnormal increase in the volume of air breathed.

C. A condition of gas bubble formation around the joints or muscles.

Answer (A) is correct. *(AIM Para 8-1-2)*
DISCUSSION: Hypoxia is oxygen deficiency in the bloodstream and may cause lack of clear thinking, fatigue, euphoria and, shortly thereafter, unconsciousness.
Answer (B) is incorrect. It describes a cause of hyperventilation. Answer (C) is incorrect. It describes decompression sickness after scuba diving.

2. Which is not a type of hypoxia?

A. Histotoxic.

B. Hypoxic.

C. Hypertoxic.

Answer (C) is correct. *(PHAK Chap 17)*
DISCUSSION: There is no such thing as hypertoxic hypoxia. The four types of hypoxia are histotoxic, hypoxic, hypemic, and stagnant hypoxia.
Answer (A) is incorrect. The four types of hypoxia are histotoxic, hypoxic, hypemic, and stagnant hypoxia. Answer (B) is incorrect. The four types of hypoxia are histotoxic, hypoxic, hypemic, and stagnant hypoxia.

3. Which of the following is a correct response to counteract the feelings of hypoxia in flight?

A. Promptly descend altitude.

B. Increase cabin air flow.

C. Avoid sudden inhalations.

Answer (A) is correct. *(PHAK Chap 17)*
DISCUSSION: The correct response to counteract feelings of hypoxia is to lower altitude or use supplemental oxygen, if the aircraft is so equipped.
Answer (B) is incorrect. Increasing the amount of air flowing inside an aircraft will not help counteract hypoxia. Because of the reduction of partial pressure at higher altitudes, there is less oxygen in the air to draw from. Answer (C) is incorrect. Breathing deeply or suddenly will not counteract feelings of hypoxia.

6.2 Hyperventilation

4. A pilot should be able to overcome the symptoms or avoid future occurrences of hyperventilation by

A. closely monitoring the flight instruments to control the airplane.

B. slowing the breathing rate, breathing into a bag, or talking aloud.

C. increasing the breathing rate in order to increase lung ventilation.

Answer (B) is correct. *(AIM Para 8-1-3)*
DISCUSSION: To recover from hyperventilation, the pilot should slow the breathing rate, breathe into a bag, or talk aloud.
Answer (A) is incorrect. Closely monitoring the flight instruments is used to overcome vertigo (spatial disorientation). Answer (C) is incorrect. Increased breathing aggravates hyperventilation.

5. Rapid or extra deep breathing while using oxygen can cause a condition known as

A. hyperventilation.

B. aerosinusitis.

C. aerotitis.

Answer (A) is correct. *(AIM Para 8-1-3)*

DISCUSSION: Hyperventilation occurs when an excessive amount of carbon dioxide is passed out of the body and too much oxygen is retained. This occurs when breathing rapidly and especially when using oxygen.

Answer (B) is incorrect. Aerosinusitis is an inflammation of the sinuses caused by changes in atmospheric pressure. Answer (C) is incorrect. Aerotitis is an inflammation of the inner ear caused by changes in atmospheric pressure.

6. When a stressful situation is encountered in flight, an abnormal increase in the volume of air breathed in and out can cause a condition known as

A. hyperventilation.

B. aerosinusitis.

C. aerotitis.

Answer (A) is correct. *(AIM Para 8-1-3)*

DISCUSSION: Hyperventilation occurs when an excessive amount of carbon dioxide is passed out of the body and too much oxygen is retained. This occurs when breathing rapidly and especially when using oxygen.

Answer (B) is incorrect. Aerosinusitis is an inflammation of the sinuses caused by changes in atmospheric pressure. Answer (C) is incorrect. Aerotitis is an inflammation of the inner ear caused by changes in atmospheric pressure.

7. Which would most likely result in hyperventilation?

A. Emotional tension, anxiety, or fear.

B. The excessive consumption of alcohol.

C. An extremely slow rate of breathing and insufficient oxygen.

Answer (A) is correct. *(AIM Para 8-1-3)*

DISCUSSION: Hyperventilation usually occurs when one becomes excited or undergoes stress, which results in an increase in one's rate of breathing.

Answer (B) is incorrect. Hyperventilation is usually caused by some type of stress, not by alcohol. Answer (C) is incorrect. The opposite is true: Hyperventilation is an extremely fast rate of breathing that produces excessive oxygen.

8. A pilot experiencing the effects of hyperventilation should be able to restore the proper carbon dioxide level in the body by

A. slowing the breathing rate, breathing into a paper bag, or talking aloud.

B. breathing spontaneously and deeply or gaining mental control of the situation.

C. increasing the breathing rate in order to increase lung ventilation.

Answer (A) is correct. *(PHAK Chap 17)*

DISCUSSION: A stressful situation can often lead to hyperventilation, which results from an increased rate and depth of respiration that leads to an abnormally low amount of carbon dioxide in the bloodstream. By slowing the breathing rate, breathing into a paper bag, or talking aloud, a pilot can overcome the effects of hyperventilation and return the carbon dioxide level in the bloodstream to normal.

Answer (B) is incorrect. Breathing deeply further aggravates the effects of hyperventilation. Answer (C) is incorrect. Increasing the rate of breathing will further aggravate the effects of hyperventilation.

6.3 Spatial Disorientation

9. Pilots are more subject to spatial disorientation if

A. they ignore the sensations of muscles and inner ear.

B. visual cues are taken away, as they are in instrument meteorological conditions (IMC).

C. eyes are moved often in the process of cross-checking the flight instruments.

Answer (B) is correct. *(AIM Para 8-1-5)*

DISCUSSION: Spatial disorientation is a state of temporary confusion resulting from misleading information being sent to the brain by various sensory organs. Thus, the pilot should ignore sensations of muscles and the inner ear and kinesthetic senses (those that sense motion), especially during flight in IMC when outside visual cues are taken away.

Answer (A) is incorrect. Ignoring the sensations of muscles and the inner ear will help overcome spatial disorientation. Answer (C) is incorrect. Cross-checking the flight instruments will help prevent spatial disorientation.

10. Pilots are more subject to spatial disorientation if

A. they ignore the sensations of muscles and inner ear.

B. body signals are used to interpret flight attitude.

C. eyes are moved often in the process of cross-checking the flight instruments.

Answer (B) is correct. *(AIM Para 8-1-5)*

DISCUSSION: Spatial disorientation is a state of temporary confusion resulting from misleading information being sent to the brain by various sensory organs. Thus, the pilot should ignore sensations of muscles and the inner ear and kinesthetic senses (those that sense motion).

Answer (A) is incorrect. Ignoring the sensations of muscles and the inner ear will help overcome spatial disorientation. Answer (C) is incorrect. Cross-checking the flight instruments will help prevent spatial disorientation.

11. If a pilot experiences spatial disorientation during flight in a restricted visibility condition, the best way to overcome the effect is to

A. rely upon the aircraft instrument indications.

B. concentrate on yaw, pitch, and roll sensations.

C. consciously slow the breathing rate until symptoms clear and then resume normal breathing rate.

Answer (A) is correct. *(AIM Para 8-1-5)*

DISCUSSION: The best way to overcome the effects of spatial disorientation is to rely entirely on the aircraft's instrument indications and not upon body sensations. Sight of the horizon also overrides inner ear sensations. Thus, in areas of poor visibility, especially, such bodily signals should be ignored.

Answer (B) is incorrect. Yaw, pitch, and roll sensations should be ignored. Answer (C) is incorrect. A decrease in breathing rate is the proper treatment for hyperventilation, not spatial disorientation.

12. A lack of orientation with regard to the position, attitude, or movement of the aircraft in space is defined as

A. spatial disorientation.

B. hyperventilation.

C. hypoxia.

Answer (A) is correct. *(PHAK Chap 17)*

DISCUSSION: Spatial disorientation is a state of temporary confusion resulting from misleading information being sent to the brain by various sensory organs. Thus, the pilot should ignore sensations of muscles and the inner ear and kinesthetic senses (those that sense motion), especially during flight in IMC when outside visual cues are taken away.

Answer (B) is incorrect. Hyperventilation occurs when an excessive amount of carbon dioxide is passed out of the body and too much oxygen is retained. This occurs when breathing rapidly and especially when using supplemental oxygen. Answer (C) is incorrect. Hypoxia is the result of an oxygen deficiency in the bloodstream and may cause lack of clear thinking, fatigue, euphoria, and, shortly thereafter, unconsciousness.

13. A state of temporary confusion resulting from misleading information being sent to the brain by various sensory organs is defined as

A. spatial disorientation.

B. hyperventilation.

C. hypoxia.

Answer (A) is correct. *(AIM Para 8-1-5)*

DISCUSSION: A state of temporary confusion resulting from misleading information being sent to the brain by various sensory organs is defined as vertigo (spatial disorientation). Put simply, the pilot cannot determine his or her relationship to the earth's horizon.

Answer (B) is incorrect. Hyperventilation causes excessive oxygen and/or a decrease in carbon dioxide in the bloodstream. Answer (C) is incorrect. Hypoxia occurs when there is insufficient oxygen in the bloodstream.

14. The danger of spatial disorientation during flight in poor visual conditions may be reduced by

A. shifting the eyes quickly between the exterior visual field and the instrument panel.

B. having faith in the instruments rather than taking a chance on the sensory organs.

C. leaning the body in the opposite direction of the motion of the aircraft.

Answer (B) is correct. *(AIM Para 8-1-5)*

DISCUSSION: Various complex motions and forces and certain visual scenes encountered in flight can create illusions of motion and position. Spatial disorientation from these illusions can be prevented only by visual reference to reliable fixed points on the ground and horizon or to flight instruments.

Answer (A) is incorrect. In poor visual conditions, reliable exterior references are not available. Answer (C) is incorrect. To avoid spatial disorientation, the pilot should avoid undue head and body movements and rely totally on the flight instruments. By moving the body in response to perceived motion, the conflicting signals reaching the brain will cause spatial disorientation.

6.4 Vision

15. Which technique should a pilot use to scan for traffic to the right and left during straight-and-level flight?

A. Systematically focus on different segments of the sky for short intervals.

B. Concentrate on relative movement detected in the peripheral vision area.

C. Continuous sweeping of the windshield from right to left.

Answer (A) is correct. *(AIM Para 8-1-6)*

DISCUSSION: Due to the fact that eyes can focus only on a narrow viewing area, effective scanning is accomplished with a series of short, regularly spaced eye movements that bring successive areas of the sky into the central vision field.

Answer (B) is incorrect. It concerns scanning for traffic at night. Answer (C) is incorrect. A pilot must continually scan successive, small portions of the sky. The eyes can focus only on a narrow viewing area and require at least 1 sec. to detect a faraway object.

16. What effect does haze have on the ability to see traffic or terrain features during flight?

A. Haze causes the eyes to focus at infinity.

B. The eyes tend to overwork in haze and do not detect relative movement easily.

C. All traffic or terrain features appear to be farther away than their actual distance.

Answer (C) is correct. *(AIM Para 8-1-5)*

DISCUSSION: Atmospheric haze can create the illusion of being at a greater distance and height from traffic or terrain than you actually are. The pilot who does not recognize this illusion will fly a lower approach.

Answer (A) is incorrect. In haze, the eyes focus at a comfortable distance, which may be only 10 to 30 ft. outside of the cockpit. Answer (B) is incorrect. In haze, the eyes relax and tend to stare outside without focusing or looking for common visual cues.

17. What preparation should a pilot make to adapt the eyes for night flying?

A. Wear sunglasses after sunset until ready for flight.

B. Avoid red lights at least 30 minutes before the flight.

C. Avoid bright white lights at least 30 minutes before the flight.

Answer (C) is correct. *(AFH Chap 10)*

DISCUSSION: Prepare for night flying by letting your eyes adapt to darkness, including avoiding bright white light for at least 30 min. prior to night flight.

Answer (A) is incorrect. Preparation does not involve wearing sunglasses but rather avoiding bright white lights. Answer (B) is incorrect. White, not red, lights impair night vision.

18. What is the most effective way to use the eyes during night flight?

A. Look only at far away, dim lights.

B. Scan slowly to permit off-center viewing.

C. Concentrate directly on each object for a few seconds.

Answer (B) is correct. *(AFH Chap 10)*

DISCUSSION: Physiologically, the eyes are most effective at seeing objects off-center at night. Accordingly, pilots should scan slowly to permit off-center viewing.

Answer (A) is incorrect. Pilots must look at their gauges and instruments, which are 2 ft. in front of them. Answer (C) is incorrect. Peripheral (off-center) vision is more effective at night.

19. The best method to use when looking for other traffic at night is to

A. look to the side of the object and scan slowly.

B. scan the visual field very rapidly.

C. look to the side of the object and scan rapidly.

Answer (A) is correct. *(AFH Chap 10)*

DISCUSSION: Physiologically, the eyes are most effective at seeing objects off-center at night. Accordingly, pilots should scan slowly to permit off-center viewing.

Answer (B) is incorrect. Scanning should always be done slowly and methodically. Answer (C) is incorrect. Scanning should always be done slowly and methodically.

6.5 Carbon Monoxide

20. Large accumulations of carbon monoxide in the human body result in

A. tightness across the forehead.

B. loss of muscular power.

C. an increased sense of well-being.

Answer (B) is correct. *(AC 20-32B)*

DISCUSSION: Carbon monoxide reduces the ability of the blood to carry oxygen. Large accumulations result in loss of muscular power.

Answer (A) is incorrect. It describes an early symptom, not the effect of large accumulations. Answer (C) is incorrect. Euphoria is a result of the lack of sufficient oxygen, not specifically an accumulation of carbon monoxide.

21. Susceptibility to carbon monoxide poisoning increases as

A. altitude increases.

B. altitude decreases.

C. air pressure increases.

Answer (A) is correct. *(AIM Para 8-1-4)*

DISCUSSION: Carbon monoxide poisoning results in an oxygen deficiency. Since there is less oxygen available at higher altitudes, carbon monoxide poisoning can occur with lesser amounts of carbon monoxide as altitude increases.

Answer (B) is incorrect. There is more available oxygen at lower altitudes. Answer (C) is incorrect. There is more available oxygen at higher air pressures.

22. What is a correct response if an exhaust leak were to be detected while in flight?

A. Increase altitude so the effects of CO would be decreased.

B. Take deep breaths so as to inhale more oxygen.

C. Open air vents or windows.

Answer (C) is correct. *(PHAK Chap 17)*

DISCUSSION: Taking corrective steps such as turning off the heater, opening air vents or windows, and using supplemental oxygen are the correct responses if a pilot smells gas fumes or otherwise detects increased amounts of CO.

Answer (A) is incorrect. An increase in altitude increases the susceptibility of CO poisoning because of the decreased oxygen available. Answer (B) is incorrect. Inhaling more CO-tainted air would be detrimental to a pilot's health and is not a positive corrective action.

23. Effects of carbon monoxide poisoning include

A. dizziness, blurred vision, and loss of muscle power.

B. sweating, increased breathing, and paleness.

C. motion sickness, tightness across the forehead, and drowsiness.

Answer (A) is correct. *(PHAK Chap 17)*

DISCUSSION: Effects of CO poisoning include headache, blurred vision, dizziness, drowsiness, and loss of muscle control.

Answer (B) is incorrect. Sweating, increased breathing, and paleness are symptoms of motion sickness, not CO poisoning. Answer (C) is incorrect. Motion sickness is not an effect or characteristic of carbon monoxide poisoning.

6.6 Aeronautical Decision Making (ADM)

24. Risk management, as part of the aeronautical decision making (ADM) process, relies on which features to reduce the risks associated with each flight?

A. Application of stress management and risk element procedures.

B. The mental process of analyzing all information in a particular situation and making a timely decision on what action to take.

C. Situational awareness, problem recognition, and good judgment.

Answer (C) is correct. *(AC 60-22)*

DISCUSSION: Risk management is that part of the ADM process that relies on situational awareness, problem recognition, and good judgment to reduce risks associated with each flight.

Answer (A) is incorrect. Risk management relies on situational awareness, problem recognition, and good judgment, not the application of stress management and risk-element procedures, to reduce the risks associated with each flight. Answer (B) is incorrect. Judgment, not risk management, is the mental process of analyzing all information in a particular situation and making a timely decision on what action to take.

25. What is it often called when a pilot pushes his or her capabilities and the aircraft's limits by trying to maintain visual contact with the terrain in low visibility and ceiling?

A. Scud running.

B. Mind set.

C. Peer pressure.

Answer (A) is correct. *(AC 60-22)*

DISCUSSION: Scud running refers to a pilot pushing his or her capabilities and the aircraft's limits by trying to maintain visual contact with the terrain while flying with a low visibility or ceiling. Scud running is a dangerous (and often illegal) practice that may lead to a mishap. This dangerous tendency must be identified and eliminated.

Answer (B) is incorrect. Mind-set may produce an inability to recognize and cope with changes in the situation requiring actions different from those anticipated or planned. Answer (C) is incorrect. Peer pressure may produce poor decision making based upon an emotional response to peers rather than an objective evaluation of a situation.

26. What often leads to spatial disorientation or collision with ground/obstacles when flying under Visual Flight Rules (VFR)?

A. Continual flight into instrument conditions.

B. Getting behind the aircraft.

C. Duck-under syndrome.

Answer (A) is correct. *(AC 60-22)*

DISCUSSION: Continuing VFR flight into instrument conditions often leads to spatial disorientation or collision with ground/obstacles due to the loss of outside visual references. It is even more dangerous if the pilot is not instrument qualified or current.

Answer (B) is incorrect. Getting behind the aircraft results in allowing events or the situation to control your actions, rather than the other way around. Answer (C) is incorrect. Duck-under syndrome is the tendency to descend below minimums during an approach based on the belief that there is always a fudge factor built in; it occurs during IFR, not VFR, flight.

27. What is one of the neglected items when a pilot relies on short and long term memory for repetitive tasks?

A. Checklists.

B. Situational awareness.

C. Flying outside the envelope.

Answer (A) is correct. *(AC 60-22)*

DISCUSSION: Neglect of checklists, flight planning, preflight inspections, etc., indicates a pilot's unjustified reliance on his or her short- and long-term memory for repetitive flying tasks.

Answer (B) is incorrect. Situational awareness suffers when a pilot gets behind the airplane, which results in an inability to recognize deteriorating circumstances and/or misjudgment on the rate of deterioration. Answer (C) is incorrect. Flying outside the envelope occurs when the pilot believes (often in error) that the aircraft's high-performance capability meets the demands imposed by the pilot's (often overestimated) flying skills.

28. Hazardous attitudes occur to every pilot to some degree at some time. What are some of these hazardous attitudes?

A. Antiauthority, impulsivity, macho, resignation, and invulnerability.

B. Poor situational awareness, snap judgments, and lack of a decision making process.

C. Poor risk management and lack of stress management.

Answer (A) is correct. *(AC 60-22)*

DISCUSSION: The five hazardous attitudes addressed in the ADM process are antiauthority, impulsivity, invulnerability, macho, and resignation.

Answer (B) is incorrect. Poor situational awareness and snap judgments are indications of the lack of a decision-making process, not hazardous attitudes. Answer (C) is incorrect. Poor risk management and lack of stress management lead to poor ADM and are not considered hazardous attitudes.

29. In the aeronautical decision making (ADM) process, what is the first step in neutralizing a hazardous attitude?

A. Recognizing hazardous thoughts.

B. Recognizing the invulnerability of the situation.

C. Making a rational judgment.

Answer (A) is correct. *(AC 60-22)*

DISCUSSION: Hazardous attitudes, which contribute to poor pilot judgment, can be effectively counteracted by redirecting that hazardous attitude so that appropriate action can be taken. Recognition of hazardous thoughts is the first step in neutralizing them in the ADM process.

Answer (B) is incorrect. Invulnerability is a hazardous attitude. The first step in neutralizing a hazardous attitude is to recognize it. Answer (C) is incorrect. Before a rational judgment can be made, the hazardous attitude must be recognized then redirected so that appropriate action can be taken.

30. What is the antidote when a pilot has a hazardous attitude, such as "Antiauthority"?

A. Rules do not apply in this situation.

B. I know what I am doing.

C. Follow the rules.

Answer (C) is correct. *(AC 60-22)*

DISCUSSION: When you recognize a hazardous thought, you should correct it by stating the corresponding antidote. The antidote for the antiauthority ("Do not tell me!") hazardous attitude is "Follow the rules. They are usually right."

Answer (A) is incorrect. "Rules do not apply in this situation" is an example of the antiauthority hazardous attitude, not its antidote. Answer (B) is incorrect. "I know what I'm doing" is an example of the macho hazardous attitude, not an antidote to the antiauthority attitude.

31. What is the antidote when a pilot has a hazardous attitude, such as "Impulsivity"?

A. It could happen to me.

B. Do it quickly to get it over with.

C. Not so fast, think first.

Answer (C) is correct. *(AC 60-22)*

DISCUSSION: When you recognize a hazardous thought, you should correct it by stating the corresponding antidote. The antidote for the impulsivity ("Do something quickly!") hazardous attitude is "Not so fast. Think first."

Answer (A) is incorrect. "It could happen to me" is the antidote for the invulnerability, not impulsivity, hazardous attitude. Answer (B) is incorrect. "Do it quickly and get it over with" is an example of the impulsivity hazardous attitude, not its antidote.

32. What is the antidote when a pilot has the hazardous attitude of "Invulnerability"?

A. It cannot be that bad.

B. It could happen to me.

C. It will not happen to me.

Answer (B) is correct. *(AC 60-22)*

DISCUSSION: The antidote to counteract the attitude of invulnerability is thinking or saying, "It could happen to me."

Answer (A) is incorrect. "It cannot be that bad" describes the hazardous macho attitude, not invulnerability. Answer (C) is incorrect. "It will not happen to me" describes the hazardous attitude of invulnerability. It is not the antidote.

33. What is the antidote when a pilot has a hazardous attitude, such as "Macho"?

A. I can do it.

B. Taking chances is foolish.

C. Nothing will happen.

Answer (B) is correct. *(AC 60-22)*

DISCUSSION: When you recognize a hazardous thought, you should correct it by stating the corresponding antidote. The antidote for the macho ("I can do it") hazardous attitude is "Taking chances is foolish."

Answer (A) is incorrect. "I can do it" is an example of the macho hazardous attitude, not its antidote. Answer (C) is incorrect. "Nothing will happen" is an example of the invulnerability hazardous attitude, not an antidote to the macho attitude.

34. What is the antidote when a pilot has a hazardous attitude, such as "Resignation"?

A. What is the use?

B. Someone else is responsible.

C. I am not helpless.

Answer (C) is correct. *(AC 60-22)*

DISCUSSION: When you recognize a hazardous thought, you should correct it by stating the corresponding antidote. The antidote for the resignation ("What is the use?") hazardous attitude is "I am not helpless. I can make a difference."

Answer (A) is incorrect. "What is the use?" is an example of the resignation hazardous attitude, not its antidote. Answer (B) is incorrect. "Someone else is responsible" is an example of the resignation hazardous attitude, not its antidote.

35. Who is responsible for determining whether a pilot is fit to fly for a particular flight, even though he or she holds a current medical certificate?

A. The FAA.

B. The medical examiner.

C. The pilot.

Answer (C) is correct. *(AC 60-22)*

DISCUSSION: A number of factors, from lack of sleep to illness, can reduce a pilot's fitness to make a particular flight. It is the responsibility of the pilot to determine whether (s)he is fit to make a particular flight, even though (s)he holds a current medical certificate. Additionally, FAR 61.53 prohibits a pilot who possesses a current medical certificate from acting as pilot in command, or in any other capacity as a required pilot flight crewmember, while the pilot has a known medical condition or an aggravation of a known medical condition that would make the pilot unable to meet the standards for a medical certificate.

Answer (A) is incorrect. The pilot, not the FAA, is responsible for determining whether (s)he is fit for a particular flight. Answer (B) is incorrect. The pilot, not the medical examiner, is responsible for determining whether (s)he is fit for a particular flight.

36. What is the one common factor which affects most preventable accidents?

A. Structural failure.

B. Mechanical malfunction.

C. Human error.

Answer (C) is correct. *(AC 60-22)*

DISCUSSION: Most preventable accidents, such as fuel starvation or exhaustion, VFR flight into IFR conditions leading to disorientation, and flight into known icing, have one common factor: human error. Pilots who are involved in accidents usually know what went wrong. In the interest of expediency, cost savings, or other often irrelevant factors, the wrong course of action (decision) was chosen.

Answer (A) is incorrect. Most preventable accidents have human error, not structural failure, as a common factor. Answer (B) is incorrect. Most preventable accidents have human error, not mechanical malfunction, as a common factor.

37. What antidotal phrase can help reverse the hazardous attitude of impulsivity?

A. Do it quickly to get it over with.

B. It could happen to me.

C. Not so fast, think first.

Answer (C) is correct. *(PHAK Chap 2)*

DISCUSSION: Impulsivity is the attitude of people who frequently feel the need to do something, anything, immediately. They do not stop to think about what they are about to do. They do not select the best alternative but instead do the first thing that comes to mind. They should recognize this attitude and state the antidote, "Not so fast. Think first," before taking action.

Answer (A) is incorrect. "Do it quickly to get it over with" is the hazardous attitude of impulsivity, not the antidote. Answer (B) is incorrect. "It could happen to me" is the antidote for the hazardous attitude of invulnerability.

END OF STUDY UNIT

STUDY UNIT SEVEN
AVIATION WEATHER

(4 pages of outline)

This study unit contains outlines of major concepts tested, sample test questions and answers regarding aviation weather, and an explanation of each answer. The table of contents above lists each subunit within this study unit, the number of questions pertaining to that particular subunit, and the pages on which the outlines and questions begin, respectively.

Recall that the **sole purpose** of this book is to expedite your passing of the FAA pilot knowledge test for the private pilot certificate. Accordingly, all extraneous material (i.e., topics or regulations not directly tested on the FAA pilot knowledge test) is omitted, even though much more knowledge is necessary to fly safely. This additional material is presented in *Pilot Handbook* and *Private Pilot Flight Maneuvers and Practical Test Prep*, available from Gleim Publications, Inc. Order online at www.GleimAviation.com.

7.1 CAUSES OF WEATHER

1. Every physical process of weather is accompanied by, or is the result of, heat exchanges.
2. Unequal heating of the Earth's surface causes differences in pressure and altimeter settings.
3. The Coriolis force deflects winds to the right in the Northern Hemisphere. It is caused by the Earth's rotation.
   a. The deflections caused by Coriolis force are less at the surface due to the slower wind speed.
   b. The wind speed is slower at the surface due to friction between wind and the Earth's surface.

7.2 CONVECTIVE CURRENTS

1. Sea breezes are caused by cool and more dense air moving inland off the water. Once inland over the warmer land, the air heats up and rises. Currents push the air over the water where it cools and descends, starting the process over again.
2. The development of thermals depends upon solar heating.

7.3 FRONTS

1. A front is the zone of transition (boundary) between two air masses of different density, e.g., the area separating a high pressure system and a low pressure system.
2. There is always a change in wind when flying across a front.
3. The most easily recognizable change when crossing a front is the change in temperature.

7.4 THUNDERSTORMS

1. Thunderstorms have three phases in their life cycle:
   a. Cumulus: The building stage of a thunderstorm when there are continuous updrafts.
   b. Mature: The time of greatest intensity when there are both updrafts and downdrafts (causing severe wind shear and turbulence).
      1) The commencing of rain on the Earth's surface indicates the beginning of the mature stage of a thunderstorm.
   c. Dissipating: When there are only downdrafts, i.e., the storm is raining itself out.
2. Thunderstorms are produced by cumulonimbus clouds. They form when there is
   a. Sufficient water vapor,
   b. An unstable lapse rate, and
   c. An initial upward boost to start the process.
3. Thunderstorms produce wind shear turbulence, a hazardous and invisible phenomenon particularly for airplanes landing and taking off.
   a. Hazardous wind shear near the ground can also be present during periods of strong temperature inversion.
4. The most severe thunderstorm conditions (heavy hail, destructive winds, tornadoes, etc.) are generally associated with squall line thunderstorms.
   a. A squall line is a nonfrontal narrow band of thunderstorms, usually ahead of a cold front.
5. A thunderstorm, by definition, has lightning because that is what causes thunder.
6. Embedded thunderstorms are obscured (i.e., pilots cannot see them) because they occur in very cloudy conditions.

7.5 ICING

1. Structural icing requires two conditions:
   a. Flight through visible moisture and
   b. The temperature at freezing or below.
2. Freezing rain usually causes the greatest accumulation of structural ice.
3. Ice pellets are caused when rain droplets freeze at a higher altitude, i.e., freezing rain exists above.

7.6 MOUNTAIN WAVE

1. Lenticular clouds are almond- or lens-shaped clouds, usually found on the leeward side of a mountain range.
   a. They may contain winds of 50 kt. or more.
   b. They appear stationary as the wind blows through them.
2. Expect mountain wave turbulence when the air is stable and winds of 40 kt. or greater blow across a mountain or ridge.

7.7 WIND SHEAR

1. Wind shear can occur at any altitude and be horizontal and/or vertical, i.e., whenever adjacent air is flowing in different directions or speeds.
2. Expect wind shear in a temperature inversion whenever wind speed at 2,000 to 4,000 ft. AGL is 25 kt. or more.
3. Hazardous wind shear may be expected in areas of low-level temperature inversions, frontal zones, and clear air turbulence.

7.8 TEMPERATURE/DEW POINT AND FOG

1. When the air temperature is within 5°F of the dew point and the spread is decreasing, you should expect fog and/or low clouds.
   a. Dew point is the temperature at which the air will have 100% humidity, i.e., be saturated.
   b. Thus, air temperature determines how much water vapor can be held by the air.
   c. Frost forms when both the collecting surface is below the dew point of the adjacent air and the dew point is below freezing. Frost is the direct sublimation of water vapor to ice crystals.
2. Water vapor becomes visible as it condenses into clouds, fog, or dew.
3. Evaporation is the conversion of liquid to water vapor.
4. Sublimation is the conversion of solids (e.g., ice) to water vapor or water vapor to solids (e.g., frost).
5. Radiation fog (shallow fog) is most likely to occur when there is a clear sky, little or no wind, and a small temperature/dew point spread.
6. Advection fog forms as a result of moist air condensing as it moves over a cooler surface.
7. Upslope fog results from warm, moist air being cooled as it is forced up sloping terrain.
8. Precipitation-induced fog occurs when warm rain or drizzle falls through cool air and evaporation from the precipitation saturates the cool air and forms fog.
   a. Precipitation-induced fog is usually associated with fronts.
   b. Because of this, it is in the proximity of icing, turbulence, and thunderstorms.
9. Steam fog forms in winter when cold, dry air passes from land areas over comparatively warm ocean waters. It is composed entirely of water droplets that often freeze quickly.
   a. Low-level turbulence can occur, and icing can become hazardous in steam fog.

7.9 CLOUDS

1. Clouds are divided into four families based on their height:
   a. High clouds
   b. Middle clouds
   c. Low clouds
   d. Clouds with extensive vertical development
2. The greatest turbulence is in cumulonimbus clouds.
3. Towering cumulus are early stages of cumulonimbus; they usually indicate convective turbulence.
4. Lifting action, unstable air, and moisture are the ingredients for the formation of cumulonimbus clouds.
5. Nimbus means rain cloud.

6. When air rises in a convective current, it cools at the rate of 5.4°F/1,000 ft., and its dew point decreases 1°F/1,000 feet. The temperature and dew point then are converging at 4.4°F/1,000 feet.
   a. Since clouds form when the temperature/dew point spread is 0°, we can use this to estimate the bases of cumulus clouds.
   b. The surface temperature/dew point spread divided by 4.4°F equals the bases of cumulus clouds in thousands of feet above ground level (AGL).
   c. EXAMPLE: A surface dew point of 56°F and a surface temperature of 69°F results in an estimate of cumulus cloud bases at 3,000 ft. AGL: 69°F – 56°F = 13°F temperature/dew point spread; 13°F/4.4°F = approximately 3,000 ft. AGL.

7.10 STABILITY OF AIR MASSES

1. Stable air characteristics
   a. Stratiform clouds
   b. Smooth air
   c. Fair-to-poor visibility in haze and smoke
   d. Continuous precipitation
2. Unstable air characteristics
   a. Cumuliform clouds
   b. Turbulent air
   c. Good visibility
   d. Showery precipitation
3. When air is warmed from below, it rises and causes instability.
4. The lapse rate is the decrease in temperature with increase in altitude. As the lapse rate increases (i.e., air cools more with increases in altitude), air is more unstable.
   a. The lapse rate can be used to determine the stability of air masses.
5. Moist, stable air moving up a mountain slope produces stratus type clouds as it cools.
6. Turbulence and clouds with extensive vertical development result when unstable air rises.
7. Steady precipitation preceding a front is usually an indication of a warm front, which results from warm air being cooled from the bottom by colder air.
   a. This results in stable air with stratiform clouds and little or no turbulence.

7.11 TEMPERATURE INVERSIONS

1. Normally, temperature decreases as altitude increases. A temperature inversion occurs when temperature increases as altitude increases.
2. Temperature inversions usually result in a stable layer of air.
3. A temperature inversion often develops near the ground on clear, cool nights when the wind is light.
   a. It is caused by terrestrial radiation.
4. Smooth air with restricted visibility is usually found beneath a low-level temperature inversion.

QUESTIONS AND ANSWER EXPLANATIONS: All of the private pilot knowledge test questions chosen by the FAA for release as well as additional questions selected by Gleim relating to the material in the previous outlines are reproduced on the following pages. These questions have been organized into the same subunits as the outlines. To the immediate right of each question are the correct answer and answer explanation. You should cover these answers and answer explanations while responding to the questions. Refer to the general discussion in the Introduction on how to take the FAA knowledge test.

Remember that the questions from the FAA knowledge test bank have been reordered by topic and organized into a meaningful sequence. Also, the first line of the answer explanation gives the citation of the authoritative source for the answer.

QUESTIONS

7.1 Causes of Weather

1. Every physical process of weather is accompanied by, or is the result of, a

A. movement of air.

B. pressure differential.

C. heat exchange.

Answer (C) is correct. *(AvW Chap 2)*
DISCUSSION: Every physical process of weather is accompanied by, or is the result of, a heat exchange. A heat differential (difference between the temperatures of two air masses) causes a differential in pressure, which in turn causes movement of air. Heat exchanges occur constantly, e.g., melting, cooling, updrafts, downdrafts, wind, etc.
Answer (A) is incorrect. Movement of air is a result of heat exchange. Answer (B) is incorrect. Pressure differential is a result of heat exchange.

2. What causes variations in altimeter settings between weather reporting points?

A. Unequal heating of the Earth's surface.

B. Variation of terrain elevation.

C. Coriolis force.

Answer (A) is correct. *(AvW Chap 3)*
DISCUSSION: Unequal heating of the Earth's surface causes differences in air pressure, which is reflected in differences in altimeter settings between weather reporting points.
Answer (B) is incorrect. Variations in altimeter settings between stations is a result of unequal heating of the Earth's surface, not variations of terrain elevations. Answer (C) is incorrect. Variations in altimeter settings between stations is a result of unequal heating of the Earth's surface, not the Coriolis force.

3. The wind at 5,000 feet AGL is southwesterly while the surface wind is southerly. This difference in direction is primarily due to

A. stronger pressure gradient at higher altitudes.

B. friction between the wind and the surface.

C. stronger Coriolis force at the surface.

Answer (B) is correct. *(AvW Chap 4)*
DISCUSSION: Winds aloft at 5,000 ft. are largely affected by Coriolis force, which deflects wind to the right, in the Northern Hemisphere. But at the surface, the winds will be more southerly (they were southwesterly aloft) because Coriolis force has less effect at the surface where the wind speed is slower. The wind speed is slower at the surface due to the friction between the wind and the surface.
Answer (A) is incorrect. Pressure gradient is a force that causes wind, not the reason for wind direction differences. Answer (C) is incorrect. The Coriolis force at the surface is weaker (not stronger) with slower wind speed.

7.2 Convective Currents

4. The development of thermals depends upon

A. a counterclockwise circulation of air.

B. temperature inversions.

C. solar heating.

Answer (C) is correct. *(AvW Chap 4)*
DISCUSSION: Thermals are updrafts in small-scale convective currents. Convective currents are caused by uneven heating of the Earth's surface. Solar heating is the means of heating the Earth's surface.
Answer (A) is incorrect. A counterclockwise circulation describes an area of low pressure in the Northern Hemisphere. Answer (B) is incorrect. A temperature inversion is an increase in temperature with height, which hinders the development of thermals.

5. Convective circulation patterns associated with sea breezes are caused by

A. warm, dense air moving inland from over the water.

B. water absorbing and radiating heat faster than the land.

C. cool, dense air moving inland from over the water.

Answer (C) is correct. *(AvW Chap 4)*

DISCUSSION: Sea breezes are caused by cool and more dense air moving inland off the water. Once over the warmer land, the air heats up and rises. Thus the cooler, more dense air from the sea forces the warmer air up. Currents push the hot air over the water where it cools and descends, starting the cycle over again. This process is caused by land heating faster than water.

Answer (A) is incorrect. The air over the water is cooler (not warmer). Answer (B) is incorrect. Water absorbs and radiates heat slower (not faster) than land.

7.3 Fronts

6. The boundary between two different air masses is referred to as a

A. frontolysis.

B. frontogenesis.

C. front.

Answer (C) is correct. *(AvW Chap 8)*

DISCUSSION: A front is a surface, interface, or transition zone of discontinuity between two adjacent air masses of different densities. It is the boundary between two different air masses.

Answer (A) is incorrect. Frontolysis is the dissipation of a front. Answer (B) is incorrect. Frontogenesis is the initial formation of a front or frontal zone.

7. One weather phenomenon which will always occur when flying across a front is a change in the

A. wind direction.

B. type of precipitation.

C. stability of the air mass.

Answer (A) is correct. *(AvW Chap 8)*

DISCUSSION: The definition of a front is the zone of transition between two air masses of different air pressure or density, e.g., the area separating high and low pressure systems. Due to the difference in changes in pressure systems, there will be a change in wind.

Answer (B) is incorrect. Frequently, precipitation will exist or not exist for both sides of the front: rain showers before and after or no precipitation before and after a dry front. Answer (C) is incorrect. Fronts separate air masses with different pressures, not stabilities; e.g., both air masses could be either stable or unstable.

8. One of the most easily recognized discontinuities across a front is

A. a change in temperature.

B. an increase in cloud coverage.

C. an increase in relative humidity.

Answer (A) is correct. *(AvW Chap 8)*

DISCUSSION: Of the many changes that take place across a front, the most easily recognized is the change in temperature. When flying through a front, you will notice a significant change in temperature, especially at low altitudes.

Answer (B) is incorrect. Although cloud formations may indicate a frontal system, they may not be present or easily recognized across the front. Answer (C) is incorrect. Precipitation is not always associated with a front.

7.4 Thunderstorms

9. If there is thunderstorm activity in the vicinity of an airport at which you plan to land, which hazardous atmospheric phenomenon might be expected on the landing approach?

A. Precipitation static.

B. Wind-shear turbulence.

C. Steady rain.

Answer (B) is correct. *(AvW Chap 11)*

DISCUSSION: The most hazardous atmospheric phenomenon near thunderstorms is wind shear turbulence.

Answer (A) is incorrect. Precipitation static is a steady, high level of noise in radio receivers, which is caused by intense corona discharges from sharp metallic points and edges of flying aircraft. This discharge may be seen at night and is also called St. Elmo's fire. Answer (C) is incorrect. Thunderstorms are usually associated with unstable air, which would produce rain showers (not steady rain).

10. A nonfrontal, narrow band of active thunderstorms that often develop ahead of a cold front is known as a

A. prefrontal system.

B. squall line.

C. dry line.

Answer (B) is correct. *(AvW Chap 11)*

DISCUSSION: A nonfrontal, narrow band of active thunderstorms that often develops ahead of a cold front is known as a squall line.

Answer (A) is incorrect. A prefrontal system is a term that has no meaning. Answer (C) is incorrect. A dry line is a front that seldom has any significant air mass contrast except for moisture.

11. What conditions are necessary for the formation of thunderstorms?

A. High humidity, lifting force, and unstable conditions.

B. High humidity, high temperature, and cumulus clouds.

C. Lifting force, moist air, and extensive cloud cover.

Answer (A) is correct. *(AvW Chap 11)*

DISCUSSION: Thunderstorms form when there is sufficient water vapor, an unstable lapse rate, and an initial upward boost (lifting) to start the storm process.

Answer (B) is incorrect. A high temperature is not required for the formation of thunderstorms. Answer (C) is incorrect. Extensive cloud cover is not necessary for the formation of thunderstorms.

12. During the life cycle of a thunderstorm, which stage is characterized predominately by downdrafts?

A. Cumulus.

B. Dissipating.

C. Mature.

Answer (B) is correct. *(AvW Chap 11)*

DISCUSSION: Thunderstorms have three life cycles: cumulus, mature, and dissipating. It is in the dissipating stage that the storm is characterized by downdrafts as the storm rains itself out.

Answer (A) is incorrect. Cumulus is the building stage when there are updrafts. Answer (C) is incorrect. The mature stage is when there are both updrafts and downdrafts, which create dangerous wind shears.

13. Thunderstorms reach their greatest intensity during the

A. mature stage.

B. downdraft stage.

C. cumulus stage.

Answer (A) is correct. *(AvW Chap 11)*

DISCUSSION: Thunderstorms reach their greatest intensity during the mature stage, where updrafts and downdrafts cause a high level of wind shear.

Answer (B) is incorrect. The downdraft stage is known as the dissipating stage, which is when the thunderstorm rains itself out. Answer (C) is incorrect. The cumulus stage is characterized by continuous updrafts and is not the most intense stage of a thunderstorm.

14. What feature is normally associated with the cumulus stage of a thunderstorm?

A. Roll cloud.

B. Continuous updraft.

C. Frequent lightning.

Answer (B) is correct. *(AvW Chap 11)*

DISCUSSION: The cumulus stage of a thunderstorm has continuous updrafts that build the storm. The water droplets are carried up until they become too heavy. Once they begin falling and creating downdrafts, the storm changes from the cumulus to the mature stage.

Answer (A) is incorrect. The roll cloud is the cloud on the ground, which is formed by the downrushing cold air pushing out from underneath the bottom of the thunderstorm. Answer (C) is incorrect. Frequent lightning is associated with the mature stage, where there is a considerable amount of wind shear and static electricity.

15. Which weather phenomenon signals the beginning of the mature stage of a thunderstorm?

A. The appearance of an anvil top.

B. Precipitation beginning to fall.

C. Maximum growth rate of the clouds.

Answer (B) is correct. *(AvW Chap 11)*

DISCUSSION: The mature stage of a thunderstorm begins when rain begins falling. This means that the downdrafts are occurring sufficiently to carry water all the way through the thunderstorm.

Answer (A) is incorrect. The appearance of an anvil top normally occurs during the dissipating stage when the upper winds blow the top of the cloud downwind. Answer (C) is incorrect. The maximum growth rate of clouds is later in the mature stage and does not necessarily mark the start of the mature stage.

16. Thunderstorms which generally produce the most intense hazard to aircraft are

A. squall line thunderstorms.

B. steady-state thunderstorms.

C. warm front thunderstorms.

Answer (A) is correct. *(AvW Chap 11)*

DISCUSSION: A squall line is a nonfrontal, narrow band of active thunderstorms. It often contains severe, steady-state thunderstorms and presents the single most intense weather hazard to airplanes.

Answer (B) is incorrect. Steady-state thunderstorms are normally associated with weather systems and often form into squall lines. Answer (C) is incorrect. Squall line (not warm front) thunderstorms generally produce the most intense hazard to aircraft.

17. Which weather phenomenon is always associated with a thunderstorm?

A. Lightning.

B. Heavy rain.

C. Hail.

Answer (A) is correct. *(AvW Chap 11)*

DISCUSSION: A thunderstorm, by definition, has lightning, because lightning causes the thunder.

Answer (B) is incorrect. While heavy rain showers usually occur, hail may occur instead. Answer (C) is incorrect. Hail is produced only when the lifting action extends above the freezing level and the supercooled water begins to freeze.

18. The mature stage of a thunderstorm begins with

A. formation of the anvil top.

B. the start of precipitation.

C. continuous downdrafts.

Answer (B) is correct. *(AvW Chap 11)*

DISCUSSION: The mature stage of a thunderstorm begins when rain begins falling. This means that the downdrafts are occurring sufficiently to carry water all the way through the thunderstorm.

Answer (A) is incorrect. The formation of an anvil top normally occurs during the dissipating stage when the upper winds blow the top of the cloud downwind. Answer (C) is incorrect. Continuous downdrafts are present during the dissipating stage of a thunderstorm, not during the mature stage.

19. The destination airport has one runway, 8-26, and the wind is calm. The normal approach in calm wind is a left-hand pattern to runway 8. There is no other traffic at the airport. A thunderstorm about 6 miles west is beginning its mature stage, and rain is starting to reach the ground. The pilot decides to

A. fly the pattern to runway 8 since the storm is too far away to affect the wind at the airport.

B. fly the normal pattern to runway 8 since the storm is west and moving north and any unexpected wind will be from the east or southeast toward the storm.

C. fly an approach to runway 26 since any unexpected wind due to the storm will be westerly.

Answer (C) is correct. *(PHAK Chap 12)*

DISCUSSION: Flying in, near, or under thunderstorms can subject an aircraft to rain, hail, lightning, and violent turbulence. It is recommended that pilots avoid severe thunderstorms by 20 NM. In this case, the storm is to the west of the airport and reaching the mature stage. The mature stage is characterized by both strong updrafts and downdrafts. The pilot of this aircraft could expect the potential of a strong wind from the west, making Runway 26 the best option. Runway 26 also keeps the aircraft on the eastern side of the airport away from the storm to the west.

Answer (A) is incorrect. Flying a left pattern for Runway 8 would put the aircraft closer to or even under the storm. Answer (B) is incorrect. Flying a left pattern for Runway 8 would put the aircraft closer to or even under the storm. The pilot can expect the winds to be from the west, not the east. Westerly winds would favor Runway 26.

7.5 Icing

20. One in-flight condition necessary for structural icing to form is

A. small temperature/dewpoint spread.

B. stratiform clouds.

C. visible moisture.

Answer (C) is correct. *(AvW Chap 10)*

DISCUSSION: Two conditions are necessary for structural icing while in flight. First, the airplane must be flying through visible moisture, such as rain or cloud droplets. Second, the temperature at the point where the moisture strikes the airplane must be freezing or below.

Answer (A) is incorrect. The temperature dew point spread is not a factor in icing as it is in the formation of fog or clouds. Answer (B) is incorrect. No special cloud formation is necessary for icing as long as visible moisture is present.

21. In which environment is aircraft structural ice most likely to have the highest accumulation rate?

A. Cumulus clouds with below freezing temperatures.

B. Freezing drizzle.

C. Freezing rain.

Answer (C) is correct. *(AvW Chap 10)*

DISCUSSION: Freezing rain usually causes the highest accumulation rate of structural icing because of the nature of the supercooled water striking the airplane.

Answer (A) is incorrect. While icing potential is great in cumulus clouds with below freezing temperatures, the highest accumulation rate is in an area with large, supercooled water drops (i.e., freezing rain). Answer (B) is incorrect. Freezing drizzle will not build up ice as quickly as freezing rain.

22. The presence of ice pellets at the surface is evidence that there

A. are thunderstorms in the area.

B. has been cold frontal passage.

C. is a temperature inversion with freezing rain at a higher altitude.

Answer (C) is correct. *(AvW Chap 5)*

DISCUSSION: Rain falling through colder air may freeze during its descent, falling as ice pellets. Ice pellets always indicate freezing rain at a higher altitude.

Answer (A) is incorrect. Ice pellets form when rain freezes during its descent, which may or may not be as a result of a thunderstorm. Answer (B) is incorrect. Ice pellets only indicate that rain is freezing at a higher altitude, not that a cold front has passed through an area.

7.6 Mountain Wave

23. An almond or lens-shaped cloud which appears stationary, but which may contain winds of 50 knots or more, is referred to as

A. an inactive frontal cloud.

B. a funnel cloud.

C. a lenticular cloud.

Answer (C) is correct. *(AvW Chap 9)*

DISCUSSION: Lenticular clouds are lens-shaped clouds, which indicate the crests of standing mountain waves. They form in the updraft and dissipate in the downdraft, so they do not move as the wind blows through them. Lenticular clouds may contain winds of 50 kt. or more and are extremely dangerous.

Answer (A) is incorrect. Frontal clouds usually do not contain winds of 50 kt. or more, and if they do, they do not appear stationary. Answer (B) is incorrect. A funnel cloud is not stationary.

24. Crests of standing mountain waves may be marked by stationary, lens-shaped clouds known as

A. mammatocumulus clouds.

B. standing lenticular clouds.

C. roll clouds.

Answer (B) is correct. *(AvW Chap 9)*

DISCUSSION: Lens-shaped clouds, which indicate crests of standing mountain waves, are called standing lenticular clouds. They form in the updraft and dissipate in the downdraft so that they do not move as the wind blows through them.

Answer (A) is incorrect. Cumulonimbus mamma clouds (also mammatocumulus) are cumulonimbus clouds with pods or circular domes on the bottom that indicate severe turbulence. Answer (C) is incorrect. Roll clouds are low-level, turbulent areas in the shear zone between the plow wind surrounding the outrushing air from a thunderstorm and the surrounding air.

25. Possible mountain wave turbulence could be anticipated when winds of 40 knots or greater blow

A. across a mountain ridge, and the air is stable.

B. down a mountain valley, and the air is unstable.

C. parallel to a mountain peak, and the air is stable.

Answer (A) is correct. *(AvW Chap 9)*

DISCUSSION: Always anticipate possible mountain wave turbulence when the air is stable and winds of 40 kt. or greater blow across a mountain or ridge.

Answer (B) is incorrect. The wind must blow across the mountain or ridge before it flows down a valley. The air must also be stable. If the air is unstable and produces convective turbulence, it will rise and disrupt the "wave." Answer (C) is incorrect. Any time the winds are 40 kt. or more and blowing across (not parallel) to the mountains, you should anticipate mountain wave turbulence.

7.7 Wind Shear

26. Where does wind shear occur?

A. Only at higher altitudes.

B. Only at lower altitudes.

C. At all altitudes, in all directions.

Answer (C) is correct. *(AvW Chap 9)*

DISCUSSION: Wind shear is the eddies in between two wind currents of differing velocities, direction, or both. Wind shear may be associated with either a wind shift or a wind speed gradient at any level in the atmosphere.

Answer (A) is incorrect. A wind shear may occur at any (not only higher) altitudes. Answer (B) is incorrect. A wind shear may occur at any (not only lower) altitudes.

27. A pilot can expect a wind-shear zone in a temperature inversion whenever the wind speed at 2,000 to 4,000 feet above the surface is at least

A. 10 knots.

B. 15 knots.

C. 25 knots.

Answer (C) is correct. *(AvW Chap 9)*

DISCUSSION: When taking off or landing in calm wind under clear skies within a few hours before or after sunset, prepare for a temperature inversion near the ground. You can be relatively certain of a shear zone in the inversion if you know the wind is 25 kt. or more at 2,000 to 4,000 feet. Allow a margin of airspeed above normal climb or approach speed to alleviate the danger of stall in the event of turbulence or sudden change in wind velocity.

Answer (A) is incorrect. A wind shear zone can be expected in a temperature inversion at 2,000 to 4,000 ft. AGL if the wind speed is at least 25 kt., not 10 kt. Answer (B) is incorrect. A wind shear zone can be expected in a temperature inversion at 2,000 to 4,000 ft. AGL if the wind speed is at least 25 kt., not 15 kt.

28. When may hazardous wind shear be expected?

A. When stable air crosses a mountain barrier where it tends to flow in layers forming lenticular clouds.

B. In areas of low-level temperature inversion, frontal zones, and clear air turbulence.

C. Following frontal passage when stratocumulus clouds form indicating mechanical mixing.

Answer (B) is correct. *(AvW Chap 9)*

DISCUSSION: Wind shear is the abrupt rate of change of wind velocity (direction and/or speed) per unit of distance and is normally expressed as vertical or horizontal wind shear. Hazardous wind shear may be expected in areas of low-level temperature inversion, frontal zones, and clear air turbulence.

Answer (A) is incorrect. A mountain wave forms when stable air crosses a mountain barrier where it tends to flow in layers forming lenticular clouds. Turbulence, not wind shear, is expected in this area. Answer (C) is incorrect. Mechanical turbulence (not wind shear) may be expected following frontal passage when clouds form, indicating mechanical mixing.

7.8 Temperature/Dew Point and Fog

29. If the temperature/dewpoint spread is small and decreasing, and the temperature is 62°F, what type weather is most likely to develop?

A. Freezing precipitation.

B. Thunderstorms.

C. Fog or low clouds.

Answer (C) is correct. *(AvW Chap 5)*

DISCUSSION: The difference between the air temperature and dew point is the temperature/dew point spread. As the temperature/dew point spread decreases, fog or low clouds tend to develop.

Answer (A) is incorrect. There cannot be freezing precipitation if the temperature is 62°F. Answer (B) is incorrect. Thunderstorms have to do with unstable lapse rates, not temperature/dew point spreads.

30. What is meant by the term "dewpoint"?

A. The temperature at which condensation and evaporation are equal.

B. The temperature at which dew will always form.

C. The temperature to which air must be cooled to become saturated.

Answer (C) is correct. *(AvW Chap 5)*

DISCUSSION: Dew point is the temperature to which air must be cooled to become saturated or have 100% humidity.

Answer (A) is incorrect. Evaporation is the change from water to water vapor and is not directly related to the dew point. Answer (B) is incorrect. Dew forms only when heat radiates from an object whose temperature lowers below the dew point of the adjacent air.

31. The amount of water vapor which air can hold depends on the

A. dewpoint.

B. air temperature.

C. stability of the air.

Answer (B) is correct. *(AvW Chap 5)*

DISCUSSION: Air temperature largely determines how much water vapor can be held by the air. Warm air can hold more water vapor than cool air.

Answer (A) is incorrect. Dew point is the temperature at which air must be cooled to become saturated by the water vapor already present in the air. Answer (C) is incorrect. Air stability is the state of the atmosphere at which vertical distribution of temperature is such that air particles will resist displacement from their initial level.

32. What are the processes by which moisture is added to unsaturated air?

A. Evaporation and sublimation.

B. Heating and condensation.

C. Supersaturation and evaporation.

Answer (A) is correct. *(AvW Chap 5)*

DISCUSSION: Evaporation is the process of converting a liquid to water vapor, and sublimation is the process of converting ice to water vapor.

Answer (B) is incorrect. Heating alone does not add moisture. Condensation is the change of water vapor to liquid water. Answer (C) is incorrect. Supersaturation is a nonsense term in this context.

33. Which conditions result in the formation of frost?

A. The temperature of the collecting surface is at or below freezing when small droplets of moisture fall on the surface.

B. The temperature of the collecting surface is at or below the dewpoint of the adjacent air and the dewpoint is below freezing.

C. The temperature of the surrounding air is at or below freezing when small drops of moisture fall on the collecting surface.

Answer (B) is correct. *(AvW Chap 5)*

DISCUSSION: Frost forms when both the collecting surface is below the dew point of the adjacent air and the dew point is below freezing. Frost is the direct sublimation of water vapor to ice crystals.

Answer (A) is incorrect. If small droplets of water fall on the collecting surface, which is at or below freezing, ice (not frost) will form. Answer (C) is incorrect. If small droplets of water fall while the surrounding air is at or below freezing, ice (not frost) will form.

34. Clouds, fog, or dew will always form when

A. water vapor condenses.

B. water vapor is present.

C. relative humidity reaches 100 percent.

Answer (A) is correct. *(AvW Chap 5)*

DISCUSSION: As water vapor condenses, it becomes visible as clouds, fog, or dew.

Answer (B) is incorrect. Water vapor is usually always present but does not form clouds, fog, or dew without condensation. Answer (C) is incorrect. Even at 100% humidity, water vapor may not condense, e.g., sufficient condensation nuclei may not be present.

35. Low-level turbulence can occur and icing can become hazardous in which type of fog?

A. Rain-induced fog.

B. Upslope fog.

C. Steam fog.

Answer (C) is correct. *(AvW Chap 14)*

DISCUSSION: Steam fog forms in winter when cold, dry air passes from land areas over comparatively warm ocean waters and is composed entirely of water droplets that often freeze quickly. Low-level turbulence can occur, and icing can become hazardous.

Answer (A) is incorrect. Precipitation- (rain-) induced fog is formed when relatively warm rain or drizzle falls through cool air and evaporation from the precipitation saturates the cool air and forms fog. While the hazards of turbulence and icing may occur in the proximity of rain-induced fog, these hazards occur as a result of the steam fog formation process. Answer (B) is incorrect. Upslope fog forms when moist, stable air is cooled as it moves up sloping terrain.

36. In which situation is advection fog most likely to form?

A. A warm, moist air mass on the windward side of mountains.

B. An air mass moving inland from the coast in winter.

C. A light breeze blowing colder air out to sea.

Answer (B) is correct. *(AvW Chap 12)*

DISCUSSION: Advection fog forms when moist air moves over colder ground or water. It is most common in coastal areas.

Answer (A) is incorrect. A warm, moist air mass on the windward side of mountains produces rain or upslope fog as it blows upward and cools. Answer (C) is incorrect. A light breeze blowing colder air out to sea causes steam fog.

37. What situation is most conducive to the formation of radiation fog?

A. Warm, moist air over low, flatland areas on clear, calm nights.

B. Moist, tropical air moving over cold, offshore water.

C. The movement of cold air over much warmer water.

Answer (A) is correct. *(AvW Chap 12)*

DISCUSSION: Radiation fog is shallow fog of which ground fog is one form. It occurs under conditions of clear skies, little or no wind, and a small temperature/dew point spread. The fog forms almost exclusively at night or near dawn as a result of terrestrial radiation cooling the ground and the ground cooling the air on contact with it.

Answer (B) is incorrect. Moist, tropical air moving over cold, offshore water causes advection fog, not radiation fog. Answer (C) is incorrect. Movement of cold, dry air over much warmer water results in steam fog.

38. What types of fog depend upon wind in order to exist?

A. Radiation fog and ice fog.

B. Steam fog and ground fog.

C. Advection fog and upslope fog.

Answer (C) is correct. *(AvW Chap 14)*

DISCUSSION: Advection fog forms when moist air moves over colder ground or water. It is most common in coastal areas. Upslope fog forms when wind blows moist air upward over rising terrain and the air cools below its dew point. Both advection fog and upslope fog require wind to move air masses.

Answer (A) is incorrect. No wind is required for the formation of either radiation (ground) or ice fog. Answer (B) is incorrect. No wind is required for the formation of ground (radiation) fog.

7.9 Clouds

39. Clouds are divided into four families according to their

A. outward shape.

B. height range.

C. composition.

Answer (B) is correct. *(AvW Chap 7)*

DISCUSSION: The four families of clouds are high clouds, middle clouds, low clouds, and clouds with extensive vertical development. Thus, they are based upon their height range.

Answer (A) is incorrect. Clouds are divided by their height range, not outward shape. Answer (C) is incorrect. Clouds are divided by their height range, not their composition.

40. The suffix "nimbus," used in naming clouds, means

A. a cloud with extensive vertical development.

B. a rain cloud.

C. a middle cloud containing ice pellets.

Answer (B) is correct. *(AvW Chap 7)*

DISCUSSION: The suffix "nimbus" or the prefix "nimbo" means a rain cloud.

Answer (A) is incorrect. Clouds with extensive vertical development are called either towering cumulus or cumulonimbus. Answer (C) is incorrect. A middle cloud has the prefix "alto."

41. The conditions necessary for the formation of cumulonimbus clouds are a lifting action and

A. unstable air containing an excess of condensation nuclei.

B. unstable, moist air.

C. either stable or unstable air.

Answer (B) is correct. *(AvW Chap 11)*

DISCUSSION: Unstable, moist air, in addition to a lifting action, i.e., convective activity, is needed to form cumulonimbus clouds.

Answer (A) is incorrect. There must be moisture available to produce the clouds and rain; e.g., in a hot, dry dust storm, there would be no thunderstorm. Answer (C) is incorrect. The air must be unstable or there will be no lifting action.

42. What clouds have the greatest turbulence?

A. Towering cumulus.

B. Cumulonimbus.

C. Nimbostratus.

Answer (B) is correct. *(AvW Chap 7)*

DISCUSSION: The greatest turbulence occurs in cumulonimbus clouds, which are thunderstorm clouds.

Answer (A) is incorrect. Towering cumulus clouds are an earlier stage of cumulonimbus clouds. Answer (C) is incorrect. Nimbostratus is a gray or dark, massive cloud layer diffused by continuous rain or ice pellets. It is a middle cloud with very little turbulence but may pose serious icing problems.

43. What cloud types would indicate convective turbulence?

A. Cirrus clouds.

B. Nimbostratus clouds.

C. Towering cumulus clouds.

Answer (C) is correct. *(AvW Chap 7)*

DISCUSSION: Towering cumulus clouds are an early stage of cumulonimbus clouds, or thunderstorms, that are based on convective turbulence, i.e., an unstable lapse rate.

Answer (A) is incorrect. Cirrus clouds are high, thin, featherlike ice crystal clouds in patches and narrow bands that are not based on any convective activity. Answer (B) is incorrect. Nimbostratus are gray or dark, massive clouds diffused by continuous rain or ice pellets with very little turbulence.

44. At approximately what altitude above the surface would the pilot expect the base of cumuliform clouds if the surface air temperature is 82°F and the dewpoint is 38°F?

A. 9,000 feet AGL.

B. 10,000 feet AGL.

C. 11,000 feet AGL.

Answer (B) is correct. *(AvW Chap 6)*

DISCUSSION: The height of cumuliform cloud bases can be estimated using surface temperature/dew point spread. Unsaturated air in a convective current cools at about 5.4°F/1,000 ft., and dew point decreases about 1°F/1,000 feet. In a convective current, temperature and dew point converge at about 4.4°F/1,000 feet. Thus, if the temperature/dew point spread is 44°F (82°F – 38°F), divide 44 by 4.4 to obtain 10,000 ft. AGL.

Answer (A) is incorrect. The approximate height of the base of cumuliform clouds is 9,000 ft. AGL if the temperature/dew point spread is 40°F. Answer (C) is incorrect. The approximate height of the base of cumuliform clouds is 11,000 ft. AGL if the temperature/dew point spread is 48°F.

45. What is the approximate base of the cumulus clouds if the surface air temperature at 1,000 feet MSL is 70°F and the dewpoint is 48°F?

A. 4,000 feet MSL.

B. 5,000 feet MSL.

C. 6,000 feet MSL.

Answer (C) is correct. *(AvW Chap 6)*

DISCUSSION: The height of cumuliform cloud bases can be estimated using surface temperature/dew point spread. Unsaturated air in a convective current cools at about 5.4°F/1,000 ft., and dew point decreases about 1°F/1,000 feet. In a convective current, temperature and dew point converge at about 4.4°F/1,000 feet. Thus, if the temperature and dew point are 70°F and 48°F, respectively, at 1,000 ft. MSL, there would be a 22°F spread that, divided by the lapse rate of 4.4, is approximately 5,000 ft. AGL, or 6,000 ft. MSL (5,000 + 1,000).

Answer (A) is incorrect. The approximate base of the cumulus clouds is 4,000 ft. MSL if the temperature at 1,000 ft. MSL is 61°F, not 70°F. Answer (B) is incorrect. The approximate base of the cumulus clouds is 5,000 ft. AGL, not MSL.

7.10 Stability of Air Masses

46. What is a characteristic of stable air?

A. Stratiform clouds.

B. Unlimited visibility.

C. Cumulus clouds.

Answer (A) is correct. *(AvW Chap 8)*

DISCUSSION: Characteristics of a stable air mass include stratiform clouds, continuous precipitation, smooth air, and fair to poor visibility in haze and smoke.

Answer (B) is incorrect. Restricted, not unlimited, visibility is an indication of stable air. Answer (C) is incorrect. Fair weather cumulus clouds indicate unstable conditions, not stable conditions.

47. When warm, moist, stable air flows upslope, it

A. produces stratus type clouds.

B. causes showers and thunderstorms.

C. develops convective turbulence.

Answer (A) is correct. *(AvW Chap 6)*

DISCUSSION: Moist, stable air flowing upslope can be expected to produce stratus type clouds as the air cools adiabatically as it moves up sloping terrain.

Answer (B) is incorrect. Showers and thunderstorms are characteristics of unstable (not stable) air. Answer (C) is incorrect. Convective turbulence is a characteristic of unstable (not stable) air.

48. If an unstable air mass is forced upward, what type clouds can be expected?

A. Stratus clouds with little vertical development.

B. Stratus clouds with considerable associated turbulence.

C. Clouds with considerable vertical development and associated turbulence.

Answer (C) is correct. *(AvW Chap 6)*

DISCUSSION: When unstable air is lifted, it usually results in considerable vertical development and associated turbulence, i.e., convective activity.

Answer (A) is incorrect. Stable rather than unstable air creates stratus clouds with little vertical development. Answer (B) is incorrect. Stratus (layer-type) clouds usually have little turbulence unless they are either lenticular clouds created by mountain waves or other high-altitude clouds associated with high winds near or in the jet stream.

49. What are characteristics of unstable air?

A. Turbulence and good surface visibility.

B. Turbulence and poor surface visibility.

C. Nimbostratus clouds and good surface visibility.

Answer (A) is correct. *(AvW Chap 8)*

DISCUSSION: Characteristics of an unstable air mass include cumuliform clouds, showery precipitation, turbulence, and good visibility, except in blowing obstructions.

Answer (B) is incorrect. Poor surface visibility is a characteristic of stable (not unstable) air. Answer (C) is incorrect. Stratus clouds are characteristic of stable (not unstable) air.

50. A stable air mass is most likely to have which characteristic?

A. Showery precipitation.

B. Turbulent air.

C. Poor surface visibility.

Answer (C) is correct. *(AvW Chap 8)*

DISCUSSION: Characteristics of a stable air mass include stratiform clouds and fog, continuous precipitation, smooth air, and fair to poor visibility in haze and smoke.

Answer (A) is incorrect. Showery precipitation is a characteristic of an unstable (not stable) air mass. Answer (B) is incorrect. Turbulent air is a characteristic of an unstable (not stable) air mass.

51. Steady precipitation preceding a front is an indication of

A. stratiform clouds with moderate turbulence.

B. cumuliform clouds with little or no turbulence.

C. stratiform clouds with little or no turbulence.

Answer (C) is correct. *(AvW Chap 8)*

DISCUSSION: Steady precipitation preceding a front is usually an indication of a warm front, which results from warm air being cooled from the bottom by colder air. This results in stratiform clouds with little or no turbulence.

Answer (A) is incorrect. Stratiform clouds usually are not turbulent. Answer (B) is incorrect. Cumuliform clouds have showery rather than steady precipitation.

52. What are characteristics of a moist, unstable air mass?

A. Cumuliform clouds and showery precipitation.

B. Poor visibility and smooth air.

C. Stratiform clouds and showery precipitation.

Answer (A) is correct. *(AvW Chap 8)*

DISCUSSION: Characteristics of an unstable air mass include cumuliform clouds, showery precipitation, turbulence, and good visibility, except in blowing obstructions.

Answer (B) is incorrect. Poor visibility and smooth air are characteristics of stable (not unstable) air. Answer (C) is incorrect. Stratiform clouds and continuous precipitation are characteristics of stable (not unstable) air.

53. What measurement can be used to determine the stability of the atmosphere?

A. Atmospheric pressure.

B. Actual lapse rate.

C. Surface temperature.

Answer (B) is correct. *(AvW Chap 6)*

DISCUSSION: The stability of the atmosphere is determined by vertical movements of air. Warm air rises when the air above is cooler. The actual lapse rate, which is the decrease of temperature with altitude, is therefore a measure of stability.

Answer (A) is incorrect. Atmospheric pressure is the pressure exerted by the atmosphere as a consequence of gravitational attraction exerted upon the "column" of air lying directly above the point in question. It cannot be used to determine stability. Answer (C) is incorrect. While the surface temperature may have some effect on temperature changes and air movements, it is the actual lapse rate that determines the stability of the atmosphere.

54. What would decrease the stability of an air mass?

A. Warming from below.

B. Cooling from below.

C. Decrease in water vapor.

Answer (A) is correct. *(AvW Chap 6)*

DISCUSSION: When air is warmed from below, even though cooling adiabatically, it remains warmer than the surrounding air. The colder, more dense surrounding air forces the warmer air upward, and an unstable condition develops.

Answer (B) is incorrect. Cooling from below means the surrounding air is warmer, which would increase (not decrease) the stability of an air mass. Answer (C) is incorrect. As water vapor in air decreases, the air mass tends to increase (not decrease) stability.

7.11 Temperature Inversions

55. What feature is associated with a temperature inversion?

A. A stable layer of air.

B. An unstable layer of air.

C. Chinook winds on mountain slopes.

Answer (A) is correct. *(AvW Chap 6)*

DISCUSSION: A temperature inversion is associated with an increase in temperature with height, a reversal of normal decrease in temperature with height. Thus, any warm air rises to where it is the same temperature and forms a stable layer of air.

Answer (B) is incorrect. Instability is a result of rising air remaining warmer than the surrounding air aloft, which would not occur with a temperature inversion. Answer (C) is incorrect. A Chinook wind is a warm, dry downslope wind blowing down the eastern slopes of the Rocky Mountains over the adjacent plains in the U.S. and Canada.

56. The most frequent type of ground or surface-based temperature inversion is that which is produced by

A. terrestrial radiation on a clear, relatively still night.

B. warm air being lifted rapidly aloft in the vicinity of mountainous terrain.

C. the movement of colder air under warm air, or the movement of warm air over cold air.

Answer (A) is correct. *(AvW Chap 2)*

DISCUSSION: An inversion often develops near the ground on clear, cool nights when wind is light. The ground loses heat and cools the air near the ground while the temperature a few hundred feet above changes very little. Thus, temperature increases in height, which is an inversion.

Answer (B) is incorrect. Warm air being lifted rapidly aloft in the vicinity of mountainous terrain describes convective activity. Answer (C) is incorrect. The movement of colder air under warm air, which causes an inversion, is caused by a cold front, not terrestrial radiation (warm air moving over cold air is a warm front).

57. When there is a temperature inversion, you would expect to experience

A. clouds with extensive vertical development above an inversion aloft.

B. good visibility in the lower levels of the atmosphere and poor visibility above an inversion aloft.

C. an increase in temperature as altitude increases.

Answer (C) is correct. *(AvW Chap 2)*

DISCUSSION: By definition, a temperature inversion is a situation in which the temperature increases as altitude increases. The normal situation is that the temperature decreases as altitude increases.

Answer (A) is incorrect. Vertical development does not occur in an inversion situation because the warm air cannot rise when the air above is warmer. Answer (B) is incorrect. The inversion traps dust, smoke, and other nuclei beneath the inversion, which reduces visibility.

58. Which weather conditions should be expected beneath a low-level temperature inversion layer when the relative humidity is high?

A. Smooth air, poor visibility, fog, haze, or low clouds.

B. Light wind shear, poor visibility, haze, and light rain.

C. Turbulent air, poor visibility, fog, low stratus type clouds, and showery precipitation.

Answer (A) is correct. *(AvW Chap 12)*

DISCUSSION: Beneath temperature inversions, there is usually smooth air because there is little vertical movement due to the inversion. There is also poor visibility due to fog, haze, and low clouds (when there is high relative humidity).

Answer (B) is incorrect. Wind shears usually do not occur below a low-level temperature inversion. They occur at or just above the inversion. Answer (C) is incorrect. Turbulent air and showery precipitation are not present with low-level temperature inversions.

END OF STUDY UNIT

STUDY UNIT EIGHT
AVIATION WEATHER SERVICES

(10 pages of outline)

This study unit contains outlines of major concepts tested, sample test questions and answers regarding aviation weather services, and an explanation of each answer. The table of contents above lists each subunit within this study unit, the number of questions pertaining to that particular subunit, and the pages on which the outlines and questions begin, respectively.

Recall that the **sole purpose** of this book is to expedite your passing of the FAA pilot knowledge test for the private pilot certificate. Accordingly, all extraneous material (i.e., topics or regulations not directly tested on the FAA pilot knowledge test) is omitted, even though much more knowledge is necessary to fly safely. This additional material is presented in *Pilot Handbook* and *Private Pilot Flight Maneuvers and Practical Test Prep*, available from Gleim Publications, Inc. Order online at www.GleimAviation.com.

8.1 WEATHER BRIEFINGS

1. When requesting a telephone weather briefing, you should identify
   a. Yourself as a pilot
   b. Your intended route
   c. Your intended destination
   d. Whether you are flying VFR or IFR
   e. Type of aircraft
   f. Proposed departure time and time en route
2. A standard briefing should be obtained before every flight. This briefing will provide all the necessary information for a safe flight.
3. An outlook briefing is provided when it is 6 or more hours before proposed departure time.
4. An abbreviated briefing will be provided when the user requests information to
   a. Supplement mass disseminated data,
   b. Update a previous briefing, or
   c. Be limited to specific information.

8.2 AVIATION ROUTINE WEATHER REPORT (METAR)

1. Aviation routine weather reports (METARs) are actual weather observations at the time indicated on the report. There are two types of reports:
   a. **METAR** is a routine weather report.
   b. **SPECI** is a nonroutine weather report.
2. Following the type of report are the elements listed below:
   a. The four-letter ICAO station identifier.
      1) In the contiguous 48 states, the three-letter domestic identifier is prefixed with a "K."
   b. Date and time of report. It is appended with a "Z" to denote Coordinated Universal Time (UTC).
   c. Modifier (if required).
   d. Wind. Wind is reported as a five-digit group (six digits if the wind speed is greater than 99 knots). It is appended with the abbreviation KT to denote the use of knots for wind speed.
      1) If the wind is gusty, it is reported as a "G" after the speed, followed by the highest gust reported.
      2) EXAMPLE: **11012G18KT** means wind from 110° true at 12 kt. with gusts to 18 knots.
   e. Visibility. Prevailing visibility is reported in statute miles with "SM" appended to it.
      1) EXAMPLE: **1 1/2SM** means visibility 1 1/2 statute miles.
   f. Runway visual range.
   g. Weather phenomena.
      1) **RA** is used to indicate rain.
   h. Sky conditions.
      1) The ceiling is the lowest broken or overcast layer, or vertical visibility into an obscuration.
      2) Cloud bases are reported with three digits in hundreds of feet AGL.
         a) EXAMPLE: **OVC007** means overcast cloud layer at 700 ft. AGL.
   i. Temperature/dew point. They are reported in a two-digit form in whole degrees Celsius separated by a solidus, "/."
   j. Altimeter.
   k. Remarks (RMK).
      1) **RAB35** means rain began at 35 min. past the hour.
3. EXAMPLE: METAR KAUS 301651Z 12008KT 4SM -RA HZ BKN010 OVC023 21/17 A3005 RMK RAB25
   a. **METAR** is a routine weather observation.
   b. **KAUS** is Austin, TX.
   c. **301651Z** means the observation was taken on the 30th day at 1651 UTC (or Z).
   d. **12008KT** means the wind is from 120° true at 8 knots.
   e. **4SM** means the visibility is 4 statute miles.
   f. **-RA HZ** means light rain and haze.
   g. **BKN010 OVC023** means ceiling 1,000 ft. broken, 2,300 ft. overcast.
   h. **21/17** means the temperature is 21°C and the dew point is 17°C.
   i. **A3005** means the altimeter setting is 30.05 in. of Hg.
   j. **RMK RAB25** means remarks, rain began at 25 min. past the hour., i.e., 1625 UTC.

8.3 PILOT WEATHER REPORT (PIREP)

1. No observation is more timely or needed than the one you make from the cockpit.
2. PIREPs are transmitted in the format illustrated below.

UUA/UA	Type of report: URGENT (UUA) - Any PIREP that contains any of the following weather phenomena: tornadoes, funnel clouds, or waterspouts; severe or extreme turbulence, including clear air turbulence (CAT); severe icing; hail; low-level wind shear (LLWS) (pilot reports air speed fluctuations of 10 knots or more within 2,000 feet of the surface); any other weather phenomena reported that are considered by the controller to be hazardous, or potentially hazardous, to flight operations. ROUTINE (UA) - Any PIREP that contains weather phenomena not listed above, including low-level wind shear reports with air speed fluctuations of less than 10 knots.
/OV	Location: Use VHF NAVAID(s) or an airport using the three- or four-letter location identifier. Position can be over a site, at some location relative to a site, or along a route. Ex: /OV KABC; /OV KABC090025; /OV KABC045020-DEF; /OV KABC-KDEF
/TM	Time: Four digits in UTC. Ex: /TM 0915
/FL	Altitude/Flight level: Three digits for hundreds of feet with no space between FL and altitude. If not known, use UNKN. Ex: /FL095; /FL310; /FLUNKN
/TP	Aircraft type: Four digits maximum; if not known, use UNKN. Ex: /TP L329; /TP B737; /TP UNKN
/SK	Sky cover: Describes cloud amount, height of cloud bases, and height of cloud tops. If unknown, use UNKN. Ex: /SK SCT040-TOP080; /SK BKNUNKN-TOP075; /SK BKN-OVC050-TOPUNKN; /SK OVCUNKN-TOP085
/WX	Flight visibility and weather: Flight visibility (FV) reported first and use standard METAR weather symbols. Intensity (– for light, no qualifier for moderate, and + for heavy) shall be coded for all precipitation types except ice crystals and hail. Ex: /WX FV05SM -RA; /WX FV01 SN BR; /WX RA
/TA	Temperature (Celsius): If below zero, prefix with an "M." Temperature should also be reported if icing is reported. Ex: /TA 15; /TA M06
/WV	Wind: Direction from which the wind is blowing, coded in tens of degrees using three digits. Directions of less than 100 degrees shall be preceded by a zero. The wind speed shall be entered as a two- or three-digit group immediately following the direction, coded in whole knots using the hundreds, tens, and units digits. Ex: /WV 27045KT; /WV 280110KT
/TB	Turbulence: Use standard contractions for intensity and type (CAT or CHOP when appropriate). Include altitude only if different from FL. Ex: /TB EXTRM; /TB OCNL LGT-MDT BLO 090; /TB MOD-SEV CHOP 080-110
/IC	Icing: Describe using standard intensity and type contractions. Include altitude only if different from FL. Ex: /IC LGT-MDT RIME; /IC SEV CLR 028-045
/RM	Remarks: Use free form to clarify the report, putting hazardous elements first. Ex: /RM LLWS –15 KT SFC-030 DURGC RY 22 JFK

3. All heights are given as MSL. To determine AGL, subtract the field height from the given height.

4. Turbulence is reported as
    a. Light = LGT
    b. Moderate = MDT
    c. Severe = SVR
5. Icing is reported as
    a. Clear = CLR
    b. Rime = RIME
6. Cloud layers are reported with heights for bases, tops, and layer type if available. "No entry" means that information was not given.
    a. EXAMPLE: SK 024 BKN 032/042 BKN-OVC decoded means a broken layer 2,400 ft. MSL to 3,200 ft. MSL. A second layer is broken to overcast starting at 4,200 ft. MSL.
7. Wind direction and velocity are given as a five- or six-digit code (e.g., **/WV 27045** means 270° at 45 knots).
8. Air temperature is expressed in degrees Celsius (°C).

8.4 AVIATION AREA FORECAST

1. Aviation area forecasts (FAs) are forecasts of visual meteorological conditions (VMC), clouds, and general weather conditions for several states and/or portions of states, generally for an area greater than 3,000 square miles. They can be used to interpolate conditions at airports that have no terminal forecasts. FAs are issued three times a day and consist of
    a. A 12-hr. forecast, and
    b. An additional 6-hr. categorical outlook.
2. FA weather format. An example is presented in Figure 16 on the next page. It is presented in abbreviations. You will see this same FA utilizing abbreviations on your pilot knowledge test.
3. There are four sections in an FA:
    a. Communication and product header section
    b. Precautionary statements section
    c. Synopsis section (for the purposes of the test, not considered a forecast)
    d. VFR clouds/weather section (VFR CLDS/WX), referred to as the forecast section
        1) Included in the VFR CLDS/WX section is a categorical outlook that is valid for an additional 6 hours. For the purposes of the test, the categorical outlook is not considered a forecast.
4. In order to get a complete weather picture, including icing, turbulence, and IFR conditions, an FA must be supplemented by In-Flight Aviation Weather Advisories (AIRMETs Zulu, Tango, and Sierra).
    a. A pilot should refer to the In-Flight Aviation Weather Advisories to determine the freezing level and areas of probable icing aloft.

```
BOSC  FA  241845
SYNOPSIS AND VFR CLDS/WX
SYNOPSIS VALID UNTIL 251300
CLDS/WX VALID UNTIL 250700...OTLK VALID 250700-251300
ME NH VT MA RI CT NY LO NJ PA OH LE WV MD DC DE VA AND CSTL WTRS
.
SEE AIRMET SIERRA FOR IFR CONDS AND MTN OBSCN.
TS IMPLY SEV OR GTR TURB SEV ICE LLWS AND IFR CONDS.
NON MSL HGTS DENOTED BY AGL OR CIG.
.
SYNOPSIS...19Z CDFNT ALG A 16NE ACK-ENE LN...CONTG AS A QSTNRY
FNT ALG AN END-50SW MSS LN. BY 13Z...CDFNT ALG A 140ESE ACK-HTO
LN...CONTG AS A QSTNRY FNT ALG A HTO-SYR-YYZ LN. TROF ACRS CNTRL
PA INTO NRN VA. ...REYNOLDS...
.
OH LE
NRN HLF OH LE...SCT-BKN025 OVC045. CLDS LYRD 150. SCT SHRA. WDLY
      SCT TSRA. CB TOPS FL350. 23-01Z OVC020-030. VIS 3SM BR. OCNL-
      RA. OTLK...IFR CIG BR FG.
SWRN QTR OH...BKN050-060 TOPS 100. OTLK...MVFR BR.
SERN QTR OH...SCT-BKN040 BKN070 TOPS 120. WDLY SCT-TSRA. 00Z
      SCT-BKN030 OVC050. WDLY SCT-TSRA. CB TOPS FL350. OTLK...VFR
      SHRA.
.
CHIC FA 241945
SYNOPSIS AND VFR CLDS/WX
SYNOPSIS VALID UNTIL 251400
CLDS/WX VALID UNTIL 250800...OTLK VALID 250800-251400
ND SD NE KS MN IA MO WI LM LS MI LH IL IN KY
.
SEE AIRMET SIERRA FOR IFR CONDS AND MTN OBSCN.
TS IMPLY SEV OR GTR TURB SEV ICE LLWS AND IFR CONDS.
NON MSL HGTS DENOTED BY AGL OR CIG.
.
SYNOPSIS...LOW PRES AREA 20Z CNTRD OVR SERN WI FCST MOV NEWD INTO
LH BY 12Z AND WKN. LOW PRES FCST DEEPEN OVR ERN CO DURG PD AND
MOV NR WRN KS BORDER BY 14Z. DVLPG CDFNT WL MOV EWD INTO S CNTRL
NE-CNTRL KS BY 14Z. ...SMITH..
.
UPR MI LS
WRN PTNS...AGL SCT030 SCT 030 SCT-BKN050. TOPS 080. 02-05Z BECMG CIG
      OVC010 VIS 3-5SM BR. OTLK...IFR CIG BR.
ERN PTNS...CIG BKN020 OVC040. OCNL VIS 3-5SM -RA BR. TOPS FL200.
      23Z CIG OVC010 VIS 3-5SM -RA BR. OTLK...IFR CIG BR.
.
LWR MI LM LH
CNTRL/NRN PTNS...CIG OVC010 VIS 3-5SM -RA BR. TOPS FL200
      OTLK...IFR CIG BR.
.
SRN THIRD...CIG OVC015-025. SCT -SHRA. TOPS 150. 00-02Z BECMG CIG
      OVC010 VIS 3-5SM BR. TOPS 060. OTLK...IFR CIG BR.
.
IN
NRN HALF...CIG BKN035 BKN080. TOPS FL200. SCT -SHRA. 00Z CIG
      BKN-SCT040 BKN-SCT080. TOPS 120. 06Z AGL SCT-BKN030. TOPS 080.
      OCNL VIS 3-5SM BR. OTLK...MVFR CIG BR.
SRN HALF...AGL SCT050 SCT-BKN100. TOPS 120. 07Z AGL SCT 030
      SCT100. OTLK...VFR.
```

Figure 16. – Area Forecast.

8.5 TERMINAL AERODROME FORECAST (TAF)

1. Terminal aerodrome forecasts (TAFs) are weather forecasts for selected airports throughout the country.
2. The elements of a TAF are listed below:
   a. Type of report
      1) **TAF** is a routine forecast.
      2) **TAF AMD** is an amended forecast.
   b. ICAO station identifier
   c. Date and time the forecast is actually prepared
   d. Valid period of the forecast
   e. Forecast meteorological conditions. This is the body of the forecast and includes the following:
      1) Wind
      2) Visibility
      3) Weather
      4) Sky condition
         a) Cumulonimbus clouds (CB) are the only cloud type forecast in TAFs.
3. EXAMPLE:
   TAF
   KBRO 300545Z 300606 VRB04KT 3SM SCT040 OVC150 TEMPO 2124 SHRA
   FM0200 10010KT P6SM OVC020 BECMG0306 NSW BKN020=
   a. **TAF** is a routine forecast.
   b. **KBRO** is Brownsville, TX.
   c. **300545Z** means the forecast was prepared on the 30th day at 0545 UTC.
   d. **300606** means the forecast is valid from the 30th day at 0600 UTC until 0600 UTC the following day.
   e. **VRB04KT 3SM SCT040 OVC150 TEMPO 2124 SHRA** means the forecast from 0600 until 0200 UTC is wind variable in direction at 4 kt., visibility 3 SM, scattered cloud layer at 4,000 ft., ceiling 15,000 ft. overcast, with occasional rain showers between 2100 and 2400 UTC.
   f. **FM0200 10010KT P6SM OVC020 BECMG0306 NSW BKN020=** means the forecast from 0200 until 0300 is wind 100° true at 10 kt., visibility greater than 6 SM, ceiling 2,000 ft. overcast then becoming no significant weather, ceiling 2,000 ft. broken between 0300 and 0600 UTC.
      1) Note that, since the becoming group (BECMG) did not forecast wind and visibility, they are the same as the previous forecast group, i.e., wind 100° true at 10 kt., visibility greater than 6 statute miles.

8.6 WEATHER DEPICTION CHARTS

1. A weather depiction chart is an outline of the United States depicting sky conditions at the time stated on the chart based on METAR reports.
   a. Reporting stations are marked with a little circle.
      1) If the sky is clear, the circle is open; if overcast, the circle is solid; if scattered, the circle is 1/4 solid; if broken, the circle is 3/4 solid. If the sky is obscured, there is an "X" in the circle.
      2) The height of clouds is expressed in hundreds of feet above ground level; e.g., 120 means 12,000 ft. AGL.

2. Areas with ceilings below 1,000 ft. and/or visibility less than 3 SM, i.e., below VFR, are bracketed with solid black contour lines and are shaded.
   a. Visibility is indicated next to the circle; e.g., 2 stands for 2 SM visibility.
      1) If the visibility is greater than 6 SM, it is not reported.
   b. Areas of marginal VFR with ceilings of 1,000 to 3,000 ft. and/or visibility at 3 to 5 SM are bracketed by solid black contour lines and are unshaded.
   c. Ceilings greater than 3,000 ft. and visibility greater than 5 SM are not indicated by contour lines on weather depiction charts.
3. Station models and significant weather are indicated by the following symbols:

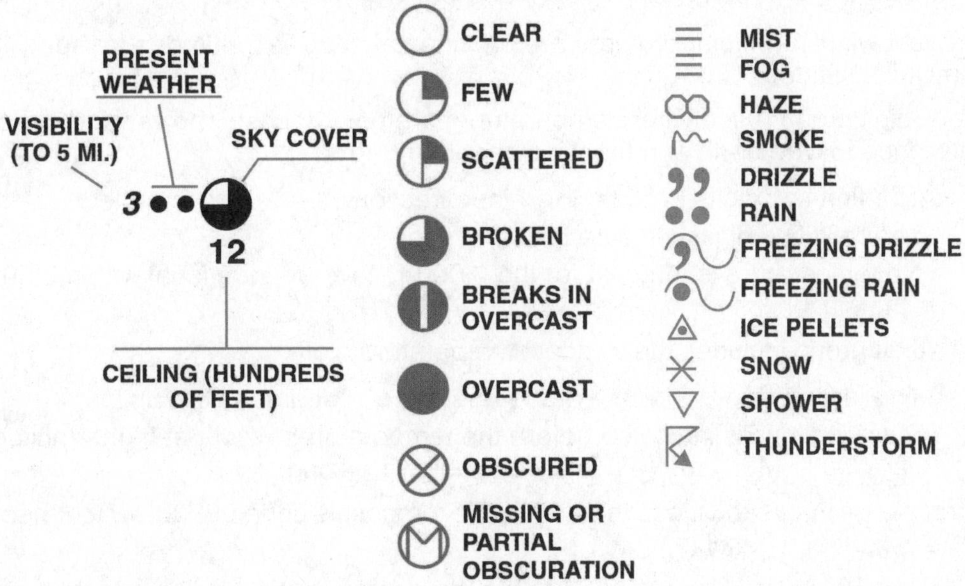

4. The weather depiction chart quickly shows pilots where weather conditions reported are above or below VFR minimums.
5. The weather depiction chart displays recent positions of frontal systems and indicates the type of front by symbols.

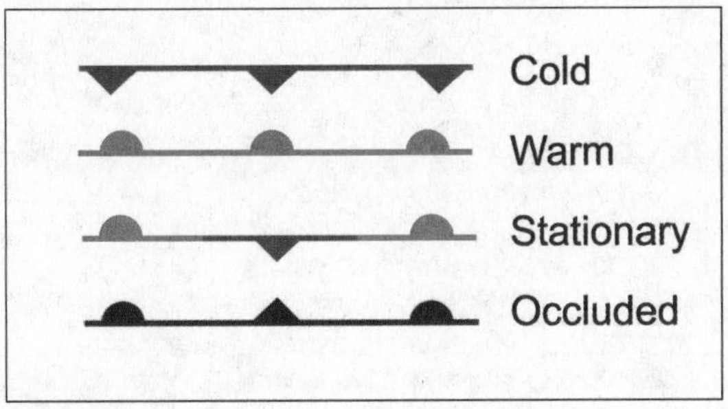

8.7 RADAR WEATHER REPORTS

1. Radar weather reports are textual reports of weather radar observations.
   a. They include the type, intensity, location, and cell movement of precipitation.
2. It is important to remember that the intensity trend (increasing or weakening) is no longer coded on the radar weather report (SD/ROB).

8.8 IN-FLIGHT WEATHER

1. Flight Service Stations (FSSs) provide weather advisories on 122.2 MHz.
   a. Generally, service is available from 6 a.m. to 10 p.m. local time.
   b. FSS provides information regarding actual weather and thunderstorm activity along a proposed route.
2. It is designed to be a continual exchange of information on winds, turbulence, visibility, icing, etc., between pilots and weather briefers.

8.9 WIND AND TEMPERATURE ALOFT FORECASTS (FB)

1. Forecast winds and temperatures are provided at specified altitudes for specific locations in the United States.
2. A four-digit group (used when temperatures are not forecast) shows wind direction with reference to **true** north and the wind speed in **knots**.
   a. The first two digits indicate the wind direction after a zero is added.
   b. The next two digits indicate the wind speed.
   c. No temperature is forecast for the 3,000-ft. level or for a level within 2,500 ft. AGL of the station.
3. A six-digit group includes the forecast temperature aloft.
   a. The last two digits indicate the temperature in degrees Celsius.
   b. Plus or minus is indicated before the temperature, except at higher altitudes (above 24,000 ft. MSL) where it is always below freezing.
4. When the wind speed is less than 5 kt., the forecast is coded 9900, which means that the wind is light and variable.
5. When the wind speed is over 100 kt., the forecaster adds 50 to the direction and subtracts 100 from the speed. To decode, you must reverse the process. For example, 730649 = 230° (73–50) at 106 kt. (100 + 06) and –49° (above 24,000 ft.).
6. An example forecast is provided in Figure 17 below.

FB WBC 151745
DATA BASED ON 151200Z
VALID 1600Z FOR USE 1800-0300Z. TEMPS NEG ABV 24000

FT	3000	6000	9000	12000	18000	24000	30000	34000	39000
ALS			2420	2635-08	2535-18	2444-30	245945	246755	246862
AMA		2714	2725+00	2625-04	2531-15	2542-27	265842	256352	256762
DEN			2321-04	2532-08	2434-19	2441-31	235347	236056	236262
HLC		1707-01	2113-03	2219-07	2330-17	2435-30	244145	244854	245561
MKC	0507	2006+03	2215-01	2322-06	2338-17	2348-29	236143	237252	238160
STL	2113	2325+07	2332+02	2339-04	2356-16	2373-27	239440	730649	731960

Figure 17. – Winds and Temperatures Aloft Forecast.

8.10 SIGNIFICANT WEATHER PROGNOSTIC CHARTS

1. Significant Weather Prognostic Charts contain four charts (panels).
   a. The two upper panels forecast significant weather from the surface up to 24,000 ft.: one for 12 hr. and the other for 24 hr. from the time of issuance.
   b. The two lower panels forecast surface conditions: one for 12 hr. and the other for 24 hr. from the time of issuance.

2. The top panels show
   a. Ceilings less than 1,000 ft. and/or visibility less than 3 SM (IFR) by a solid line around the area
   b. Ceilings 1,000 to 3,000 ft. and/or visibility 3 to 5 SM (MVFR) by a scalloped line around the area
   c. Moderate or greater turbulence by a broken line around the area
      1) A peaked hat  indicates moderate turbulence.
      2) Altitudes are indicated on the chart; e.g., 180 means from surface to 18,000 feet.
   d. Freezing levels, given by a dashed line corresponding to the height of the freezing level
3. The bottom panels show the location of
   a. Highs, lows, fronts
   b. Other areas of significant weather
      1) Unshaded outlined areas indicate precipitation covering half or less of the area.
      2) Shaded outlined areas indicate precipitation covering more than half of the area.
      3) Precipitation type and intensity is reported with standard symbols. Examples include
         a)  thunderstorms embedded in a larger area of continuous moderate rain
         b)  thunderstorms embedded in a larger area of intermittent moderate rain
         c)  continuous light to moderate snow
         d)  intermittent light to moderate snow
      4) Precipitation symbols may be connected to an area of precipitation by an arrow if there is not sufficient room to place them in that area.
4. These charts are used to determine areas to avoid (freezing levels and turbulence).

8.11 AIRMETs AND SIGMETs

1. SIGMETs and AIRMETs are issued to notify pilots en route of the possibility of encountering hazardous flying conditions.
2. SIGMET advisories include weather phenomena that are potentially hazardous to all aircraft.
   a. Convective SIGMETs include
      1) Tornadoes
      2) Lines of thunderstorms
      3) Embedded thunderstorms
      4) Thunderstorm areas greater than or equal to thunderstorm intensity level 4 with an area coverage of 40% or more
      5) Hail greater than or equal to 3/4 in. diameter
   b. SIGMETs include
      1) Severe or extreme turbulence or clear air turbulence (CAT) not associated with thunderstorms
      2) Severe icing not associated with thunderstorms
      3) Duststorms, sandstorms, or volcanic ash lowering visibility to less than 3 SM
      4) Volcanic eruption

3. AIRMETs apply to light (e.g., small single-engine) aircraft to notify of
   a. Moderate icing
   b. Moderate turbulence
   c. Visibility less than 3 SM or ceilings less than 1,000 ft.
   d. Sustained winds of 30 kt. or more at the surface
   e. Extensive mountain obscurement

QUESTIONS AND ANSWER EXPLANATIONS: All of the private pilot knowledge test questions chosen by the FAA for release as well as additional questions selected by Gleim relating to the material in the previous outlines are reproduced on the following pages. These questions have been organized into the same subunits as the outlines. To the immediate right of each question are the correct answer and answer explanation. You should cover these answers and answer explanations while responding to the questions. Refer to the general discussion in the Introduction on how to take the FAA knowledge test.

Remember that the questions from the FAA knowledge test bank have been reordered by topic and organized into a meaningful sequence. Also, the first line of the answer explanation gives the citation of the authoritative source for the answer.

QUESTIONS

8.1 Weather Briefings

1. To get a complete weather briefing for the planned flight, the pilot should request

A. a general briefing.

B. an abbreviated briefing.

C. a standard briefing.

Answer (C) is correct. *(AWS Sect 1)*

DISCUSSION: To get a complete briefing before a planned flight, the pilot should request a standard briefing. This will include all pertinent information needed for a safe flight.

Answer (A) is incorrect. A general briefing is not standard terminology for any type of weather briefing. Answer (B) is incorrect. An abbreviated briefing is provided as a supplement to mass disseminated data or a previous briefing. It can also be used to obtain specific information.

2. Which type weather briefing should a pilot request, when departing within the hour, if no preliminary weather information has been received?

A. Outlook briefing.

B. Abbreviated briefing.

C. Standard briefing.

Answer (C) is correct. *(AWS Sect 1)*

DISCUSSION: A pilot should request a standard briefing anytime (s)he is planning a flight and has not received a previous briefing or has not received preliminary information through mass dissemination media (e.g., PATWAS, etc.).

Answer (A) is incorrect. Outlook briefings are for flights 6 hr. or more in the future. Answer (B) is incorrect. Abbreviated briefings are to update previous briefings, supplement other data, or answer a specific inquiry.

3. Which type of weather briefing should a pilot request to supplement mass disseminated data?

A. An outlook briefing.

B. A supplemental briefing.

C. An abbreviated briefing.

Answer (C) is correct. *(AWS Sect 1)*

DISCUSSION: An abbreviated briefing will be provided when the user requests information to supplement mass disseminated data, to update a previous briefing, or to obtain specific information.

Answer (A) is incorrect. An outlook briefing should be requested if the proposed departure time is 6 hr. or more in the future. Answer (B) is incorrect. A supplemental briefing is not a standard type of briefing.

4. A weather briefing that is provided when the information requested is 6 or more hours in advance of the proposed departure time is

A. an outlook briefing.

B. a forecast briefing.

C. a prognostic briefing.

Answer (A) is correct. *(AWS Sect 1)*

DISCUSSION: An outlook briefing is given when the briefing is 6 or more hours before the proposed departure time.

Answer (B) is incorrect. A forecast briefing is not a type of weather briefing. Answer (C) is incorrect. A prognostic briefing is not a type of weather briefing.

5. What should pilots state initially when telephoning a weather briefing facility for preflight weather information?

A. Tell the number of occupants on board.

B. State their total flight time.

C. Identify themselves as pilots.

Answer (C) is correct. *(AWS Sect 1)*

DISCUSSION: When telephoning for a weather briefing, you should identify yourself as a pilot so the person can give you an aviation-oriented briefing. Many nonpilots call weather briefing facilities to get the weather for other activities.

Answer (A) is incorrect. The number of occupants on board is information needed for a flight plan, not for a weather briefing. Answer (B) is incorrect. Total flight time is a question asked by insurance companies, not information needed for a weather briefing.

6. What should pilots state initially when telephoning a weather briefing facility for preflight weather information?

A. The intended route of flight radio frequencies.

B. The intended route of flight and destination.

C. The address of the pilot in command.

Answer (B) is correct. *(AWS Sect 1)*

DISCUSSION: By telling the briefer your intended route and destination, the briefer will be able to provide you a more relevant briefing.

Answer (A) is incorrect. The radio frequencies to be used are the pilot's preflight responsibility, not the weather briefer's. Answer (C) is incorrect. The address of the pilot in command is information needed for a flight plan, not for a weather briefing.

7. When telephoning a weather briefing facility for preflight weather information, pilots should state

A. the aircraft identification or the pilot's name.

B. true airspeed.

C. fuel on board.

Answer (A) is correct. *(AWS Sect 1)*

DISCUSSION: When requesting a briefing, you should provide the briefer with the following information: VFR or IFR, aircraft identification or the pilot's name, aircraft type, departure point, route of flight, destination, altitude, estimated time of departure, and time en route or estimated time of arrival.

Answer (B) is incorrect. True airspeed is information provided on a flight plan. Answer (C) is incorrect. Fuel on board is information provided on a flight plan.

8. When speaking to a flight service weather briefer, you should state

A. the pilot in command's full name and address.

B. a summary of your qualifications.

C. whether the flight is VFR or IFR.

Answer (C) is correct. *(AWS Sect 1)*

DISCUSSION: When speaking to an AFSS weather briefer, you should identify yourself as a pilot and state the route, destination, type of airplane, and whether you intend to fly VFR or IFR to permit the weather briefer to give you the most complete briefing.

Answer (A) is incorrect. The full name and address of the pilot in command is information provided on a flight plan. Answer (B) is incorrect. You should state that you are a pilot, not that you possess a current pilot certificate, or a summary of your qualifications.

9. To update a previous weather briefing, a pilot should request

A. an abbreviated briefing.

B. a standard briefing.

C. an outlook briefing.

Answer (A) is correct. *(AWS Sect 1)*

DISCUSSION: An abbreviated briefing will be provided when the user requests information (1) to supplement mass disseminated data, (2) to update a previous briefing, or (3) to be limited to specific information.

Answer (B) is incorrect. A standard briefing is a complete preflight briefing to include all (not update) information pertinent to a safe flight. Answer (C) is incorrect. An outlook briefing is for a flight at least 6 hr. in the future.

10. When requesting weather information for the following morning, a pilot should request

A. an outlook briefing.

B. a standard briefing.

C. an abbreviated briefing.

Answer (A) is correct. *(AWS Sect 1)*

DISCUSSION: An outlook briefing should be requested when the briefing is 6 or more hours in advance of the proposed departure.

Answer (B) is incorrect. A standard briefing should be requested if the proposed departure time is less than 6 hr. in the future and if you have not received a previous briefing or have received information through mass dissemination media. Answer (C) is incorrect. An abbreviated briefing is provided as a supplement to mass disseminated data, to update a previous briefing, or to obtain specific information.

11. You plan to phone a weather briefing facility for preflight weather information. You should

A. provide the number of occupants on board.

B. identify yourself as a pilot.

C. begin with your route of flight.

Answer (B) is correct. *(AWS Sect 1)*

DISCUSSION: When calling for a weather briefing, you should identify yourself as a pilot so the person can give you an aviation-oriented briefing. Nonpilots may call weather briefing facilities to get the weather for other activities. It is best to tell them what kind of pilot you are, e.g., student pilot, private pilot, instrument pilot.

Answer (A) is incorrect. You will not include the number of occupants on board the aircraft until you are at the end of the flight plan filing process. Answer (C) is incorrect. The briefer needs to know other information before the route of your flight, such as what kind of pilot you are, departure time, etc. Moreover, the briefer may want to know your aircraft tail number and type to include the equipment suffix before wanting your route of flight.

8.2 Aviation Routine Weather Report (METAR)

12. For aviation purposes, ceiling is defined as the height above the Earth's surface of the

A. lowest reported obscuration and the highest layer of clouds reported as overcast.

B. lowest broken or overcast layer or vertical visibility into an obscuration.

C. lowest layer of clouds reported as scattered, broken, or thin.

Answer (B) is correct. *(AWS Sect 3)*

DISCUSSION: A ceiling layer is not designated in the METAR code. For aviation purposes, the ceiling is the lowest broken or overcast layer, or vertical visibility into an obscuration.

Answer (A) is incorrect. A ceiling is the lowest, not highest, broken or overcast layer, or the vertical visibility into an obscuration, not the lowest obscuration. Answer (C) is incorrect. A ceiling is the lowest broken or overcast, not scattered, layer. Also, there is no provision for reporting thin layers in the METAR code.

13. (Refer to Figure 12 on page 263.) What are the current conditions depicted for Chicago Midway Airport (KMDW)?

A. Sky 700 feet overcast, visibility 1-1/2 SM, rain.

B. Sky 7000 feet overcast, visibility 1-1/2 SM, heavy rain.

C. Sky 700 feet overcast, visibility 11, occasionally 2 SM, with rain.

Answer (A) is correct. *(AWS Sect 3)*

DISCUSSION: At KMDW a special METAR (SPECI) taken at 1856Z reported wind 320° at 5 kt., visibility 1 1/2 SM in moderate rain, overcast clouds at 700 ft., temperature 17°C, dew point 16°C, altimeter 29.80 in. Hg, remarks follow, rain began at 35 min. past the hour.

Answer (B) is incorrect. The intensity of the rain is moderate, not heavy. Heavy rain would be coded +RA. Answer (C) is incorrect. Visibility is 1 1/2 SM, not 11 SM with an occasional 2 statute miles.

14. (Refer to Figure 12 on page 263.) Which of the reporting stations have VFR weather?

A. All.

B. KINK, KBOI, and KJFK.

C. KINK, KBOI, and KLAX.

Answer (C) is correct. *(AWS Sect 3)*

DISCUSSION: KINK is reporting visibility of 15 SM and sky clear (15SM SKC); KBOI is reporting visibility of 30 SM and a scattered cloud layer base at 15,000 ft. (30SM SCT150); and KLAX is reporting visibility of 6SM in mist (foggy conditions > 5/8 SM visibility) with a scattered cloud layer at 700 ft. and another one at 25,000 ft. (6SM BR SCT007 SCT250). All of these conditions are above VFR weather minimums of 1,000-ft. ceiling and/or 3-SM visibility.

Answer (A) is incorrect. KMDW is reporting a visibility of 1 1/2 SM in rain and a ceiling of 700 ft. overcast (1 1/2SM RA OVC007), and KJFK is reporting a visibility of 1/2SM in fog and a ceiling of 500 ft. overcast (1/2SM FG OVC005). Both of these are below VFR weather minimums of 1,000-ft. ceiling and/or 3-SM visibility. Answer (B) is incorrect. KJFK is reporting a visibility of 1/2 SM in fog and a ceiling of 500 ft. overcast (1/2SM FG OVC005), which is below the VFR weather minimums of 1,000-ft. ceiling and/or 3-SM visibility.

METAR KINK 121845Z 11012G18KT 15SM SKC 25/17 A3000
METAR KBOI 121854Z 13004KT 30SM SCT150 17/6 A3015
METAR KLAX 121852Z 25004KT 6SM BR SCT007 SCT250 16/15 A2991
SPECI KMDW 121856Z 32005KT 1 1/2SM RA OVC007 17/16 A2980 RMK RAB35
SPECI KJFK 121853Z 18004KT 1/2SM FG R04/2200 OVC005 20/18 A3006

Figure 12. – Aviation Routine Weather Reports (METAR).

15. (Refer to Figure 12 above.) The wind direction and velocity at KJFK is from

A. 180° true at 4 knots.

B. 180° magnetic at 4 knots.

C. 040° true at 18 knots.

Answer (A) is correct. *(AWS Sect 3)*

DISCUSSION: The wind group at KJFK is coded as 18004KT. The first three digits are the direction the wind is blowing from referenced to true north. The next two digits are the speed in knots. Thus, the wind direction and speed at KJFK are 180° true at 4 knots.

Answer (B) is incorrect. Wind direction is referenced to true, not magnetic, north. Answer (C) is incorrect. The wind direction is 180° true, not 040° true, at 4 knots, not 18 knots.

16. (Refer to Figure 12 above.) What are the wind conditions at Wink, Texas (KINK)?

A. Calm.

B. 110° at 12 knots, gusts 18 knots.

C. 111° at 2 knots, gusts 18 knots.

Answer (B) is correct. *(AWS Sect 3)*

DISCUSSION: The wind group at KINK is coded as 11012G18KT. The first three digits are the direction the wind is blowing from referenced to true north. The next two digits are the wind speed in knots. If the wind is gusty, it is reported as a "G" after the speed followed by the highest (or peak) gust reported. Thus, the wind conditions at KINK are 110° true at 12 knots, peak gust at 18 knots.

Answer (A) is incorrect. A calm wind would be reported as 00000KT, not 11012G18KT. Answer (C) is incorrect. The wind conditions at KINK are 110°, not 111°, at 12 knots, not 2 knots.

17. (Refer to Figure 12 above.) The remarks section for KMDW has RAB35 listed. This entry means

A. blowing mist has reduced the visibility to 1-1/2 SM.

B. rain began at 1835Z.

C. the barometer has risen .35" Hg.

Answer (B) is correct. *(AWS Sect 3)*

DISCUSSION: In the remarks (RMK) section for KMDW, RAB35 means that rain began at 35 min. past the hour. Since the report was taken at 1856Z, rain began at 35 min. past the hour, or 1835Z.

Answer (A) is incorrect. RAB35 means that rain began at 35 min. past the hour, not that blowing mist has reduced the visibility to 1 1/2 statute miles. Answer (C) is incorrect. RAB35 means that rain began at 35 min. past the hour, not that the barometer has risen .35 in. Hg.

8.3 Pilot Weather Report (PIREP)

18. (Refer to Figure 14 below.) If the terrain elevation is 1,295 feet MSL, what is the height above ground level of the base of the ceiling?

A. 505 feet AGL.

B. 1,295 feet AGL.

C. 6,586 feet AGL.

Answer (A) is correct. *(AWS Sect 3)*

DISCUSSION: Refer to the PIREP (identified by the letters UA) in Fig. 14. The base of the ceiling is reported in the sky cover (SK) section. The first layer is considered a ceiling (i.e., broken), and the base is 1,800 ft. MSL. The height above ground of the broken base is 505 ft. AGL (1,800 ft. – 1,295 ft.).

Answer (B) is incorrect. The figure of 1,295 ft. MSL (not AGL) is the terrain elevation. Answer (C) is incorrect. The ceiling base is 505 ft. (not 6,586 ft.) AGL.

19. (Refer to Figure 14 below.) The base and tops of the overcast layer reported by a pilot are

A. 1,800 feet MSL and 5,500 feet MSL.

B. 5,500 feet AGL and 7,200 feet MSL.

C. 7,200 feet MSL and 8,900 feet MSL.

Answer (C) is correct. *(AWS Sect 3)*

DISCUSSION: Refer to the PIREP (identified by the letters UA) in Fig. 14. The base and tops of the overcast layer are reported in the sky conditions (identified by the letters SK). This pilot has reported the base of the overcast layer at 7,200 ft. and the top of the overcast layer at 8,900 ft. (072 OVC 089). All altitudes are stated in MSL unless otherwise noted. Thus, the base and top of the overcast layer are reported as 7,200 ft. MSL and 8,900 ft. MSL, respectively.

Answer (A) is incorrect. The figures of 1,800 ft. MSL and 5,500 ft. MSL are the base and top of the broken (BKN), not overcast (OVC), layer. Answer (B) is incorrect. The figure of 5,500 ft. MSL (not AGL) is the top of the broken (BKN) layer, not the base of the overcast (OVC) layer.

20. (Refer to Figure 14 below.) The wind and temperature at 12,000 feet MSL as reported by a pilot are

A. 080° at 21 knots and –7°C.

B. 090° at 21 MPH and –9°F.

C. 090° at 21 knots and –9°C.

Answer (A) is correct. *(AWS Sect 3)*

DISCUSSION: Refer to the PIREP (identified by the letters UA) in Fig. 14. The wind is reported in the section identified by the letters WV and is presented in five or six digits. The temperature is reported in the section identified by the letters TA in degrees Celsius, and if below 0°C, prefixed with an "M." The wind is reported as 080° at 21 kt. with a temperature of –7°C.

Answer (B) is incorrect. Speed is given in kt., not MPH. Temperature is given in degrees Celsius (not Fahrenheit) and is reported as –7, not –9. Answer (C) is incorrect. The wind is reported as being from 080°, not 090°, and the temperature is reported as –7°C, not –9°C.

21. (Refer to Figure 14 below.) The intensity of the turbulence reported at a specific altitude is

A. moderate at 5,500 feet and at 7,200 feet.

B. moderate from 5,500 feet to 7,200 feet.

C. light from 5,500 feet to 7,200 feet.

Answer (C) is correct. *(AWS Sect 3)*

DISCUSSION: Refer to the PIREP (identified by the letters UA) in Fig. 14. The turbulence is reported in the section identified by the letters TB. In the PIREP the turbulence is reported as light from 5,500 ft. to 7,200 ft. (TB LGT 055-072).

Answer (A) is incorrect. Turbulence is reported from 5,500 to 7,200 ft. MSL, not only at 5,500 ft. and 7,200 feet. Answer (B) is incorrect. Rime ice (not turbulence) is reported as light to moderate from 7,200 to 8,900 ft. MSL (not 5,500 to 7,200 ft. MSL).

22. (Refer to Figure 14 below.) The intensity and type of icing reported by a pilot is

A. light to moderate.

B. light to moderate clear.

C. light to moderate rime.

Answer (C) is correct. *(AWS Sect 3)*

DISCUSSION: Refer to the PIREP (identified by the letters UA) in Fig. 14. The icing conditions are reported following the letters IC. In this report, icing is reported as light to moderate rime (LGT-MDT RIME) from 7,200 to 8,900 ft. MSL (072-089).

Answer (A) is incorrect. The question asks not only for the intensity of the icing (light to moderate) but also the type, which is rime (RIME) ice. Answer (B) is incorrect. The type is rime (not clear) ice.

UA/OV KOKC-KTUL/TM 1800/FL 120/TP BE90//SK BKN018-TOP055/OVC072-TOP089/CLR ABV/TA M7/WV 08021/TB LGT 055-072/IC LGT-MOD RIME 072-089

Figure 14. – Pilot Weather Report.

8.4 Aviation Area Forecast

23. To best determine general forecast weather conditions covering a flight information region, the pilot should refer to

A. aviation area forecasts.

B. weather depiction charts.

C. satellite maps.

Answer (A) is correct. *(AWS Sect 7)*

DISCUSSION: An aviation area forecast is a prediction of general weather conditions covering a flight information region. It is used to obtain expected en route weather conditions and also to provide an insight to weather conditions that might be expected at airports where weather reports or forecasts are not issued.

Answer (B) is incorrect. Weather depiction charts are compiled from METAR reports of observed, not forecast, areas. Answer (C) is incorrect. Satellite pictures (maps) are observed pictures used to determine the presence and types of clouds, not forecast conditions.

24. To determine the freezing level and areas of probable icing aloft, the pilot should refer to the

A. inflight aviation weather advisories.

B. weather depiction chart.

C. area forecast.

Answer (A) is correct. *(AWS Sect 7)*

DISCUSSION: To determine the freezing level and areas of probable icing aloft, you should refer to the inflight aviation weather advisories (AIRMET Zulu for icing and freezing level; AIRMET Tango for turbulence, strong winds/low-level wind shear; and AIRMET Sierra for IFR conditions and mountain obscuration.) Inflight aviation weather advisories supplement the area forecast.

Answer (B) is incorrect. The weather depiction chart does not include any icing information. Answer (C) is incorrect. The area forecast alone contains no icing information; it must be supplemented by inflight aviation weather advisories.

25. The section of the Area Forecast entitled "VFR CLDS/WX" contains a general description of

A. cloudiness and weather significant to flight operations broken down by states or other geographical areas.

B. area and route briefings, as well as airspace procedures and special announcements.

C. clouds and weather which cover an area greater than 3,000 square miles and is significant to VFR flight operations.

Answer (C) is the best answer. *(AWS Sect 7)*

DISCUSSION: The VFR CLDS/WX section contains a 12-hr. specific forecast plus a 6-hour categorical outlook section. The specific forecast section gives a general description of clouds and weather that covers an area greater than 3,000 square miles and is significant to VFR flight operations.

Answer (A) is incorrect. While the VFR CLDS/WX section may be broken down by states or well-known geographical areas, the area of coverage will always be greater than 3,000 square miles. Answer (B) is incorrect. TIBS (Telephone Information Briefing Service) is a continuous telephone recording of area and route briefings, as well as airspace procedures and special announcements. It is designed to be a preliminary briefing tool and is available 24 hours a day.

26. From which primary source should information be obtained regarding expected weather at the estimated time of arrival if your destination has no Terminal Forecast?

A. Low-Level Prognostic Chart.

B. Weather Depiction Chart.

C. Area Forecast.

Answer (C) is correct. *(AWS Sect 7)*

DISCUSSION: An area forecast (FA) is a forecast of general weather conditions over an area the size of several states. It is used to determine forecast en route weather and to interpolate conditions at airports that do not have a TAF issued.

Answer (A) is incorrect. A Low-Level Prognostic Chart forecasts weather conditions expected to exist 12 hr. and 24 hr. in the future for the entire U.S. Answer (B) is incorrect. A Weather Depiction Chart is a national map prepared from METAR reports that give a broad overview of observed weather conditions as of the time on the chart. It is not a forecast.

```
BOSC FA 241845
SYNOPSIS AND VFR CLDS/WX
SYNOPSIS VALID UNTIL 251300
CLDS/WX VALID UNTIL 250700...OTLK VALID 250700-251300
ME NH VT MA RI CT NY LO NJ PA OH LE WV MD DC DE VA AND CSTL WTRS
.
SEE AIRMET SIERRA FOR IFR CONDS AND MTN OBSCN.
TS IMPLY SEV OR GTR TURB SEV ICE LLWS AND IFR CONDS.
NON MSL HGTS DENOTED BY AGL OR CIG.
.
SYNOPSIS...19Z CDFNT ALG A 16NE ACK-ENE LN...CONTG AS A QSTNRY
FNT ALG AN END-50SW MSS LN. BY 13Z...CDFNT ALG A 140ESE ACK-HTO
LN...CONTG AS A QSTNRY FNT ALG A HTO-SYR-YYZ LN. TROF ACRS CNTRL
PA INTO NRN VA. ...REYNOLDS...
.
OH LE
NRN HLF OH LE...SCT-BKN025 OVC045. CLDS LYRD 150. SCT SHRA. WDLY
     SCT TSRA. CB TOPS FL350. 23-01Z OVC020-030. VIS 3SM BR. OCNL-
     RA. OTLK...IFR CIG BR FG.
SWRN QTR OH...BKN050-060 TOPS 100. OTLK...MVFR BR.
SERN QTR OH...SCT-BKN040 BKN070 TOPS 120. WDLY SCT-TSRA. 00Z
     SCT-BKN030 OVC050. WDLY SCT-TSRA. CB TOPS FL350. OTLK...VFR
     SHRA.
.
CHIC FA 241945
SYNOPSIS AND VFR CLDS/WX
SYNOPSIS VALID UNTIL 251400
CLDS/WX VALID UNTIL 250800...OTLK VALID 250800-251400
ND SD NE KS MN IA MO WI LM LS MI LH IL IN KY
.
SEE AIRMET SIERRA FOR IFR CONDS AND MTN OBSCN.
TS IMPLY SEV OR GTR TURB SEV ICE LLWS AND IFR CONDS.
NON MSL HGTS DENOTED BY AGL OR CIG.
.
SYNOPSIS...LOW PRES AREA 20Z CNTRD OVR SERN WI FCST MOV NEWD INTO
LH BY 12Z AND WKN. LOW PRES FCST DEEPEN OVR ERN CO DURG PD AND
MOV NR WRN KS BORDER BY 14Z. DVLPG CDFNT WL MOV EWD INTO S CNTRL
NE-CNTRL KS BY 14Z. ...SMITH..
.
UPR MI LS
WRN PTNS...AGL SCT030 SCT 030 SCT-BKN050. TOPS 080. 02-05Z BECMG CIG
     OVC010 VIS 3-5SM BR. OTLK...IFR CIG BR.
ERN PTNS...CIG BKN020 OVC040. OCNL VIS 3-5SM -RA BR. TOPS FL200.
     23Z CIG OVC010 VIS 3-5SM -RA BR. OTLK...IFR CIG BR.
.
LWR MI LM LH
CNTRL/NRN PTNS...CIG OVC010 VIS 3-5SM -RA BR. TOPS FL200
     OTLK...IFR CIG BR.
.
SRN THIRD...CIG OVC015-025. SCT -SHRA. TOPS 150. 00-02Z BECMG CIG
     OVC010 VIS 3-5SM BR. TOPS 060. OTLK...IFR CIG BR.
.
IN
NRN HALF...CIG BKN035 BKN080. TOPS FL200. SCT -SHRA. 00Z CIG
     BKN-SCT040 BKN-SCT080. TOPS 120. 06Z AGL SCT-BKN030. TOPS 080.
     OCNL VIS 3-5SM BR. OTLK...MVFR CIG BR.
SRN HALF...AGL SCT050 SCT-BKN100. TOPS 120. 07Z AGL SCT 030
     SCT100. OTLK...VFR.
```

Figure 16. – Area Forecast.

27. (Refer to Figure 16 on page 266.) The Chicago FA forecast section is valid until the twenty-fifth at

A. 1945Z.

B. 0800Z.

C. 1400Z.

Answer (B) is correct. *(AWS Sect 7)*

DISCUSSION: The Chicago area forecast (FA) is the second of two FAs depicted in Fig. 16. There is a note in the communication and product header section that says "CLDS/WX VALID UNTIL 250800," which means that the VFR clouds and weather section of the FA (the forecast section) is valid until 0800Z on the 25th.

Answer (A) is incorrect. The note "CHIC FA 241945" in the communication and product header section means that the FA was issued at 1945Z on the 24th, not that it is valid until 1945Z on the 25th. Answer (C) is incorrect. The synopsis and categorical outlook (which are not considered to be forecasts), not the forecast section, are valid until 1400Z on the 25th, as indicated by the notes "SYNOPSIS VALID UNTIL 251400" and "OTLK VALID 250800-251400."

28. (Refer to Figure 16 on page 266.) What sky condition and visibility are forecast for upper Michigan in the eastern portions after 2300Z?

A. Ceiling 100 feet overcast and 3 to 5 statute miles visibility.

B. Ceiling 1,000 feet overcast and 3 to 5 nautical miles visibility.

C. Ceiling 1,000 feet overcast and 3 to 5 statute miles visibility.

Answer (C) is correct. *(AWS Sect 7)*

DISCUSSION: The Chicago area forecast (FA) is the second of two FAs depicted in Fig. 16. It contains an entry labeled "UPR MI LS," meaning "upper Michigan and Lake Superior." Under this heading is a section labeled "ERN PTNS," meaning "eastern portions." The entry "23Z CIG OVC010 VIS 3-5SM -RA BR" means that from 2300Z, the forecast weather is an overcast ceiling at 1,000 ft. AGL, with 3 to 5 statute miles visibility in light rain and mist.

Answer (A) is incorrect. The ceiling is forecast to be overcast at 1,000 ft., not 100 ft., which would be coded as "OVC001." Answer (B) is incorrect. Visibilities are always given in statute, not nautical, miles.

29. (Refer to Figure 16 on page 266.) What is the outlook for the southern half of Indiana after 0700Z?

A. VFR.

B. IFR.

C. Marginal VFR.

Answer (A) is correct. *(AWS Sect 7)*

DISCUSSION: The question asks for the outlook for the southern half of Indiana after 0700Z. Indiana (IN) is covered by the Chicago area forecast (FA), which is the second of two FAs depicted in Fig. 16. There is a heading under "IN" labeled "SRN HALF," meaning "southern half." Under this heading is an entry, "OTLK...VFR," meaning that the categorical outlook is for VFR conditions. Note in the communication and product header section that there is a note, "OTLK VALID 250800-251400," meaning that the categorical outlook is valid from 0800Z to 1400Z on the 25th. Therefore, the outlook does not become valid until 1 hour after 0700Z. You should still select "VFR" as the answer for this question because it specifically asks for the outlook after 0700Z, not at 0700Z; 0800Z is after 0700Z.

Answer (B) is incorrect. IFR would be indicated under the heading as "OTLK...IFR." Answer (C) is incorrect. Marginal VFR would be indicated under the heading as "OTLK...MVFR."

30. (Refer to Figure 16 on page 266.) What sky conditions and obstructions to visibility are forecast for upper Michigan in the western portions from 0200Z until 0500Z?

A. Ceiling becoming 1,000 feet overcast with visibility 3 to 5 statute miles in mist.

B. Ceiling becoming 100 feet overcast with visibility 3 to 5 statute miles in mist.

C. Ceiling becoming 1,000 feet overcast with visibility 3 to 5 nautical miles in mist.

Answer (A) is correct. *(AWS Sect 7)*

DISCUSSION: The Chicago area forecast (FA) is the second of two FAs depicted in Fig. 16. It contains an entry labeled "UPR MI LS," meaning "upper Michigan and Lake Superior." Under this heading is a section labeled "WRN PTNS," meaning "western portions." The entry "02-05Z BECMG CIG OVC 010 VIS 3-5SM BR" means that between 0200Z and 0500Z, the weather conditions are forecast to become an overcast ceiling at 1,000 ft., with 3-5 statute miles visibility in mist.

Answer (B) is incorrect. The ceiling is forecast to become overcast at 1,000 ft., not 100 ft., which would be coded as "OVC001." Answer (C) is incorrect. Visibilities are always given in statute, not nautical, miles.

8.5 Terminal Aerodrome Forecast (TAF)

31. (Refer to Figure 15 on page 269.) In the TAF for KMEM, what does "SHRA" stand for?

A. Rain showers.

B. A shift in wind direction is expected.

C. A significant change in precipitation is possible.

Answer (A) is correct. *(AWS Sect 7)*

DISCUSSION: SHRA is a coded group of forecast weather. SH is a descriptor that means showers. RA is a type of precipitation that means rain. Thus, SHRA means rain showers.

Answer (B) is incorrect. SHRA means rain showers, not that a shift in wind direction is expected. A change in wind direction would be reflected by a forecast wind. Answer (C) is incorrect. SHRA means rain showers, not that a significant change in precipitation is possible.

32. (Refer to Figure 15 on page 269.) During the time period from 0600Z to 0800Z, what visibility is forecast for KOKC?

A. Greater than 6 statute miles.

B. Possibly 6 statute miles.

C. Not forecasted.

Answer (A) is correct. *(AWS Sect 7)*

DISCUSSION: At KOKC, between 0600Z and 0800Z, conditions are forecast to become wind 210° at 15 kt., visibility greater than 6 SM (P6SM), scattered clouds at 4,000 ft. with conditions continuing until the end of the forecast (1200Z).

Answer (B) is incorrect. Between 0600Z and 0800Z, the visibility is forecast to be greater than, not possibly, 6 statute miles. Answer (C) is incorrect. Between 0600Z and 0800Z, the visibility is forecast to be greater than 6 statute miles (P6SM).

33. (Refer to Figure 15 on page 269.) In the TAF from KOKC, the clear sky becomes

A. overcast at 2,000 feet during the forecast period between 2200Z and 2400Z.

B. overcast at 200 feet with a 40 percent probability of becoming overcast at 600 feet during the forecast period between 2200Z and 2400Z.

C. overcast at 200 feet with the probability of becoming overcast at 400 feet during the forecast period between 2200Z and 2400Z.

Answer (A) is correct. *(AWS Sect 7)*

DISCUSSION: In the TAF for KOKC, from 2200Z to 2400Z, the conditions are forecast to gradually become wind 200° at 13 kt. with gusts to 20 kt., visibility 4 SM in moderate rain showers, overcast clouds at 2,000 feet. Between the hours of 0000Z and 0600Z, a chance (40 percent) exists of visibility 2 SM in thunderstorm with moderate rain, and 800 ft. overcast, cumulus clouds.

Answer (B) is incorrect. Between 2200Z and 2400Z, the coded sky condition of OVC020 means overcast clouds at 2,000 ft., not 200 feet. Answer (C) is incorrect. Between 2200Z and 2400Z, the coded sky condition of OVC020 means overcast clouds at 2,000 ft., not 200 feet.

34. (Refer to Figure 15 on page 269.) What is the valid period for the TAF for KMEM?

A. 1200Z to 1800Z.

B. 1200Z to 2400Z.

C. 1800Z to 2400Z.

Answer (C) is correct. *(AWS Sect 7)*

DISCUSSION: The valid period of a TAF follows the four-letter location identifier and the six-digit issuance date/time. The valid period group is a two-digit date followed by the two-digit beginning hour and the two-digit ending hour. The valid period of the TAF for KMEM is 1218/1324, which means the forecast is valid from the 12th day at 1800Z until the 13th at 2400Z.

Answer (A) is incorrect. The valid period of the TAF for KOKC, not KMEM, is from 1200Z to 1800Z. Answer (B) is incorrect. The valid period of the TAF for KMEM is from the 12th day, not 1200Z, at 1800Z until the 13th at 2400Z.

35. (Refer to Figure 15 on page 269.) Between 1000Z and 1200Z the visibility at KMEM is forecast to be?

A. 1/2 statute mile.

B. 3 statute miles.

C. 6 statute miles.

Answer (B) is correct. *(AWS Sect 7)*

DISCUSSION: Between 1000Z and 1200Z, the conditions at KMEM are forecast to gradually become wind calm, visibility 3 SM in mist, sky clear with temporary (occasional) visibility 1/2 SM in fog between 1200Z and 1400Z. Conditions are expected to continue until 1600Z.

Answer (A) is incorrect. Between the hours of 1200Z and 1400Z, not between 1000Z and 1200Z, the forecast is for temporary (occasional) visibility of 1/2 SM in fog. Answer (C) is incorrect. Between 1000Z and 1200Z, the forecast visibility for KMEM is 3 SM, not 6 SM.

36. (Refer to Figure 15 below.) What is the forecast wind for KMEM from 1600Z until the end of the forecast?

A. No significant wind.

B. Variable in direction at 6 knots.

C. Variable in direction at 4 knots.

Answer (B) is correct. *(AWS Sect 7)*

DISCUSSION: The forecast for KMEM from 1600Z until the end of the forecast (1800Z) is wind direction variable at 6 kt. (VRB06KT), visibility greater than 6 SM, and sky clear.

Answer (A) is incorrect. The wind is forecast to be variable in direction at 6 knots. Answer (C) is incorrect. The wind is forecast to be variable in direction at 6 kt., not 4 knots. KMEM of 020° at 8 kt. is for 0600Z until 0800Z, not from 1600Z until the end of the forecast.

37. (Refer to Figure 15 below.) In the TAF from KOKC, the "FM (FROM) Group" is forecast for the hours from 1600Z to 2200Z with the wind from

A. 160° at 10 knots.

B. 180° at 10 knots.

C. 180° at 10 knots, becoming 200° at 13 knots.

Answer (B) is correct. *(AWS Sect 7)*

DISCUSSION: The FM group states that, from 1600Z until 2200Z (time of next change group), the forecast wind is 180° at 10 knots.

Answer (A) is incorrect. The forecast wind is 180°, not 160°, at 10 knots. Answer (C) is incorrect. The BECMG (becoming) group is a change group and is not part of the FM forecast group. The wind will gradually become 200° at 13 kt. with gusts to 20 kt., between 2200Z and 2400Z.

38. (Refer to Figure 15 below.) The only cloud type forecast in TAF reports is

A. Nimbostratus.

B. Cumulonimbus.

C. Scattered cumulus.

Answer (B) is correct. *(AWS Sect 7)*

DISCUSSION: Cumulonimbus clouds are the only cloud type forecast in TAFs. If cumulonimbus clouds are expected at the airport, the contraction CB is appended to the cloud layer that represents the base of the cumulonimbus cloud(s).

Answer (A) is incorrect. The only cloud type forecast in TAFs is cumulonimbus, not nimbostratus, clouds. Answer (C) is incorrect. The only cloud type forecast in TAFs is cumulonimbus, not scattered cumulus, clouds.

TAF	
KMEM	121720Z 1218/1324 20012KT 5SM HZ BKN030 PROB40 2022 1SM TSRA OVC008CB FM2200 33015G20KT P6SM BKN015 OVC025 PROB40 2202 3SM SHRA FM0200 35012KT OVC008 PROB40 0205 2SM-RASN BECMG 0608 02008KT BKN012 BECMG 1310/1312 00000KT 3SM BR SKC TEMPO 1212/1214 1/2SM FG FM131600 VRB06KT P6SM SKC=
KOKC	051130Z 0512/0618 14008KT 5SM BR BKN030 TEMPO 0513/0516 1 1/2SM BR FM051600 18010KT P6SM SKC BECMG 0522/0524 20013G20KT 4SM SHRA OVC020 PROB40 0600/0606 2SM TSRA OVC008CB BECMG 0606/0608 21015KT P6SM SCT040=

Figure 15. – Terminal Aerodrome Forecasts (TAF).

8.6 Weather Depiction Charts

39. Of what value is the Weather depiction chart to the pilot?

A. For determining general weather conditions on which to base flight planning.

B. For a forecast of cloud coverage, visibilities, and frontal activity.

C. For determining frontal trends and air mass characteristics.

Answer (A) is correct. *(AWS Sect 5)*

DISCUSSION: The Weather depiction chart is prepared from surface aviation weather reports giving a quick picture of weather conditions as of the time stated on the chart. Thus, it presents general weather conditions on which to base flight planning.

Answer (B) is incorrect. A significant weather prognostic chart can provide a forecast of cloud coverage, visibilities, and frontal activity. A weather depiction chart shows actual, not forecast, conditions. Answer (C) is incorrect. A lifted index chart would be used to determine the characteristics of an air mass.

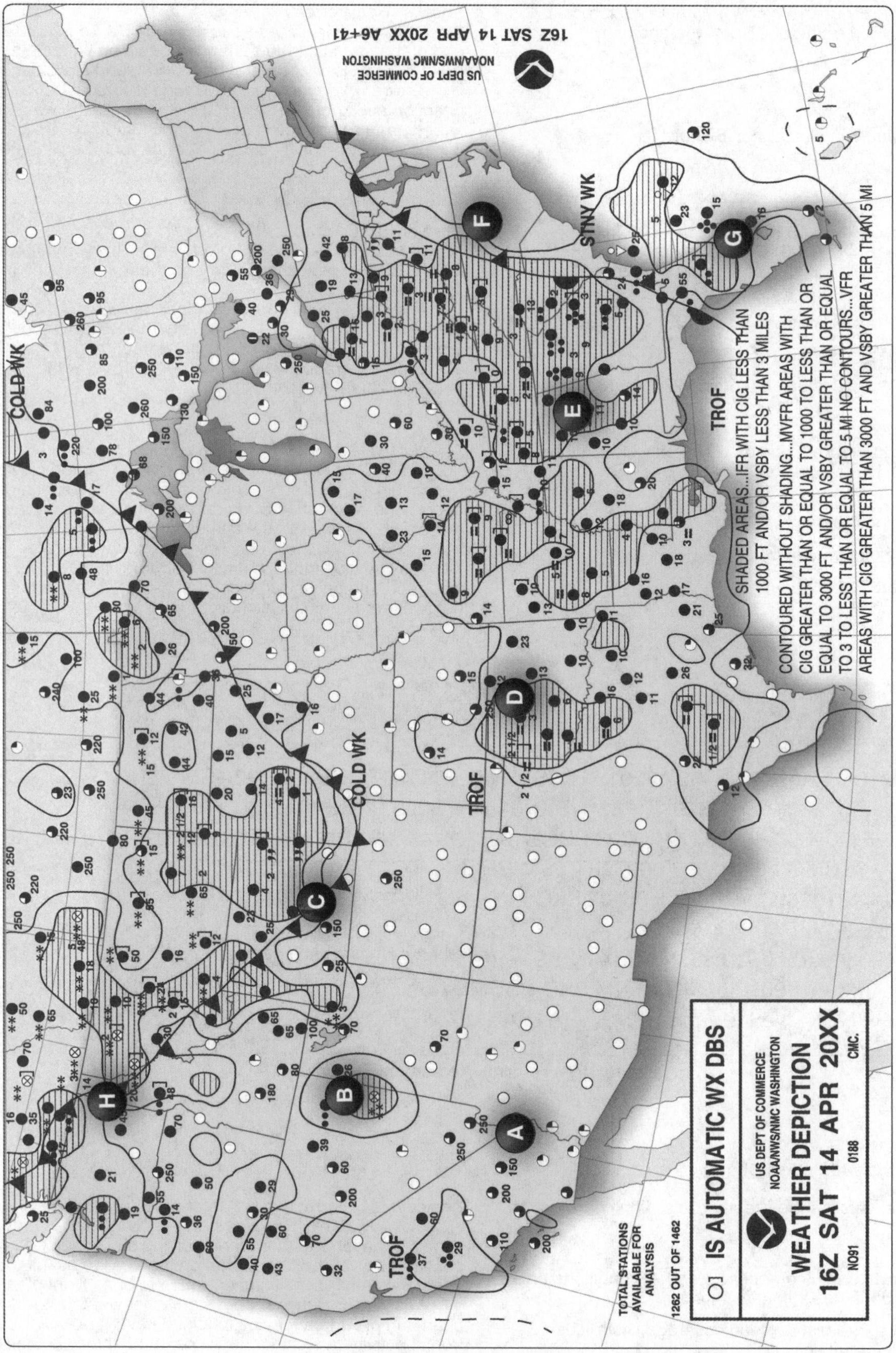

Figure 18. – Weather Depiction Chart.

40. (Refer to Figure 18 on page 270.) The IFR weather in northern Texas is due to

A. intermittent rain.

B. low ceilings.

C. dust devils.

Answer (B) is correct. *(AWS Sect 5)*

DISCUSSION: Refer to the Weather Depiction Chart in Fig. 18. The shaded area around northern Texas and central Oklahoma indicates that IFR conditions exist. The symbol =6 means mist (=) and the sky is overcast at 600 ft. (6) AGL. Thus, low ceilings at 600 ft. are the source of IFR weather conditions.

Answer (A) is incorrect. A solid round dot (•) indicates intermittent rain. Answer (C) is incorrect. The symbol § indicates dust devils, which are small vigorous whirlwinds, usually of short duration, made visible by dust, sand, or debris picked up from the ground. This symbol is not seen on this chart in northern Texas.

41. (Refer to Figure 18 on page 270.) What weather phenomenon is causing IFR conditions in central Oklahoma?

A. Low visibility only.

B. Low ceilings and visibility.

C. Heavy rain showers.

Answer (B) is correct. *(AWS Sect 5)*

DISCUSSION: Refer to the Weather Depiction Chart in Fig. 18. In central Oklahoma, the IFR conditions are caused by low ceilings and visibility. In the shaded area over central Oklahoma and northern Texas, there are five darkened circles with numbers 2 1/2 beside them, signifying visibilities between 2 1/2 and 3 statute miles. The IFR conditions are therefore due to low ceilings and visibility.

Answer (A) is incorrect. There are also low ceilings in the area from 300 to 600 feet. Answer (C) is incorrect. Heavy rain showers are shown by the symbol ▽.

42. (Refer to Figure 18 on page 270.) What is the status of the front that extends from Nebraska through the upper peninsula of Michigan?

A. Cold.

B. Stationary.

C. Warm.

Answer (A) is correct. *(AWS Sect 5)*

DISCUSSION: Refer to the Weather depiction chart in Fig. 18. The front that extends from Nebraska through the upper peninsula of Michigan is a cold front, as shown by the pointed scallops on the southern side of the frontal line.

Answer (B) is incorrect. A stationary front has pointed scallops on one side of the frontal line and rounded scallops on the other. Answer (C) is incorrect. A warm front has rounded scallops, not pointed scallops.

43. (Refer to Figure 18 on page 270.) According to the weather depiction chart, the weather for a flight from southern Michigan to north Indiana is ceilings

A. 1,000 to 3,000 feet and/or visibility 3 to 5 miles.

B. less than 1,000 feet and/or visibility less than 3 miles.

C. greater than 3,000 feet and visibility greater than 5 miles.

Answer (C) is correct. *(AWS Sect 5)*

DISCUSSION: Refer to the Weather depiction chart in Fig. 18. The weather from southern Michigan to north Indiana is shown by the lack of shading or contours to have ceilings greater than 3,000 ft. and visibilities greater than 5 miles.

Answer (A) is incorrect. Ceilings from 1,000 to 3,000 ft. and/or visibilities between 3 and 5 statute miles (MVFR conditions) are indicated on Weather depiction charts by an unshaded area surrounded by a contour. Answer (B) is incorrect. Ceilings less than 1,000 ft. and/or visibilities less than 3 statute miles (IFR conditions) are indicated on Weather depiction charts by a shaded area surrounded by a contour.

44. (Refer to Figure 18 on page 270.) The marginal weather in central Kentucky is due to low

A. ceiling.

B. ceiling and visibility.

C. visibility.

Answer (A) is correct. *(AWS Sect 5)*

DISCUSSION: Refer to the Weather depiction chart in Fig. 18. The MVFR weather in central Kentucky is indicated by the contour line without shading. The station symbol indicates an overcast ceiling at 1,000 feet. MVFR is ceiling 1,000 ft. to 3,000 ft. and/or visibility 3 to 5 statute miles. Thus, the marginal weather is due to a low ceiling.

Answer (B) is incorrect. The marginal weather is caused by low ceilings only. Answer (C) is incorrect. The visibility is greater than 6 SM (indicated by the lack of a report). Therefore, the visibility is not a cause of the marginal conditions.

8.7 Radar Weather Reports

45. Radar weather reports are of special interest to pilots because they indicate

A. large areas of low ceilings and fog.

B. location of precipitation along with type, intensity, and cell movement of precipitation.

C. location of precipitation along with type, intensity, and trend.

Answer (B) is correct. *(AWS Sect 3)*

DISCUSSION: Radar weather reports are of special interest to pilots because they report the location of precipitation along with type, intensity, and cell movement.

Answer (A) is incorrect. Weather radar cannot detect clouds or fog, only precipitation size particles. Answer (C) is incorrect. Radar weather reports no longer include trend information.

8.8 In-Flight Weather

46. How should contact be established with a Flight Service Station, and what service would be expected?

A. Call Flight Service on 122.2 for routine weather, current reports on hazardous weather, and altimeter settings.

B. Call flight assistance on 122.5 for advisory service pertaining to severe weather.

C. Call Flight Service on 122.0 for information regarding actual weather and thunderstorm activity along proposed route.

Answer (A) is correct. *(AIM Para 7-1-4, 4-2-14)*

DISCUSSION: You would call FSS on 122.2 MHz for routine weather, current reports on hazardous weather, and altimeter settings.

Answer (B) is incorrect. You would possibly call FSS on 122.2 MHz for advisory service pertaining to severe weather. Answer (C) is incorrect. You would call FSS on 122.2 MHz, not 122.0 MHz.

47. What service should a pilot normally expect from Flight Service?

A. Actual weather information and thunderstorm activity along the route.

B. Preferential routing and radar vectoring to circumnavigate severe weather.

C. Local information about restaurants, hotels, and rental car services.

Answer (A) is correct. *(AIM Para 7-1-4, 4-2-14)*

DISCUSSION: Flight Service is designed to provide en route traffic with timely and meaningful weather advisories pertinent to the type of flight intended. It is designed to be a continuous exchange of information on winds, turbulence, visibility, icing, etc., between pilots and Flight Service specialists on the ground.

Answer (B) is incorrect. Preferential routing and radar vectoring is provided by approach control and ATC center. Answer (C) is incorrect. Local information can be obtained from a Fixed Base Operator (FBO) or various online and directory services.

48. En route weather advisories should be obtained from an FSS on

A. 122.2 MHz.

B. 122.1 MHz.

C. 123.6 MHz.

Answer (A) is correct. *(AIM Para 7-1-4, 4-2-14)*

DISCUSSION: To receive weather advisories along your route, you should contact Flight Service on 122.2 MHz.

Answer (B) is incorrect. This is the pilot-to-FSS frequency used on duplex remote communication facilities. Answer (C) is incorrect. This is the common FSS frequency for airport advisory service.

8.9 Wind and Temperature Aloft Forecasts (FB)

49. What values are used for Winds Aloft Forecasts?

A. Magnetic direction and knots.

B. Magnetic direction and miles per hour.

C. True direction and knots.

Answer (C) is correct. *(AWS Sect 7)*

DISCUSSION: For Winds Aloft Forecasts, the wind direction is given in true direction and the wind speed is in knots.

Answer (A) is incorrect. ATC (not Winds Aloft Forecasts) will provide winds in magnetic direction and knots. Answer (B) is incorrect. Winds Aloft Forecast will provide winds based on true (not magnetic) direction and speed in kt. (not MPH).

50. (Refer to Figure 17 on page 273.) What wind is forecast for STL at 12,000 feet?

A. 230° magnetic at 39 knots.

B. 230° true at 39 knots.

C. 230° true at 106 knots.

Answer (B) is correct. *(AWS Sect 7)*

DISCUSSION: Refer to the FB forecast in Fig. 17. Locate STL on the left side of the chart and move to the right to the 12,000-ft. column. The wind forecast (first four digits) is coded as 2339. The forecast is decoded as 230° true at 39 knots.

Answer (A) is incorrect. The wind is from 230° true, not magnetic. Answer (C) is incorrect. This is the forecast wind speed and direction for 34,000 ft., not 12,000 ft. (coded as 7306).

51. (Refer to Figure 17 below.) Determine the wind and temperature aloft forecast for MKC at 6,000 ft.

A. 050° true at 7 knots, temperature missing.

B. 200° magnetic at 6 knots, temperature +3°C.

C. 200° true at 6 knots, temperature +3°C.

Answer (C) is correct. *(AWS Sect 7)*

DISCUSSION: Refer to the FB forecast in Fig. 17. Locate MKC on the left side of the chart and move to the right to the 6,000-ft. column. The wind and temperature forecast is coded as 2006+03, which translates as the forecast wind at 200° true at 6 kt. and a temperature of 3°C.

Answer (A) is incorrect. This is the forecast for MKC at 3,000 ft., not 6,000 feet. Answer (B) is incorrect. Wind direction is given in true degrees, not magnetic degrees.

52. (Refer to Figure 17 below.) What wind is forecast for STL at 9,000 feet?

A. 230° magnetic at 25 knots.

B. 230° true at 32 knots.

C. 230° true at 25 knots.

Answer (B) is correct. *(AWS Sect 7)*

DISCUSSION: Refer to the FB forecast in Fig. 17. Locate STL on the left side of the chart and move right to the 9,000-ft. column. The coded wind forecast (first four digits) is 2332. Thus, the forecast wind is 230° true at 32 knots.

Answer (A) is incorrect. Wind direction is forecast in true (not magnetic) direction. Wind forecast of 230° true at 25 kt. is for STL at 6,000 ft., not 9,000 feet. Answer (C) is incorrect. This is the wind forecast for STL at 6,000 ft., not 9,000 feet.

FB WBC 151745
DATA BASED ON 151200Z
VALID 1600Z FOR USE 1800-0300Z. TEMPS NEG ABV 24000

FT	3000	6000	9000	12000	18000	24000	30000	34000	39000
ALS			2420	2635-08	2535-18	2444-30	245945	246755	246862
AMA		2714	2725+00	2625-04	2531-15	2542-27	265842	256352	256762
DEN			2321-04	2532-08	2434-19	2441-31	235347	236056	236262
HLC		1707-01	2113-03	2219-07	2330-17	2435-30	244145	244854	245561
MKC	0507	2006+03	2215-01	2322-06	2338-17	2348-29	236143	237252	238160
STL	2113	2325+07	2332+02	2339-04	2356-16	2373-27	239440	730649	731960

Figure 17. – Winds and Temperatures Aloft Forecast.

53. (Refer to Figure 17 above.) What wind is forecast for STL at 12,000 feet?

A. 230° true at 39 knots.

B. 230° true at 56 knots.

C. 230° magnetic at 56 knots.

Answer (A) is correct. *(AWS Sect 7)*

DISCUSSION: Refer to the FB forecast in Fig. 17. Locate STL and move right to the 12,000-ft. column. The wind forecast (first four digits) is coded as 2339, which means the wind is 230° true at 39 knots.

Answer (B) is incorrect. This is the forecast wind direction and speed for 18,000 ft., not 12,000 feet. Answer (C) is incorrect. The first two digits are direction referenced to true (not magnetic) north. Thus, 2356 is 230° true (not magnetic) at 56 kt., which is the forecast wind direction and speed for 18,000 ft., not 12,000 feet.

54. (Refer to Figure 17 above.) Determine the wind and temperature aloft forecast for DEN at 9,000 feet.

A. 230° magnetic at 53 knots, temperature 47°C.

B. 230° true at 53 knots, temperature –47°C.

C. 230° true at 21 knots, temperature –4°C.

Answer (C) is correct. *(AWS Sect 7)*

DISCUSSION: Refer to the FB forecast in Fig. 17. Locate DEN on the left side of the chart and move to the right to the 9,000-ft. column. The wind and temperature forecast is coded as 2321-04. The forecast is decoded as 230° true at 21 kt., temperature –4°C.

Answer (A) is incorrect. The correct measurement is 230° true (not magnetic), and the temperature is –4°C, not 47°C. Answer (B) is incorrect. The temperature is –4°C, not –47°C, which is the temperature for DEN at 30,000 ft., not 9,000 feet.

55. When the term "light and variable" is used in reference to a Winds Aloft Forecast, the coded group and windspeed is

A. 0000 and less than 7 knots.

B. 9900 and less than 5 knots.

C. 9999 and less than 10 knots.

Answer (B) is correct. *(AWS Sect 7)*

DISCUSSION: When winds are light and variable on a Winds Aloft Forecast (FB), it is coded 9900 and wind speed is less than 5 knots.

Answer (A) is incorrect. When winds are light and variable, it is coded 9900 (not 0000) and wind speed is less than 5 (not 7) knots. Answer (C) is incorrect. When winds are light and variable, it is coded 9900 (not 9999) and wind speed is less than 5 (not 10) knots.

8.10 Significant Weather Prognostic Charts

56. (Refer to Figure 19 on page 275.) What weather is forecast for the Florida area just ahead of the stationary front during the first 12 hours?

A. Ceiling 1,000 to 3,000 feet and/or visibility 3 to 5 miles with intermittent precipitation.

B. Ceiling 1,000 to 3,000 feet and/or visibility 3 to 5 miles with continuous precipitation.

C. Ceiling less than 1,000 feet and/or visibility less than 3 miles with continuous precipitation.

Answer (B) is correct. *(AWS Sect 8)*

DISCUSSION: Refer to the Significant weather prognostic chart in Fig. 19. During the first 12 hr. (bottom and top left panels), the weather just ahead of the stationary front that extends from coastal Virginia into the Gulf of Mexico is forecast to have ceilings from 1,000 to 3,000 ft. and/or visibility 3 to 5 SM (as indicated by the scalloped lines) with continuous light to moderate rain covering more than half the area (as indicated by the shading).

Answer (A) is incorrect. Thunderstorms embedded in an area of moderate continuous, not intermittent, precipitation are forecast just ahead of the stationary front, as indicated by the following symbol: ∴/R . Thunderstorms embedded in an area of intermittent rain would be indicated with this symbol: :/R . Answer (C) is incorrect. Marginal VFR conditions (ceilings from 1,000 to 3,000 ft. and/or visibility from 3 to 5 SM), not IFR conditions (ceilings less than 1,000 ft. and/or visibility less than 3 miles) are forecast, as indicated by the scalloped line surrounding the southeastern states on the top left panel.

57. (Refer to Figure 19 on page 275.) Interpret the weather symbol depicted in Utah on the 12-hour Significant weather prognostic chart.

A. Moderate turbulence, surface to 18,000 feet.

B. Thunderstorm tops at 18,000 feet.

C. Base of clear air turbulence, 18,000 feet.

Answer (A) is correct. *(AWS Sect 8)*

DISCUSSION: Refer to the upper left panel of the Significant weather prognostic chart in Fig. 19. In Utah, the weather symbol indicates moderate turbulence as designated by the symbol of a small peaked hat. Note that the broken line indicates moderate or greater turbulence. The peaked hat is the symbol for moderate turbulence. The 180 means the moderate turbulence extends from the surface upward to 18,000 feet.

Answer (B) is incorrect. The peaked hat symbol denotes moderate turbulence, not thunderstorms. The symbol for thunderstorms is shown by what looks like the letter "R," as shown on the 12-hr. surface prog in the Gulf of Mexico. Answer (C) is incorrect. This is not the base of the clear air turbulence. A line over a number indicates a base.

58. (Refer to Figure 19 on page 275.) At what altitude is the freezing level over the middle of Florida on the 12-hour significant weather prognostic chart?

A. 4,000 feet.

B. 8,000 feet.

C. 12,000 feet.

Answer (C) is correct. *(AWS Sect 8)*

DISCUSSION: Refer to the upper left panel of the Significant weather prognostic chart in Fig. 19. On prog charts, the freezing level is indicated by a dashed line, with the height given in hundreds of feet MSL. In Fig. 19, there is a dashed line across the middle of Florida, marked with "120." This signifies that the freezing level is 12,000 ft. MSL.

Answer (A) is incorrect. The freezing level is at 4,000 ft. MSL across the northern U.S. and Canada, not over the middle of Florida. Answer (B) is incorrect. The freezing level is at 8,000 ft. MSL extending from southern California, upward and across the northern U.S., and into New Jersey, not over the middle of Florida.

59. (Refer to Figure 19 on page 275.) The enclosed shaded area associated with the low pressure system over northern Utah is forecast to have

A. continuous snow.

B. intermittent snow.

C. continuous snow showers.

Answer (A) is correct. *(AWS Sect 8)*

DISCUSSION: In the lower left panel of Fig. 19, the low pressure center over northern Utah is indicated by a bold "L." The shaded area to the left of the "L" indicates precipitation covering more than half the area. The symbol ∗∗/∗∗ is just to the right of the "L" with an arrow pointing to the shaded area. This means that the shaded area is forecast to have continuous light snow.

Answer (B) is incorrect. Intermittent snow would be indicated by a symbol with vertical snowflakes, not horizontal ones. Answer (C) is incorrect. Continuous snow showers are indicated for the unshaded area in southern Utah, not the shaded area in northern Utah, by the symbol ∗∗/∗▽ .

Figure 19. – Low-Level Significant Weather (SIGWX) Prognostic Charts.

60. How are significant weather prognostic charts best used by a pilot?

A. For overall planning at all altitudes.

B. For determining areas to avoid (freezing levels and turbulence).

C. For analyzing current frontal activity and cloud coverage.

Answer (B) is correct. *(AWS Sect 8)*

DISCUSSION: Weather prognostic charts forecast conditions that exist 12 and 24 hr. in the future. They include two types of forecasts: low level significant weather, such as IFR and marginal VFR areas, and moderate or greater turbulence areas and freezing levels.

Answer (A) is incorrect. A complete set of weather forecasts for overall planning includes terminal forecasts, area forecasts, etc. Answer (C) is incorrect. The weather depiction chart shows analysis of frontal activities, cloud coverage, areas of precipitation, ceilings, etc.

8.11 AIRMETs and SIGMETs

61. SIGMETs are issued as a warning of weather conditions hazardous to which aircraft?

A. Small aircraft only.

B. Large aircraft only.

C. All aircraft.

Answer (C) is correct. *(AWS Sect 6)*

DISCUSSION: SIGMETs (significant meteorological information) warn of weather considered potentially hazardous to all aircraft. SIGMET advisories cover severe and extreme turbulence; severe icing; and widespread duststorms, sandstorms, or volcanic ash that reduce visibility to less than 3 statute miles.

Answer (A) is incorrect. SIGMETs apply to all aircraft, not just to small aircraft. Answer (B) is incorrect. SIGMETs apply to all aircraft, not just to large aircraft.

62. AIRMETs are advisories of significant weather phenomena but of lower intensities than SIGMETs and are intended for dissemination to

A. only IFR pilots.

B. all pilots.

C. only VFR pilots.

Answer (B) is correct. *(AWS Sect 6)*

DISCUSSION: AIRMETs are advisories of significant weather phenomena that describe conditions at intensities lower than those which require the issuance of SIGMETs. They are intended for dissemination to all pilots.

Answer (A) is incorrect. AIRMETs are intended for dissemination to all pilots, not just IFR pilots. Answer (C) is incorrect. AIRMETs are intended for dissemination to all pilots, not just VFR pilots.

63. Which in-flight advisory would contain information on severe icing not associated with thunderstorms?

A. Convective SIGMET.

B. SIGMET.

C. AIRMET.

Answer (B) is correct. *(AWS Sect 6)*

DISCUSSION: SIGMET advisories cover severe icing not associated with thunderstorms; severe or extreme turbulence or clear air turbulence not associated with thunderstorms; duststorms, sandstorms, or volcanic ash that reduce visibility to less than 3 SM; and volcanic eruption.

Answer (A) is incorrect. A convective SIGMET is issued concerning convective activity such as tornadoes and severe thunderstorms. Any convective SIGMET implies severe icing, which is associated with thunderstorms. Answer (C) is incorrect. AIRMETs are issued for moderate, not severe, icing.

64. What information is contained in a CONVECTIVE SIGMET?

A. Tornadoes, embedded thunderstorms, and hail 3/4 inch or greater in diameter.

B. Severe icing, severe turbulence, or widespread dust storms lowering visibility to less than 3 miles.

C. Surface winds greater than 40 knots or thunderstorms equal to or greater than video integrator processor (VIP) level 4.

Answer (A) is correct. *(AWS Sect 6)*

DISCUSSION: Convective SIGMETs are issued for tornadoes, lines of thunderstorms, embedded thunderstorms of any intensity level, areas of thunderstorms greater than or equal to VIP level 4 with an area coverage of 40% or more, and hail 3/4 in. or greater.

Answer (B) is incorrect. A SIGMET, not a convective SIGMET, is issued for severe icing, severe turbulence, or widespread duststorms lowering visibility to less than 3 statute miles. Answer (C) is incorrect. A severe thunderstorm having surface winds of 50 kt. or greater, not 40 kt., will be contained in a convective SIGMET.

65. What is indicated when a current CONVECTIVE SIGMET forecasts thunderstorms?

A. Moderate thunderstorms covering 30 percent of the area.

B. Moderate or severe turbulence.

C. Thunderstorms obscured by massive cloud layers.

Answer (C) is correct. *(AWS Sect 6)*

DISCUSSION: Convective SIGMETs are issued for tornadoes, lines of thunderstorms, embedded (i.e., obscured by massive cloud layers) thunderstorms of any intensity level, areas of thunderstorms greater than or equal to VIP level 4 with an area coverage of 40% or more, and hail 3/4 in. or greater.

Answer (A) is incorrect. Thunderstorms would be very strong (VIP level 4) or greater, not moderate, and cover 40%, not 30%, of the area for a convective SIGMET. Answer (B) is incorrect. A convective SIGMET that is issued for thunderstorms implies severe or greater, not moderate, turbulence.

END OF STUDY UNIT

STUDY UNIT NINE
NAVIGATION: CHARTS AND PUBLICATIONS

(24 pages of outline)

This study unit contains outlines of major concepts tested, sample test questions and answers regarding navigation charts and publications, and an explanation of each answer. The table of contents above lists each subunit within this study unit, the number of questions pertaining to that particular subunit, and the pages on which the outlines and questions begin, respectively.

Many of the questions in this study unit ask about sectional (aeronautical) charts, which appear as Legend 1 and Figures 20 through 26, 59, 69 through 71, 74 through 76, 78, and 80.

Important Note about FAA Charts

The FAA prints the charts published in their Airman Knowledge Testing Supplements to the wrong scale. If you were to measure a distance on one of these charts with the plotter, do the calculations based on that information, and enter that answer, you would be wrong every time.

Accurately calculating distance is a part of the testing process. By printing the charts to the wrong scale, the FAA is testing to see if you checked your plotter to the scale printed on the chart to make sure the chart is accurate. Because our goal at Gleim is to prepare you for your Knowledge Test, our reproductions of the charts are also not to scale.

To answer questions related to these charts, you must transfer the chart's scale to a scrap of paper, which is supplied to you at the testing site. You will use this scale as an accurate measuring tool in place of your plotter.

Also, the second subunit, "Airspace and Altitudes," is long (50 questions) and covers a number of diverse topics regarding interpretation of sectional charts. Be prepared.

Note that a number of questions in Study Unit 10, "Navigation Systems," and Study Unit 11, "Cross-Country Flight Planning," will refer you to these same figures. These questions require you to determine your position and compute magnetic heading, true course, time en route, etc.

GLEIM SUCCESS TIPS®

Recall that the **sole purpose** of this book is to expedite your passing of the FAA pilot knowledge test for the private pilot certificate. Accordingly, all extraneous material (i.e., topics or regulations not directly tested on the FAA pilot knowledge test) is omitted, even though much more knowledge is necessary to fly safely. This additional material is presented in *Pilot Handbook* and *Private Pilot Flight Maneuvers and Practical Test Prep*, available from Gleim Publications, Inc. Order online at www.GleimAviation.com.

9.1 LONGITUDE AND LATITUDE

1. The location of an airport can be determined by the intersection of the lines of latitude and longitude.
   a. Lines of latitude are parallel to the equator, and those north of the equator are numbered from 0° to 90° north latitude.
   b. Lines of longitude extend from the north pole to the south pole. The prime meridian (which passes through Greenwich, England) is 0° longitude with 180° on both the east and west sides of the prime meridian.
2. The lines of latitude and longitude are printed on aeronautical charts (e.g., sectional) with each degree subdivided into 60 equal segments called minutes; i.e., 1/2° is 30' (the min. symbol is " ' ").

9.2 AIRSPACE AND ALTITUDES

Cloud Clearance and Visibility Required for VFR

Airspace	Flight Visibility	Distance from Clouds
Class A	Not Applicable	Not applicable
Class B	3 SM	Clear of clouds
Class C	3 SM	500 ft. below 1,000 ft. above 2,000 ft. horiz.
Class D	3 SM	500 ft. below 1,000 ft. above 2,000 ft. horiz.
Class E		
Less than 10,000 ft. MSL	3 SM	500 ft. below 1,000 ft. above 2,000 ft. horiz.
At or above 10,000 ft. MSL	5 SM	1,000 ft. below 1,000 ft. above 1 SM horiz.

Airspace	Flight Visibility	Distance from Clouds
Class G:		
1,200 ft. or less above the surface (regardless of MSL altitude)		
Day	1 SM	Clear of clouds
Night, except as provided in 1. below	3 SM	500 ft. below 1,000 ft. above 2,000 ft. horiz.
More than 1,200 ft. above the surface but less than 10,000 ft. MSL		
Day	1 SM	500 ft. below 1,000 ft. above 2,000 ft. horiz.
Night	3 SM	500 ft. below 1,000 ft. above 2,000 ft. horiz.
More than 1,200 ft. above the surface and at or above 10,000 ft. MSL	5 SM	1,000 ft. below 1,000 ft. above 1 SM horiz.

1. An airplane may be operated clear of clouds in Class G airspace at night below 1,200 ft. AGL when the visibility is less than 3 SM but more than 1 SM in an airport traffic pattern and within 1/2 NM of the runway.

2. Class G airspace is all navigable airspace that is not classified as Class A, Class B, Class C, Class D, or Class E airspace.
3. On sectional charts, blue airport symbols indicate that the airport has a control tower on the field. Magenta airport symbols indicate non-towered airports.
4. Class E airspace is controlled airspace that is not defined as Class A, Class B, Class C, or Class D.
    a. The lower limits of Class E airspace are specified by markings on terminal and sectional charts.
        1) The surface in areas marked by segmented (dashed) magenta lines.
        2) 700 ft. AGL in areas marked by shaded magenta lines.
        3) 1,200 ft. AGL in areas marked by shaded blue lines.
        4) 1,200 ft. AGL in areas defined as Federal Airways. Blue lines between VOR facilities labeled with the letter "V" followed by numbers, e.g., V-120.
        5) A specific altitude depicted in En Route Domestic Areas denoted by blue "zipper" marks.
    b. If not defined, the floor of Class E airspace begins at 14,500 ft. MSL or 1,200 ft. AGL, whichever is higher.
    c. Class E airspace extends up to, but does not include, 18,000 ft. MSL.
5. Class D airspace is an area of controlled airspace surrounding an airport with an operating control tower, not associated with Class B or Class C airspace areas.
    a. Class D airspace is depicted by a segmented (dashed) blue line on sectional charts.
    b. The height of the Class D airspace is shown in a broken box and is expressed in hundreds of feet MSL.
        1) EXAMPLE: [**29**] means the height of the Class D airspace is 2,900 ft. MSL.
6. Class C airspace areas are depicted by solid magenta lines on sectional charts.
    a. The surface area (formerly called the inner circle) of Class C airspace, the area within 5 NM from the primary airport, begins at the surface and goes up to 4,000 ft. above the airport. The shelf area (formerly called the outer circle) of a Class C airspace area, the area from 5 NM to 10 NM from the primary airport, begins at about 1,200 ft. AGL and extends to the same altitude as the surface area.

b. The vertical limits are indicated on the chart within each circle and are expressed in hundreds of feet MSL. The top limit is shown above a straight line and the bottom limit beneath the line.

1) EXAMPLE: See Figure 23 on the previous page. At the bottom right (area 3) is the Savannah Class C airspace.

a) $\frac{41}{SFC}$ in the surface area means Class C airspace extends from the surface (SFC) to 4,100 ft. MSL.

b) $\frac{41}{13}$ in the shelf area means Class C airspace extends from 1,300 ft. MSL to 4,100 ft. MSL.

c. The minimum equipment needed to operate in Class C airspace

1) 4096-code transponder
2) Mode C (altitude encoding) capability
3) Two-way radio communication capability

d. You must establish and maintain two-way radio communication with ATC prior to entering Class C airspace.

7. Class B airspace areas are depicted by heavy blue lines on sectional charts.

a. The vertical limits are shown on the chart in the same manner as the vertical limits for Class C airspace discussed in item 6.b. above.

b. Satellite airports underlying Class B airspace may have different floor and ceiling altitude limitation markings, such as those indicated in the red circles in the figure below. These markings and their explanations can be found in the FAA Aeronautical Chart User's Guide. They may not be on all sectional chart legends.

1) For Class B airspace, these markings are numbers in light blue and appear to be written as a fraction. An example can be seen between the two floor and ceiling altitude limitation markings (circled in red) above area 6 in the figure below.

2) There may be what appears to be a "T" substituted for a number in the altitude.

a) This symbol is not actually a "T" but a line going from the lower, indicated altitude, up to the bottom of the overlying Class B airspace. The horizontal line represents the bottom of the overlying airspace. For example, the markings (circled in red) in the upper-left and bottom-right of the figure below are from 1,500 MSL up to the bottom (or floor) of the overlying Class B airspace of 2,100 MSL.

b) It may be easier to remember this as the "top of the bottom" of the overlying airspace.

NOTE: These red circles have been added to the figure excerpt for ease of reference and instructive purposes only. They will not appear on the actual FAA Figure 70.

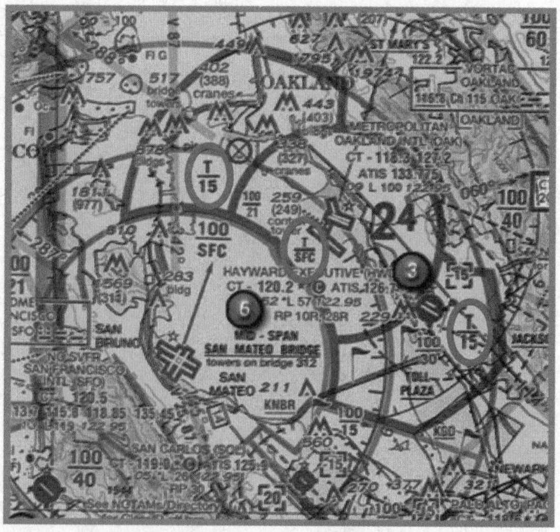

Excerpt from Figure 70.

c. The minimum equipment to operate in Class B airspace is

1) A 4096-code transponder
2) Mode C capability
3) Two-way radio communication capability

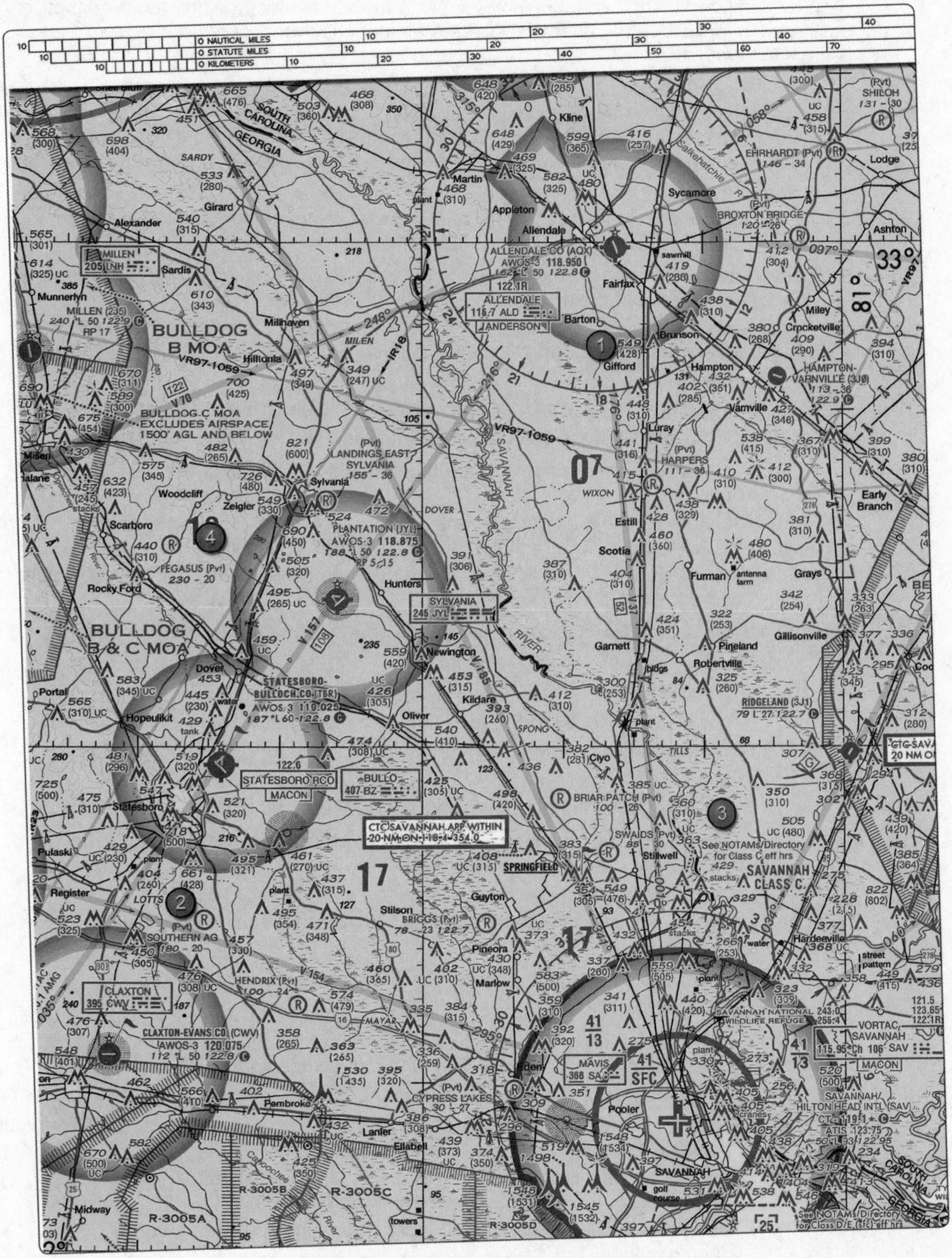

Figure 23. – Sectional Chart Excerpt.
NOTE: Chart is not to scale and should not be used for navigation. Use associated scale.

8. When overlapping airspace designations apply to the same airspace, the more restrictive designation applies. Remember that Class A airspace is the most restrictive, and Class G is the least restrictive.
    a. EXAMPLE: The primary airport of a Class D airspace area underlies Class B airspace. The ceiling of the Class D airspace is 3,100 ft. MSL, and the floor of the Class B airspace is 3,000 ft. MSL. Since Class B is more restrictive than Class D, the overlapping airspace between 3,000 ft. and 3,100 ft. MSL is considered to be Class B airspace.
9. Special use airspace includes prohibited, restricted, warning, military operations, alert, national security, and controlled firing areas.
    a. **Restricted areas** denote the existence of unusual, often invisible hazards to aircraft such as military firing, aerial gunnery, or guided missiles.
    b. **Warning areas** contain activity that may be hazardous to nonparticipating aircraft, e.g., aerial gunnery, guided missiles, etc.
        1) Warning areas extend from 3 NM outward from the U.S. coast.
        2) A warning area may be located over domestic air or international waters or both.
    c. **Military operations areas (MOAs)** denote areas of military training activities.
        1) Pilots should contact any FSS within 100 NM to determine the MOA hours of operation.
        2) If it is active, the pilot should contact the controlling agency prior to entering the MOA for traffic advisories because of high-density military training.
        3) When operating in an MOA, exercise extreme caution when military activity is being conducted.
10. **Military training routes (MTR)** are established below 10,000 ft. MSL for operations at speeds in excess of 250 kt.
    a. IR means the routes are made in accordance with IFRs.
        1) VR means the routes are made in accordance with VFRs.
    b. MTRs that include one or more segments above 1,500 ft. AGL are identified by a three-digit number.
        1) MTRs with no segment above 1,500 ft. AGL are identified by a four-digit number.
11. Information about parachute jumping areas and glider operations is contained in the Chart Supplement. Parachute jumping areas are marked on sectional charts with a parachute symbol.
12. Over national wildlife refuges, pilots are requested to maintain a minimum altitude of 2,000 ft. AGL.
13. Airport data on sectional charts include the following information:
    a. The name of the airport.
    b. The elevation of the airport, followed by the length of the longest hard-surfaced runway. An L between the altitude and length indicates lighting.
        1) EXAMPLE: 1008 L 70 means 1,008 ft. MSL airport elevation, L is for lighting sunset to sunrise, and 70 indicates that the length of the longest hard-surfaced runway is 7,000 ft.
        2) If the L has an asterisk beside it (*L), airport lighting limitations exist, and you should refer to the Chart Supplement for information.
        3) Private, or "**(Pvt)**," indicating a nonpublic-use airport having emergency or landmark value.
    c. The UNICOM frequency if one has been assigned (e.g., 122.8) is shown after or underneath the runway length.

d. At controlled airports, the tower frequency is usually under the airport name and above the runway information. It is preceded by CT.

   1) If not a federal control tower, NFCT precedes the CT frequency.

e. A small, star-shaped symbol immediately above the airport symbol indicates a rotating beacon from sunset to sunrise.

f. The notation "NO SVFR" above the airport name means that fixed-wing special VFR operations are prohibited.

14. Obstructions on sectional charts

a. Obstructions of a height less than 1,000 ft. AGL have the symbol Λ.

   1) A group of such obstructions has the symbol ΛΛ.

b. Obstructions of a height of 1,000 ft. or more AGL have the symbol **Λ**.

   1) A group of such obstructions has the symbol **ΛΛ**.

c. Obstructions with high-intensity lights have arrows, or lightning bolts, projecting from the top of the obstruction symbol.

d. The actual height of the top of obstructions is listed near the obstruction by two numbers: one in bold print over another in light print with parentheses around it.

   1) The bold number is the elevation of the top of the obstruction in feet above MSL.
   2) The light number in parentheses is the height of the obstruction in feet AGL.
   3) The elevation (MSL) at the base of the obstruction is the bold figures minus the light figures.

      a) Use this computation to compute terrain elevation.
      b) Terrain elevation is also given in the airport identifier for each airport and by the contour lines and color shading on the chart.

e. You must maintain at least 1,000 ft. above obstructions in congested areas and 500 ft. above obstructions in other areas.

NOTE: The red circle has been added to the figure excerpt for ease of reference and instructive purposes only. It will not appear on the actual Figure 70.

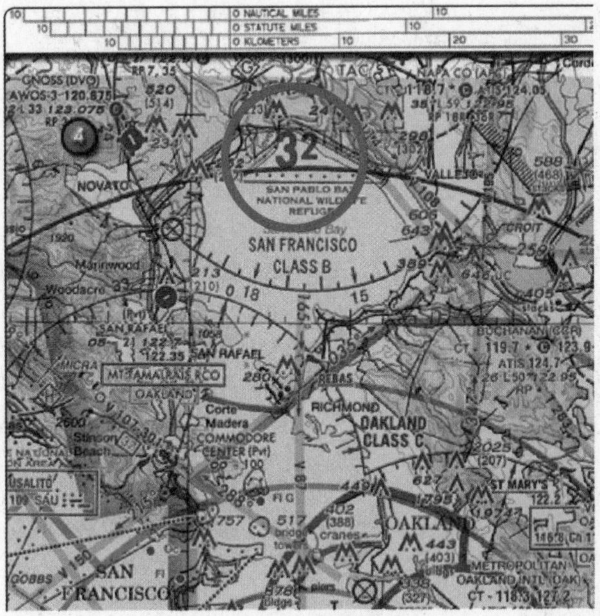

Excerpt from Figure 70.

f. The maximum elevation figure (MEF) represents the highest elevation within a quadrant, including terrain and other vertical obstacles (towers, trees, etc.). A quadrant on sectional charts is an area bound by ticked lines every 30 minutes of latitude and 30 minutes of longitude. MEF figures are rounded up to the nearest 100-foot value and the last two digits of the number are not shown.

15. Navigational facilities are depicted on sectional charts with various symbols depending on type and services available. These symbols are shown in Legend 1 on page 288.
    a. A VORTAC is depicted as a hexagon with a dot in the center and a small solid rectangle attached to three of the six sides.
    b. A VOR/DME is depicted as a hexagon within a square.
    c. A VOR is depicted as a hexagon with a dot in the center

9.3 IDENTIFYING LANDMARKS

1. On aeronautical charts, magenta (red) flags denote prominent landmarks that may be used as visual reporting checkpoints for VFR traffic when contacting ATC.
2. The word "CAUTION" on aeronautical charts usually has an accompanying explanation of the hazard.
3. Airports with a rotating beacon will have a star at the top of the airport symbol on sectional charts.
4. Airports attended during normal business hours and having fuel service are indicated on airport symbols by the presence of small solid squares at the top and bottom and on both sides (9 o'clock and 3 o'clock) on the airport symbol.

9.4 RADIO FREQUENCIES

1. At airports without operating control towers, you should use the Common Traffic Advisory Frequency (CTAF), marked with a letter C in the airport data on the sectional chart.
    a. The control tower (CT) frequency is usually used for CTAF when the control tower is closed.
    b. At airports without control towers but with FSS at the airport, the FSS airport advisory frequency is usually the CTAF.
    c. At airports without a tower or FSS, the UNICOM frequency is the CTAF.
    d. At airports without a tower, FSS, or UNICOM, the CTAF is MULTICOM, i.e., 122.9.
    e. Inbound and outbound traffic should communicate position and monitor CTAF within a 10-NM radius of the airport and give position reports when in the traffic pattern.
    f. At airports with operating control towers the UNICOM frequency listed on the sectional chart and Chart Supplement can be used to request services such as fuel, phone calls, and catering.
2. Flight Service Stations (FSSs) specifically provide en route aircraft with current weather along their route of flight.
    a. Flight Service is available throughout the country on 122.2 MHz or the frequencies listed on aeronautical charts and the Chart Supplement.
    b. The name of the nearest FSS facility is sometimes indicated in communications boxes.
3. Hazardous Inflight Weather Advisory Service (HIWAS) is available from navigation facilities that have a small "H" indicated inside of a solid black circle at the upper right corner of the navigation aid identifier box.

9.5 FAA ADVISORY CIRCULARS

1. The FAA issues advisory circulars to provide a systematic means for the issuance of nonregulatory material of interest to the aviation public.
2. The circulars are issued in a numbered system of general subject matter areas to correspond with the subject areas in Federal Aviation Regulations (e.g., 60 Airmen, 70 Airspace, and 90 Air Traffic and General Operating Rules).
3. FAA Advisory Circulars are available from the FAA's website at www.faa.gov.
   a. An Advisory Circular Checklist is available for download at www.faa.gov.

9.6 CHART SUPPLEMENTS

1. Chart Supplements are published by Aeronautical Navigation Products (AeroNav Products) every 56 days for each of seven geographical districts of the United States.
   a. Chart Supplements provide information on services available, runways, special conditions at the airport, communications, navigation aids, etc.
2. The airport name comes first, followed by the alternate name, if any, and then the location identifier.
3. The airport location is expressed as a distance and direction of the airport from the city.
   a. EXAMPLE: **4 NW** means 4 NM northwest of the city.
4. Right-turn traffic is indicated by "Rgt tfc" following a runway number.
5. When a control tower is not in operation, the CTAF frequency (found in the section titled **Communications**) should be used for traffic advisories.
6. Initial communication should be with Approach Control if available where you are landing. The frequency is listed following "APP/DEP CON."
   a. It may be different for approaches from different headings.
   b. It may be operational only for certain hours of the day.
7. In Class C airspace, VFR aircraft are provided the following radar services:
   a. Sequencing to the primary Class C airport
   b. Approved separation between IFR and VFR aircraft
   c. Basic radar services, including safety alerts, limited vectoring, and traffic advisories
8. For more information on the Chart Supplement legend explanations, refer to Legends 2 through 9 and 13 through 17.
9. All of the applicable FAA legends from Appendix 1 of *Airman Knowledge Testing Supplement for Sport Pilot, Recreational Pilot, and Private Pilot* are reproduced beginning on the next page. The legends not included (Legends 10 through 12, Legend 18, and Legend 19) pertain to military topics, helicopters, gyroplanes, and/or gliders. Gleim does not believe you will be tested on these legends on your Private Knowledge Test.

GLEIM SUCCESS TIPS®

As you practice answering questions, keep in mind that you will need to refer to Appendix 1 of the testing supplement to find these legends on test day.

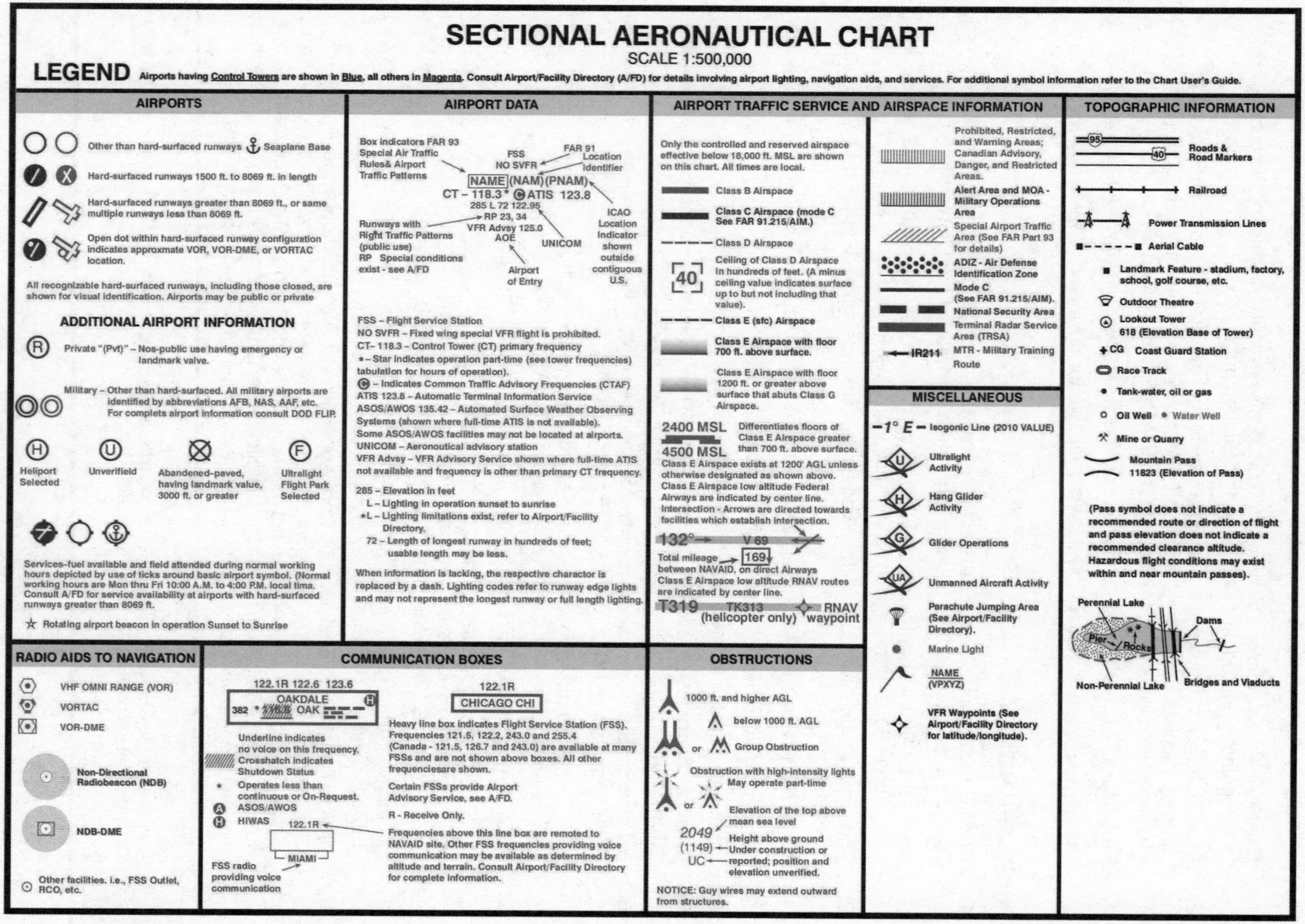

Legend 1. – Sectional Aeronautical Chart.

4 **DIRECTORY LEGEND**

SAMPLE

1 2 3 4 5 6 7 8

CITY NAME

AIRPORT NAME (ALTERNATE NAME) (LTS) (KLTS) CIV/MIL 3 N UTC–6(–5DT) N34°41.93′ W99°20.20′ **JACKSONVILLE**

200 B S4 **FUEL** 100 OX 1 TPA—1000(800) AOE Class IV, ARFF Index A NOTAM FILE ORL Not insp. **COPTER**

H–4G, L–19C

11 12 13 14 15 16 17 18 19 20 **IAP, DIAP, AD**

9

21 **RWY 18–36:** H12004X200 (ASPH–CONC–GRVD)

S–90, D–160, 2D–300 PCN 80 R/B/W/T HIRL CL

RWY 18: LDIN. MALSF. TDZL. REIL. PAPI(P2R)—GA 3.0° TCH 36′.

Thld dsplcd 300′. Trees. Rgt tfc. 0.3% up.

RWY 36: ALSF1. 0.4% down.

RWY 09–27: H6000X150 (ASPH) MIRL

RWY 173–353: H3515X150 (ASPH–PFC) AUW PCN 59 F/A/W/T

LAND AND HOLD SHORT OPERATIONS

LANDING	HOLD SHORT POINT	DIST AVBL
RWY 18	09–27	6500
RWY 36	09–27	5400

RUNWAY DECLARED DISTANCE INFORMATION

RWY 18: TORA–12004 TODA–12704 ASDA–11704 LDA–11504

RWY 36: TORA–12004 TODA–12004 ASDA–12004 LDA–11704

22 **ARRESTING GEAR/SYSTEM**

RWY 18 → HOOK E5 (65′ OVRN) BAK–14 BAK–12B (1650′)

BAK–14 BAK–12 (B) (1087′) HOOK E5 (74′ OVRN) ← **RWY 36**

23 **MILITARY SERVICE: A–GEAR** E–5 connected on dep end, disconnected on apch end. **JASU** 3(AM32A–60) 2(A/M32A–86)

24

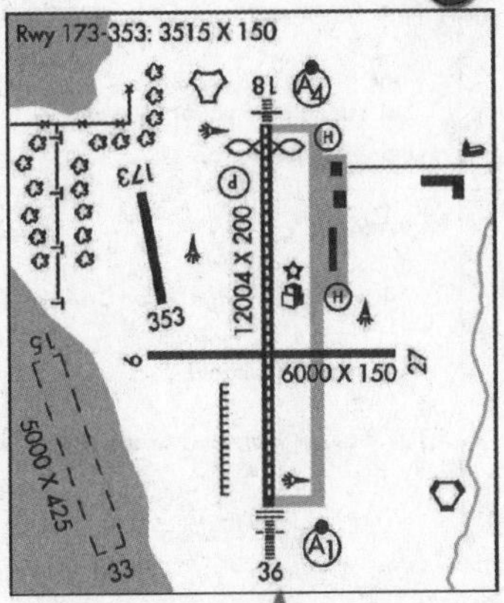

10

25 **FUEL** J8(Mil) (NC–100, A) **FLUID** W SP PRESAIR LOX 26

OIL O–128 **TRAN ALERT** Avbl 1300–0200Z‡, svc limited weekends.

27 28

29 **AIRPORT REMARKS:** Special Air Traffic Rules—Part 93, see Regulatory Notices. Attended 1200–0300Z‡. Parachute Jumping. Deer invof arpt. Heavy jumbo jet training surface to 9000′. Twy A clsd indef. Flight Notification Service (ADCUS) avbl.

30 **MILITARY REMARKS: ANG** PPR/Official Business Only. Base OPS DSN 638–4390, C503–335–4222. Ctc Base OPS 15 minutes prior to ldg and after dep. Limited tran parking.

31 **WEATHER DATA SOURCES:** AWOS–1 120.3 (202) 426–8000. LLWAS.

32 **COMMUNICATIONS: SFA ATIS** 127.25 273.5 (202) 426–8003 **UNICOM** 122.95 **PTD** 372.2

NAME FSS (ORL) on arpt. 123.65 122.65 122.2

NAME RCO 112.2T 112.1R (NAME RADIO)

Ⓡ **NAME APP/DEP CON** 128.35 257.725 (1200–0400Z‡)

TOWER 119.65 255.6 (1200–0400Z‡) **GND CON** 121.7 **GCO** 135.075 (ORLANDO CLNC) **CLNC DEL** 125.55

NAME COMD POST (GERONIMO) 311.0 321.4 6761 **PMSV METRO** 239.8 **NAME OPS** 257.5

33 **AIRSPACE: CLASS B** See VFR Terminal Area Chart.

34 **RADIO AIDS TO NAVIGATION:** NOTAM FILE ORL. VHF/DF ctc FSS.

(H) VORTAC 112.2 MCO Chan 59 N28°32.55′ W81°20.12′ at fld. 1110/8E.

(H) TACAN Chan 29 CBU (109.2) N28°32.65′ W81°21.12′ at fld. 1115/8E.

HERNY NDB (LOM) 221 OR N28°37.40′ W81°21.05′ 177° 5.4 NM to fld.

ILS/DME 108.5 I–ORL Chan 22 Rwy 18. Class IIE. LOM HERNY NDB.

ASR/PAR (1200–0400Z‡)

35 **COMM/NAV/WEATHER REMARKS:** Emerg frequency 121.5 not avbl at twr.

• •

HELIPAD H1: H100X75 (ASPH)

HELIPAD H2: H60X60 (ASPH)

HELIPORT REMARKS: Helipad H1 lctd on general aviation side and H2 lctd on air carrier side of arpt. 1

• •

187 TPA 1000(813)

WATERWAY 15–33: 5000X425 (WATER)

SEAPLANE REMARKS: Birds roosting and feeding areas along river banks. Seaplanes operating adjacent to SW side of arpt not visible from twr and are required to ctc twr.

All bearings and radials are magnetic unless otherwise specified.
All mileages are nautical unless otherwise noted.
All times are Coordinated Universal Time (UTC) except as noted.
All elevations are in feet above/below Mean Sea Level (MSL) unless otherwise noted.
The horizontal reference datum of this publication is North American Datum of 1983 (NAD83), which for charting purposes is considered equivalent to World Geodetic System 1984 (WGS 84).

NE, 09 FEB 20XX to 05 APR 20XX

Legend 2. – Chart Supplements U.S. (formerly Airport/Facility Directory).

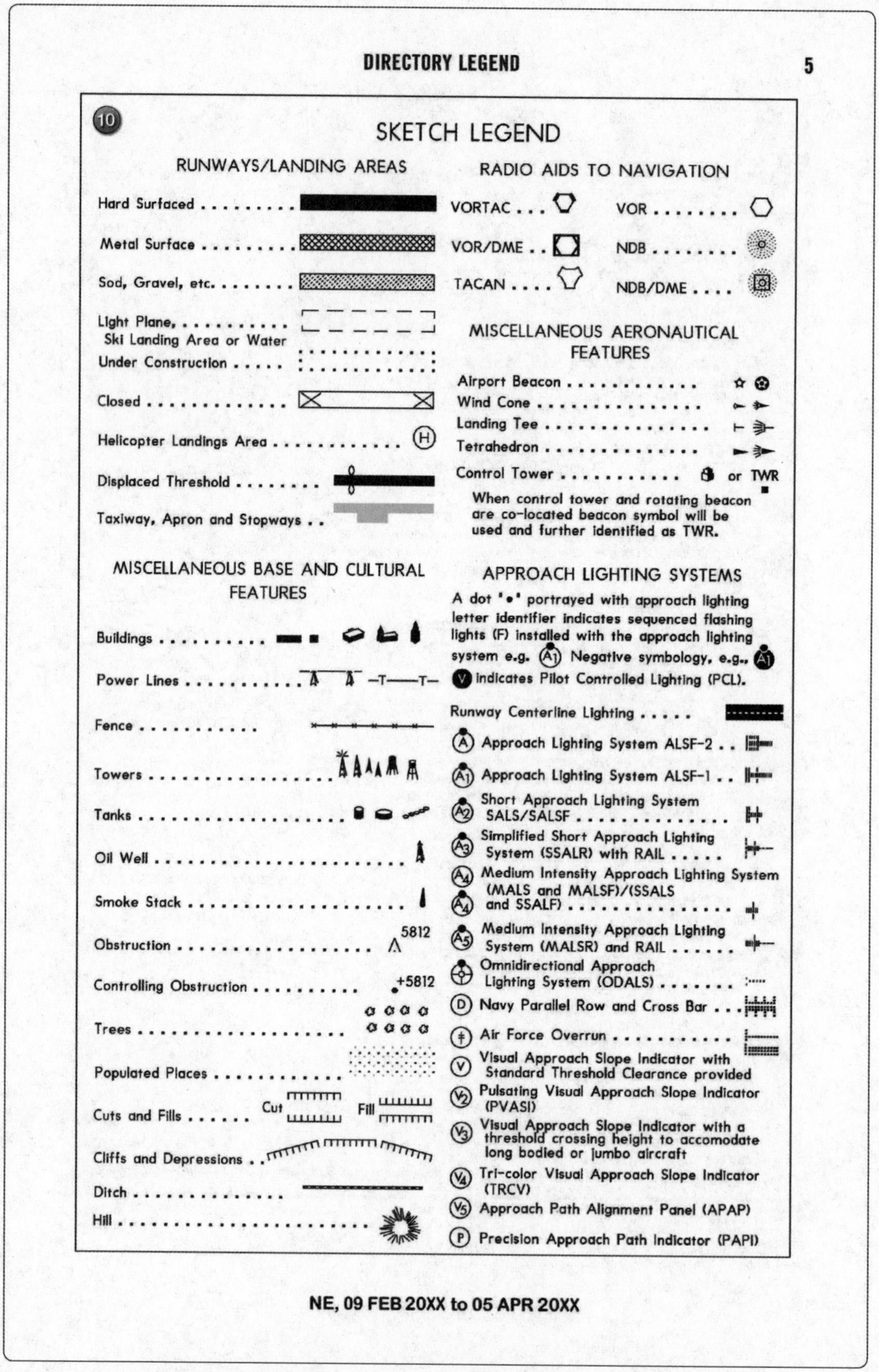

DIRECTORY LEGEND 5

10

SKETCH LEGEND

RUNWAYS/LANDING AREAS

Hard Surfaced ....
Metal Surface ....
Sod, Gravel, etc. ....
Light Plane, Ski Landing Area or Water ....
Under Construction .....
Closed ....
Helicopter Landings Area ....
Displaced Threshold ....
Taxiway, Apron and Stopways . .

RADIO AIDS TO NAVIGATION

VORTAC . . .
VOR ....
VOR/DME . .
NDB ....
TACAN . . . .
NDB/DME . . . .

MISCELLANEOUS AERONAUTICAL FEATURES

Airport Beacon ....
Wind Cone ....
Landing Tee ....
Tetrahedron ....
Control Tower .... or TWR

When control tower and rotating beacon are co-located beacon symbol will be used and further identified as TWR.

MISCELLANEOUS BASE AND CULTURAL FEATURES

Buildings ....
Power Lines .... —T——T—
Fence ....
Towers ....
Tanks ....
Oil Well ....
Smoke Stack ....
Obstruction 5812
Controlling Obstruction .... +5812
Trees ....
Populated Places ....
Cuts and Fills ..... Cut Fill
Cliffs and Depressions . .
Ditch ....
Hill ....

APPROACH LIGHTING SYSTEMS

A dot "•" portrayed with approach lighting letter identifier indicates sequenced flashing lights (F) installed with the approach lighting system e.g. (A1) Negative symbology, e.g., (A1) (V) indicates Pilot Controlled Lighting (PCL).

Runway Centerline Lighting .....

(A) Approach Lighting System ALSF-2 . .
(A1) Approach Lighting System ALSF-1 . .
(A2) Short Approach Lighting System SALS/SALSF ....
(A3) Simplified Short Approach Lighting System (SSALR) with RAIL .....
(A4) Medium Intensity Approach Lighting System (MALS and MALSF)/(SSALS and SSALF) ....
(A5) Medium Intensity Approach Lighting System (MALSR) and RAIL ......
Omnidirectional Approach Lighting System (ODALS) ....
(D) Navy Parallel Row and Cross Bar . . .
Air Force Overrun ....
(V) Visual Approach Slope Indicator with Standard Threshold Clearance provided
(V2) Pulsating Visual Approach Slope Indicator (PVASI)
(V3) Visual Approach Slope Indicator with a threshold crossing height to accomodate long bodied or jumbo aircraft
(V4) Tri-color Visual Approach Slope Indicator (TRCV)
(V5) Approach Path Alignment Panel (APAP)
(P) Precision Approach Path Indicator (PAPI)

NE, 09 FEB 20XX to 05 APR 20XX

Legend 3. – Chart Supplements U.S. (formerly Airport/Facility Directory).

6

DIRECTORY LEGEND

LEGEND

This directory is a listing of data on record with the FAA on all open to the public airports, military facilities and selected private use facilities specifically requested by the Department of Defense (DoD) for which a DoD Instrument Approach Procedure has been published in the U.S. Terminal Procedures Publication. Additionally this listing contains data for associated terminal control facilities, air route traffic control centers, and radio aids to navigation within the conterminous United States, Puerto Rico and the Virgin Islands. Joint civil/military and civil airports are listed alphabetically by state, associated city and airport name and cross-referenced by airport name. Military facilities are listed alphabetically by state and official airport name and cross-referenced by associated city name. Navaids, flight service stations and remote communication outlets that are associated with an airport, but with a different name, are listed alphabetically under their own name, as well as under the airport with which they are associated.

The listing of an open to the public airport in this directory merely indicates the airport operator's willingness to accommodate transient aircraft, and does not represent that the facility conforms with any Federal or local standards, or that it has been approved for use on the part of the general public. Military and private use facilities published in this directory are open to civil pilots only in an emergency or with prior permission. See Special Notice Section, Civil Use of Military Fields.

The information on obstructions is taken from reports submitted to the FAA. Obstruction data has not been verified in all cases. Pilots are cautioned that objects not indicated in this tabulation (or on the airports sketches and/or charts) may exist which can create a hazard to flight operation. Detailed specifics concerning services and facilities tabulated within this directory are contained in the Aeronautical Information Manual, Basic Flight Information and ATC Procedures.

The legend items that follow explain in detail the contents of this Directory and are keyed to the circled numbers on the sample on the preceding pages.

1 CITY/AIRPORT NAME

Civil and joint civil/military airports and facilities in this directory are listed alphabetically by state and associated city. Where the city name is different from the airport name the city name will appear on the line above the airport name. Airports with the same associated city name will be listed alphabetically by airport name and will be separated by a dashed rule line. A solid rule line will separate all others. FAA approved helipads and seaplane landing areas associated with a land airport will be separated by a dotted line. Military airports are listed alphabetically by state and official airport name.

2 ALTERNATE NAME

Alternate names, if any, will be shown in parentheses.

3 LOCATION IDENTIFIER

The location identifier is a three or four character FAA code followed by a four-character ICAO code assigned to airports. ICAO codes will only be published at joint civil/military, and military facilities. If two different military codes are assigned, both codes will be shown with the primary operating agency's code listed first. These identifiers are used by ATC in lieu of the airport name in flight plans, flight strips and other written records and computer operations. Zeros will appear with a slash to differentiate them from the letter "O".

4 OPERATING AGENCY

Airports within this directory are classified into two categories, Military/Federal Government and Civil airports open to the general public, plus selected private use airports. The operating agency is shown for military, private use and joint civil/military airports. The operating agency is shown by an abbreviation as listed below. When an organization is a tenant, the abbreviation is enclosed in parenthesis. No classification indicates the airport is open to the general public with no military tenant.

A	US Army	MC	Marine Corps
AFRC	Air Force Reserve Command	N	Navy
AF	US Air Force	NAF	Naval Air Facility
ANG	Air National Guard	NAS	Naval Air Station
AR	US Army Reserve	NASA	National Air and Space Administration
ARNG	US Army National Guard	P	US Civil Airport Wherein Permit Covers Use by Transient Military Aircraft
CG	US Coast Guard		
CIV/MIL	Joint Use Civil/Military	PVT	Private Use Only (Closed to the Public)
DND	Department of National Defense Canada		

5 AIRPORT LOCATION

Airport location is expressed as distance and direction from the center of the associated city in nautical miles and cardinal points, e.g., 4 NE.

6 TIME CONVERSION

Hours of operation of all facilities are expressed in Coordinated Universal Time (UTC) and shown as "Z" time. The directory indicates the number of hours to be subtracted from UTC to obtain local standard time and local daylight saving time UTC–5(–4DT). The symbol ‡ indicates that during periods of Daylight Saving Time effective hours will be one hour earlier than shown. In those areas where daylight saving time is not observed the (–4DT) and ‡ will not be shown. Daylight saving time is in effect from 0200 local time the second Sunday in March to 0200 local time the first Sunday in November. Canada and all U.S. Conterminous States observe daylight saving time except Arizona and Puerto Rico, and the Virgin Islands. If the state observes daylight saving time and the operating times are other than daylight saving times, the operating hours will include the dates, times and no ‡ symbol will be shown, i.e., April 15–Aug 31 0630–1700Z, Sep 1–Apr 14 0600–1700Z.

NE, 09 FEB 20XX to 05 APR 20XX

Legend 4. – Chart Supplements U.S. (formerly Airport/Facility Directory).

DIRECTORY LEGEND 7

7 GEOGRAPHIC POSITION OF AIRPORT—AIRPORT REFERENCE POINT (ARP)

Positions are shown as hemisphere, degrees, minutes and hundredths of a minute and represent the approximate geometric center of all usable runway surfaces.

8 CHARTS

Charts refer to the Sectional Chart and Low and High Altitude Enroute Chart and panel on which the airport or facility is located. Helicopter Chart locations will be indicated as COPTER. IFR Gulf of Mexico West and IFR Gulf of Mexico Central will be depicted as GOMW and GOMC.

9 INSTRUMENT APPROACH PROCEDURES, AIRPORT DIAGRAMS

IAP indicates an airport for which a prescribed (Public Use) FAA Instrument Approach Procedure has been published. DIAP indicates an airport for which a prescribed DoD Instrument Approach Procedure has been published in the U.S. Terminal Procedures. See the Special Notice Section of this directory, Civil Use of Military Fields and the Aeronautical Information Manual 5–4–5 Instrument Approach Procedure Charts for additional information. AD indicates an airport for which an airport diagram has been published. Airport diagrams are located in the back of each A/FD volume alphabetically by associated city and airport name.

10 AIRPORT SKETCH

The airport sketch, when provided, depicts the airport and related topographical information as seen from the air and should be used in conjunction with the text. It is intended as a guide for pilots in VFR conditions. Symbology that is not self-explanatory will be reflected in the sketch legend. The airport sketch will be oriented with True North at the top. Airport sketches will be added incrementally.

11 ELEVATION

The highest point of an airport's usable runways measured in feet from mean sea level. When elevation is sea level it will be indicated as "00". When elevation is below sea level a minus "–" sign will precede the figure.

12 ROTATING LIGHT BEACON

B indicates rotating beacon is available. Rotating beacons operate sunset to sunrise unless otherwise indicated in the AIRPORT REMARKS or MILITARY REMARKS segment of the airport entry.

13 SERVICING—CIVIL

S1: Minor airframe repairs.
S2: Minor airframe and minor powerplant repairs.
S3: Major airframe and minor powerplant repairs.
S4: Major airframe and major powerplant repairs.
S5: Major airframe repairs.
S6: Minor airframe and major powerplant repairs.
S7: Major powerplant repairs.
S8: Minor powerplant repairs.

14 FUEL

CODE	FUEL
80	Grade 80 gasoline (Red)
100	Grade 100 gasoline (Green)
100LL	100LL gasoline (low lead) (Blue)
115	Grade 115 gasoline (115/145 military specification) (Purple)
A	Jet A, Kerosene, without FS–II*, FP** minus 40° C.
A+	Jet A, Kerosene, with FS–II*, FP** minus 40°C.
A1	Jet A–1, Kerosene, without FS–II*, FP** minus 47°C.
A1+	Jet A–1, Kerosene with FS–II*, FP** minus 47° C.
B	Jet B, Wide-cut, turbine fuel without FS–II*, FP** minus 50° C.
B+	Jet B, Wide-cut, turbine fuel with FS–II*, FP** minus 50° C.
J4 (JP4)	(JP–4 military specification) FP** minus 58° C.
J5 (JP5)	(JP–5 military specification) Kerosene with FS–11, FP** minus 46°C.
J8 (JP8)	(JP–8 military specification) Jet A–1, Kerosene with FS–II*, FP** minus 47°C.
J8+100	(JP–8 military specification) Jet A–1, Kerosene with FS–II*, FP** minus 47°C, with-fuel additive package that improves thermo stability characteristics of JP–8.
J	(Jet Fuel Type Unknown)
MOGAS	Automobile gasoline which is to be used as aircraft fuel.

*(Fuel System Icing Inhibitor)
**(Freeze Point)

NOTE: Certain automobile gasoline may be used in specific aircraft engines if a FAA supplemental type certificate has been obtained. Automobile gasoline, which is to be used in aircraft engines, will be identified as "MOGAS", however, the grade/type and other octane rating will not be published.

Data shown on fuel availability represents the most recent information the publisher has been able to acquire. Because of a variety of factors, the fuel listed may not always be obtainable by transient civil pilots. Confirmation of availability of fuel should be made directly with fuel suppliers at locations where refueling is planned.

15 OXYGEN—CIVIL

OX 1 High Pressure
OX 2 Low Pressure
OX 3 High Pressure—Replacement Bottles
OX 4 Low Pressure—Replacement Bottles

16 TRAFFIC PATTERN ALTITUDE

Traffic Pattern Altitude (TPA)—The first figure shown is TPA above mean sea level. The second figure in parentheses is TPA above airport elevation. Multiple TPA shall be shown as "TPA—See Remarks" and detailed information shall be shown in the Airport or Military Remarks Section. Traffic pattern data for USAF bases, USN facilities, and U.S. Army airports (including those on which ACC or U.S. Army is a tenant) that deviate from standard pattern altitudes shall be shown in Military Remarks.

NE, 09 FEB 20XX to 05 APR 20XX

Legend 5. – Chart Supplements U.S. (formerly Airport/Facility Directory).

8

DIRECTORY LEGEND

17 AIRPORT OF ENTRY, LANDING RIGHTS, AND CUSTOMS USER FEE AIRPORTS

U.S. CUSTOMS USER FEE AIRPORT—Private Aircraft operators are frequently required to pay the costs associated with customs processing.

AOE—Airport of Entry. A customs Airport of Entry where permission from U.S. Customs is not required to land. However, at least one hour advance notice of arrival is required.

LRA—Landing Rights Airport. Application for permission to land must be submitted in advance to U.S. Customs. At least one hour advance notice of arrival is required.

NOTE: Advance notice of arrival at both an AOE and LRA airport may be included in the flight plan when filed in Canada or Mexico. Where Flight Notification Service (ADCUS) is available the airport remark will indicate this service. This notice will also be treated as an application for permission to land in the case of an LRA. Although advance notice of arrival may be relayed to Customs through Mexico, Canada, and U.S. Communications facilities by flight plan, the aircraft operator is solely responsible for ensuring that Customs receives the notification. (See Customs, Immigration and Naturalization, Public Health and Agriculture Department requirements in the International Flight Information Manual for further details.)

US Customs Air and Sea Ports, Inspectors and Agents	
Northeast Sector (New England and Atlantic States—ME to MD)	407–975–1740
Southeast Sector (Atlantic States—DC, WV, VA to FL)	407–975–1780
Central Sector (Interior of the US, including Gulf states—MS, AL, LA)	407–975–1760
Southwest East Sector (OK and eastern TX)	407–975–1840
Southwest West Sector (Western TX, NM and AZ)	407–975–1820
Pacific Sector (WA, OR, CA, HI and AK)	407–975–1800

18 CERTIFICATED AIRPORT (14 CFR PART 139)

Airports serving Department of Transportation certified carriers and certified under 14 CFR part 139 are indicated by the Class and the ARFF Index; e.g. Class I, ARFF Index A, which relates to the availability of crash, fire, rescue equipment. Class I airports can have an ARFF Index A through E, depending on the aircraft length and scheduled departures. Class II, III, and IV will always carry an Index A.

14 CFR PART 139 CERTIFICATED AIRPORTS
AIRPORT CLASSIFICATIONS

Type of Air Carrier Operation	Class I	Class II	Class III	Class IV
Scheduled Air Carrier Aircraft with 31 or more passenger seats	X			
Unscheduled Air Carrier Aircraft with 31 or more passengers seats	X	X		X
Scheduled Air Carrier Aircraft with 10 to 30 passenger seats	X	X	X	

14 CFR–PART 139 CERTIFICATED AIRPORTS

INDICES AND AIRCRAFT RESCUE AND FIRE FIGHTING EQUIPMENT REQUIREMENTS

Airport Index	*Required No. Vehicles*	*Aircraft Length*	*Scheduled Departures*	*Agent + Water for Foam*
A	1	<90′	≥1	500#DC or HALON 1211 or 450#DC + 100 gal H_2O
B	1 or 2	≥90′, <126′	≥5	Index A + 1500 gal H_2O
		≥126′, <159′	<5	
C	2 or 3	≥126′, <159′	≥5	Index A + 3000 gal H_2O
		≥159′, <200′	<5	
D	3	≥159′, <200′		Index A + 4000 gal H_2O
		>200′	<5	
E	3	≥200′	≥5	Index A + 6000 gal H_2O

> Greater Than; < Less Than; ≥ Equal or Greater Than; ≤ Equal or Less Than; H_2O–Water; DC–Dry Chemical.

NOTE: The listing of ARFF index does not necessarily assure coverage for non-air carrier operations or at other than prescribed times for air carrier. ARFF Index Ltd.—indicates ARFF coverage may or may not be available, for information contact airport manager prior to flight.

19 NOTAM SERVICE

All public use landing areas are provided NOTAM service. A NOTAM FILE identifier is shown for individual langing areas, e.g., "NOTAM FILE BNA". See the AIM, Basic Flight Information and ATC Procedures for a detailed description of NOTAMs.

NE, 09 FEB 20XX to 05 APR 20XX

Legend 6. – Chart Supplements U.S. (formerly Airport/Facility Directory).

DIRECTORY LEGEND

Current NOTAMs are available from flight service stations at 1–800–WX–BRIEF (992–7433) or online through the FAA PilotWeb at https://pilotweb.nas.faa.gov. Military NOTAMs are available using the Defense Internet NOTAM Service (DINS) at https://www.notams.jcs.mil.
Pilots flying to or from airports not available through the FAA PilotWeb or DINS can obtain assistance from Flight Service.

20 FAA INSPECTION

All airports not inspected by FAA will be identified by the note: Not insp. This indicates that the airport information has been provided by the owner or operator of the field.

21 RUNWAY DATA

Runway information is shown on two lines. That information common to the entire runway is shown on the first line while information concerning the runway ends is shown on the second or following line. Runway direction, surface, length, width, weight bearing capacity, lighting, and slope, when available are shown for each runway. Multiple runways are shown with the longest runway first. Direction, length, width, and lighting are shown for sea-lanes. The full dimensions of helipads are shown, e.g., 50X150. Runway data that requires clarification will be placed in the remarks section.

RUNWAY DESIGNATION

Runways are normally numbered in relation to their magnetic orientation rounded off to the nearest 10 degrees. Parallel runways can be designated L (left)/R (right)/C (center). Runways may be designated as Ultralight or assault strips. Assault strips are shown by magnetic bearing.

RUNWAY DIMENSIONS

Runway length and width are shown in feet. Length shown is runway end to end including displaced thresholds, but excluding those areas designed as overruns.

RUNWAY SURFACE AND LENGTH

Runway lengths prefixed by the letter "H" indicate that the runways are hard surfaced (concrete, asphalt, or part asphalt–concrete). If the runway length is not prefixed, the surface is sod, clay, etc. The runway surface composition is indicated in parentheses after runway length as follows:

(AFSC)—Aggregate friction seal coat
(AMS)—Temporary metal planks coated with nonskid material
(ASPH)—Asphalt
(CONC)—Concrete
(DIRT)—Dirt
(GRVD)—Grooved
(GRVL)—Gravel, or cinders
(MATS)—Pierced steel planking, landing mats, membranes
(PEM)—Part concrete, part asphalt
(PFC)—Porous friction courses
(PSP)—Pierced steel plank
(RFSC)—Rubberized friction seal coat
(TURF)—Turf
(TRTD)—Treated
(WC)—Wire combed

RUNWAY WEIGHT BEARING CAPACITY

Runway strength data shown in this publication is derived from available information and is a realistic estimate of capability at an average level of activity. It is not intended as a maximum allowable weight or as an operating limitation. Many airport pavements are capable of supporting limited operations with gross weights in excess of the published figures. Permissible operating weights, insofar as runway strengths are concerned, are a matter of agreement between the owner and user. When desiring to operate into any airport at weights in excess of those published in the publication, users should contact the airport management for permission. Runway strength figures are shown in thousand of pounds, with the last three figures being omitted. Add 000 to figure following S, D, 2S, 2T, AUW, SWL, etc., for gross weight capacity. A blank space following the letter designator is used to indicate the runway can sustain aircraft with this type landing gear, although definite runway weight bearing capacity figures are not available, e.g., S, D. Applicable codes for typical gear configurations with S=Single, D=Dual, T=Triple and Q=Quadruple:

CURRENT	NEW	NEW DESCRIPTION
S	S	Single wheel type landing gear (DC3), (C47), (F15), etc.
D	D	Dual wheel type landing gear (BE1900), (B737), (A319), etc.
T	D	Dual wheel type landing gear (P3, C9).
ST	2S	Two single wheels in tandem type landing gear (C130).
TRT	2T	Two triple wheels in tandem type landing gear (C17), etc.
DT	2D	Two dual wheels in tandem type landing gear (B707), etc.
TT	2D	Two dual wheels in tandem type landing gear (B757, KC135).
SBTT	2D/D1	Two dual wheels in tandem/dual wheel body gear type landing gear (KC10).
None	2D/2D1	Two dual wheels in tandem/two dual wheels in tandem body gear type landing gear (A340–600).
DDT	2D/2D2	Two dual wheels in tandem/two dual wheels in double tandem body gear type landing gear (B747, E4).
TTT	3D	Three dual wheels in tandem type landing gear (B777), etc.
TT	D2	Dual wheel gear two struts per side main gear type landing gear (B52).
TDT	C5	Complex dual wheel and quadruple wheel combination landing gear (C5).

Legend 7. – Chart Supplements U.S. (formerly Airport/Facility Directory).

10 **DIRECTORY LEGEND**

AUW—All up weight. Maximum weight bearing capacity for any aircraft irrespective of landing gear configuration.

SWL—Single Wheel Loading. (This includes information submitted in terms of Equivalent Single Wheel Loading (ESWL) and Single Isolated Wheel Loading).

PSI—Pounds per square inch. PSI is the actual figure expressing maximum pounds per square inch runway will support, e.g., (SWL 000/PSI 535).

Omission of weight bearing capacity indicates information unknown.

The ACN/PCN System is the ICAO standard method of reporting pavement strength for pavements with bearing strengths greater than 12,500 pounds. The Pavement Classification Number (PCN) is established by an engineering assessment of the runway. The PCN is for use in conjunction with an Aircraft Classification Number (ACN). Consult the Aircraft Flight Manual, Flight Information Handbook, or other appropriate source for ACN tables or charts. Currently, ACN data may not be available for all aircraft. If an ACN table or chart is available, the ACN can be calculated by taking into account the aircraft weight, the pavement type, and the subgrade category. For runways that have been evaluated under the ACN/PCN system, the PCN will be shown as a five-part code (e.g. PCN 80 R/B/W/T). Details of the coded format are as follows:

(1) The PCN NUMBER—The reported PCN indicates that an aircraft with an ACN equal or less than the reported PCN can operate on the pavement subject to any limitation on the tire pressure.

(2) The type of pavement:
R — Rigid
F — Flexible

(3) The pavement subgrade category:
A — High
B — Medium
C — Low
D — Ultra-low

(4) The maximum tire pressure authorized for the pavement:
W — High, no limit
X — Medium, limited to 217 psi
Y — Low, limited to 145 psi
Z — Very low, limited to 73 psi

(5) Pavement evaluation method:
T — Technical evaluation
U — By experience of aircraft using the pavement

NOTE: Prior permission from the airport controlling authority is required when the ACN of the aircraft exceeds the published PCN or aircraft tire pressure exceeds the published limits.

RUNWAY LIGHTING

Lights are in operation sunset to sunrise. Lighting available by prior arrangement only or operating part of the night and/or pilot controlled lighting with specific operating hours are indicated under airport or military remarks. At USN/USMC facilities lights are available only during airport hours of operation. Since obstructions are usually lighted, obstruction lighting is not included in this code. Unlighted obstructions on or surrounding an airport will be noted in airport or military remarks. Runway lights nonstandard (NSTD) are systems for which the light fixtures are not FAA approved L-800 series: color, intensity, or spacing does not meet FAA standards. Nonstandard runway lights, VASI, or any other system not listed below will be shown in airport remarks or military service. Temporary, emergency or limited runway edge lighting such as flares, smudge pots, lanterns or portable runway lights will also be shown in airport remarks or military service. Types of lighting are shown with the runway or runway end they serve.

NSTD—Light system fails to meet FAA standards.
LIRL—Low Intensity Runway Lights.
MIRL—Medium Intensity Runway Lights.
HIRL—High Intensity Runway Lights.
RAIL—Runway Alignment Indicator Lights.
REIL—Runway End Identifier Lights.
CL—Centerline Lights.
TDZL—Touchdown Zone Lights.
ODALS—Omni Directional Approach Lighting System.
AF OVRN—Air Force Overrun 1000′ Standard Approach Lighting System.
LDIN—Lead-In Lighting System.
MALS—Medium Intensity Approach Lighting System.
MALSF—Medium Intensity Approach Lighting System with Sequenced Flashing Lights.
MALSR—Medium Intensity Approach Lighting System with Runway Alignment Indicator Lights.
SALS—Short Approach Lighting System.
SALSF—Short Approach Lighting System with Sequenced Flashing Lights.
SSALS—Simplified Short Approach Lighting System.
SSALF—Simplified Short Approach Lighting System with Sequenced Flashing Lights.
SSALR—Simplified Short Approach Lighting System with Runway Alignment Indicator Lights.
ALSAF—High Intensity Approach Lighting System with Sequenced Flashing Lights.
ALSF1—High Intensity Approach Lighting System with Sequenced Flashing Lights, Category I, Configuration.
ALSF2—High Intensity Approach Lighting System with Sequenced Flashing Lights, Category II, Configuration.
SF—Sequenced Flashing Lights.
OLS—Optical Landing System.
WAVE-OFF.

NOTE: Civil ALSF2 may be operated as SSALR during favorable weather conditions. When runway edge lights are positioned more than 10 feet from the edge of the usable runway surface a remark will be added in the "Remarks" portion of the airport entry. This is applicable to Air Force, Air National Guard and Air Force Reserve Bases, and those joint civil/military airfields on which they are tenants.

NE, 09 FEB 20XX to 05 APR 20XX

Legend 8. – Chart Supplements U.S. (formerly Airport/Facility Directory).

DIRECTORY LEGEND 11

VISUAL GLIDESLOPE INDICATORS

APAP—A system of panels, which may or may not be lighted, used for alignment of approach path.

PNIL	APAP on left side of runway	PNIR	APAP on right side of runway

PAPI—Precision Approach Path Indicator

P2L	2-identical light units placed on left side of runway	P4L	4-identical light units placed on left side of runway
P2R	2-identical light units placed on right side of runway	P4R	4-identical light units placed on right side of runway

PVASI—Pulsating/steady burning visual approach slope indicator, normally a single light unit projecting two colors.

PSIL	PVASI on left side of runway	PSIR	PVASI on right side of runway

SAVASI—Simplified Abbreviated Visual Approach Slope Indicator

S2L	2-box SAVASI on left side of runway	S2R	2-box SAVASI on right side of runway

TRCV—Tri-color visual approach slope indicator, normally a single light unit projecting three colors.

TRIL	TRCV on left side of runway	TRIR	TRCV on right side of runway

VASI—Visual Approach Slope Indicator

V2L	2-box VASI on left side of runway	V6L	6-box VASI on left side of runway
V2R	2-box VASI on right side of runway	V6R	6-box VASI on right side of runway
V4L	4-box VASI on left side of runway	V12	12-box VASI on both sides of runway
V4R	4-box VASI on right side of runway	V16	16-box VASI on both sides of runway

NOTE: Approach slope angle and threshold crossing height will be shown when available; i.e., –GA 3.5° TCH 37′.

PILOT CONTROL OF AIRPORT LIGHTING

Key Mike	Function
7 times within 5 seconds	Highest intensity available
5 times within 5 seconds	Medium or lower intensity (Lower REIL or REIL-Off)
3 times within 5 seconds	Lowest intensity available (Lower REIL or REIL-Off)

Available systems will be indicated in the airport or military remarks, e.g., ACTIVATE HIRL Rwy 07–25, MALSR Rwy 07, and VASI Rwy 07—122.8.

Where the airport is not served by an instrument approach procedure and/or has an independent type system of different specification installed by the airport sponsor, descriptions of the type lights, method of control, and operating frequency will be explained in clear text. See AIM, "Basic Flight Information and ATC Procedures," for detailed description of pilot control of airport lighting.

RUNWAY SLOPE

When available, runway slope data will only be provided for those airports with an approved FAA instrument approach procedure. Runway slope will be shown only when it is 0.3 percent or greater. On runways less than 8000 feet, the direction of the slope up will be indicated, e.g., 0.3% up NW. On runways 8000 feet or greater, the slope will be shown (up or down) on the runway end line, e.g., RWY 13: 0.3% up., RWY 21: Pole. Rgt tfc. 0.4% down.

RUNWAY END DATA

Information pertaining to the runway approach end such as approach lights, touchdown zone lights, runway end identification lights, visual glideslope indicators, displaced thresholds, controlling obstruction, and right hand traffic pattern, will be shown on the specific runway end. "Rgt tfc"—Right traffic indicates right turns should be made on landing and takeoff for specified runway end.

LAND AND HOLD SHORT OPERATIONS (LAHSO)

LAHSO is an acronym for "Land and Hold Short Operations." These operations include landing and holding short of an intersection runway, an intersecting taxiway, or other predetermined points on the runway other than a runway or taxiway. Measured distance represents the available landing distance on the landing runway, in feet.

Specific questions regarding these distances should be referred to the air traffic manager of the facility concerned. The Aeronautical Information Manual contains specific details on hold–short operations and markings.

RUNWAY DECLARED DISTANCE INFORMATION

TORA—Take-off Run Available. The length of runway declared available and suitable for the ground run of an aeroplane take–off.

TODA—Take-off Distance Available. The length of the take–off run available plus the length of the clearway, if provided.

ASDA—Accelerate-Stop Distance Available. The length of the take–off run available plus the length of the stopway, if provided.

LDA—Landing Distance Available. The length of runway which is declared available and suitable for the ground run of an aeroplane landing.

22 ARRESTING GEAR/SYSTEMS

Arresting gear is shown as it is located on the runway. The a–gear distance from the end of the appropriate runway (or into the overrun) is indicated in parentheses. A–Gear which has a bi–direction capability and can be utilized for emergency approach end engagement is indicated by a (B). The direction of engaging device is indicated by an arrow. Up to 15 minutes advance notice may be required for rigging A–Gear for approach and engagement. Airport listing may show availability of other than US Systems. This information is provided for emergency requirements only. Refer to current aircraft operating manuals for specific engagement weight and speed criteria based on aircraft structural restrictions and arresting system limitations.

Following is a list of current systems referenced in this publication identified by both Air Force and Navy terminology:

NE, 09 FEB 20XX to 05 APR 20XX

Legend 9. – Chart Supplements U.S. (formerly Airport/Facility Directory).

DIRECTORY LEGEND 15

aircraft. When transient alert services are not shown, facilities are unknown. NO PRIORITY BASIS—means that transient alert services will be provided only after all the requirements for mission/tactical assigned aircraft have been accomplished.

29 AIRPORT REMARKS

The Attendance Schedule is the months, days and hours the airport is actually attended. Airport attendance does not mean watchman duties or telephone accessibility, but rather an attendant or operator on duty to provide at least minimum services (e.g., repairs, fuel, transportation).

Airport Remarks have been grouped in order of applicability. Airport remarks are limited to those items of information that are determined essential for operational use, i.e., conditions of a permanent or indefinite nature and conditions that will remain in effect for more than 30 days concerning aeronautical facilities, services, maintenance available, procedures or hazards, knowledge of which is essential for safe and efficient operation of aircraft. Information concerning permanent closing of a runway or taxiway will not be shown. A note "See Special Notices" shall be applied within this remarks section when a special notice applicable to the entry is contained in the Special Notices section of this publication.

Parachute Jumping indicates parachute jumping areas associated with the airport. See Parachute Jumping Area section of this publication for additional Information.

Landing Fee indicates landing charges for private or non-revenue producing aircraft. In addition, fees may be charged for planes that remain over a couple of hours and buy no services, or at major airline terminals for all aircraft.

Note: Unless otherwise stated, remarks including runway ends refer to the runway's approach end.

30 MILITARY REMARKS

Military Remarks published at a joint Civil/Military facility are remarks that are applicable to the Military. At Military Facilities all remarks will be published under the heading Military Remarks. Remarks contained in this section may not be applicable to civil users. The first group of remarks is applicable to the primary operator of the airport. Remarks applicable to a tenant on the airport are shown preceded by the tenant organization, i.e., (A) (AF) (N) (ANG), etc. Military airports operate 24 hours unless otherwise specified. Airport operating hours are listed first (airport operating hours will only be listed if they are different than the airport attended hours or if the attended hours are unavailable) followed by pertinent remarks in order of applicability. Remarks will include information on restrictions, hazards, traffic pattern, noise abatement, customs/agriculture/immigration, and miscellaneous information applicable to the Military.

Type of restrictions:

CLOSED: When designated closed, the airport is restricted from use by all aircraft unless stated otherwise. Any closure applying to specific type of aircraft or operation will be so stated. USN/USMC/USAF airports are considered closed during non–operating hours. Closed airports may be utilized during an emergency provided there is a safe landing area.

OFFICIAL BUSINESS ONLY: The airfield is closed to all transient military aircraft for obtaining routine services such as fueling, passenger drop off or pickup, practice approaches, parking, etc. The airfield may be used by aircrews and aircraft if official government business (including civilian) must be conducted on or near the airfield and prior permission is received from the airfield manager.

AF OFFICIAL BUSINESS ONLY OR NAVY OFFICIAL BUSINESS ONLY: Indicates that the restriction applies only to service indicated.

PRIOR PERMISSION REQUIRED (PPR): Airport is closed to transient aircraft unless approval for operation is obtained from the appropriate commander through Chief, Airfield Management or Airfield Operations Officer. Official Business or PPR does not preclude the use of US Military airports as an alternate for IFR flights. If a non–US military airport is used as a weather alternate and requires a PPR, the PPR must be requested and confirmed before the flight departs. The purpose of PPR is to control volume and flow of traffic rather than to prohibit it. Prior permission is required for all aircraft requiring transient alert service outside the published transient alert duty hours. All aircraft carrying hazardous materials must obtain prior permission as outlined in AFJI 11–204, AR 95–27, OPNAVINST 3710.7.

Note: OFFICIAL BUSINESS ONLY AND PPR restrictions are not applicable to Special Air Mission (SAM) or Special Air Resource (SPAR) aircraft providing person or persons on aboard are designated Code 6 or higher as explained in AFJMAN 11–213, AR 95–11, OPNAVINST 3722–8J. Official Business Only or PPR do not preclude the use of the airport as an alternate for IFR flights.

31 WEATHER DATA SOURCES

Weather data sources will be listed alphabetically followed by their assigned frequencies and/or telephone number and hours of operation.

ASOS—Automated Surface Observing System. Reports the same as an AWOS–3 plus precipitation identification and intensity, and freezing rain occurrence;

AWOS—Automated Weather Observing System

AWOS–A—reports altimeter setting (all other information is advisory only).

AWOS–AV—reports altimeter and visibility.

AWOS–1—reports altimeter setting, wind data and usually temperature, dew point and density altitude.

AWOS–2—reports the same as AWOS–1 plus visibility.

AWOS–3—reports the same as AWOS–1 plus visibility and cloud/ceiling data.

AWOS–3P reports the same as the AWOS–3 system, plus a precipitation identification sensor.

AWOS–3PT reports the same as the AWOS–3 system, plus precipitation identification sensor and a thunderstorm/lightning reporting capability.

AWOS–3T reports the same as AWOS–3 system and includes a thunderstorm/lightning reporting capability.

NE, 09 FEB 20XX to 05 APR 20XX

Legend 13. – Chart Supplements U.S. (formerly Airport/Facility Directory).

DIRECTORY LEGEND

See AIM, Basic Flight Information and ATC Procedures for detailed description of Weather Data Sources.

AWOS–4—reports same as AWOS–3 system, plus precipitation occurence, type and accumulation, freezing rain, thunderstorm, and runway surface sensors.

HIWAS—See RADIO AIDS TO NAVIGATION

LAWRS—Limited Aviation Weather Reporting Station where observers report cloud height, weather, obstructions to vision, temperature and dewpoint (in most cases), surface wind, altimeter and pertinent remarks.

LLWAS—indicates a Low Level Wind Shear Alert System consisting of a center field and several field perimeter anemometers.

SAWRS—identifies airports that have a Supplemental Aviation Weather Reporting Station available to pilots for current weather information.

SWSL—Supplemental Weather Service Location providing current local weather information via radio and telephone.

TDWR—indicates airports that have Terminal Doppler Weather Radar.

WSP—indicates airports that have Weather System Processor.

When the automated weather source is broadcast over an associated airport NAVAID frequency (see NAVAID line), it shall be indicated by a bold ASOS, AWOS, or HIWAS followed by the frequency, identifier and phone number, if available.

32 COMMUNICATIONS

Airport terminal control facilities and radio communications associated with the airport shall be shown. When the call sign is not the same as the airport name the call sign will be shown. Frequencies shall normally be shown in descending order with the primary frequency listed first. Frequencies will be listed, together with sectorization indicated by outbound radials, and hours of operation. Communications will be listed in sequence as follows:

Single Frequency Approach (SFA), Common Traffic Advisory Frequency (CTAF), Automatic Terminal Information Service (ATIS) and Aeronautical Advisory Stations (UNICOM) or (AUNICOM) along with their frequency is shown, where available, on the line following the heading "COMMUNICATIONS." When the CTAF and UNICOM frequencies are the same, the frequency will be shown as CTAF/UNICOM 122.8.

The FSS telephone nationwide is toll free 1–800–WX–BRIEF (1–800–992–7433). When the FSS is located on the field it will be indicated as "on arpt". Frequencies available at the FSS will follow in descending order. Remote Communications Outlet (RCO) providing service to the airport followed by the frequency and FSS RADIO name will be shown when available.

FSS's provide information on airport conditions, radio aids and other facilities, and process flight plans. Airport Advisory Service (AAS) is provided on the CTAF by FSS's for select non-tower airports or airports where the tower is not in operation.

(See AIM, Para 4–1–9 Traffic Advisory Practices at Airports Without Operating Control Towers or AC 90–42C.)

Aviation weather briefing service is provided by FSS specialists. Flight and weather briefing services are also available by calling the telephone numbers listed.

Remote Communications Outlet (RCO)—An unmanned air/ground communications facility that is remotely controlled and provides UHF or VHF communications capability to extend the service range of an FSS.

Civil Communications Frequencies-Civil communications frequencies used in the FSS air/ground system are operated on 122.0, 122.2, 123.6; emergency 121.5; plus receive-only on 122.1.

a. 122.0 is assigned as the Enroute Flight Advisory Service frequency at selected FSS RADIO outlets.
b. 122.2 is assigned as a common enroute frequency.
c. 123.6 is assigned as the airport advisory frequency at select non-tower locations. At airports with a tower, FSS may provide airport advisories on the tower frequency when tower is closed.
d. 122.1 is the primary receive-only frequency at VOR's.
e. Some FSS's are assigned 50 kHz frequencies in the 122–126 MHz band (eg. 122.45). Pilots using the FSS A/G system should refer to this directory or appropriate charts to determine frequencies available at the FSS or remoted facility through which they wish to communicate.

Emergency frequency 121.5 and 243.0 are available at all Flight Service Stations, most Towers, Approach Control and RADAR facilities.

Frequencies published followed by the letter "T" or "R", indicate that the facility will only transmit or receive respectively on that frequency. All radio aids to navigation (NAVAID) frequencies are transmit only.

TERMINAL SERVICES

SFA—Single Frequency Approach.

CTAF—A program designed to get all vehicles and aircraft at airports without an operating control tower on a common frequency.

ATIS—A continuous broadcast of recorded non-control information in selected terminal areas.

D–ATIS—Digital ATIS provides ATIS information in text form outside the standard reception range of conventional ATIS via landline & data link communications and voice message within range of existing transmitters.

AUNICOM—Automated UNICOM is a computerized, command response system that provides automated weather, radio check capability and airport advisory information selected from an automated menu by microphone clicks.

UNICOM—A non-government air/ground radio communications facility which may provide airport information.

PTD—Pilot to Dispatcher.

APP CON—Approach Control. The symbol Ⓡ indicates radar approach control.

TOWER—Control tower.

GCA—Ground Control Approach System.

GND CON—Ground Control.

GCO—Ground Communication Outlet—An unstaffed, remotely controlled, ground/ground communications facility. Pilots at

Legend 14. – Chart Supplements U.S. (formerly Airport/Facility Directory).

DIRECTORY LEGEND 17

uncontrolled airports may contact ATC and FSS via VHF to a telephone connection to obtain an instrument clearance or close a VFR or IFR flight plan. They may also get an updated weather briefing prior to takeoff. Pilots will use four "key clicks" on the VHF radio to contact the appropriate ATC facility or six "key clicks" to contact the FSS. The GCO system is intended to be used only on the ground.
DEP CON—Departure Control. The symbol ® indicates radar departure control.
CLNC DEL—Clearance Delivery.
PRE TAXI CLNC—Pre taxi clearance.

VFR ADVSY SVC—VFR Advisory Service. Service provided by Non-Radar Approach Control.
Advisory Service for VFR aircraft (upon a workload basis) ctc APP CON.
COMD POST—Command Post followed by the operator call sign in parenthesis.
PMSV—Pilot-to-Metro Service call sign, frequency and hours of operation, when full service is other than continuous. PMSV installations at which weather observation service is available shall be indicated, following the frequency and/or hours of operation as "Wx obsn svc 1900–0000Z‡" or "other times" may be used when no specific time is given. PMSV facilities manned by forecasters are considered "Full Service". PMSV facilities manned by weather observers are listed as "Limited Service".
OPS—Operations followed by the operator call sign in parenthesis.
CON
RANGE
FLT FLW—Flight Following
MEDIVAC
NOTE: Communication frequencies followed by the letter "X" indicate frequency available on request.

33 AIRSPACE

Information concerning Class B, C, and part-time D and E surface area airspace shall be published with effective times. Class D and E surface area airspace that is continuous as established by Rulemaking Docket will not be shown.
CLASS B—Radar Sequencing and Separation Service for all aircraft in CLASS B airspace.
CLASS C—Separation between IFR and VFR aircraft and sequencing of VFR arrivals to the primary airport.
TRSA—Radar Sequencing and Separation Service for participating VFR Aircraft within a Terminal Radar Service Area.
Class C, D, and E airspace described in this publication is that airspace usually consisting of a 5 NM radius core surface area that begins at the surface and extends upward to an altitude above the airport elevation (charted in MSL for Class C and Class D). Class E surface airspace normally extends from the surface up to but not including the overlying controlled airspace.
When part-time Class C or Class D airspace defaults to Class E, the core surface area becomes Class E. This will be formatted as:
AIRSPACE: CLASS C svc "times" ctc **APP CON** other times CLASS E:
or
AIRSPACE: CLASS D svc "times" other times CLASS E.
When a part-time Class C, Class D or Class E surface area defaults to Class G, the core surface area becomes Class G up to, but not including, the overlying controlled airspace. Normally, the overlying controlled airspace is Class E airspace beginning at either 700′ or 1200′ AGL and may be determined by consulting the relevant VFR Sectional or Terminal Area Charts. This will be formatted as:
AIRSPACE: CLASS C svc "times" ctc **APP CON** other times CLASS G, with CLASS E 700′ (or 1200′) AGL & abv:
or
AIRSPACE: CLASS D svc "times" other times CLASS G with CLASS E 700′ (or 1200′) AGL & abv:
or
AIRSPACE: CLASS E svc "times" other times CLASS G with CLASS E 700′ (or 1200′) AGL & abv.
NOTE: AIRSPACE SVC "TIMES" INCLUDE ALL ASSOCIATED ARRIVAL EXTENSIONS. Surface area arrival extensions for instrument approach procedures become part of the primary core surface area. These extensions may be either Class D or Class E airspace and are effective concurrent with the times of the primary core surface area. For example, when a part-time Class C, Class D or Class E surface area defaults to Class G, the associated arrival extensions will default to Class G at the same time. When a part-time Class C or Class D surface area defaults to Class E, the arrival extensions will remain in effect as Class E airspace.
NOTE: CLASS E AIRSPACE EXTENDING UPWARD FROM 700 FEET OR MORE ABOVE THE SURFACE, DESIGNATED IN CONJUNCTION WITH AN AIRPORT WITH AN APPROVED INSTRUMENT PROCEDURE.
Class E 700′ AGL (shown as magenta vignette on sectional charts) and 1200′ AGL (blue vignette) areas are designated when necessary to provide controlled airspace for transitioning to/from the terminal and enroute environments. Unless otherwise specified, these 700′/1200′ AGL Class E airspace areas remain in effect continuously, regardless of airport operating hours or surface area status. These transition areas should not be confused with surface areas or arrival extensions.
(See Chapter 3, AIRSPACE, in the Aeronautical Information Manual for further details)

NE, 09 FEB 20XX to 05 APR 20XX

Legend 15. – Chart Supplements U.S. (formerly Airport/Facility Directory).

18 **DIRECTORY LEGEND**

34 RADIO AIDS TO NAVIGATION

The Airport/Facility Directory lists, by facility name, all Radio Aids to Navigation that appear on FAA, AeroNav Products Visual or IFR Aeronautical Charts and those upon which the FAA has approved an Instrument Approach Procedure, with exception of selected TACANs. Military TACAN information will be published for Military facilities contained in this publication. All VOR, VORTAC, TACAN, ILS and MLS equipment in the National Airspace System has an automatic monitoring and shutdown feature in the event of malfunction. Unmonitored, as used in this publication, for any navigational aid, means that monitoring personnel cannot observe the malfunction or shutdown signal. The NAVAID NOTAM file identifier will be shown as "NOTAM FILE IAD" and will be listed on the Radio Aids to Navigation line. When two or more NAVAIDS are listed and the NOTAM file identifier is different from that shown on the Radio Aids to Navigation line, it will be shown with the NAVAID listing. NOTAM file identifiers for ILSs and its components (e.g., NDB (LOM) are the same as the associated airports and are not repeated. Automated Surface Observing System (ASOS), Automated Weather Observing System (AWOS), and Hazardous Inflight Weather Advisory Service (HIWAS) will be shown when this service is broadcast over selected NAVAIDs.

NAVAID information is tabulated as indicated in the following sample:

TACAN/DME Channel — Geographical Position — Site Elevation

NAME (L) ABVORTAC 117.55 ABE Chan 122(Y) N40°43.60′ W75°27.30′ 180°4.1 NM to fld. 1110/8E. **AWOS. HIWAS.**

Class — Frequency — Identifier — Bearing and distance facility to center of airport — Magnetic Variation — Automated Weather Observing System — Hazardous Inflight Weather Advisory Service

VOR unusable 020°–060° byd 26 NM blo 3,500′

Restriction within the normal altitude/range of the navigational aid (See primary alphabetical listing for restrictions on VORTAC and VOR/DME).

Note: Those DME channel numbers with a (Y) suffix require TACAN to be placed in the "Y" mode to receive distance information.

HIWAS—Hazardous Inflight Weather Advisory Service is a continuous broadcast of inflight weather advisories including summarized SIGMETs, convective SIGMETs, AIRMETs and urgent PIREPs. HIWAS is presently broadcast over selected VOR's throughout the U.S.

ASR/PAR—Indicates that Surveillance (ASR) or Precision (PAR) radar instrument approach minimums are published in the U.S. Terminal Procedures. Only part-time hours of operation will be shown.

RADIO CLASS DESIGNATIONS

VOR/DME/TACAN Standard Service Volume (SSV) Classifications

SSV Class	Altitudes	Distance (NM)
(T) Terminal	1000′ to 12,000′	25
(L) Low Altitude	1000′ to 18,000′	40
(H) High Altitude	1000′ to 14,500′	40
	14,500′ to 18,000′	100
	18,000′ to 45,000′	130
	45,000′ to 60,000′	100

NOTE: Additionally, (H) facilities provide (L) and (T) service volume and (L) facilities provide (T) service. Altitudes are with respect to the station's site elevation. Coverage is not available in a cone of airspace directly above the facility.

CONTINUED ON NEXT PAGE

NE, 09 FEB 20XX to 05 APR 20XX

Legend 16. – Chart Supplements U.S. (formerly Airport/Facility Directory).

DIRECTORY LEGEND 19

CONTINUED FROM PRECEDING PAGE

The term VOR is, operationally, a general term covering the VHF omnidirectional bearing type of facility without regard to the fact that the power, the frequency protected service volume, the equipment configuration, and operational requirements may vary between facilities at different locations.

AB	Automatic Weather Broadcast.
DF	Direction Finding Service.
DME	UHF standard (TACAN compatible) distance measuring equipment.
DME(Y)	UHF standard (TACAN compatible) distance measuring equipment that require TACAN to be placed in the "Y" mode to receive DME.
GS	Glide slope.
H	Non-directional radio beacon (homing), power 50 watts to less than 2,000 watts (50 NM at all altitudes).
HH	Non-directional radio beacon (homing), power 2,000 watts or more (75 NM at all altitudes).
H-SAB	Non-directional radio beacons providing automatic transcribed weather service.
ILS	Instrument Landing System (voice, where available, on localizer channel).
IM	Inner marker.
ISMLS	Interim Standard Microwave Landing System.
LDA	Localizer Directional Aid.
LMM	Compass locator station when installed at middle marker site (15 NM at all altitudes).
LOM	Compass locator station when installed at outer marker site (15 NM at all altitudes).
MH	Non-directional radio beacon (homing) power less than 50 watts (25 NM at all altitudes).
MLS	Microwave Landing System.
MM	Middle marker.
OM	Outer marker.
S	Simultaneous range homing signal and/or voice.
SABH	Non-directional radio beacon not authorized for IFR or ATC. Provides automatic weather broadcasts.
SDF	Simplified Direction Facility.
TACAN	UHF navigational facility-omnidirectional course and distance information.
VOR	VHF navigational facility-omnidirectional course only.
VOR/DME	Collocated VOR navigational facility and UHF standard distance measuring equipment.
VORTAC	Collocated VOR and TACAN navigational facilities.
W	Without voice on radio facility frequency.
Z	VHF station location marker at a LF radio facility.

NE, 09 FEB 20XX to 05 APR 20XX

Legend 17. – Chart Supplements U.S. (formerly Airport/Facility Directory).

9.7 *NOTICES TO AIRMEN PUBLICATION (NTAP)*

1. The Notices to Airmen (NOTAM) system disseminates time-critical aeronautical information that either is of a temporary nature or is not sufficiently known in advance to permit publication on aeronautical charts or in other operational publications.
   a. NOTAMs contain aeronautical information that could affect your decision to make a flight.
2. NOTAMs are grouped into five types:
   a. **NOTAM (D)** includes information such as airport or primary runway closures; changes in the status of navigational aids, ILSs, and radar service availability; and other information essential to planned en route, terminal, or landing operations. Also included is information on airport taxiways, aprons, ramp areas, and associated lighting.
   b. **FDC NOTAMs** are issued by the Flight Data Center and contain regulatory information such as amendments to published instrument approach charts and other current aeronautical charts.
   c. **Pointer NOTAMs** reduce total NOTAM volume by pointing to other NOTAM (D) and FDC NOTAMs rather than duplicating potentially unnecessary information for an airport or NAVAID. They allow pilots to reference NOTAMs that might not be listed under a given airport or NAVAID identifier.
   d. **SAA NOTAMs** are issued when Special Activity Airspace (SAA) will be active outside the published schedule times and when required by the published schedule, although pilots must still check published schedule times for SAA as well as any other NOTAMs for that airspace.
   e. **Military NOTAMs** reference military airports and NAVAIDs and are rarely of any interest to civilian pilots.
3. The ***Notices to Airmen Publication (NTAP)*** is issued every 28 days and is an integral part of the NOTAM system. Once a NOTAM is published in the *NTAP*, the NOTAM is not provided during pilot weather briefings unless specifically requested.
   a. The *NTAP* contains (D) NOTAMs that are expected to remain in effect for an extended period and FDC NOTAMs that are current at the time of publication.

QUESTIONS AND ANSWER EXPLANATIONS: All of the private pilot knowledge test questions chosen by the FAA for release as well as additional questions selected by Gleim relating to the material in the previous outlines are reproduced on the following pages. These questions have been organized into the same subunits as the outlines. To the immediate right of each question are the correct answer and answer explanation. You should cover these answers and answer explanations while responding to the questions. Refer to the general discussion in the Introduction on how to take the FAA knowledge test.

Remember that the questions from the FAA knowledge test bank have been reordered by topic and organized into a meaningful sequence. Also, the first line of the answer explanation gives the citation of the authoritative source for the answer.

QUESTIONS

9.1 Longitude and Latitude

1. (Refer to Figure 22 on page 303.) (Refer to area 3.) Determine the approximate latitude and longitude of Shoshone County Airport.

A. 47°02'N – 116°11'W.

B. 47°33'N – 116°11'W.

C. 47°32'N – 116°41'W.

Answer (B) is correct. *(PHAK Chap 16)*

DISCUSSION: Shoshone County Airport is below 3, just west of the 116° line of longitude (find the 116° line in the 8,000 MSL northeast of Shoshone). There are 60 min. between the 116° line and the 117° line, depicted in 1-min. tick marks. Shoshone is 11 tick marks (11 min.) past the 116° line. Find the labeled 48° latitude line just northeast of the 116° line. The latitude and longitude lines are presented each 30 min. Since lines of latitude are also divided into 1 min. tick marks, the airport is three tick marks above the 47°30' line or 47°33'N. The correct latitude and longitude is thus 47°33'N – 116°11'W.

Answer (A) is incorrect. Shoshone Airport is just north of the 47°30' line of latitude (not the 47°00' line). Answer (C) is incorrect. Shoshone Airport is 11 ticks past the 116°00' line of longitude (not the 116°30' line).

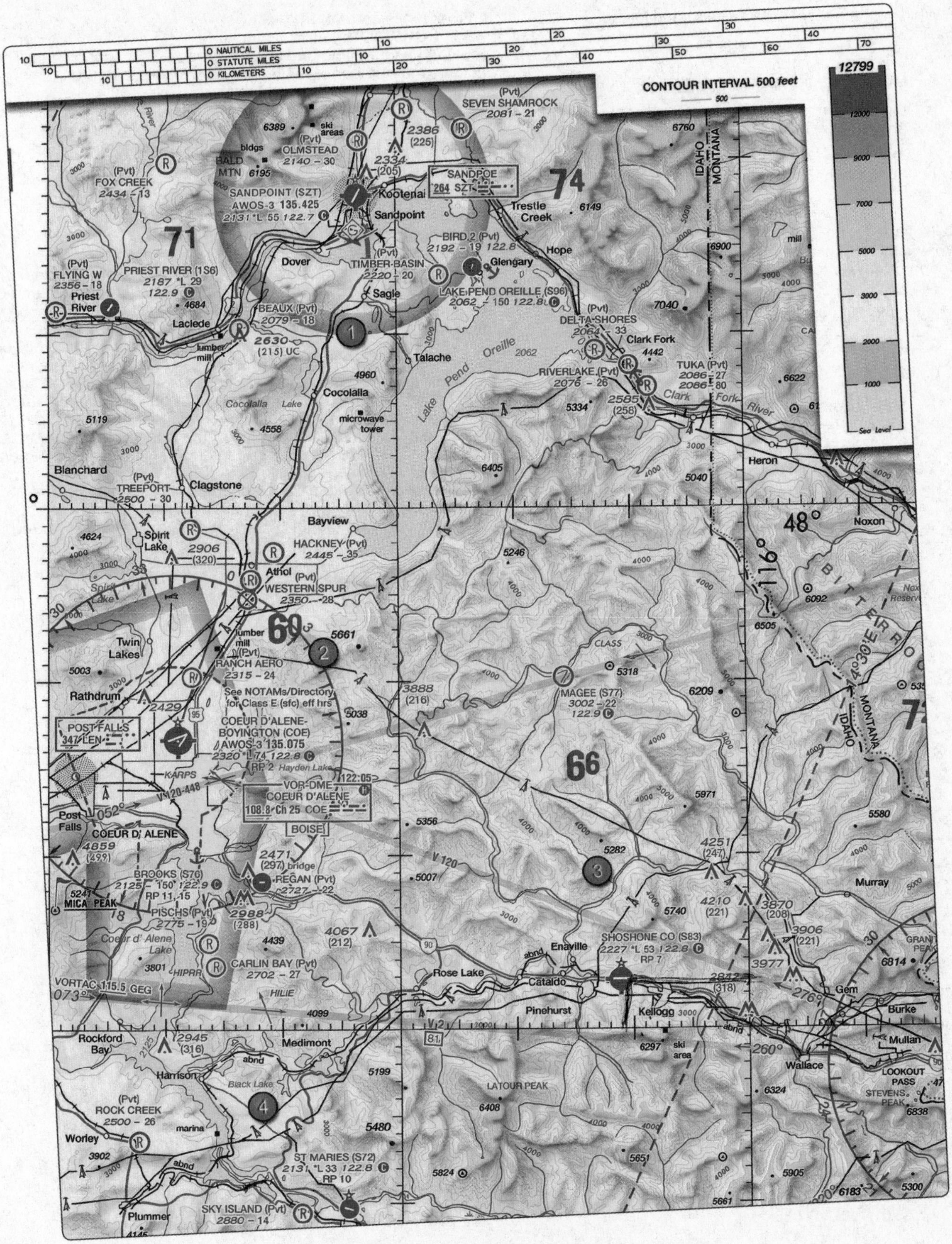

Figure 22. – Sectional Chart Excerpt.
NOTE: Chart is not to scale and should not be used for navigation. Use associated scale.

2. Which statement about longitude and latitude is true?

A. Lines of longitude are parallel to the Equator.

B. Lines of longitude cross the Equator at right angles.

C. The 0° line of latitude passes through Greenwich, England.

Answer (B) is correct. *(PHAK Chap 16)*

DISCUSSION: Lines of longitude are drawn from the north pole to the south pole and cross the equator at right angles. They indicate the number of degrees east and west of the 0° line of longitude, which passes through Greenwich, England.

Answer (A) is incorrect. Lines of latitude, not longitude, are parallel to the equator. Answer (C) is incorrect. The 0° line of longitude, not latitude, passes through Greenwich, England.

3. (Refer to Figure 26 on page 305.) (Refer to area 2.) What is the approximate latitude and longitude of Cooperstown Airport?

A. 47°25'N – 98°06'W.

B. 47°25'N – 99°54'W.

C. 47°55'N – 98°06'W.

Answer (A) is correct. *(PHAK Chap 16)*

DISCUSSION: First locate the Cooperstown Airport on Fig. 26. It is just above 2, middle right of chart. Note that it is to the left (west) of the 98° line of longitude. The line of longitude on the left side of the chart is 99°. Thus, the longitude is a little bit more than 98°W, but not near 99°W.

With respect to latitude, note that Cooperstown Airport is just below a line of latitude that is not marked in terms of degrees. However, the next line of latitude below is 47° (see the left side of the chart, northwest of Jamestown Airport). As with longitude, there are two lines of latitude for every degree of latitude; i.e., each line is 30 min. Thus, latitude of the Cooperstown Airport is almost 47°30'N, but not quite. Accordingly, Cooperstown Airport's latitude is 47°25'N and longitude is 98°06'W.

Answer (B) is incorrect. Cooperstown is just west of the 98° line of longitude (not just east of 99°). Answer (C) is incorrect. Cooperstown is just south of the 47°30' line of latitude (not the 48°00' line).

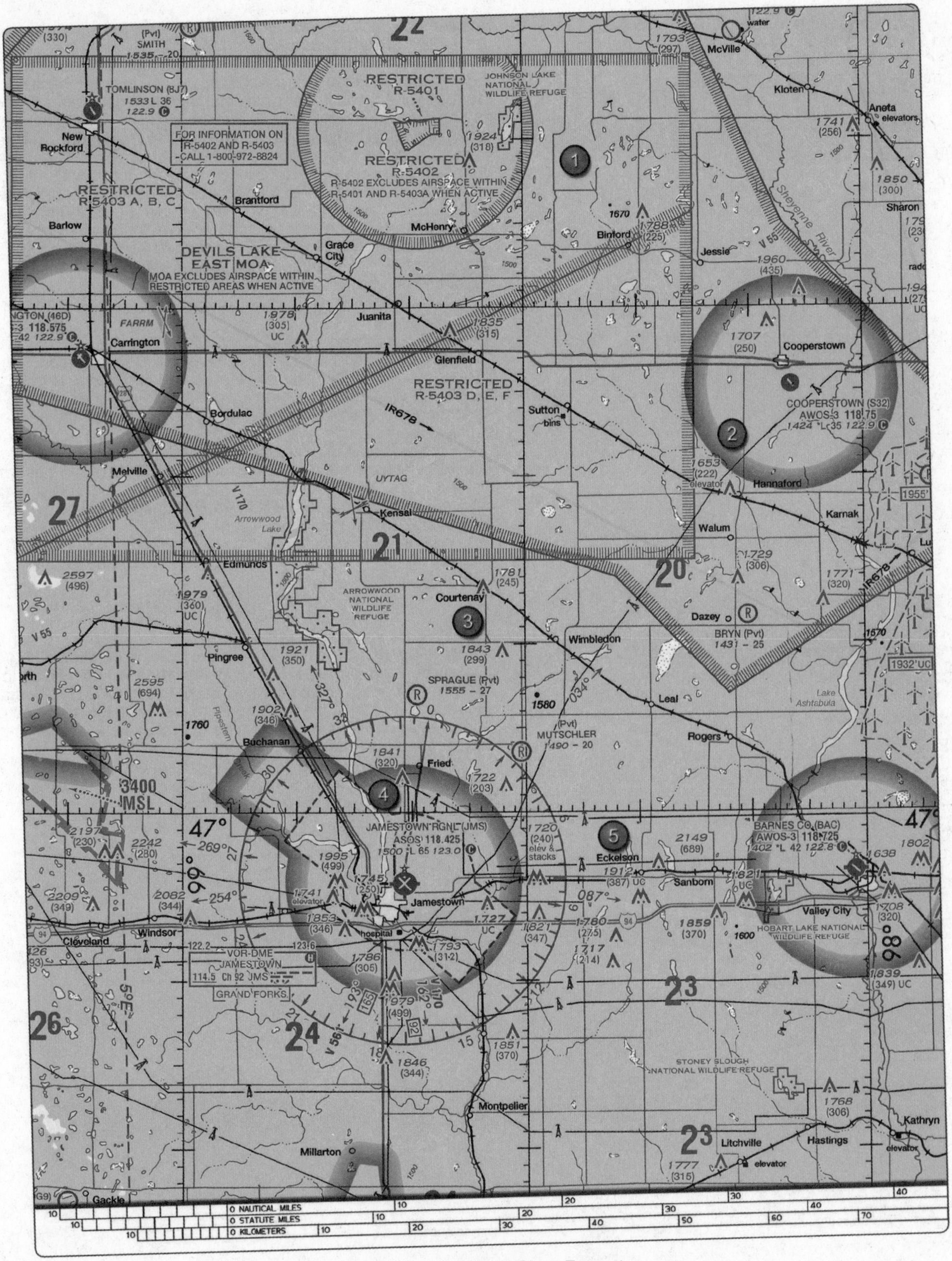

Figure 26. – Sectional Chart Excerpt.
NOTE: Chart is not to scale and should not be used for navigation. Use associated scale.

4. (Refer to Figure 21 on page 307.) (Refer to area 2.) Which airport is located at approximately 47° 41 minutes 00 seconds N latitude and 101° 36 minutes 00 seconds W longitude?

A. Fischer.

B. Crooked Lake.

C. Johnson.

Answer (A) is correct. *(PH SU 9)*

DISCUSSION: You are asked to locate an airport at 47°41'00"N latitude and 101°36'00"W longitude. Referring to the chart, find the longitude (vertical) 101° W line (increases to the west) and the latitude (horizontal) 48° line (decreases to the south). The longitude line to the west of 101° is 101° 30 min. (each additional crossline is 1 min.). Find 101°36 min. by moving west six additional crosslines. The latitude line south of 48° is 47° 30 min. (each additional crossline is 1 min.). Find 47° 41 min. by moving north an additional 11 crosslines. These two coordinates (101°36'00"W and 47°30'00"N) intersect over Fischer Airfield.

Answer (B) is incorrect. It is not shown on the referenced chart. Answer (C) is incorrect. The coordinates for Johnson are approximately 47° 27 minutes 00 seconds N latitude and 100° 50 minutes 00 seconds W.

5. (Refer to Figure 21 on page 307.) (Refer to area 2.) Which airport is located at approximately 47°34'30"N latitude and 100°43'00"W longitude?

A. Linrud.

B. Makeeff.

C. Johnson.

Answer (B) is correct. *(PHAK Chap 16)*

DISCUSSION: On Fig. 21, you are asked to locate an airport at 47°34'30"N latitude and 100°43'W longitude. Note that the 101°W longitude line runs down the middle of the figure. Accordingly, the airport you are seeking is 17 min. to the east of that line.

Each crossline is 1 min. on the latitude and longitude lines. The 48°N latitude line is approximately two-thirds of the way up the chart. The 47°30'N latitude line is about one-fourth of the way up. One-third up from 47°30'N to 48°N latitude would be 47°39'N. At this spot is Makeeff Airport.

Answer (A) is incorrect. Linrud is north of the 48°N latitude line. Answer (C) is incorrect. Johnson is south of the 47°30'N latitude line.

6. (Refer to Figure 21 on page 307.) (Refer to area 3.) Which airport is located at approximately 47°21'N latitude and 101°01'W longitude?

A. Underwood.

B. Pietsch.

C. Washburn.

Answer (C) is correct. *(PHAK Chap 16)*

DISCUSSION: On Fig. 21, find the 48° line of latitude (2/3 up the figure). Start at the 47°30' line of latitude (the line below the 48° line) and count down nine tick marks to the 47°21'N tick mark and draw a horizontal line on the chart. Next find the 101° line of longitude and go left one tick mark and draw a vertical line. The closest airport is Washburn.

Answer (A) is incorrect. Underwood is a city (not an airport) northwest of Washburn by about 1 in. Answer (B) is incorrect. Pietsch is north of the 48°00' latitude line.

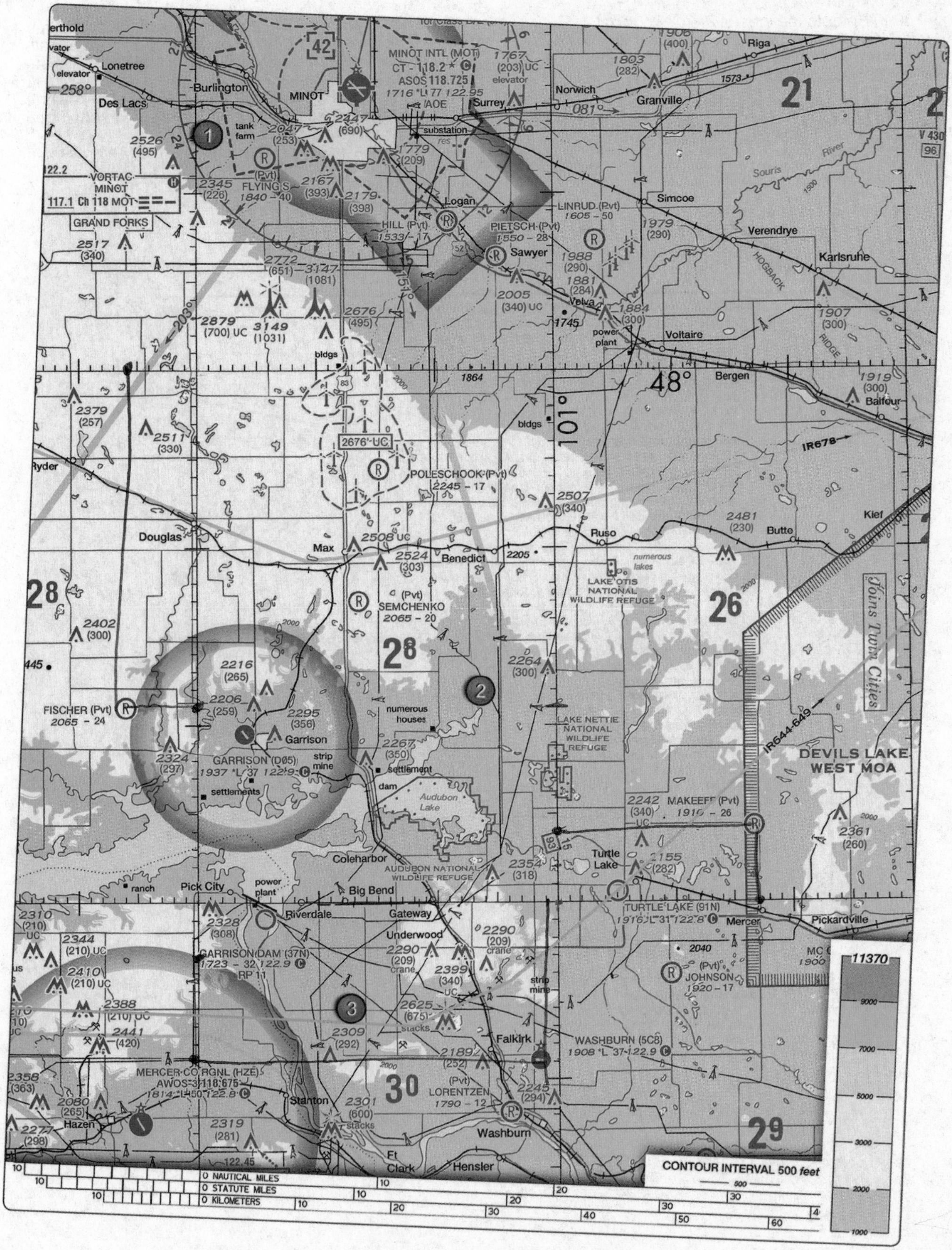

Figure 21. – Sectional Chart Excerpt.
NOTE: Chart is not to scale and should not be used for navigation. Use associated scale.

7. (Refer to Figure 77 below, and Figure 76 on page 309.) Refer to the area of Pierre Regional Airport (N44°22.96' W100°17.16"). What frequency can be monitored for Hazardous Inflight Weather Advisory Service in this area?

A. 119.025 MHz.

B. 112.5 MHz.

C. 122.2 MHz.

Answer (B) is correct. *(Chart Supplement)*

DISCUSSION: Fig. 77 is the Chart Supplement excerpt for Pierre Regional Airport. Look for the section titled "Weather Data Sources." In that line, you will see "HIWAS." This is the Hazardous Inflight Weather Advisory Service frequency, 112.5. It is also located on Fig. 76 in the Pierre VOR frequency and identifier box. It is depicted by the "H" within a darkened circle in the top right corner of the box.

Answer (A) is incorrect. This is the ASOS (Automated Surface Observing System) frequency, not the HIWAS frequency. Answer (C) is incorrect. The RCO (Remote Communications Outlet) frequency is 122.2.

340 **SOUTH DAKOTA**

PIERRE RGNL (PIR) 3 E UTC–6(–5DT) N44°22.96′ W100°17.16′ **OMAHA**
1744 B S4 **FUEL** 100LL, JET A OX 1, 2, 3, 4 Class I, ARFF Index A NOTAM FILE PIR **H–2I, L–12H**
RWY 13–31: H6900X100 (ASPH-GRVD) S-91, D-108, 2S-137, 2D-168 HIRL **IAP**
RWY 13: REIL. PAPI(P4L)—GA 3.0 ° TCH 52′.
RWY 31: MALSR. PAPI(P4L)—GA 3.0 ° TCH 52′.
RWY 07–25: H6881X150 (ASPH-GRVD) S-91, D-114, 2S-145, 2D-180 HIRL 0.6% up W
RWY 07: REIL. PAPI(P4L)—GA 3.0 ° TCH 47′. Tank.
RWY 25: REIL. PAPI(P4L)—GA 3.0 ° TCH 54′.

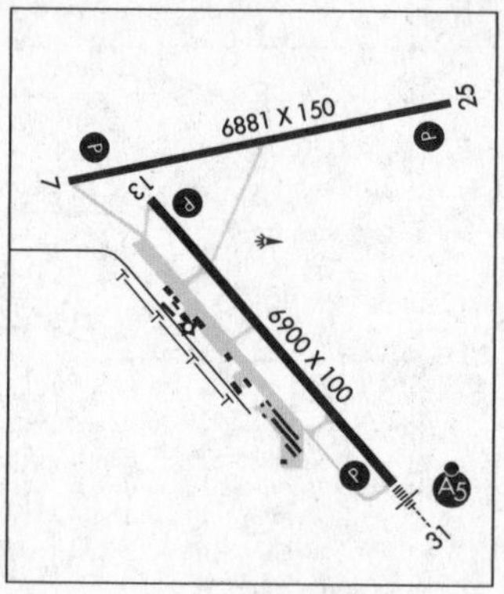

RUNWAY DECLARED DISTANCE INFORMATION

RWY 07:	TORA-6881	TODA-6881	ASDA-6830	LDA-6830
RWY 13:	TORA-6900	TODA-6900	ASDA-6900	LDA-6900
RWY 25:	TORA-6881	TODA-6881	ASDA-6881	LDA-6881
RWY 31:	TORA-6900	TODA-6900	ASDA-6900	LDA-6900

AIRPORT REMARKS: Attended Mon–Fri 1100–0600Z‡, Sat–Sun 1100–0400Z‡. For attendant other times call 605-224-9000/8621. Arpt conditions unmonitored during 0530–1000Z‡. Numerous non-radio acft operating in area. Birds on and invof arpt and within a 25 NM radius. No line of sight between rwy ends of Rwy 07–25. ARFF provided for part 121 air carrier ops only. 48 hr PPR for unscheduled acr ops involving acft designed for 31 or more passenger seats call 605-773-7447 or 605-773-7405. Taxiway C is 50 ′ wide and restricted to acft 75,000 pounds or less. ACTIVATE HIRL Rwy 13-31 and Rwy 07-25, MALSR Rwy 31, REIL Rwy 07, Rwy 13 and Rwy 25, PAPI Rwy 07, Rwy 25, Rwy 13 and Rwy 31—CTAF 122.7. NOTE: See Special Notices Section—Aerobatic Practice Areas.
WEATHER DATA SOURCES: ASOS 119.025 (605) 224-6087. **HIWAS** 112.5 PIR.
COMMUNICATIONS: CTAF 122.7 **UNICOM** 122.95
RCO 122.2 (HURON RADIO)
® **MINNEAPOLIS CENTER APP/DEP CON** 125.1
RADIO AIDS TO NAVIGATION: NOTAM FILE PIR.
(L) VORTACW 112.5 PIR Chan 72 N44 °23.67′ W100°09.77′ 251° 5.3 NM to fld. 1789/11E. **HIWAS.**
ILS/DME 111.9 I-PIR Chan 56 Rwy 31. Class IA ILS GS unusable for coupled apch blo 2,255 ′. GS unusable blo 2135 ′.

PINE RIDGE (IEN) 2 E UTC –7(–6DT) N43°01.35′ W102°30.66′ **CHEYENNE**
3333 B NOTAM FILE IEN **H–5B, L–12G**
RWY 12–30: H5000X60 (ASPH) S-12 MIRL 0.7% up SE **IAP**
RWY 12: P-line.
RWY 30: PAPI(P2L)—GA 3.0 ° TCH 26′. Fence.
RWY 06–24: H3003X50 (ASPH) S-12 0.7% up NE
RWY 24: Fence.
AIRPORT REMARKS: Unattended. Rwy 06-24 CLOSED indef. MIRL Rwy 12-30 and PAPI Rwy 30 opr dusk–0530Z‡, after 0530Z‡ ACTIVATE—CTAF.
WEATHER DATA SOURCES: ASOS 126.775 (605) 867-1584.
COMMUNICATIONS: CTAF 122.9
DENVER CENTER APP/DEP CON 127.95
RADIO AIDS TO NAVIGATION: NOTAM FILE RAP.
RAPID CITY (H) VORTAC 112.3 RAP Chan 70 N43 °58.56′ W103°00.74′ 146° 61.3 NM to fld. 3160/13E.

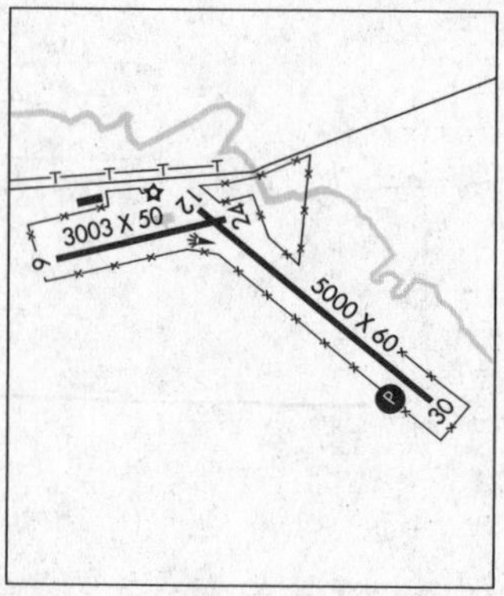

Figure 77. – Chart Supplements U.S. (formerly Airport/Facility Directory).

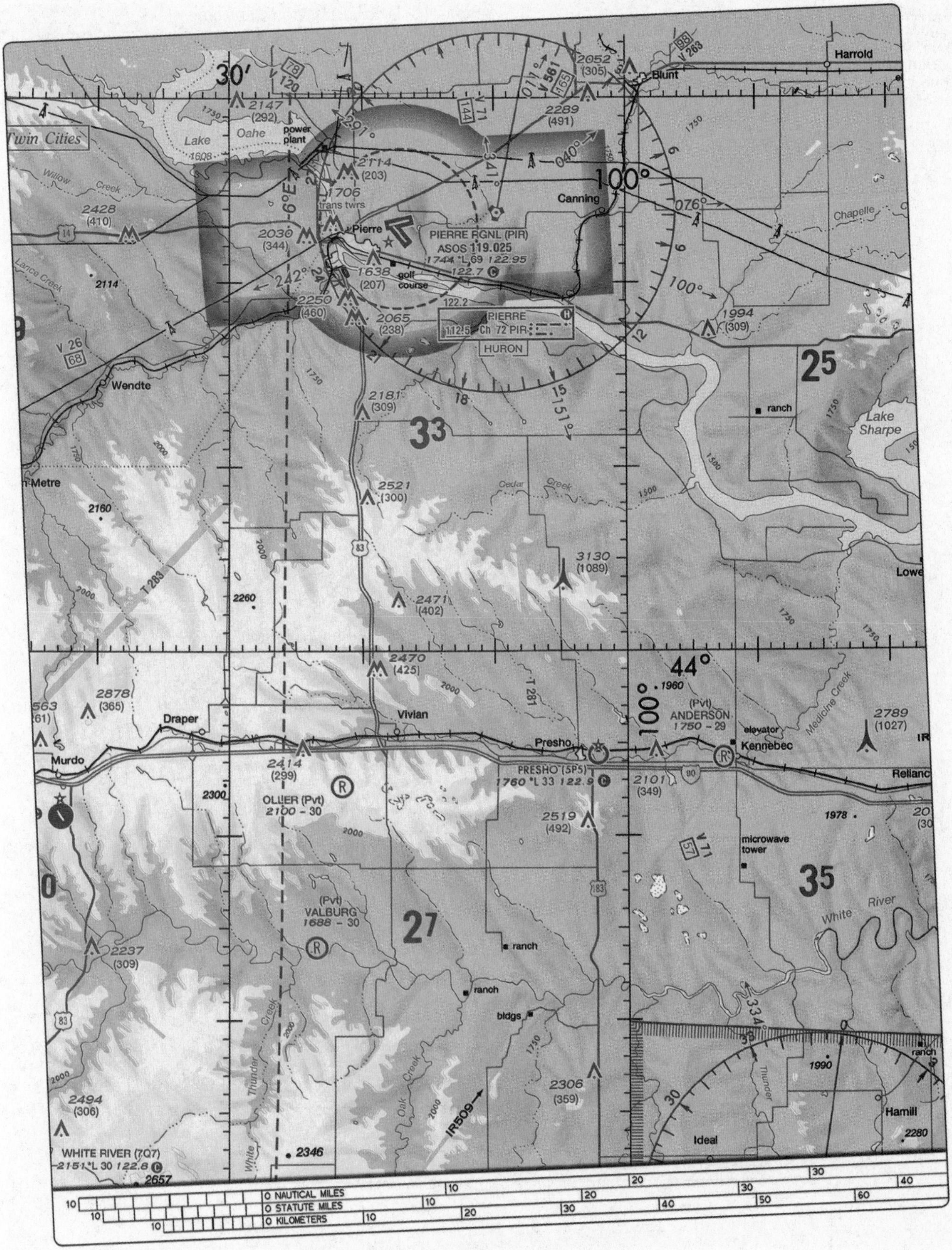

Figure 76. – Sectional Chart Excerpt.
NOTE: Chart is not to scale and should not be used for navigation. Use associated scale.

8. (Refer to Figure 79 below, and Figure 78 on page 311.) At Sioux Gateway/Col Day (N42°20.67' W96°19.42'), which frequency should be used as a Common Traffic Advisory Frequency (CTAF) to self-announce position and intentions when the control tower is closed?

A. 122.95 MHz.

B. 119.45 MHz.

C. 118.7 MHz.

Answer (C) is correct. *(Chart Supplement)*

DISCUSSION: Fig. 79 is the Chart Supplement excerpt for Sioux Gateway/Col Day Airport. Look for the section titled “Communications.” On that same line, it states that the CTAF frequency is 118.7. It is also located on Fig. 78 in the Sioux Gateway Airport Data Description, indicated by a “C” surrounded by a shaded blue circle.

Answer (A) is incorrect. This is the UNICOM frequency, not the CTAF frequency. Answer (B) is incorrect. The ATIS (Automatic Terminal Information Service) frequency is 119.45 and is not the CTAF frequency.

64 **IOWA**

SIOUX CITY N42°20.67′ W96°19.42′ NOTAM FILE SUX **OMAHA**
(L) VORTAC 116.5 SUX Chan 112 313 ° 4.4 NM to Sioux Gateway/Col Bud Day Fld. 1087/9E. **HIWAS.** **L–12I**
VOR unusable:
280°–292° byd 25 NM
293°–305° byd 20 NM blo 4,500′
293°–305° byd 35 NM
306°–350° byd 20 NM blo 3,000′
350°–280° byd 30 NM blo 3,000′
RCO 122.45 122.1R 116.5T (FORT DODGE RADIO)

SIOUX CITY
SIOUX GATEWAY/COL BUD DAY FLD (SUX) 6 S UTC –6(–5DT) N42°24.16′ W96°23.06′ **OMAHA**
1098 B S4 **FUEL** 100LL, 115, JET A OX 1, 2, 3, 4 Class I, ARFF Index–See Remarks **H–5C, L–12I**
NOTAM FILE SUX **IAP, AD**
RWY 13–31: H9002X150 (CONC–GRVD) S–100, D–120, 2S–152, 2D–220 HIRL
RWY 13: MALS. VASI(V4L)—GA 3.0 ° TCH 49′. Tree.
RWY 31: MALSR. VASI(V4L)—GA 3.0 ° TCH 50′.
RWY 17–35: H6600X150 (ASPH–PFC) S–65, D–80, 2S–102, 2D–130 MIRL
RWY 17: REIL. VASI(V4R)—GA 3.0 ° TCH 50′. Trees.
RWY 35: PAPI(P4L)—GA 3.0 ° TCH 54′. Pole.
LAND AND HOLD SHORT OPERATIONS

LANDING	HOLD SHORT POINT	DIST AVBL
RWY 13	17–35	5400
RWY 17	13–31	5650

ARRESTING GEAR/SYSTEM
RWY 13 ←BAK–14 BAK–12B(B) (1392′) BAK–14 BAK–12B(B) (1492′) →**RWY 31**

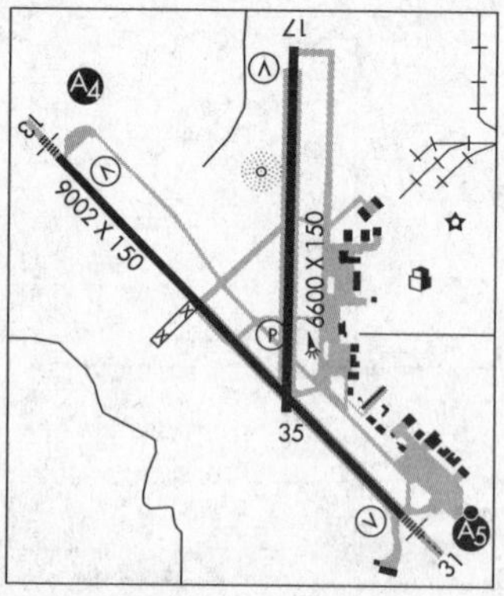

AIRPORT REMARKS: Attended continuously. PAEW 0330–1200Z ‡ during inclement weather Nov–Apr. AER 31–BAK–12/14 located (1492 ′) from thld. Airfield surface conditions not monitored by arpt management between 0600–1000Z ‡ daily. Rwy 13–BAK–12/14 located (1392 ′) from thld. All A–gear avbl only during ANG flying ops. Twr has limited visibility southeast of ramp near ARFF bldg and northeast of Rwy 31 touchdown zone. Rwy 31 is calm wind rwy. Class I, ARFF Index B. ARFF Index E fire fighting equipment avbl on request. Twy F unlit, retro–reflective markers in place. Portions of Twy A SE of Twy B not visible by twr and is designated a non–movement area. Rwy 13–31 touchdown and rollout rwy visual range avbl. When twr clsd, ACTIVATE HIRL Rwy 13–31; MIRL Rwy 17–35; MALS Rwy 13; MALSR Rwy 31; and REIL Rwy 17—CTAF.
WEATHER DATA SOURCES: ASOS (712) 255–6474. **HIWAS** 116.5 SUX. LAWRS.
COMMUNICATIONS: CTAF 118.7 **ATIS** 119.45 **UNICOM** 122.95
SIOUX CITY RCO 122.45 122.1R 116.5T (FORT DODGE RADIO)
Ⓡ **SIOUX CITY APP/DEP CON** 124.6 (1200–0330Z‡)
Ⓡ **MINNEAPOLIS CENTER APP/DEP CON** 124.1 (0330–1200Z‡)
SIOUX CITY TOWER 118.7 (1200–0330Z‡) **GND CON** 121.9
AIRSPACE: CLASS D svc 1200–0330Z‡ other times CLASS E.
RADIO AIDS TO NAVIGATION: NOTAM FILE SUX.
SIOUX CITY (L) VORTAC 116.5 SUX Chan 112 N42 °20.67′ W96°19.42′ 313° 4.4 NM to fld. 1087/9E. **HIWAS.**
NDB (MHW) 233 GAK N42°24.49′ W96°23.16′ at fld.
SALIX NDB (MHW/LOM) 414 SU N42°19.65′ W96°17.43′ 311° 6.1 NM to fld. Unmonitored.
TOMMI NDB (MHW/LOM) 305 OI N42°27.61′ W96°27.73′ 128° 4.9 NM to fld. Unmonitored.
ILS 109.3 I–SUX Rwy 31 Class IT. LOM SALIX NDB. ILS Unmonitored when twr clsd. Glide path unusable coupled approach (CPD) blo 1805 ′.
ILS 111.3 I–OIQ Rwy 13 LOM TOMMI NDB. Localizer shutdown when twr clsd.
ASR (1200–0330Z‡)

SNORE N43°13.96′ W95°19.66′ NOTAM FILE SPW. **OMAHA**
NDB (LOM) 394 SP 121° 6.8 NM to Spencer Muni.

SOUTHEAST IOWA RGNL (See BURLINGTON)

Figure 79. – Chart Supplements U.S. (formerly Airport/Facility Directory).

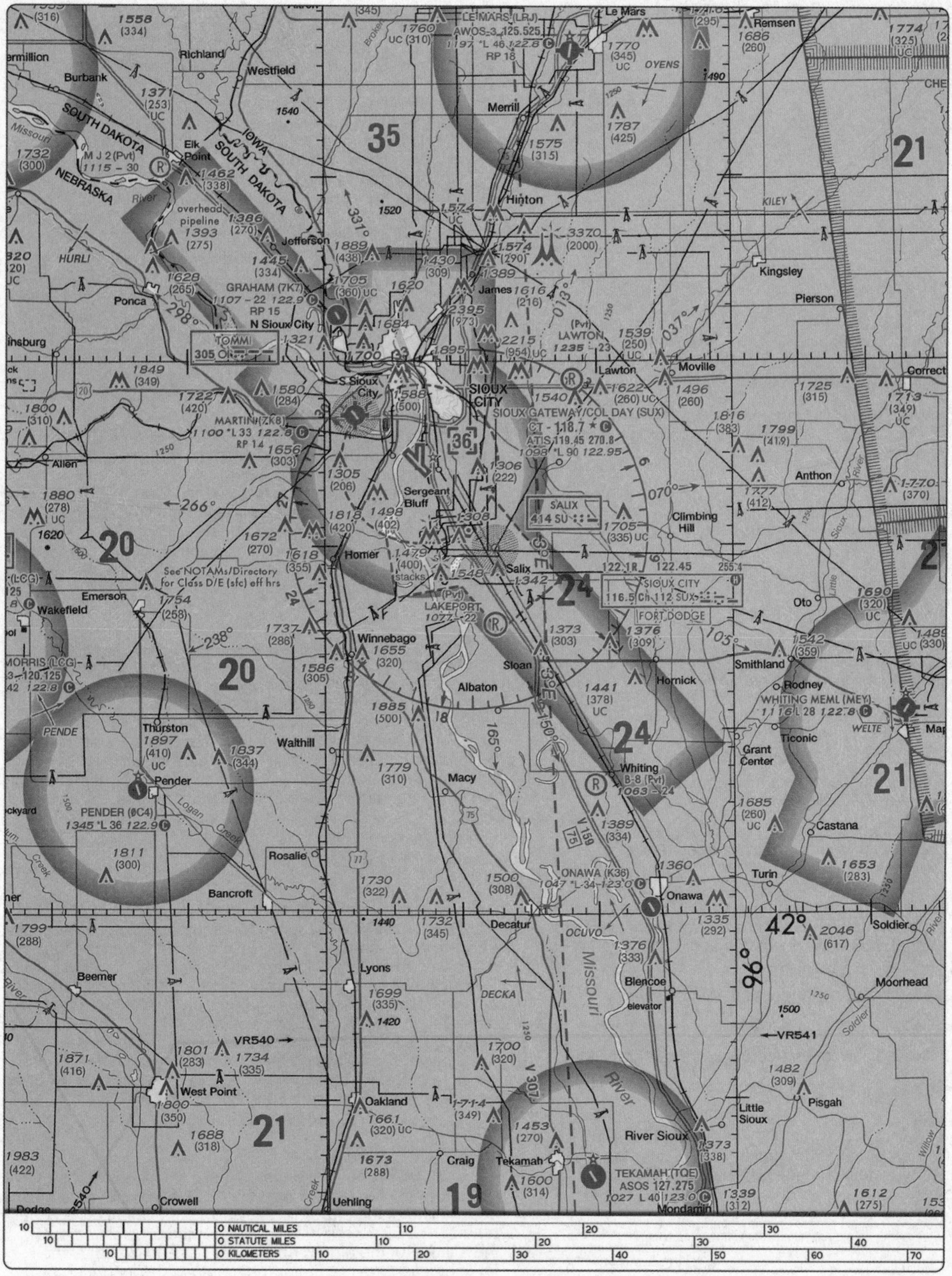

Figure 78. – Sectional Chart Excerpt.
NOTE: Chart is not to scale and should not be used for navigation. Use associated scale.

9. (Refer to Figure 20 on page 313.) (Refer to area 3.) Determine the approximate latitude and longitude of Currituck County Airport.

A. 36°24'N – 76°01'W.

B. 36°48'N – 76°01'W.

C. 47°24'N – 75°58'W.

Answer (A) is correct. *(PHAK Chap 16)*

DISCUSSION: On Fig. 20, find the Currituck County Airport, which is northeast of area 3. Note that the airport symbol is just to the west of 76° longitude (find 76° just north of Virginia Beach). There are 60 min. between the 76°W and 77°W lines of longitude, with each tick mark depicting 1 min. The airport is one tick mark to the west of the 76° line, or 76°01'W.

The latitude is below the 30-min. latitude line across the center of the chart. See the numbered latitude lines at the top (37°) of the chart. Since each tick mark represents 1 min. of latitude, and the airport is approximately six tick marks south of the 36°30'N latitude, the airport is at 36°24'N latitude. Thus, Currituck County Airport is at approximately 36°24'N – 76°01'W.

Answer (B) is incorrect. Currituck County Airport is south of the 36°30'N (not 37°00'N) line of latitude. Answer (C) is incorrect. Currituck County Airport is west (not east) of the 76°W line of longitude and 47°24'N is 11°N of the airport.

9.2 Airspace and Altitudes

10. (Refer to Figure 20 on page 313.) (Refer to area 1.) The NALF Fentress (NFE) Airport is in what type of airspace?

A. Class C.

B. Class E.

C. Class G.

Answer (B) is correct. *(ACL)*

DISCUSSION: The NALF Fentress (NFE) Airport is surrounded by a dashed magenta line, indicating Class E airspace from the surface.

Answer (A) is incorrect. Class C airspace is surrounded by a solid magenta line. The line surrounding NFE airport is dashed magenta. Answer (C) is incorrect. The dashed magenta line surrounding NFE Airport indicates Class E begins at the surface. A shaded magenta line would be required to indicate Class G airspace from the surface up to 700 ft. AGL.

11. (Refer to Figure 20 on page 313.) (Refer to area 4.) What hazards to aircraft may exist in restricted areas such as R-5302A?

A. Unusual, often invisible, hazards such as aerial gunnery or guided missiles.

B. High volume of pilot training or an unusual type of aerial activity.

C. Military training activities that necessitate acrobatic or abrupt flight maneuvers.

Answer (A) is correct. *(AIM Para 3-4-3)*

DISCUSSION: See Fig. 20. Restricted areas denote the existence of unusual, often invisible, hazards to aircraft such as military firing, aerial gunnery, or guided missiles.

Answer (B) is incorrect. A high volume of pilot training or an unusual type of aerial activity describes an alert area, not a warning area. Answer (C) is incorrect. Military training activities that necessitate acrobatic or abrupt flight maneuvers are characteristic of MOAs, not restricted areas.

12. (Refer to Figure 20 on page 313.) (Refer to area 1.) What minimum radio equipment is required to land and take off at Norfolk International?

A. Mode C transponder and omnireceiver.

B. Mode C transponder and two-way radio.

C. Mode C transponder, omnireceiver, and DME.

Answer (B) is correct. *(AIM Para 3-2-4)*

DISCUSSION: The minimum equipment to land and take off at Norfolk International (Fig. 20) is a Mode C transponder and a two-way radio. Norfolk International is located within Class C airspace. Unless otherwise authorized, a pilot must establish and maintain radio communication with ATC prior to and while operating in the Class C airspace area. Mode C transponders are also required in and above all Class C airspace areas.

Answer (A) is incorrect. An omnireceiver (VOR) is not required in Class C airspace. Answer (C) is incorrect. Neither an omnireceiver (VOR) nor a DME is required in Class C airspace.

13. (Refer to Figure 20 on page 313.) (Refer to area 2.) The elevation of the Chesapeake Regional Airport is

A. 19 feet.

B. 36 feet.

C. 360 feet.

Answer (A) is correct. *(ACL)*

DISCUSSION: The question asks for the elevation of the Chesapeake Regional Airport (Fig. 20). East of 2, note that the second line of the airport identifier for Chesapeake Regional reads “19 L 55 123.075.” The first number, in bold type, is the altitude of the airport above MSL. It is followed by the L for lighted runway(s), 55 for the length of the longest runway (5,500 ft.), and the CTAF frequency (123.075).

Answer (B) is incorrect. This is not listed as the elevation of anything near Chesapeake Regional Airport. Answer (C) is incorrect. This is the height above ground of the group obstructions approximately 6 NM southeast of Chesapeake Regional Airport, not the elevation of the airport.

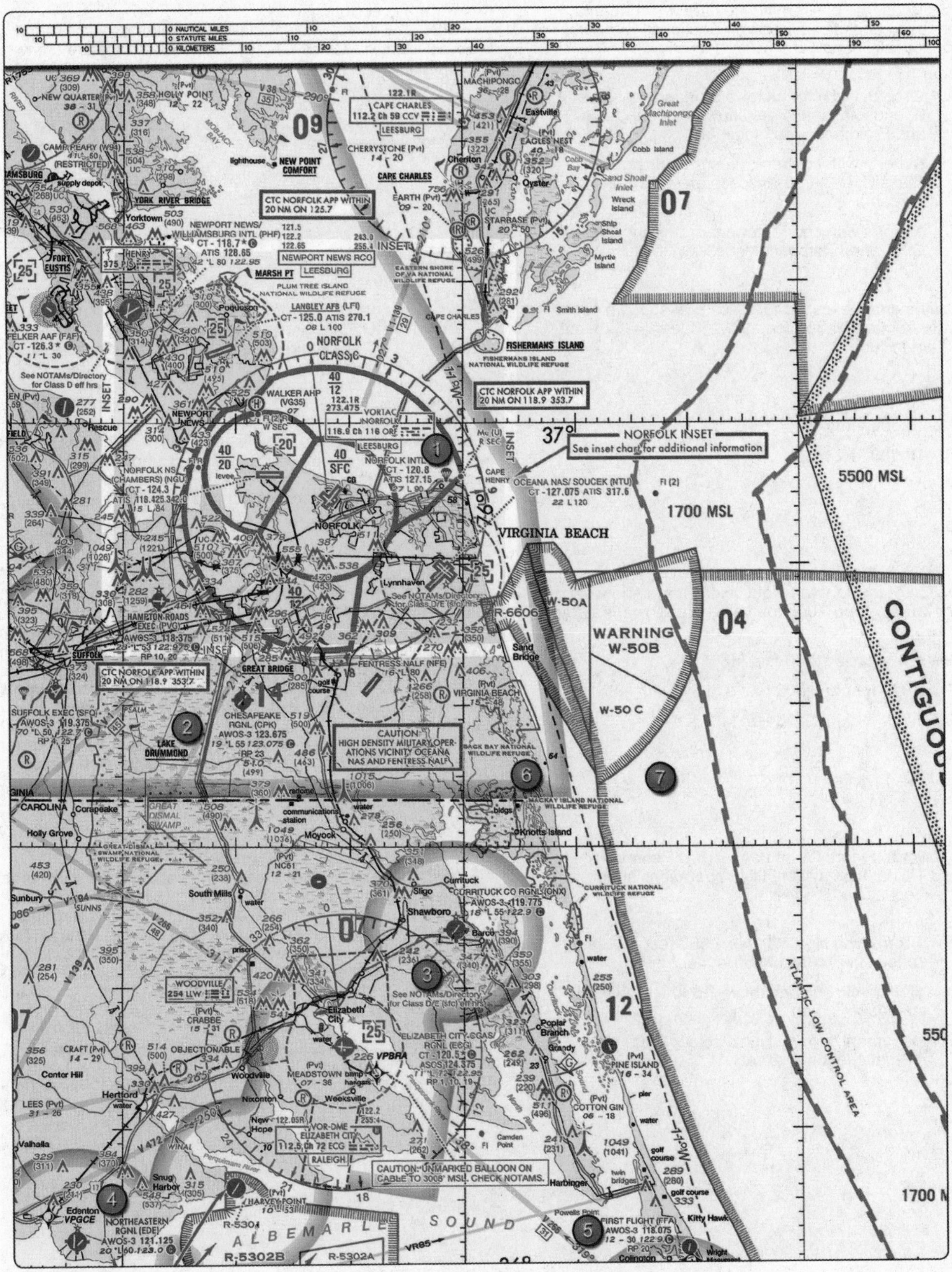

Figure 20. – Sectional Chart Excerpt.
NOTE: Chart is not to scale and should not be used for navigation. Use associated scale.

14. Which is true concerning the blue and magenta colors used to depict airports on Sectional Aeronautical Charts?

A. Airports with control towers underlying Class A, B, and C airspace are shown in blue; Class D and E airspace are magenta.

B. Airports with control towers underlying Class C, D, and E airspace are shown in magenta.

C. Airports with control towers underlying Class B, C, D, and E airspace are shown in blue.

Answer (C) is correct. *(ACL)*

DISCUSSION: On sectional charts, airports with control towers underlying Class B, C, D, E, or G airspace are shown in blue. Airports with no control towers are shown in magenta.

Answer (A) is incorrect. There are no airports in Class A airspace. Airports with control towers are shown in blue, and all others are in magenta. Answer (B) is incorrect. Airports with control towers are shown in blue, not magenta.

15. With certain exceptions, Class E airspace extends upward from either 700 feet or 1,200 feet AGL to, but does not include,

A. 10,000 feet MSL.

B. 14,500 feet MSL.

C. 18,000 feet MSL.

Answer (C) is correct. *(AIM Para 3-2-6)*

DISCUSSION: Beginning at either 700 ft. AGL or 1,200 ft. AGL, Class E airspace extends up to, but not including, the base of the overlying controlled airspace. With the exception of Class B and Class C airspace, Class E airspace extends up to, but not including, 18,000 ft. MSL, i.e., the floor of Class A airspace.

Answer (A) is incorrect. This is the base of increased VFR visibility and cloud distance requirements and the Mode C requirement. Answer (B) is incorrect. Class G, not Class E, airspace may extend from the surface up to, but not including, 14,500 ft. MSL.

16. (Refer to Figure 21 on page 315.) The terrain elevation of the light tan (light colored) area between Minot (area 1) and Audubon Lake (area 2) varies from

A. sea level to 2,000 feet MSL.

B. 2,000 feet to 2,500 feet MSL.

C. 2,000 feet to 2,700 feet MSL.

Answer (B) is correct. *(ACL)*

DISCUSSION: The tan area indicates terrain between 2,000 ft. and 3,000 ft. The elevation contours on sectionals vary by 500 ft. increments. The 2,000 ft. contour line is located where the color changes from light green to light tan. Since there is no other contour line in the light tan area, the terrain elevation is between 2,000 ft. and 2,500 ft. MSL. Also, Poleschook Airport (halfway between 1 and 2) indicates an elevation above MSL of 2,245.

Answer (A) is incorrect. The light tan area indicates terrain elevation from 2,000 ft. to 3,000 ft. MSL, not from sea level to 2,000 ft. MSL. Answer (C) is incorrect. Elevation contours vary by 500 ft., not 700 ft.

17. (Refer to Figure 21 on page 315.) (Refer to area 3.) What type military flight operations should a pilot expect along IR 644?

A. IFR training flights above 1,500 feet AGL at speeds in excess of 250 knots.

B. VFR training flights above 1,500 feet AGL at speeds less than 250 knots.

C. Instrument training flights below 1,500 feet AGL at speeds in excess of 150 knots.

Answer (A) is correct. *(AIM Para 3-5-2)*

DISCUSSION: In Fig. 21, IR 644 is below area 3. Military training flights are established to promote proficiency of military pilots in the interest of national defense. Military flight routes below 1,500 ft. are charted with four-digit numbers; those above 1,500 ft. have three-digit numbers. IR means the flights are made in accordance with IFR. (VR would mean they use VFR.) Thus, IR 644, a three-digit number, is above 1,500 ft., and flights will be flown under IFR rules.

Answer (B) is incorrect. VFR flights are coded VR (not IR), and the speeds are in excess of (not less than) 250 kt. Answer (C) is incorrect. Military training flights below 1,500 ft. AGL have four-digit (not three-digit) identifier numbers, and the airspeed is in excess of 250 kt. (not 150 kt.).

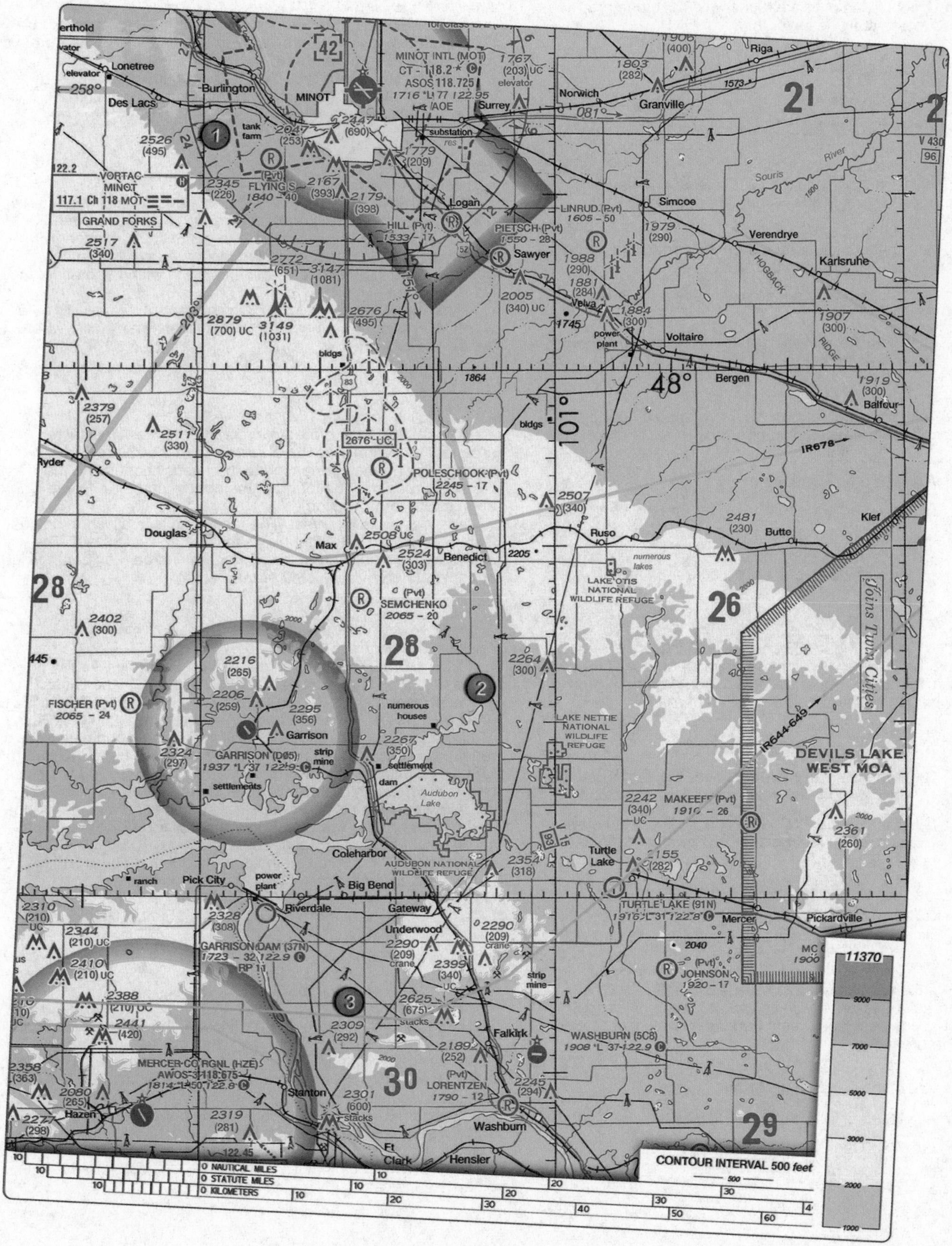

Figure 21. – Sectional Chart Excerpt.
NOTE: Chart is not to scale and should not be used for navigation. Use associated scale.

18. Pilots flying over a national wildlife refuge are requested to fly no lower than

A. 1,000 feet AGL.

B. 2,000 feet AGL.

C. 3,000 feet AGL.

Answer (B) is correct. *(AIM Para 7-4-6)*

DISCUSSION: The Fish and Wildlife Service requests that pilots maintain a minimum altitude of 2,000 ft. above the terrain of national wildlife refuge areas.

Answer (A) is incorrect. This is the required distance above obstructions over congested areas. Answer (C) is incorrect. This has no significance to wildlife refuges.

19. What action should a pilot take when operating under VFR in a Military Operations Area (MOA)?

A. Obtain a clearance from the controlling agency prior to entering the MOA.

B. Operate only on the airways that transverse the MOA.

C. Exercise extreme caution when military activity is being conducted.

Answer (C) is correct. *(AIM Para 3-4-5)*

DISCUSSION: Military operations areas consist of airspace established for separating military training activities from IFR traffic. VFR traffic should exercise extreme caution when flying within an MOA. Information regarding MOA activity can be obtained from flight service stations (FSSs) within 100 mi. of the MOA.

Answer (A) is incorrect. A clearance is not required to enter an MOA. Answer (B) is incorrect. VFR flights may fly anywhere in the MOA.

20. Flight through a restricted area should not be accomplished unless the pilot has

A. filed a IFR flight plan.

B. received prior authorization from the controlling agency.

C. received prior permission from the commanding officer of the nearest military base.

Answer (B) is correct. *(AIM Para 3-4-3)*

DISCUSSION: Before an aircraft penetrates a restricted area, authorization must be obtained from the controlling agency. Information pertaining to the agency controlling the restricted area may be found at the bottom of the En Route Chart appropriate to navigation.

Answer (A) is incorrect. The restriction is to all flight, not just flights without an IFR flight plan. Answer (C) is incorrect. The commanding officer is not necessarily in charge (i.e., controlling agency) of nearby restricted areas.

21. (Refer to Figure 22 on page 317.) (Refer to area 1.) The visibility and cloud clearance requirements to operate VFR during daylight hours over Sandpoint Airport at 1,200 feet AGL are

A. 1 mile and clear of clouds.

B. 1 mile and 1,000 feet above, 500 feet below, and 2,000 feet horizontally from each cloud.

C. 3 miles and 1,000 feet above, 500 feet below, and 2,000 feet horizontally from each cloud.

Answer (C) is correct. *(14 CFR 91.155)*

DISCUSSION: The airspace around Sandpoint Airport is Class G airspace from the surface to 700 ft. AGL and Class E airspace from 700 ft. AGL up to, but not including, 18,000 ft. MSL (indicated by the magenta shading). Therefore, 1,200 ft. AGL is within Class E airspace. The VFR visibility and cloud clearance requirements for operations in Class E airspace below 10,000 ft. MSL are 3 miles and a distance of 1,000 ft. above, 500 ft. below, and 2,000 ft. horizontally from each cloud.

Answer (A) is incorrect. One mile and clear of clouds are the visibility and cloud clearance requirements for VFR operations in Class G, not Class E, airspace at or below 1,200 ft. AGL. Answer (B) is incorrect. One mile and 1,000 ft. above, 500 ft. below, and 2,000 ft. horizontally are the visibility and cloud clearance requirements for VFR operations in Class G, not Class E, airspace at more than, not at, 1,200 ft. AGL but less than 10,000 ft. MSL.

22. (Refer to Figure 22 on page 317.) (Refer to area 3.) The vertical limits of that portion of Class E airspace designated as a Federal Airway over Magee Airport are

A. 1,200 feet AGL to 17,999 feet MSL.

B. 700 feet MSL to 12,500 feet MSL.

C. 7,500 feet MSL to 17,999 feet MSL.

Answer (A) is correct. *(ACL)*

DISCUSSION: Magee Airport on Fig. 22 is northwest of 3. The question asks for the vertical limits of the Class E airspace over the airport. Class E airspace areas extend upwards but do not include 18,000 ft. MSL (base of Class A airspace). The floor of a Class E airspace designated as an airway is 1,200 ft. AGL, unless otherwise indicated.

Answer (B) is incorrect. This airway begins at 1,200 ft. AGL and extends upward to 17,999 ft. MSL, not 12,500 ft. MSL. Answer (C) is incorrect. Class E airspace designated as a Federal Airway begins at 1,200 ft. AGL, not 7,500 ft. MSL, unless otherwise indicated.

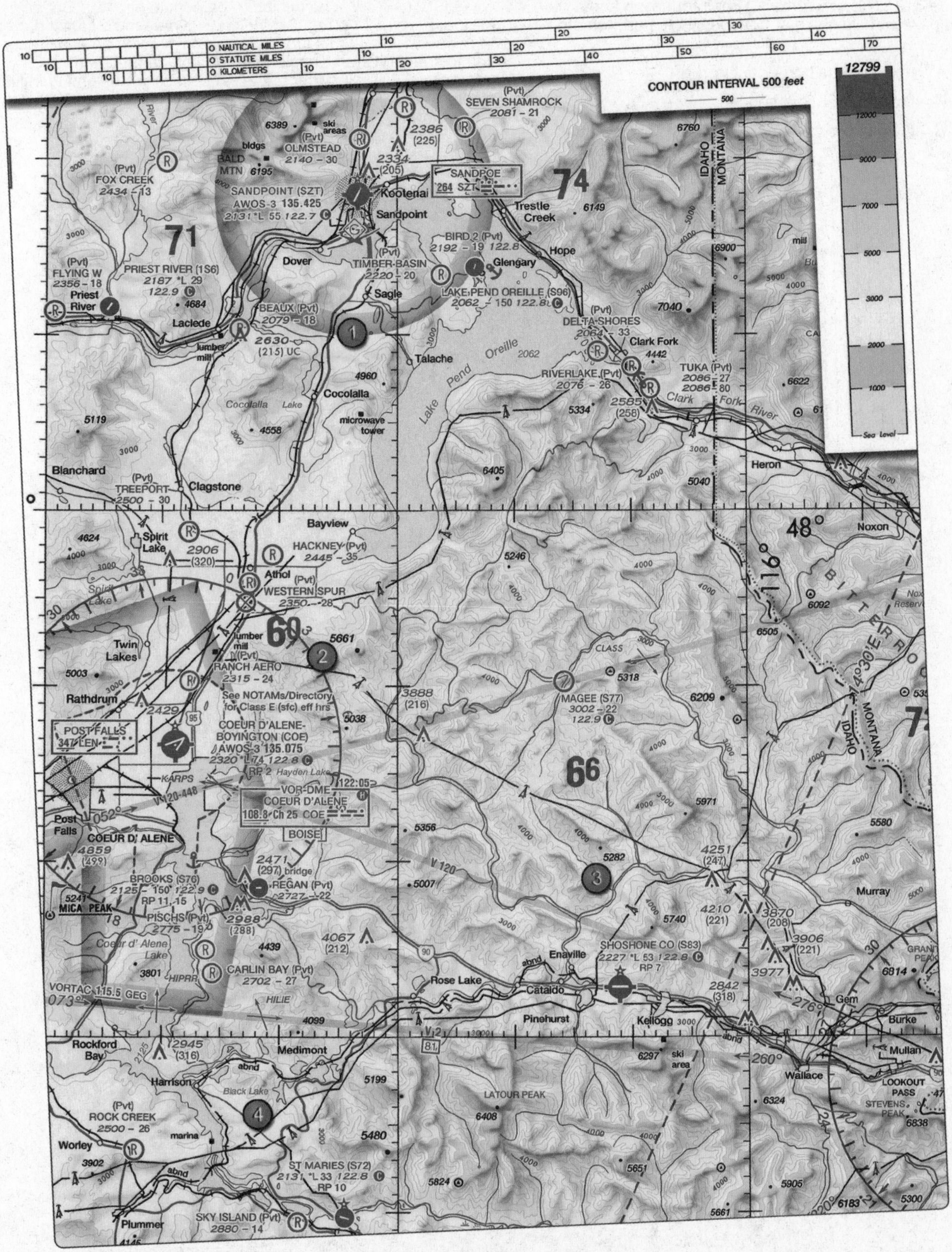

Figure 22. – Sectional Chart Excerpt.
NOTE: Chart is not to scale and should not be used for navigation. Use associated scale.

23. (Refer to Figure 24 below, and Legend 1 on page 319.) (Refer to area 1.) For information about the parachute jumping at Caddo Mills Airport, refer to

A. notes on the border of the chart.

B. the Chart Supplement.

C. the Notices to Airmen (NOTAM) publication.

Answer (B) is correct. *(ACL)*

DISCUSSION: The miniature parachute near the Caddo Mills Airport (at 1 on Fig. 24) indicates a parachute jumping area. In Legend 1, the symbol for a parachute jumping area instructs you to see the Chart Supplement for more information.

Answer (A) is incorrect. The sectional chart legend identifies symbols only. Answer (C) is incorrect. NOTAMs are issued only for hazards to flight.

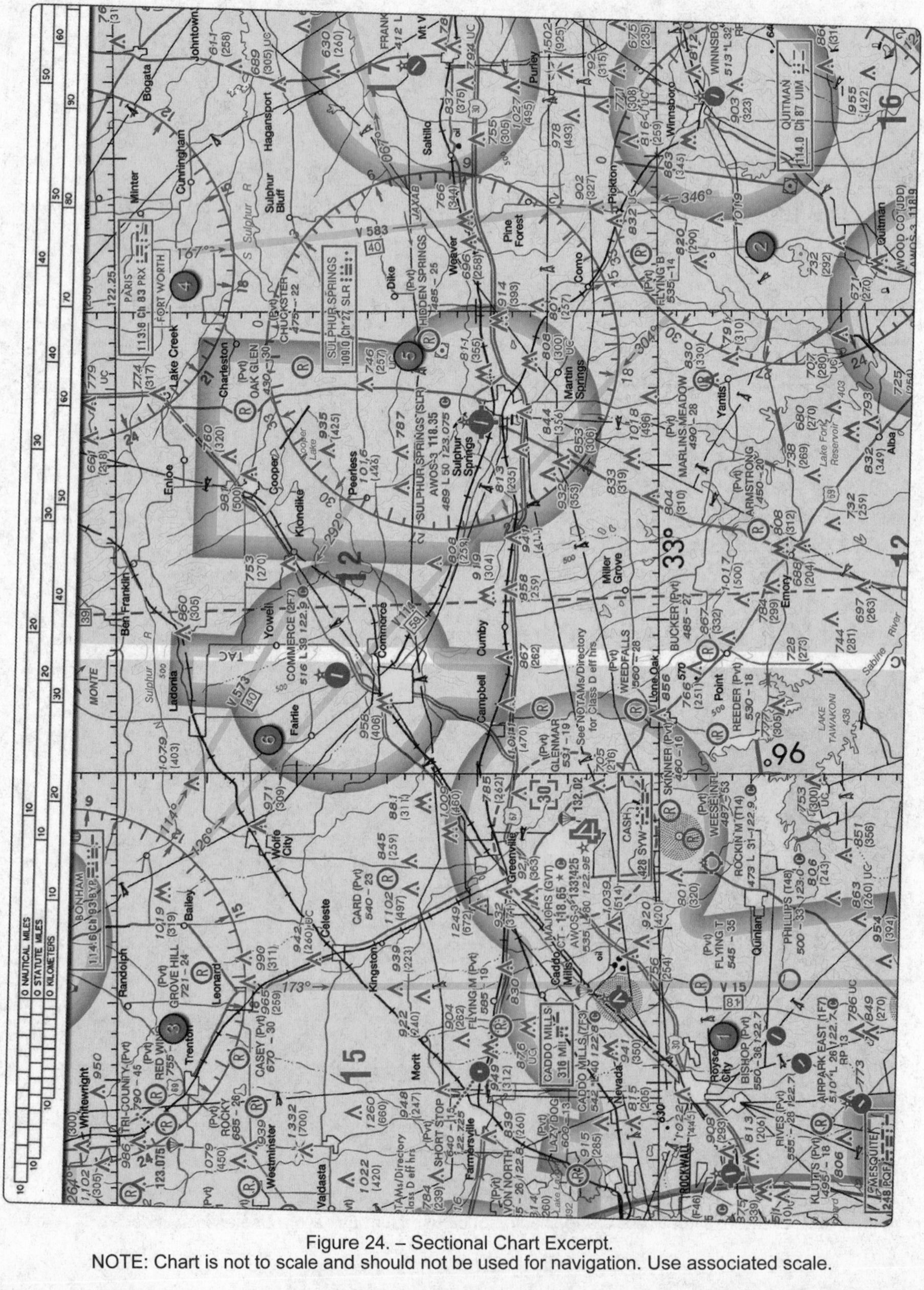

Figure 24. – Sectional Chart Excerpt.

NOTE: Chart is not to scale and should not be used for navigation. Use associated scale.

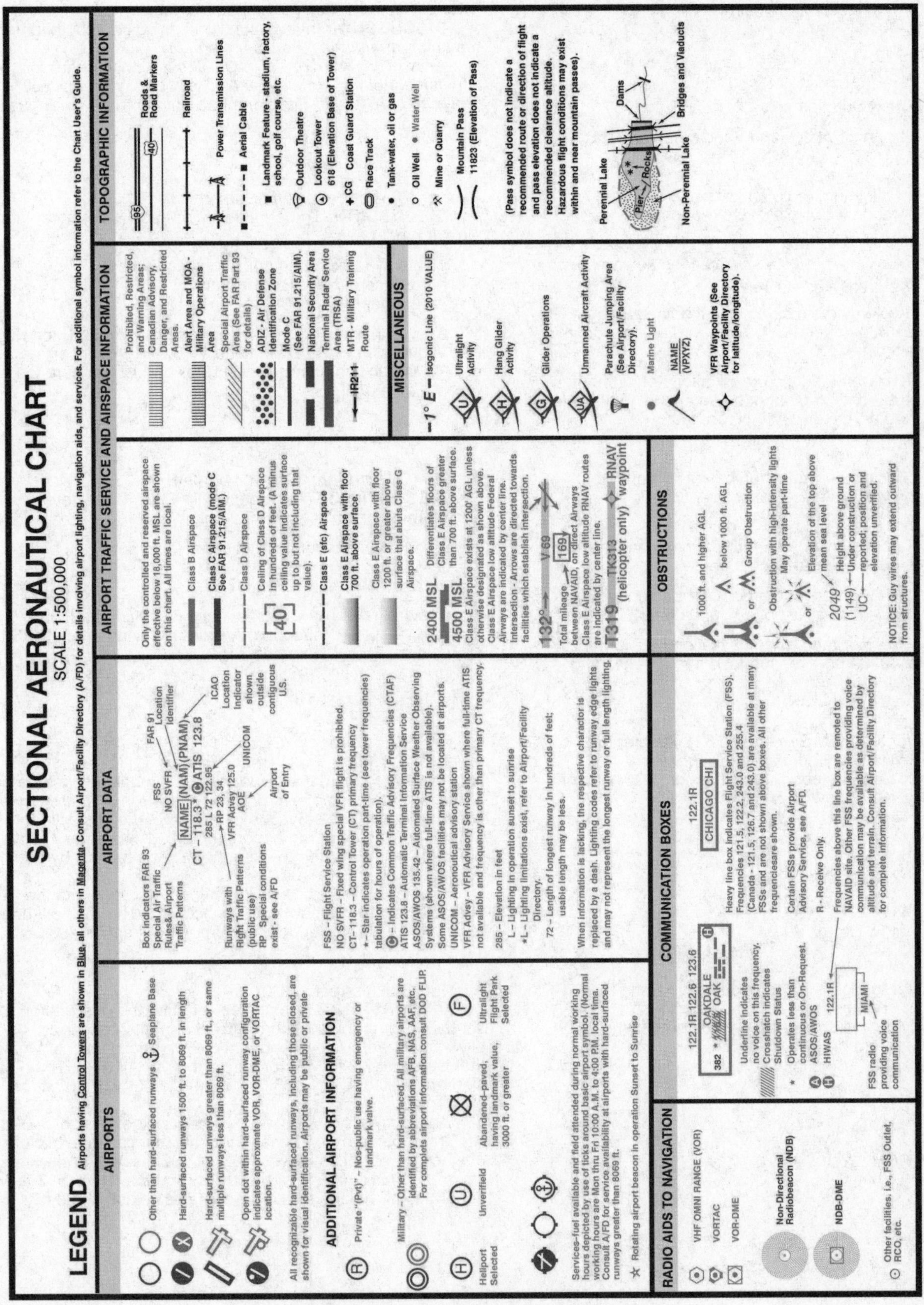

Legend 1. – Sectional Aeronautical Chart.

24. Information concerning parachute jumping sites may be found in the

A. NOTAMs.

B. Chart Supplement.

C. Graphic Notices and Supplemental Data.

Answer (B) is correct. *(Chart Supplement)*

DISCUSSION: Information concerning parachute jump sites may be found in the Chart Supplement.

Answer (A) is incorrect. NOTAMs are only issued for special situations, not routine jump sites. Answer (C) is incorrect. Graphic Notices and Supplemental Data are no longer published.

25. What minimum radio equipment is required for VFR operation within Class B airspace?

A. Two-way radio communications equipment and a 4096-code transponder.

B. Two-way radio communications equipment, a 4096-code transponder, and an encoding altimeter.

C. Two-way radio communications equipment, a 4096-code transponder, an encoding altimeter, and a VOR or TACAN receiver.

Answer (B) is correct. *(AIM Para 3-2-3)*

DISCUSSION: To operate within Class B airspace, the aircraft must have

1. Two-way radio communications equipment,
2. A 4096-code transponder, and
3. An encoding altimeter.

Answer (A) is incorrect. An encoding altimeter (Mode C) is also required in Class B airspace. Answer (C) is incorrect. A VOR or TACAN receiver is required for IFR, not VFR, operation within Class B airspace.

26. What minimum radio equipment is required for operation within Class C airspace?

A. Two-way radio communications equipment and a 4096-code transponder.

B. Two-way radio communications equipment, a 4096-code transponder, and DME.

C. Two-way radio communications equipment, a 4096-code transponder, and an encoding altimeter.

Answer (C) is correct. *(AIM Para 3-2-4)*

DISCUSSION: To operate within Class C airspace, the aircraft must have

1. Two-way radio communications equipment,
2. A 4096-code transponder, and
3. An encoding altimeter.

Answer (A) is incorrect. An encoding altimeter (Mode C) is required in Class C airspace. Answer (B) is incorrect. DME is not required in Class C airspace.

27. (Refer to Figure 24 on page 321.) (Refer to area 1.) What minimum altitude is necessary to vertically clear the obstacle on the northeast side of Airpark East Airport by 500 feet?

A. 1,010 feet MSL.

B. 1,273 feet MSL.

C. 1,283 feet MSL.

Answer (B) is correct. *(ACL and 14 CFR 91.119)*

DISCUSSION: Find Airpark East, which is near 1 in Fig. 24. Remember to locate the actual airport symbol, not just the name of the airport. It is the third of three airports in a southwesterly line from the 1. The elevation of the top of the obstacle on the northeast side of the airport is marked in bold as 773 ft. MSL. Minimum altitude to clear the 773-ft. obstacle by 500 ft. is 1,273 ft. MSL.

Answer (A) is incorrect. The airport elevation, not the obstacle, is 510 ft. Answer (C) is incorrect. The AGL altitude of a tower 1 in. west of Caddo Mills Airport appears as 283.

28. (Refer to Figure 24 on page 321.) (Refer to area 2.) What minimum altitude is necessary to vertically clear the obstacle on the southeast side of Winnsboro Airport by 500 feet?

A. 823 feet MSL.

B. 1,013 feet MSL.

C. 1,403 feet MSL.

Answer (C) is correct. *(ACL)*

DISCUSSION: The first step is to find the obstacle on the southeast side of Winnsboro Airport on Fig. 24, near 2. The elevation numbers to the right of the obstruction symbol indicate that its top is 903 ft. MSL or a height of 323 ft. AGL. Thus, the clearance altitude is 1,403 ft. MSL (903 ft. MSL + 500 ft. of clearance).

Answer (A) is incorrect. Since the obstacle height is 323 ft. AGL (number in parentheses), the minimum altitude to clear the obstacle by 500 ft. is 823 ft. AGL, not 823 ft. MSL. Answer (B) is incorrect. This is 500 ft. above the airport elevation (513 ft. MSL), not 500 ft. above the top of the obstacle height of 903 ft.

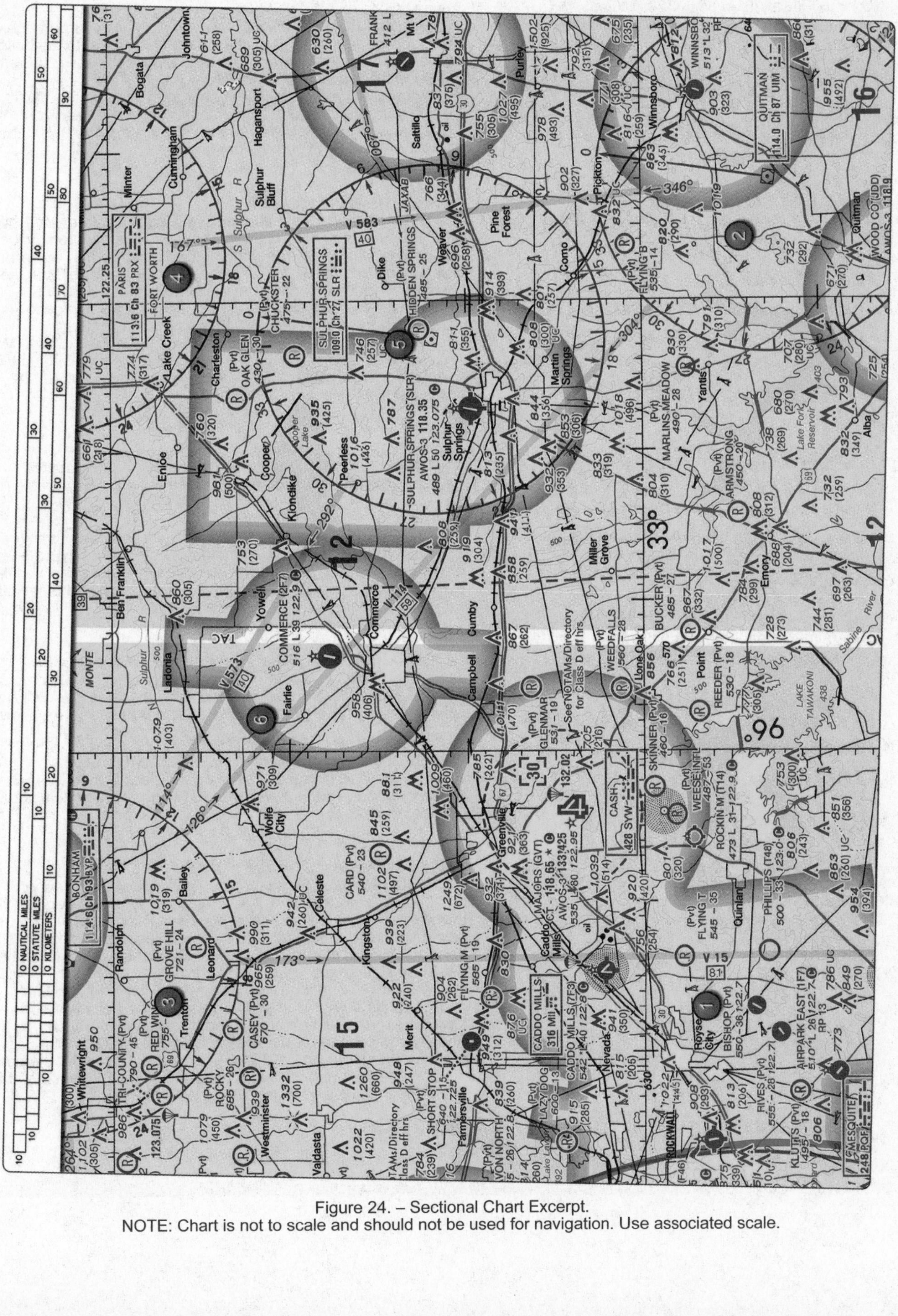

Figure 24. – Sectional Chart Excerpt.

NOTE: Chart is not to scale and should not be used for navigation. Use associated scale.

29. (Refer to Figure 25 on page 323.) What is the base of Class B airspace at Lakeview (30F) Airport (area 2)?

A. 4,000

B. 3,000

C. 1,700

Answer (B) is correct. *(AIM Chap 3)*

DISCUSSION: To the southwest of Lakeview Airport, there are numbers 110 over 30 in blue color. This indicates the base of Class B airspace between the blue airspace lines is 3,000 ft. MSL and the top is 11,000 ft. MSL.

Answer (A) is incorrect. The base is indicated at 4,000 ft. MSL beyond the blue line located north of Lakeview Airport. Answer (C) is incorrect. A base of 1,700 ft. would be below the maximum elevation figure in that quadrant.

30. (Refer to Figure 25 on page 323.) (Refer to area 4.) The airspace directly overlying Fort Worth Meacham is

A. Class B airspace to 10,000 feet MSL.

B. Class C airspace to 5,000 feet MSL.

C. Class D airspace to 3,200 feet MSL.

Answer (C) is correct. *(ACL)*

DISCUSSION: The airspace overlying Fort Worth Meacham (Fig. 25, southeast of 4) is Class D airspace as denoted by the segmented blue lines. The upper limit is depicted in a broken box in hundreds of feet MSL northeast of the airport. Thus, the Class D airspace extends from the surface to 3,200 ft. MSL.

Answer (A) is incorrect. Class D, not Class B, airspace extends from the surface of Ft. Worth Meacham. Class B airspace overlies the airport from 4,000 ft. MSL to 11,000 ft. MSL. Answer (B) is incorrect. Class D, not Class C, airspace directly overlies Ft. Worth Meacham from the surface to 3,200 ft. MSL, not 5,000 ft. MSL.

31. (Refer to Figure 25 on page 323.) At which airports is fixed-wing Special VFR not authorized?

A. Fort Worth Meacham and Fort Worth Spinks.

B. Dallas-Fort Worth International and Dallas Love Field.

C. Addison and Dallas Executive.

Answer (B) is correct. *(ACL)*

DISCUSSION: The first (top) line of the airport data for Dallas-Ft. Worth Int'l. and Dallas Love Field (Fig. 25, areas 5 and 6) indicates NO SVFR, which means no special VFR permitted for a fixed-wing aircraft.

Answer (A) is incorrect. Ft. Worth Meacham and Fort Worth Spinks permit special VFR operations since it is not indicated otherwise. Answer (C) is incorrect. Addison and Dallas Executive permit special VFR operations since it is not indicated otherwise.

32. (Refer to Figure 25 on page 323.) (Refer to area 2.) The floor of Class B airspace at Addison Airport is

A. at the surface.

B. 3,000 feet MSL.

C. 3,100 feet MSL.

Answer (B) is correct. *(ACL, 14 CFR 71.9)*

DISCUSSION: Addison Airport (Fig. 25, area 2) has a segmented blue circle around it depicting Class D airspace. Addison Airport also underlies Class B airspace as depicted by solid blue lines. The altitudes of the Class B airspace are shown as $\frac{110}{30}$ to the east of the airport. The bottom number denotes the floor of the Class B airspace to be 3,000 ft. MSL.

Answer (A) is incorrect. The floor of Class D, not Class B, airspace is at the surface. Answer (C) is incorrect. This is not a defined limit of any airspace over Addison airport.

33. (Refer to Figure 25 on page 323.) (Refer to area 7.) The airspace overlying Mc Kinney (TKI) is controlled from the surface to

A. 700 feet AGL.

B. 2,900 feet MSL.

C. 2,500 feet MSL.

Answer (B) is correct. *(ACL)*

DISCUSSION: The airspace overlying Mc Kinney airport (TKI) (Fig. 25, northeast of 7) is Class D airspace as denoted by the segmented blue lines. The upper limit is depicted in a broken box in hundreds of feet MSL to the left of the airport symbol. The box contains the number "29," meaning that the vertical limit of the Class D airspace is 2,900 ft. MSL.

Answer (A) is incorrect. This is normally the vertical limit of uncontrolled, not controlled, airspace in the vicinity of non-towered airports with an authorized instrument approach. Answer (C) is incorrect. The height of 2,500 ft. AGL, not MSL, is normally the upper limit of Class D airspace. This is not the case here, where the upper limit is somewhat lower, at about 2,300 ft. AGL [2,900 ft. MSL – 586 ft. AGL (field elevation) = 2,314 ft. AGL].

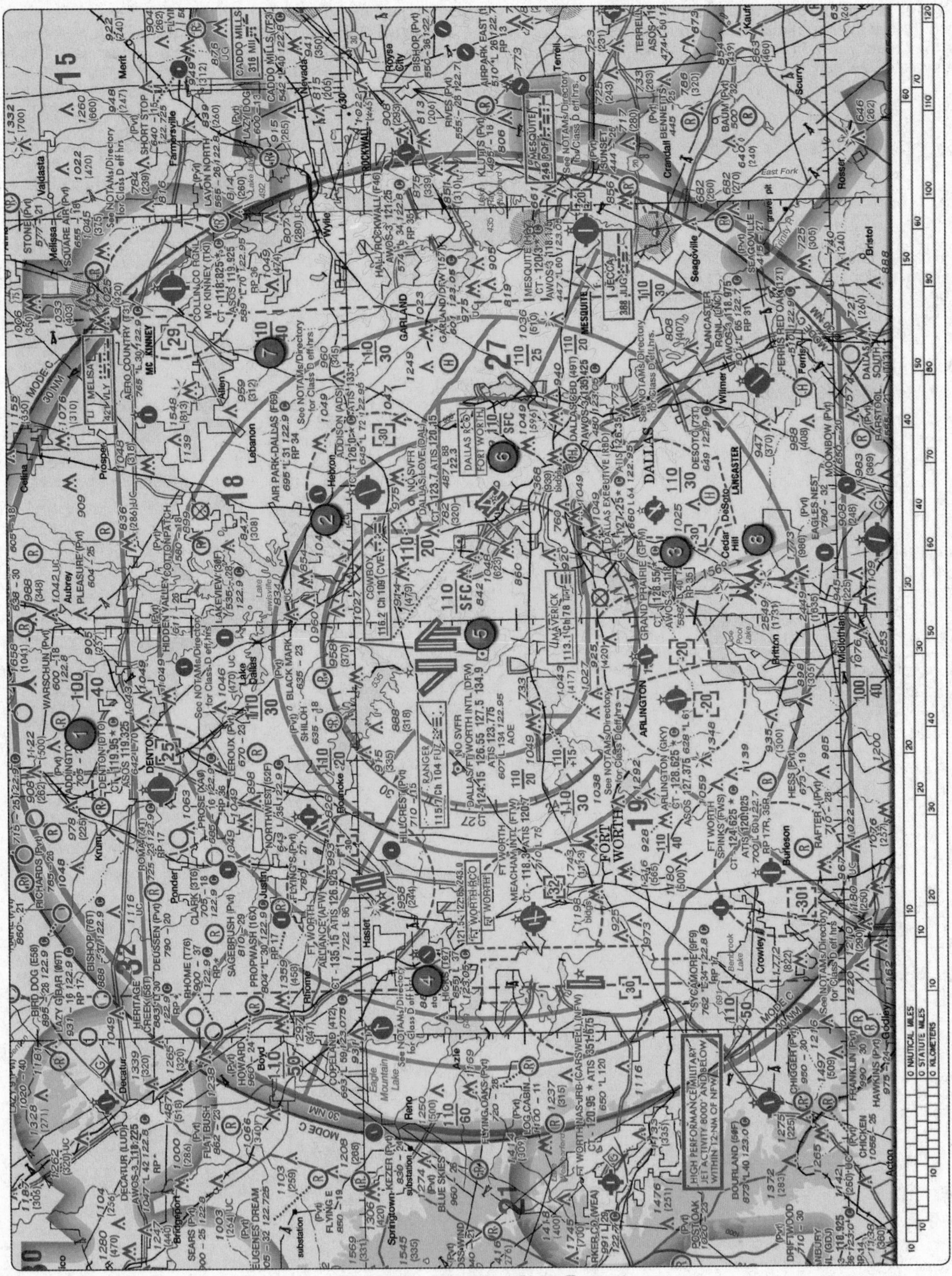

Figure 25. – Sectional Chart Excerpt.
NOTE: Chart is not to scale and should not be used for navigation. Use associated scale.

34. (Refer to Figure 25 on page 325.) (Refer to area 8.) What minimum altitude is required to fly over the Cedar Hill TV towers in the congested area southwest of Dallas Executive?

A. 2,731 feet MSL.

B. 3,549 feet MSL.

C. 3,349 feet MSL.

Answer (B) is correct. *(14 CFR 91.119)*

DISCUSSION: The Cedar Hill TV towers (Fig. 25, west of 8) have an elevation of 2,549 ft. MSL. The minimum safe altitude over a congested area is 1,000 ft. above the highest obstacle within a horizontal radius of 2,000 ft. of the aircraft. Thus, to vertically clear the towers, the minimum altitude is 3,549 ft. MSL (2,549 + 1,000).

Answer (A) is incorrect. The figure of 2,731 ft. AGL, not MSL, is the minimum height to fly over the shortest, not the tallest, of the obstructions in the group. Answer (C) is incorrect. This is only 800 ft., not 1,000 ft., above the tallest structure.

35. (Refer to Figure 25 on page 325.) (Refer to area 4.) The floor of Class B airspace overlying Hicks Airport (T67) north-northwest of Fort Worth Meacham Field is

A. at the surface.

B. 3,200 feet MSL.

C. 4,000 feet MSL.

Answer (C) is correct. *(ACL)*

DISCUSSION: Hicks Airport (T67) on Fig. 25 is northeast of 4. Class B airspace is depicted by a solid blue line, as shown just west of the airport. Follow the blue line toward the bottom of the chart until you find a number over a number in blue, $\frac{110}{40}$. The bottom number denotes the floor of the Class B airspace as 4,000 ft. MSL.

Answer (A) is incorrect. The floor of the Class B airspace would be at the surface if SFC, not 40, was below the 100, as depicted just south of Dallas-Ft. Worth International Airport. Answer (B) is incorrect. This is the upper limit of the Class D airspace for the Ft. Worth/Meacham Airport, not the floor of Class B airspace overlying Hicks Airport.

36. (Refer to Figure 25 on page 325.) (Refer to area 5.) The navigation facility at Dallas-Ft. Worth International (DFW) is a

A. VOR.

B. VORTAC.

C. VOR/DME.

Answer (C) is correct. *(ACL)*

DISCUSSION: On Fig. 25, DFW is located at the center of the chart and the navigation facility is 1 NM south of the right set of parallel runways. The symbol is a hexagon with a dot in the center within a square. This is the symbol for a VOR/DME navigation facility.

Answer (A) is incorrect. A VOR facility symbol is a hexagon with a dot in the center, but is not located within a square. Answer (B) is incorrect. A VORTAC symbol is a hexagon with a dot in the center and a small rectangle attached to three of the six sides. The Ranger VORTAC is depicted approximately 7 NM to the west of DFW airport.

Figure 25. – Sectional Chart Excerpt.
NOTE: Chart is not to scale and should not be used for navigation. Use associated scale.

37. (Refer to Figure 26 on page 327.) The Devils Lake East MOA (area 1) is a

A. meteorological observation area.

B. military observation area.

C. military operations area.

Answer (C) is correct. *(AIM Chap 3)*

DISCUSSION: Military operations areas are shown on the sectional chart surrounded by magenta hashed lines. Devils Lake East MOA is labeled in the top left of Fig. 26. All the magenta hashed lines around the label are the boundaries of the MOA.

Answer (A) is incorrect. There are no meteorological observation areas on the chart. Answer (B) is incorrect. There are no military observation areas on the chart.

38. (Refer to Figure 26 on page 327.) (Refer to area 2.) What hazards to aircraft may exist in areas such as Devils Lake East MOA?

A. Unusual, often invisible, hazards to aircraft such as artillery firing, aerial gunnery, or guided missiles.

B. Military training activities that necessitate acrobatic or abrupt flight maneuvers.

C. High volume of pilot training or an unusual type of aerial activity.

Answer (B) is correct. *(AIM Para 3-4-5)*

DISCUSSION: Military Operations Areas (MOAs), such as Devils Lake East in Fig. 26 consist of defined lateral and vertical limits that are designated for the purpose of separating military training activities from IFR traffic. Most training activities necessitate acrobatic or abrupt flight maneuvers. Therefore, the likelihood of a collision is increased inside an MOA. VFR traffic is permitted, but extra vigilance should be exercised in seeing and avoiding military aircraft.

Answer (A) is incorrect. Unusual, often invisible, hazards to aircraft, such as artillery firing, aerial gunnery, or guided missiles, are characteristic of restricted areas, not MOAs. Answer (C) is incorrect. A high volume of pilot training or an unusual type of aerial activity is characteristic of alert areas, not MOAs.

39. (Refer to Figure 26 on page 327.) (Refer to area 2.) Identify the airspace over Bryn Airport.

A. Class G airspace -- surface up to but not including 1,200 feet AGL; Class E airspace -- 1,200 feet AGL up to but not including 18,000 feet MSL.

B. Class G airspace -- surface up to but not including 18,000 feet MSL.

C. Class G airspace -- surface up to but not including 700 feet MSL; Class E airspace -- 700 feet to 14,500 feet MSL.

Answer (A) is correct. *(ACL)*

DISCUSSION: Bryn Airport is located 1.5 inches south of 2 on Fig. 26. In the lower left-hand corner of the figure, there is a portion of a blue shaded ring. According to the chart legend, this indicates that Class E airspace begins at 1,200 ft. AGL within this ring. Therefore, the Class G airspace would extend from the surface to 1,200 ft. AGL, followed by Class E airspace up to, but not including, 18,000 ft. MSL.

Answer (B) is incorrect. The Class G airspace above Bryn Airport ends at 1,200 ft. AGL (the beginning of Class E airspace), not 18,000 ft. MSL. Answer (C) is incorrect. Class G airspace above Bryn Airport extends to 1,200 ft. AGL, indicated by the shaded blue line in the bottom left corner of the chart excerpt. Class G airspace up to 700 ft. AGL (not MSL) would be indicated by magenta shading surrounding Bryn Airport. Additionally, Class E airspace above Bryn Airport extends to 18,000 ft. MSL, not 14,500 ft. MSL.

40. (Refer to Figure 26 on page 327.) (Refer to area 2.) The visibility and cloud clearance requirements to operate VFR during daylight hours over the town of Cooperstown between 1,200 feet AGL and 10,000 feet MSL are

A. 1 mile and clear of clouds.

B. 1 mile and 1,000 feet above, 500 feet below, and 2,000 feet horizontally from clouds.

C. 3 miles and 1,000 feet above, 500 feet below, and 2,000 feet horizontally from clouds.

Answer (C) is correct. *(14 CFR 91.155)*

DISCUSSION: The airspace over the town of Cooperstown (Fig. 26, north of 2) is Class G airspace up to 700 ft. AGL, and Class E airspace from 700 ft. AGL up to, but not including, 18,000 ft. MSL (indicated by the magenta shading). Therefore, the visibility and cloud clearance requirements for daylight VFR operation over the town of Cooperstown between 1,200 ft. AGL and 10,000 ft. MSL are 3 miles and 1,000 ft. above, 500 ft. below, and 2,000 ft. horizontally.

Answer (A) is incorrect. One mile and clear of clouds are the visibility and cloud clearance requirements for daylight VFR operation over the town of Cooperstown up to, but not above, 700 ft. AGL (i.e., the visibility and cloud clearance requirements for Class G airspace below 1,200 ft. AGL). Answer (B) is incorrect. One mile and 1,000 ft. above, 500 ft. below, and 2,000 ft. horizontally from clouds are the visibility and cloud clearance requirements for daylight VFR operations at or above 1,200 ft. AGL, but below 10,000 ft. MSL, in Class G airspace. The airspace above Cooperstown is Class E above 700 ft. AGL.

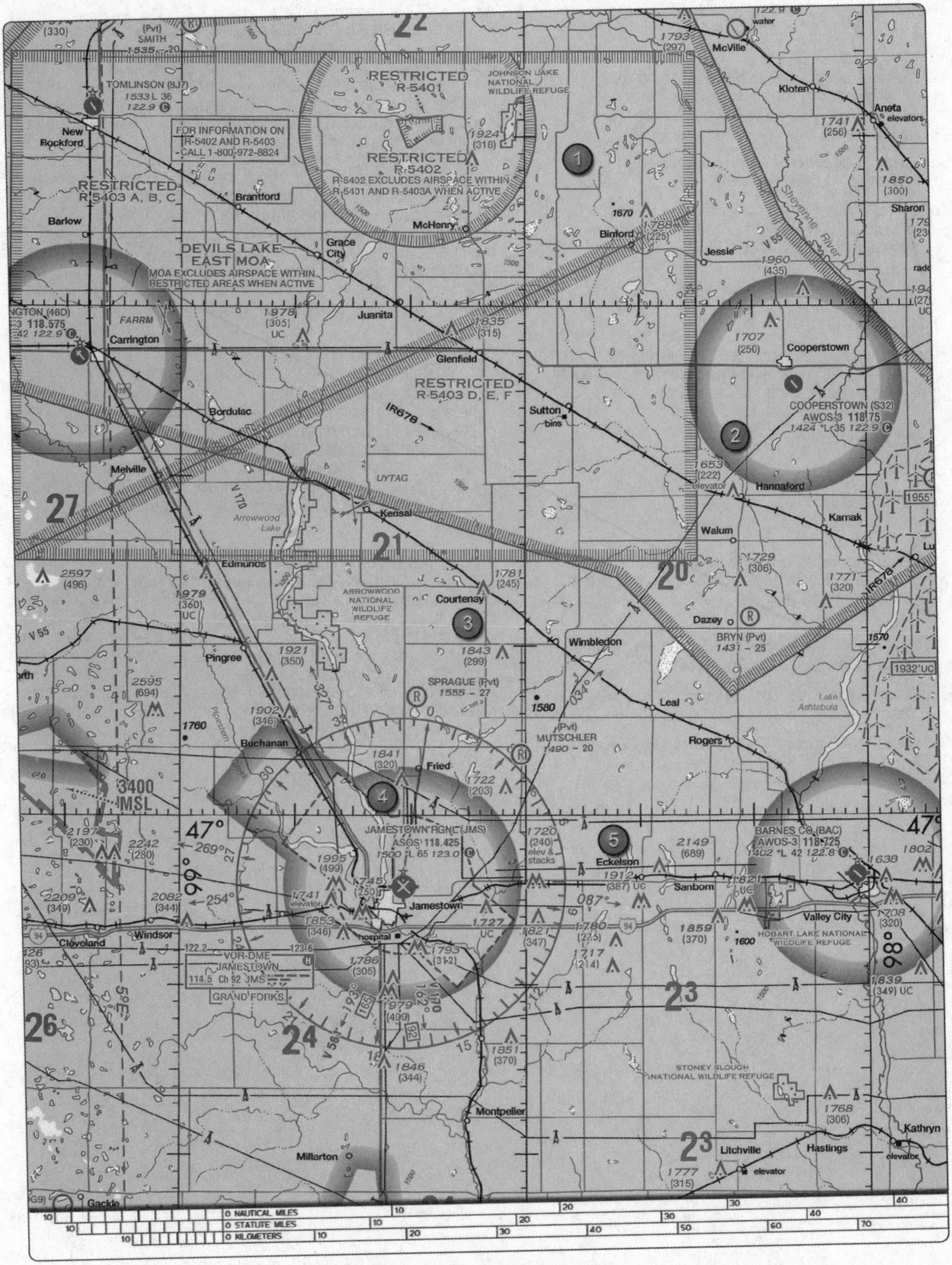

Figure 26. – Sectional Chart Excerpt.
NOTE: Chart is not to scale and should not be used for navigation. Use associated scale.

41. (Refer to Figure 26 on page 329.) (Refer to area 3.) Identify the airspace over Sprague Airport.

A. Class G airspace -- surface up to but not including 1,200 feet AGL; Class E airspace - 1,200 feet AGL up to but not including 18,000 feet MSL.

B. Class G airspace -- surface up to but not including 18,000 feet MSL.

C. Class G airspace -- surface up to but not including 700 feet MSL; Class E airspace - 700 feet to 14,500 feet MSL.

Answer (A) is correct. *(ACL)*

DISCUSSION: Sprague Airport is located between areas 3 and 4 on Fig. 26. In the lower left-hand corner of the figure, there is a portion of a blue shaded ring. According to the chart legend, this indicates that Class E airspace begins at 1,200 ft. AGL within this ring. Therefore, the Class G airspace would extend from the surface to 1,200 ft. AGL, followed by Class E airspace up to, but not including, 18,000 ft. MSL.

Answer (B) is incorrect. The Class G airspace above Sprague Airport ends at 1,200 ft. AGL (the beginning of Class E airspace), not 18,000 ft. MSL. Answer (C) is incorrect. Class G airspace above Sprague Airport extends to 1,200 ft. AGL, indicated by the shaded blue line in the bottom left corner of the chart excerpt. Class G airspace up to 700 ft. AGL (not MSL) would be indicated by magenta shading surrounding Sprague Airport. Additionally, Class E airspace above Sprague Airport extends to 18,000 ft. MSL, not 14,500 ft. MSL.

42. (Refer to Figure 26 on page 329.) (Refer to area 3.) When flying over Arrowwood National Wildlife Refuge, a pilot should fly no lower than

A. 2,000 feet AGL.

B. 2,500 feet AGL.

C. 3,000 feet AGL.

Answer (A) is correct. *(AIM Para 7-4-6)*

DISCUSSION: On Fig. 26, Arrowwood National Wildlife Refuge is to the west of area 3. All aircraft are requested to maintain a minimum altitude of 2,000 ft. above the surface of a national wildlife refuge except if forced to land by emergency, landing at a designated site, or on official government business.

Answer (B) is incorrect. This flight altitude has no significance to wildlife refuges. Answer (C) is incorrect. This flight altitude has no significance to wildlife refuges.

43. (Refer to Figure 26 on page 329.) (Refer to east of area 5.) The airspace overlying and within 5 miles of Barnes County Airport is

A. Class D airspace from the surface to the floor of the overlying Class E airspace.

B. Class E airspace from the surface to 1,200 feet MSL.

C. Class G airspace from the surface to 700 feet AGL.

Answer (C) is correct. *(ACL)*

DISCUSSION: The magenta band surrounding Barnes County Airport indicates that Class G airspace is from the surface to 700 ft. surrounding that 5 SM ring.

Answer (A) is incorrect. Class D airspace requires a control tower. The Barnes County Airport does not have a control tower, since the airport identifier is magenta, not blue. Answer (B) is incorrect. An airport located in Class E airspace would be marked by magenta dashed lines, such as the ones surrounding Jamestown Airport to the left. Barnes has no such lines.

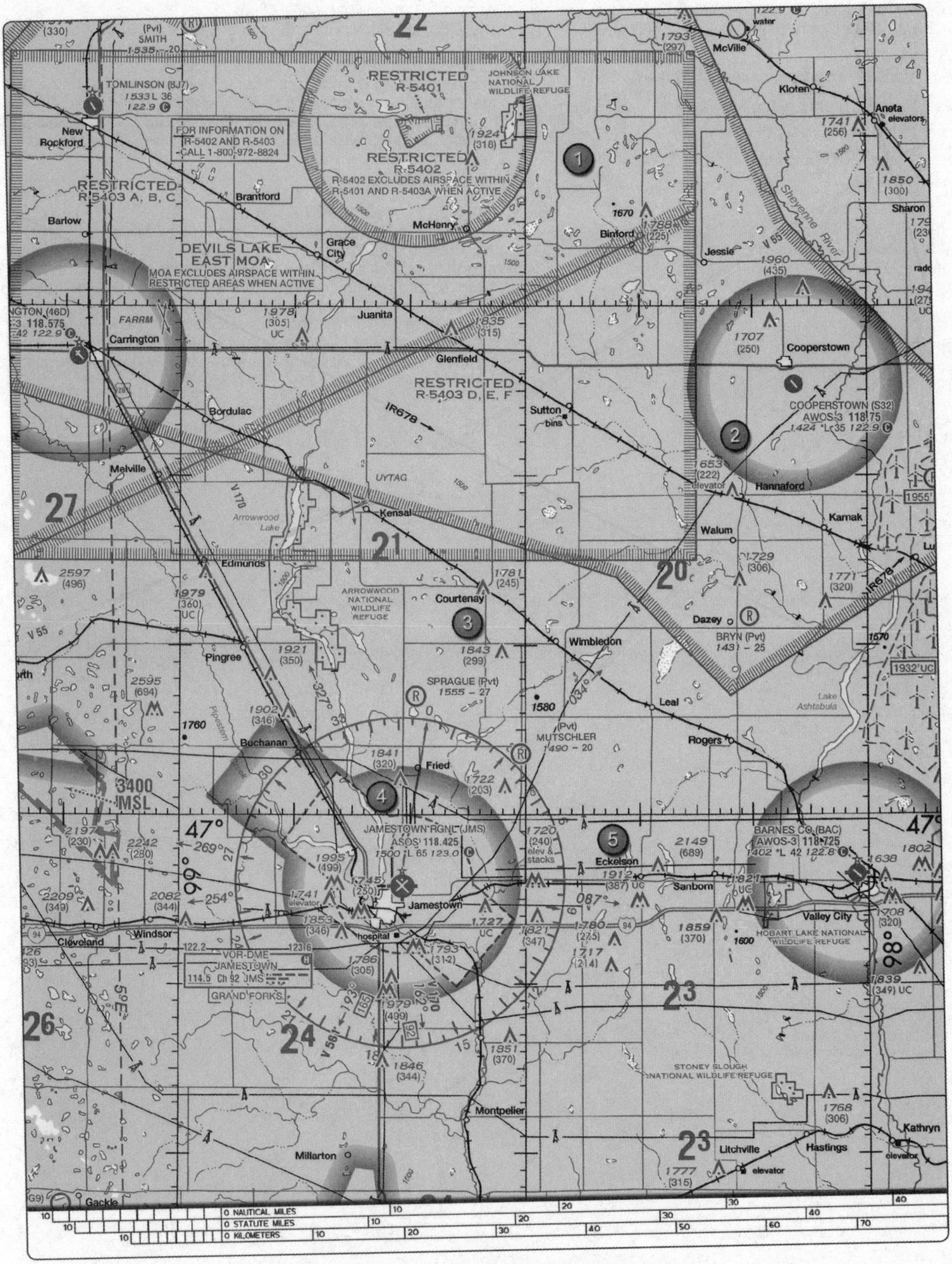

Figure 26. – Sectional Chart Excerpt.
NOTE: Chart is not to scale and should not be used for navigation. Use associated scale.

44. (Refer to Figure 59 on page 331.) (Refer to area 2.) What kind of airport is Deshler (6D7)?

A. A private airport with a grass runway.

B. A public airport with a runway that is not a hard surface.

C. An abandoned paved airport having landmark value.

Answer (B) is correct. *(AIM Chap 3)*

DISCUSSION: According to the Sectional Chart Legend, a magenta circle with nothing indicated on the inside of the circle indicates that airport is not hard-surfaced.

Answer (A) is incorrect. There is not a letter “R” inside the magenta circle indicating it is a private airport. Answer (C) is incorrect. There is no “X” inside the magenta circle to indicate it is an abandoned paved airport having landmark value.

45. (Refer to Figure 59 on page 331.) (Refer to area 3.) What is the airspace classification around Findlay (FDY) airport?

A. C.

B. D.

C. E.

Answer (C) is correct. *(PHAK Chap 16 and Sectional Chart)*

DISCUSSION: A magenta dashed line surrounding an airport identifies it as Class E airspace that extends to the surface. The presence of this dashed magenta line indicates that this airport offers a precision instrument approach.

Answer (A) is incorrect. Class C airspace is identified by two solid magenta lines surrounding the airport. Answer (B) is incorrect. Class D airspace is surrounded by dashed blue lines.

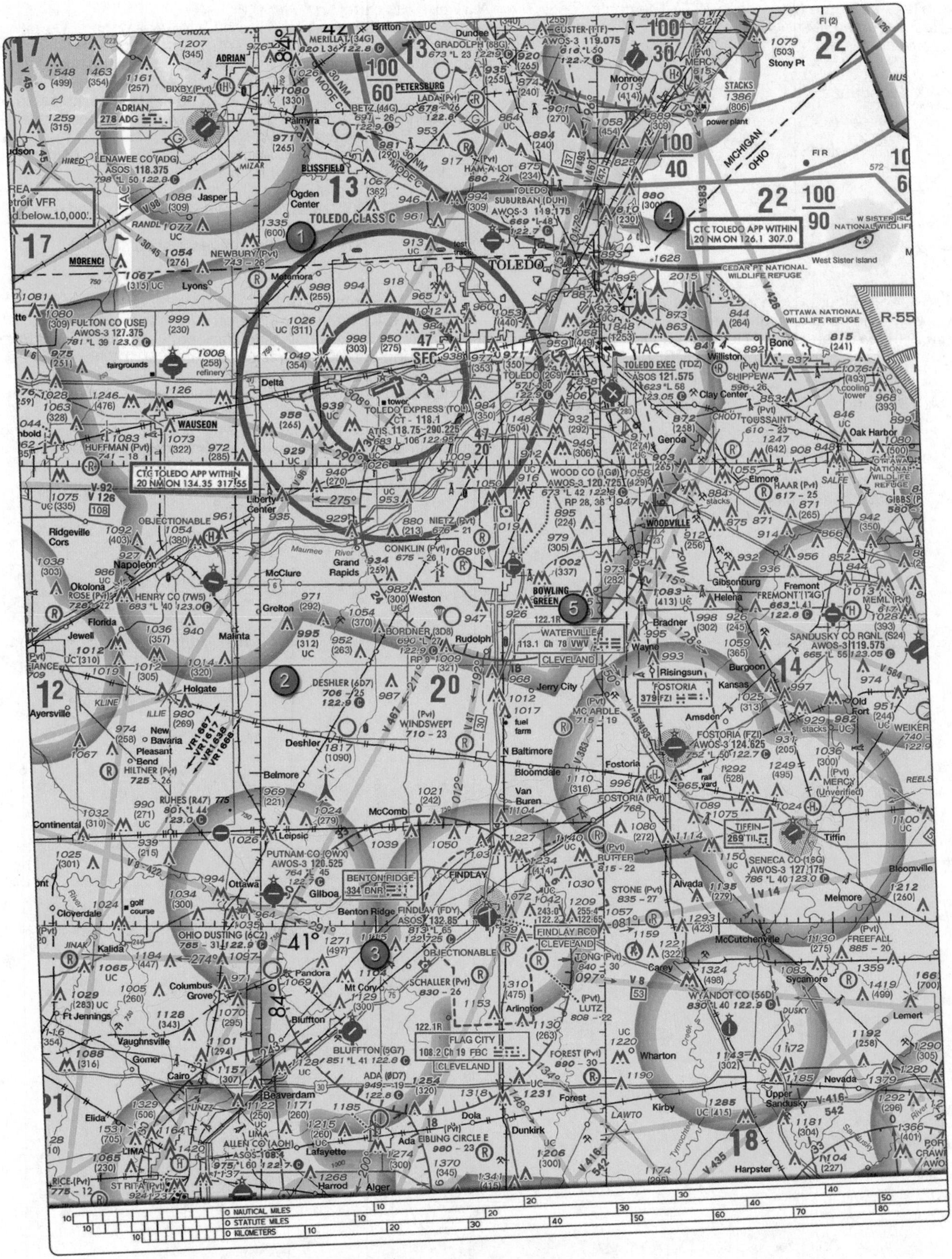

Figure 59. – Sectional Chart Excerpt.
NOTE: Chart is not to scale and should not be used for navigation. Use associated scale.

46. (Refer to Figure 69 on page 333.) The controlled airspace located at the Corpus Christi VORTAC (area 5) begins at

A. the surface.

B. 700 feet AGL.

C. 1,200 feet MSL.

Answer (B) is correct. *(ACL)*

DISCUSSION: On Fig. 69, area 5 is 9 NM north of Corpus Christi. The Corpus Christi VORTAC is just inside the magenta-shaded area. This indicates that Class E (controlled) airspace extends upward from 700 ft. AGL to the base of the overlying airspace [here Class C airspace at 1,200 ft. MSL, as indicated by the magenta solid lines and the "40" above the "12" (separated by a line), 5 NM west of the VORTAC].

Answer (A) is incorrect. A magenta-shaded area indicates that Class E extends upward from 700 ft. AGL, not the surface. Answer (C) is incorrect. Although Class C airspace extending upward from 1,200 ft. MSL to 4,000 ft. MSL is indicated by the magenta solid lines, Class E airspace extends upward from 700 ft. AGL, as indicated by the magenta shading.

47. (Refer to Figure 69 on page 333.) When are two-way radio communications required on a flight from Bishop Airport (area 4) to McCampbell Airport (area 1) at an altitude of 2,000 feet MSL?

A. Entering the Corpus Christi Class C airspace.

B. Leaving and entering the alert areas and entering the Corpus Christi Class C airspace.

C. Leaving and entering the alert areas, entering the Corpus Christi Class C airspace, and passing through the Cabaniss Field Class D airspace.

Answer (A) is correct. *(ACL)*

DISCUSSION: On Fig. 69, area 4 is near the center and area 1 is in the upper right-hand corner of the chart. A flight from Bishop Airport to McCampbell Airport at 2,000 ft. MSL will pass through the Corpus Christi Class C airspace. Two-way radio communications and transponder with encoding altimeter are required when operating within Class C airspace.

Answer (B) is incorrect. Two-way radio communication is not required in alert areas. Answer (C) is incorrect. Two-way radio communication is not required in alert areas, and a direct flight will not pass through the Cabaniss Field Class D airspace.

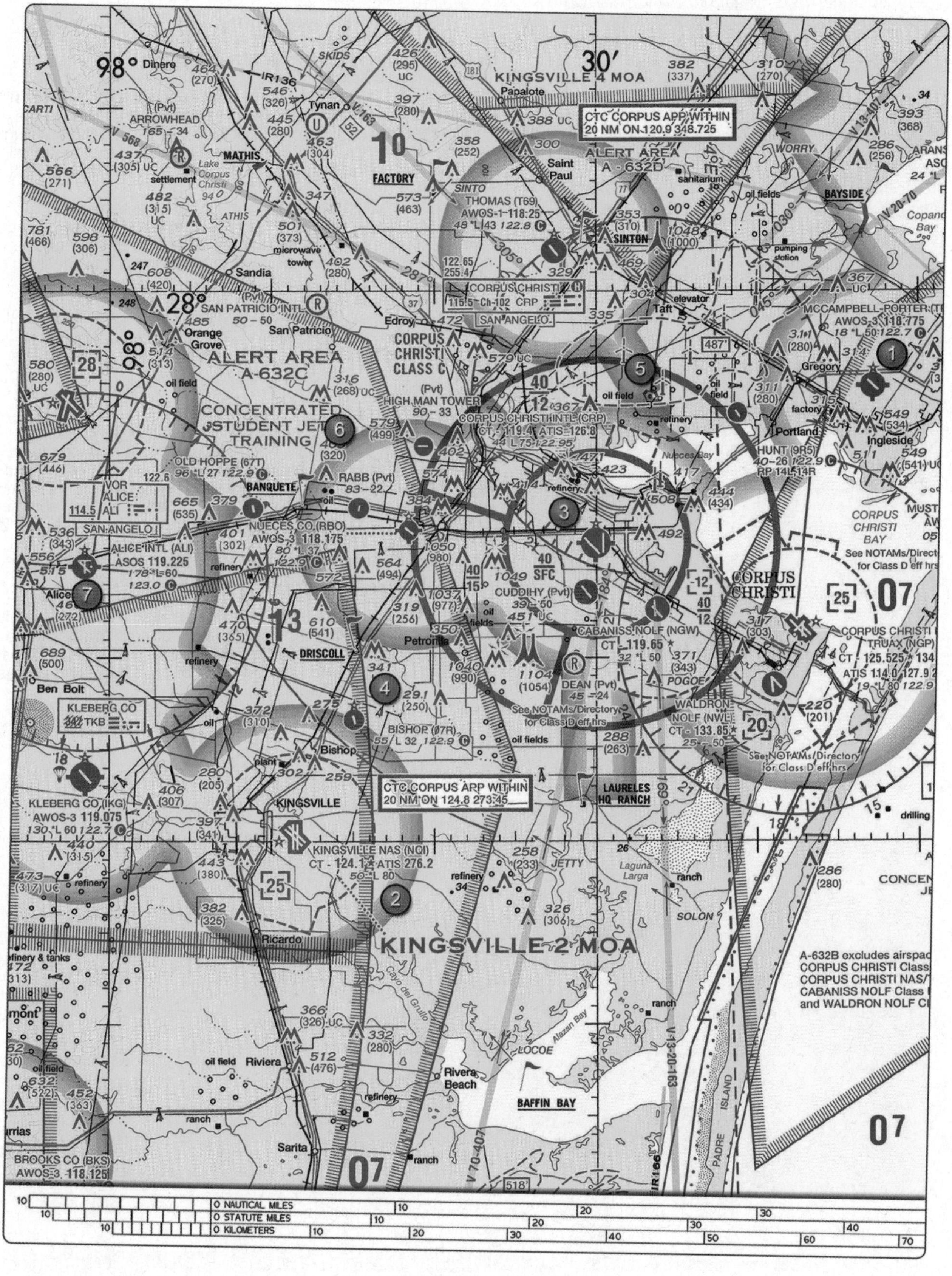

Figure 69. – Sectional Chart Excerpt.
NOTE: Chart is not to scale and should not be used for navigation. Use associated scale.

48. (Refer to Figure 70 on page 335.) When are two-way radio communications required on a flight from Gnoss Airport (area 4) to Livermore Airport (area 5) at an altitude of 3,500 ft. AGL? When entering

A. the Class B airspace.

B. the Livermore Airport Class D airspace.

C. both the Class B airspace and the Livermore Airport Class D airspace.

Answer (B) is correct. *(ACL)*

DISCUSSION: Area 4 is in the upper left hand-corner, and area 5 is in the center of the right-hand side of Fig. 70. A flight from Gnoss Airport to Livermore Airport will pass beneath the sections of Class B airspace extending upward from 4,000 ft. MSL and 6,000 ft. MSL, as indicated by the "100" above the "40" (separated by a line) and the "100" above the "60" (separated by a line), respectively. (Note that the cruising altitude is given as 3,500 ft. AGL, not MSL, and that the terrain elevation along the route of flight appears to be 1,000 ft. MSL or less.)

Livermore Airport is encircled by blue dashed lines, indicating Class D airspace extending upward from the surface to a specified altitude (here 2,900 ft. MSL). Two-way radio communications are required when operating within Class D airspace.

Answer (A) is incorrect. The flight will pass beneath the Class B airspace, and two-way radio communications are required when operating within Class D airspace. Answer (C) is incorrect. The flight will pass beneath the Class B airspace.

49. (Refer to Figure 70 on page 335.) An aircraft takes off from Gnoss Airport (area 4) and flies southeast 25.4 NM to Buchanan Airport. What maximum elevation figure would assure obstruction clearance during the flight?

A. 6,000 feet MSL.

B. 4,200 feet MSL.

C. 3,200 feet MSL.

Answer (C) is correct. *(ACL)*

DISCUSSION: The maximum elevation figure (MEF) is shown in each quadrangle bounded by latitude and longitude tick marks. The MEF in the quadrangle that is just east of Gnoss Airport consists of a large "3" and a somewhat smaller "2," which mean the MEF is 3,200 ft. MSL. In the quadrangle that contains Buchanan Airport, the MEF is south of the airport. The large "2" and the somewhat smaller "4" mean the MEF is 2,400 ft. MSL. Thus, on a flight from Gnoss Airport to Buchanan Airport, the MEF that would ensure obstacle clearance is 3,200 ft.

Answer (A) is incorrect. The shelf of Class B airspace is 6,000 ft. MSL. That portion of Class B airspace is from 6,000 ft. MSL to 10,000 ft. MSL. Answer (B) is incorrect. This would be the MEF to ensure obstruction clearance on a flight from Gnoss Airport to Livermore Airport (area 5), not on a flight from Gnoss Airport to Buchanan Airport.

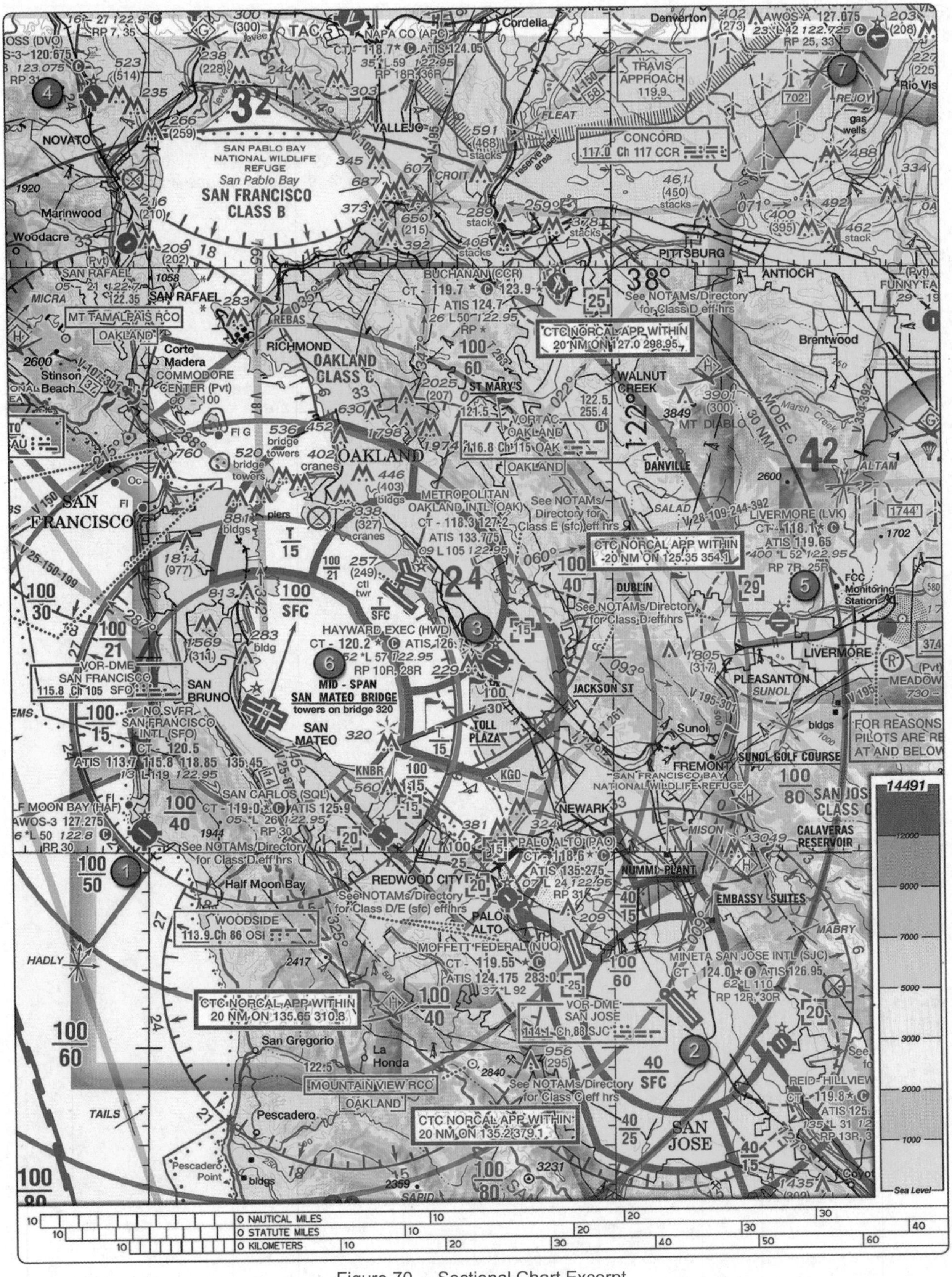

Figure 70. – Sectional Chart Excerpt.
NOTE: Chart is not to scale and should not be used for navigation. Use associated scale.

50. (Refer to Figure 71 on page 337.) (Refer to area 1.) Dubey Airport is

A. a privately owned airport restricted to use.

B. a restricted military stage field within restricted airspace.

C. an airport restricted to use by sport pilots only.

Answer (A) is correct. *(ACL)*

DISCUSSION: Dubey Airport (south of 1) is a private, i.e., nonpublic-use, airport as indicated by the term "(Pvt)" after the airport name. Private airports that are shown on the sectional charts have an emergency or landmark value. The airport symbol with the letter "R" in the center means it is a nonpublic-use airport.

Answer (B) is incorrect. Military airfields are labeled as AFB, NAS, AAF, NAAS, NAF, MCAS, or DND. Answer (C) is incorrect. Dubey is restricted by its use according to its owners and management.

51. (Refer to Figure 71 on page 337.) (Refer to area 6.) Sky Way Airport is

A. an airport restricted to use by private and recreational pilots.

B. a restricted military stage field within restricted airspace.

C. a nonpublic-use airport.

Answer (C) is correct. *(ACL)*

DISCUSSION: Sky Way Airport (west of 6) is a private, i.e., nonpublic-use, airport as indicated by the term "(Pvt)" after the airport name. Private airports that are shown on the sectional charts have an emergency or landmark value.

Answer (A) is incorrect. The airport symbol with the letter "R" in the center means it is a nonpublic-use airport, not that only private and recreational pilots may use the airport. Answer (B) is incorrect. Military airfields are labeled as AFB, NAS, AAF, NAAS, NAF, MCAS, or DND.

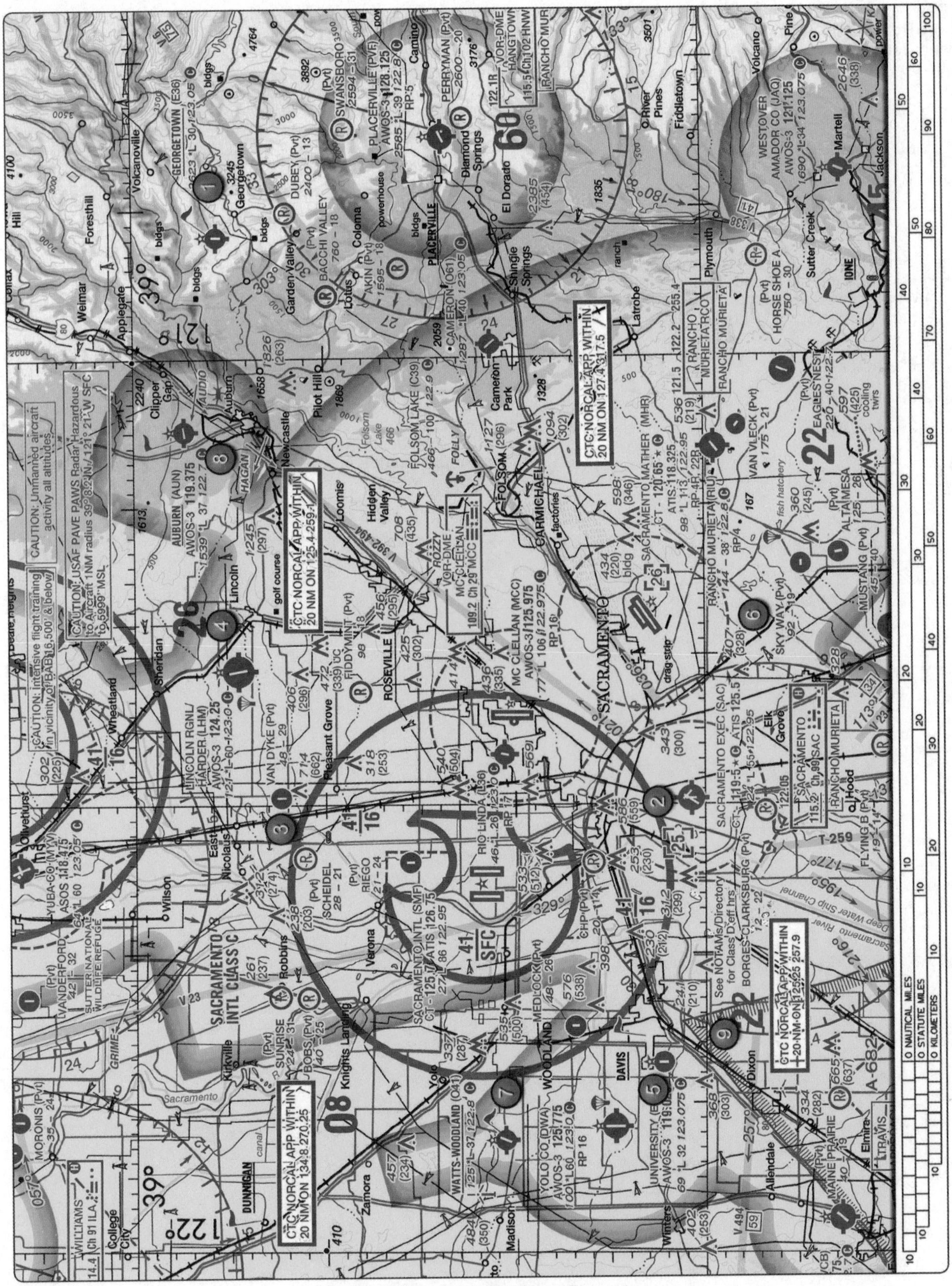

Figure 71. – Sectional Chart Excerpt.

NOTE: Chart is not to scale and should not be used for navigation. Use associated scale.

52. (Refer to Figure 74 on page 339.) (Refer to area 6.) The Class C airspace at Metropolitan Oakland International (OAK) which extends from the surface upward has a ceiling of

A. both 2,100 feet and 3,000 feet MSL.

B. 8,000 feet MSL.

C. 2,100 feet AGL.

Answer (A) is correct. *(ACL)*

DISCUSSION: The Class C airspace at OAK (area 6) is shown in solid magenta lines. The surface area over the airport indicates the Class C airspace extends from the surface (SFC) upward to T, which means the ceiling ends at the base of the San Francisco Class B airspace. The base of the Class B airspace changes over OAK. To the left of OAK the base is 2,100 ft. MSL and to the right of OAK the base is 3,000 ft. MSL.

Answer (B) is incorrect. This is the ceiling of the Class B, not the Class C, airspace over OAK. Answer (C) is incorrect. This is the approximate ceiling of the Class C airspace on the west side of OAK, but the ceiling on the east side is 3,000 ft. MSL.

53. (Refer to Figure 74 on page 339.) (Refer to area 1.) What minimum altitude is required to avoid the Livermore Airport (LVK) Class D airspace?

A. 2,503 feet MSL.

B. 2,901 feet MSL.

C. 3,297 feet MSL.

Answer (B) is correct. *(ACL)*

DISCUSSION: The Class D airspace at Livermore Airport extends from the surface to 2,900 ft. MSL, as indicated by the [29] within the blue segmented circle. Thus, the minimum altitude to fly over and avoid the Livermore Airport Class D airspace is 2,901 ft. MSL.

Answer (A) is incorrect. At 2,503 ft. MSL, you would be in Class D airspace. Answer (C) is incorrect. Although at 3,297 ft. MSL you would be above the Class D airspace, it is not the minimum altitude at which you could avoid the airspace.

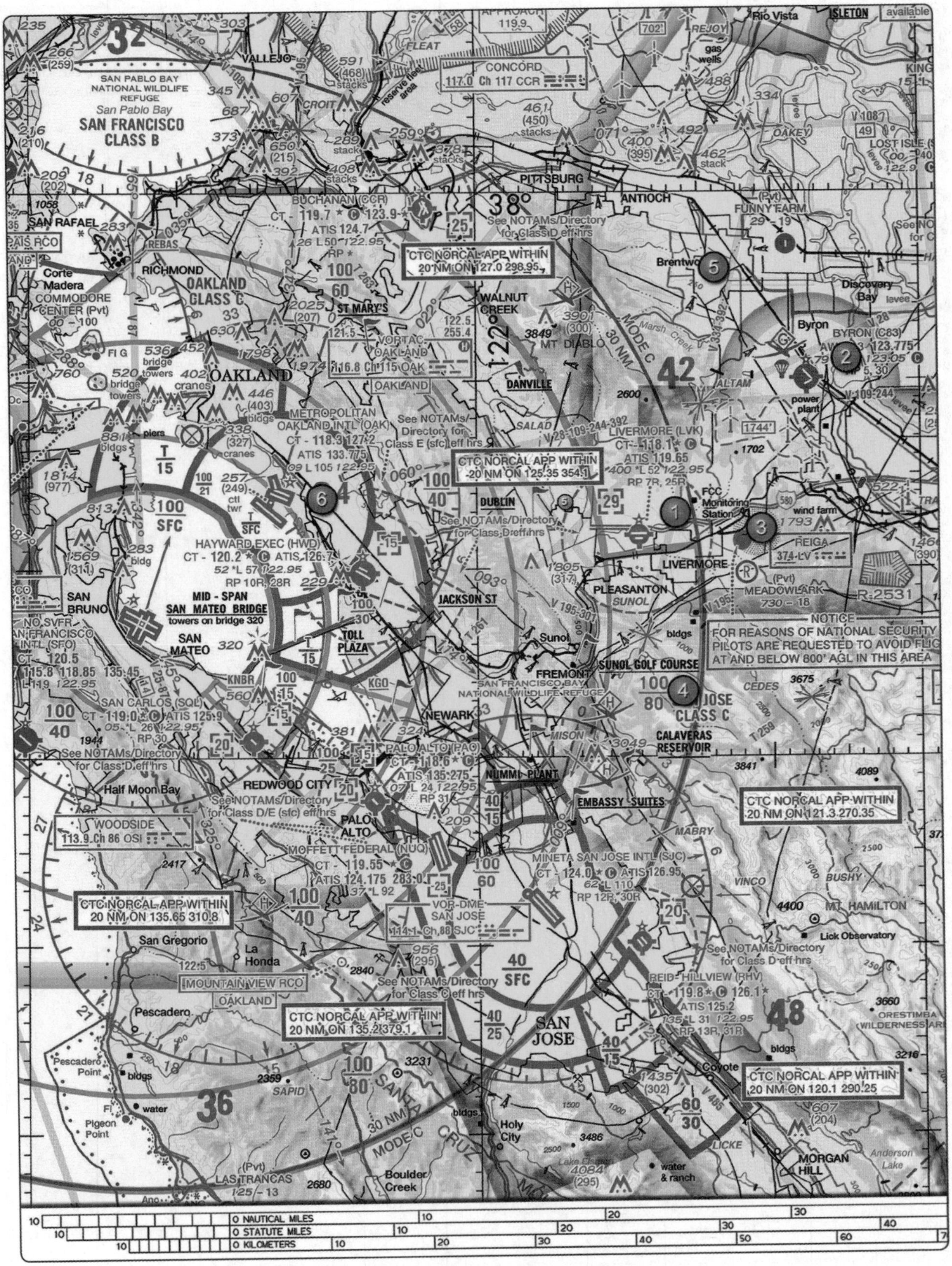

Figure 74. – Sectional Chart Excerpt.
NOTE: Chart is not to scale and should not be used for navigation. Use associated scale.

54. (Refer to Figure 75 on page 341.) The airspace surrounding the Gila Bend AF AUX Airport (GBN) (area 6) is classified as Class

A. B.

B. C.

C. D.

Answer (C) is correct. *(AIM Chap 3)*

DISCUSSION: The GBN airport is surrounded by a dashed blue line, which indicates it is within Class D airspace.

Answer (A) is incorrect. Class B airspace is surrounded by a solid blue line. Answer (B) is incorrect. Class C airspace is surrounded by a solid magenta line.

55. (Refer to Figure 75 on page 341.) What is the dotted outlined area northeast of Gila Bend Airport, near area 3?

A. Restricted airspace.

B. Military operations area.

C. Wilderness area.

Answer (C) is correct. *(PHAK Chap 16)*

DISCUSSION: The area just to the west of area 3 represents an area that is a national park, wildlife refuge, primitive and wilderness area, etc. To the northwest of this area is the name, North Maricopa Mountains Wilderness Area.

Answer (A) is incorrect. A restricted area on a sectional chart is outlined with a hashed blue border and labeled with an "R" followed by a numbered (e.g., R-1234). Answer (B) is incorrect. A military operations area (MOA) is outlined with a hashed magenta border. MOAs are named rather than numbered (e.g., Snowbird MOA) and further defined on the back of sectional charts.

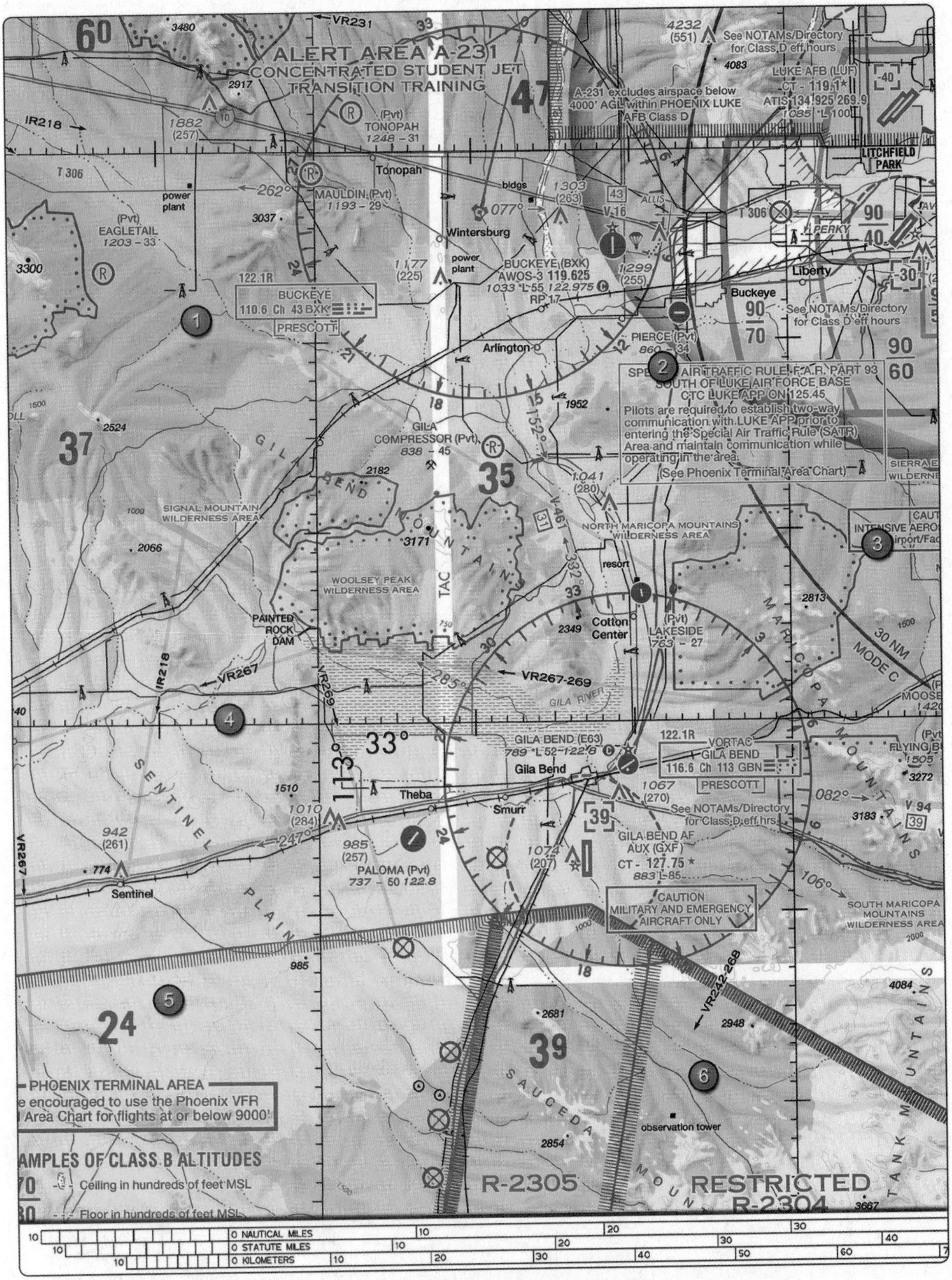

Figure 75. – Sectional Chart Excerpt.
NOTE: Chart is not to scale and should not be used for navigation. Use associated scale.

56. (Refer to Figure 22 below, and Legend 1 on page 343.) (Refer to area 3.) For information about glider operations at Ridgeland Airport, refer to

A. notes on the border of the chart.

B. the Chart Supplement.

C. the Notices to Airmen (NOTAM) publication.

Answer (B) is correct. *(ACL)*

DISCUSSION: The miniature glider near the Ridgeland Airport (at 3 on Fig. 22) indicates a glider operations area. The Chart Supplement will have information on the glider operations at Ridgeland Airport.

Answer (A) is incorrect. The sectional chart legend identifies symbols only. Answer (C) is incorrect. NOTAMs are issued only for hazards to flight.

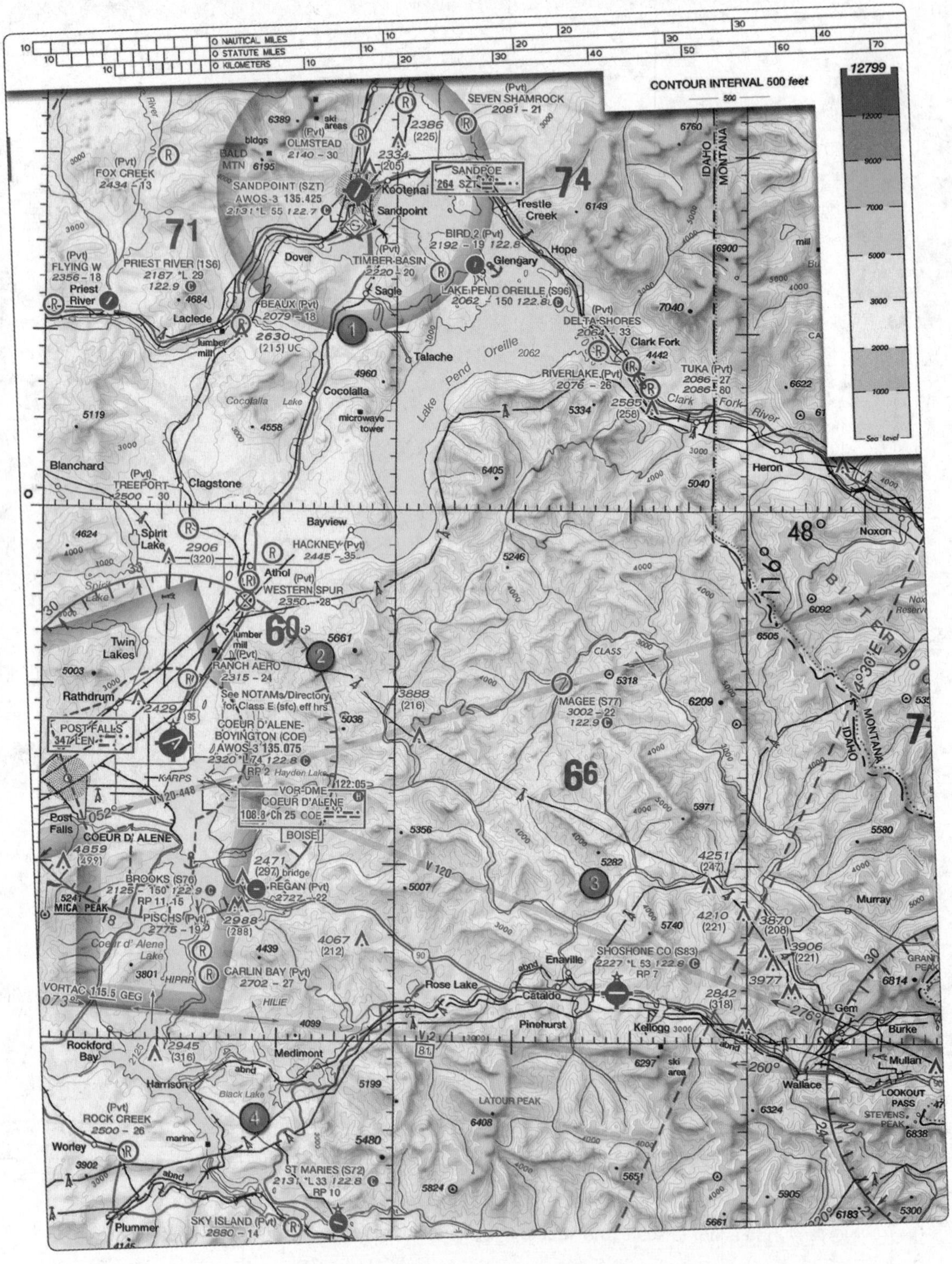

Figure 22. – Sectional Chart Excerpt.

NOTE: Chart is not to scale and should not be used for navigation. Use associated scale.

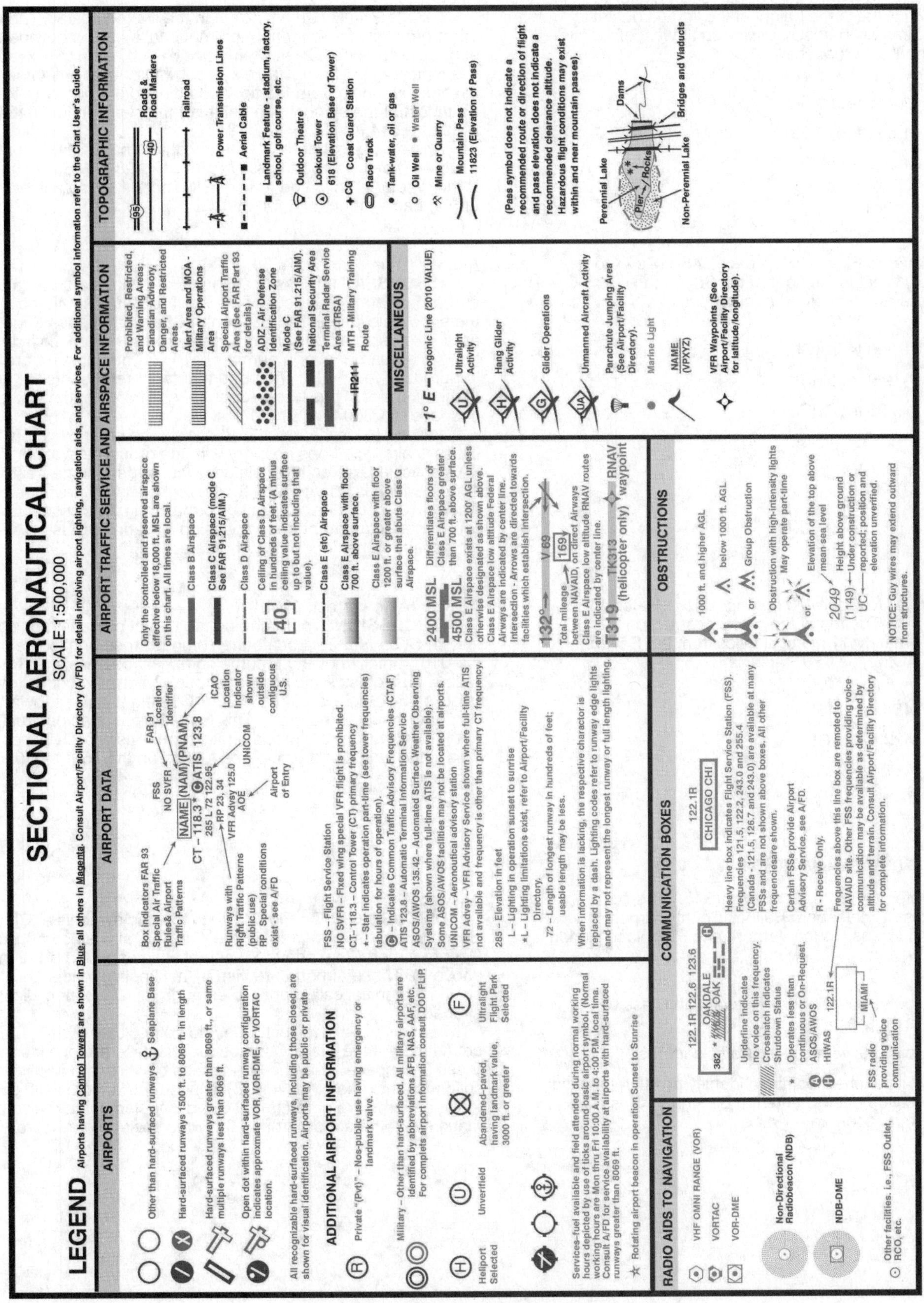

Legend 1. – Sectional Aeronautical Chart.

57. (Refer to Figure 23 on page 345.) (Refer to area 3.) What is the height of the lighted obstacle approximately 6 nautical miles southwest of Savannah International?

A. 1,498 feet MSL.

B. 1,531 feet AGL.

C. 1,548 feet MSL.

Answer (C) is correct. *(ACL)*

DISCUSSION: On Fig. 23, find the lighted obstacle noted by its proximity to Savannah International by being outside the surface area of the Class C airspace, which has a 5-NM radius. It is indicated by the obstacle symbol with arrows or lightning flashes extending from the tip. According to the numbers to the northeast of the symbol, the height of the obstacle is 1,548 ft. MSL or 1,534 ft. AGL.

Answer (A) is incorrect. The unlighted tower 8 NM, not 6 NM, southwest of the airport has a height of 1,498 ft. MSL. Answer (B) is incorrect. An unlighted tower 9 NM, not 6 NM, southwest of the airport has a height of 1,531 ft. AGL.

58. (Refer to Figure 23 on page 345.) (Refer to area 3.) What is the floor of the Savannah Class C airspace at the shelf area (outer circle)?

A. 1,200 feet AGL.

B. 1,300 feet MSL.

C. 1,700 feet MSL.

Answer (B) is correct. *(ACL)*

DISCUSSION: Class C airspace consists of a surface area and a shelf area. The floor of the shelf area is 1,200 ft. above the airport elevation. The Savannah Class C airspace (Fig. 23, area 3) is depicted by solid magenta circles. For each circle there is a number over a number or SFC. The numbers are in hundreds of feet MSL. The bottom number represents the floor of the airspace. Thus, the floor of the shelf area of the Class C airspace is 1,300 ft. MSL (41/13).

Answer (A) is incorrect. The floor of the outer circle of Class C airspace does not vary with the ground elevation. The FAA specifies a fixed MSL altitude, rounded to the nearest 100 ft., which is about 1,200 ft. above the airport elevation. Answer (C) is incorrect. This is the maximum elevation figure (MEF) of the quadrant encompassing Savannah Class C airspace, not the floor of the shelf area.

59. (Refer to Figure 23 on page 345.) (Refer to area 3.) The top of the group obstruction approximately 11 nautical miles from the Savannah VORTAC on the 010° radial is

A. 454 feet MSL.

B. 429 feet AGL.

C. 417 feet MSL.

Answer (A) is correct. *(ACL)*

DISCUSSION: To determine the height of the lighted stack, first find it on Fig. 23. Locate the compass rose and look along the 010° radial, knowing that the compass rose has a 10 NM radius. Just outside the compass rose is a group obstruction (stacks). Its height is 454 ft. MSL; AGL height is not shown.

Answer (B) is incorrect. This is the height of an obstruction to the northeast of the group obstruction. Answer (C) is incorrect. This is the height of a group obstruction on the 355°, not 010°, radial.

9.3 Identifying Landmarks

60. (Refer to Figure 23 on page 345.) The flag symbols at Statesboro Bullock County Airport, Claxton-Evans County Airport, and Ridgeland Airport are

A. outer boundaries of Savannah Class C airspace.

B. airports with special traffic patterns.

C. visual checkpoints to identify position for initial callup prior to entering Savannah Class C airspace.

Answer (C) is correct. *(ACL)*

DISCUSSION: On Fig. 23, note the flag symbols at Claxton-Evans County Airport (1 in. to the left of 2), at Statesboro Bullock County Airport (2 in. above 2), and at Ridgeland Airport (2 in. above 3). These airports are visual checkpoints to identify position for initial callup prior to entering the Savannah Class C airspace.

Answer (A) is incorrect. They do not indicate outer boundaries of the Class C airspace. The flags are outside the Class C airspace area, the boundaries of which are marked by solid magenta lines. Answer (B) is incorrect. Airports with special traffic patterns are noted in the Chart Supplement and also by markings at the airport around the wind sock or tetrahedron.

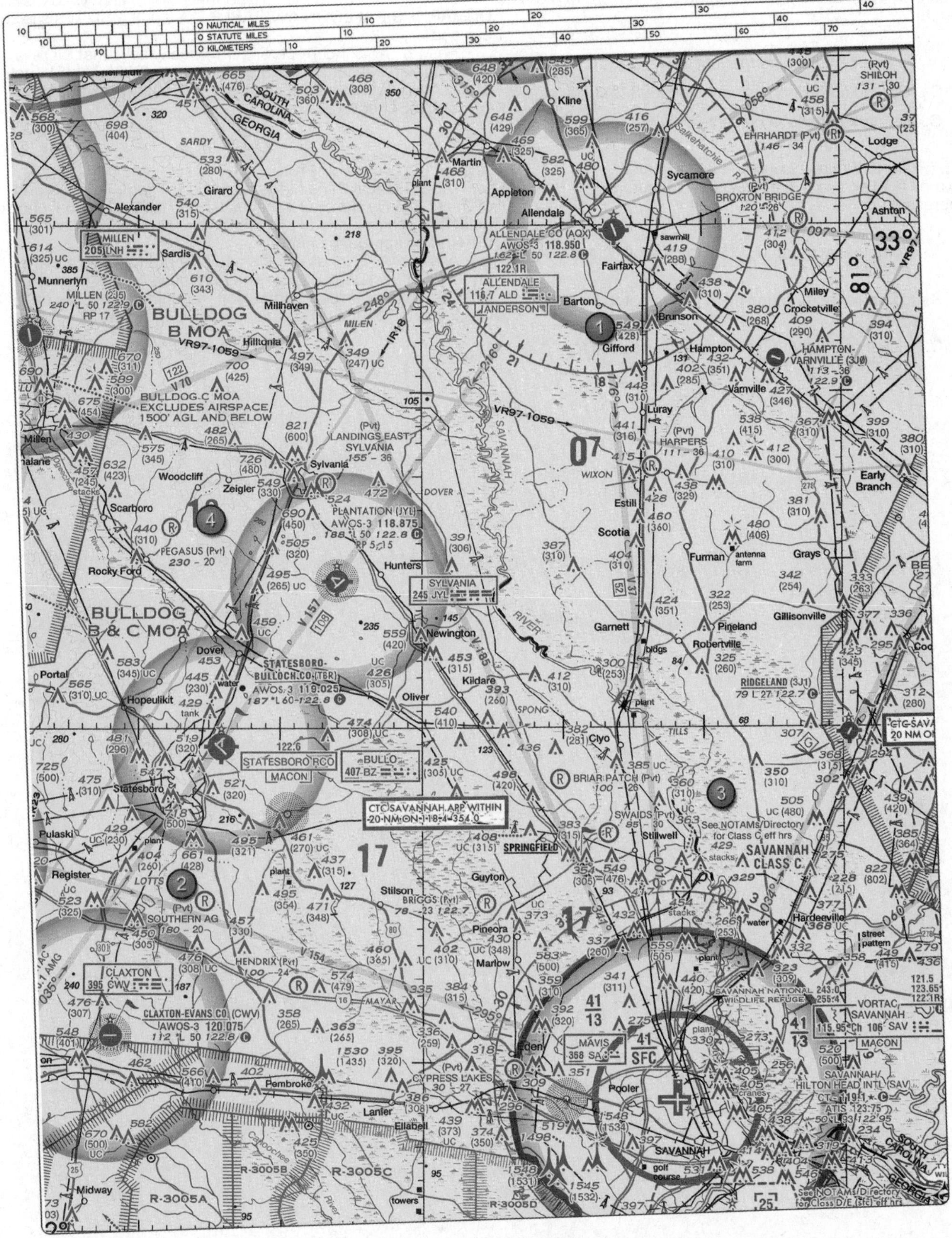

Figure 23. – Sectional Chart Excerpt.
NOTE: Chart is not to scale and should not be used for navigation. Use associated scale.

61. (Refer to Figure 20 on page 347.) (Refer to area 5.) The CAUTION box denotes what hazard to aircraft?

A. Unmarked blimp hangars at 308 feet MSL.

B. Unmarked balloon on cable to 3,008 feet AGL.

C. Unmarked balloon on cable to 3,008 feet MSL.

Answer (C) is correct. *(ACL)*

DISCUSSION: On Fig. 20, northwest of 5, find "CAUTION: UNMARKED BALLOON ON CABLE TO 3,008 MSL." This is self-explanatory.

Answer (A) is incorrect. The box clearly says that there is an unmarked balloon, not blimp hangars, to 3,008 ft. MSL, not 308 ft. MSL. Answer (B) is incorrect. The balloon extends to 3,008 ft. MSL, not AGL.

62. (Refer to Figure 20 on page 347.) (Refer to area 2.) The flag symbol at Lake Drummond represents a

A. compulsory reporting point for Norfolk Class C airspace.

B. compulsory reporting point for Hampton Roads Airport.

C. visual checkpoint used to identify position for initial callup to Norfolk Approach Control.

Answer (C) is correct. *(ACL)*

DISCUSSION: The magenta (reddish) flag (Fig. 20, north of 2) at Lake Drummond signifies that the lake is a visual checkpoint that can be used to identify the position for initial callup to the Norfolk approach control.

Answer (A) is incorrect. Compulsory reporting points are on IFR, not sectional, charts. They are used on IFR flights. Answer (B) is incorrect. Compulsory reporting points are on IFR, not sectional, charts. They are used on IFR flights.

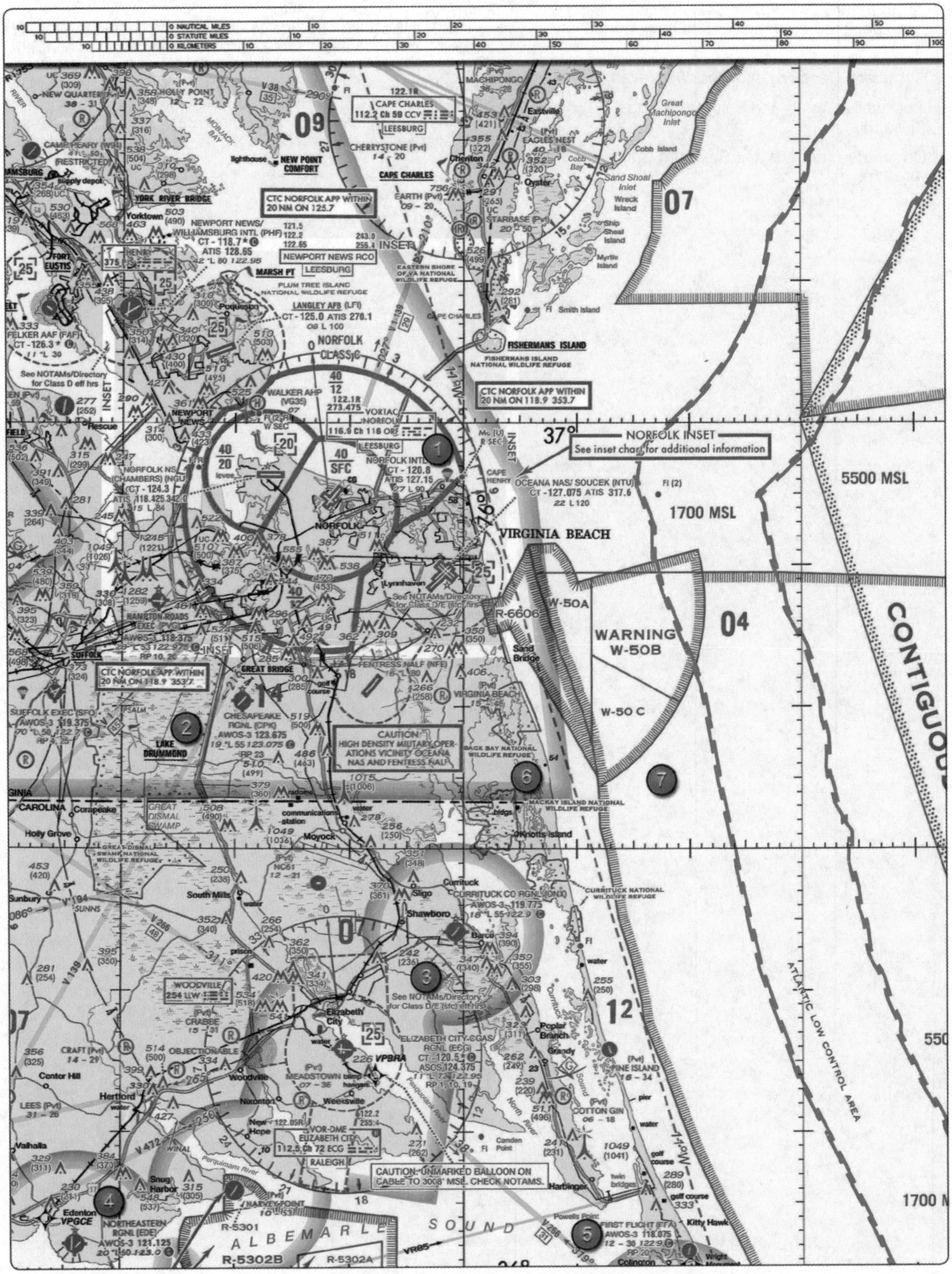

Figure 20. – Sectional Chart Excerpt.
NOTE: Chart is not to scale and should not be used for navigation. Use associated scale.

63. (Refer to Figure 24 on page 349.) Which public use airports depicted are indicated as having fuel?

A. Commerce (area 6) and Rockwall (area 1).

B. Rockwall (area 1) and Sulphur Springs (area 5).

C. Commerce (area 6) and Sulphur Springs (area 5).

Answer (B) is correct. *(ACL)*

DISCUSSION: On Fig. 24, the requirement is to identify the airports having fuel available. Airports having fuel available are designated by small squares extending from the top, bottom, and both sides of the airport symbol. Only Rockwall (area 1) and Sulphur Springs (area 5) have such symbols.

Answer (A) is incorrect. Commerce does not indicate it has fuel. Answer (C) is incorrect. Commerce does not indicate it has fuel.

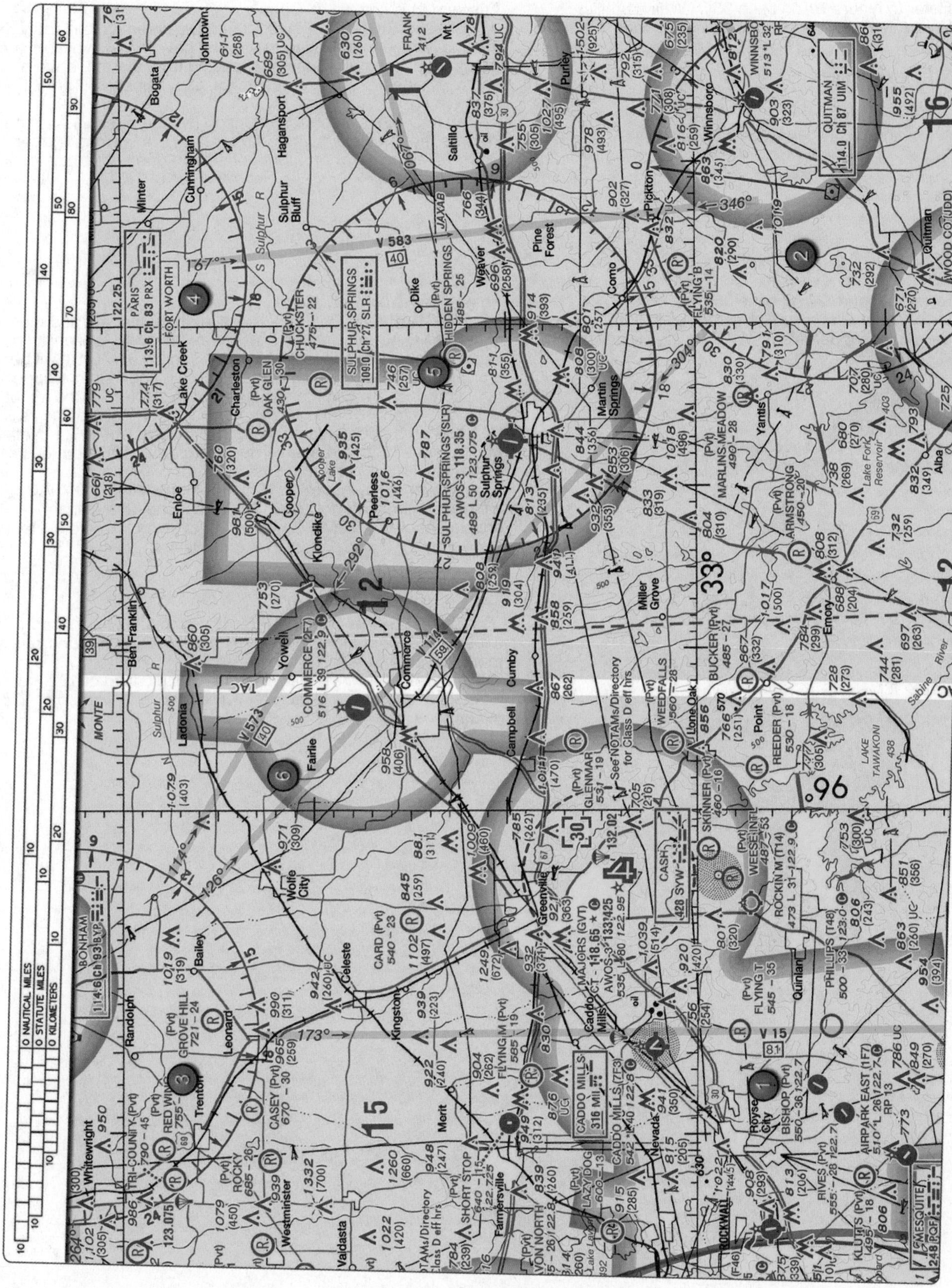

Figure 24. – Sectional Chart Excerpt.
NOTE: Chart is not to scale and should not be used for navigation. Use associated scale.

64. (Refer to Figure 21 on page 351.) Which public use airport depicted is indicated as having fuel?

A. Minot Int'l (area 1).

B. Garrison (area 2).

C. Mercer County Regional Airport (area 3).

Answer (A) is correct. *(ACL)*

DISCUSSION: On Fig. 21, the requirement is to identify the airports having fuel available. Airports having fuel available are designated by small squares extending from the top, bottom, and both sides of the airport symbol. Only Minot Int'l (area 1) has such a symbol.

Answer (B) is incorrect. Garrison (west of area 2) does not indicate that fuel is available. Answer (C) is incorrect. Mercer County Regional Airport (south of area 3) does not indicate that fuel is available.

9.4 Radio Frequencies

65. (Refer to Figure 21 on page 351.) On what frequency can a pilot receive Hazardous Inflight Weather Advisory Service (HIWAS) in the vicinity of area 1?

A. 117.1 MHz.

B. 118.0 MHz.

C. 122.2 MHz.

Answer (A) is correct. *(ACL)*

DISCUSSION: On Fig. 21, 1 is on the upper left and the Minot VORTAC information box is 1 in. below 1. Availability of Hazardous Inflight Weather Advisory Service (HIWAS) will be indicated by a circle which contains an "H," found in the upper right corner of a navigation frequency box. Note that the Minot VORTAC information box has such a symbol. Accordingly, a HIWAS can be obtained on the VOR frequency of 117.1. Notice the 1 before 17.1 is truncated by the excerpt. VOR frequencies all begin with a 1, so a 1 can be inferred.

Answer (B) is incorrect. "Ch 118" in the Minot VORTAC information box refers to the TACAN channel (the military equivalent of VOR/DME). Answer (C) is incorrect. The universal frequency for Flight Service is 122.2 MHz.

66. (Refer to Figure 21 on page 351.) (Refer to area 2.) The CTAF/MULTICOM frequency for Garrison Airport is

A. 122.8 MHz.

B. 122.9 MHz.

C. 123.0 MHz.

Answer (B) is correct. *(ACL)*

DISCUSSION: The CTAF for Garrison Municipal Airport (west of area 2 in Fig. 21) is 122.9, because that frequency is marked with a C.

Answer (A) is incorrect. There is no indication of 122.8 at Garrison. Answer (C) is incorrect. There is no indication of 123.0 at Garrison.

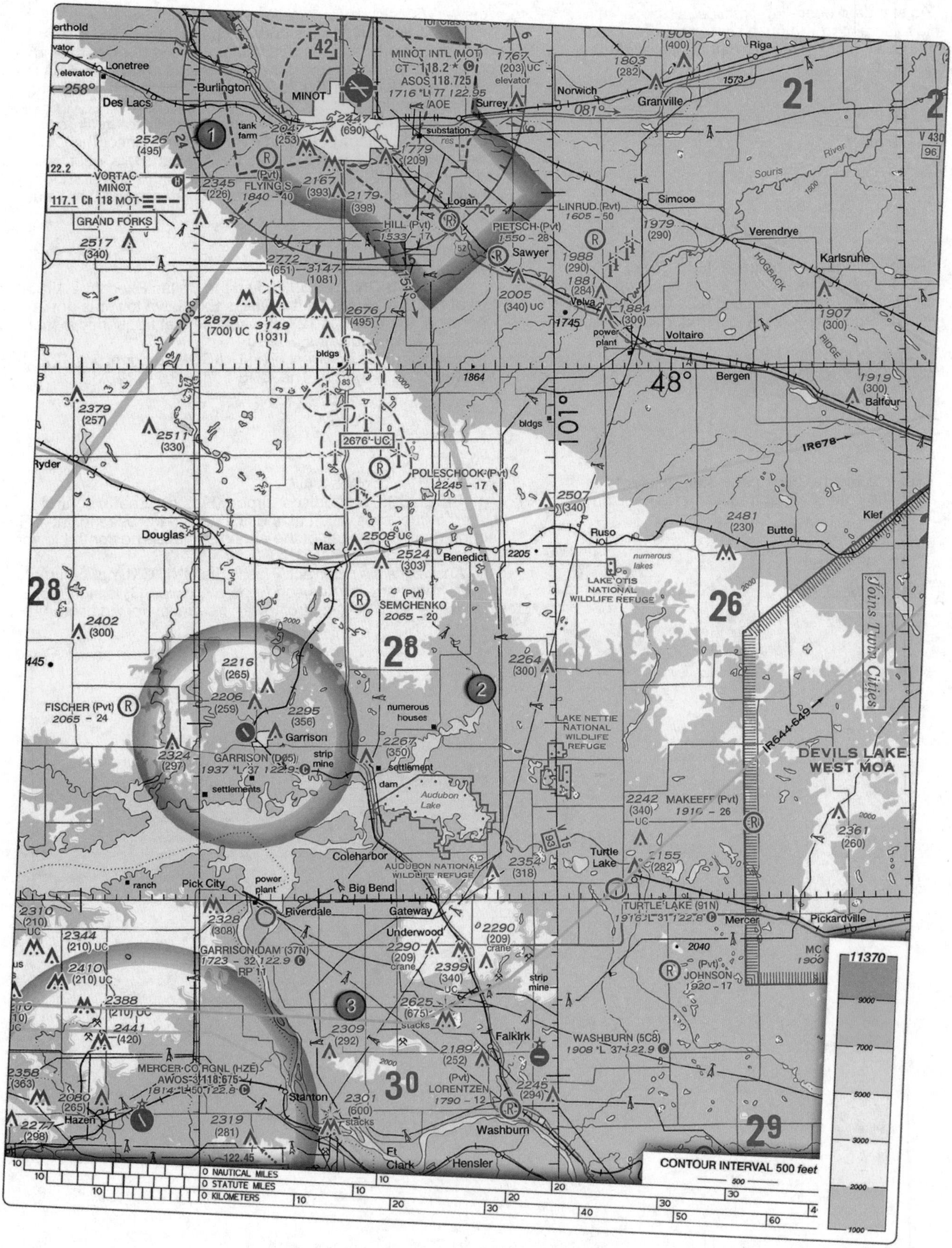

Figure 21. – Sectional Chart Excerpt.
NOTE: Chart is not to scale and should not be used for navigation. Use associated scale.

67. As standard operating practice, all inbound traffic to an airport without a control tower should continuously monitor the appropriate facility from a distance of

A. 25 miles.

B. 20 miles.

C. 10 miles.

Answer (C) is correct. *(AIM Para 4-1-9)*

DISCUSSION: As a standard operating practice, pilots of inbound traffic to an airport without a control tower should continuously monitor and communicate, as appropriate, on the designated Common Traffic Advisory Frequency (CTAF) from 10 mi. to landing.

Answer (A) is incorrect. All inbound traffic to an airport without a control tower should continuously monitor the CTAF from a distance of 10 mi., not 25 mi. Answer (B) is incorrect. All inbound traffic to an airport without a control tower should continuously monitor the CTAF from a distance of 10 mi., not 20 mi.

68. (Refer to Figure 25 on page 353.) (Refer to area 3.) If Dallas Executive Tower is not in operation, which frequency should be used as a Common Traffic Advisory Frequency (CTAF) to monitor airport traffic?

A. 127.25 MHz.

B. 122.95 MHz.

C. 126.35 MHz.

Answer (A) is correct. *(ACL)*

DISCUSSION: In Fig. 25, find the Dallas Executive Airport just above area 3. When the Dallas Executive tower is not in operation, the CTAF is 127.25 because that frequency is marked with a C, which indicates a CTAF.

Answer (B) is incorrect. The UNICOM frequency is 122.95. Answer (C) is incorrect. The ATIS frequency is 126.35.

69. (Refer to Figure 25 on page 353.) (Refer to area 2.) The control tower frequency for Addison Airport is

A. 122.95 MHz.

B. 126.0 MHz.

C. 133.4 MHz.

Answer (B) is correct. *(ACL)*

DISCUSSION: Addison Airport (Fig. 25, area 2) control tower frequency is given as the first item in the second line of the airport data to the right of the airport symbol. The control tower (CT) frequency is 126.0 MHz.

Answer (A) is incorrect. This is the UNICOM, not control tower, frequency for Addison Airport. Answer (C) is incorrect. This is the ATIS, not control tower, frequency for Addison Airport.

Figure 25. – Sectional Chart Excerpt.
NOTE: Chart is not to scale and should not be used for navigation. Use associated scale.

70. (Refer to Figure 26 on page 355.) (Refer to area 2.) What is the recommended communication procedure when inbound to land at Cooperstown Airport?

A. Broadcast intentions when 10 miles out on the CTAF/MULTICOM frequency, 122.9 MHz.

B. Contact UNICOM when 10 miles out on 122.8 MHz.

C. Circle the airport in a left turn prior to entering traffic.

Answer (A) is correct. *(AIM Para 4-1-9)*

DISCUSSION: Find Cooperstown Airport, which is at the top of Fig. 26, just north of 2. You should broadcast your intentions when 10 NM out on the CTAF/MULTICOM frequency, 122.9 MHz.

Answer (B) is incorrect. There is no UNICOM indicated at Cooperstown, and the CTAF is 122.9, not 122.8. Answer (C) is incorrect. A left turn is not a communication procedure.

71. (Refer to Figure 26 on page 355.) (Refer to area 4.) The CTAF/UNICOM frequency at Jamestown Airport is

A. 122.2 MHz.

B. 123.0 MHz.

C. 123.6 MHz.

Answer (B) is correct. *(ACL)*

DISCUSSION: The UNICOM frequency is printed in bold italics in the airport identifier. At Jamestown it is 123.0 MHz. The C next to it indicates it as the CTAF.

Answer (A) is incorrect. This is the Flight Service frequency, not UNICOM. Answer (C) is incorrect. This is an FSS frequency, not UNICOM.

72. (Refer to Figure 26 on page 355.) (Refer to area 5.) What is the CTAF/UNICOM frequency at Barnes County Airport?

A. 122.2 MHz.

B. 122.8 MHz.

C. 123.6 MHz.

Answer (B) is correct. *(ACL)*

DISCUSSION: In Fig. 26, Barnes County Airport is to the west of area 5. The CTAF at Barnes County Airport is marked as the UNICOM frequency for the airport, i.e., 122.8.

Answer (A) is incorrect. This is the Flight Service frequency. Answer (C) is incorrect. This is an FSS frequency.

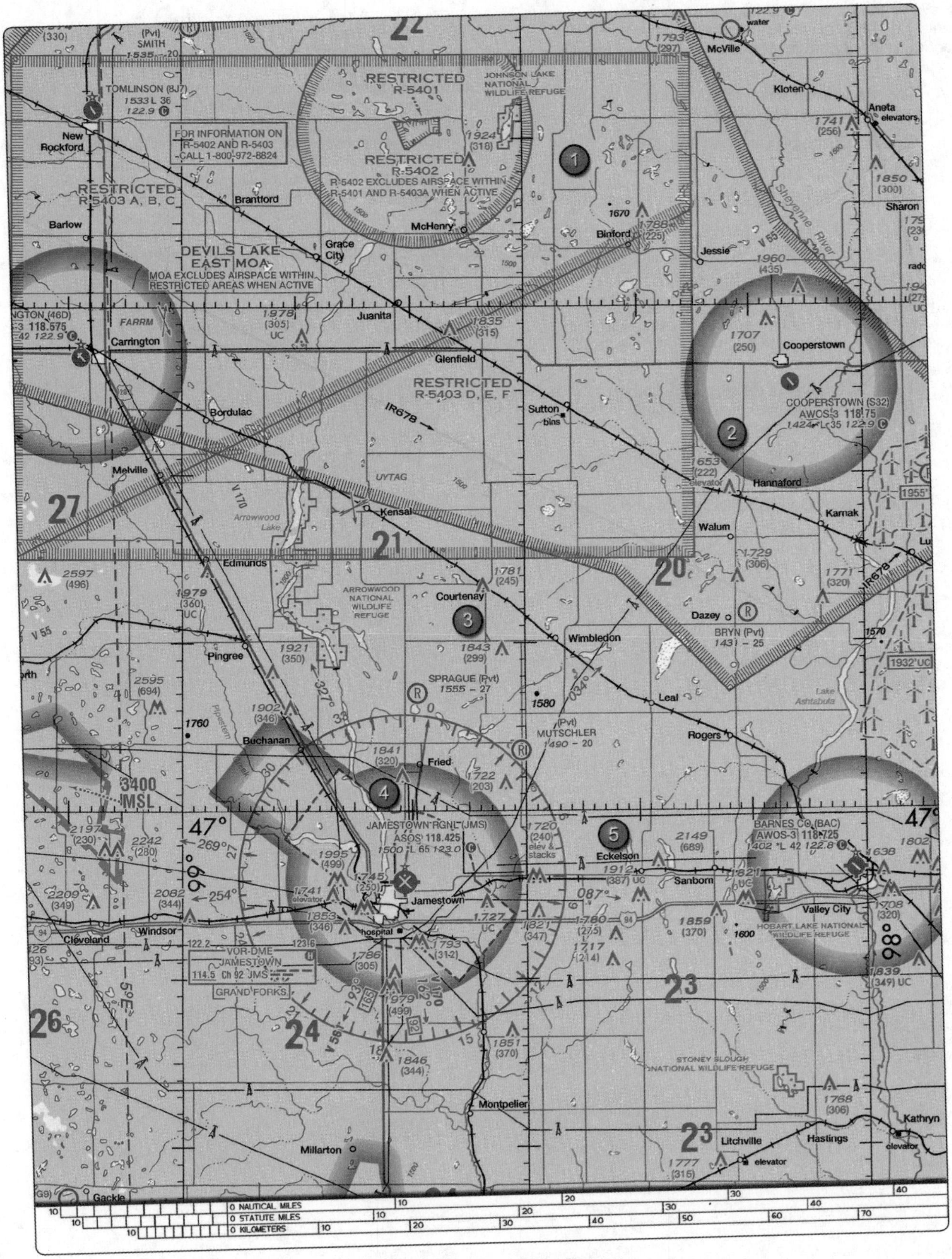

Figure 26. – Sectional Chart Excerpt.

NOTE: Chart is not to scale and should not be used for navigation. Use associated scale.

73. (Refer to Figure 20 on page 357.) (Refer to area 3.) What is the recommended communications procedure for departure at Currituck County Airport?

A. Broadcast intentions prior to taxi and announcing runway of departure.

B. Contact Elizabeth City tower on 120.5.

C. Radio need not be used.

Answer (A) is correct. *(AIM Para 4-1-9)*

DISCUSSION: Find Currituck County Airport, which is northeast of area 3 in Fig. 20. Currituck County Airport is a non-towered airport with the specified CTAF 122.9. The recommended procedure for departure at a non-towered airport is to self-announce intentions on the CTAF prior to taxi and before taxiing on runway for departure.

Answer (B) is incorrect. The recommended communications procedure for departure at a non-towered airport is to broadcast intentions on the CTAF for that airport, not another airport's designated frequency. Answer (C) is incorrect. Although two-way radio communications are not required, it is good operating practice for pilots to transmit their intentions on the specified frequency for the benefit of other traffic in the area.

74. (Refer to Figure 20 on page 357.) (Refer to area 3.) What is the recommended communications procedure for a landing at Currituck County Airport?

A. Transmit intentions on 122.9 MHz when 10 miles out and give position reports in the traffic pattern.

B. Contact Elizabeth City FSS for airport advisory service.

C. Contact New Bern FSS for area traffic information.

Answer (A) is correct. *(AIM Para 4-1-9)*

DISCUSSION: Find the symbol for Currituck County Airport, northeast of area 3 in Fig. 20. Incoming flights should use MULTICOM, 122.9, as the CTAF, because it is marked with a C. The recommended procedure is to report 10 NM out and then give position reports in the airport traffic pattern.

Answer (B) is incorrect. There is no Elizabeth City FSS. Elizabeth City is serviced by the Raleigh FSS, as indicated by "Raleigh" just below the identifier box for Elizabeth City VOR. Answer (C) is incorrect. The controlling FSS is Raleigh, not New Bern, and Raleigh FSS does not monitor 122.9, which is marked as the CTAF at Currituck County Airport.

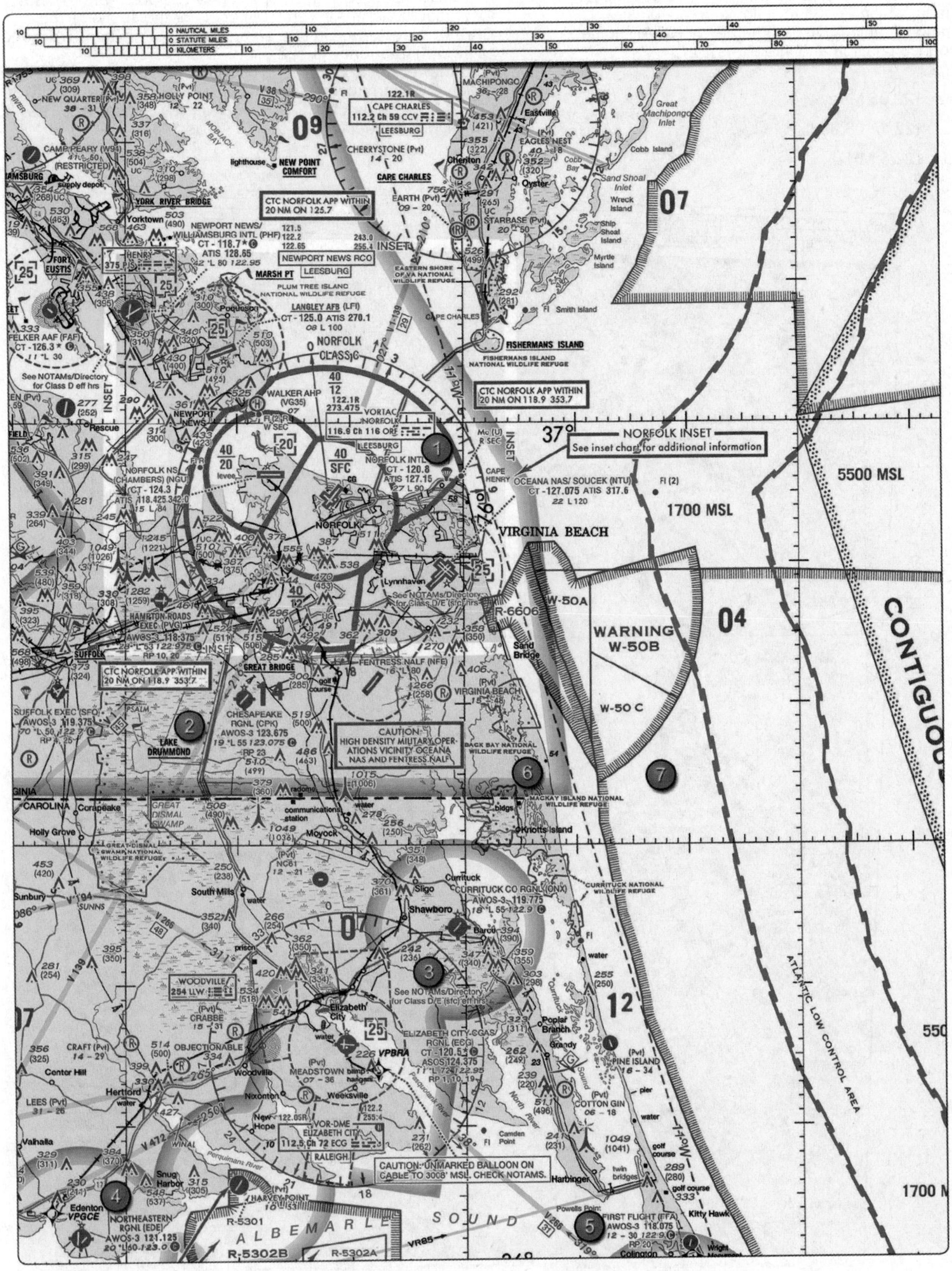

Figure 20. – Sectional Chart Excerpt.

NOTE: Chart is not to scale and should not be used for navigation. Use associated scale.

75. (Refer to Figure 22 below, and Figure 31 on page 359.) (Refer to area 2 in Figure 22.) At Coeur D'Alene, which frequency should be used as a Common Traffic Advisory Frequency (CTAF) to self-announce position and intentions?

A. 122.05 MHz.

B. 122.1/108.8 MHz.

C. 122.8 MHz.

Answer (C) is correct. *(Chart Supplement)*

DISCUSSION: Fig. 31 is the Chart Supplement excerpt for Coeur D'Alene Air Terminal. Look for the section titled **Communications**. On that same line, it states the CTAF (and UNICOM) frequency is 122.8.

Answer (A) is incorrect. This is the remote communications outlet (RCO) frequency to contact Boise FSS in the vicinity of Coeur D'Alene, not the CTAF. Answer (B) is incorrect. The COE VOR/DME frequency, not the CTAF, is 108.8.

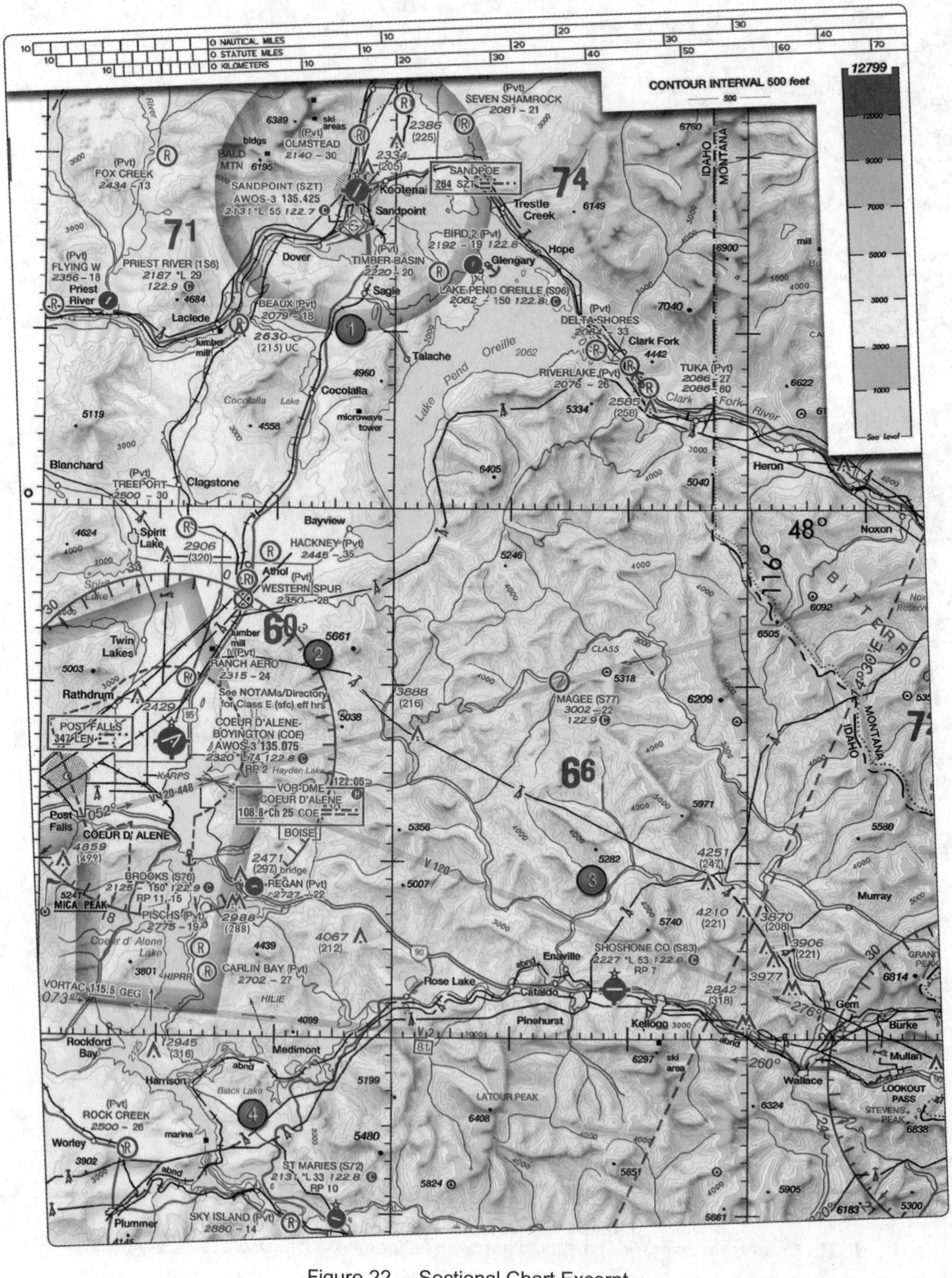

Figure 22. – Sectional Chart Excerpt.
NOTE: Chart is not to scale and should not be used for navigation. Use associated scale.

IDAHO **31**

COEUR D'ALENE–PAPPY BOYINGTON FLD (COE) 9 NW UTC–8(–7DT)
N47°46.46′ W116°49.18′ **GREAT FALLS**
2320 B S4 **FUEL** 100, JET A OX 1, 2, 3, 4 Class IV, ARFF Index A NOTAM FILE COE **H–1C, L–13B**
RWY 05–23: H7400X100 (ASPH–GRVD) S–57, D–95, 2S–121, 2D–165 HIRL 0.6% up NE **IAP**

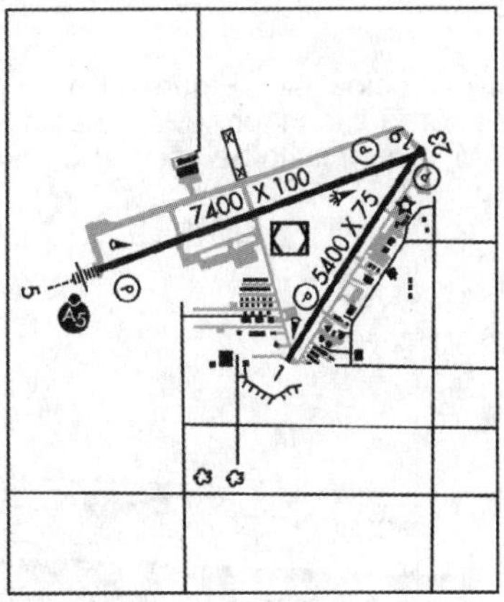

RWY 05: MALSR (NSTD). PAPI(P4R)—GA 3.0° TCH 56′.
RWY 23: REIL. PAPI(P4R)—GA 3.0° TCH 50′.
RWY 01–19: H5400X75 (ASPH) S–50, D–83, 2S–105, 2D–150
MIRL 0.3% up N
RWY 01: REIL. PAPI(P2L)—GA 3.0° TCH 39′. Rgt tfc.
RWY 19: PAPI(P2L)—GA 3.0° TCH 41′.
RUNWAY DECLARED DISTANCE INFORMATION

RWY 01:	TORA–5400	TODA–5400	ASDA–5400	LDA–5400
RWY 05:	TORA–7400	TODA–7400	ASDA–7400	LDA–7400
RWY 19:	TORA–5400	TODA–5400	ASDA–5400	LDA–5400
RWY 23:	TORA–7400	TODA–7400	ASDA–7400	LDA–7400

AIRPORT REMARKS: Attended Mon–Fri 1500–0100Z‡. For after hrs fuel-self svc avbl or call 208–772–6404, 208–661–4174, 208–661–7449, 208–699–5433. Self svc fuel avbl with credit card. 48 hr PPR for unscheduled ops with more than 30 passenger seats call arpt manager 208–446–1860. Migratory birds on and invof arpt Oct–Nov. Remote cntl airstrip is 2.3 miles west AER 05. Arpt conditions avbl on AWOS. Rwy 05 NSTD MALSR, thld bar extends 5′ byd rwy edge lgts each side. ACTIVATE MIRL Rwy 01–19, HIRL Rwy 05–23, REIL Rwy 01 and Rwy 23, MALSR Rwy 05—CTAF. PAPI Rwy 01, Rwy 19, Rwy 05, and Rwy 23 opr continuously.
WEATHER DATA SOURCES: AWOS–3 135.075 (208) 772–8215.
HIWAS 108.8 COE.
COMMUNICATIONS: CTAF/UNICOM 122.8
RCO 122.05 (BOISE RADIO)
Ⓡ **SPOKANE APP/DEP CON** 132.1
AIRSPACE: CLASS E svc continuous.
RADIO AIDS TO NAVIGATION: NOTAM FILE COE.
(T) VORW/DME 108.8 COE Chan 25 N47°46.42′ W116°49.24′ at fld. 2320/19E. **HIWAS.**
DME portion unusable:
220°–240° byd 15 NM 280°–315° byd 15 NM blo 11,000′.
POST FALLS NDB (MHW) 347 LEN N47°44.57′ W116°57.66′ 053° 6.0 NM to fld.
ILS 110.7 I–COE Rwy 05 Class ID. Localizer unusable 25° left and right of course.

Figure 31. – Chart Supplements U.S. (formerly Airport/Facility Directory).

76. (Refer to Figure 22 below, and Figure 31 on page 361.) (Refer to area 2 in Figure 22.) At Coeur D'Alene, which frequency should be used as a Common Traffic Advisory Frequency (CTAF) to monitor airport traffic?

A. 122.05 MHz.

B. 135.075 MHz.

C. 122.8 MHz.

Answer (C) is correct. *(Chart Supplement)*

DISCUSSION: Fig. 31 is the Chart Supplement excerpt for Coeur D'Alene Air Terminal. Look for the section titled **Communications**. On that same line, it states that the CTAF (and UNICOM) frequency is 122.8. The CTAF can also be found in the airport information on the sectional chart.

Answer (A) is incorrect. This is the remote communication outlet (RCO) frequency to contact Boise FSS in the vicinity of Coeur D'Alene, not the CTAF. Answer (B) is incorrect. This is the AWOS frequency, not the CTAF.

77. (Refer to Figure 22 below, and Figure 31 on page 361.) (Refer to area 2 in Figure 22.) What is the correct UNICOM frequency to be used at Coeur D'Alene to request fuel?

A. 135.075 MHz.

B. 122.1/108.8 MHz.

C. 122.8 MHz.

Answer (C) is correct. *(ACL)*

DISCUSSION: The correct frequency to request fuel at the Coeur D'Alene Airport is the UNICOM frequency 122.8. It is given in Fig. 22, after "L74" in the airport information on the sectional chart. Radio frequencies are also given in Fig. 31, the Chart Supplement, under "Communications."

Answer (A) is incorrect. This is the AWOS frequency for Coeur D'Alene Airport. Answer (B) is incorrect. The COE VOR/DME frequency, not the UNICOM, is 108.8, and 122.1 is not a frequency associated with Coeur D'Alene Airport.

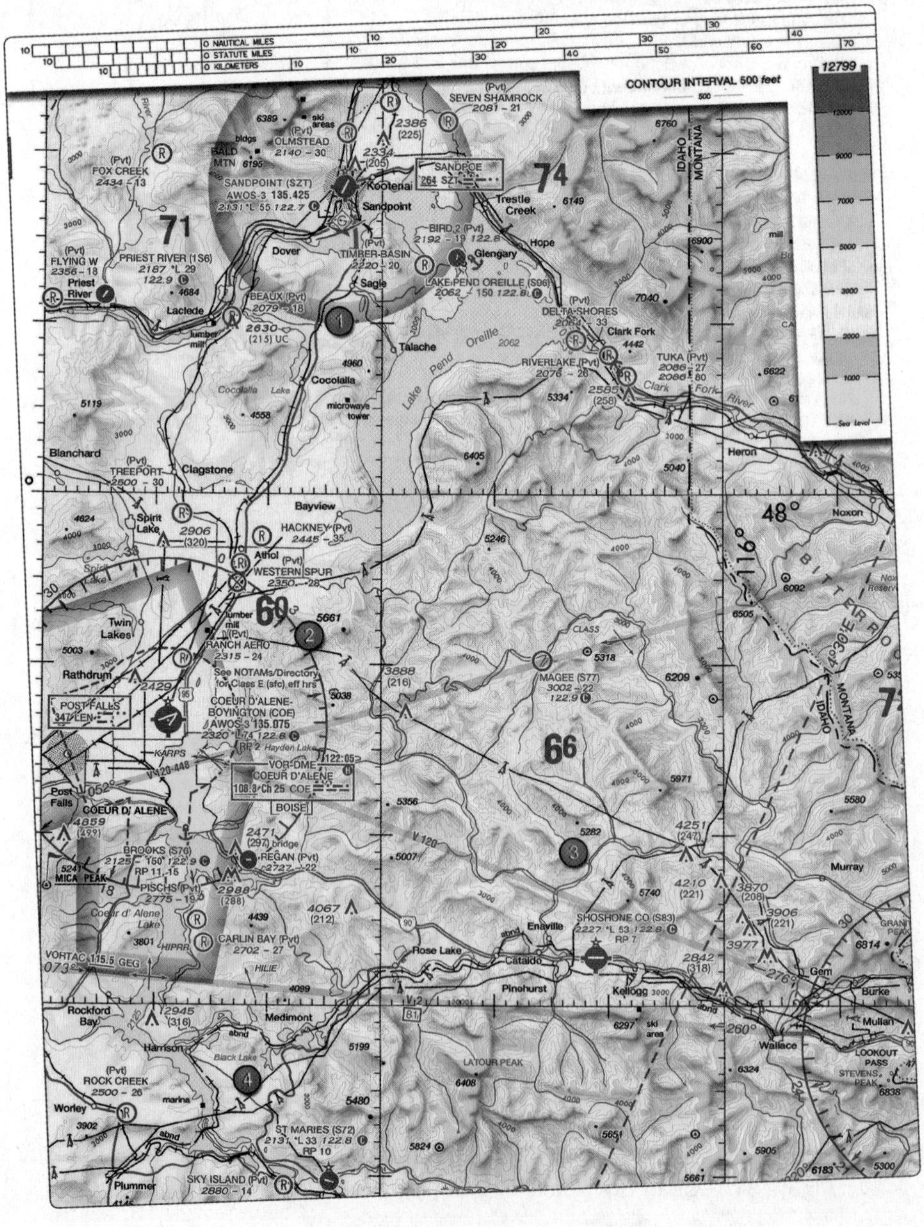

Figure 22. – Sectional Chart Excerpt.
NOTE: Chart is not to scale and should not be used for navigation. Use associated scale.

IDAHO **31**

COEUR D'ALENE–PAPPY BOYINGTON FLD (COE) 9 NW UTC–8(–7DT)
N47°46.46′ W116°49.18′ **GREAT FALLS**
2320 B S4 **FUEL** 100, JET A OX 1, 2, 3, 4 Class IV, ARFF Index A NOTAM FILE COE **H–1C, L–13B**
RWY 05–23: H7400X100 (ASPH–GRVD) S–57, D–95, 2S–121, 2D–165 HIRL 0.6% up NE **IAP**
RWY 05: MALSR (NSTD). PAPI(P4R)—GA 3.0° TCH 56′.
RWY 23: REIL. PAPI(P4R)—GA 3.0° TCH 50′.
RWY 01–19: H5400X75 (ASPH) S–50, D–83, 2S–105, 2D–150
MIRL 0.3% up N
RWY 01: REIL. PAPI(P2L)—GA 3.0° TCH 39′. Rgt tfc.
RWY 19: PAPI(P2L)—GA 3.0° TCH 41′.

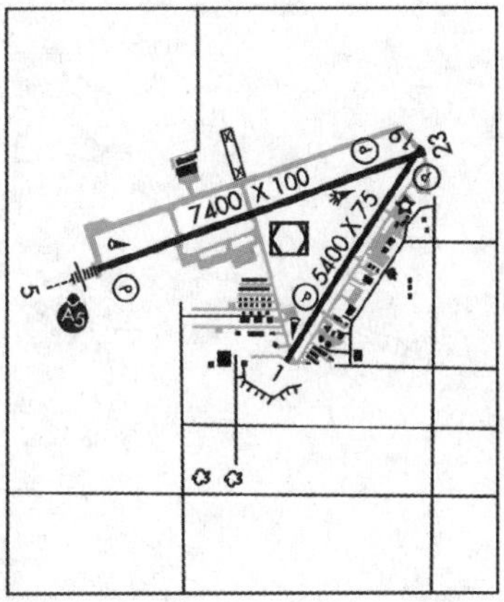

RUNWAY DECLARED DISTANCE INFORMATION

RWY 01:	TORA–5400	TODA–5400	ASDA–5400	LDA–5400
RWY 05:	TORA–7400	TODA–7400	ASDA–7400	LDA–7400
RWY 19:	TORA–5400	TODA–5400	ASDA–5400	LDA–5400
RWY 23:	TORA–7400	TODA–7400	ASDA–7400	LDA–7400

AIRPORT REMARKS: Attended Mon–Fri 1500–0100Z‡. For after hrs fuel-self svc avbl or call 208–772–6404, 208–661–4174, 208–661–7449, 208–699–5433. Self svc fuel avbl with credit card. 48 hr PPR for unscheduled ops with more than 30 passenger seats call arpt manager 208–446–1860. Migratory birds on and invof arpt Oct–Nov. Remote cntl airstrip is 2.3 miles west AER 05. Arpt conditions avbl on AWOS. Rwy 05 NSTD MALSR, thld bar extends 5′ byd rwy edge lgts each side. ACTIVATE MIRL Rwy 01–19, HIRL Rwy 05–23, REIL Rwy 01 and Rwy 23, MALSR Rwy 05—CTAF. PAPI Rwy 01, Rwy 19, Rwy 05, and Rwy 23 opr continuously.
WEATHER DATA SOURCES: AWOS–3 135.075 (208) 772–8215.
HIWAS 108.8 COE.
COMMUNICATIONS: CTAF/UNICOM 122.8
RCO 122.05 (BOISE RADIO)
Ⓡ **SPOKANE APP/DEP CON** 132.1
AIRSPACE: CLASS E svc continuous.
RADIO AIDS TO NAVIGATION: NOTAM FILE COE.
(T) VORW/DME 108.8 COE Chan 25 N47°46.42′ W116°49.24′ at fld. 2320/19E. **HIWAS.**
DME portion unusable:
220°–240° byd 15 NM 280°–315° byd 15 NM blo 11,000′.
POST FALLS NDB (MHW) 347 LEN N47°44.57′ W116°57.66′ 053° 6.0 NM to fld.
ILS 110.7 I–COE Rwy 05 Class ID. Localizer unusable 25° left and right of course.

Figure 31. – Chart Supplements U.S. (formerly Airport/Facility Directory).

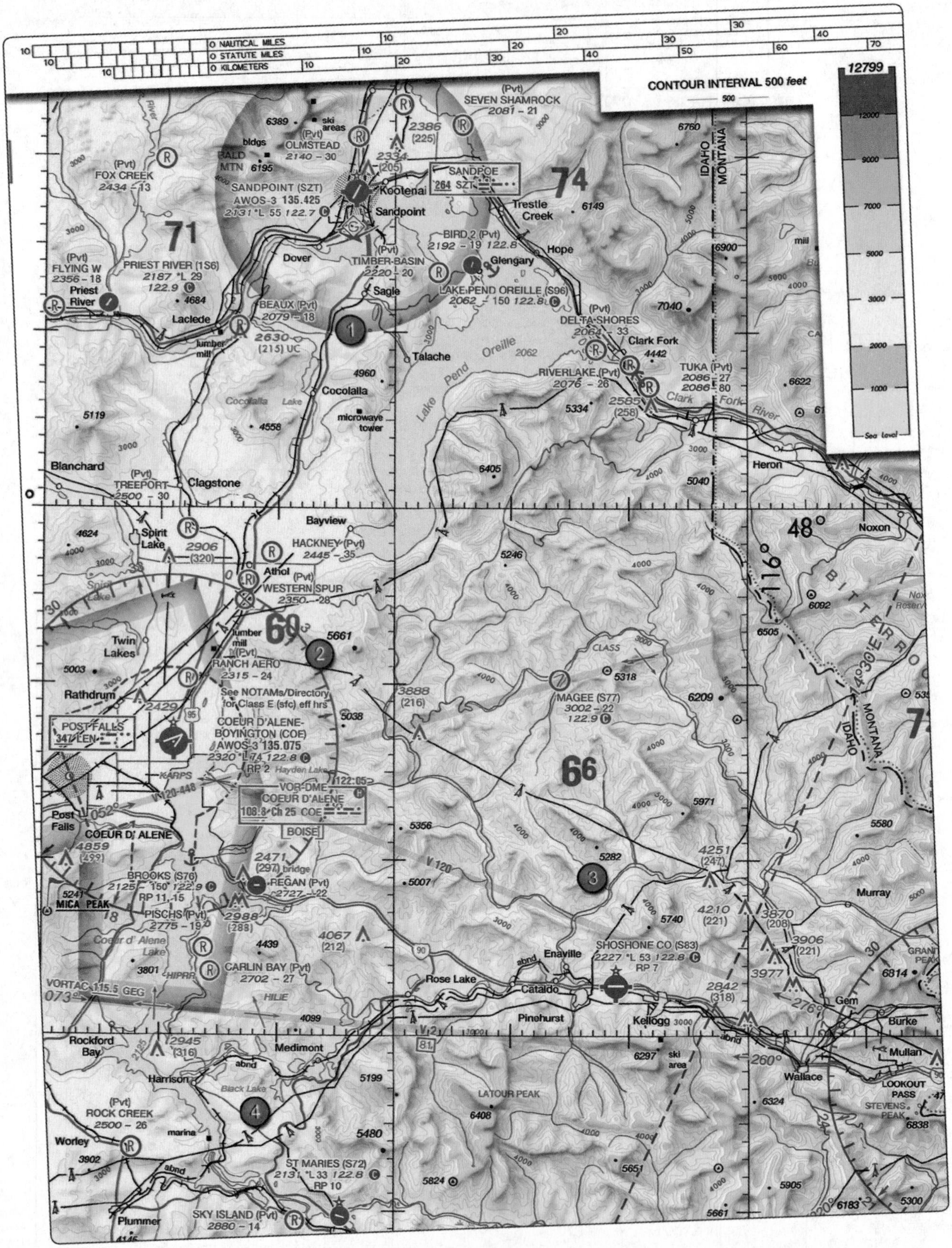

Figure 22. – Sectional Chart Excerpt.
NOTE: Chart is not to scale and should not be used for navigation. Use associated scale.

78. (Refer to Figure 22 on page 362.) Weather information is available at the Coeur d'Alene (COE) Airport (area 2)

A. at the flight service station on the field.
B. from AWOS 3 135.075.
C. from UNICOM (CTAF) on 122.8.

Answer (B) is correct. *(PHAK Chap 13 and Sectional Chart)*
DISCUSSION: On the sectional chart excerpt, to the right of the airport, you will find in the information for the airport weather in the third line. It states the type of Automated Weather Observation System (AWOS) and the frequency of 135.075.
Answer (A) is incorrect. There is no flight service station on the field. This would be found in the Chart Supplement as FSS "on arpt" in the Communications section for this airport. Answer (C) is incorrect. The UNICOM (CTAF) is the Common Traffic Advisory Frequency.

9.5 FAA Advisory Circulars

79. FAA advisory circulars are available to all pilots and are obtained by

A. distribution from the nearest FAA district office.
B. downloading them from the FAA website.
C. subscribing to the Federal Register.

Answer (B) is correct. *(www.faa.gov)*
DISCUSSION: FAA Advisory Circulars are issued with the purpose of informing the public of nonregulatory material of interest. Free advisory circulars can be downloaded from the FAA website at www.faa.gov.
Answer (A) is incorrect. FAA offices have their own copies but none for distribution to the public. Answer (C) is incorrect. The *Federal Register* contains Notices of Proposed Rulemaking (NPRM) and final rules. It is a federal government publication.

80. FAA advisory circulars containing subject matter specifically related to Air Traffic and General Operating Rules are issued under which subject number?

A. 60
B. 70
C. 90

Answer (C) is correct. *(www.faa.gov)*
DISCUSSION: FAA advisory circulars are numbered based on the numbering system used in the FARs:

60 -- Airmen
70 -- Airspace
90 -- Air Traffic and General Operating Rules

Answer (A) is incorrect. This subject number refers to Airmen. Answer (B) is incorrect. This subject number refers to Airspace.

81. FAA advisory circulars containing subject matter specifically related to Airmen are issued under which subject number?

A. 60
B. 70
C. 90

Answer (A) is correct. *(www.faa.gov)*
DISCUSSION: FAA advisory circulars are numbered based on the numbering system used in the FARs:

60 -- Airmen
70 -- Airspace
90 -- Air Traffic and General Operating Rules

Answer (B) is incorrect. This subject number relates to Airspace. Answer (C) is incorrect. This subject number relates to Air Traffic and General Operating Rules.

82. FAA advisory circulars containing subject matter specifically related to Airspace are issued under which subject number?

A. 60
B. 70
C. 90

Answer (B) is correct. *(www.faa.gov)*
DISCUSSION: FAA advisory circulars are numbered based on the numbering system used in the FARs:

60 -- Airmen
70 -- Airspace
90 -- Air Traffic and General Operating Rules

Answer (A) is incorrect. This subject number relates to Airmen. Answer (C) is incorrect. This subject number relates to Air Traffic and General Operating Rules.

9.6 Chart Supplements

83. (Refer to Figure 52 on page 365.) When approaching Lincoln Municipal from the west at noon for the purpose of landing, initial communications should be with

A. Lincoln Approach Control on 124.0 MHz.

B. Minneapolis Center on 128.75 MHz.

C. Lincoln Tower on 118.5 MHz.

Answer (A) is correct. *(Chart Supplement)*

DISCUSSION: Fig. 52 contains the Chart Supplement excerpt for Lincoln Municipal. Locate the section titled Airspace and note that Lincoln Municipal is located in Class C airspace. The Class C airspace is in effect from 0530-0000 local time (1130-0600Z). You should contact approach control (app con) during that time before entering. Move up two lines to App/Dep Con and note that aircraft arriving from the west of Lincoln (i.e., 170° – 349°) at noon should initially contact Lincoln Approach Control on 124.0.

Answer (B) is incorrect. The frequencies shown in the communications section for App/Dep Con do not include 128.75 MHz. Answer (C) is incorrect. When approaching Lincoln Municipal at noon, your initial contact should be with approach control, not the tower.

84. (Refer to Figure 52 on page 365.) Traffic patterns in effect at Lincoln Municipal are

A. to the right on Runway 14 and Runway 32; to the left on Runway 18 and Runway 35.

B. to the left on Runway 14 and Runway 32; to the right on Runway 18 and Runway 35.

C. to the right on Runways 14 - 32.

Answer (B) is correct. *(Chart Supplement)*

DISCUSSION: Fig. 52 contains the Chart Supplement excerpt for Lincoln Municipal. For this question, you need to locate the runway end data elements, i.e., Rwy 18, Rwy 14, Rwy 32, Rwy 17, Rwy 35, and Rwy 36. Traffic patterns are to the left unless right traffic is noted by the contraction "Rgt tfc." The only runways with right traffic are Rwy 18 and Rwy 35.

Answer (A) is incorrect. Traffic patterns are to the left, not right, for Rwy 14 and Rwy 32. Traffic patterns are to the right, not left, for Rwy 18 and Rwy 35. Answer (C) is incorrect. The traffic pattern for Rwy 14 and Rwy 32 is to the left, not right.

85. (Refer to Figure 52 on page 365.) Which type radar service is provided to VFR aircraft at Lincoln Municipal?

A. Sequencing to the primary Class C airport and standard separation.

B. Sequencing to the primary Class C airport and conflict resolution so that radar targets do not touch, or 1,000 feet vertical separation.

C. Sequencing to the primary Class C airport, traffic advisories, conflict resolution, and safety alerts.

Answer (C) is correct. *(Chart Supplement, AIM Para 4-1-17)*

DISCUSSION: Fig. 52 contains the Chart Supplement excerpt for Lincoln Municipal. Locate the section titled Airspace to determine that Lincoln Municipal is located in Class C airspace. Once communications and radar contact are established, VFR aircraft are provided the following services:

1. Sequencing to the primary airport
2. Approved separation between IFR and VFR aircraft
3. Basic radar services, i.e., safety alerts, limited vectoring, and traffic advisories

The FAA should change "conflict resolution" to "limited vectoring" in the future.

Answer (A) is incorrect. In addition to sequencing to the primary Class C airport and standard separation, Class C radar service also includes basic radar services, i.e., traffic advisories and safety alerts. Answer (B) is incorrect. One radar service provided to VFR aircraft in Class C airspace provides for traffic advisories and conflict resolution so that radar targets do not touch, or 500 ft., not 1,000 ft., vertical separation.

86. (Refer to Figure 52 on page 365.) What is the recommended communications procedure for landing at Lincoln Municipal during the hours when the tower is not in operation?

A. Monitor airport traffic and announce your position and intentions on 118.5 MHz.

B. Contact UNICOM on 122.95 MHz for traffic advisories.

C. Monitor ATIS for airport conditions, then announce your position on 122.95 MHz.

Answer (A) is correct. *(Chart Supplement)*

DISCUSSION: When the Lincoln Municipal tower is closed, you should monitor airport traffic and announce your position and intentions on the CTAF. Fig. 52 contains the Chart Supplement excerpt for Lincoln Municipal. Locate the section titled Communications and note that on that same line the CTAF frequency is 118.5.

Answer (B) is incorrect. When the tower is not in operation, you should monitor other traffic and announce your position and intentions on the specified CTAF. At Lincoln Municipal, the CTAF is the tower frequency of 118.5, not the UNICOM frequency of 122.95. Answer (C) is incorrect. When the tower is not in operation, you should monitor other traffic and announce your position and intentions on the specified CTAF. At Lincoln Municipal, the CTAF is the tower frequency of 118.5, not the UNICOM frequency of 122.95.

87. (Refer to Figure 52 below.) Where is Loup City Municipal located with relation to the city?

A. Northwest approximately 4 miles.

B. Northwest approximately 1 mile.

C. East approximately 7 miles.

Answer (B) is correct. *(Chart Supplement)*

DISCUSSION: Fig. 52 contains the Chart Supplement excerpt for Loup City Municipal. On the first line, the third item listed, 1 NW, means that Loup City Municipal is located approximately 1 NM northwest of the associated city.

Answer (A) is incorrect. 4 NW is the approximate location of LNK airport to the associated city, not Loup City Municipal airport. Answer (C) is incorrect. The airport is approximately 1 NM northwest, not 7 NM east, of the associated city.

NEBRASKA **271**

LINCOLN (LNK) 4 NW UTC–6(–5DT) N40°51.05′ W96°45.55′ **OMAHA**
1219 B S4 **FUEL** 100LL, JET A TPA—See Remarks ARFF Index—See Remarks **H–5C, L–10I**
NOTAM FILE LNK **IAP, AD**
RWY 18–36: H12901X200 (ASPH–CONC–GRVD) S–100, D–200, 2S–175, 2D–400 HIRL
RWY 18: MALSR. PAPI(P4L)—GA 3.0° TCH 55′. Rgt tfc. 0.4% down.
RWY 36: MALSR. PAPI(P4L)—GA 3.0° TCH 57′.
RWY 14–32: H8649X150 (ASPH–CONC–GRVD) S–80, D–170, 2S–175, 2D–280 MIRL
RWY 14: REIL. VASI(V4L)—GA 3.0° TCH 48′. Thld dsplcd 363′.
RWY 32: VASI(V4L)—GA 3.0° TCH 50′. Thld dsplcd 470′. Pole. 0.3% up.
RWY 17–35: H5800X100 (ASPH–CONC–AFSC) S–49, D–60 HIRL 0.8% up S
RWY 17: REIL. PAPI(P4L)—GA 3.0° TCH 44′.
RWY 35: ODALS. PAPI(P4L)—GA 3.0° TCH 30′. Rgt tfc.

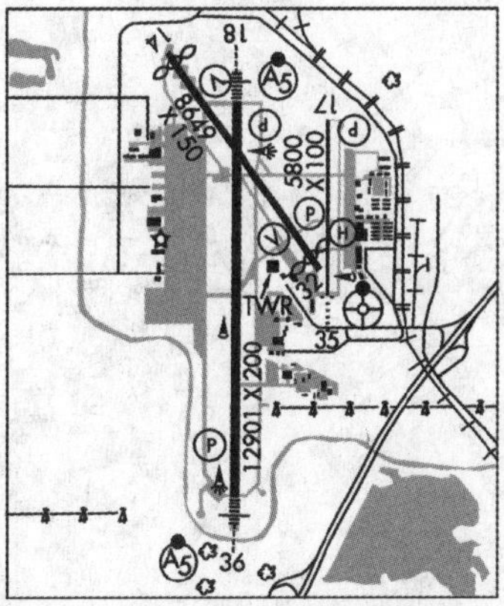

RUNWAY DECLARED DISTANCE INFORMATION

RWY 14:	TORA–8649	TODA–8649	ASDA–8649	LDA–8286
RWY 17:	TORA–5800	TODA–5800	ASDA–5400	LDA–5400
RWY 18:	TORA–12901	TODA–12901	ASDA–12901	LDA–12901
RWY 32:	TORA–8649	TODA–8649	ASDA–8286	LDA–7816
RWY 35:	TORA–5800	TODA–5800	ASDA–5800	LDA–5800
RWY 36:	TORA–12901	TODA–12901	ASDA–12901	LDA–12901

AIRPORT REMARKS: Attended continuously. Birds invof arpt. Rwy 18 designated calm wind rwy. Rwy 32 apch holdline on South A twy. TPA–2219 (1000), heavy military jet 3000 (1781). Class I, ARFF Index B. ARFF Index C level equipment provided. Rwy 18–36 touchdown and rollout rwy visual range avbl. When twr clsd MIRL Rwy 14–32 preset on low ints, HIRL Rwy 18–36 and Rwy 17–35 preset on med ints, ODALS Rwy 35 operate continuously on med ints, MALSR Rwy 18 and Rwy 36 operate continuously and REIL Rwy 14 and Rwy 17 operate continuously on low ints. VASI Rwy 14 and Rwy 32, PAPI Rwy 17, Rwy 35, Rwy 18 and Rwy 36 on continuously.
WEATHER DATA SOURCES: ASOS (402) 474–9214. LLWAS
COMMUNICATIONS: CTAF 118.5 **ATIS** 118.05 **UNICOM** 122.95
RCO 122.65 (COLUMBUS RADIO)
Ⓡ **APP/DEP CON** 124.0 (180°–359°) 124.8 (360°–179°)
TOWER 118.5 125.7 (1130–0600Z‡) **GND CON** 121.9 **CLNC DEL** 120.7
AIRSPACE: CLASS C svc 1130–0600Z‡ ctc **APP CON** other times CLASS E.
RADIO AIDS TO NAVIGATION: NOTAM FILE LNK.
(H) VORTACW 116.1 LNK Chan 108 N40°55.43′ W96°44.52′ 181° 4.4 NM to fld. 1370/9E
POTTS NDB (MHW/LOM) 385 LN N40°44.83′ W96°45.75′ 355° 6.2 NM to fld. Unmonitored when twr clsd.
ILS 111.1 I–OCZ Rwy 18. Class IB OM unmonitored.
ILS 109.9 I–LNK Rwy 36 Class IA LOM POTTS NDB. MM unmonitored. LOM unmonitored when twr clsd.
COMM/NAV/WEATHER REMARKS: Emerg frequency 121.5 not available at twr.

LOUP CITY MUNI (ØF4) 1 NW UTC–6(–5DT) N41°17.20′ W98°59.41′ **OMAHA**
2071 B **FUEL** 100LL NOTAM FILE OLU **L–10H, 12H**
RWY 16–34: H3200X60 (CONC) S–12.5 MIRL
RWY 34: Trees.
RWY 04–22: 2040X100 (TURF)
RWY 04: Tree. **RWY 22:** Road.
AIRPORT REMARKS: Unattended. For svc call 308–745–1344/1244/0664.
COMMUNICATIONS: CTAF 122.9
RADIO AIDS TO NAVIGATION: NOTAM FILE OLU.
WOLBACH (H) VORTAC 114.8 OBH Chan 95 N41°22.54′ W98°21.22′ 253° 29.3 NM to fld. 2010/7E.

MARTIN FLD (See SO SIOUX CITY)

Figure 52. – Chart Supplements U.S. (formerly Airport/Facility Directory).

88. (Refer to Figure 80 below, and Figure 81 on page 367.) Refer to Crawford Airport (N38°42.25' W107°38.62'). Is fuel ever available at Crawford Airport?

A. Yes, whenever the airport is attended by airport personnel.

B. No, as there is no “star” symbol near the airport on the chart, there is no fuel available at this airport.

C. Yes, 100LL fuel is available for emergency use only.

Answer (C) is correct. *(Chart Supplement)*

DISCUSSION: Look at Fig. 81, the Chart Supplement excerpt for Crawford Airport, located at the given coordinates. Locate the Airport Remarks; you will see on the second line that 100LL fuel is available (avbl) for emergency use only.

Answer (A) is incorrect. There are no regular fuel services available. Answer (B) is incorrect. There are no regular fuel services available, but there is 100LL available for emergency use only.

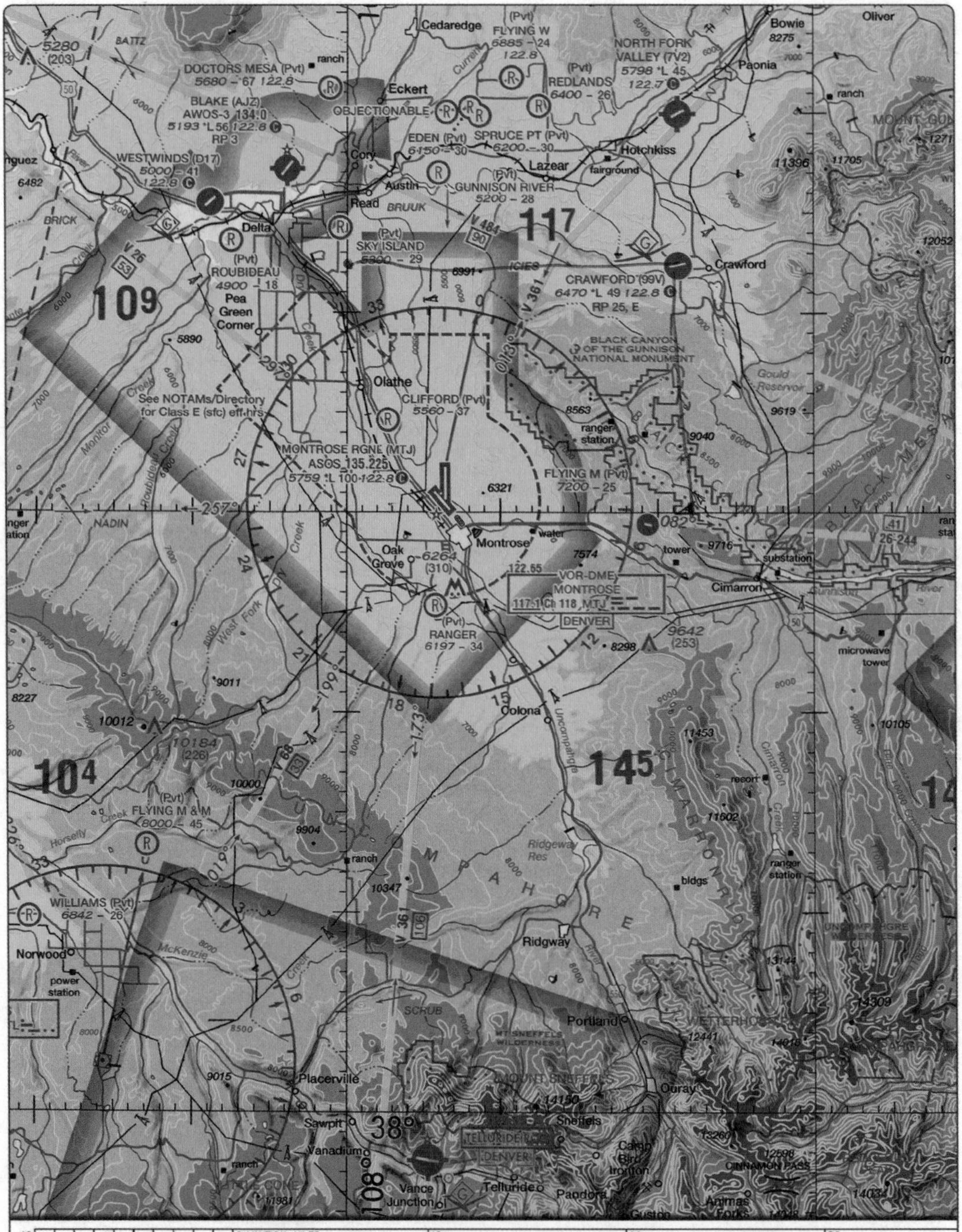

Figure 80. – Sectional Chart Excerpt.
NOTE: Chart is not to scale and should not be used for navigation. Use associated scale.

216 **COLORADO**

CRAWFORD (99V) 2 W UTC –7(–6DT) N38°42.25′ W107°38.62′ **DENVER**
6470 S2 OX 4 TPA–7470(1000) NOTAM FILE DEN **L–9E**
RWY 07–25: H4900X20 (ASPH) LIRL (NSTD)
RWY 07: VASI (NSTD). Trees. **RWY 25:** VASI (NSTD) Tank. Rgt tfc.
RWY E–W: 2500X125 (TURF)
RWY E: Rgt tfc. **RWY W:** Trees.
AIRPORT REMARKS: Attended continuously. Rwy 07-25 west 1300 ′ only 25′ wide. Heavy glider ops at arpt. Land to the east tkf to the west winds permitting. 100LL fuel avbl for emergency use only. Pedestrians, motor vehicles, deer and wildlife on and invof arpt. Unlimited vehicle use on arpt. Rwy West has +15 ′ building 170′ from thld 30′ left, +10′ road 100′ from thld centerline. +45′ tree 100′ L of Rwy 07 extended centerline 414 ′ from rwy end. –8′ to –20′ terrain off both sides of first 674 ′ of Rwy 25 end. E-W rwy occasionally has 6 inch diameter irrigation pipes crossing rwy width in various places. Rwy 07 has 20 ′ trees and -10′ to 20′ terrain 20′ right of rwy first 150′. E-W rwy consists of +12 inch alfalfa vegetation during various times of the year. Arpt lgts opr dusk-0800Z‡. Rwy 07 1 box VASI left side for local operators only or PPR call 970-921-7700 or 970-921-3018. Rwy 07-25 LIRL on N side from Rwy 25 end W 3800 ′. Rwy 07 1300′ from end E 300′. No thld lgts Rwy 07-25 3800′ usable for ngt ops.
COMMUNICATIONS: CTAF/UNICOM 122.8
RADIO AIDS TO NAVIGATION: NOTAM FILE MTJ.
MONTROSE (H) VORW/DME 117.1 MTJ Chan 118 N38 °30.39′ W107°53.96′ 033° 16.9 NM to fld. 5713/12E.

CREEDE
MINERAL CO MEM (C24) 2 E UTC –7(–6DT) N37°49.33′ W106°55.79′ **DENVER**
8680 NOTAM FILE DEN **H–3E, L–9E**
RWY 07–25: H6880X60 (ASPH) S–12.5, D–70, 2D–110
RWY 07: Thld dsplcd 188′. **RWY 25:** Road.
AIRPORT REMARKS: Unattended. Elk and deer on and invof arpt. Glider and hang glider activity on and in vicinity of arpt. Mountains in all directions. Departure to NE avoid over flight of trailers and resident homes, climb to 200 ′ above ground level on centerline extended prior to turn. Acft stay to right of valley on apch and/or departure route. 2′ cable fence around apron.
COMMUNICATIONS: CTAF 122.9
RADIO AIDS TO NAVIGATION: NOTAM FILE DEN.
BLUE MESA (H) VORW/DME 114.9 HBU Chan 96 N38 °27.13′ W107°02.39′ 158° 38.1 NM to fld. 8730/14E.

CUCHARA VALLEY AT LA VETA (See LA VETA)

DEL NORTE
ASTRONAUT KENT ROMINGER (8V1) 3 N UTC –7(–6DT) N37°42.83′ W106°21.11′ **DENVER**
7949 NOTAM FILE DEN **H–3E, L–9E**
RWY 06–24: 6050X75 (ASPH) 1.1% up SW
RWY 03–21: 4670X60 (TURF-DIRT)
RWY 21: Mountain.
AIRPORT REMARKS: Unattended. Wildlife on and invof arpt. Unlimited vehicle access on arpt. Mountainous terrain surrounds arpt in all directions.
COMMUNICATIONS: CTAF 122.9
RADIO AIDS TO NAVIGATION: NOTAM FILE ALS.
ALAMOSA (H) VORTACW 113.9 ALS Chan 86 N37 °20.95′ W105°48.93′ 298° 33.7 NM to fld. 7535/13E.

Figure 81. – Chart Supplements U.S. (formerly Airport/Facility Directory).

89. (Refer to Figure 80 below, and Figure 81 on page 369.) Refer to Crawford Airport (N38°42.25' W107°38.62'). What is the traffic pattern for Runway 25?

A. Right hand traffic pattern.

B. Left hand traffic pattern.

C. It does not matter because it is an uncontrolled airport.

Answer (A) is correct. *(Chart Supplement)*

DISCUSSION: The traffic pattern for runway 25 is a right-hand pattern. It is noted on the sectional chart excerpt (Fig. 80). Under the airport information, near Crawford Airport, the third line displays the letters "RP 25." On the Chart Supplement excerpt in Fig. 81, the section titled RWY 25 has "Rgt tfc" (right traffic) written to give pilots the pattern direction of the west runway.

Answer (B) is incorrect. It is a left-hand traffic pattern for the east runway (RWY 07), not for Runway 25. Answer (C) is incorrect. Standard traffic patterns are left turns, unless otherwise noted. If there is nothing that states which direction the pattern is, it is left patterns.

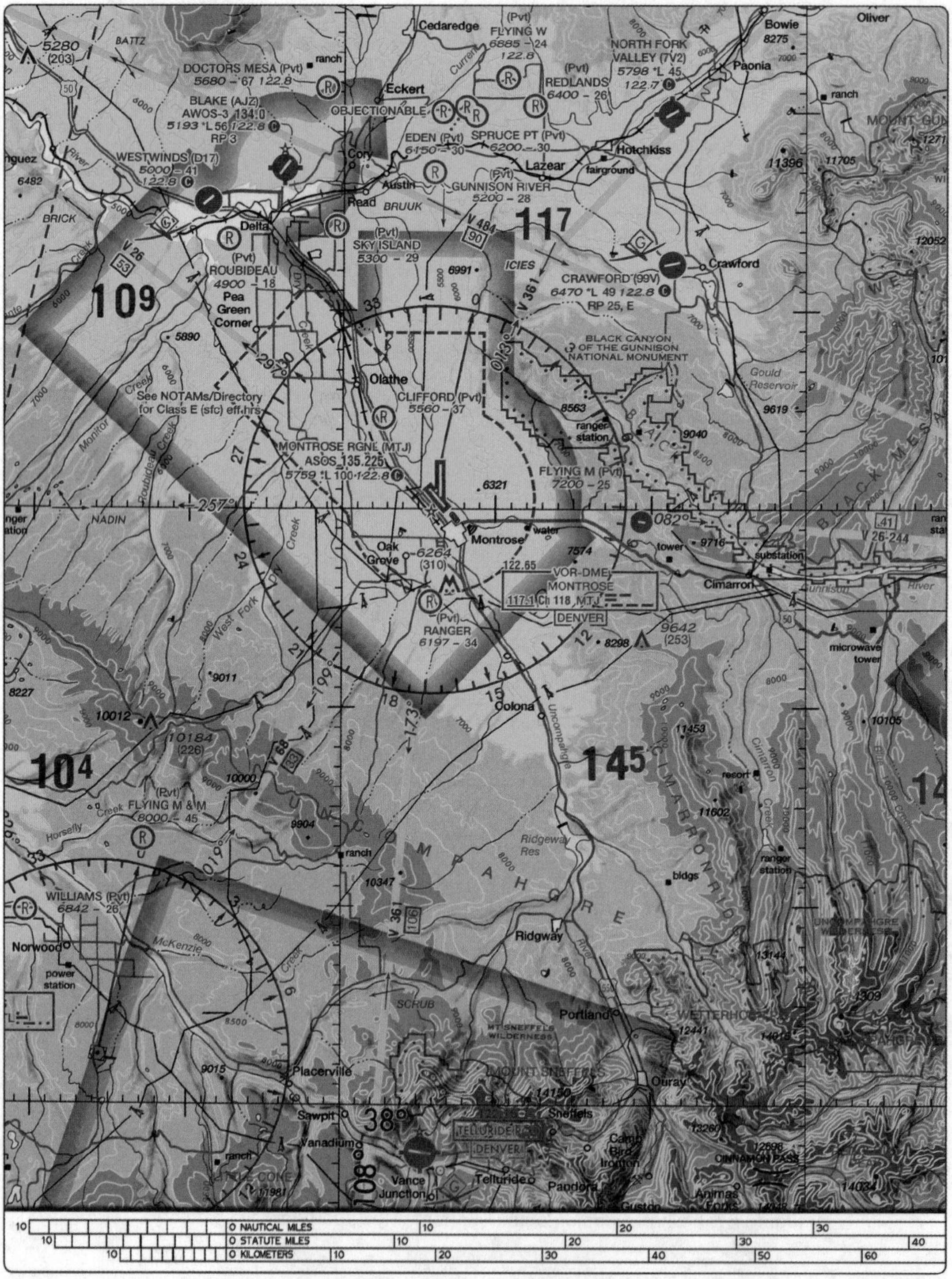

Figure 80. – Sectional Chart Excerpt.

NOTE: Chart is not to scale and should not be used for navigation. Use associated scale.

216 **COLORADO**

CRAWFORD (99V) 2 W UTC –7(–6DT) N38°42.25′ W107°38.62′ **DENVER**
6470 S2 OX 4 TPA–7470(1000) NOTAM FILE DEN **L–9E**
RWY 07–25: H4900X20 (ASPH) LIRL (NSTD)
RWY 07: VASI (NSTD). Trees. **RWY 25:** VASI (NSTD) Tank. Rgt tfc.
RWY E–W: 2500X125 (TURF)
RWY E: Rgt tfc. **RWY W:** Trees.
AIRPORT REMARKS: Attended continuously. Rwy 07–25 west 1300 ′ only 25′ wide. Heavy glider ops at arpt. Land to the east tkf to the west winds permitting. 100LL fuel avbl for emergency use only. Pedestrians, motor vehicles, deer and wildlife on and invof arpt. Unlimited vehicle use on arpt. Rwy West has +15 ′ building 170′ from thld 30′ left, +10′ road 100′ from thld centerline. +45′ tree 100′ L of Rwy 07 extended centerline 414 ′ from rwy end. –8′ to –20′ terrain off both sides of first 674 ′ of Rwy 25 end. E–W rwy occasionally has 6 inch diameter irrigation pipes crossing rwy width in various places. Rwy 07 has 20 ′ trees and -10′ to 20′ terrain 20′ right of rwy first 150′. E–W rwy consists of +12 inch alfalfa vegetation during various times of the year. Arpt lgts opr dusk–0800Z‡. Rwy 07 1 box VASI left side for local operators only or PPR call 970-921-7700 or 970-921-3018. Rwy 07-25 LIRL on N side from Rwy 25 end W 3800 ′. Rwy 07 1300′ from end E 300′. No thld lgts Rwy 07-25 3800′ usable for ngt ops.
COMMUNICATIONS: CTAF/UNICOM 122.8
RADIO AIDS TO NAVIGATION: NOTAM FILE MTJ.
MONTROSE (H) VORW/DME 117.1 MTJ Chan 118 N38 °30.39′ W107°53.96′ 033° 16.9 NM to fld. 5713/12E.

CREEDE
MINERAL CO MEM (C24) 2 E UTC –7(–6DT) N37°49.33′ W106°55.79′ **DENVER**
8680 NOTAM FILE DEN **H–3E, L–9E**
RWY 07–25: H6880X60 (ASPH) S-12.5, D-70, 2D-110
RWY 07: Thld dsplcd 188′. **RWY 25:** Road.
AIRPORT REMARKS: Unattended. Elk and deer on and invof arpt. Glider and hang glider activity on and in vicinity of arpt. Mountains in all directions. Departure to NE avoid over flight of trailers and resident homes, climb to 200 ′ above ground level on centerline extended prior to turn. Acft stay to right of valley on apch and/or departure route. 2′ cable fence around apron.
COMMUNICATIONS: CTAF 122.9
RADIO AIDS TO NAVIGATION: NOTAM FILE DEN.
BLUE MESA (H) VORW/DME 114.9 HBU Chan 96 N38 °27.13′ W107°02.39′ 158° 38.1 NM to fld. 8730/14E.

CUCHARA VALLEY AT LA VETA (See LA VETA)

DEL NORTE
ASTRONAUT KENT ROMINGER (8V1) 3 N UTC –7(–6DT) N37°42.83′ W106°21.11′ **DENVER**
7949 NOTAM FILE DEN **H–3E, L–9E**
RWY 06–24: 6050X75 (ASPH) 1.1% up SW
RWY 03–21: 4670X60 (TURF-DIRT)
RWY 21: Mountain.
AIRPORT REMARKS: Unattended. Wildlife on and invof arpt. Unlimited vehicle access on arpt. Mountainous terrain surrounds arpt in all directions.
COMMUNICATIONS: CTAF 122.9
RADIO AIDS TO NAVIGATION: NOTAM FILE ALS.
ALAMOSA (H) VORTACW 113.9 ALS Chan 86 N37 °20.95′ W105°48.93′ 298° 33.7 NM to fld. 7535/13E.

Figure 81. – Chart Supplements U.S. (formerly Airport/Facility Directory).

90. (Refer to Figure 63 below.) According to the Chart Supplement, what times can a pilot obtain fuel and services in September at Toledo Express (TOL) Airport?

A. 1400 - 0600 hr. local time.

B. 1300 - 0500 hr. local time.

C. 0900 - 0100 hr. local time.

Answer (C) is correct. *(Chart Supplement)*

DISCUSSION: In the Airport Remarks of the Toledo Express (TOL) section of the Chart Supplement, you will see that fuel and services are available from 1300-0500Z‡. The ‡ symbol specifies that the location observes daylight savings time and will be 1 hour earlier than shown. Daylight savings time is in effect from 0200 hr. local time the second Sunday in March to 0200 hr. local time the first Sunday in November. September is during daylight savings time.

Answer (A) is incorrect. It is an hour ahead instead of an hour behind for daylight savings time. Answer (B) is incorrect. This is the time of availability during standard time.

OHIO 263

TOLEDO

TOLEDO EXECUTIVE (TDZ) 6 SE UTC–5(–4DT) N41°33.90′ W83°28.93′ **DETROIT H–10G, L–28J IAP**
623 B S4 **FUEL** 100LL, JET A OX 1, 3 NOTAM FILE TDZ
RWY 14–32: H5829X100 (ASPH–GRVD) S–63, D–85, 2S–107 MIRL
RWY 14: REIL. PAPI(P4L)—GA 3.0° TCH 34′. Thld dsplcd 225′. Tower.
RWY 32: VASI(V4L)—GA 3.0° TCH 43′. Thld dsplcd 351′. Road.
RWY 04–22: H3799X75 (ASPH) S–63, D–85, 2S–107 MIRL
RWY 04: REIL. PAPI(P4L)—GA 3.5° TCH 35′. Thld dsplcd 100′. Road.
RWY 22: REIL. PAPI(P4L)—GA 3.0° TCH 25′. Thld dsplcd 380′. Railroad.
AIRPORT REMARKS: Attended Mon–Fri continuously, Sat–Sun 1300–0100Z‡. Parallel twy Rwy 04–22 and Rwy 14–32 35′ wide. Seagulls on and invof arpt. Ldg fee. ACTIVATE MIRL Rwy 04–22 and Rwy 14–32, REIL and PAPI Rwy 04, Rwy 22, Rwy 14 and VASI Rwy 32—CTAF.
WEATHER DATA SOURCES: ASOS 121.575 (419) 838–5034.
COMMUNICATIONS: CTAF/UNICOM 123.05
Ⓡ **APP/DEP CON** 126.1 **CLNC DEL** 125.6
RADIO AIDS TO NAVIGATION: NOTAM FILE CLE.
WATERVILLE (L) VOR/DME 113.1 VWV Chan 78 N41°27.09′ W83°38.32′ 048° 9.8 NM to fld. 664/2W.

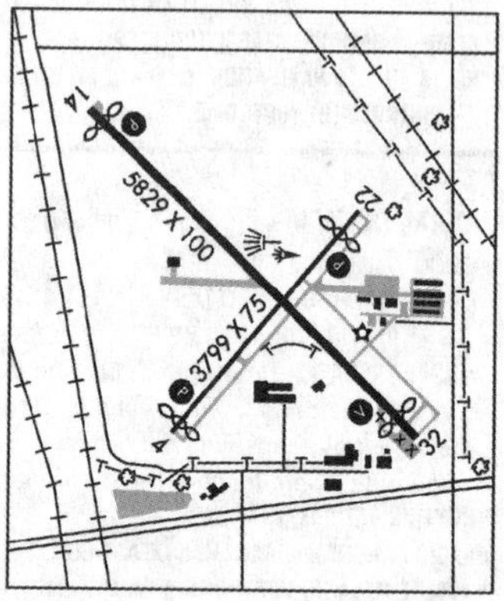

TOLEDO EXPRESS (TOL) 10 W UTC–5(–4DT) N41°35.21′ W83°48.47′ **DETROIT H–10G, L–28J IAP, AD**
683 B S4 **FUEL** 100LL, JET A OX 3 LRA Class I, ARFF Index B NOTAM FILE TOL
RWY 07–25: H10599X150 (ASPH–GRVD) S–100, D–174, 2S–175, 2D–300, 2D/2D2–550 HIRL CL
RWY 07: ALSF2. TDZL. Trees.
RWY 25: MALSR. VASI(V4L)—GA 3.0° TCH 51′. Trees. 0.3% up.
RWY 16–34: H5599X150 (ASPH–GRVD) S–100, D–174, 2S–175, 2D–300 MIRL
RWY 16: REIL. PAPI(P4L)—GA 3.0° TCH 48′. Trees.
RWY 34: REIL.
RUNWAY DECLARED DISTANCE INFORMATION
RWY 07: TORA 10599 TODA 10599 ASDA 10599 LDA 10599
RWY 16: TORA 5599 TODA 5599 ASDA 5599 LDA 5599
RWY 25: TORA 10599 TODA 10599 ASDA 10599 LDA 10599
RWY 34: TORA 5599 TODA 5599 ASDA 5599 LDA 5599
ARRESTING GEAR/SYSTEM
RWY 07 ←BAK–12 BAK–12 →**RWY 25**
AIRPORT REMARKS: Attended continuously. Fuel and svc avbl 1300–0500Z‡. Birds on and invof arpt. Twy A west of Rwy 16 and the ramp between Twy B9 and B13 not visible from twr. Twy D intersection of Twy D1, heavy acft use minimal power to reduce foreign object damage on Air National Guard ramp. Customs: Sat–Sun req must be made prior to 2200Z‡ on Fri, phone 419–259–6424.
WEATHER DATA SOURCES: ASOS (419) 865–8351.
COMMUNICATIONS: ATIS 118.75 **UNICOM** 122.95
Ⓡ **APP/DEP CON** 126.1 (360°–179°) 134.35 (180°–359°) 123.975
TOWER 118.1 **GND CON** 121.9 **CLNC DEL** 121.75
AIRSPACE: CLASS C svc continuous ctc **APP CON**
RADIO AIDS TO NAVIGATION: NOTAM FILE CLE.
WATERVILLE (L) VOR/DME 113.1 VWV Chan 78 N41°27.09′ W83°38.32′ 319° 11.1 NM to fld. 664/2W.
TOPHR NDB (LOM) 219 TO N41°33.21′ W83°55.27′ 074° 5.5 NM to fld. Unmonitored. NOTAM FILE TOL.
ILS 109.7. I–TOL Rwy 07. Class IE. LOM TOPHR NDB.
ILS 108.7 I–BQE Rwy 25. Class IA. LOC unusable 0.4 NM inbound. ILS unmonitored when twr clsd.
ASR

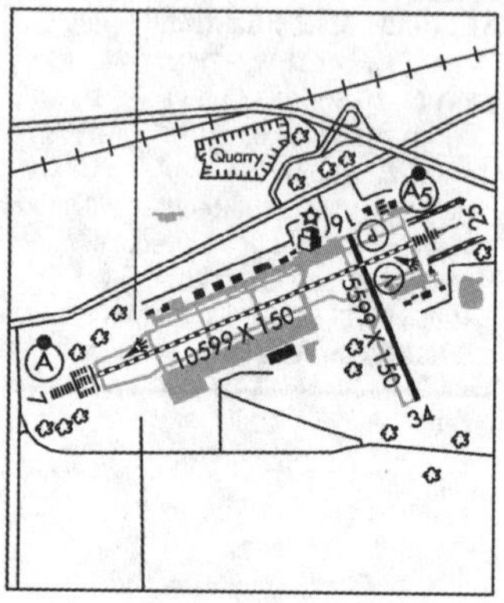

SEAGATE HELISTOP (6T2) 00 N UTC–5(–4DT) N41°39.25′ W83°31.88′ **DETROIT**
650 NOTAM FILE CLE
HELIPAD H1: H50X50 (CONC)
HELIPORT REMARKS: Unattended. ACTIVATE orange perimeter lgts—CTAF. Helipad H1 NSTD 1–box (2 VASIS). Helipad H1 not marked with "H." Helipad H1 perimeter lgts.
COMMUNICATIONS: CTAF/UNICOM 123.05

Figure 63. – Chart Supplements U.S. (formerly Airport/Facility Directory).

91. (Refer to Legend 13 below.) Where in the Chart Supplement can you find information where a pilot would need prior authorization from other than ATC to land at certain airports?

A. Under Airport Remarks.

B. Under Military Remarks.

C. Under Weather Data Sources.

Answer (B) is correct. *(Chart Supplement)*

DISCUSSION: Any civilian pilot who wants to land at a military airport must have a Prior Permission Request (PPR) authorized (usually by the Air Operations Commander) before being authorized to land.

Answer (A) is incorrect. Airport Remarks contain information of what the airport offers to the pilot and what cautions need to be taken whenever at or in the vicinity of the airport. Answer (C) is incorrect. The Weather Data Sources section gives information about weather sources available at airports.

DIRECTORY LEGEND 15

aircraft. When transient alert services are not shown, facilities are unknown. NO PRIORITY BASIS—means that transient alert services will be provided only after all the requirements for mission/tactical assigned aircraft have been accomplished.

(29) AIRPORT REMARKS

The Attendance Schedule is the months, days and hours the airport is actually attended. Airport attendance does not mean watchman duties or telephone accessibility, but rather an attendant or operator on duty to provide at least minimum services (e.g., repairs, fuel, transportation).

Airport Remarks have been grouped in order of applicability. Airport remarks are limited to those items of information that are determined essential for operational use, i.e., conditions of a permanent or indefinite nature and conditions that will remain in effect for more than 30 days concerning aeronautical facilities, services, maintenance available, procedures or hazards, knowledge of which is essential for safe and efficient operation of aircraft. Information concerning permanent closing of a runway or taxiway will not be shown. A note "See Special Notices" shall be applied within this remarks section when a special notice applicable to the entry is contained in the Special Notices section of this publication.

Parachute Jumping indicates parachute jumping areas associated with the airport. See Parachute Jumping Area section of this publication for additional Information.

Landing Fee indicates landing charges for private or non-revenue producing aircraft. In addition, fees may be charged for planes that remain over a couple of hours and buy no services, or at major airline terminals for all aircraft.

Note: Unless otherwise stated, remarks including runway ends refer to the runway's approach end.

(30) MILITARY REMARKS

Military Remarks published at a joint Civil/Military facility are remarks that are applicable to the Military. At Military Facilities all remarks will be published under the heading Military Remarks. Remarks contained in this section may not be applicable to civil users. The first group of remarks is applicable to the primary operator of the airport. Remarks applicable to a tenant on the airport are shown preceded by the tenant organization, i.e., (A) (AF) (N) (ANG), etc. Military airports operate 24 hours unless otherwise specified. Airport operating hours are listed first (airport operating hours will only be listed if they are different than the airport attended hours or if the attended hours are unavailable) followed by pertinent remarks in order of applicability. Remarks will include information on restrictions, hazards, traffic pattern, noise abatement, customs/agriculture/immigration, and miscellaneous information applicable to the Military.

Type of restrictions:

CLOSED: When designated closed, the airport is restricted from use by all aircraft unless stated otherwise. Any closure applying to specific type of aircraft or operation will be so stated. USN/USMC/USAF airports are considered closed during non-operating hours. Closed airports may be utilized during an emergency provided there is a safe landing area.

OFFICIAL BUSINESS ONLY: The airfield is closed to all transient military aircraft for obtaining routine services such as fueling, passenger drop off or pickup, practice approaches, parking, etc. The airfield may be used by aircrews and aircraft if official government business (including civilian) must be conducted on or near the airfield and prior permission is received from the airfield manager.

AF OFFICIAL BUSINESS ONLY OR NAVY OFFICIAL BUSINESS ONLY: Indicates that the restriction applies only to service indicated.

PRIOR PERMISSION REQUIRED (PPR): Airport is closed to transient aircraft unless approval for operation is obtained from the appropriate commander through Chief, Airfield Management or Airfield Operations Officer. Official Business or PPR does not preclude the use of US Military airports as an alternate for IFR flights. If a non-US military airport is used as a weather alternate and requires a PPR, the PPR must be requested and confirmed before the flight departs. The purpose of PPR is to control volume and flow of traffic rather than to prohibit it. Prior permission is required for all aircraft requiring transient alert service outside the published transient alert duty hours. All aircraft carrying hazardous materials must obtain prior permission as outlined in AFJI 11–204, AR 95–27, OPNAVINST 3710.7.

Note: OFFICIAL BUSINESS ONLY AND PPR restrictions are not applicable to Special Air Mission (SAM) or Special Air Resource (SPAR) aircraft providing person or persons on aboard are designated Code 6 or higher as explained in AFJMAN 11–213, AR 95–11, OPNAVINST 3722–8J. Official Business Only or PPR do not preclude the use of the airport as an alternate for IFR flights.

(31) WEATHER DATA SOURCES

Weather data sources will be listed alphabetically followed by their assigned frequencies and/or telephone number and hours of operation.

ASOS—Automated Surface Observing System. Reports the same as an AWOS–3 plus precipitation identification and intensity, and freezing rain occurrence;

AWOS—Automated Weather Observing System

AWOS–A—reports altimeter setting (all other information is advisory only).

AWOS–AV—reports altimeter and visibility.

AWOS–1—reports altimeter setting, wind data and usually temperature, dew point and density altitude.

AWOS–2—reports the same as AWOS–1 plus visibility.

AWOS–3—reports the same as AWOS–1 plus visibility and cloud/ceiling data.

AWOS–3P reports the same as the AWOS–3 system, plus a precipitation identification sensor.

AWOS–3PT reports the same as the AWOS–3 system, plus precipitation identification sensor and a thunderstorm/lightning reporting capability.

AWOS–3T reports the same as AWOS–3 system and includes a thunderstorm/lightning reporting capability.

NE, 09 FEB 20XX to 05 APR 20XX

Legend 13. – Chart Supplements U.S. (formerly Airport/Facility Directory).

92. (Refer to Legend 14 below.) What is the acronym for a computerized command response system that provides automated weather, radio check capability, and airport advisory information selected from an automated menu by microphone clicks?

A. GCA.

B. AUNICOM.

C. UNICOM.

Answer (B) is correct. *(Chart Supplement)*

DISCUSSION: The AUNICOM provides automated weather, radio check capability, and airport advisory information selected from an automated menu by microphone clicks.

Answer (A) is incorrect. A GCA is a Ground Control Approach system. Answer (C) is incorrect. A UNICOM is a nongovernment air/ground radio communications facility that may or may not provide airport information.

16 **DIRECTORY LEGEND**

See AIM, Basic Flight Information and ATC Procedures for detailed description of Weather Data Sources.

AWOS–4—reports same as AWOS–3 system, plus precipitation occurence, type and accumulation, freezing rain, thunderstorm, and runway surface sensors.

HIWAS—See RADIO AIDS TO NAVIGATION

LAWRS—Limited Aviation Weather Reporting Station where observers report cloud height, weather, obstructions to vision, temperature and dewpoint (in most cases), surface wind, altimeter and pertinent remarks.

LLWAS—indicates a Low Level Wind Shear Alert System consisting of a center field and several field perimeter anemometers.

SAWRS—identifies airports that have a Supplemental Aviation Weather Reporting Station available to pilots for current weather information.

SWSL—Supplemental Weather Service Location providing current local weather information via radio and telephone.

TDWR—indicates airports that have Terminal Doppler Weather Radar.

WSP—indicates airports that have Weather System Processor.

When the automated weather source is broadcast over an associated airport NAVAID frequency (see NAVAID line), it shall be indicated by a bold ASOS, AWOS, or HIWAS followed by the frequency, identifier and phone number, if available.

32 COMMUNICATIONS

Airport terminal control facilities and radio communications associated with the airport shall be shown. When the call sign is not the same as the airport name the call sign will be shown. Frequencies shall normally be shown in descending order with the primary frequency listed first. Frequencies will be listed, together with sectorization indicated by outbound radials, and hours of operation. Communications will be listed in sequence as follows:

Single Frequency Approach (SFA), Common Traffic Advisory Frequency (CTAF), Automatic Terminal Information Service (ATIS) and Aeronautical Advisory Stations (UNICOM) or (AUNICOM) along with their frequency is shown, where available, on the line following the heading "COMMUNICATIONS." When the CTAF and UNICOM frequencies are the same, the frequency will be shown as CTAF/UNICOM 122.8.

The FSS telephone nationwide is toll free 1–800–WX–BRIEF (1–800–992–7433). When the FSS is located on the field it will be indicated as "on arpt". Frequencies available at the FSS will follow in descending order. Remote Communications Outlet (RCO) providing service to the airport followed by the frequency and FSS RADIO name will be shown when available.

FSS's provide information on airport conditions, radio aids and other facilities, and process flight plans. Airport Advisory Service (AAS) is provided on the CTAF by FSS's for select non-tower airports or airports where the tower is not in operation.

(See AIM, Para 4–1–9 Traffic Advisory Practices at Airports Without Operating Control Towers or AC 90–42C.)

Aviation weather briefing service is provided by FSS specialists. Flight and weather briefing services are also available by calling the telephone numbers listed.

Remote Communications Outlet (RCO)—An unmanned air/ground communications facility that is remotely controlled and provides UHF or VHF communications capability to extend the service range of an FSS.

Civil Communications Frequencies-Civil communications frequencies used in the FSS air/ground system are operated on 122.0, 122.2, 123.6; emergency 121.5; plus receive-only on 122.1.

a. 122.0 is assigned as the Enroute Flight Advisory Service frequency at selected FSS RADIO outlets.
b. 122.2 is assigned as a common enroute frequency.
c. 123.6 is assigned as the airport advisory frequency at select non-tower locations. At airports with a tower, FSS may provide airport advisories on the tower frequency when tower is closed.
d. 122.1 is the primary receive-only frequency at VOR's.
e. Some FSS's are assigned 50 kHz frequencies in the 122–126 MHz band (eg. 122.45). Pilots using the FSS A/G system should refer to this directory or appropriate charts to determine frequencies available at the FSS or remoted facility through which they wish to communicate.

Emergency frequency 121.5 and 243.0 are available at all Flight Service Stations, most Towers, Approach Control and RADAR facilities.

Frequencies published followed by the letter "T" or "R", indicate that the facility will only transmit or receive respectively on that frequency. All radio aids to navigation (NAVAID) frequencies are transmit only.

TERMINAL SERVICES

SFA—Single Frequency Approach.

CTAF—A program designed to get all vehicles and aircraft at airports without an operating control tower on a common frequency.

ATIS—A continuous broadcast of recorded non-control information in selected terminal areas.

D-ATIS—Digital ATIS provides ATIS information in text form outside the standard reception range of conventional ATIS via landline & data link communications and voice message within range of existing transmitters.

AUNICOM—Automated UNICOM is a computerized, command response system that provides automated weather, radio check capability and airport advisory information selected from an automated menu by microphone clicks.

UNICOM—A non-government air/ground radio communications facility which may provide airport information.

PTD—Pilot to Dispatcher.

APP CON—Approach Control. The symbol Ⓡ indicates radar approach control.

TOWER—Control tower.

GCA—Ground Control Approach System.

GND CON—Ground Control.

GCO—Ground Communication Outlet—An unstaffed, remotely controlled, ground/ground communications facility. Pilots at

NE, 09 FEB 20XX to 05 APR 20XX

Legend 14. – Chart Supplements U.S. (formerly Airport/Facility Directory).

93. (Refer to Legend 15 below.) What depicts a Class E airspace that begins at 700 feet AGL?

A. A dashed blue circle around an airport.

B. A solid magenta circle around an airport.

C. A magenta vignette that goes around an airport.

Answer (C) is correct. *(PHAK Chap 15)*

DISCUSSION: Class E airspace floor begins at 700 ft. AGL. It is depicted by a magenta vignette circle or area around an airport.

Answer (A) is incorrect. A dashed blue circle around an airport depicts a Class D airspace. Answer (B) is incorrect. A solid magenta circle going around an airport depicts Class C airspace.

DIRECTORY LEGEND **17**

uncontrolled airports may contact ATC and FSS via VHF to a telephone connection to obtain an instrument clearance or close a VFR or IFR flight plan. They may also get an updated weather briefing prior to takeoff. Pilots will use four "key clicks" on the VHF radio to contact the appropriate ATC facility or six "key clicks" to contact the FSS. The GCO system is intended to be used only on the ground.
DEP CON—Departure Control. The symbol Ⓡ indicates radar departure control.
CLNC DEL—Clearance Delivery.
PRE TAXI CLNC—Pre taxi clearance.

VFR ADVSY SVC—VFR Advisory Service. Service provided by Non-Radar Approach Control.
Advisory Service for VFR aircraft (upon a workload basis) ctc APP CON.
COMD POST—Command Post followed by the operator call sign in parenthesis.
PMSV—Pilot-to-Metro Service call sign, frequency and hours of operation, when full service is other than continuous. PMSV installations at which weather observation service is available shall be indicated, following the frequency and/or hours of operation as "Wx obsn svc 1900–0000Z‡" or "other times" may be used when no specific time is given. PMSV facilities manned by forecasters are considered "Full Service". PMSV facilities manned by weather observers are listed as "Limited Service".
OPS—Operations followed by the operator call sign in parenthesis.
CON
RANGE
FLT FLW—Flight Following
MEDIVAC
NOTE: Communication frequencies followed by the letter "X" indicate frequency available on request.

33 AIRSPACE

Information concerning Class B, C, and part–time D and E surface area airspace shall be published with effective times. Class D and E surface area airspace that is continuous as established by Rulemaking Docket will not be shown.
CLASS B—Radar Sequencing and Separation Service for all aircraft in CLASS B airspace.
CLASS C—Separation between IFR and VFR aircraft and sequencing of VFR arrivals to the primary airport.
TRSA—Radar Sequencing and Separation Service for participating VFR Aircraft within a Terminal Radar Service Area.
Class C, D, and E airspace described in this publication is that airspace usually consisting of a 5 NM radius core surface area that begins at the surface and extends upward to an altitude above the airport elevation (charted in MSL for Class C and Class D). Class E surface airspace normally extends from the surface up to but not including the overlying controlled airspace.
When part–time Class C or Class D airspace defaults to Class E, the core surface area becomes Class E. This will be formatted as:
AIRSPACE: CLASS C svc "times" ctc **APP CON** other times CLASS E:
or
AIRSPACE: CLASS D svc "times" other times CLASS E.
When a part–time Class C, Class D or Class E surface area defaults to Class G, the core surface area becomes Class G up to, but not including, the overlying controlled airspace. Normally, the overlying controlled airspace is Class E airspace beginning at either 700′ or 1200′ AGL and may be determined by consulting the relevant VFR Sectional or Terminal Area Charts. This will be formatted as:
AIRSPACE: CLASS C svc "times" ctc **APP CON** other times CLASS G, with CLASS E 700′ (or 1200′) AGL & abv:
or
AIRSPACE: CLASS D svc "times" other times CLASS G with CLASS E 700′ (or 1200′) AGL & abv:
or
AIRSPACE: CLASS E svc "times" other times CLASS G with CLASS E 700′ (or 1200′) AGL & abv.
NOTE: AIRSPACE SVC "TIMES" INCLUDE ALL ASSOCIATED ARRIVAL EXTENSIONS. Surface area arrival extensions for instrument approach procedures become part of the primary core surface area. These extensions may be either Class D or Class E airspace and are effective concurrent with the times of the primary core surface area. For example, when a part–time Class C, Class D or Class E surface area defaults to Class G, the associated arrival extensions will default to Class G at the same time. When a part–time Class C or Class D surface area defaults to Class E, the arrival extensions will remain in effect as Class E airspace.
NOTE: CLASS E AIRSPACE EXTENDING UPWARD FROM 700 FEET OR MORE ABOVE THE SURFACE, DESIGNATED IN CONJUNCTION WITH AN AIRPORT WITH AN APPROVED INSTRUMENT PROCEDURE.
Class E 700′ AGL (shown as magenta vignette on sectional charts) and 1200′ AGL (blue vignette) areas are designated when necessary to provide controlled airspace for transitioning to/from the terminal and enroute environments. Unless otherwise specified, these 700′/1200′ AGL Class E airspace areas remain in effect continuously, regardless of airport operating hours or surface area status. These transition areas should not be confused with surface areas or arrival extensions.
(See Chapter 3, AIRSPACE, in the Aeronautical Information Manual for further details)

NE, 09 FEB 20XX to 05 APR 20XX

Legend 15. – Chart Supplements U.S. (formerly Airport/Facility Directory).

94. (Refer to Legend 16 below.) If the SSV Class of VORTAC is listed as a Terminal Class, the altitudes and distance to adequately receive the signal of the VORTAC is

A. 1,000 feet to 12,000 feet and 25 NM.

B. 1,000 feet to 18,000 feet and 40 NM.

C. 1,000 feet up to 60,000 feet and up to 130 NM.

Answer (A) is correct. *(Chart Supplement)*

DISCUSSION: The (T) or Terminal Class VORTAC can be received at 1,000 ft. to 12,000 ft. and 25 NM.

Answer (B) is incorrect. The (L) or Low Altitude Class VORTAC can be received at 1,000 ft. to 18,000 ft. and 40 NM. Answer (C) is incorrect. The (H) or High Altitude Class VORTAC can be received at 1,000 ft. up to 18,000 ft. and up to 130 NM.

18 **DIRECTORY LEGEND**

34 RADIO AIDS TO NAVIGATION

The Airport/Facility Directory lists, by facility name, all Radio Aids to Navigation that appear on FAA, AeroNav Products Visual or IFR Aeronautical Charts and those upon which the FAA has approved an Instrument Approach Procedure, with exception of selected TACANs. Military TACAN information will be published for Military facilities contained in this publication. All VOR, VORTAC, TACAN, ILS and MLS equipment in the National Airspace System has an automatic monitoring and shutdown feature in the event of malfunction. Unmonitored, as used in this publication, for any navigational aid, means that monitoring personnel cannot observe the malfunction or shutdown signal. The NAVAID NOTAM file identifier will be shown as "NOTAM FILE IAD" and will be listed on the Radio Aids to Navigation line. When two or more NAVAIDS are listed and the NOTAM file identifier is different from that shown on the Radio Aids to Navigation line, it will be shown with the NAVAID listing. NOTAM file identifiers for ILSs and its components (e.g., NDB (LOM) are the same as the associated airports and are not repeated. Automated Surface Observing System (ASOS), Automated Weather Observing System (AWOS), and Hazardous Inflight Weather Advisory Service (HIWAS) will be shown when this service is broadcast over selected NAVAIDs.

NAVAID information is tabulated as indicated in the following sample:

TACAN/DME Channel — Geographical Position — Site Elevation

NAME (L) ABVORTAC 117.55 ABE Chan 122(Y) N40°43.60′ W75°27.30′ 180°4.1 NM to fld. 1110/8E. **AWOS. HIWAS.**

Class — Frequency — Identifier — Bearing and distance facility to center of airport — Magnetic Variation — Automated Weather Observing System — Hazardous Inflight Weather Advisory Service

VOR unusable 020°–060° byd 26 NM blo 3,500′

Restriction within the normal altitude/range of the navigational aid (See primary alphabetical listing for restrictions on VORTAC and VOR/DME).

Note: Those DME channel numbers with a (Y) suffix require TACAN to be placed in the "Y" mode to receive distance information.

HIWAS—Hazardous Inflight Weather Advisory Service is a continuous broadcast of inflight weather advisories including summarized SIGMETs, convective SIGMETs, AIRMETs and urgent PIREPs. HIWAS is presently broadcast over selected VOR's throughout the U.S.

ASR/PAR—Indicates that Surveillance (ASR) or Precision (PAR) radar instrument approach minimums are published in the U.S. Terminal Procedures. Only part-time hours of operation will be shown.

RADIO CLASS DESIGNATIONS

VOR/DME/TACAN Standard Service Volume (SSV) Classifications

SSV Class	Altitudes	Distance (NM)
(T) Terminal	1000′ to 12,000′	25
(L) Low Altitude	1000′ to 18,000′	40
(H) High Altitude	1000′ to 14,500′	40
	14,500′ to 18,000′	100
	18,000′ to 45,000′	130
	45,000′ to 60,000′	100

NOTE: Additionally, (H) facilities provide (L) and (T) service volume and (L) facilities provide (T) service. Altitudes are with respect to the station's site elevation. Coverage is not available in a cone of airspace directly above the facility.

CONTINUED ON NEXT PAGE

NE, 09 FEB 20XX to 05 APR 20XX

Legend 16. – Chart Supplements U.S. (formerly Airport/Facility Directory).

95. (Refer to Legend 17 below.) According to the Chart Supplement, what are the operational requirements of a VORTAC?

A. VHF navigational facility with omnidirectional course only.

B. Collocated VOR navigational facility and UHF standard distance measuring equipment.

C. Collocated VOR and TACAN navigational facilities.

Answer (C) is correct. *(Chart Supplement)*

DISCUSSION: According to the Chart Supplement, a VORTAC has the operational requirements of collocated VOR and TACAN navigational facilities.

Answer (A) is incorrect. This is describing the operational requirement of a VOR. Answer (B) is incorrect. This is describing the operational requirement of a VOR/DME.

DIRECTORY LEGEND 19

CONTINUED FROM PRECEDING PAGE

The term VOR is, operationally, a general term covering the VHF omnidirectional bearing type of facility without regard to the fact that the power, the frequency protected service volume, the equipment configuration, and operational requirements may vary between facilities at different locations.

AB	Automatic Weather Broadcast.
DF	Direction Finding Service.
DME	UHF standard (TACAN compatible) distance measuring equipment.
DME(Y)	UHF standard (TACAN compatible) distance measuring equipment that require TACAN to be placed in the "Y" mode to receive DME.
GS	Glide slope.
H	Non-directional radio beacon (homing), power 50 watts to less than 2,000 watts (50 NM at all altitudes).
HH	Non-directional radio beacon (homing), power 2,000 watts or more (75 NM at all altitudes).
H-SAB	Non-directional radio beacons providing automatic transcribed weather service.
ILS	Instrument Landing System (voice, where available, on localizer channel).
IM	Inner marker.
ISMLS	Interim Standard Microwave Landing System.
LDA	Localizer Directional Aid.
LMM	Compass locator station when installed at middle marker site (15 NM at all altitudes).
LOM	Compass locator station when installed at outer marker site (15 NM at all altitudes).
MH	Non-directional radio beacon (homing) power less than 50 watts (25 NM at all altitudes).
MLS	Microwave Landing System.
MM	Middle marker.
OM	Outer marker.
S	Simultaneous range homing signal and/or voice.
SABH	Non-directional radio beacon not authorized for IFR or ATC. Provides automatic weather broadcasts.
SDF	Simplified Direction Facility.
TACAN	UHF navigational facility-omnidirectional course and distance information.
VOR	VHF navigational facility-omnidirectional course only.
VOR/DME	Collocated VOR navigational facility and UHF standard distance measuring equipment.
VORTAC	Collocated VOR and TACAN navigational facilities.
W	Without voice on radio facility frequency.
Z	VHF station location marker at a LF radio facility.

NE, 09 FEB 20XX to 05 APR 20XX

Legend 17. – Chart Supplements U.S. (formerly Airport/Facility Directory).

9.7 Notices to Airmen Publication (NTAP)

96. What information is contained in the *Notices to Airmen Publication (NTAP)*?

A. Current NOTAM (D) and FDC NOTAMs.

B. All current NOTAMs only.

C. Current Chart Supplement information and FDC NOTAMs.

Answer (A) is correct. *(AIM Para 5-1-3)*

DISCUSSION: The *NTAP* contains (D) NOTAMs that are expected to remain in effect for an extended period and FDC NOTAMs that are current at the time of publication.

Answer (B) is incorrect. Military NOTAMs are not published in the *NTAP*. Answer (C) is incorrect. While current FDC NOTAMs are published in the *NTAP*, current Chart Supplement information is not.

97. When NOTAMs are published in the *Notices to Airmen Publication (NTAP)*, they are

A. Still a part of a standard weather briefing.

B. Only available in a standard weather briefing if the pilot requests published NOTAMs.

C. Canceled and are no longer valid.

Answer (B) is correct. *(AIM Para 5-1-3)*

DISCUSSION: Once a NOTAM is published in the *NTAP*, the NOTAM is not provided during pilot weather briefings unless specifically requested.

Answer (A) is incorrect. Published NOTAMs are only available in a pilot weather briefing if the pilot makes a specific request for them. NOTAMs that have not been published are a part of a standard weather briefing. Answer (C) is incorrect. A published NOTAM remains in effect until its expiration date or until an additional NOTAM is issued to cancel it.

END OF STUDY UNIT

STUDY UNIT TEN
NAVIGATION SYSTEMS

(5 pages of outline)

This study unit contains outlines of major concepts tested, sample test questions and answers regarding navigation systems, and an explanation of each answer. The table of contents above lists each subunit within this study unit, the number of questions pertaining to that particular subunit, and the pages on which the outlines and questions begin, respectively.

Many of the questions in this study unit ask about the sectional (aeronautical) charts, which appear as Figures 20 and 23 through 26. The acronym ACL is the question source code used to refer to this aeronautical chart legend.

Recall that the **sole purpose** of this book is to expedite your passing of the FAA pilot knowledge test for the private pilot certificate. Accordingly, all extraneous material (i.e., topics or regulations not directly tested on the FAA pilot knowledge test) is omitted, even though much more knowledge is necessary to fly safely. This additional material is presented in *Pilot Handbook* and *Private Pilot Flight Maneuvers and Practical Test Prep*, available from Gleim Publications, Inc. Order online at www.GleimAviation.com.

10.1 VOR TEST FACILITY (VOT)

1. VOR Test Facilities (VOTs) are available on a specific frequency at certain airports. The facility permits you to check the accuracy of your VOR receiver while you are on the ground.
   a. The airborne use of a VOT is permitted; however, its use is strictly limited to those areas and altitudes specifically authorized by the Chart Supplement.
   b. In each Chart Supplement, there is a section, listed by state, of VOT ground locations and airborne checkpoints.
      1) Frequencies, identifiers, distances, and descriptions, if appropriate, are given to determine where these tests can be conducted.
2. Tune the navigation radio to the specified VOT frequency, and center the course deviation indicator.
   a. The OBS should read either 0° or 180°, regardless of your position at the airport.
   b. If 0°, the TO/FROM indicator should indicate FROM.
   c. If 180°, the TO/FROM indicator should indicate TO.
   d. Accuracy of the VOR should be ±4° for ground checks or ±6° for airborne checks.

10.2 DETERMINING POSITION USING VORs

1. Several FAA exam questions require you to identify your position based on the intersection of given radials of two VORs.
   a. To locate a position based on VOR radials, draw the radials on your chart or on the plastic overlay during the FAA knowledge test.
   b. Remember that radials are from the VOR, or leaving the VOR.
   c. Make sure you have located the correct radial on the compass rose before drawing your line.
   d. Recheck yourself by counting in 10° or 5° intervals from each of the closest 30° intervals that are numbered and marked with an arrow.
2. Other FAA exam questions require you to identify your position based upon the indications of a single VOR.
   a. You must compare the OBS setting and the TO/FROM indicator with the aircraft heading. To indicate correctly, the OBS (top) setting must correspond roughly with the aircraft heading [e.g., 180° OBS (top) setting, 180° aircraft heading].
   b. The TO/FROM indicator must correspond to the aircraft's flight path in relation to the VOR. Flying TO a VOR with a FROM indication and flying FROM a VOR with a TO indication will result in reverse sensing.
   c. When flying directly from a station, the heading and the radial being flown will correspond (i.e., 360° heading FROM will be the 360° radial).
   d. When flying directly TO a station, the heading flown and the radial being flown will be reciprocals (i.e., 180° heading TO will be on the 360° radial).
   e. With regard to CDI deflection, you must pretend your airplane has the same heading as the OBS setting. A left deviation means you are right of course, and a right deviation means you are left of course.
      1) If your heading and the OBS setting are not roughly the same, the CDI **will not** indicate correctly.
   f. If no TO or FROM flag indication appears, the aircraft is in the area of ambiguity, i.e., 90° away from the radial dialed up on the OBS. To know the side of the station on which the aircraft is located, consult the CDI. The needle points toward the station.
3. Interpreting VOR indications (see the diagram below).

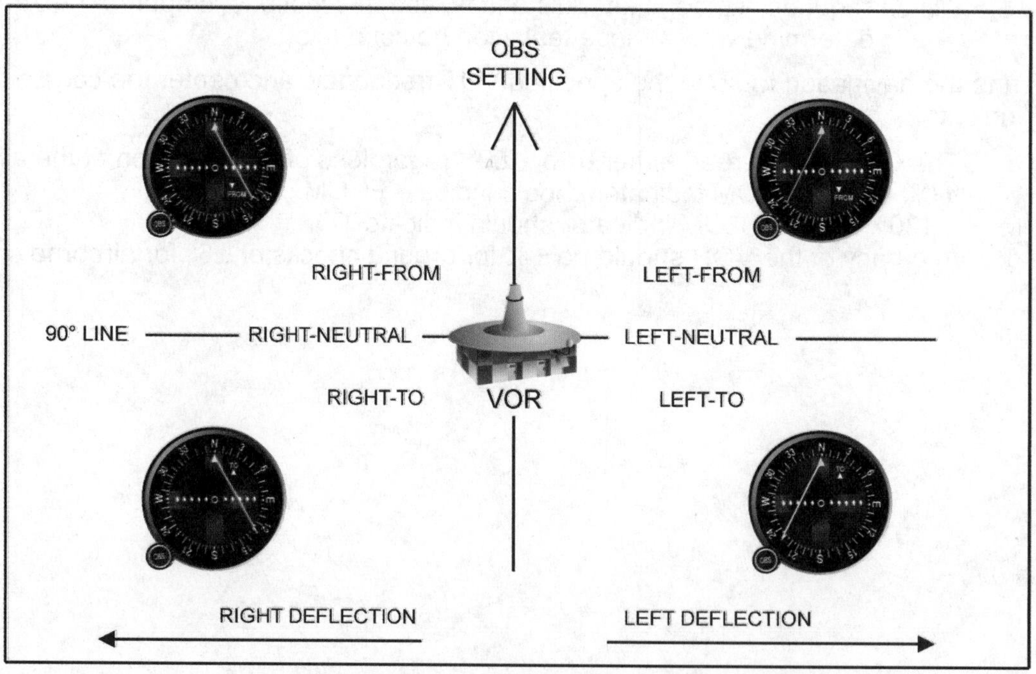

a. When you select a course in the OBS, imagine that you have drawn a line through the VOR station in the direction of the course.
   1) The line should extend outward from the VOR in both the direction of the selected course and the direction of its reciprocal.
   2) Imagine an arrowhead at the end of the line in the direction of the desired course, as in the diagram.
   3) Now look at the diagram and imagine the VOR in the center.
      a) Rotate the diagram until the arrowhead points in the direction of your OBS setting.
      b) Note that, when you are facing in the direction of the OBS setting, the CDI needle points to the right if you are left of the course and points to the left if you are right of the course.
      c) If you are directly on the course line, the CDI needle will be centered.
b. Imagine also a line drawn through the VOR perpendicular to the selected course, as shown in the figure on the previous page.
   1) Again, rotate the diagram until the arrowhead points in the direction of the OBS setting, and imagine that you are facing in that same direction.
      a) If you are below the 90° line, the TO/FROM indicator will read TO.
      b) If you are above the 90° line, it will read FROM.
      c) If you are anywhere on the 90° line, you will see a neutral (i.e., a blank TO/FROM window, NAV, OFF, or red flag) indication.
         i) You will also see a neutral indication if the VOR signal is too weak for reliable navigation.
c. The diagram should be used to understand how to interpret VOR indications in flight. Remember that you must rotate the diagram so the omnibearing direction is pointed in the direction in which your OBS is set (i.e., the selected course).
   1) When flying, interpret the needle by envisioning your airplane being on a heading indicated by the OBS.
      a) You can immediately tell which quadrant you are in -- TO or FROM, left or right.

d. Note that the airplane's heading does not affect the VOR navigation instrument.

1) The airplane's position (not heading) relative to the VOR determines the CDI and TO/FROM indications.

a) The following diagram illustrates this point:

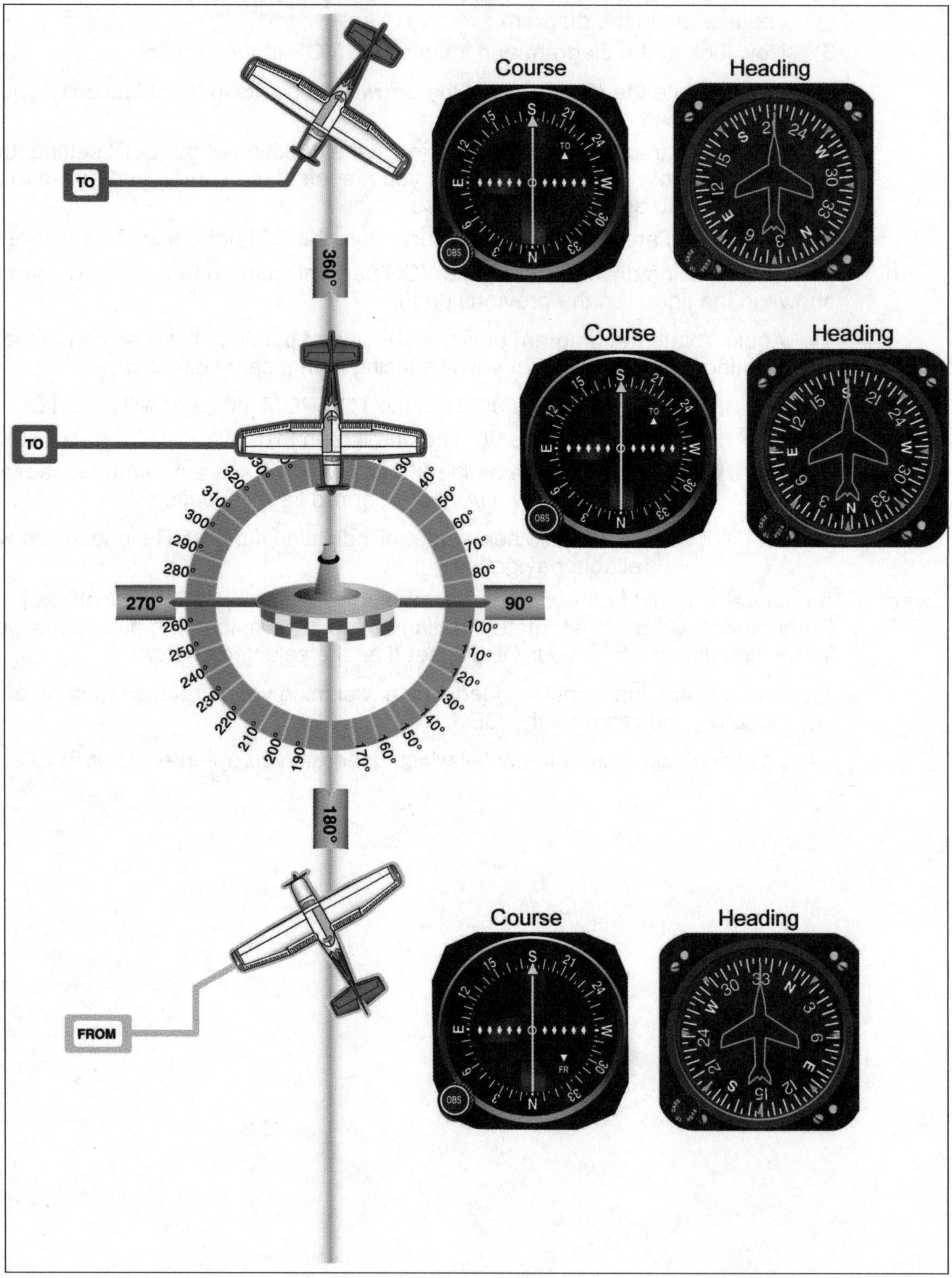

2) Thus, to obtain a useful indication, your airplane must be heading in the same general direction as your OBS setting.
   a) A right CDI deflection will indicate that the desired course is to your right, and a left deflection will indicate that it is to your left.
   b) A TO indication will show that your present course will move you closer to the station, and a FROM indication means that it will take you farther from the station.
3) Always be sure that your OBS setting agrees with the direction in which you intend to fly.

10.3 GLOBAL POSITIONING SYSTEM (GPS)

1. The Global Positioning System (GPS) is a satellite-based radio navigation system.
2. The GPS receiver needs at least four satellites to yield a three-dimensional position (latitude, longitude, and altitude) and time solution.
   a. The GPS receiver computes navigational data, such as distance and bearing to a waypoint (e.g., an airport), groundspeed, etc., by using the airplane's known latitude/longitude (position) and referencing this to a database built into the receiver.
3. GPS receivers
   a. Contain chart databases, moving maps, traffic, and weather overlays;
   b. Can contain VOR/DME/localizer/glideslope receivers; and
   c. Can compute groundspeed, time, and fuel burn.
4. To effectively navigate by means of GPS, pilots should
   a. Determine the GPS unit is approved for their planned flight,
   b. Understand how to make and cancel all appropriate entries,
   c. Determine the status of the databases,
   d. Program and review the programmed route, and
   e. Ensure the track flown is approved by ATC.
5. Navigating by GPS must be integrated with other forms of electronic navigation as well as pilotage and dead reckoning.
   a. Pilots should never rely solely on one system of navigation.
6. Always check to see if the unit has Receiver Autonomous Integrity Monitoring (RAIM) capability.
   a. If no RAIM capability exists, be suspicious of a GPS-displayed position when any disagreement exists with the position derived from other radio navigation systems, pilotage, or dead reckoning.
   b. If RAIM is lost during flight, the pilot has no assurance of the accuracy of the GPS position.
   c. With three satellites, you narrow the possible location down to one of two points, meaning that you could be at only one of those points.
      1) Four satellites are required for navigation.
      2) At least one satellite, in addition to those required for navigation, must be in view for the receiver to perform the RAIM function. Thus, RAIM needs a minimum of five satellites in view, or four satellites and a barometric altimeter (baro-aiding), to detect an integrity anomaly.

QUESTIONS AND ANSWER EXPLANATIONS: All of the private pilot knowledge test questions chosen by the FAA for release as well as additional questions selected by Gleim relating to the material in the previous outlines are reproduced on the following pages. These questions have been organized into the same subunits as the outlines. To the immediate right of each question are the correct answer and answer explanation. You should cover these answers and answer explanations while responding to the questions. Refer to the general discussion in the Introduction on how to take the FAA knowledge test.

Remember that the questions from the FAA knowledge test bank have been reordered by topic and organized into a meaningful sequence. Also, the first line of the answer explanation gives the citation of the authoritative source for the answer.

QUESTIONS

10.1 VOR Test Facility (VOT)

1. Where can locations for VOR test facilities be found?

A. *Aeronautical Information Manual.*

B. Sectional charts.

C. Chart Supplement.

Answer (C) is correct. *(AIM Para 1-1-4)*
DISCUSSION: In each Chart Supplement, there is a section, listed by state, of VOT ground locations and airborne checkpoints.
Answer (A) is incorrect. The *Aeronautical Information Manual* does not list locations of VOR test facilities. Answer (B) is incorrect. Sectional charts, while showing locations of VORs, do not include locations of VOR test facilities.

2. What should the airborne accuracy of a VOR be?

A. ±4°

B. ±5°

C. ±6°

Answer (C) is correct. *(AIM Para 1-1-4)*
DISCUSSION: The accuracy of the VOR should be ±4° for ground checks or ±6° for airborne checks.
Answer (A) is incorrect. The accuracy of an airborne VOR check should be ±6°, not ±4°. Answer (B) is incorrect. The accuracy of an airborne VOR check should be ±6°, not ±5°.

3. When the course deviation indicator (CDI) needle is centered using a VOR test signal (VOT), the omnibearing selector (OBS) and the TO/FROM indicator should read

A. 180° FROM, only if the pilot is due north of the VOT.

B. 0° TO or 180° FROM, regardless of the pilot's position from the VOT.

C. 0° FROM or 180° TO, regardless of the pilot's position from the VOT.

Answer (C) is correct. *(AIM Para 1-1-4)*
DISCUSSION: To use the VOT service, tune in to the VOT frequency (108.0-117.95 MHz) on the VOR receiver. With the CDI centered, the OBS should read 0° with the TO/FROM indication showing FROM, or the OBS should read 180° with the TO/FROM indication showing TO.
Answer (A) is incorrect. Regardless of your heading, with the CDI centered, the OBS should read 0° with the TO/FROM indication showing FROM, or the OBS should read 180° with the TO/FROM indication showing TO. Answer (B) is incorrect. This answer selection is backwards. With the CDI centered, the OBS should read 0° with the TO/FROM indication showing FROM, or the OBS should read 180° with the TO/FROM indication showing TO.

10.2 Determining Position Using VORs

4. (Refer to Figure 23 on page 383.) What is the approximate position of the aircraft if the VOR receivers indicate the 340° radial of Savannah VORTAC (area 3) and the 184° radial of Allendale VOR (area 1)?

A. Town of Guyton.

B. Town of Springfield.

C. 3 miles east of Briggs.

Answer (B) is correct. *(PHAK Chap 16)*
DISCUSSION: To locate a position based on VOR radials, draw the radials on your map or on the plastic overlay during the FAA pilot knowledge test. Remember that radials are from the VOR, or leaving the VOR. On Fig. 23, the 340° radial from Savannah extends northwest, and the 184° radial from Allendale extends south. They intersect over the town of Springfield.
Answer (A) is incorrect. Guyton is on the 325° radial (not the 340° radial of Savannah VORTAC) and the 188° radial (not the 184° radial of Allendale VOR). Answer (C) is incorrect. The position of 3 NM east of Briggs is on the 330° radial, not the 340° radial of Savannah VORTAC and the 184° radial of Allendale VOR.

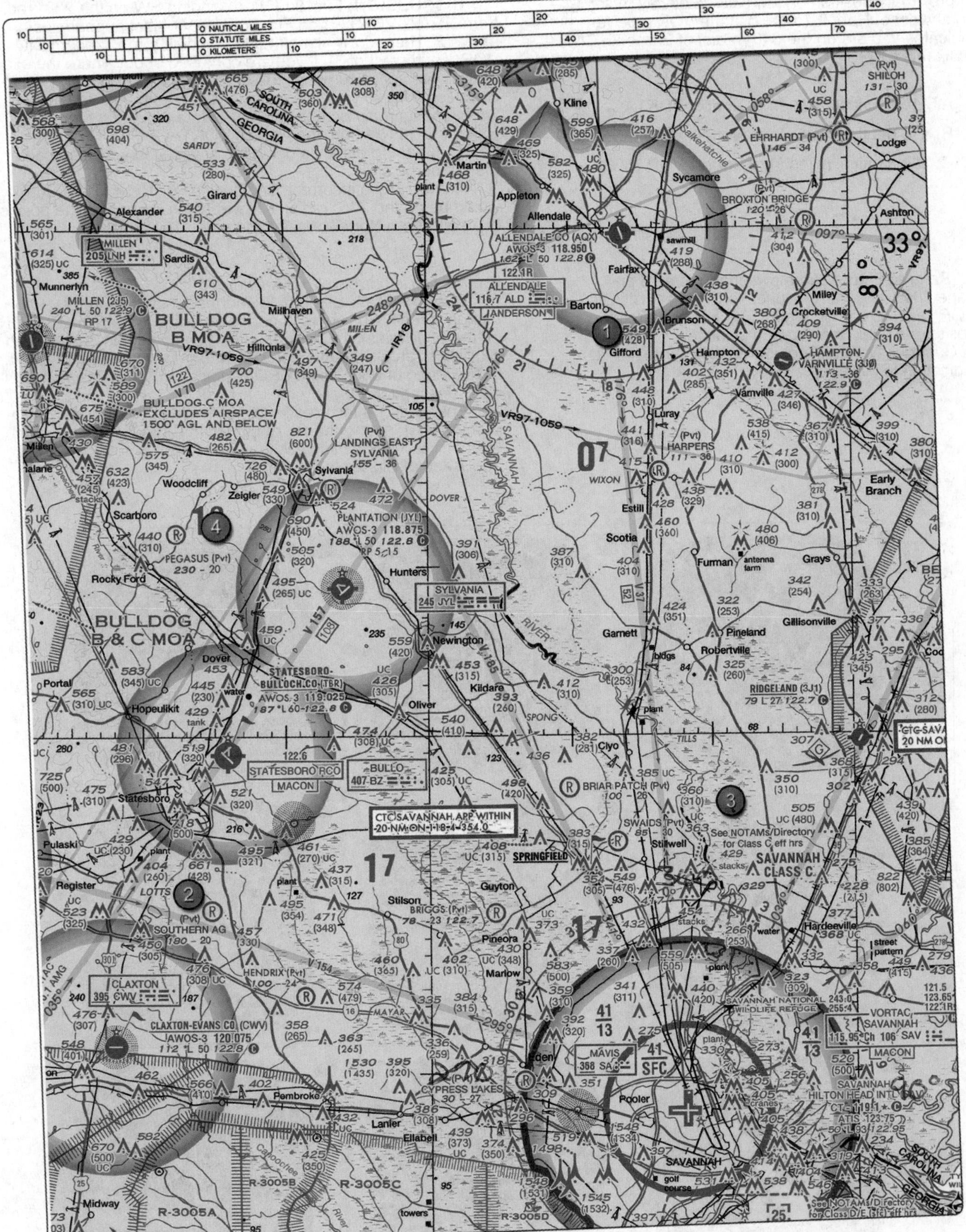

Figure 23. – Sectional Chart Excerpt.

NOTE: Chart is not to scale and should not be used for navigation. Use associated scale.

180

5. (Refer to Figure 20 on page 385.) What is your approximate position on low altitude airway Victor 1, southwest of Norfolk (area 1), if the VOR receiver indicates you are on the 340° radial of Elizabeth City VOR (area 3)?

A. 15 nautical miles from Norfolk VORTAC.

B. 18 nautical miles from Norfolk VORTAC.

C. 23 nautical miles from Norfolk VORTAC.

Answer (B) is correct. *(PHAK Chap 15)*

DISCUSSION: First find V1 extending SW on the 233° radial from Norfolk VORTAC on Fig. 20. The V1 label appears just above 2. Then, draw along the 340° radial from Elizabeth City VOR (southwest of 3). If you are confused about where the exact VOR is (center of compass rose), draw a line through the entire compass rose so your line coincides with both your radial (here 340°) and its reciprocal (here 160°). Note that the intersection with V1 is 18 NM from the Norfolk VORTAC.

NOTE: Measure distance using the associated scale located at the top of the chart.

Answer (A) is incorrect. The position of 15 NM from Norfolk would be on the 345° radial. Answer (C) is incorrect. The position of 23 NM from Norfolk would be on the 330° radial.

6. (Refer to Figure 28 below, and Figure 20 on page 385.) The VOR is tuned to Elizabeth City VOR/DME (area 3 in Figure 20), and the aircraft is positioned over Shawboro, a small town 3 NM west of Currituck County Regional (ONX). Which VOR indication is correct?

A. 5

B. 9

C. 2

Answer (C) is correct. *(PHAK Chap 16)*

DISCUSSION: See Fig. 20, northeast of 3 along the compass rose. Shawboro is northeast of the Elizabeth City VOR on the 030° radial. To be over it, the needle should be centered with either an OBS setting of 210° and a TO indication or with an OBS setting of 030° and a FROM indication. VOR 2 matches the latter description.

Answer (A) is incorrect. VOR 5 indicates that the aircraft is southwest, not northeast, of Elizabeth City VOR. Answer (B) is incorrect. VOR 9 indicates that the aircraft is southwest, not northeast, of Elizabeth City VOR.

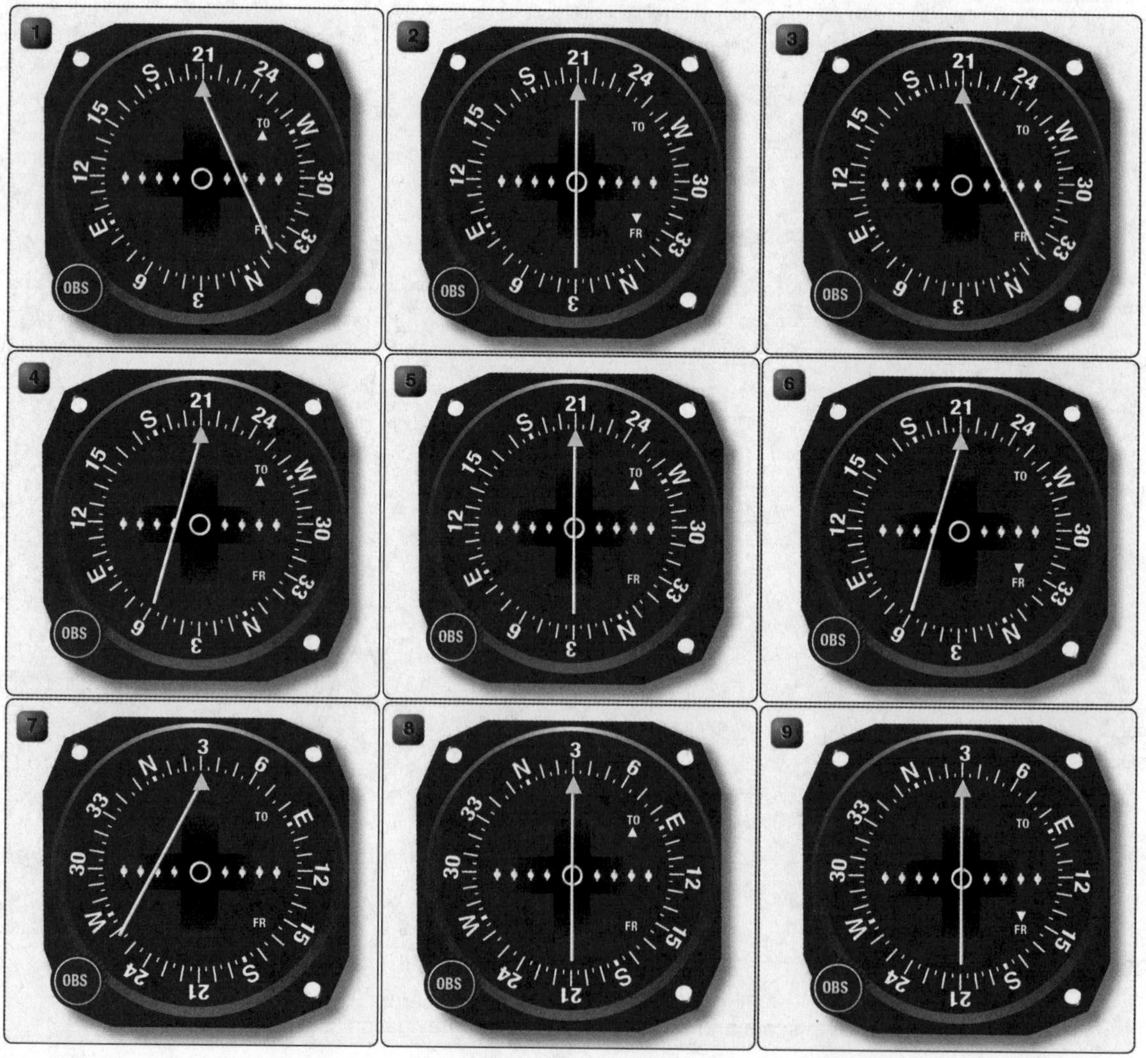

Figure 28. – VOR.

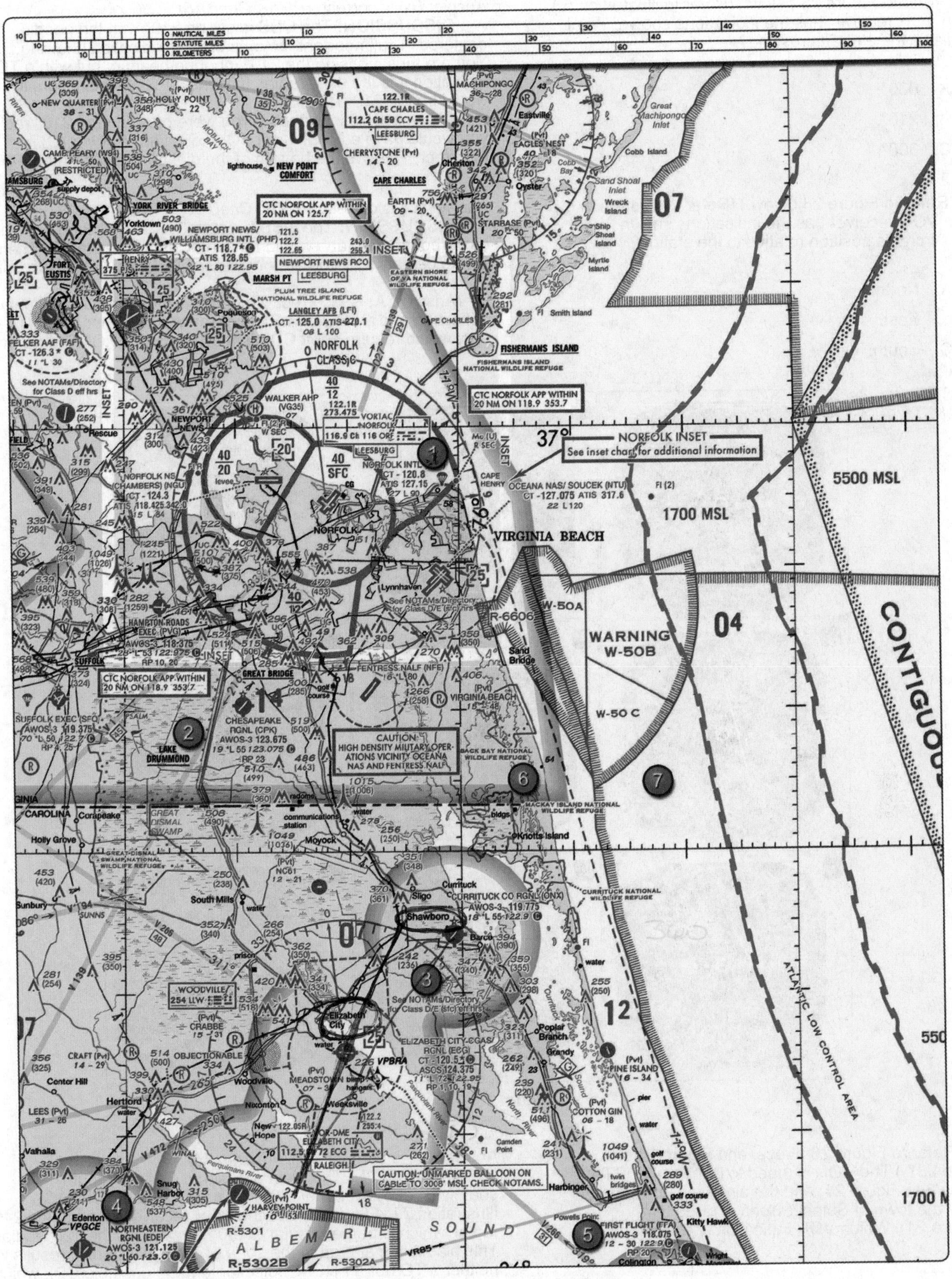

Figure 20. – Sectional Chart Excerpt.

NOTE: Chart is not to scale and should not be used for navigation. Use associated scale.

7. (Refer to Figure 28 below.) (Refer to illustration 5.) The VOR receiver has the indications shown. What radial is the aircraft crossing?

A. 030°.

B. 210°.

C. 300°.

Answer (A) is correct. *(PHAK Chap 16)*

DISCUSSION: The OBS is set on 210° with the needle centered. The important factor is the TO indication showing. You are thus crossing the 210° inbound bearing, but with a TO indication it is the 030° radial. If it was a FROM indication, it would be the 210° radial.

Answer (B) is incorrect. If you were crossing the 210° radial, you would have a FROM (not TO) indication. Answer (C) is incorrect. The 3 at the bottom of the dial means 030° (not 300°).

8. (Refer to Figure 28 below.) (Refer to illustration 8.) The VOR receiver has the indications shown. What is the aircraft's position relative to the station?

A. North.

B. East.

C. South.

Answer (C) is correct. *(PHAK Chap 16)*

DISCUSSION: The OBS is set to 030°. If the needle were centered, the airplane would be southwest of the station. The CDI is centered so you are on course. Thus, you are south of the VORTAC.

Answer (A) is incorrect. To be north would require a right CDI deflection and a FROM indication. Answer (B) is incorrect. To be east would require a left CDI deflection and a FROM indication.

Figure 28. – VOR.

9. (Refer to Figure 28 above, and Figure 24 on page 387.) The VOR is tuned to Bonham VORTAC (area 3 in Figure 24) and the aircraft is positioned over the town of Sulphur Springs (area 5 in Figure 24). Which VOR indication is correct?

A. 1

B. 8

C. 7

Answer (C) is correct. *(PHAK Chap 16)*

DISCUSSION: The town of Sulphur Springs (south-southwest of 5) is on the 120° radial of Bonham VORTAC. Illustration 7 in Fig. 28 shows the VOR receiver tuned to the 210° radial, which is perpendicular to (90° away from) the 120° radial. This places the aircraft in the zone of ambiguity, which results in neither a TO nor a FROM indication and an unstable CDI, which can be deflected left or right.

Answer (A) is incorrect. With indication 1, the aircraft would have to be west of Sulphur Springs. Answer (B) is incorrect. It shows the aircraft on the 030° radial, which is well to the north of Sulphur Springs.

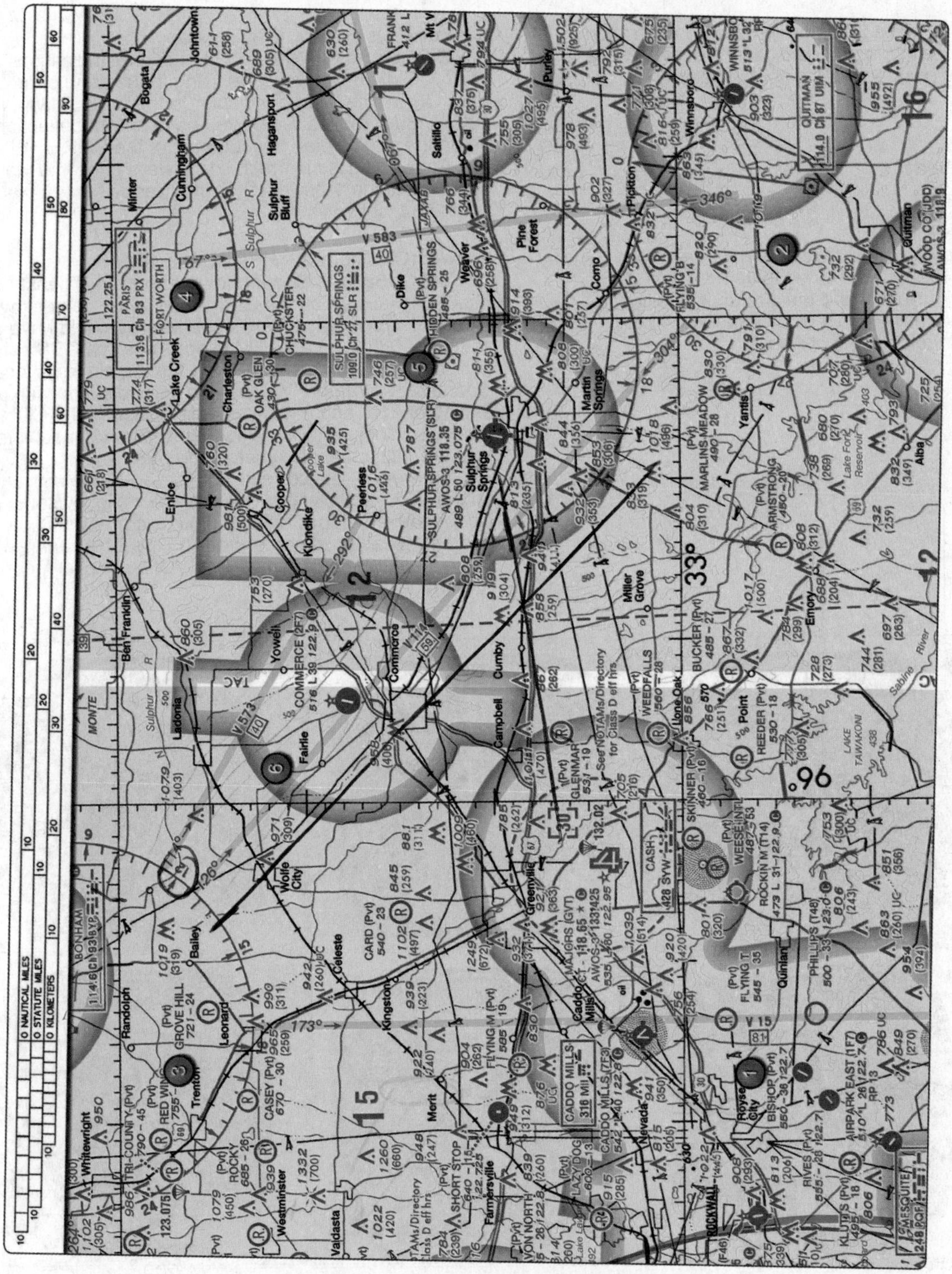

Figure 24. – Sectional Chart Excerpt.
NOTE: Chart is not to scale and should not be used for navigation. Use associated scale.

10. (Refer to Figure 24 above.) What is the approximate position of the aircraft if the VOR receivers indicate the 245° radial of Sulphur Springs VOR-DME (area 5) and the 140° radial of Bonham VORTAC (area 3)?

A. Glenmar Airport.

B. Caddo Mills Airport.

C. Majors Airport.

Answer (A) is correct. *(PHAK Chap 16)*

DISCUSSION: To locate a position based on VOR radials, draw the radials on your map or on the plastic overlay during the FAA knowledge test. Remember that radials are from the VOR, or leaving the VOR. On Fig. 24, the 245° radial from Sulphur Springs VOR-DME extends southwest, and the 140° radial from Bonham VORTAC extends southeast. They intersect about 1 mi. east of Glenmar Airport.

Answer (B) is incorrect. Caddo Mills Airport is on the 247°, not 245°, radial of Sulphur Springs VOR-DME and the 174°, not 140°, radial of Bonham VORTAC. Answer (C) is incorrect. Majors Airport is on the 157°, not 140°, radial of Bonham VORTAC.

11. (Refer to Figure 28 below.) (Refer to illustration 3.) The VOR receiver has the indications shown. What is the aircraft's position relative to the station?

A. East.

B. Southeast.

C. West.

Answer (B) is correct. *(PHAK Chap 16)*

DISCUSSION: With no TO or FROM indications showing on VOR 3, Fig. 28, you must be flying in the zone of ambiguity from the VOR, which is perpendicular to the OBS setting, i.e., on the 120° or 300° radials. Since you have a right deflection, you would be on the 120° radial, or southeast of the VOR.

Answer (A) is incorrect. If you were east, you would have a TO indication. Answer (C) is incorrect. The 120° radial is southeast, not west.

12. (Refer to Figure 28 below, and Figure 26 on page 389.) The VOR is tuned to Jamestown VOR (area 4 in Figure 26), and the aircraft is positioned over Cooperstown Airport (area 2 in Figure 26.). Which VOR indication is correct?

A. 9

B. 2

C. 4

Answer (C) is correct. *(PHAK Chap 16)*

DISCUSSION: Cooperstown Airport (northeast of 2 in Fig. 26) is located on the 028° radial of the Jamestown VOR (south of 4). With a centered needle, you could have an OBS setting of 028° and a FROM indication or an OBS setting of 208° and a TO indication. VOR 4 fits the aircraft's location over Cooperstown Airport. You have a TO indication with an OBS setting of 210° and a half-scale deflection of the CDI to the left (because Cooperstown Airport is north of your selected course). You are thus on approximately the 028° radial.

Answer (A) is incorrect. VOR 9 shows the aircraft's location on the 030° radial, which would place it slightly south of Cooperstown Airport. Answer (B) is incorrect. VOR 2 shows the aircraft's location as somewhere on the 210° radial, which would place it southwest of Jamestown VOR, not over Cooperstown Airport.

Figure 28. – VOR.

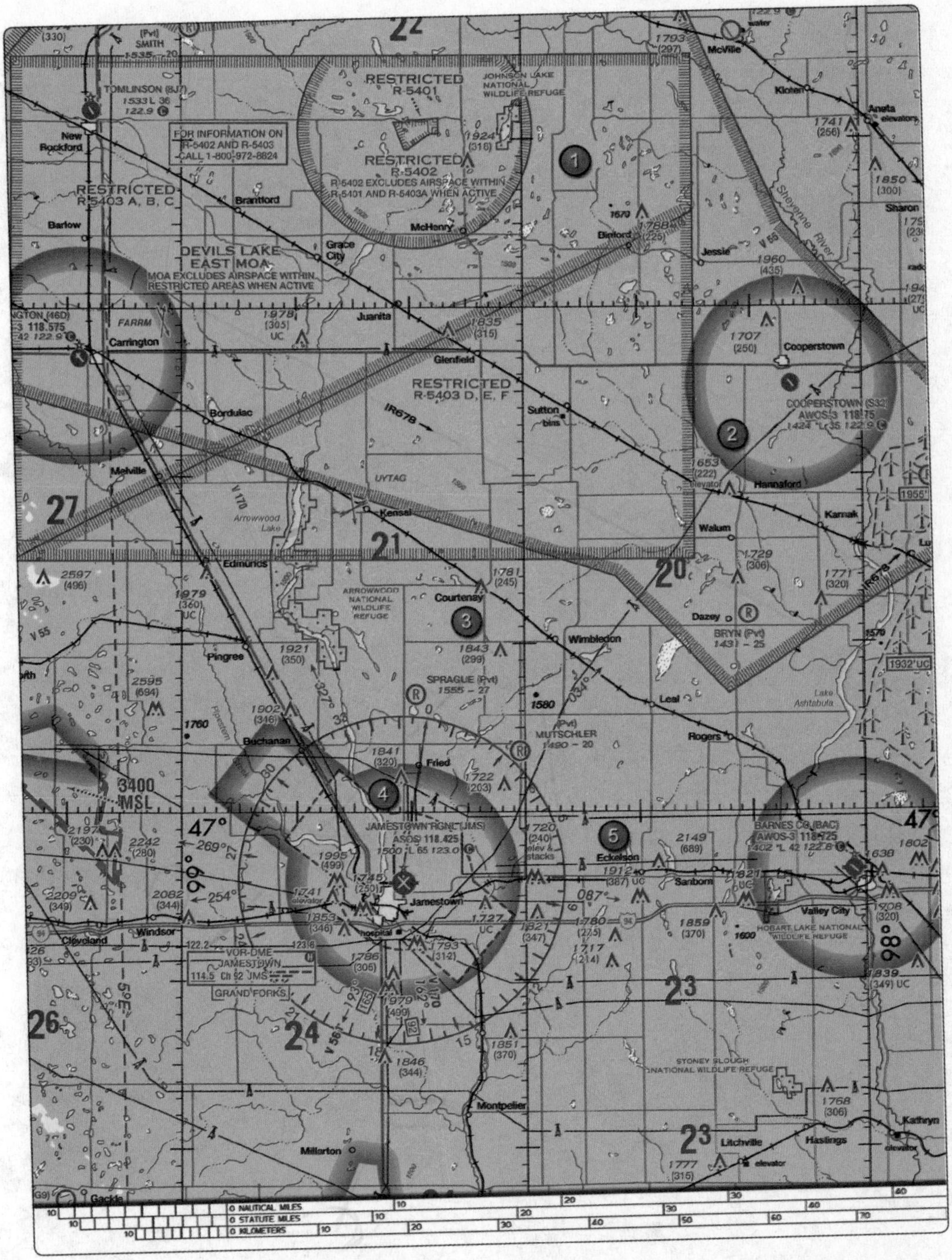

Figure 26. – Sectional Chart Excerpt.
NOTE: Chart is not to scale and should not be used for navigation. Use associated scale.

13. (Refer to Figure 26 above, and Figure 28 on page 388.) The VOR is tuned to Jamestown VOR (area 4 in Figure 26), and the aircraft is positioned over Cooperstown Airport (area 2 in Figure 26). Which VOR indication is correct?

A. 1

B. 6

C. 4

Answer (C) is correct. *(PHAK Chap 16)*

DISCUSSION: Cooperstown Airport (northeast of 2 in Fig. 26) is located on the 028° radial of the Jamestown VOR (south of 4). With a centered needle you could have an OBS setting of 028° and a FROM indication or an OBS setting of 208° and a TO indication. VOR 4 fits the aircraft's location over Cooperstown Airport. You have a TO indication with an OBS setting of 210° and a half-scale deflection of the CDI to the left (because Cooperstown Airport is north of your selected course). You are thus on approximately the 028° radial.

Answer (A) is incorrect. VOR 1 shows the aircraft's location as somewhere southeast of the 030° radial, which would place it south of, not over Cooperstown Airport. Answer (B) is incorrect. VOR 6 shows the aircraft's location as southwest of the VOR, not over Cooperstown Airport.

Figure 25. – Sectional Chart Excerpt.
NOTE: Chart is not to scale and should not be used for navigation. Use associated scale.

14. (Refer to Figure 25 on page 390.) (Refer to area 5.) The VOR is tuned to the Dallas/Fort Worth VOR. The omnibearing selector (OBS) is set on 253°, with a TO indication, and a right course deviation indicator (CDI) deflection. What is the aircraft's position from the VOR?

A. East-northeast.

B. North-northeast.

C. West-southwest.

Answer (A) is correct. *(PHAK Chap 16)*

DISCUSSION: It is not necessary to refer to Fig. 25 to solve this problem. Write the word VOR on a piece of paper. Now draw a line through it, representing the 253° radial and its reciprocal. Now imagine you are flying along this line on a heading of 253°. With a TO indication and a right CDI deflection, you are northeast of the VOR but south of the course.

Answer (B) is incorrect. You are south, not north, of the course. Answer (C) is incorrect. You have a TO, not FROM, indication.

10.3 Global Positioning System (GPS)

15. How many Global Positioning System (GPS) satellites are required to yield a three-dimensional position (latitude, longitude, and altitude) and time solution?

A. 5

B. 6

C. 4

Answer (C) is correct. *(AIM Para 1-1-19)*

DISCUSSION: GPS satellites broadcast radio signals that are decoded by a receiver in order to triangulate a three-dimensional position by calculating distances based on the amount of time it takes the radio signals to reach the receiver. At least four GPS satellites are required to yield a three-dimensional position (latitude, longitude, and altitude) and time solution.

Answer (A) is incorrect. Four, not five, satellites are required for a three-dimensional position and time solution. Answer (B) is incorrect. Four, not six, satellites are required for a three-dimensional position and time solution.

16. If Receiver Autonomous Integrity Monitoring (RAIM) capability is lost in-flight,

A. the pilot may still rely on GPS derived altitude for vertical information.

B. the pilot has no assurance of the accuracy of the GPS position.

C. GPS position is reliable provided at least 3 GPS satellites are available.

Answer (B) is correct. *(AIM Para 1-1-18, PHAK Chap 16)*

DISCUSSION: Always check to see if the unit has RAIM capability. If no RAIM capability exists, be suspicious of a GPS displayed position when any disagreement exists with the position derived from other radio navigation systems, pilotage, or dead reckoning. If RAIM is lost during flight, the pilot has no assurance of the accuracy of the GPS position.

Answer (A) is incorrect. Without RAIM capability, the pilot has no assurance of the accuracy of the GPS position. Answer (C) is incorrect. With three satellites, you narrow the possible location down to one of two points, meaning that you could be at only one of those points. Four satellites are required for navigation. At least one satellite in addition to those required for navigation must be in view for the receiver to perform the RAIM function. Thus, RAIM needs a minimum of five satellites in view, or four satellites and a barometric altimeter (baro-aiding), to detect an integrity anomaly.

17. Which of the following is a true statement concerning the Global Positioning System?

A. Advances in technology make it possible to rely completely on GPS units.

B. GPS databases and paper navigational charts are updated at the same time.

C. Navigating by GPS must be integrated with other forms of navigation.

Answer (C) is correct. *(AAH Chap 3)*

DISCUSSION: Navigating by GPS must be integrated with other forms of electronic navigation as well as pilotage and dead reckoning.

Answer (A) is incorrect. There is always the possibility for equipment failure, so pilots should never rely solely on one system of navigation. Answer (B) is incorrect. GPS databases and paper navigational charts are not necessarily updated on the same schedule.

18. The Global Positioning System is

A. ground based.

B. satellite based.

C. antenna based.

Answer (B) is correct. *(PHAK Chap 16)*

DISCUSSION: The Global Positioning System (GPS) is a satellite-based radio navigation system.

Answer (A) is incorrect. GPS is satellite based, not ground based. Answer (C) is incorrect. GPS is satellite based, not antenna based.

STUDY UNIT ELEVEN
CROSS-COUNTRY FLIGHT PLANNING

(9 pages of outline)

This study unit contains outlines of major concepts tested, sample test questions and answers regarding cross-country flight planning, and an explanation of each answer. The table of contents above lists each subunit within this study unit, the number of questions pertaining to that particular subunit, and the pages on which the outlines and questions begin, respectively.

This book assumes that you are familiar with the standard flight computer. Full discussion with examples can be found in *Pilot Handbook*, Study Unit 9.

Many of the questions in this study unit ask about the sectional (aeronautical) charts, which appear as Figures 20 through 26. The acronym ACL is the question source code used to refer to this aeronautical chart legend.

Important Note about FAA Charts

The FAA prints the charts published in their Airman Knowledge Testing Supplements to the wrong scale. If you were to measure a distance on one of these charts with the plotter, do the calculations based on that information, and enter that answer, you would be wrong every time.

Accurately calculating distance is a part of the testing process. By printing the charts to the wrong scale, the FAA is testing to see if you checked your plotter to the scale printed on the chart to make sure the chart is accurate. Because our goal at Gleim is to prepare you for your Knowledge Test, our reproductions of the charts are also not to scale.

To answer questions related to these charts, you must transfer the chart's scale to a scrap of paper, which is supplied to you at the testing site. You will use this scale as an accurate measuring tool in place of your plotter.

GLEIM SUCCESS TIPS®

Recall that the **sole purpose** of this book is to expedite your passing of the FAA pilot knowledge test for the private pilot certificate. Accordingly, all extraneous material (i.e., topics or regulations not directly tested on the FAA pilot knowledge test) is omitted, even though much more knowledge is necessary to fly safely. This additional material is presented in *Pilot Handbook* and *Private Pilot Flight Maneuvers and Practical Test Prep*, available from Gleim Publications, Inc. Order online at www.GleimAviation.com.

11.1 VFR FLIGHT PLAN

Form Approved OMB No. 2120-0026
09/30/2006

U S Department of Transportation
Federal Aviation Administration

International Flight Plan

PRIORITY ADDRESSEE(S)

<=FF

<=

FILING TIME ORIGINATOR **<=**

SPECIFIC IDENTIFICATION OF ADDRESSEE(S) AND / OR ORIGINATOR

3 MESSAGE TYPE 7 AIRCRAFT IDENTIFICATION 8 FLIGHT RULES TYPE OF FLIGHT

<=(FPL — — — **<=**

9 NUMBER TYPE OF AIRCRAFT WAKE TURBULENCE CAT. 10 EQUIPMENT

— / — / **<=**

13 DEPARTURE AERODROME TIME

— **<=**

15 CRUISING SPEED LEVEL ROUTE

—

<=

TOTAL EET

16 DESTINATION AERODROME HR MIN ALTN AERODROME 2ND ALTN AERODROME

— **<=**

18 OTHER INFORMATION

—

<=

SUPPLEMENTARY INFORMATION (NOT TO BE TRANSMITTED IN FPL MESSAGES)

19 ENDURANCE EMERGENCY RADIO

HR MIN PERSONS ON BOARD UHF VHF ELBA

—E/ **P/** **R/**

SURVIVAL EQUIPMENT JACKETS

POLAR DESERT MARITIME JUNGLE LIGHT FLUORES UHF VHF

/ **/**

DINGHIES

NUMBER CAPACITY COVER COLOR

D / **<=**

AIRCRAFT COLOR AND MARKINGS

A/

REMARKS

N / **<=**

PILOT-IN-COMMAND

C/ **)<=**

FILED BY ACCEPTED BY ADDITIONAL INFORMATION

FAA Form 7233-4 (7-93)

Figure 51A. – ICAO Flight Plan Form (not in supplement).

NOTE: As of the publication date of this text, pilots may file flight plans in the U.S. under either the domestic or International Civil Aviation Organization (ICAO) format. The FAA is planning to exclusively use the ICAO format for civil aircraft as of October 1, 2016. The FAA previously removed all questions from its test bank referring to flight plans; however, new questions regarding ICAO flight plans are expected to be added by January 2017. The questions in Subunit 11.1, VFR Flight Plan, are written based on previous questions using the domestic flight plan format, with updates referring to the equivalent ICAO flight plan form entries. Please check www.gleim.com/updates for edits and updates, if applicable.

1. The ICAO international flight plan form may be used for domestic and international operations under VFR or IFR.
   a. If an instrument rated pilot wants to conduct a flight partially under VFR and then change to IFR, a separate flight plan should be filed for each portion.
   b. For complete guidance on filling out the ICAO flight plan form, refer to the *Aeronautical Information Manual (AIM)* paragraph 5-1-9.
   c. Item 15, “Level.” Use only your initial requested altitude on your VFR flight plan.
   d. Item 16, “Destination Aerodrome,” should include the ICAO four-letter indicator for the airport or place at which you plan to make your last landing for this flight.
      1) An exception is if you plan a stopover of more than 1 hr. elsewhere en route. In this instance, you need to file a flight plan for each leg because, practically, the FAA views this as two flights. Otherwise, stopovers that are 1 hr. or less should be mentioned in the remaining section.
   e. Item 19, “Endurance” (in hours and minutes), requires the amount of usable fuel in the airplane at the time of departure, expressed in hours of flying time.
2. You should close your flight plan with the nearest FSS, or, if one is not available, you may request any ATC facility to relay your cancelation to the FSS.
   a. Control towers (and ground control) do not automatically close VFR or DVFR flight plans since they do not know if a particular VFR aircraft is on a flight plan.
   b. You may close your flight plan after landing by contacting a FSS via a remote communications outlet, or by calling 1-800-WX-BRIEF (1-800-992-7433).

GLEIM SUCCESS TIPS®

It is essential for each student to own an approved E6B flight computer (manual or electronic) and a navigation plotter. These tools are necessary to answer some questions on the knowledge test and to use during your check ride. Go to www.gleim.com/E6B to access complete instructions on the use of the Gleim E6B flight computer.

11.2 PREFLIGHT INSPECTION

1. During the preflight inspection, the pilot in command is responsible for determining that the airplane is safe for flight.
2. The owner or operator is responsible for maintaining the airplane in an airworthy condition.
3. For the first flight of the day, the preflight inspection should be accomplished by a thorough and systematic means recommended by the manufacturer.

11.3 MISCELLANEOUS AIRSPEED QUESTIONS

1. When turbulence is encountered, the airplane’s airspeed should be reduced to design maneuvering speed (V_A).
   a. The pilot should attempt to maintain a level flight attitude.
   b. Constant altitude and constant airspeed are usually impossible and result in additional control pressure, which adds stress to the airplane.

2. In the event of a power failure after becoming airborne, the most important thing to do is to immediately establish and maintain the best glide airspeed.
   a. Do not maintain altitude at the expense of airspeed or a stall/spin will result.
   b. The maximum gliding distance of an aircraft is obtained when the total drag on the aircraft is minimized. The best glide speed is calculated by determining when the aircraft produces the least amount of total drag. This occurs at a point where all of the sources of drag add up to a minimum total drag -- any airspeed above or below this point will result in an **increase** in drag.
   c. A constant gliding speed should be maintained because variations in gliding speed will nullify your ability to accurately determine gliding distance and choose a landing spot.
3. Approaches and landings at night should be the same as in daylight (i.e., at same airspeeds and altitudes).

11.4 TAXIING TECHNIQUE

1. When taxiing in strong quartering headwinds, the aileron should be up on the side from which the wind is blowing.
   a. The elevator should be in the neutral position for tricycle-geared airplanes.
   b. The elevator should be in the up position for tailwheel airplanes.
2. When taxiing during strong quartering tailwinds, the aileron should be down on the side from which the wind is blowing.
   a. The elevator should be in the down position (for both tricycle and tailwheel airplanes).
3. When taxiing high-wing, nosewheel-equipped airplanes, the most critical wind condition is a quartering tailwind.

11.5 MAGNETIC COURSE

1. Because magnetic north and true north are not equal, pilots have to account for the differences between what the compass reads and the true course (TC) of the flight path. Therefore, magnetic course (MC) takes into account the difference between true north and magnetic north.
2. To determine the MC from one airport to another, correct the TC only for magnetic variation; i.e., make no allowance for wind correction angle.
   a. Determine the TC by placing the straight edge of a navigational plotter or protractor along the route, with the hole in the plotter on the intersection of the route and a meridian, or line of longitude (the vertical line with little crosslines).
      1) The TC is measured by the numbers on the protractor portion of the plotter (semi-circle) at the meridian.
      2) Note that up to four numbers (90° apart) are provided on the plotter. You must determine which is the direction of the flight, using a common sense approximation of your direction.
   b. Alternatively, you can use a line of latitude (horizontal line with little crosslines) if your course is in a north or south direction.
      1) This is why there are four numbers on the plotter. You may be using either a meridian or line of latitude to measure your course and be going in either direction along the course line.
   c. Determine the MC by adjusting the TC for magnetic variation (angle between true north and magnetic north).
      1) On sectional charts, a long dashed line provides the number of degrees of magnetic variation. The variation is either east or west and is signified by “E” or “W,” e.g., 3°E or 5°W.

2) If the variation is east, subtract; if west, add (memory aid: east is least and west is best). This is from TC to MC.

3. If your course is to or from a VOR, use the compass rose to determine the MC; i.e., no adjustment is needed from TC to MC.
   a. Compass roses have about a 3-in. diameter on sectional charts.
   b. Every 30° is labeled, as well as marked with an arrow inside the rose pointing out.
   c. Use the reciprocal to radials when flying toward the VOR.
      1) EXAMPLE: If your course is toward an airport on the 180° radial rather than from the airport, your MC is 360°, not 180°.

11.6 MAGNETIC HEADING

1. Magnetic heading (MH) is a step beyond the computation of MC because MH is MC adjusted for wind correction and your aircraft's specific compass deviation due to your avionics.
2. Simply put, to compute MH from MC, you must adjust for the wind and compass error (deviation).
3. There are two methods to compute MH. We suggest that you use the most efficient method, but if you already have your MC or an FAA problem provides MC, then you should use the longer method.
   a. In brief, Gleim's reasoning is as follows: in the left column of the table below, many pilots forget to correct for the magnetic variation of wind because they already corrected for magnetic variation when they found magnetic course. This method makes you correct for magnetic variation twice. Therefore, Gleim believes you should use the most efficient method in the right column of the table below for your actual flight planning and everyday use.

If MC Already Determined	**Most Efficient Method**
Determine True Course	Determine True Course
+/- Add/Subtract Magnetic Variation	Determine Wind Correction (E6-B)
= Magnetic Course	+/- Add/Subtract Wind Correction Angle (WCA)
+/- Add/Subtract Magnetic Variation to Wind	+/- Add/Subtract Magnetic Variation (same for course and wind)
Determine Wind Correction (E6-B)	+/- Add/Subtract Deviation of Compass Error
+/- Add/Subtract Wind Correction Angle (WCA)	= Magnetic Heading
+/- Add/Subtract Deviation of Compass Error	
= Magnetic Heading	

4. The following directions explain each of the components above using the most efficient method.
   a. <u>Determine Wind Correction:</u> To compute wind effect, use the wind side of the computer.
      1) Align the true wind direction on the inner scale under the true index (top of the computer).
      2) Slide the grid through the computer until the grommet (the hole in the center) is on the 100-kt. wind line. Measure up the vertical line the amount of wind speed in knots and put a pencil mark on the plastic.
      3) Rotate the inner scale so the TC lies under the true index.
      4) Slide the grid so that your pencil dot is superimposed over the true airspeed (TAS). The location of the grommet will indicate the groundspeed. This is needed for time en route calculations.
      5) The pencil mark will indicate the wind correction angle (WCA). If to the left, it is a negative wind correction. If to the right, it is a positive wind correction.

b. WCA: Adjust the TC for the wind correction.

   1) Add the number of degrees the pencil mark is to the right of the centerline or subtract the number of degrees to the left.

c. Magnetic Variation: Now, further adjust the TC for magnetic variation.

   1) Review Subunit 11.5 for how to determine magnetic variation.

d. Compass Error: Add/subtract deviation for your plane's specific compass error. This is found on the compass deviation card inside your cockpit.

   1) Add or subtract the number of degrees from the calculation to arrive at magnetic heading.

If MC Already Determined

a) Wind direction is normally given in true, not magnetic, direction. Thus, you must first adjust the wind direction from true to magnetic.

b) Find the magnetic variation on the navigation chart. As with course corrections, add westerly variation and subtract easterly variation.

c) See the discussion of magnetic variation under item 2.c. in Subunit 11.5, "Magnetic Course."

d) EXAMPLE: Given wind of 330° and a 20°E variation, the magnetic direction of the wind is 310° (330° – 20°).

e) When using magnetic wind direction, you should use magnetic course (MC) in items a.3) on the previous page and b. above. Also skip item c. because variation is already applied.

5. On your E6-B, you will find directions such as

   a. Set Wind Direction opposite True Index.
   b. Mark Wind Dot up from Grommet.
   c. Place TC under True Index.
   d. Slide TAS under Wind Dot.
   e. Read GS under Grommet.
   f. Read WCA under Wind Dot.
   g. Complete the problem by use of the formulas.

6. The formulas given are

   TH = TC ± WCA (wind correction angle)
   MH = TH ± magnetic variation (E–, W+)
   CH = MH ± compass deviation

7. These E6-B instructions should also get you to the same answer as our more efficient method.

8. If the FAA provides no information in a question on compass error, then assume the aircraft does not have any. It is one less calculation you need to make.

11.7 COMPASS HEADING

1. If a question asks for a compass heading (CH), the MH is converted to a CH by adding or subtracting deviation (installation error), which is indicated on a compass correction card usually mounted on the compass.

   a. Compass correction cards are needed because the metal, electric motors, and other instruments in each airplane affect the compass causing compass deviation.

   b. Compass correction cards usually indicate corrections for every 30°.

      1) For each 30°, you are given the corresponding MH and the heading you should follow, i.e., the CH.

      2) The difference between these two headings is the amount to add or subtract.

3) EXAMPLE: Using the compass correction card below, your CH would be 085° if your MH were due east, and 332° if your MH were 330°.

4) If your MH does not coincide with a heading on the correction card, use the nearest one, i.e., interpolate.

FOR (MAGNETIC)	N	30	60	E	120	150
STEER (COMPASS)	0	28	57	85	117	148
FOR (MAGNETIC)	S	210	240	W	300	330
STEER (COMPASS)	180	212	243	274	303	332

Typical Compass Correction Card

11.8 TIME EN ROUTE

NOTE: When using a navigation plotter, always use the "Sectional" side of the plotter and the "NM" scale. Make sure the plotter and the chart scale are the same. If the scales do not match, use your plotter to reference the distance, mark that distance on your plotter with a pencil or marker, then place your plotter over the NM scale on the chart and find the distance. You will find all the new FAA sectional charts used for the actual knowledge test are **not** to scale.

1. A number of questions require you to determine the time of arrival at some specified point on a sectional chart given the times that two other points on the chart were crossed. You must
   a. Compute your groundspeed based upon the distance already traveled (i.e., between the two given points) in the given time.
   b. Measure the additional distance to go.
   c. Compute the time required to travel to the next point.
2. First, measure the distances (a) already gone and (b) remaining to go with a navigational plotter or a ruler.
   a. Remember that the scale at the bottom of sectional charts is 1:500,000.
   b. Because the questions give data in NM instead of SM (e.g., wind speed is given in knots), use NM.
3. To compute speed, place the distance already gone on the outer scale of the flight computer adjacent to the number of minutes it took on the inner scale.
   a. Read the number on the outer scale adjacent to the solid triangular pointer (i.e., at 60 min.). This is your groundspeed in knots.
   b. For numbers less than 10 on either scale, add a zero.
   c. EXAMPLE: If you travel 3 NM in 3 min., you are going 60 kt. Place 30 on the outer scale adjacent to 30 on the inner scale. Then the outer scale shows 60 kt. above the solid triangular pointer.
4. To compute the time required to fly to the next point, start with the speed on the outer scale adjacent to 60 min. on the inner scale (just as you had it in the preceding step). Find the remaining NM to go on the outer scale. The adjacent number on the inner scale is the number of minutes to go.
   a. EXAMPLE: Place 12 (for 120 kt.) on the outer scale over the solid triangular pointer (i.e., at 60 min.). Look along the outer scale and find 4 (for 40 NM). It should be directly above 2 (for 20 min.) on the inner scale.
5. Another type of time en route question has you compute the magnetic course, heading, and groundspeed.
   a. Determine the groundspeed as explained previously in this subunit.
   b. Recall that groundspeed appears under the grommet when you slide the grid on the wind side of your flight computer such that your pencil mark is on the TAS arc.

c. Once you determine groundspeed, put it over 60 min. on the inner scale. Find the distance to go on the outer scale, and read the time en route on the inner scale.

6. Some problems require the use of a wind triangle to compute speed, distance, and wind corrections.
   a. The line connecting Point A to Point B represents the true heading and airspeed line.
   b. The line connecting Point C to Point A represents the wind direction and velocity line.
   c. The line connecting Point C to Point B represents the true course and groundspeed line.

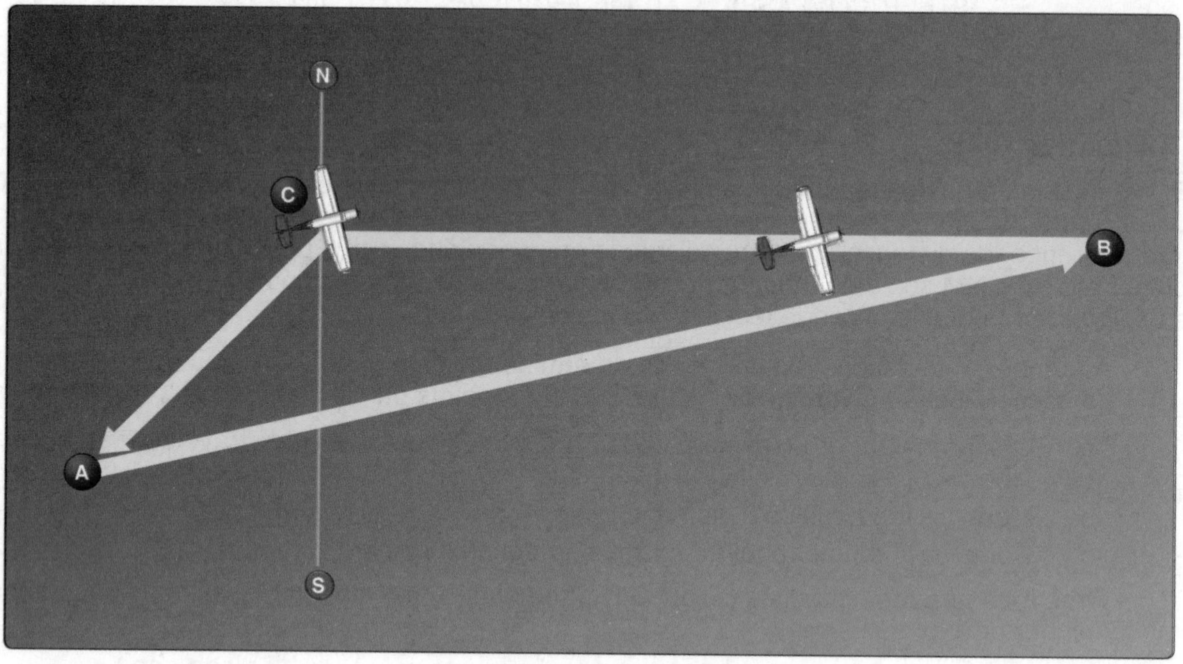

Figure 68. – Wind Triangle.

11.9 TIME ZONE CORRECTIONS

1. To correct for time zones, remember that there is a 1-hr. difference between each time zone, i.e., from the Eastern Time Zone to the Central Time Zone, from the Central Time Zone to the Mountain Time Zone, and from the Mountain Time Zone to the Pacific Time Zone.
   a. Subtract 1 hr. for each time zone when traveling east to west, and add 1 hr. for each time zone when traveling west to east.
   b. Additionally, there may be daylight saving time (in the summer) or standard time in effect.
2. The number of hours to adjust to or from Coordinated Universal Time (UTC) are 4-5-6-7 in the summer and 5-6-7-8 in the winter (for the four zones from east to west).
   a. EXAMPLE: To compute UTC, add 4 hr. to Eastern Daylight Saving Time and 5 hr. to Eastern Standard Time.
      1) Add 5 and 6 hr. respectively to Central Time.
      2) Add 6 and 7 hr. respectively to Mountain Time.
      3) Add 7 and 8 hr. respectively to Pacific Time.
   b. Remember, there is always a longer lag in standard than in daylight saving time.
3. For questions requiring the time of arrival at a destination airport, you should
   a. First add the hours en route to the time of departure and determine the time of arrival based on the time zone of departure.

b. Then adjust the time to the time zone requested, i.e., UTC or time zone of arrival.
c. Alternatively, convert the departure time to UTC, add hours en route, and convert to local time.

11.10 FUNDAMENTALS OF FLIGHT

1. The four fundamentals involved in maneuvering an aircraft are
   a. Straight-and-level,
   b. Turns,
   c. Climbs, and
   d. Descents.

11.11 RECTANGULAR COURSE

1. When beginning a rectangular course, the determining factor in deciding the distance from the field boundary at which an aircraft should be flown is the steepness of the bank desired in the turns.
2. The same techniques of a rectangular course apply when flying an airport traffic pattern.
   a. On the turn from downwind to base, one goes from a steep to a medium bank.
   b. On the turn from base to final, one goes from a medium to a shallow bank.
   c. On a turn from upwind to crosswind, one goes from a shallow to a medium bank.
   d. On a turn from crosswind to downwind, one goes from a medium to a steep bank.
3. The corners that require less than a 90° turn in a rectangular course are
   a. The turn to final and
   b. The turn to crosswind.
4. The corners that require more than a 90° turn in a rectangular course are
   a. The turn to downwind and
   b. The turn to base.
5. To properly compensate for a crosswind during straight-and-level cruising flight, the pilot should establish a proper heading into the wind by coordinated use of the controls.

11.12 S-TURNS ACROSS A ROAD

1. Groundspeed will be equal when the headwind or tailwind components are the same, e.g., direct crosswind, downwind just out of crosswind and just into crosswind, and the same for upwind.
2. The angle of bank will be steepest when flying in a tailwind.
3. In S-turns, you must be crabbed into the wind the most when you have a full crosswind component.
4. In S-turns, a consistently smaller half-circle will be made on the upwind side of the road when the bank is increased too rapidly during the early part of the turn.

11.13 LANDINGS

1. Under normal conditions, a proper crosswind landing on a runway requires that, at the moment of touchdown, the direction of motion of the aircraft and its longitudinal axis be parallel to the runway.
   a. This minimizes the side load placed on the landing gear during touchdown.

QUESTIONS AND ANSWER EXPLANATIONS: All of the private pilot knowledge test questions chosen by the FAA for release as well as additional questions selected by Gleim relating to the material in the previous outlines are reproduced on the following pages. These questions have been organized into the same subunits as the outlines. To the immediate right of each question are the correct answer and answer explanation. You should cover these answers and answer explanations while responding to the questions. Refer to the general discussion in the Introduction on how to take the FAA knowledge test.

Remember that the questions from the FAA knowledge test bank have been reordered by topic and organized into a meaningful sequence. Also, the first line of the answer explanation gives the citation of the authoritative source for the answer.

QUESTIONS

11.1 VFR Flight Plan

1. (Refer to Figure 51A on page 403.) If more than one cruising altitude is intended, which should be entered in item 15, "Level," of the flight plan?

A. Initial cruising altitude.

B. Highest cruising altitude.

C. Lowest cruising altitude.

Answer (A) is correct. *(AIM Para 5-1-9)*

DISCUSSION: Use only your initial requested altitude on your VFR flight plan to assist briefers in providing weather and wind information.

Answer (B) is incorrect. The initial, not highest, altitude should be filed on your VFR flight plan. Answer (C) is incorrect. The initial, not lowest, altitude should be filed on your VFR flight plan.

2. (Refer to Figure 51A on page 403.) What information should be entered in item 15, "Level," for a VFR day flight?

A. The altitude assigned by the FSS.

B. The initial altitude assigned by ATC.

C. The appropriate VFR cruising altitude.

Answer (C) is correct. *(AIM Para 5-1-9)*

DISCUSSION: Item 15, "Level," should contain the appropriate VFR altitude so the weather briefer can provide you with a more accurate weather advisory.

Answer (A) is incorrect. FSS does not assign altitudes. Answer (B) is incorrect. You will have not yet been assigned an altitude by ATC.

3. (Refer to Figure 51A on page 403.) What information should be entered into item 16, "Destination Aerodrome," for a VFR day flight?

A. The destination airport identifier code and name of the FBO where the airplane will be parked.

B. The destination airport identifier code and city name.

C. The destination city and state.

Answer (B) is correct. *(AIM Para 5-1-9)*

DISCUSSION: In item 16, "Destination Aerodrome," of the flight plan form in Fig. 51A, enter the identifier or name of the airport of last intended landing for that flight, as long as no stopover exceeds 1 hr.

Answer (A) is incorrect. The name of the FBO is not required. Answer (C) is incorrect. The ICAO four-letter indicator should be entered, not the city and state.

4. (Refer to Figure 51A on page 403.) What information should be entered in item 19, "Endurance," for a VFR day flight?

A. The estimated time en route plus 30 minutes.

B. The estimated time en route plus 45 minutes.

C. The amount of usable fuel on board expressed in time.

Answer (C) is correct. *(AIM Para 5-1-9)*

DISCUSSION: Item 19, "Endurance," of the flight plan requires the amount of usable fuel in the airplane at the time of departure. It should be expressed in hours and minutes of flying time.

Answer (A) is incorrect. It states the VFR fuel requirement for day flight. Answer (B) is incorrect. It states the VFR fuel requirement for night flight.

5. (Refer to Figure 51A on page 403.) What information should be entered in item 19, "Endurance," for a VFR day flight?

A. The actual time en route expressed in hours and minutes.

B. The estimated time en route expressed in hours and minutes.

C. The total amount of usable fuel onboard expressed in hours and minutes.

Answer (C) is correct. *(AIM Para 5-1-9)*

DISCUSSION: Item 19, "Endurance," of the flight plan requires the amount of usable fuel in the airplane at the time of departure. It should be expressed in hours and minutes of flying time.

Answer (A) is incorrect. Item 19 requires the amount of fuel on board expressed in time. Answer (B) is incorrect. Item 19 requires the amount of fuel on board expressed in time.

6. (Refer to Figure 51A below.) What information should be entered in item 16, "Destination Aerodrome," for a VFR day flight?

A. The ICAO four-letter indicator of the airport of first intended landing.

B. The ICAO four-letter indicator of destination airport if no stopover for more than 1 hour is anticipated.

C. The ICAO four-letter indicator of the airport where the aircraft is based.

Answer (B) is correct. *(AIM Para 5-1-9)*

DISCUSSION: In item 16 of the flight plan form in Fig. 51A, enter the ICAO four-letter indicator of the airport of last intended landing for that flight, as long as no stopover exceeds 1 hr.

Answer (A) is incorrect. The first intended landing, i.e., the end of the first leg of the flight, is included in the route of flight (item 15). Answer (C) is incorrect. The ICAO four-letter indicator of the airport where the airplane is based is not entered on the ICAO flight plan form.

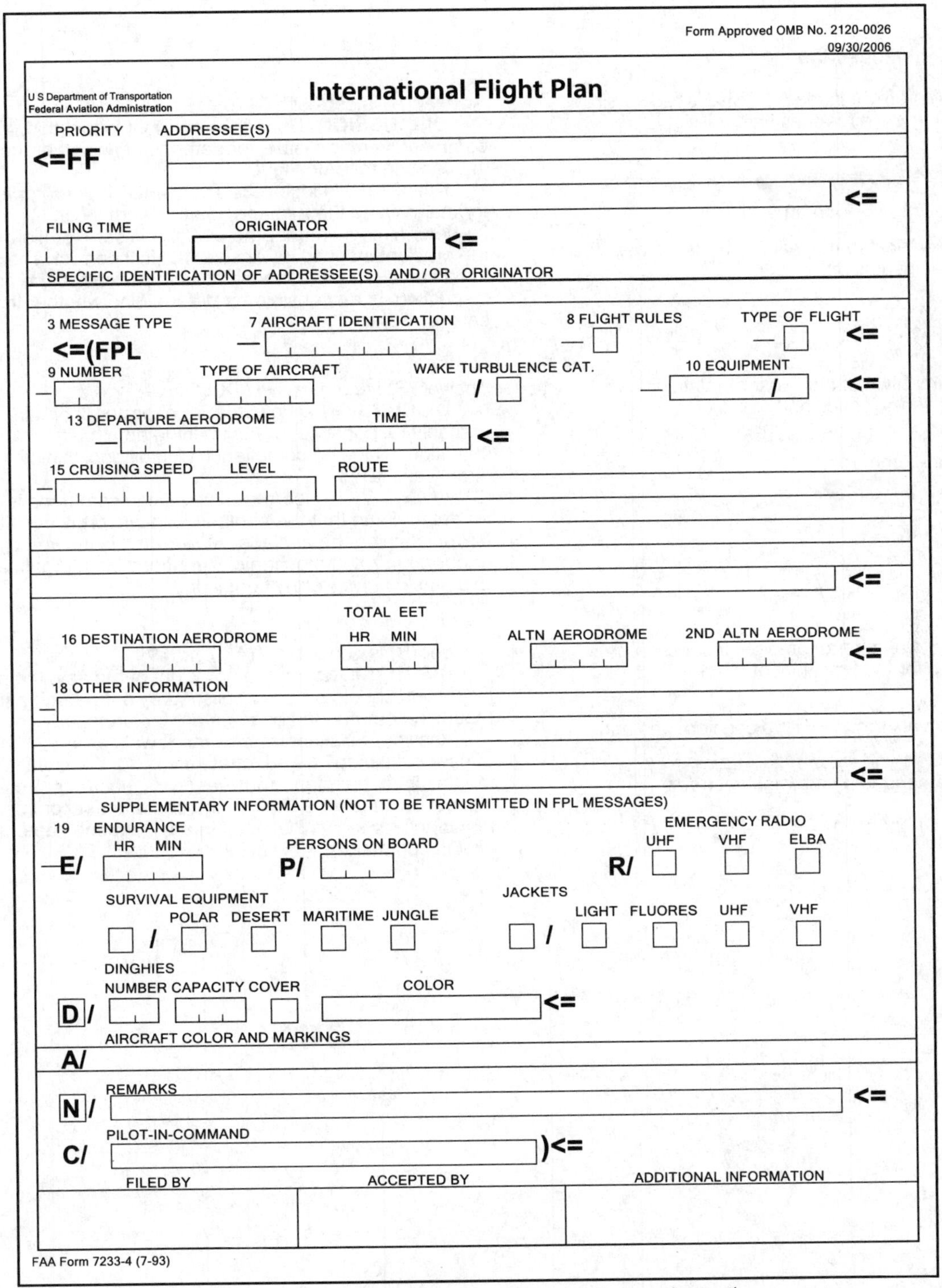

Form Approved OMB No. 2120-0026
09/30/2006

U S Department of Transportation
Federal Aviation Administration

International Flight Plan

PRIORITY ADDRESSEE(S)
<=FF
<=
FILING TIME ORIGINATOR <=
SPECIFIC IDENTIFICATION OF ADDRESSEE(S) AND / OR ORIGINATOR
3 MESSAGE TYPE 7 AIRCRAFT IDENTIFICATION 8 FLIGHT RULES TYPE OF FLIGHT <=
<=(FPL
9 NUMBER TYPE OF AIRCRAFT WAKE TURBULENCE CAT. 10 EQUIPMENT <=
13 DEPARTURE AERODROME TIME <=
15 CRUISING SPEED LEVEL ROUTE
<=
16 DESTINATION AERODROME TOTAL EET HR MIN ALTN AERODROME 2ND ALTN AERODROME <=
18 OTHER INFORMATION
<=
SUPPLEMENTARY INFORMATION (NOT TO BE TRANSMITTED IN FPL MESSAGES)
19 ENDURANCE HR MIN
PERSONS ON BOARD
EMERGENCY RADIO UHF VHF ELBA
E/ P/ R/
SURVIVAL EQUIPMENT POLAR DESERT MARITIME JUNGLE
JACKETS LIGHT FLUORES UHF VHF
DINGHIES
NUMBER CAPACITY COVER COLOR
D/ <=
AIRCRAFT COLOR AND MARKINGS
A/
REMARKS
N/ <=
PILOT-IN-COMMAND
C/)<=
FILED BY ACCEPTED BY ADDITIONAL INFORMATION
FAA Form 7233-4 (7-93)

Figure 51A. – ICAO Flight Plan Form (not in supplement).

7. How should a VFR flight plan be closed at the completion of the flight at a controlled airport?

A. The tower will automatically close the flight plan when the aircraft turns off the runway.

B. The pilot must close the flight plan with the nearest FSS or other FAA facility upon landing.

C. The tower will relay the instructions to the nearest FSS when the aircraft contacts the tower for landing.

Answer (B) is correct. *(AIM Para 5-1-14)*

DISCUSSION: A pilot is responsible for ensuring that the VFR or DVFR flight plan is canceled (FAR 91.153). You should close your flight plan with the nearest FSS or, if one is not available, you may request any ATC facility to relay your cancelation to the FSS.

Answer (A) is incorrect. The tower will automatically close an IFR (not VFR) flight plan. Answer (C) is incorrect. The tower will relay to the nearest FSS only if requested.

11.2 Preflight Inspection

8. During the preflight inspection who is responsible for determining the aircraft as safe for flight?

A. The pilot in command.

B. The owner or operator.

C. The certificated mechanic who performed the annual inspection.

Answer (A) is correct. *(14 CFR 91.7)*

DISCUSSION: During the preflight inspection, the pilot in command is responsible for determining whether the airplane is in condition for safe flight.

Answer (B) is incorrect. The owner or operator is responsible for maintaining the airplane in an airworthy condition, not for determining whether the airplane is safe for flight during the preflight inspection. Answer (C) is incorrect. The pilot in command, not the mechanic who performed the annual inspection, is responsible for determining whether the airplane is safe for flight.

9. Who is primarily responsible for maintaining an aircraft in airworthy condition?

A. Pilot-in-command.

B. Owner or operator.

C. Mechanic.

Answer (B) is correct. *(PHAK Chap 9)*

DISCUSSION: The owner or operator of an airplane is primarily responsible for maintaining an airplane in an airworthy condition, including compliance with all applicable airworthiness directives (ADs).

Answer (A) is incorrect. The pilot in command is responsible for determining that the airplane is in airworthy condition, not for maintaining the airplane. Answer (C) is incorrect. The owner or operator, not a mechanic, is responsible for maintaining an airplane in an airworthy condition.

10. How should an aircraft preflight inspection be accomplished for the first flight of the day?

A. Quick walk around with a check of gas and oil.

B. Thorough and systematic means recommended by the manufacturer.

C. Any sequence as determined by the pilot-in-command.

Answer (B) is correct. *(PHAK Chap 9)*

DISCUSSION: For the first flight of the day, the preflight inspection should be accomplished by a thorough and systematic means recommended by the manufacturer.

Answer (A) is incorrect. A quick walk around with a check of gas and oil may be adequate if it is not the first flight of the day in that airplane. Answer (C) is incorrect. A preflight inspection should be done in the sequence recommended by the manufacturer in the POH, not in any sequence determined by the pilot in command.

11.3 Miscellaneous Airspeed Questions

11. Upon encountering severe turbulence, which flight condition should the pilot attempt to maintain?

A. Constant altitude and airspeed.

B. Constant angle of attack.

C. Level flight attitude.

Answer (C) is correct. *(AC 00-24B)*

DISCUSSION: Attempting to hold altitude and airspeed in severe turbulence can lead to overstressing the airplane. Rather, you should set power to what normally will maintain V_A and simply attempt to maintain a level flight attitude.

Answer (A) is incorrect. Maintaining a constant altitude will require additional control movements, adding stress to the airplane. Answer (B) is incorrect. In severe turbulence, the angle of attack will fluctuate due to the wind shears and wind shifts that cause the turbulence.

12. The most important rule to remember in the event of a power failure after becoming airborne is to

A. immediately establish the proper gliding attitude and airspeed.

B. quickly check the fuel supply for possible fuel exhaustion.

C. determine the wind direction to plan for the forced landing.

Answer (A) is correct. *(AFH Chap 8)*

DISCUSSION: In the event of a power failure after becoming airborne, the most important rule to remember is to maintain best glide airspeed. This will usually require a pitch attitude slightly higher than level flight. Invariably, with a power failure, one returns to ground, but emphasis should be put on a controlled return rather than a crash return. Many pilots attempt to maintain altitude at the expense of airspeed, resulting in a stall or stall/spin.

Answer (B) is incorrect. Checking the fuel supply should only be done after a glide has been established and a landing site has been selected. Answer (C) is incorrect. Landing into the wind may not be possible, depending upon altitude and field availability.

13. When executing an emergency approach to land in a single-engine airplane, it is important to maintain a constant glide speed because variations in glide speed will

A. increase the chances of shock cooling the engine.

B. assure the proper descent angle is maintained until entering the flare.

C. nullify all attempts at accuracy in judgment of gliding distance and landing spot.

Answer (C) is correct. *(AFH Chap 8)*

DISCUSSION: A constant gliding speed should be maintained because variations of gliding speed nullify all attempts at accuracy in judgment of gliding distance and the landing spot.

Answer (A) is incorrect. Shock cooling the engine can occur when you significantly increase the speed beyond the best glide speed. Answer (B) is incorrect. A constant glide speed may not guarantee a certain descent angle. The angle of descent will be based on many environmental factors. While this statement is potentially valid, it is not the best answer option available for this question.

14. VFR approaches to land at night should be accomplished

A. at a higher airspeed.

B. with a steeper descent.

C. the same as during daytime.

Answer (C) is correct. *(AFH Chap 10)*

DISCUSSION: Every effort should be made to execute approaches and landings at night in the same manner as they are made in the day. Inexperienced pilots often have a tendency to make approaches and landings at night with excessive airspeed.

Answer (A) is incorrect. Approaching at a higher airspeed could result in floating into unseen obstacles at the far end of the runway. Answer (B) is incorrect. A steeper descent is not necessary. You should use the visual glide slope indicators at night whenever they are available.

11.4 Taxiing Technique

15. (Refer to Figure 9 below.) (Refer to area A.) How should the flight controls be held while taxiing a tricycle-gear equipped airplane into a left quartering headwind?

A. Left aileron up, elevator neutral.
B. Left aileron down, elevator neutral.
C. Left aileron up, elevator down.

Answer (A) is correct. *(AFH Chap 2)*
DISCUSSION: Given a left quartering headwind, the left aileron should be kept up to spoil the excess lift on the left wing that the crosswind is creating. The elevator should be neutral to keep from putting too much or too little weight on the nosewheel.
Answer (B) is incorrect. Lowering the left aileron will increase the lift on the left wing. Answer (C) is incorrect. It describes the control setting for a right tailwind in a tailwheel airplane.

16. (Refer to Figure 9 below.) (Refer to area C.) How should the flight controls be held while taxiing a tricycle-gear equipped airplane with a left quartering tailwind?

A. Left aileron up, elevator neutral.
B. Left aileron down, elevator down.
C. Left aileron up, elevator down.

Answer (B) is correct. *(AFH Chap 2)*
DISCUSSION: With a left quartering tailwind, the left aileron should be down so the wind does not get under the left wing and flip the airplane over. Also, the elevator should be down, i.e., controls forward, so the wind does not get under the tail and blow the airplane tail over front.
Answer (A) is incorrect. It describes the control setting for a left headwind. Answer (C) is incorrect. It describes the control setting for a right tailwind.

17. (Refer to Figure 9 below.) (Refer to area B.) How should the flight controls be held while taxiing a tailwheel airplane into a right quartering headwind?

A. Right aileron up, elevator up.
B. Right aileron down, elevator neutral.
C. Right aileron up, elevator down.

Answer (A) is correct. *(AFH Chap 2)*
DISCUSSION: When there is a right quartering headwind, the right aileron should be up to spoil the excess lift on the right wing that the crosswind is creating. The elevator should be up to keep weight on the tailwheel to help maintain maneuverability.
Answer (B) is incorrect. The elevator should be up (not neutral) and the right aileron up (not down) when taxiing a tailwheel airplane in a right quartering headwind. Answer (C) is incorrect. The elevator should be up (not down) when taxiing in a right quartering headwind.

18. (Refer to Figure 9 below.) (Refer to area C.) How should the flight controls be held while taxiing a tailwheel airplane with a left quartering tailwind?

A. Left aileron up, elevator neutral.
B. Left aileron down, elevator neutral.
C. Left aileron down, elevator down.

Answer (C) is correct. *(AFH Chap 2)*
DISCUSSION: When there is a left quartering tailwind, the left aileron should be held down so the wind does not get under the left wing and flip the airplane over. Also, the elevator should be down, i.e., controls forward, so the wind does not get under the tail and blow the airplane tail over front.
Answer (A) is incorrect. The left aileron should be down (not up) and the elevator down (not neutral). Answer (B) is incorrect. The elevator should be down when taxiing with a tailwind.

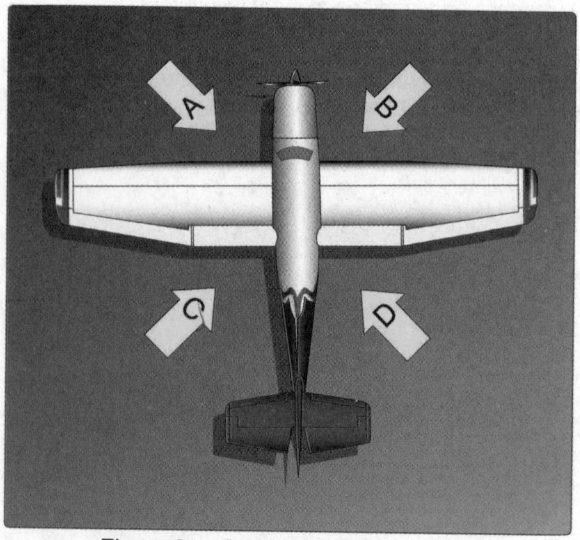

Figure 9. – Control Position for Taxi.

19. When taxiing with strong quartering tailwinds, which aileron positions should be used?

A. Aileron down on the downwind side.

B. Ailerons neutral.

C. Aileron down on the side from which the wind is blowing.

Answer (C) is correct. *(AFH Chap 2)*

DISCUSSION: When there is a strong quartering tailwind, the aileron should be down on the side from which the wind is blowing (when taxiing away from the wind, turn away from the wind) to help keep the wind from getting under that wing and flipping the airplane over.

Answer (A) is incorrect. The aileron should be down on the upwind (not downwind) side. Answer (B) is incorrect. The aileron positions help control the airplane while taxiing in windy conditions.

20. Which aileron positions should a pilot generally use when taxiing in strong quartering headwinds?

A. Aileron up on the side from which the wind is blowing.

B. Aileron down on the side from which the wind is blowing.

C. Ailerons neutral.

Answer (A) is correct. *(AFH Chap 2)*

DISCUSSION: When there is a strong quartering headwind, the aileron should be up on the side from which the wind is blowing to help keep the wind from getting under that wing and blowing the aircraft over. (When taxiing into the wind, turn into the wind.)

Answer (B) is incorrect. The aileron should be up (not down) on the side from which the wind is blowing (i.e., upwind). Answer (C) is incorrect. The aileron positions help control the airplane while taxiing in windy conditions.

21. Which wind condition would be most critical when taxiing a nosewheel equipped high-wing airplane?

A. Quartering tailwind.

B. Direct crosswind.

C. Quartering headwind.

Answer (A) is correct. *(AFH Chap 2)*

DISCUSSION: The most critical wind condition when taxiing a nosewheel-equipped high-wing airplane is a quartering tailwind, which can flip a high-wing airplane over on its top. This should be prevented by holding the elevator in the down position, i.e., controls forward, and the aileron down on the side from which the wind is coming.

Answer (B) is incorrect. A direct crosswind will probably not flip an airplane over. However, it may weathervane the airplane into the wind. Answer (C) is incorrect. A headwind is aerodynamically the condition an airplane is designed for, i.e., wind from the front.

11.5 Magnetic Course

22. The angular difference between true north and magnetic north is

A. magnetic deviation.

B. magnetic variation.

C. compass acceleration error.

Answer (B) is correct. *(PHAK Chap 16)*

DISCUSSION: The angular difference between true and magnetic north is referred to as magnetic variation.

Answer (A) is incorrect. Deviation is the deflection of the compass needle in the airplane because of magnetic influences within the airplane. Answer (C) is incorrect. Compass acceleration error results from accelerating the aircraft.

23. (Refer to Figure 23 on page 409.) On what course should the VOR receiver (OBS) be set to navigate direct from Hampton Varnville Airport (area 1) to Savannah VORTAC (area 3)?

A. 015°.

B. 195°.

C. 201°.

Answer (B) is correct. *(PHAK Chap 16)*

DISCUSSION: You are to find the OBS course setting from Hampton Varnville Airport (right of 1) to Savannah VORTAC (below 3). Since compass roses are based on magnetic courses, you can find that a straight line from Hampton Varnville Airport to Savannah VORTAC coincides the Savannah VORTAC compass rose at 015°. Since the route is south to (not north from) Savannah, compute the reciprocal direction as 195° magnetic (015° + 180°). To use the VOR properly when flying to a VOR station, the course you select with the OBS should be the reciprocal of the radial you will be tracking. If this is not done, reverse sensing occurs.

Answer (A) is incorrect. This would be the course north from, not south to, Savannah. Answer (C) is incorrect. Compass roses are based on magnetic course, so you do not need to correct for magnetic variation.

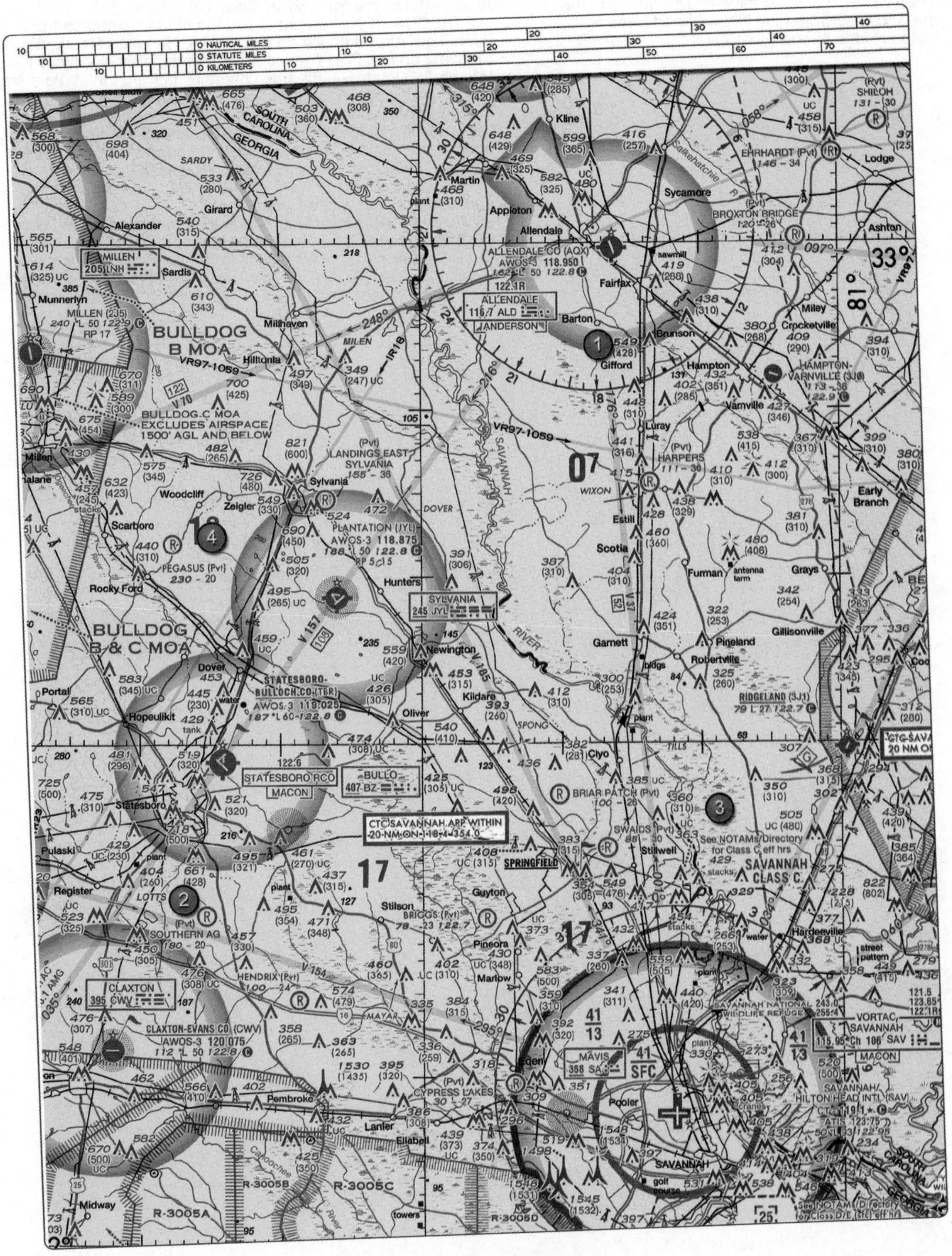

Figure 23. – Sectional Chart Excerpt.
NOTE: Chart is not to scale and should not be used for navigation. Use associated scale.

24. (Refer to Figure 20 on page 411.) Determine the magnetic course from First Flight Airport (area 5) to Hampton Roads Airport (area 2).

A. 141°.

B. 321°.

C. 331°.

Answer (C) is correct. *(PHAK Chap 16)*

DISCUSSION: You are to find the magnetic course from First Flight Airport (lower right corner) to Hampton Roads Airport (above 2 on Fig. 20). True course is the degrees clockwise from true north. Determine the true course by placing the straight edge of your plotter along the given route with the grommet at the intersection of your route and a meridian (the north/south line with crosslines). Here, TC is 320°. To convert this to a magnetic course, add the 11° westerly variation (indicated by the slanted dashed line across the upper right of the sectional), and find the magnetic course of 331°. Remember to subtract easterly variation and add westerly variation.

Answer (A) is incorrect. This is the approximate true, not magnetic, course for a flight from Hampton Roads Airport to First Flight Airport, not for a flight from First Flight to Hampton Roads. Answer (B) is incorrect. This is the approximate true, not magnetic, course.

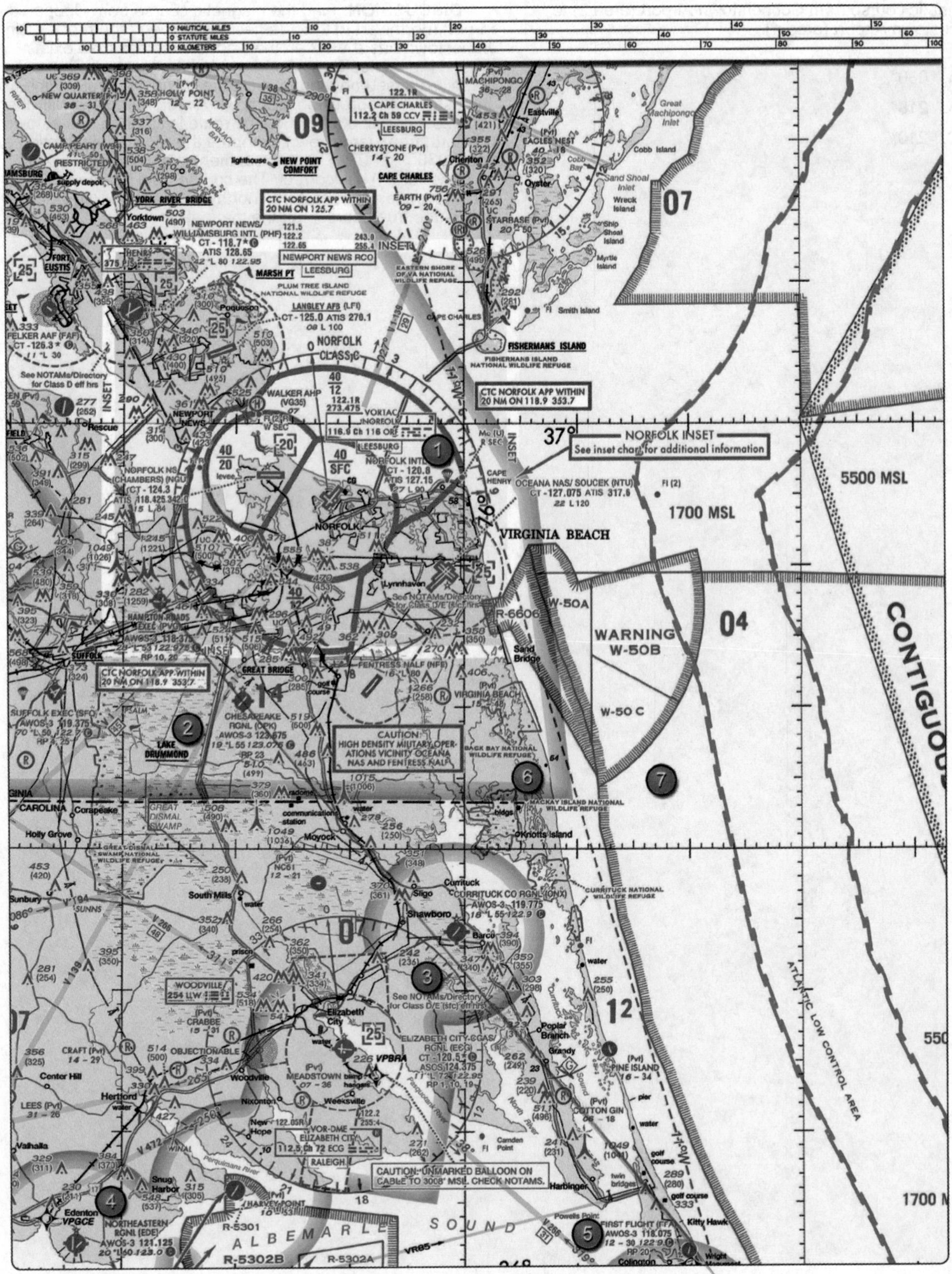

Figure 20. – Sectional Chart Excerpt.
NOTE: Chart is not to scale and should not be used for navigation. Use associated scale.

25. (Refer to Figure 26 on page 413.) Determine the magnetic course from Cooperstown Airport (area 2) to Jamestown Airport (area 4).

A. 030°.

B. 218°.

C. 210°.

Answer (C) is correct. *(PHAK Chap 16)*

DISCUSSION: Find the magnetic course from Cooperstown Airport (northeast of 2) to Jamestown Airport (south of 4). Since Jamestown has a VOR on the field, a compass rose exists around the Jamestown Airport symbol on the chart. Compass roses are based on magnetic courses. Thus, a straight line from Jamestown Airport to Cooperstown Airport coincides with the compass rose at 030°. Since the route is south to Jamestown, not north from Jamestown, compute the reciprocal direction as 210° (030° + 180°). The course, then, is approximately 210°.

Answer (A) is incorrect. The course from Cooperstown to Jamestown is southwest (not northwest). Answer (B) is incorrect. This is the true course, not the magnetic course.

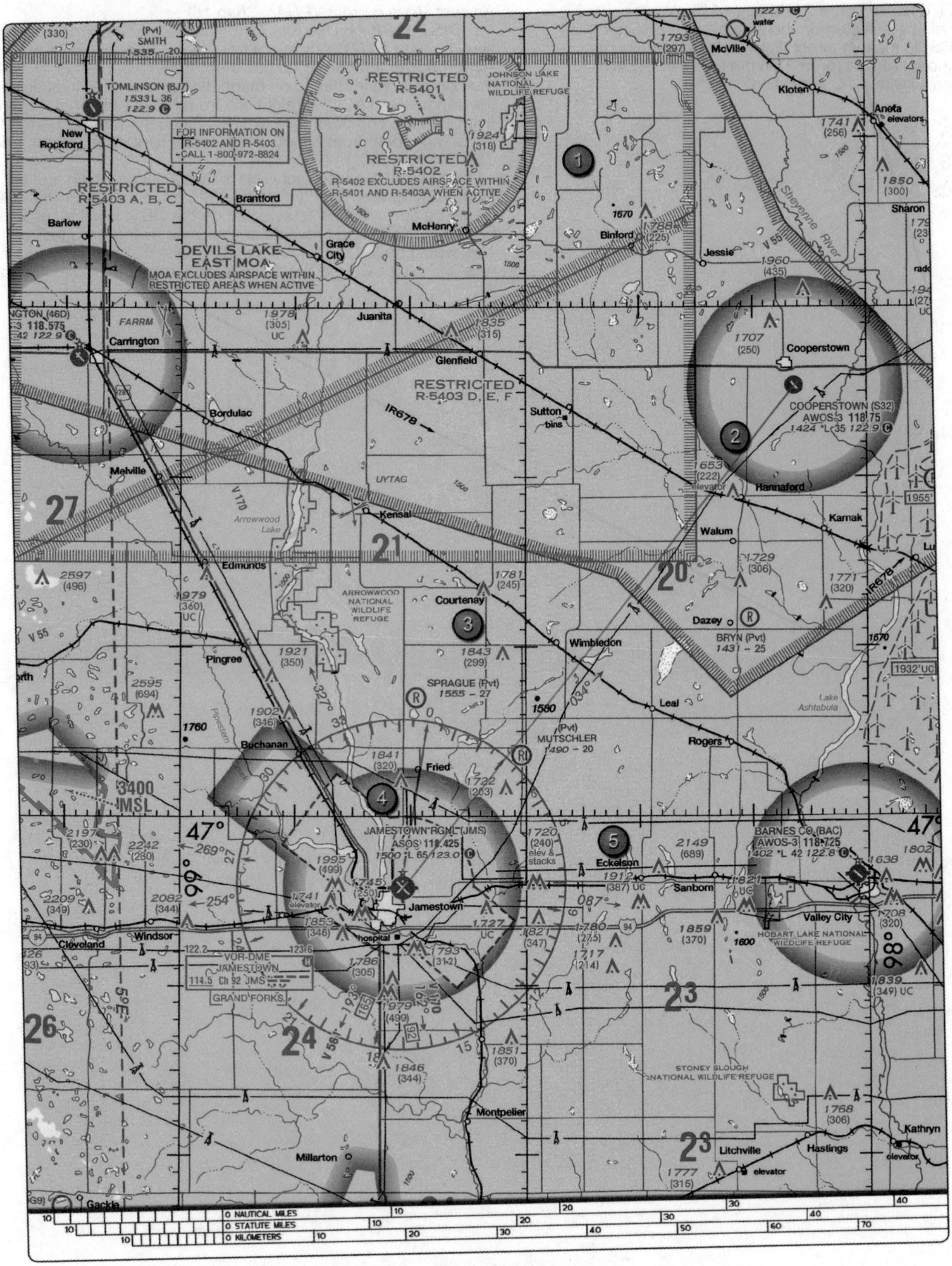

Figure 26. – Sectional Chart Excerpt.
NOTE: Chart is not to scale and should not be used for navigation. Use associated scale.

26. (Refer to Figure 21 on page 415.) What course should be selected on the omnibearing selector (OBS) to make a direct flight from Mercer County Regional Airport (area 3) to the Minot VORTAC (area 1) with a TO indication?

A. 359°.

B. 179°.

C. 001°.

Answer (A) is correct. *(PHAK Chap 16)*

DISCUSSION: Use Fig. 21 to find the course (omnibearing selector with a "TO" indication) from Mercer County Regional Airport (lower left corner) to the Minot VORTAC (right of 1). Note the compass rose (based on magnetic courses) that indicates the Minot VORTAC. A straight line from Mercer to Minot Airport coincides the compass rose at 179°. Since the route is north TO Minot, not south from Minot, compute the reciprocal direction as 359° (179° + 180°).

Answer (B) is incorrect. This is the radial on which a direct flight from Mercer County Regional Airport to the Minot VORTAC would be flown. If 179° is selected on the OBS, it will result in a FROM indication and reverse sensing. Answer (C) is incorrect. This would be the proper OBS setting for a flight originating 5 NM west of Mercer County Regional Airport, rather than directly from it.

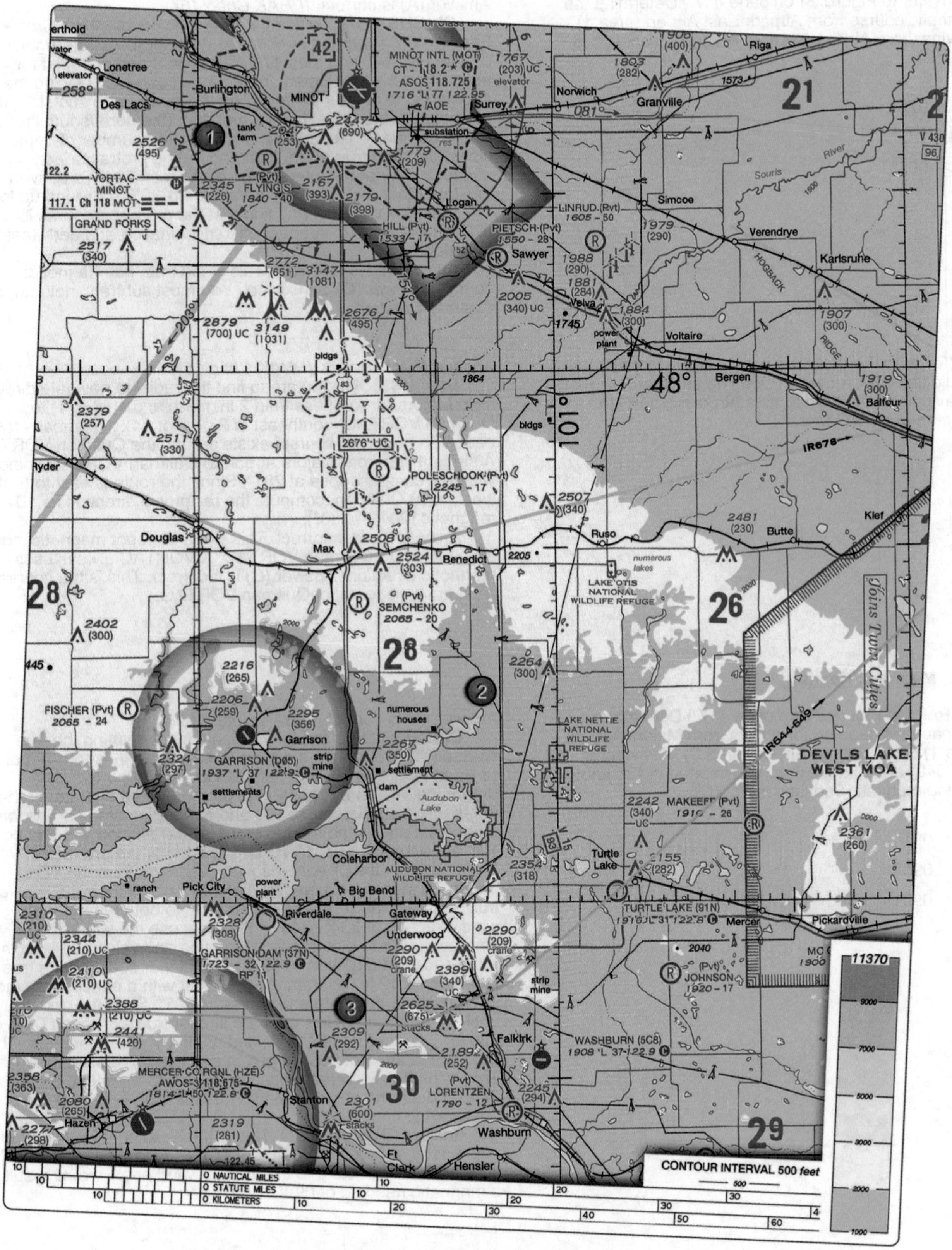

Figure 21. – Sectional Chart Excerpt.
NOTE: Chart is not to scale and should not be used for navigation. Use associated scale.

27. (Refer to Figure 24 on page 417.) Determine the magnetic course from Airpark East Airport (area 1) to Winnsboro Airport (area 2). Magnetic variation is 6°30'E.

A. 075°.

B. 082°.

C. 091°.

Answer (A) is correct. *(PHAK Chap 16)*

DISCUSSION: To find the magnetic course from Airpark East Airport (lower left of chart) to Winnsboro Airport (right of 2 on Fig. 24), you must find true course and correct it for magnetic variation. Determine the true course by placing the straight edge of your plotter along the given route such that the grommet (center hole) is on a meridian (the north/south line with crosslines). True course of 082° is the number of degrees clockwise from true north. It is read on the protractor portion of your plotter at the intersection of the meridian. To convert this to a magnetic course, subtract the 6°30'E (or round up to 7°E) easterly variation and find that the magnetic course is 075°. Remember to subtract easterly variation and add westerly variation.

Answer (B) is incorrect. This is the true, not magnetic, course. Answer (C) is incorrect. You must subtract, not add, an easterly variation.

28. (Refer to Figure 24 on page 417.) On what course should the VOR receiver (OBS) be set in order to navigate direct from Majors Airport (area 1) to Quitman VORTAC (area 2)?

A. 101°.

B. 108°.

C. 281°.

Answer (A) is correct. *(PHAK Chap 16)*

DISCUSSION: You are to find the radial to navigate direct from Majors Airport (less than 2 in. north and east of 1) to Quitman VORTAC (southeast of 2 on Fig. 24). A compass rose, based on magnetic course, exists around the Quitman VORTAC. A straight line from Majors Airport to Quitman VORTAC coincides with this compass rose at 281°. Since the route is east to (not west from) Quitman, compute the reciprocal direction as 101° magnetic (281° – 180°).

Answer (B) is incorrect. This is the true, not magnetic, course from Majors to Quitman VORTAC. A VORTAC always uses magnetic direction. Answer (C) is incorrect. This is the course west from, not east to, Quitman VORTAC.

11.6 Magnetic Heading

29. (Refer to Figure 24 on page 417.) Determine the magnetic heading for a flight from Majors Airport (area 1) to Winnsboro Airport (area 2). The wind is from 340° at 12 knots, the true airspeed is 136 knots, and the magnetic variation is 6° 30'E.

A. 091°.

B. 095°.

C. 099°.

Answer (A) is correct. *(PHAK Chap 16)*

DISCUSSION: On Fig. 24, begin by computing the true course (TC) from Majors Airport (area 1) to Winnsboro Airport (area 2) by drawing a line between the two airports. Next, determine the TC by placing the grommet on the plotter at the intersection on the course line and a meridian (vertical line with cross-hatchings) and the top of the plotter aligned with the course line. Note the TC of 101° TC on the edge of the protractor. Next, subtract the 6° east magnetic variation from the TC to obtain a magnetic course (MC) of 095°. Since the wind is given true, subtract the 6° magnetic variation to obtain a magnetic wind direction of 334° (340° – 6°). Now use the wind side of your computer to plot the wind direction and velocity. Place the magnetic wind direction of 334° on the inner scale on the true index. Mark 12 kt. up from the grommet with a pencil. Turn the inner scale to the magnetic course of 095°. Slide the grid up until the pencil mark lies over the line for true airspeed (TAS) of 136 kt. Correct for the 4° left wind angle by subtracting from the magnetic course of 095° to obtain a magnetic heading of 091°. This is intuitively correct because, given the magnetic course of 095° and a northwesterly wind, you must turn to the left (crab into the wind) to correct for it.

Answer (B) is incorrect. This is the heading you would get if you did not subtract the wind angle of 4° to the left. Answer (C) is incorrect. Correcting to the right for wind angle would result in a magnetic heading of 099°.

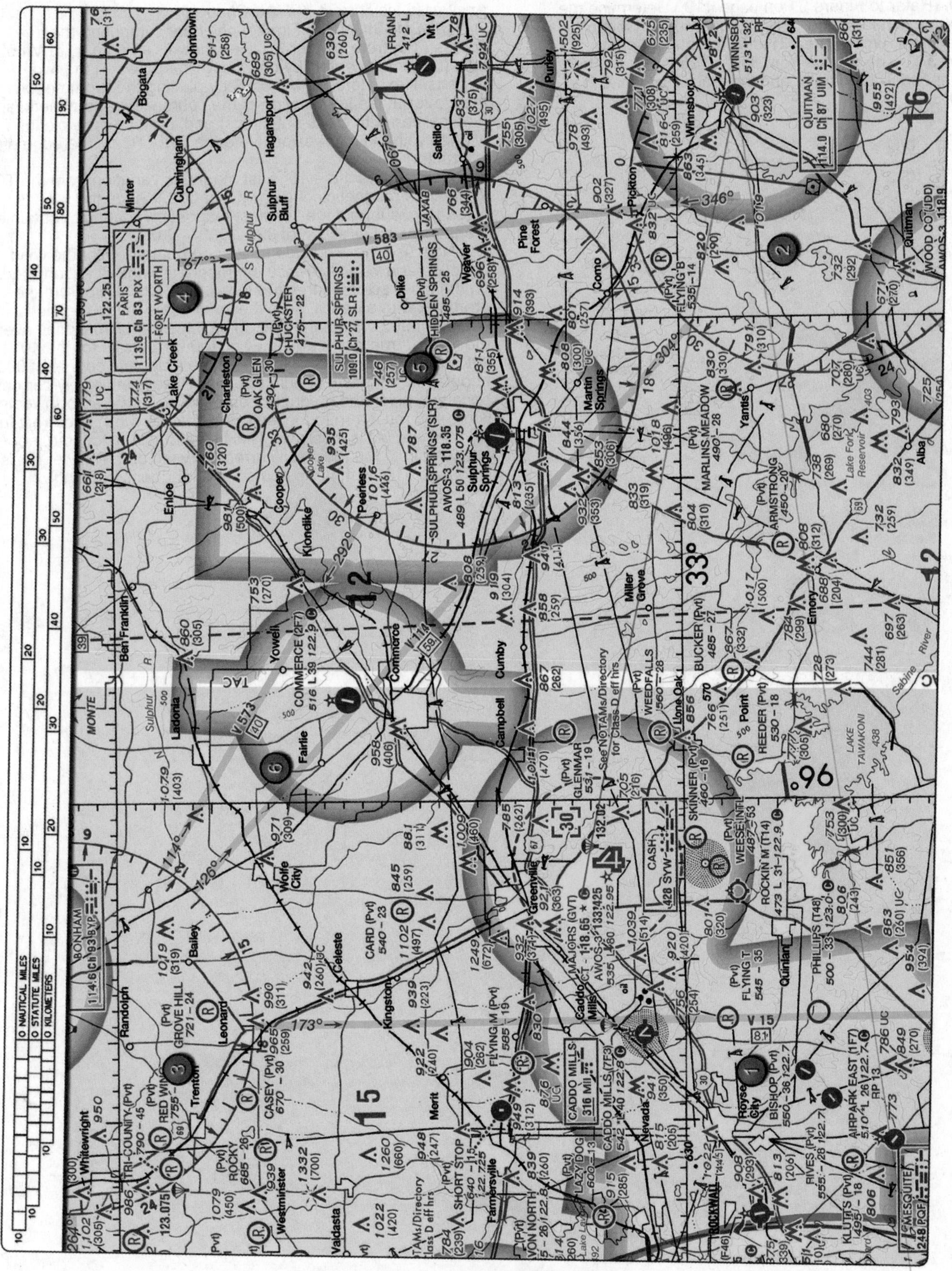

Figure 24. – Sectional Chart Excerpt.
NOTE: Chart is not to scale and should not be used for navigation. Use associated scale.

30. (Refer to Figure 21 on page 419.) Determine the magnetic heading for a flight from Mercer County Regional Airport (area 3) to Minot International (area 1). The wind is from 330° at 25 knots, the true airspeed is 100 knots, and the magnetic variation is 10°E.

A. 002°.

B. 012°.

C. 352°.

Answer (C) is correct. *(PHAK Chap 16)*

DISCUSSION: On Fig. 21, begin by computing the true course (TC) from Mercer Co. Reg. (lower left corner) to Minot Int'l. (upper left center) by drawing a line between the two airports. Next, determine the TC by placing the grommet on the plotter at the intersection of the course line and a meridian (vertical line with cross-hatchings) and the top of the plotter aligned with the course line. Note the 012° TC on the edge of the protractor.

Next, subtract the 10° east magnetic variation from the TC to obtain a magnetic course (MC) of 002°. Since the wind is given true, subtract the 10° east magnetic variation to obtain a magnetic wind direction of 320° (330° – 10°).

Now use the wind side of your computer to plot the wind direction and velocity. Place the magnetic wind direction of 320° on the inner scale on the true index. Mark 25 kt. up from the grommet with a pencil. Turn the inner scale to the magnetic course of 002°. Slide the grid up until the pencil mark lies over the line for true airspeed (TAS) of 100 kt. Correct for the 10° left wind angle by subtracting from the magnetic course of 002° to obtain a magnetic heading of 352°. This is intuitively correct because, given the magnetic course of 002° and a northwesterly wind, you must turn to the left (crab into the wind) to correct for it.

Answer (A) is incorrect. This is the magnetic course, not heading; i.e., you must still correct for wind drift. Answer (B) is incorrect. This is the true course, not magnetic heading.

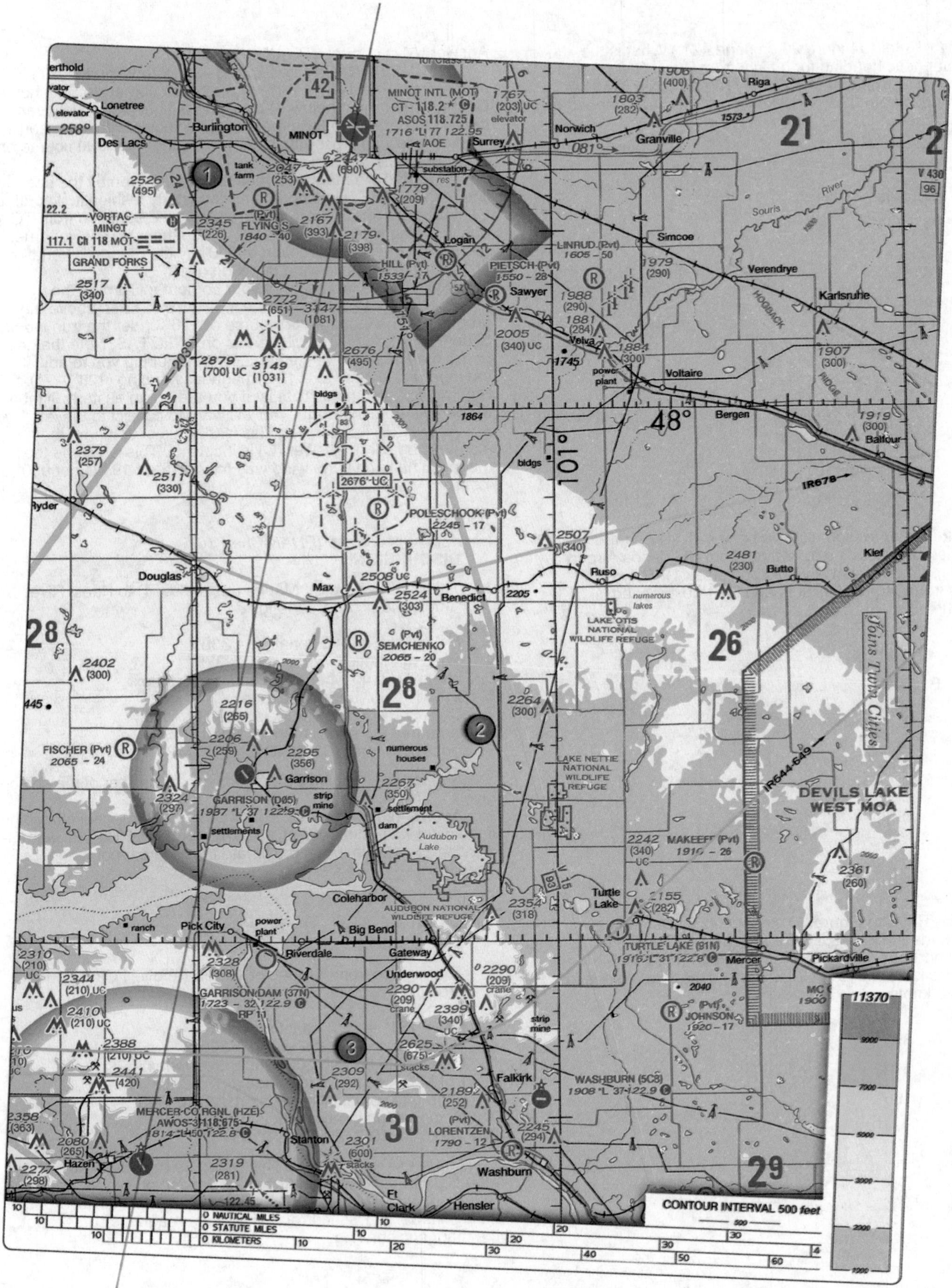

Figure 21. – Sectional Chart Excerpt.
NOTE: Chart is not to scale and should not be used for navigation. Use associated scale.

31. (Refer to Figure 22 on page 421.) What is the magnetic heading for a flight from Priest River Airport (area 1) to Shoshone County Airport (area 3)? The wind is from 030° at 12 knots and the true airspeed is 95 knots.

A. 121°.

B. 143°.

C. 136°.

Answer (A) is correct. *(PHAK Chap 16)*

DISCUSSION: On Fig. 22, begin by computing the true course from Priest River Airport (upper left corner) to Shoshone County Airport (just below 3) by laying a flight plotter between the two airports. The grommet should coincide with the meridian (vertical line with cross-hatchings). Note the 143° true course on the edge of the protractor.

Next, find the magnetic variation that is given by the dashed line marked 15°E, slanting in a northeasterly fashion just south of Carlin Bay Private Airport. Subtract the 15°E variation from TC to obtain a magnetic course of 128°. Since the wind is given true, reduce the true wind direction of 030° by the magnetic variation of 15°E to a magnetic wind direction of 15°.

Now use the wind side of your computer. Turning the inner circle to 15° under the true index, mark 12 kt. above the grommet. Set the magnetic course of 128° under the true index. Slide the grid so the pencil mark is on 95 kt. TAS. Note that the pencil mark is 7° left of the center line, requiring you to adjust the magnetic course to a 121° magnetic heading (128° – 7°). Subtract left, add right. That is, if you are on an easterly flight and the wind is from the north, you will want to correct to the left.

Answer (B) is incorrect. This is the true course, not the magnetic heading. Answer (C) is incorrect. This would be the magnetic heading if the wind was from 215° at 19 kt., not 030° at 12 kt.

32. (Refer to Figure 22 on page 421.) Determine the magnetic heading for a flight from St. Maries Airport (area 4) to Priest River Airport (area 1). The wind is from 340° at 10 knots and the true airspeed is 90 knots.

A. 330°.

B. 325°.

C. 345°.

Answer (A) is correct. *(PHAK Chap 16)*

DISCUSSION:

1. This flight is from St. Maries (just below 4) to Priest River (upper left corner) on Fig. 22.
2. TC is 345°.
3. MC = 345° – 15°E variation = 330°.
4. Wind magnetic = 340° – 15° = 325°.
5. Mark 10 kt. up when 325° under true index.
6. Put MC 330° under true index.
7. Slide grid so pencil mark is on 90 kt. TAS.
8. Note that the pencil mark is 1° left.
9. Subtract 1° from 330° MC for 329° MH.

A magnetic heading of 330° is the best answer of the choices given.

Answer (B) is incorrect. This would be the magnetic heading if the wind was from 300° at 14 kt., not 340° at 10 kt. Answer (C) is incorrect. This is the approximate true course, not magnetic heading.

33. (Refer to Figure 22 on page 421.) Determine the magnetic heading for a flight from Sandpoint Airport (area 1) to St. Maries Airport (area 4). The wind is from 215° at 25 knots and the true airspeed is 125 knots.

A. 352°.

B. 172°.

C. 166°.

Answer (B) is correct. *(PHAK Chap 16)*

DISCUSSION:

1. This flight is from Sandpoint Airport (above 1), to St. Maries (below 4) on Fig. 22
2. TC = 181°.
3. MC = 181° – 15°E variation = 166°.
4. Wind magnetic = 215° – 15° = 200°.
5. Mark up 25 kt. with 200° under true index.
6. Put MC 166° under true index.
7. Slide grid so pencil mark is on 125 kt. TAS.
8. Note that the pencil mark is 6° right.
9. Add 6° to 166° MC for 172° MH.

Answer (A) is incorrect. This would be the magnetic heading for a flight from St. Maries Airport to Sandpoint Airport, not from Sandpoint to St. Maries, with the wind from 145°, not 215°, at 25 kt. Answer (C) is incorrect. This is the magnetic course, not the magnetic heading.

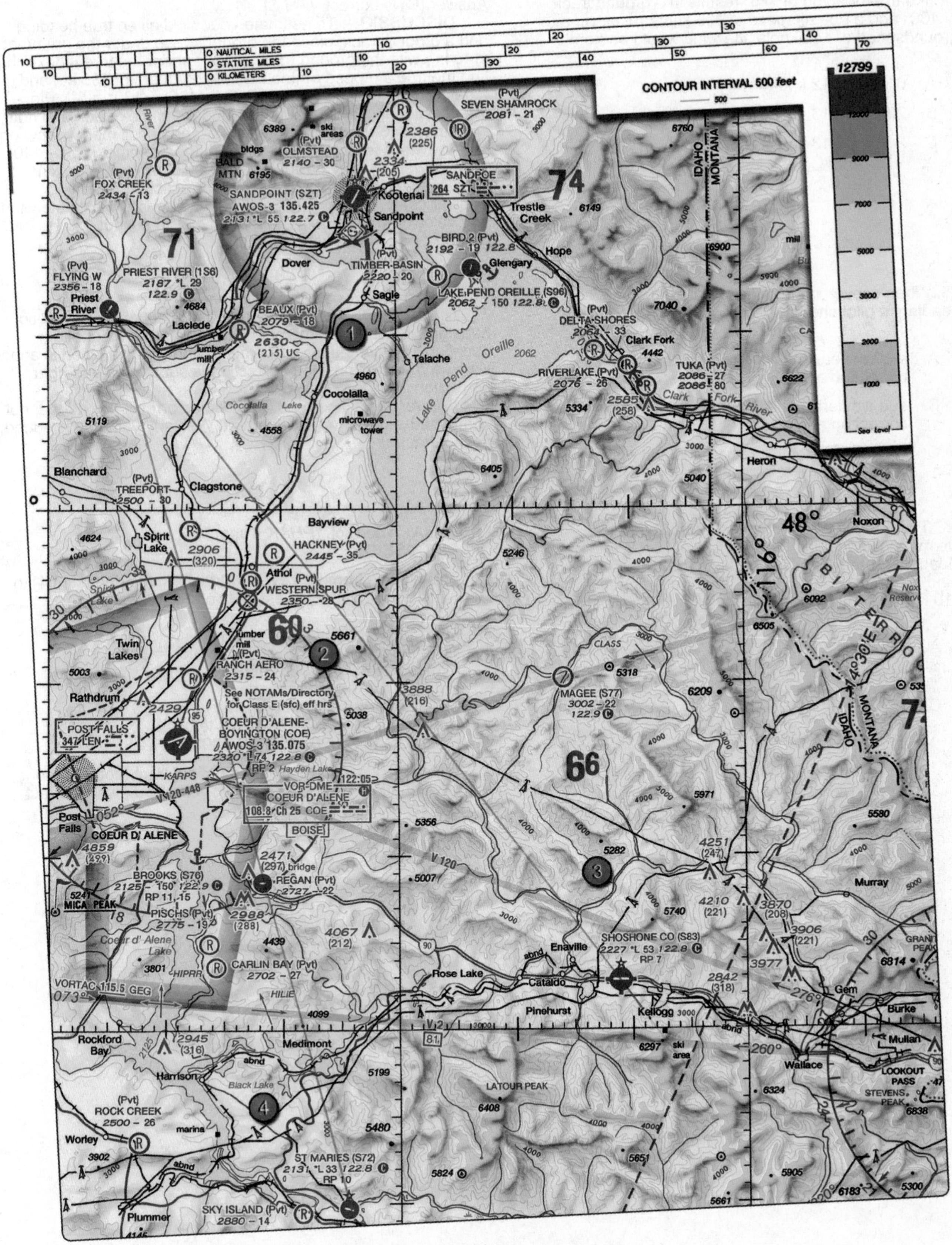

Figure 22. – Sectional Chart Excerpt.
NOTE: Chart is not to scale and should not be used for navigation. Use associated scale.

34. If a true heading of 135° results in a ground track of 130° and a true airspeed of 135 knots results in a groundspeed of 140 knots, the wind would be from

A. 019° and 12 knots.

B. 200° and 13 knots.

C. 246° and 13 knots.

Answer (C) is correct. *(PH SU 9)*

DISCUSSION: To estimate your wind given true heading and a ground track, place the groundspeed under the grommet (140 kt.) with the ground track of 130° under the true index. Then find the true airspeed on the true airspeed arc of 135 kt., and put a pencil mark for a 5° right deviation (135° – 130° = 5°). Place the pencil mark on the centerline under the true index and note a wind from 246° under the true index. The pencil mark is now on 153 kt., which is about 13 kt. up from the grommet (153 – 140).

Answer (A) is incorrect. These would be your approximate wind and velocity for a 5° left wind correction, not right. Answer (B) is incorrect. These would be your approximate wind and velocity when at a true airspeed of 140 kt., not 135 kt., and a groundspeed of 135 kt., not 140 kt.

35. When converting from true course to magnetic heading, a pilot should

A. subtract easterly variation and right wind correction angle.

B. add westerly variation and subtract left wind correction angle.

C. subtract westerly variation and add right wind correction angle.

Answer (B) is correct. *(PHAK Chap 16)*

DISCUSSION: When converting true course to magnetic heading, you should remember two rules. With magnetic variation, east variation is subtracted and west variation is added. With wind corrections, left correction is subtracted and right correction is added.

Answer (A) is incorrect. Right wind correction is added, not subtracted. Answer (C) is incorrect. Westerly variation is added, not subtracted.

36. (Refer to Figure 25 on page 423.) Determine the magnetic heading for a flight from Fort Worth Meacham (area 4) to Denton Muni (area 1). The wind is from 330° at 25 knots, the true airspeed is 110 knots, and the magnetic variation is 7°E.

A. 003°.

B. 017°.

C. 023°.

Answer (A) is correct. *(PHAK Chap 16)*

DISCUSSION:

1. This flight is from Fort Worth Meacham (southeast of 4) to Denton Muni (southwest of 1) on Fig. 25.
2. TC = 021°.
3. MC = 021° – 7°E variation = 014°.
4. Wind magnetic = 330° – 7°E variation = 323°.
5. Mark up 25 kt. with 323° under true index.
6. Put MC 014° under true index.
7. Slide grid so pencil mark is on 110 kt. TAS.
8. Note that the pencil mark is 11° left.
9. Subtract 11° from 014° MC for 003° MH.

Answer (B) is incorrect. You must subtract (not add) an easterly variation. Answer (C) is incorrect. You must subtract (not add) a left wind correction.

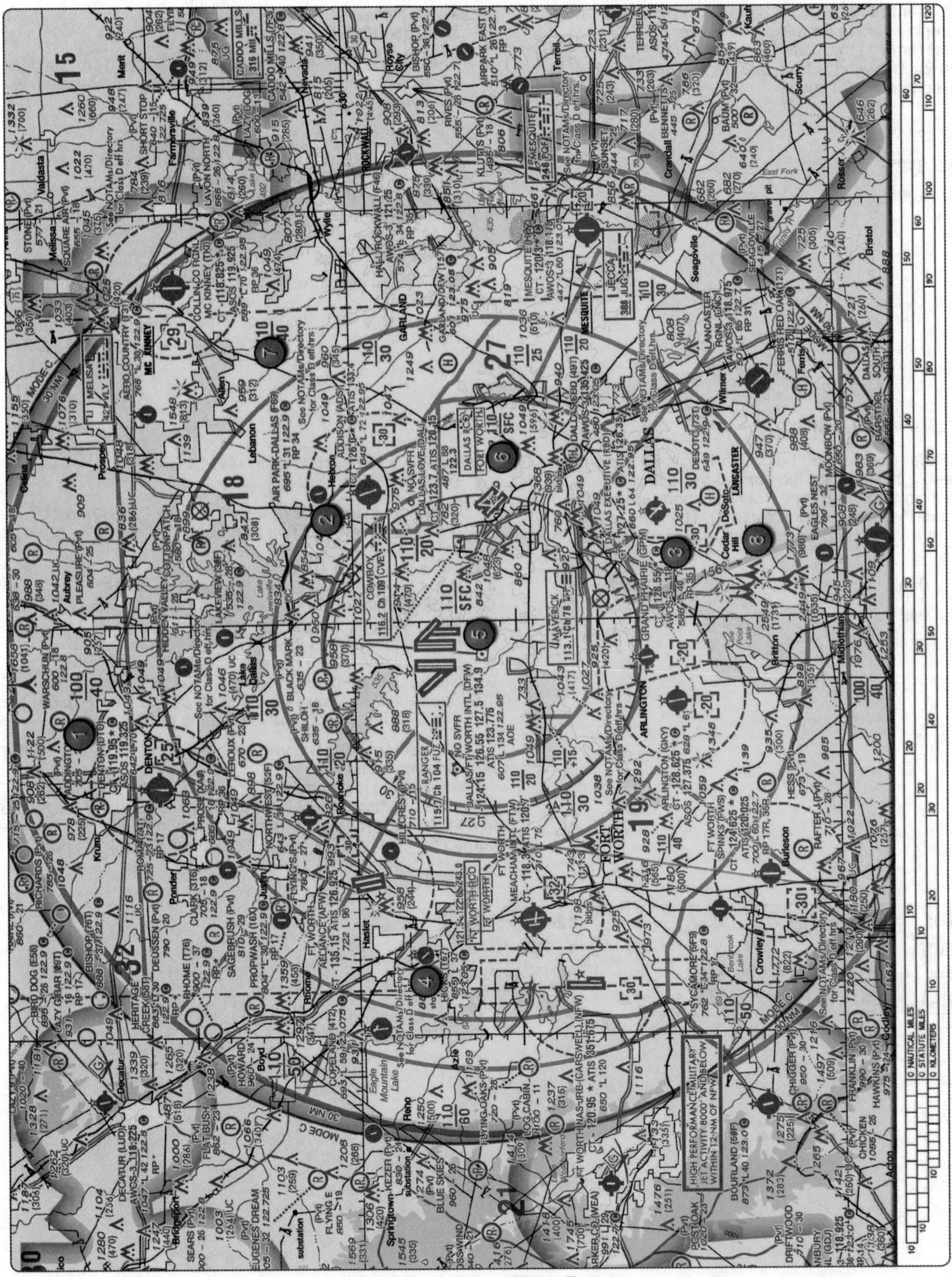

Figure 25. – Sectional Chart Excerpt.
NOTE: Chart is not to scale and should not be used for navigation. Use associated scale.

37. (Refer to Figure 23 on page 425.) Determine the magnetic heading for a flight from Allendale County Airport (area 1) to Claxton-Evans County Airport (area 2). The wind is from 090° at 16 knots and the true airspeed is 90 knots.

A. 230°.

B. 212°.

C. 209°.

Answer (C) is correct. *(PHAK Chap 16)*

DISCUSSION:

1. This flight is from Allendale County (above 1) to Claxton-Evans County Airport (left of 2) on Fig. 23. Variation is shown on Fig. 23 as 6°W.
2. TC = 212°.
3. MC = 212° TC + 6°W variation = 218°.
4. Wind magnetic = 090° + 6°W variation = 096°.
5. Mark up 16 kt. with 096° under true index.
6. Place MC 218° under true index.
7. Move wind mark to 90 kt. TAS arc.
8. Note that the pencil mark is 9° left.
9. Subtract 9° from 218° MC for 209° MH.

Answer (A) is incorrect. This would be the approximate magnetic heading if the wind was out of 330° at 23 kt., not 090° at 16 kt. Answer (B) is incorrect. This is the true heading, not the magnetic heading.

11.7 Compass Heading

38. (Refer to Figure 58 below, and Figure 23 on page 425.) Determine the compass heading for a flight from Claxton-Evans County Airport (area 2) to Hampton Varnville Airport (area 1). The wind is from 280° at 8 knots, and the true airspeed is 85 knots.

A. 033°.

B. 042°.

C. 038°.

Answer (B) is the best answer. *(PHAK Chap 16)*

DISCUSSION:

1. This flight is from Claxton-Evans (left of 2) to Hampton Varnville (right of 1) on Fig. 23.
2. TC = 045°.
3. MC = 045° TC + 6°W variation = 051°.
4. Wind magnetic = 280° + 6°W variation = 286°.
5. Mark up 8 kt. with 286° under true index.
6. Place MC 051° under true index.
7. Move wind mark to 85 kt. TAS arc.
8. Note that the pencil mark is 4° left.
9. Subtract 4° from 051° MC for 047° MH.
10. Subtract 4° compass variation (obtained from Fig. 58) from 047° to find the compass heading of 043°.

After determining a compass heading of 043°, 042° is the best answer available.

Answer (A) is incorrect. This would be the approximate compass heading if the wind were out of 295° at 22 kt., not 280° at 8 kt. Answer (C) is incorrect. This would be the approximate compass heading if the wind were out of 295° at 12 knots.

For	N	30	60	E	120	150
Steer	0	27	56	85	116	148
For	S	210	240	W	300	330
Steer	181	214	244	274	303	332

Figure 58. – Compass Card.

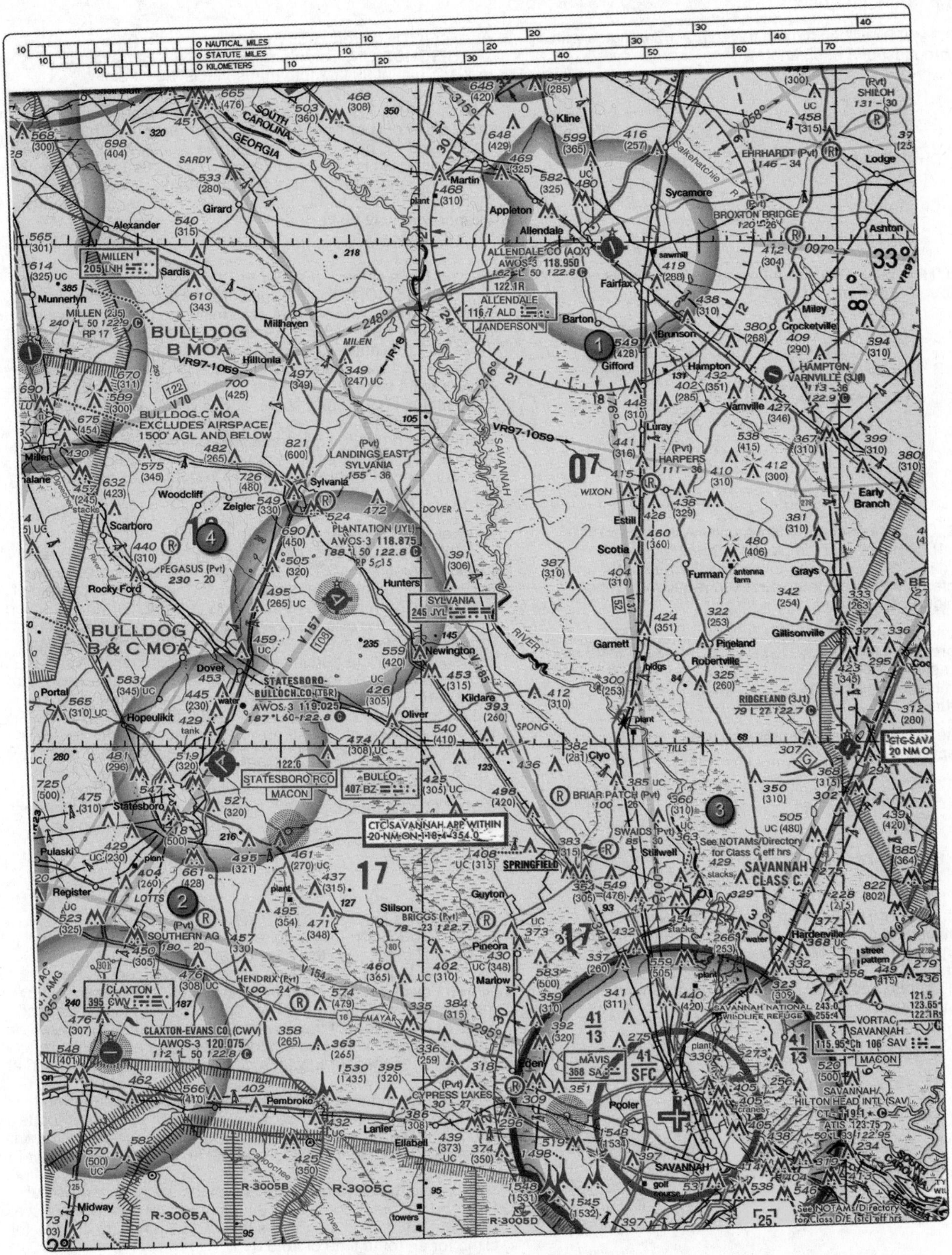

Figure 23. – Sectional Chart Excerpt.
NOTE: Chart is not to scale and should not be used for navigation. Use associated scale.

11.8 Time En Route

39. How far will an aircraft travel in 2-1/2 minutes with a groundspeed of 98 knots?

A. 2.45 NM.

B. 3.35 NM.

C. 4.08 NM.

Answer (C) is correct. *(PH SU 9)*

DISCUSSION: To determine the distance traveled in 2-1/2 min. at 98 kt., note that 98 kt. is 1.6 NM/min. (98 ÷ 60 = 1.633). Thus, in 2-1/2 min., you will have traveled a total of 4.08 NM (1.633 × 2.5 = 4.08). Alternatively, put 98 on the outer scale of your flight computer over the index on the inner scale. Find 2.5 min. on the inner scale, above which is 4.1 NM.

Answer (A) is incorrect. For 2.45 NM to be true, you would need a groundspeed of approximately 59 kt. Answer (B) is incorrect. For 3.35 NM to be true, you would need a groundspeed of approximately 80 kt.

40. How far will an aircraft travel in 7.5 minutes with a ground speed of 114 knots?

A. 14.25 NM.

B. 15.00 NM.

C. 14.50 NM.

Answer (A) is correct. *(PH SU 9)*

DISCUSSION: To determine the distance traveled in 7-1/2 minutes at 114 kt., first determine the distance traveled per minute (114 ÷ 60 = 1.9). In 1 minute, the aircraft travels 1.9 NM. Thus, in 7.5 minutes, the plane will have traveled 14.25 NM (1.9 × 7.5 = 14.25). Alternatively, put 114 on the outer scale of your flight computer over the index on the inner scale. Find 7.5 minutes on the inner scale, above which is 14.25 miles.

Answer (B) is incorrect. The airplane would require a groundspeed of 120 kt. to travel 15.00 NM in 7.5 minutes. Answer (C) is incorrect. The airplane would require a groundspeed of 116 kt. to travel 14.50 NM in 7.5 minutes.

41. On a cross-country flight, point A is crossed at 1500 hours and the plan is to reach point B at 1530 hours. Use the following information to determine the indicated airspeed required to reach point B on schedule.

Distance between A and B.................. 70 NM
Forecast wind.................................... 310° at 15 kts
Pressure altitude................................ 8,000 ft
Ambient temperature .... –10°C
True course.. 270°

The required indicated airspeed would be approximately

A. 126 knots.

B. 137 knots.

C. 152 knots.

Answer (B) is correct. *(PH SU 9)*

DISCUSSION: First determine the required groundspeed to reach point B at 1530 by placing 70 NM on the outer scale over 30 min. on the inner scale to determine a groundspeed of 140 kt. On the wind side of the computer, put the wind direction of 310° under the true index and put a pencil mark 15 kt. up from the grommet. Next, turn the inner scale so the 270° true course is under the true index and put the grommet over the groundspeed. Note that to obtain the 140-kt. groundspeed, you need a 152-kt. true airspeed. Next, on the computer side, put the air temperature of –10°C over 8,000 ft. altitude. Then find the true airspeed of 152 kt. on the outer scale, which lies over approximately 137 kt. indicated airspeed on the inner scale.

Answer (A) is incorrect. This would be your indicated airspeed if you had a true airspeed of 140 kt. Note that 140 kt. is your groundspeed, not true airspeed. Answer (C) is incorrect. This is your required true airspeed, not indicated airspeed.

42. (Refer to Figure 21 on page 427.) What is the estimated time en route from Mercer County Regional Airport (area 3) to Minot International (area 1)? The wind is from 330° at 25 knots and the true airspeed is 100 knots. Add 3-1/2 minutes for departure and climb-out.

A. 45 minutes.

B. 48 1/2 minutes.

C. 52 minutes.

Answer (B) is correct. *(PHAK Chap 15)*

DISCUSSION: The requirement is time en route and not magnetic heading, so there is no need to convert TC to MC.

Using Fig. 21, the time en route from Mercer Co. Reg. Airport (lower left corner) to Minot (right of 1) is determined by measuring the distance (60 NM measured with the associated scale at the bottom of the chart), determining the time based on groundspeed, and adding 3.5 min. for takeoff and climb. The TC is 012° as measured with a plotter. The wind is from 330° at 25 kt.

On the wind side of your flight computer, place the wind direction 330° under the true index and mark 25 kt. up. Rotate TC of 012° under the true index. Slide the grid so the pencil mark is on the arc for TAS of 100 kt. Read 80 kt. groundspeed under the grommet.

Turn to the calculator side and place the groundspeed of 80 kt. on the outer scale over 60 min. Find 60 NM on outer scale and note 45 min. on the inner scale. Add 3.5 min. to 45 min. for climb for en route time of 48.5 min.

Answer (A) is incorrect. You must add 3.5 min. for departure and climbout. Answer (C) is incorrect. The time en route is 48.5 min. (not 52 min.).

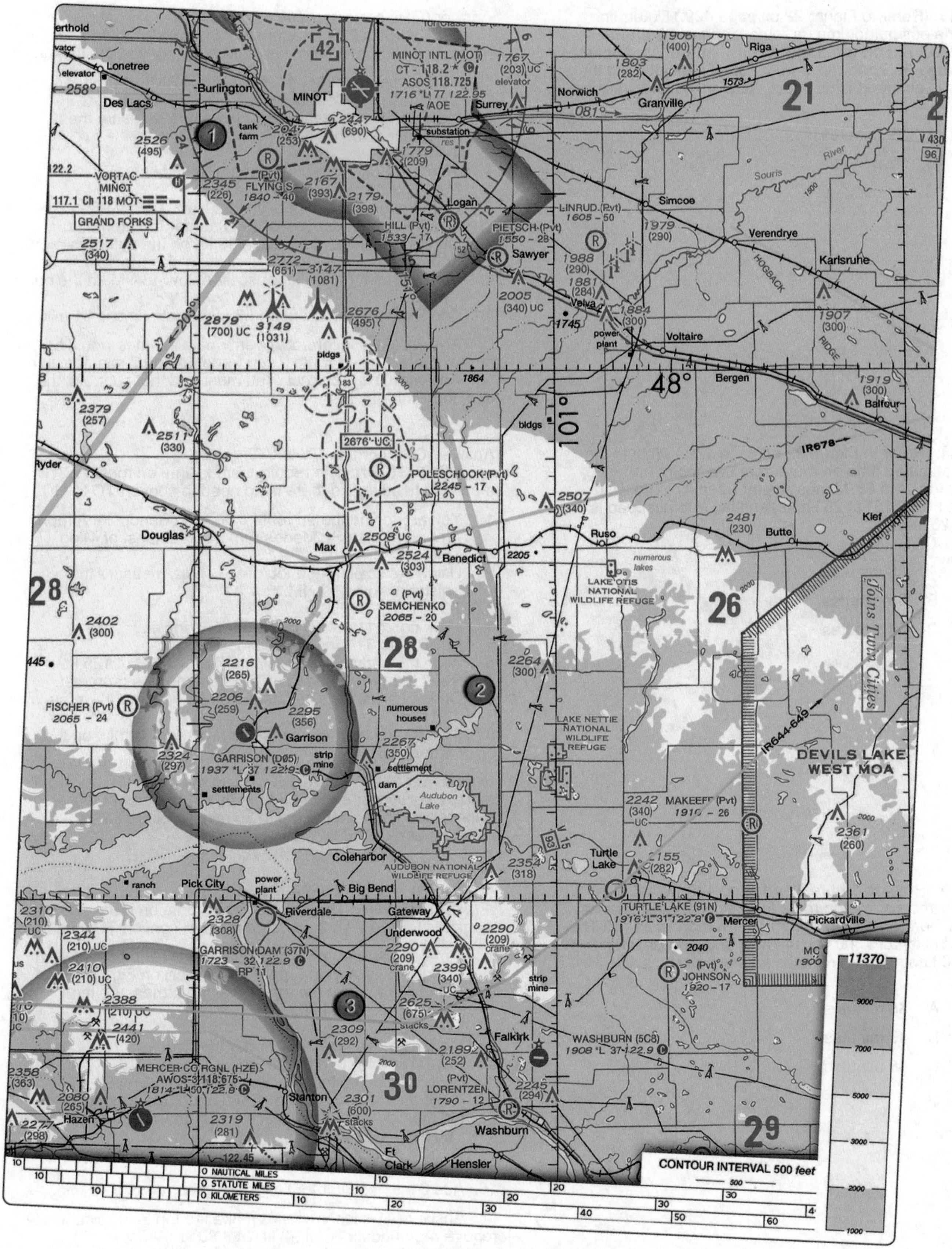

Figure 21. – Sectional Chart Excerpt.
NOTE: Chart is not to scale and should not be used for navigation. Use associated scale.

43. (Refer to Figure 22 on page 429.) Determine the estimated time en route for a flight from Priest River Airport (area 1) to Shoshone County Airport (area 3). The wind is from 030 at 12 knots and the true airspeed is 95 knots. Add 2 minutes for climb-out.

A. 29 minutes.

B. 27 minutes.

C. 31 minutes.

TC: 143
-15
MC: 128

Answer (C) is correct. *(PHAK Chap 16)*

DISCUSSION: The requirement is time en route and not magnetic heading, so there is no need to convert TC to MC.

1. To find the en route time from Priest River Airport (area 1) to Shoshone County Airport (area 3) use Fig. 22.
2. Using the scale at the top of the chart, measure the distance to be 48 NM.
3. TC = 143°.
4. Mark up 12 kt. with 030° under true index.
5. Put TC of 143° under true index.
6. Slide the grid so the pencil mark is on TAS of 95 kt.
7. Read the groundspeed of 99 kt. under the grommet.
8. On the calculator side, place 99 kt. on the outer scale over 60 min.
9. Read 29 min. on the inner scale below 48 NM on the outer scale.
10. Add 2 min for climb-out and the en route time is 31 min.

Answer (A) is incorrect. Twenty-nine minutes would be the approximate time en route if you forgot to add 2 min. for climb-out. Answer (B) is incorrect. You must add, not subtract, the 2 min. for climb-out.

44. (Refer to Figure 22 on page 429.) What is the estimated time en route from Sandpoint Airport (area 1) to St. Maries Airport (area 4)? The wind is from 215° at 25 knots, and the true airspeed is 125 knots.

A. 38 minutes.

B. 30 minutes.

C. 34 minutes.

Answer (C) is correct. *(PHAK Chap 16)*

DISCUSSION: The requirement is time en route and not magnetic heading, so there is no need to convert TC to MC.

1. You are to find the en route time from Sandpoint Airport (north of 1) to St. Maries Airport (southeast of 4) on Fig. 22.
2. Using the scale at the top of the chart, measure the distance to be 59 NM.
3. TC = 181°.
4. Mark up 25 kt. with 215° under true index.
5. Put TC of 181° under true index.
6. Slide the grid so the pencil mark is on TAS of 125 kt.
7. Read the groundspeed of 104 kt. under the grommet.
8. On the calculator side, place 104 kt. on the outer scale over 60 min.
9. Find 59 NM on the outer scale and read 34 min. on the inner scale.

Answer (A) is incorrect. To make the trip in 38 min. would require a groundspeed of 93 kt., not 104 kt. Answer (B) is incorrect. To make the trip in 30 min. would require a groundspeed of 118 kt., not 104 kt.

45. (Refer to Figure 22 on page 429.) What is the estimated time en route for a flight from St. Maries Airport (area 4) to Priest River Airport (area 1)? The wind is from 300° at 14 knots and the true airspeed is 90 knots. Add 3 minutes for climb-out.

A. 38 minutes.

B. 43 minutes.

C. 48 minutes.

Answer (B) is correct. *(PHAK Chap 16)*

DISCUSSION: The requirement is time en route and not magnetic heading, so there is no need to convert TC to MC.

1. Time en route from St. Maries Airport (southeast of 4) to Priest River Airport (upper left corner) on Fig. 22.
2. Using the scale at the top of the chart, measure the distance to be 54 NM.
3. TC = 346°.
4. Mark up 14 kt. with 300° under true index.
5. Put TC of 346° under true index.
6. Slide the grid so the pencil mark is on TAS of 90 kt.
7. Read the groundspeed of 80 kt. under the grommet.
8. On the calculator side, place 80 kt. on the outer scale over 60 min.
9. Find 54 NM on the outer scale and read 40 min. on the inner scale.
10. Add 3 min for climb-out to get time en route of 43 min.

Answer (A) is incorrect. To make the trip in 38 min. would require a groundspeed of 92 kt. (not 80 kt.). Answer (C) is incorrect. To make the trip in 48 min. would require a groundspeed of 72 kt. (not 80 kt.).

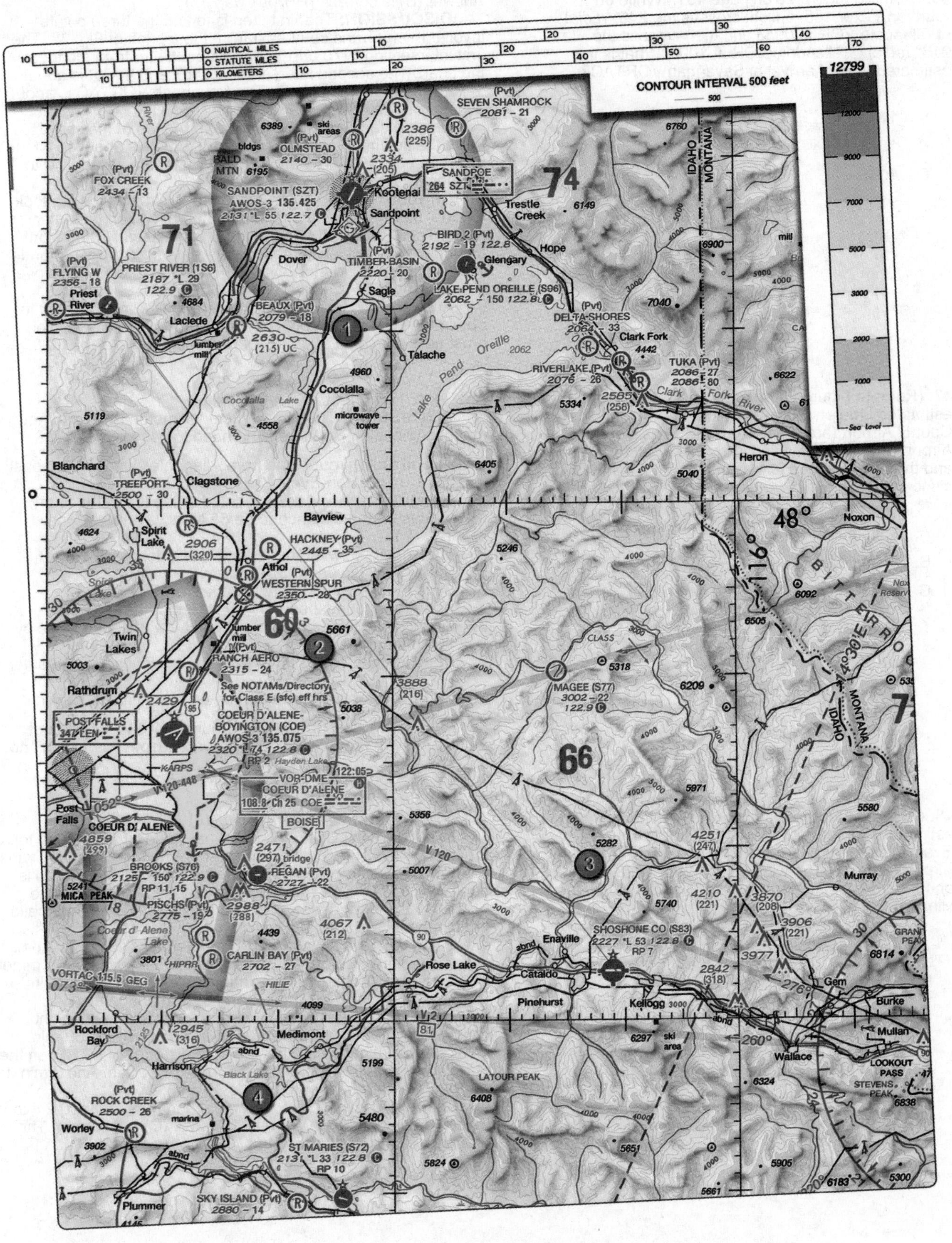

Figure 22. – Sectional Chart Excerpt.
NOTE: Chart is not to scale and should not be used for navigation. Use associated scale.

46. (Refer to Figure 23 on page 431.) While en route on Victor 185, a flight crosses the 248° radial of Allendale VOR at 0953 and then crosses the 216° radial of Allendale VOR at 1000. What is the estimated time of arrival at Savannah VORTAC?

A. 1023.

B. 1028.

C. 1036.

Answer (B) is correct. *(PHAK Chap 16)*

DISCUSSION: The first step is to find the three points involved. V185 runs southeast from the top left of Fig. 23. The first intersection (V70 and V185) is about 1 in. from the top of the chart. The second intersection (V157 and V185) is about 1-1/2 in. farther along V185. The Savannah VORTAC is about 6 in. farther down V185.

Use the sectional scale located at the top of the chart. From the first intersection (V70 and V185), it is about 10 NM to the intersection of V185 and V157. From there it is 40 NM to Savannah VORTAC.

On your flight computer, place the 7 min. the first leg took (1000 – 0953) on the inner scale under 10 NM on the outer scale. Then find 40 NM on the outer scale. Read 28 min. on the inner scale, which is the time en route from the V185 and V157 intersection to the Savannah VORTAC. Arrival time over Savannah VORTAC is therefore 1028.

Answer (A) is incorrect. You must add 28 min. to 1000 to obtain the correct ETA of 1028. Answer (C) is incorrect. You must add 28 min. to 1000 to obtain the correct ETA of 1028.

47. (Refer to Figure 23 on page 431.) What is the estimated time en route for a flight from Allendale County Airport (area 1) to Claxton-Evans County Airport (area 2)? The wind is from 100° at 18 knots and the true airspeed is 115 knots. Add 2 minutes for climb-out.

A. 33 minutes.

B. 27 minutes.

C. 30 minutes.

Answer (C) is correct. *(PHAK Chap 16)*

DISCUSSION: The requirement is time en route and not magnetic heading, so there is no need to convert TC to MC.

1. To find the en route time from Allendale County (northeast of 1) to Claxton-Evans (southeast of 2), use Fig. 23.
2. Using the sectional scale located at the top of the chart, measure the distance to be 55 NM.
3. TC = 212°.
4. Mark up 18 kt. with 100° under true index.
5. Put TC of 212° under true index.
6. Slide the grid so the pencil mark is on TAS of 115 kt.
7. Read the groundspeed of 120 kt. under the grommet.
8. On the calculator side, place 120 kt. on the outer scale over 60 min.
9. Read 28 min. on the inner scale below 55 NM on the outer scale.
10. Add 2 min for climb-out and the en route time is 30 min.

Answer (A) is incorrect. The groundspeed is 120 kt., not 105 kt. Answer (B) is incorrect. The groundspeed is 120 kt., not 130 kt.

48. (Refer to Figure 23 on page 431.) What is the estimated time en route for a flight from Claxton-Evans County Airport (area 2) to Hampton Varnville Airport (area 1)? The wind is from 290° at 18 knots and the true airspeed is 85 knots. Add 2 minutes for climb-out.

A. 35 minutes.

B. 39 minutes.

C. 43 minutes.

Answer (B) is correct. *(PHAK Chap 16)*

DISCUSSION: Using the sectional scale located at the top of the chart, you will find the distance en route from Claxton-Evans (southwest of 2) to Hampton Varnville (east of 1 on Fig. 23) is approximately 57 NM. Use your plotter to determine that the TC is 045°. The requirement is time en route and not magnetic heading, so there is no need to convert TC to MC.

Using the wind side of your computer, turn your true index to the wind direction of 290° and mark 18 kt. above the grommet with your pencil. Then turn the inner scale so that the true index is above the TC of 045°. Place the pencil mark on the TAS of 85 kt. and note the groundspeed of 91 kt. Turn your flight computer over and set the speed of 91 kt. above the 60-min. index on the inner scale. Then find the distance of 57 NM on the outer scale to determine a time en route of 37 min. Add 2 min. for climb-out, and the en route time is 39 min.

Answer (A) is incorrect. You must add (not subtract) 2 min. for climb-out to the time en route. Answer (C) is incorrect. The groundspeed is 91 kt. (not 81 kt.).

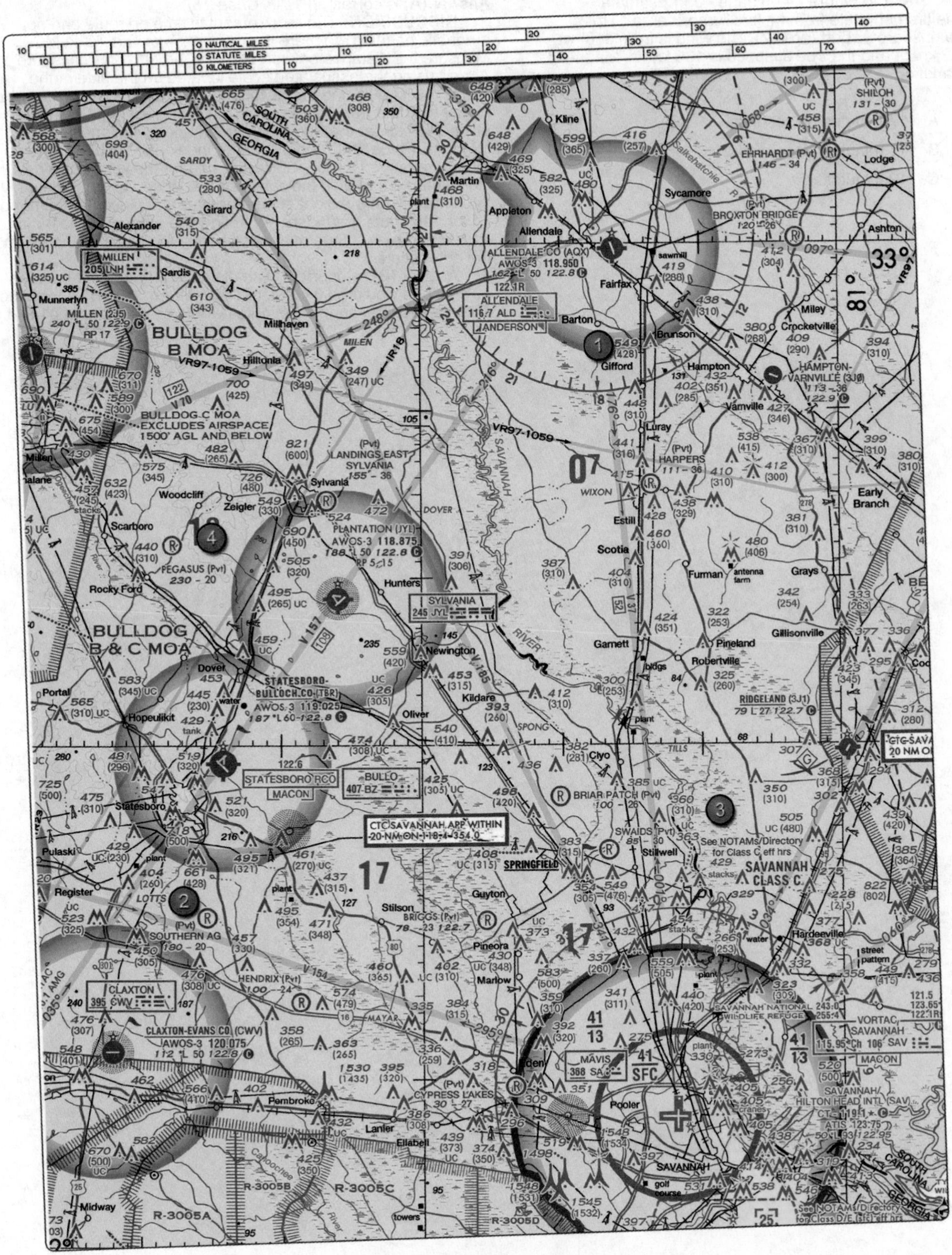

Figure 23. – Sectional Chart Excerpt.
NOTE: Chart is not to scale and should not be used for navigation. Use associated scale.

49. (Refer to Figure 24 on page 433.) Estimate the time en route from Majors Airport (area 1) to Winnsboro Airport (area 2). The wind is from 340° at 12 knots and the true airspeed is 136 knots. Magnetic variation is 5° east.

A. 17 minutes 30 seconds.

B. 14 minutes 30 seconds.

C. 19 minutes.

Answer (A) is correct. *(PHAK Chap 16)*

DISCUSSION: The requirement is time en route and not magnetic heading, so there is no need to convert TC to MC. Measure the distance between Majors Airport and Winnsboro Airport using the associated scale located on the side of the chart. You should find the distance to be about 41 NM. Use your plotter to find a true course of 100°. Using your flight computer, place 340° under the true index and mark a wind speed of 12 knots. Place 100° under the true index and slide the card so the true airspeed arc of 136 knots is under the wind dot. The flight computer should indicate a groundspeed of approximately 140 knots. Turn the flight computer over and place the pointer on 14 for 140 knots groundspeed. Follow the outer scale to 41 for 41 NM and read a time of approximately 17:30 below the 41 on the outer scale.

Answer (B) is incorrect. The distance requiring 14 minutes 30 seconds would be 34 NM, not 41 NM. Answer (C) is incorrect. The distance requiring 19 minutes would be 45 NM, not 41 NM.

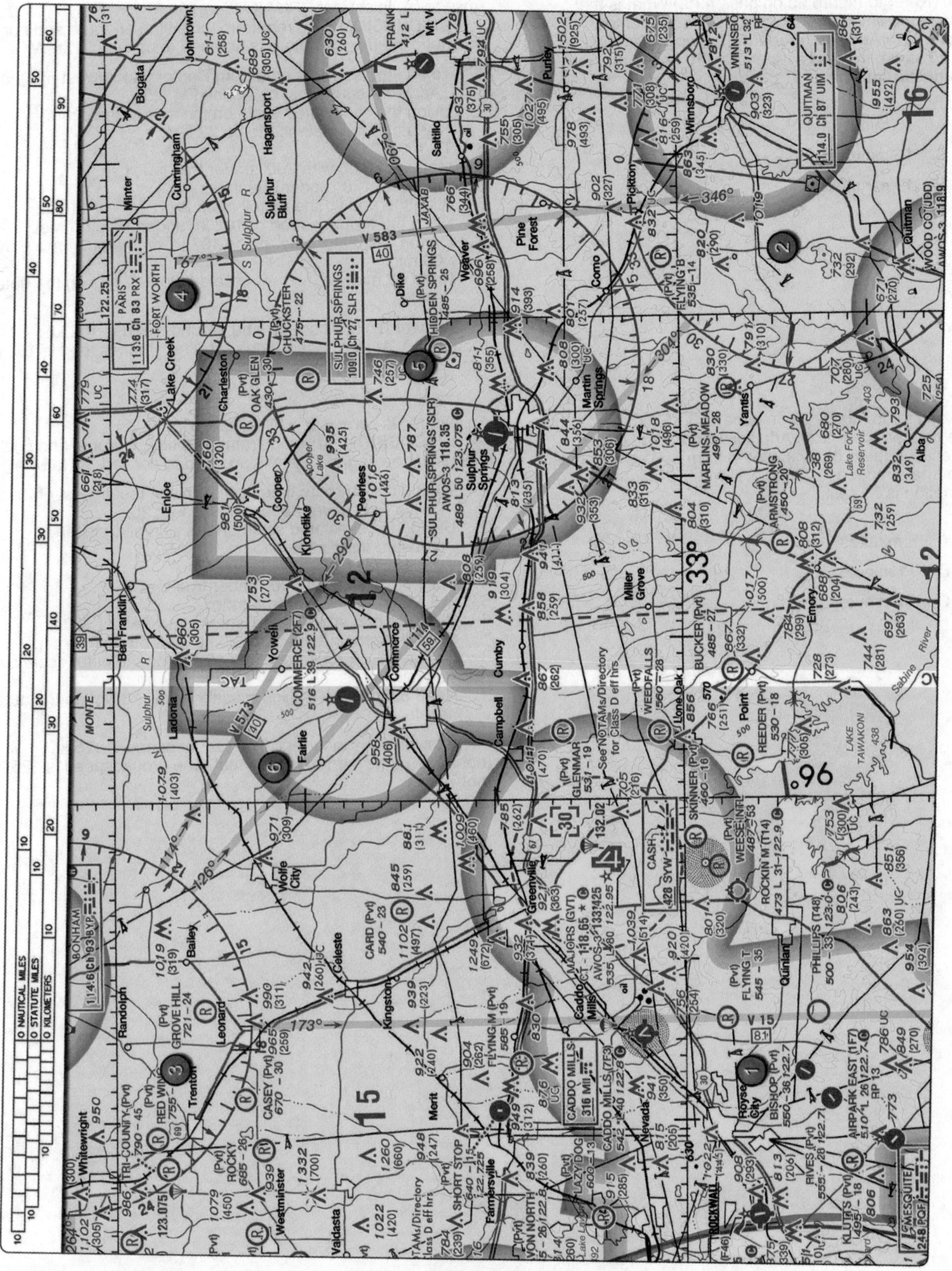

Figure 24. – Sectional Chart Excerpt.
NOTE: Chart is not to scale and should not be used for navigation. Use associated scale.

50. (Refer to Figure 25 on page 435.) What is the estimated time en route for a flight from Denton (area 1) to Addison (area 2)? The wind is from 200° at 20 knots, the true airspeed is 110 knots, and the magnetic variation is 7° east.

A. 13 minutes.

B. 16 minutes.

C. 19 minutes.

Answer (A) is correct. *(PHAK Chap 16)*

DISCUSSION: The requirement is time en route and not magnetic heading, so there is no need to convert TC to MC.

1. To find the en route time from Denton (southwest of 1) to Addison (southwest of 2), use Fig. 25.
2. Using the associated scale on the side of the chart, measure the distance to be 22 NM.
3. TC = 128°.
4. Mark up 20 kt. with 200° under true index.
5. Put TC of 128° under true index.
6. Slide the grid so the pencil mark is on TAS of 110 kt.
7. Read the groundspeed of 102 kt. under the grommet.
8. On the calculator side, place 102 kt. on the outer scale over 60 min.
9. Read 13 min. on the inner scale below 22 NM on the outer scale.

Answer (B) is incorrect. The groundspeed is 102 kt. (not 86 kt.). Answer (C) is incorrect. The groundspeed is 102 kt. (not 73 kt.).

51. (Refer to Figure 25 on page 435.) Estimate the time en route from Addison (area 2) to Dallas Executive (area 3). The wind is from 300° at 15 knots, the true airspeed is 120 knots, and the magnetic variation is 7° east.

A. 8 minutes.

B. 11 minutes.

C. 14 minutes.

Answer (A) is correct. *(PHAK Chap 16)*

DISCUSSION: The requirement is time en route and not magnetic heading, so there is no need to convert TC to MC.

1. To find the en route time from Addison (southwest of 2) to Dallas Executive (above 3), use Fig. 25.
2. Using the associated scale on the side of the chart, measure the distance to be 18 NM.
3. TC = 186°.
4. Mark up 15 kt. with 300° under true index.
5. Put TC of 186° under true index.
6. Slide the grid so the pencil mark is on TAS of 120 kt.
7. Read the groundspeed of 125 kt. under the grommet.
8. On the calculator side, place 125 kt. on the outer scale over 60 min.
9. Read 8.5 min. on the inner scale below 18 NM on the outer scale.

Answer (B) is incorrect. The groundspeed is 125 kt. (not 98 kt.). Answer (C) is incorrect. The groundspeed is 125 kt. (not 77 kt.).

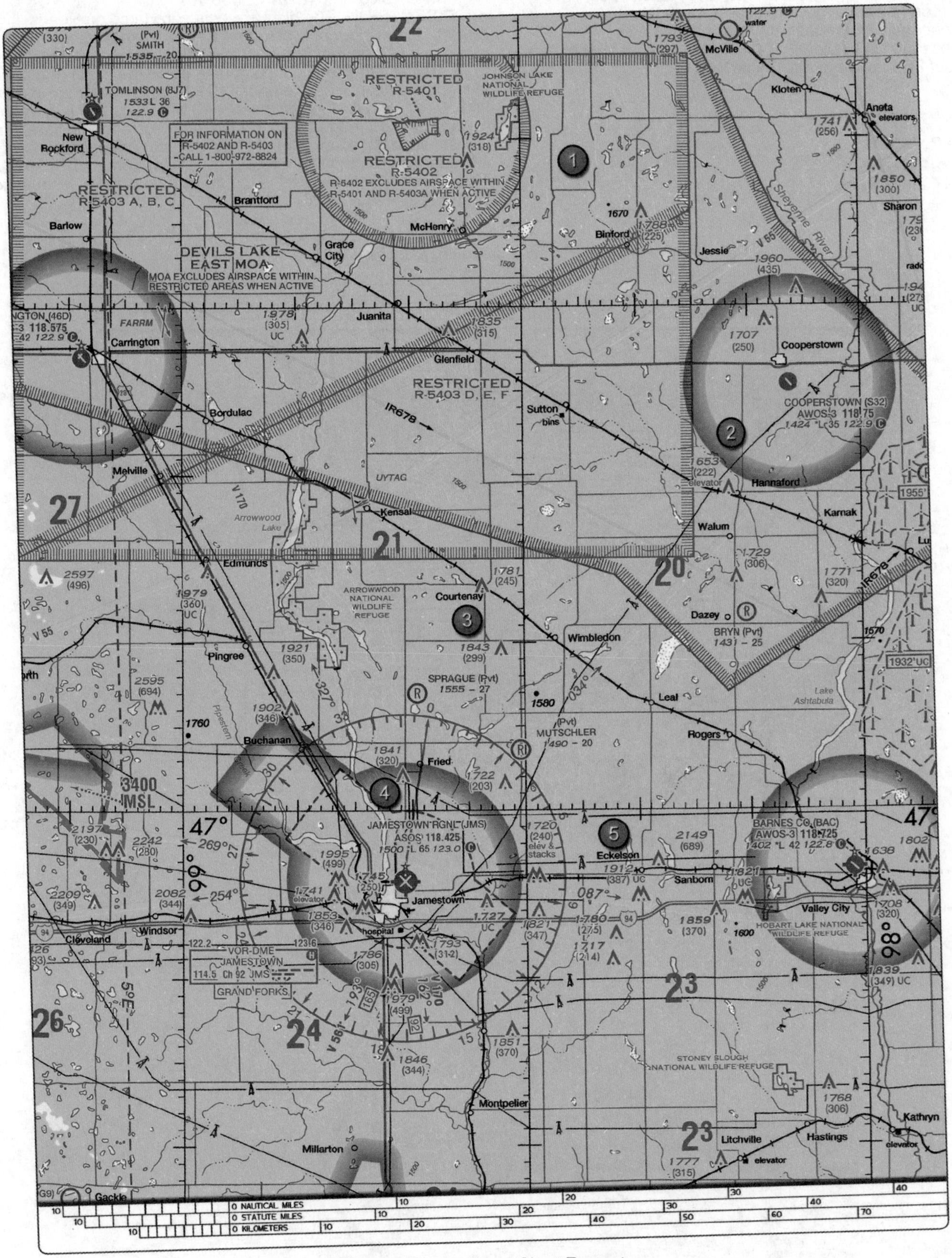

Figure 25. – Sectional Chart Excerpt.
NOTE: Chart is not to scale and should not be used for navigation. Use associated scale.

52. (Refer to Figure 20 below.) En route to First Flight Airport (area 5), your flight passes over Hampton Roads Airport (area 2) at 1456 and then over Chesapeake Regional at 1501. At what time should your flight arrive at First Flight?

A. 1516.

B. 1521.

C. 1526.

Answer (C) is correct. *(PHAK Chap 16)*

DISCUSSION: The distance between Hampton Roads Airport (about 2 in. north of 2) and Chesapeake Regional (northeast of 2 on Fig. 20) is 10 NM. It took 5 min. (1501 – 1456) to go 10 NM. On your flight computer, place the 5 min. the first leg took on the inner scale under 10 NM on the outer scale. Then find 50 NM (60 NM total distance – 10 NM of the first leg) on the outer scale and read 25 min. on the inner scale for the time from Chesapeake Regional to First Flight Airport. The distance from Chesapeake Regional to First Flight Airport (right of 5) is 50 NM. Twenty-five minutes added to the time you passed Chesapeake Regional (1501) is 1526.

Answer (A) is incorrect. At 2 NM per min., it will take 25 min., not 15 min., to reach first flight. Answer (B) is incorrect. The 25 min. must be added to 1501, not 1456.

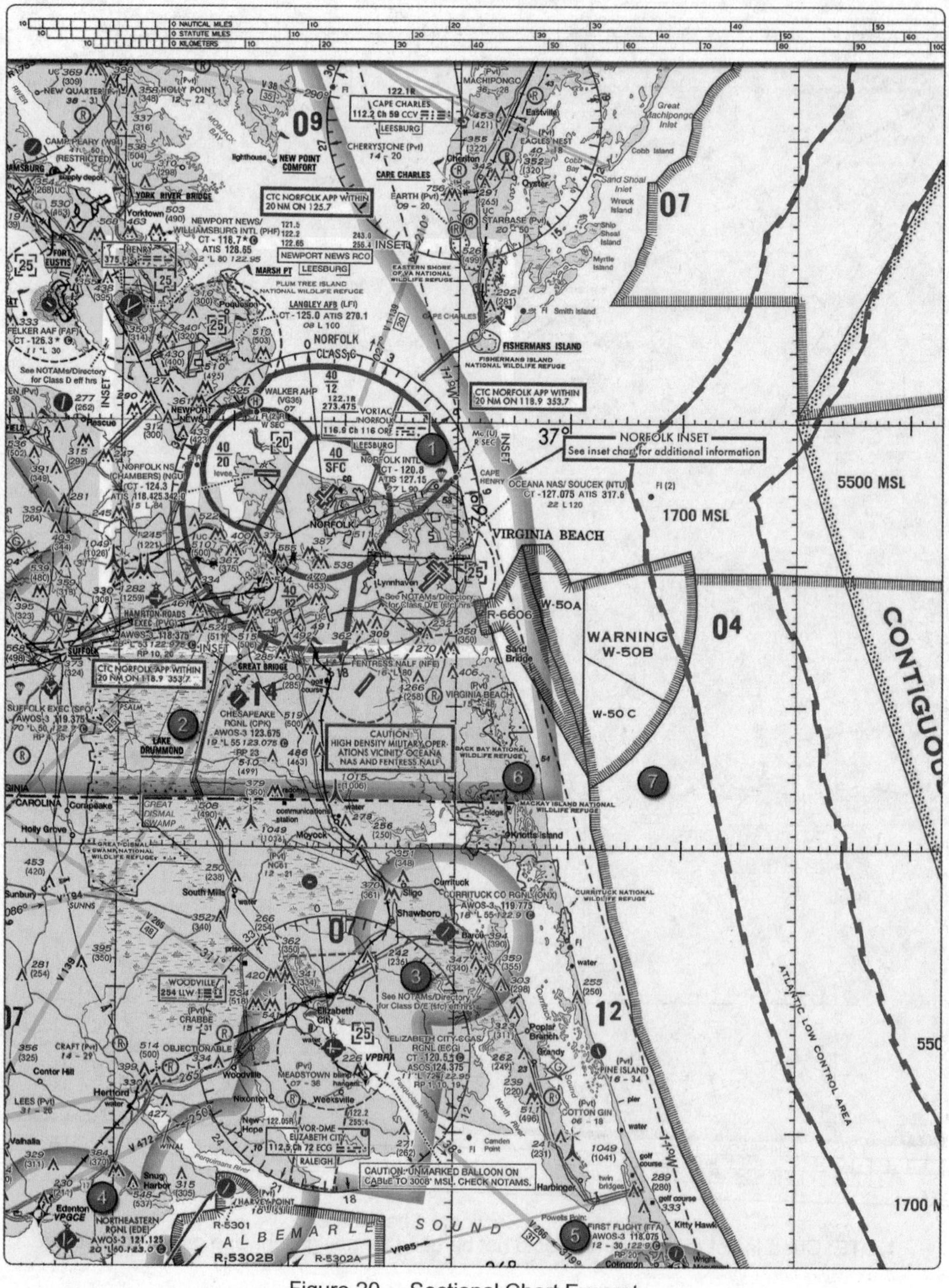

Figure 20. – Sectional Chart Excerpt.
NOTE: Chart is not to scale and should not be used for navigation. Use associated scale.

53. (Refer to Figure 68 below.) The line from point A to point B of the wind triangle represents

A. true heading and airspeed.
B. true course and groundspeed.
C. groundspeed and true heading.

Answer (A) is correct. *(PHAK Chap 16)*
DISCUSSION: The line connecting point A to point B on the wind triangle represents the true heading and airspeed line.
Answer (B) is incorrect. The line from point B to point C, not point A, represents the true course and groundspeed line. Answer (C) is incorrect. These are values obtained through using a wind triangle. Groundspeed is obtained by measuring the length of the TC line using the same scale as the chart (point B to point C). True heading is the direction, measured in degrees clockwise from true north, in which the nose of the plane should point to make good the desired course (point A to point B).

54. (Refer to Figure 68 below.) The line from point C to point B of the wind triangle represents

A. airspeed and heading.
B. groundspeed and true course.
C. true heading and groundspeed.

Answer (B) is correct. *(PHAK Chap 16)*
DISCUSSION: The line from point C to point B, on the wind triangle, represents the true course and groundspeed line.
Answer (A) is incorrect. The line from point A, not point C, to point B represents the true heading and airspeed line. Answer (C) is incorrect. These are values obtained through using a wind triangle. Groundspeed is obtained by measuring the length of the TC line using the same scale as the chart (point C to point B). True heading is the direction, measured in degrees clockwise from true north, in which the nose of the plane should point to make good the desired course (point A to point B).

55. (Refer to Figure 68 below.) The line from point C to point A of the wind triangle represents

A. wind direction and velocity.
B. true course and groundspeed.
C. true heading and groundspeed.

Answer (A) is correct. *(PHAK Chap 16)*
DISCUSSION: The line from point C to point A on the wind triangle represents the wind direction and velocity line.
Answer (B) is incorrect. The line from point C to point B, not point A, represents the true course and groundspeed line. Answer (C) is incorrect. These are values obtained through using a wind triangle. Groundspeed is obtained by measuring the length of the TC line using the same scale as the chart (point C to point B). True heading is the direction, measured in degrees clockwise from true north, in which the nose of the plane should point to make good the desired course (point A to point B).

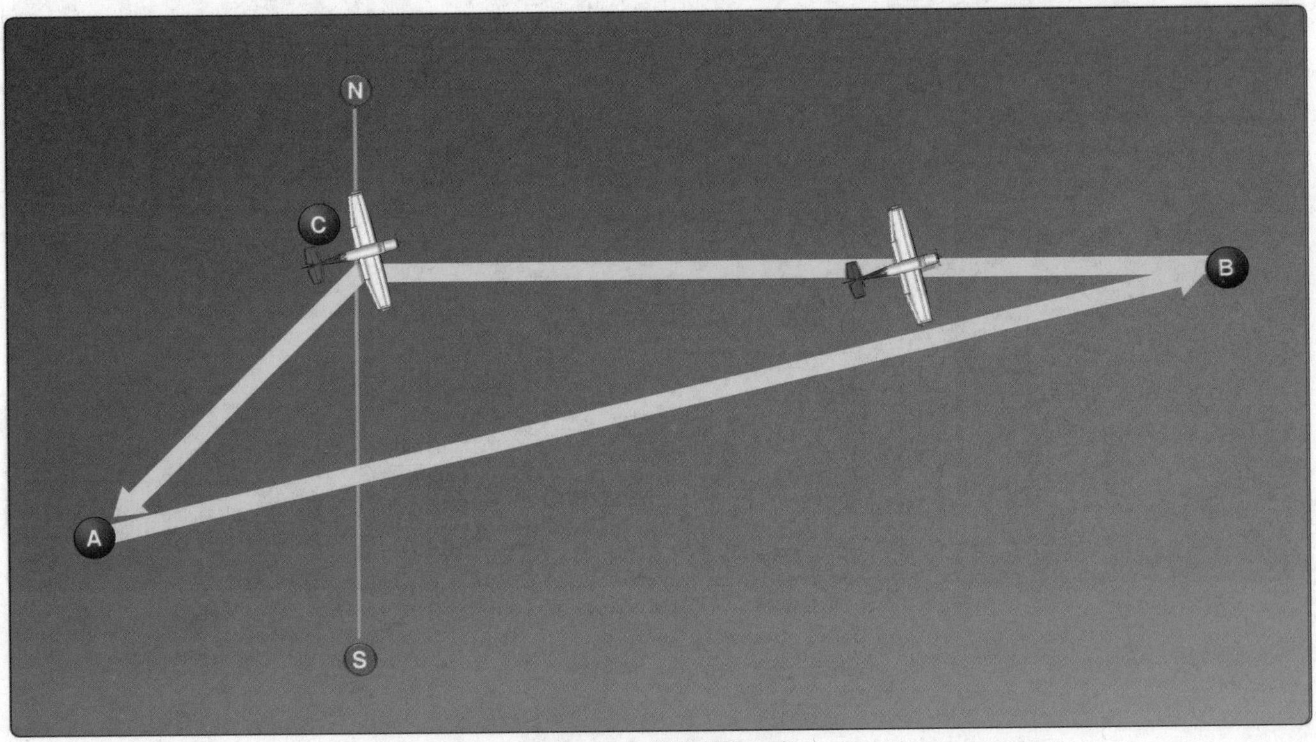

Figure 68. – Wind Triangle.

11.9 Time Zone Corrections

56. (Refer to Figure 27 below.) An aircraft departs an airport in the eastern daylight time zone at 0945 EDT for a 2-hour flight to an airport located in the central daylight time zone. The landing should be at what coordinated universal time?

A. 1345Z.

B. 1445Z.

C. 1545Z.

Answer (C) is correct. *(PHAK Chap 16)*

DISCUSSION: First convert the departure time to coordinated universal time (Z) by using the time conversion table in Fig. 27. To convert from eastern daylight time (EDT), add 4 hr. to get 1345Z (0945 + 4 hr). A 2-hr. flight would have you arriving at your destination airport at 1545Z.

Answer (A) is incorrect. This is the departure time.
Answer (B) is incorrect. You would arrive at an airport at 1445Z if the flight were 1 (not 2) hr.

57. (Refer to Figure 27 below.) An aircraft departs an airport in the Pacific standard time zone at 1030 PST for a 4-hour flight to an airport located in the central standard time zone. The landing should be at what coordinated universal time?

A. 2030Z.

B. 2130Z.

C. 2230Z.

Answer (C) is correct. *(PHAK Chap 16)*

DISCUSSION: First, convert the departure time to coordinated universal time (Z) by using the time conversion table in Fig. 27. To convert from PST to Z, you must add 8 hr.; thus, 1030 PST is 1830Z (1030 + 8 hr.). A 4-hr. flight would make the proposed landing time at 2230Z (1830 + 4 hr.).

Answer (A) is incorrect. This is for a flight of 2 (not 4) hr.
Answer (B) is incorrect. This is the proposed landing time if the departure time were 1030 PDT, not PST.

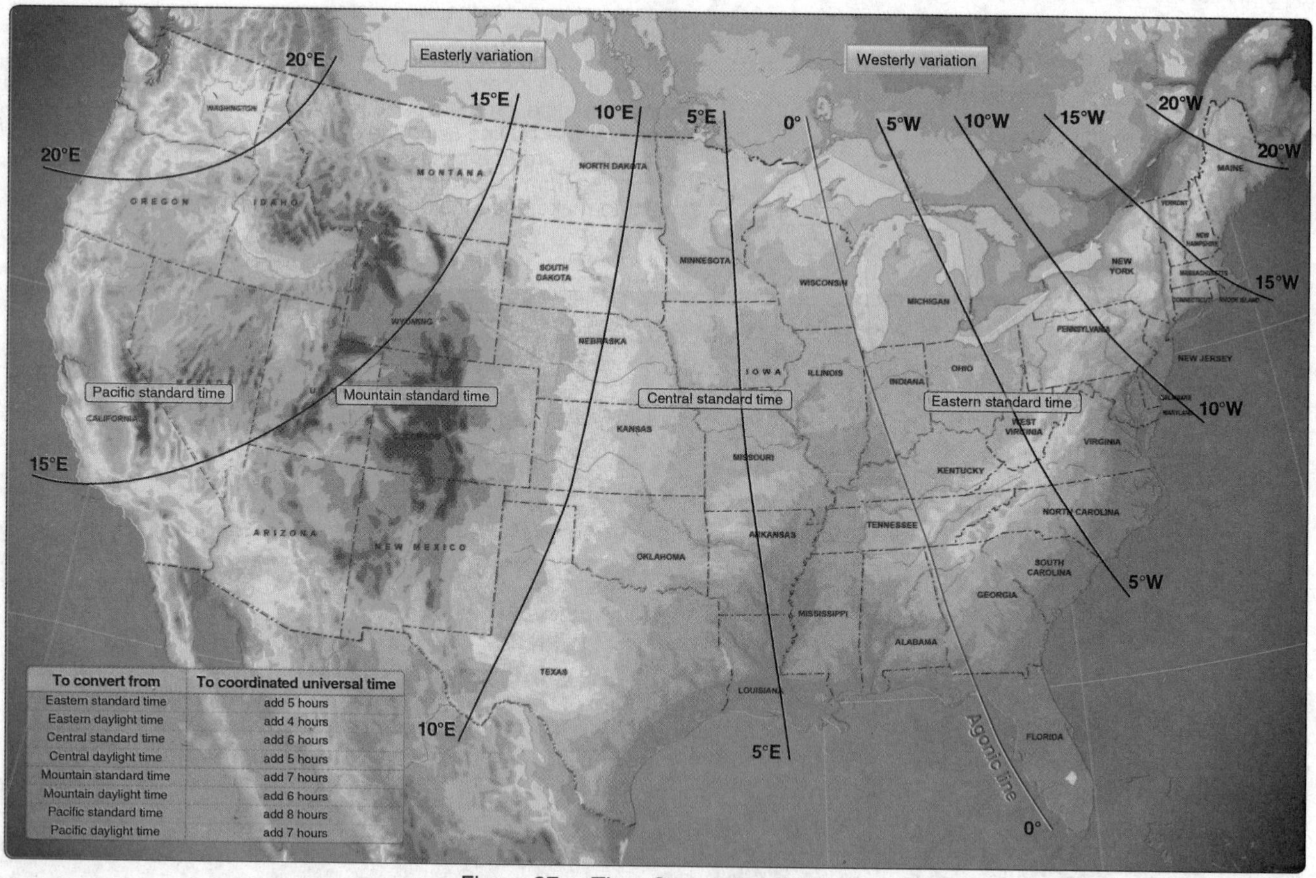

To convert from	To coordinated universal time
Eastern standard time	add 5 hours
Eastern daylight time	add 4 hours
Central standard time	add 6 hours
Central daylight time	add 5 hours
Mountain standard time	add 7 hours
Mountain daylight time	add 6 hours
Pacific standard time	add 8 hours
Pacific daylight time	add 7 hours

Figure 27. – Time Conversion Table.

58. (Refer to Figure 27 on page 438.) An aircraft departs an airport in the central standard time zone at 0930 CST for a 2-hour flight to an airport located in the mountain standard time zone. The landing should be at what time?

A. 0930 MST.

B. 1030 MST.

C. 1130 MST.

Answer (B) is correct. *(PHAK Chap 16)*

DISCUSSION: Flying from the Central Standard Time Zone to the Mountain Standard Time Zone results in a 1-hr. gain due to time zone changes. A 2-hr. flight leaving at 0930 CST will arrive in the Mountain Standard Time Zone at 1130 CST, which is 1030 MST.

Answer (A) is incorrect. The aircraft departed at 0930 CST (not MST). Answer (C) is incorrect. A landing at 1130 MST would be correct for a 3-hr. (not 2-hr.) flight departing from the CST zone at 0930 CST to the MST zone.

59. (Refer to Figure 27 on page 438.) An aircraft departs an airport in the central standard time zone at 0845 CST for a 2-hour flight to an airport located in the mountain standard time zone. The landing should be at what coordinated universal time?

A. 1345Z.

B. 1445Z.

C. 1645Z.

Answer (C) is correct. *(PHAK Chap 16)*

DISCUSSION: First convert the departure time to coordinated universal time (Z) by using the time conversion table in Fig. 27. To convert from CST to Z, you must add 6 hr. Thus, 0845 CST is 1445Z (0845 + 6 hr.). A 2-hr. flight would make the estimated landing time at 1645Z (1445 + 2 hr.).

Answer (A) is incorrect. This is the departure time at 0845 CDT, not CST. Answer (B) is incorrect. This is the departure (not landing) time.

60. (Refer to Figure 27 on page 438.) An aircraft departs an airport in the mountain standard time zone at 1615 MST for a 2-hour 15-minute flight to an airport located in the Pacific standard time zone. The estimated time of arrival at the destination airport should be

A. 1630 PST.

B. 1730 PST.

C. 1830 PST.

Answer (B) is correct. *(PHAK Chap 16)*

DISCUSSION: Departing the Mountain Standard Time Zone at 1615 MST for a 2-hr. 15-min. flight would result in arrival in the Pacific Standard Time Zone at 1830 MST. Because there is a 1-hr. difference between Mountain Standard Time and Pacific Standard Time, 1 hr. must be subtracted from the 1830 MST arrival to determine the 1730 PST arrival.

Answer (A) is incorrect. An arrival time of 1630 PST would be for a 1-hr. 15-min. (not a 2-hr. 15-min.) flight. Answer (C) is incorrect. The time of 1830 MST (not PST) is the estimated time of arrival at the destination airport.

61. (Refer to Figure 27 on page 438.) An aircraft departs an airport in the mountain standard time zone at 1515 MST for a 2-hour 30-minute flight to an airport located in the Pacific standard time zone. What is the estimated time of arrival at the destination airport?

A. 1645 PST.

B. 1745 PST.

C. 1845 PST.

Answer (A) is correct. *(PHAK Chap 16)*

DISCUSSION: Departing the Mountain Standard Time (MST) Zone at 1515 MST for a 2-hr. 30-min. flight would result in arrival in the Pacific Standard Time (PST) Zone at 1745 MST. Because there is a 1-hr. difference between MST and PST, 1 hr. must be subtracted from the 1745 MST arrival to determine the 1645 PST estimated time of arrival at the destination airport.

Answer (B) is incorrect. The estimated time of arrival at the destination airport is 1745 MST, not PST. Answer (C) is incorrect. This would be the estimated arrival time for a 3-hr. 30-min. (not 2-hr. 30-min.) flight from the MST zone.

11.10 Fundamentals of Flight

62. Select the four flight fundamentals involved in maneuvering an aircraft.

A. Aircraft power, pitch, bank, and trim.

B. Starting, taxiing, takeoff, and landing.

C. Straight-and-level flight, turns, climbs, and descents.

Answer (C) is correct. *(AFH Chap 3)*

DISCUSSION: Maneuvering an airplane is generally divided into four flight fundamentals: straight-and-level flight, turns, climbs, and descents. All controlled flight consists of one or a combination of more than one of these basic maneuvers.

Answer (A) is incorrect. It lists variable factors necessary for the performance of the flight fundamentals. Answer (B) is incorrect. It lists a combination of basic maneuvers, not flight fundamentals.

11.11 Rectangular Course

63. (Refer to Figure 62 below.) In flying the rectangular course, when would the aircraft be turned less than 90°?

A. Corners 1 and 4.

B. Corners 1 and 2.

C. Corners 2 and 4.

Answer (A) is correct. *(AFH Chap 6)*

DISCUSSION: When doing a rectangular course, think in terms of traffic pattern descriptions of the various legs. In Fig. 62, note that the airplane is going counterclockwise about the rectangular pattern. While on the base leg (between corners 3 and 4), the airplane is crabbed to the inside of the course. Thus, on corner 4, less than a 90° turn is required. Similarly, when the airplane proceeds through corner 1, it should roll out such that it is crabbed into the wind, and, again, a less-than-90° angle is required.

Answer (B) is incorrect. On corner 2, you would have to turn more than 90° (you must roll out of your crab angle plus 90° to be heading downwind). Answer (C) is incorrect. Corner 2 is more than 90° (you start with the airplane crabbed to the outside of the rectangular course).

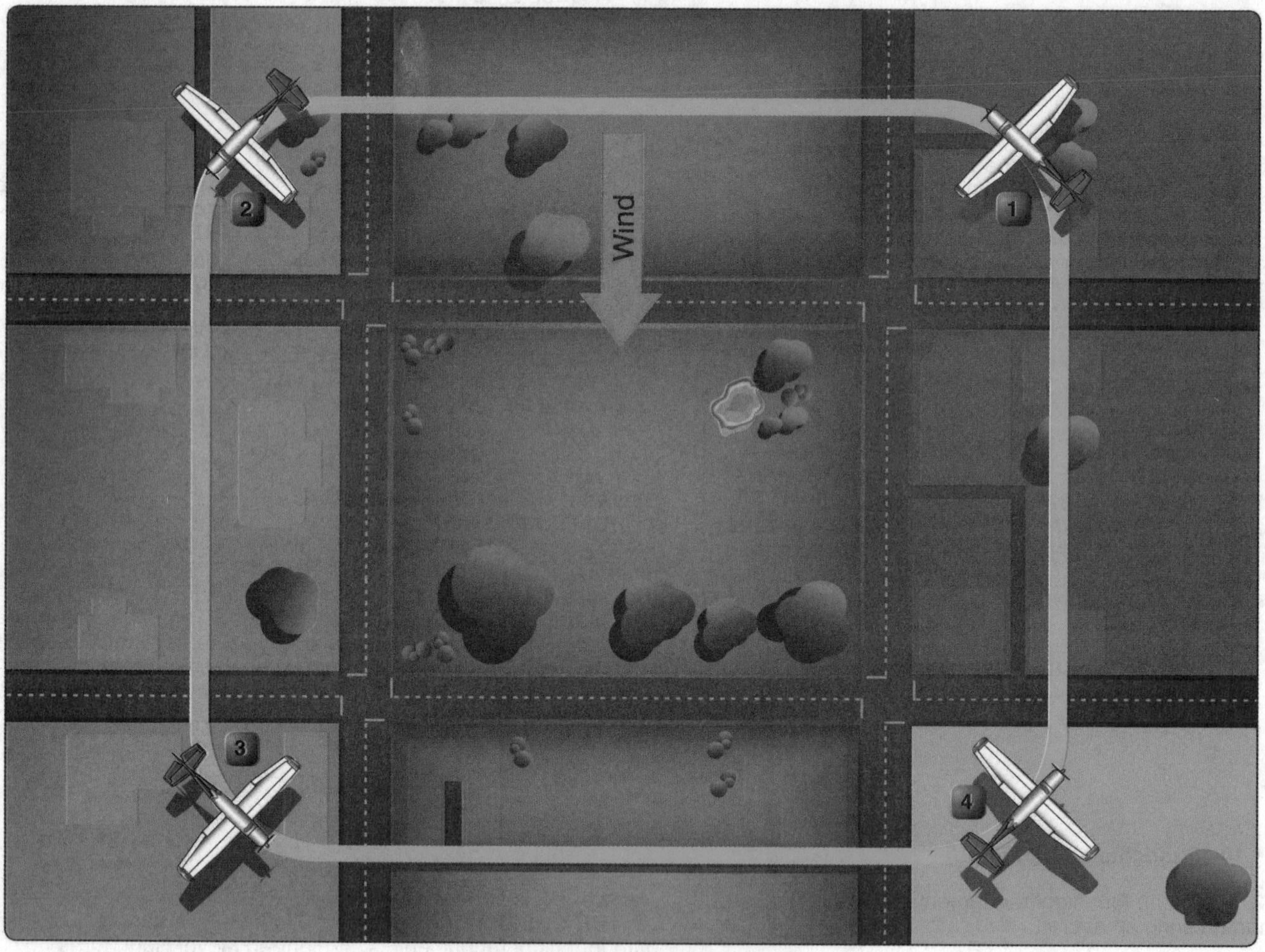

Figure 62. – Rectangular Course.

64. (Refer to Figure 62 above.) In flying the rectangular course, when should the aircraft bank vary from a steep bank to a medium bank?

A. Corner 1.

B. Corner 3.

C. Corner 2 and 3.

Answer (B) is correct. *(AFH Chap 6)*

DISCUSSION: When flying a rectangular course, imagine that the course is a traffic pattern at an airport. On the downwind leg, the wind is a tailwind and results in an increased groundspeed. Accordingly, the turn on the next leg requires a fast roll-in with a steep bank. When the tailwind component diminishes, the bank angle is reduced.

Answer (A) is incorrect. Corner 1 requires a turn that varies from shallow to medium. Answer (C) is incorrect. Corner 2 requires a turn that varies from medium to steep.

11.12 S-Turns across a Road

65. (Refer to Figure 66 below.) While practicing S-turns, a consistently smaller half-circle is made on one side of the road than on the other, and this turn is not completed before crossing the road or reference line. This would most likely occur in turn

A. 1-2-3 because the bank is decreased too rapidly during the latter part of the turn.

B. 4-5-6 because the bank is increased too rapidly during the early part of the turn.

C. 4-5-6 because the bank is increased too slowly during the latter part of the turn.

Answer (B) is correct. *(AFH Chap 6)*

DISCUSSION: Note that the wind in Fig. 66 is coming up from the bottom rather than from the top as in Fig. 62. The consistently smaller half-circle is made when on the upwind side of the road, i.e., 4-5-6. The initial bank is increased too rapidly, resulting in a smaller half-circle. Then an attempt is made to widen the turn out in the latter stages. Thus, the recrossing of the road is done at less than a 90° angle.

Answer (A) is incorrect. Decreasing the bank too rapidly in the latter stages of 1, 2, and 3 on the downwind side of the road increases, not decreases, the size of that half-circle. Answer (C) is incorrect. Increasing the bank too slowly at the latter stages of 4, 5, and 6 would make the half-circle larger, not smaller.

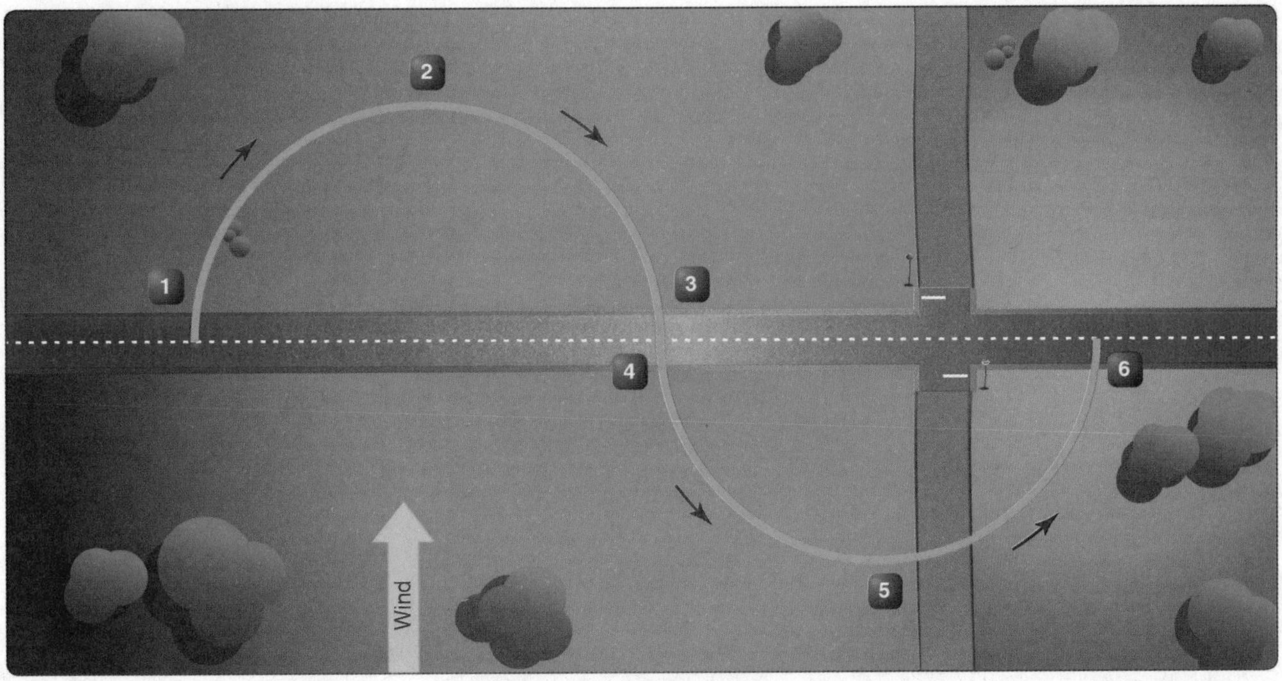

Figure 66. – S-Turn Diagram.

11.13 Landings

66. To minimize the side loads placed on the landing gear during touchdown, the pilot should keep the

A. direction of motion of the aircraft parallel to the runway.

B. longitudinal axis of the aircraft parallel to the direction of its motion.

C. downwind wing lowered sufficiently to eliminate the tendency for the aircraft to drift.

Answer (B) is correct. *(AFH Chap 8)*

DISCUSSION: At touchdown when landing, the longitudinal axis of the airplane should be parallel to the direction of its motion, i.e., no side loads to stress the landing gear.

Answer (A) is incorrect. It is important that the longitudinal axis also parallels the runway to avoid side loads on the landing gear. Answer (C) is incorrect. The upwind wing, not the downwind wing, needs to be lowered.

END OF STUDY UNIT

APPENDIX A
PRIVATE PILOT PRACTICE TEST

The following 60 questions have been randomly selected from the airplane questions in our private pilot test bank. You will be referred to figures (charts, tables, etc.) throughout this book. Be careful not to consult the answers or answer explanations when you look for and at the figures. Topical coverage in this practice test is similar to that of the FAA pilot knowledge test. Use the correct answer listing on page 448 to grade your practice test.

NOTE: Our **FAA Test Prep Online** provides unlimited Study and Test Sessions for your personal use. See the discussion on pages 17 through 18 in the introduction of this book.

1. (Refer to Figure 8 on page 193.) What is the effect of a temperature increase from 25 to 50° F on the density altitude if the pressure altitude remains at 5,000 feet?

A — 1,200-foot increase.
B — 1,400-foot increase.
C — 1,650-foot increase.

2. (Refer to Figure 40 on page 194.) Determine the total distance required for takeoff to clear a 50-foot obstacle.

OAT	Std
Pressure altitude	4,000 ft
Takeoff weight	2,800 lb
Headwind component	Calm

A — 1,500 feet.
B — 1,750 feet.
C — 2,000 feet.

3. (Refer to Figure 24 on page 417.) Determine the magnetic course from Airpark East Airport (area 1) to Winnsboro Airport (area 2). Magnetic variation is 6°30'E.

A — 075°.
B — 082°.
C — 091°.

4. (Refer to Figure 36 on page 198.) With a reported wind of south at 20 knots, which runway is appropriate for an airplane with a 13-knot maximum crosswind component?

A — Runway 10.
B — Runway 14.
C — Runway 24.

5. If an aircraft is loaded 90 pounds over maximum certificated gross weight and fuel (gasoline) is drained to bring the aircraft weight within limits, how much fuel should be drained?

A — 10 gallons.
B — 12 gallons.
C — 15 gallons.

6. (Refer to Figure 32 on page 223 and Figure 33 on page 223.) Which action can adjust the airplane's weight to maximum gross weight and the CG within limits for takeoff?

Front seat occupants	425 lb
Rear seat occupants	300 lb
Fuel, main tanks	44 gal

A — Drain 12 gallons of fuel.
B — Drain 9 gallons of fuel.
C — Transfer 12 gallons of fuel from the main tanks to the auxiliary tanks.

7. What is true altitude?

A — The vertical distance of the aircraft above sea level.
B — The vertical distance of the aircraft above the surface.
C — The height above the standard datum plane.

8. (Refer to Figure 25 on page 323.) (Refer to area 4.) The airspace directly overlying Fort Worth Meacham is

A — Class B airspace to 10,000 feet MSL.
B — Class C airspace to 5,000 feet MSL.
C — Class D airspace to 3,200 feet MSL.

9. (Refer to Figure 12 on page 263.) Which of the reporting stations have VFR weather?

A — All.
B — KINK, KBOI, and KJFK.
C — KINK, KBOI, and KLAX.

10. (Refer to Figure 14 on page 264.) If the terrain elevation is 1,295 feet MSL, what is the height above ground level of the base of the ceiling?

A — 505 feet AGL.
B — 1,295 feet AGL.
C — 6,586 feet AGL.

11. (Refer to Figure 20 on page 313.) (Refer to area 3.) Determine the approximate latitude and longitude of Currituck County Airport.

A — 36°24'N – 76°01'W.
B — 36°48'N – 76°01'W.
C — 47°24'N – 75°58'W.

12. (Refer to Figure 25 on page 323.) (Refer to area 2.) The floor of Class B airspace at Addison Airport is

A — at the surface.
B — 3,000 feet MSL.
C — 3,100 feet MSL.

13. (Refer to Figure 23 on page 345.) (Refer to area 3.) What is the height of the lighted obstacle approximately 6 nautical miles southwest of Savannah International?

A — 1,498 feet MSL.
B — 1,531 feet AGL.
C — 1,548 feet MSL.

14. (Refer to Figure 25 on page 353.) (Refer to area 2.) The control tower frequency for Addison Airport is

A — 122.95 MHz.
B — 126.0 MHz.
C — 133.4 MHz.

15. (Refer to Figure 26 on page 355.) (Refer to area 2.) What is the recommended communication procedure when inbound to land at Cooperstown Airport?

A — Broadcast intentions when 10 miles out on the CTAF/MULTICOM frequency, 122.9 MHz.
B — Contact UNICOM when 10 miles out on 122.8 MHz.
C — Circle the airport in a left turn prior to entering traffic.

16. (Refer to Figure 15 on page 269.) The only cloud type forecast in TAF reports is

A — Nimbostratus.
B — Cumulonimbus.
C — Scattered cumulus.

17. (Refer to Figure 4 on page 48.) What is the full flap operating range for the airplane?

A — 55 to 100 kts.
B — 55 to 208 kts.
C — 55 to 165 kts.

18. (Refer to Figure 28 on page 386.) (Refer to illustration 3.) The VOR receiver has the indications shown. What is the aircraft's position relative to the station?

A — East.
B — Southeast.
C — West.

19. (Refer to Figure 24 on page 387.) What is the approximate position of the aircraft if the VOR receivers indicate the 245° radial of Sulphur Springs VOR-DME (area 5) and the 140° radial of Bonham VORTAC (area 3)?

A — Glenmar Airport.
B — Caddo Mills Airport.
C — Majors Airport.

20. What is the one common factor which affects most preventable accidents?

A — Structural failure.
B — Mechanical malfunction.
C — Human error.

21. (Refer to Figure 9 on page 406) (Refer to area C.) How should the flight controls be held while taxiing a tailwheel airplane with a left quartering tailwind?

A — Left aileron up, elevator neutral.
B — Left aileron down, elevator neutral.
C — Left aileron down, elevator down.

22. Detonation occurs in a reciprocating aircraft engine when

A — the spark plugs are fouled or shorted out or the wiring is defective.
B — hot spots in the combustion chamber ignite the fuel/air mixture in advance of normal ignition.
C — the unburned charge in the cylinders explodes instead of burning normally.

23. During a night flight, you observe a steady red light and a flashing red light ahead and at the same altitude. What is the general direction of movement of the other aircraft?

A — The other aircraft is crossing to the left.
B — The other aircraft is crossing to the right.
C — The other aircraft is approaching head-on.

24. What is the effect of advancing the throttle in flight?

A — Both aircraft groundspeed and angle of attack will increase.
B — Airspeed will remain relatively constant but the aircraft will climb.
C — The aircraft will accelerate, which will cause a turn to the right.

25. (Refer to Figure 47 on page 92.) Illustration A indicates that the aircraft is

A — below the glide slope.
B — on the glide slope.
C — above the glide slope.

26. Prior to entering an Airport Advisory Area, a pilot should

A — monitor ATIS for weather and traffic advisories.
B — contact approach control for vectors to the traffic pattern.
C — contact the local FSS for airport and traffic advisories.

27. What ATC facility should the pilot contact to receive a special VFR departure clearance in Class D airspace?

A — Automated Flight Service Station.
B — Air Traffic Control Tower.
C — Air Route Traffic Control Center.

28. During operations within controlled airspace at altitudes of less than 1,200 feet AGL, the minimum horizontal distance from clouds requirement for VFR flight is

A — 1,000 feet.
B — 1,500 feet.
C — 2,000 feet.

29. Which condition would cause the altimeter to indicate a lower altitude than true altitude?

A — Air temperature lower than standard.
B — Atmospheric pressure lower than standard.
C — Air temperature warmer than standard.

30. Which condition is most favorable to the development of carburetor icing?

A — Any temperature below freezing and a relative humidity of less than 50 percent.
B — Temperature between 32°F and 50°F and low humidity.
C — Temperature between 20°F and 70°F and high humidity.

31. Prior to starting each maneuver, pilots should

A — check altitude, airspeed, and heading indications.
B — visually scan the entire area for collision avoidance.
C — announce their intentions on the nearest CTAF.

32. (Refer to Figure 25 on page 423.) Determine the magnetic heading for a flight from Fort Worth Meacham (area 4) to Denton Muni (area 1). The wind is from 330° at 25 knots, the true airspeed is 110 knots, and the magnetic variation is 7°E.

A — 003°.
B — 017°.
C — 023°.

33. What determines the longitudinal stability of an airplane?

A — The location of the CG with respect to the center of lift.
B — The effectiveness of the horizontal stabilizer, rudder, and rudder trim tab.
C — The relationship of thrust and lift to weight and drag.

34. In the Northern Hemisphere, the magnetic compass will normally indicate a turn toward the south when

A — a left turn is entered from an east heading.
B — a right turn is entered from a west heading.
C — the aircraft is decelerated while on a west heading.

35. VFR approaches to land at night should be accomplished

A — at a higher airspeed.
B — with a steeper descent.
C — the same as during daytime.

36. Each pilot of an aircraft approaching to land on a runway served by a visual approach slope indicator (VASI) shall

A — maintain a 3° glide to the runway.
B — maintain an altitude at or above the glide slope.
C — stay high until the runway can be reached in a power-off landing.

37. When are the four forces that act on an airplane in equilibrium?

A — During unaccelerated level flight.
B — When the aircraft is accelerating.
C — When the aircraft is at rest on the ground.

38. What is an important airspeed limitation that is not color coded on airspeed indicators?

A — Never-exceed speed.
B — Maximum structural cruising speed.
C — Maneuvering speed.

39. Which in-flight advisory would contain information on severe icing not associated with thunderstorms?

A — Convective SIGMET.
B — SIGMET.
C — AIRMET.

40. The presence of ice pellets at the surface is evidence that there

A — are thunderstorms in the area.
B — has been cold frontal passage.
C — is a temperature inversion with freezing rain at a higher altitude.

41. Which statement best defines hypoxia?

A — A state of oxygen deficiency in the body.
B — An abnormal increase in the volume of air breathed.
C — A condition of gas bubble formation around the joints or muscles.

42. If the pitot tube and outside static vents become clogged, which instruments would be affected?

A — The altimeter, airspeed indicator, and turn-and-slip indicator.
B — The altimeter, airspeed indicator, and vertical speed indicator.
C — The altimeter, attitude indicator, and turn-and-slip indicator.

43. What action can a pilot take to aid in cooling an engine that is overheating during a climb?

A — Reduce rate of climb and increase airspeed.
B — Reduce climb speed and increase RPM.
C — Increase climb speed and increase RPM.

44. Which incident requires an immediate notification be made to the nearest NTSB field office?

A — An overdue aircraft that is believed to be involved in an accident.
B — An in-flight radio communications failure.
C — An in-flight generator or alternator failure.

45. With respect to the certification of airmen, which are categories of aircraft?

A — Gyroplane, helicopter, airship, free balloon.
B — Airplane, rotorcraft, glider, lighter-than-air.
C — Single-engine land and sea, multiengine land and sea.

46. A 100-hour inspection was due at 3302.5 hours. The 100-hour inspection was actually done at 3309.5 hours. When is the next 100-hour inspection due?

A — 3312.5 hours.
B — 3402.5 hours.
C — 3395.5 hours.

47. Prior to takeoff, the altimeter should be set to which altitude or altimeter setting?

A — The current local altimeter setting, if available, or the departure airport elevation.
B — The corrected density altitude of the departure airport.
C — The corrected pressure altitude for the departure airport.

48. When must a current pilot certificate be in the pilot's personal possession or readily accessible in the aircraft?

A — When acting as a crew chief during launch and recovery.
B — Only when passengers are carried.
C — Anytime when acting as pilot in command or as a required crewmember.

49. An airplane and an airship are converging. If the airship is left of the airplane's position, which aircraft has the right-of-way?

A — The airship.
B — The airplane.
C — Each pilot should alter course to the right.

50. Unless each occupant is provided with supplemental oxygen, no person may operate a civil aircraft of U.S. registry above a maximum cabin pressure altitude of

A — 12,500 feet MSL.
B — 14,000 feet MSL.
C — 15,000 feet MSL.

51. The three takeoffs and landings that are required to act as pilot in command at night must be done during the time period from

A — sunset to sunrise.
B — 1 hour after sunset to 1 hour before sunrise.
C — the end of evening civil twilight to the beginning of morning civil twilight.

52. In regard to privileges and limitations, a private pilot may

A — act as pilot in command of an aircraft carrying a passenger for compensation if the flight is in connection with a business or employment.
B — not pay less than the pro rata share of the operating expenses of a flight with passengers provided the expenses involve only fuel, oil, airport expenditures, or rental fees.
C — not be paid in any manner for the operating expenses of a flight.

53. Under what condition, if any, may a pilot allow a person who is obviously under the influence of drugs to be carried aboard an aircraft?

A — In an emergency or if the person is a medical patient under proper care.
B — Only if the person does not have access to the cockpit or pilot's compartment.
C — Under no condition.

54. What is one purpose of wing flaps?

A — To enable the pilot to make steeper approaches to a landing without increasing the airspeed.
B — To relieve the pilot of maintaining continuous pressure on the controls.
C — To decrease wing area to vary the lift.

55. Thunderstorms reach their greatest intensity during the

A — mature stage.
B — downdraft stage.
C — cumulus stage.

56. Where can locations for VOR test facilities be found?

A — *Aeronautical Information Manual.*
B — Sectional charts.
C — Chart Supplement.

57. A stable air mass is most likely to have which characteristic?

A — Showery precipitation.
B — Turbulent air.
C — Poor surface visibility.

58. Every physical process of weather is accompanied by, or is the result of, a

A — movement of air.
B — pressure differential.
C — heat exchange.

59. Convective circulation patterns associated with sea breezes are caused by

A — warm, dense air moving inland from over the water.
B — water absorbing and radiating heat faster than the land.
C — cool, dense air moving inland from over the water.

60. Where does wind shear occur?

A — Only at higher altitudes.
B — Only at lower altitudes.
C — At all altitudes, in all directions.

PRACTICE TEST LIST OF ANSWERS

Listed below are the answers to the practice test. To the immediate right of each answer is the page number on which the question, as well as correct and incorrect answer explanations, can be found.

Q. #	Answer	Page	Q. #	Answer	Page	Q. #	Answer	Page	Q. #	Answer	Page
1.	C	192	16.	B	269	31.	B	97	46.	B	168
2.	B	195	17.	A	48	32.	A	422	47.	A	153
3.	A	416	18.	B	388	33.	A	32	48.	C	130
4.	B	199	19.	A	387	34.	C	46	49.	A	150
5.	C	203	20.	C	234	35.	C	405	50.	C	164
6.	B	222	21.	C	406	36.	B	93	51.	B	135
7.	A	53	22.	C	63	37.	A	27	52.	B	137
8.	C	322	23.	A	96	38.	C	50	53.	A	147
9.	C	262	24.	A	33	39.	B	276	54.	A	25
10.	A	264	25.	B	92	40.	C	243	55.	A	241
11.	A	312	26.	C	100	41.	A	228	56.	C	382
12.	B	322	27.	B	161	42.	B	47	57.	C	248
13.	C	344	28.	C	161	43.	A	59	58.	C	239
14.	B	352	29.	C	55	44.	A	171	59.	C	240
15.	A	354	30.	C	60	45.	B	126	60.	C	244

APPENDIX B
INTERPOLATION

The following is a tutorial based on information that has appeared in the FAA's *Pilot's Handbook of Aeronautical Knowledge*. Interpolation is required in questions found in the following two subunits:

Study Unit 5 - "Airplane Performance and Weight and Balance"
Subunit 5.2, "Density Altitude Computations" (pages 174, 190)
Subunit 5.4, "Cruise Power Settings" (pages 177, 196)

A. To interpolate means to compute intermediate values between a series of given values.

1. In many instances when performance is critical, an accurate determination of the performance values is the only acceptable means to enhance safe flight.
2. Guessing to determine these values should be avoided.

B. Interpolation is simple to perform if the method is understood. The following are examples of how to interpolate, or accurately determine the intermediate values, between a series of given values.

C. The numbers in column A range from 10 to 30, and the numbers in column B range from 50 to 100. Determine the intermediate numerical value in column B that would correspond with an intermediate value of 20 placed in column A.

A	B
10	50
20	X = Unknown
30	100

1. It can be visualized that 20 is halfway between 10 and 30; therefore, the corresponding value of the unknown number in column B would be halfway between 50 and 100, or 75.

D. Many interpolation problems are more difficult to visualize than the preceding example; therefore, a systematic method must be used to determine the required intermediate value. The following describes one method that can be used.

1. The numbers in column A range from 10 to 30 with intermediate values of 15, 20, and 25. Determine the intermediate numerical value in column B that would correspond with 15 in column A.

A	B
10	50
15	
20	
25	
30	100

2. First, in column A, determine the relationship of 15 to the range between 10 and 30 as follows:

$$\frac{15-10}{30-10} = \frac{5}{20} \text{ or } 1/4$$

a. It should be noted that 15 is 1/4 of the range between 10 and 30.

3. Now determine 1/4 of the range of column B between 50 and 100 as follows:

$$100 - 50 = 50$$
$$1/4 \text{ of } 50 = 12.5$$

   a. The answer 12.5 represents the number of units, but to arrive at the correct value, 12.5 must be added to the lower number in column B as follows:

$$50 + 12.5 = 62.5$$

4. The interpolation has been completed and 62.5 is the actual value which is 1/4 of the range of column B.

E. Another method of interpolation is shown below:

1. Using the same numbers as in the previous example, a proportion problem based on the relationship of the number can be set up.

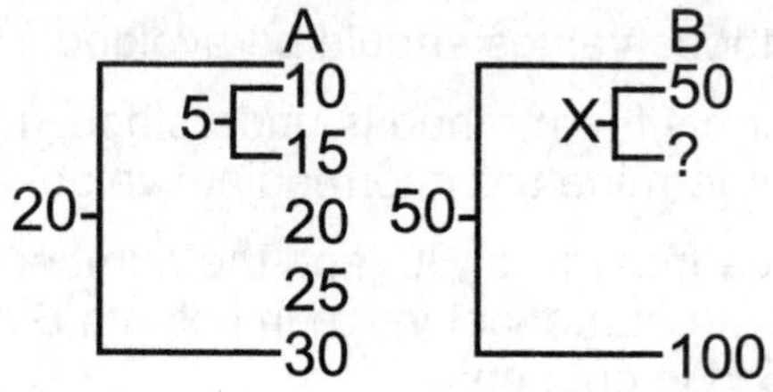

$$\text{Proportion:}\quad \frac{5}{20} = \frac{X}{50}$$
$$20X = 250$$
$$X = 12.5$$

   a. The answer, 12.5, must be added to 50 to arrive at the actual value of 62.5.

F. The following example illustrates the use of interpolation applied to a problem dealing with one aspect of airplane performance:

Temperature (°F)	Takeoff Distance (ft.)
70	1,173
80	1,356

1. If a distance of 1,173 feet is required for takeoff when the temperature is 70°F and 1,356 feet is required at 80°F, what distance is required when the temperature is 75°F? The solution to the problem can be determined as follows:

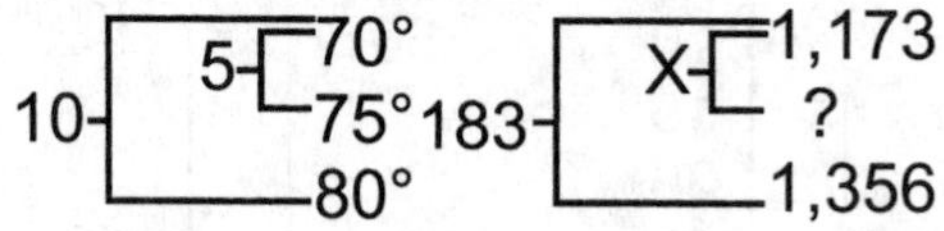

$$\frac{5}{10} = \frac{X}{183}$$
$$10X = 915$$
$$X = 91.5$$

   a. The answer, 91.5, must be added to 1,173 to arrive at the actual value of 1,264.5 ft.

FAA LISTING OF LEARNING STATEMENT CODES

Reprinted below and on the following pages are all of the FAA's learning statement codes for pilots. These are the codes that will appear on your Airman Computer Test Report. See the example on page 14. Your test report will list the learning statement code of each question answered incorrectly. The statements are designed to represent the knowledge test topic areas in clear verbal terms and encourage applicants to study the entire area of identified weakness instead of merely studying a specific question area. You should discuss your test results with your CFI.

When you receive your Airman Computer Test Report, you can trace the learning statement codes listed on it to these pages to find out which topics you had difficulty with. To determine the knowledge area in which a particular question was incorrectly answered, compare the learning statement code(s) on your Airman Computer Test Report to the listing that follows. The total number of test items missed may differ from the number of learning statement codes shown on your test report because you may have missed more than one question in a certain knowledge area.

Additionally, you should trace the learning statement codes on your Airman Computer Test Report to our cross-reference listing of questions beginning on page 457. Determine which Gleim subunits you need to review.

The FAA will periodically revise the existing learning codes and add new ones. As Gleim learns about any changes, we will update our materials.

PLT001 Calculate a course intercept
PLT002 Calculate aircraft performance - airspeed
PLT003 Calculate aircraft performance - center of gravity
PLT004 Calculate aircraft performance - climb / descent / maneuvering
PLT005 Calculate aircraft performance - density altitude
PLT006 Calculate aircraft performance - glide
PLT007 Calculate aircraft performance - IAS
PLT008 Calculate aircraft performance - landing
PLT009 Calculate aircraft performance - turbine temperatures (MGT, EGT, ITT, T4, etc) / torque / horsepower
PLT010 Calculate aircraft performance - STAB TRIM
PLT011 Calculate aircraft performance - takeoff
PLT012 Calculate aircraft performance - time/speed/ distance/course/fuel/wind
PLT013 Calculate crosswind / headwind components
PLT014 Calculate distance / bearing to a station
PLT015 Calculate flight performance / planning - range
PLT016 Calculate fuel - dump time / weight / volume / quantity / consumption
PLT017 Calculate L/D ratio
PLT018 Calculate load factor / stall speed / velocity / angle of attack
PLT019 Calculate pressure altitude
PLT020 Calculate turbulent air penetration
PLT021 Calculate weight and balance
PLT022 Define Aeronautical Decision Making (ADM)
PLT023 Define altitude - absolute / true / indicated / density / pressure
PLT024 Define atmospheric adiabatic process
PLT025 Define Bernoulli's principle
PLT026 Define ceiling
PLT027 Define coning
PLT028 Define crewmember
PLT029 Define critical phase of flight
PLT030 Define false lift
PLT031 Define isobars / associated winds
PLT032 Define MACH speed regimes
PLT033 Define MEA / MOCA / MRA
PLT034 Define stopway / clearway
PLT035 Define Vne / Vno
PLT036 Interpret a MACH meter reading
PLT037 Interpret a Radar Weather Report / National Convective Weather Forecast
PLT038 Interpret aircraft Power Schedule Chart
PLT039 Interpret airport landing indicator
PLT040 Interpret airspace classes - charts / diagrams
PLT041 Interpret altimeter - readings / settings
PLT042 Interpret Constant Pressure charts / Isotachs Chart
PLT043 Interpret Analysis Heights / Temperature Chart
PLT044 Interpret ATC communications / instructions / terminology
PLT045 Interpret Descent Performance Chart
PLT046 Interpret drag ratio from charts
PLT047 Interpret/Program Flight Director/FMS/ Automation - modes / operation / indications / errors
PLT048 Interpret Hovering Ceiling Chart
PLT049 Interpret ILS - charts / RMI / CDI / indications
PLT050 Interpret information on a Brake Energy Limit Chart
PLT051 Interpret information on a Convective Outlook
PLT052 Interpret information on a Departure Procedure Chart
PLT053 Interpret information on a Flight Plan
PLT054 Interpret information on a Glider Performance Graph
PLT055 Interpret information on a High Altitude Chart
PLT056 Interpret information on a Horizontal Situation Indicator (HSI)
PLT057 Interpret information on a Hot Air Balloon Performance Graph
PLT058 Interpret information on a Low Altitude Chart
PLT059 Interpret information on a METAR / SPECI report
PLT060 Interpret information on a Performance Curve Chart
PLT061 Interpret information on a PIREP
PLT062 Interpret information on a Pseudo-Adiabatic Chart / K Index / Lifted Index
PLT063 *Removed by the FAA*
PLT064 Interpret information on a Sectional Chart
PLT065 Interpret information on a Service Ceiling Engine Inoperative Chart

PLT066 Interpret information on a Convective Outlook Chart
PLT067 Interpret information on a SIGMET
PLT068 Interpret information on a Significant Weather Prognostic Chart
PLT069 Interpret information on a Slush/Standing Water Takeoff Chart
PLT070 Interpret information on a Stability Chart
PLT071 Interpret information on a Surface Analysis Chart
PLT072 Interpret information on a Terminal Aerodrome Forecast (TAF)
PLT073 Interpret information on a Tower Enroute Control (TEC)
PLT074 Interpret information on a Velocity/Load Factor Chart
PLT075 Interpret information on a Weather Depiction Chart
PLT076 Interpret information on a Winds and Temperatures Aloft Forecast (FB)
PLT077 Interpret information on an Airport Diagram
PLT078 Interpret information in an Airport Facility Directory (AFD)
PLT079 Interpret information on an Airways Chart
PLT080 Interpret information on an Arrival Chart
PLT081 Interpret information on an Aviation Area Forecast (FA)
PLT082 Interpret information on an IFR Alternate Airport Minimums Chart
PLT083 Interpret information on an Instrument Approach Procedures (IAP)
PLT084 Interpret information on an Observed Winds Aloft Chart
PLT085 Interpret information on Takeoff Obstacle / Field / Climb Limit Charts
PLT086 Interpret readings on a Turn and Slip Indicator
PLT087 Interpret readings on an Aircraft Course and DME Indicator
PLT088 Interpret speed indicator readings
PLT089 Interpret Takeoff Speeds Chart
PLT090 Interpret VOR - charts / indications / CDI / NAV
PLT091 Interpret VOR / CDI - illustrations / indications / procedures
PLT092 Interpret weight and balance - diagram
PLT093 Recall administration of medical oxygen
PLT094 Recall aerodynamics - airfoil design / pressure distribution / effects of altitude
PLT095 Recall aerodynamics - longitudinal axis / lateral axis
PLT096 Recall aeromedical factors - effects of altitude
PLT097 Recall aeromedical factors - effects of carbon monoxide poisoning
PLT098 Recall aeromedical factors - fitness for flight
PLT099 Recall aeromedical factors - scanning procedures
PLT100 Recall aeronautical charts - IFR En Route Low Altitude
PLT101 Recall aeronautical charts - pilotage
PLT102 Recall aeronautical charts - terminal procedures
PLT103 Recall Aeronautical Decision Making (ADM) - hazardous attitudes
PLT104 Recall Aeronautical Decision Making (ADM) - human factors / CRM
PLT105 Recall airborne radar / thunderstorm detection equipment - use / limitations
PLT106 Recall aircraft air-cycle machine
PLT107 Recall aircraft alternator / generator system
PLT108 Recall aircraft anti-icing / deicing - methods / fluids
PLT109 Recall aircraft batteries - capacity / charging / types / storage / rating / precautions
PLT110 Recall aircraft brake system
PLT111 Recall aircraft circuitry - series / parallel
PLT112 Recall aircraft controls - proper use / techniques
PLT113 Recall aircraft design - categories / limitation factors
PLT114 Recall aircraft design - construction / function
PLT115 Recall aircraft engine - detonation/backfiring/ after firing, cause/characteristics
PLT116 Recall aircraft general knowledge / publications / AIM / navigational aids
PLT117 Recall aircraft heated windshields
PLT118 Recall aircraft instruments - gyroscopic
PLT119 Recall aircraft lighting - anti-collision / landing / navigation
PLT120 Recall aircraft limitations - turbulent air penetration
PLT121 Recall aircraft loading - computations
PLT122 Recall aircraft operations - checklist usage
PLT123 Recall aircraft performance - airspeed
PLT124 Recall aircraft performance - atmospheric effects
PLT125 Recall aircraft performance - climb / descent
PLT126 Recall aircraft performance - cold weather operations
PLT127 Recall aircraft performance - density altitude
PLT128 Recall aircraft performance - effects of icing
PLT129 Recall aircraft performance - effects of runway slope / slope landing
PLT130 Recall aircraft performance - fuel
PLT131 Recall aircraft performance - ground effect
PLT132 Recall aircraft performance - instrument markings / airspeed / definitions / indications
PLT133 Recall aircraft performance - normal climb / descent rates
PLT134 Recall aircraft performance - takeoff
PLT135 Recall aircraft pressurization - system / operation
PLT136 Recall aircraft systems - anti-icing / deicing
PLT137 Recall aircraft systems - environmental control
PLT138 Recall aircraft landing gear/tires - types / characteristics
PLT139 Recall aircraft warning systems - stall / fire / retractable gear / terrain awareness
PLT140 Recall airport operations - LAHSO
PLT141 Recall airport operations - markings / signs / lighting
PLT142 Recall airport operations - noise avoidance routes
PLT143 Recall airport operations - rescue / fire fighting vehicles and types of agents
PLT144 Recall airport operations - runway conditions
PLT145 Recall airport operations - runway lighting
PLT146 Recall airport operations - traffic pattern procedures / communication procedures
PLT147 Recall airport operations - visual glideslope indicators
PLT148 Recall airport operations lighting - MALS / ALSF / RCLS / TDZL
PLT149 Recall airport preflight / taxi operations - procedures
PLT150 Recall airport traffic patterns - entry procedures
PLT151 Recall airship - buoyancy
PLT152 Recall airship - flight characteristics / controllability
PLT153 Recall airship - flight operations
PLT154 Recall airship - ground weigh-off / static / trim condition
PLT155 Recall airship - maintaining pressure
PLT156 Recall airship - maximum headway / flight at equilibrium
PLT157 Recall airship - pressure height / dampers / position
PLT158 Recall airship - pressure height / manometers
PLT159 Recall airship - pressure height / super heat / valving gas

PLT160 Recall airship - stability / control / positive superheat
PLT161 Recall airspace classes - limits / requirements / restrictions / airspeeds / equipment
PLT162 Recall airspace requirements - operations
PLT163 Recall airspace requirements - visibility / cloud clearance
PLT164 Recall airspeed - effects during a turn
PLT165 Recall altimeter - effect of temperature changes
PLT166 Recall altimeter - settings / setting procedures
PLT167 Recall altimeters - characteristics / accuracy
PLT168 Recall angle of attack - characteristics / forces / principles
PLT169 Recall antitorque system - components / functions
PLT170 Recall approach / landing / taxiing techniques
PLT171 Recall ATC - reporting
PLT172 Recall ATC - system / services
PLT173 Recall atmospheric conditions - measurements / pressure / stability
PLT174 Recall autopilot / yaw damper - components / operating principles / characteristics / failure modes
PLT175 Recall autorotation
PLT176 Recall balance tab - purpose / operation
PLT177 Recall balloon - flight operations
PLT178 Recall balloon - flight operations / gas
PLT179 Recall balloon - ground weigh-off / static equilibrium / load
PLT180 Recall balloon gas/hot air - lift / false lift / characteristics
PLT181 Recall balloon - hot air / physics
PLT182 Recall balloon - inspecting the fabric
PLT183 Recall balloon flight operations - ascent / descent
PLT184 Recall balloon flight operations - launch / landing
PLT185 Recall basic instrument flying - fundamental skills
PLT186 Recall basic instrument flying - pitch instruments
PLT187 Recall basic instrument flying - turn coordinator / turn and slip indicator
PLT188 Recall cabin atmosphere control
PLT189 Recall carburetor - effects of carburetor heat / heat control
PLT190 Recall carburetor ice - factors affecting / causing
PLT191 Recall carburetors - types / components / operating principles / characteristics
PLT192 Recall clouds - types / formation / resulting weather
PLT193 Recall cockpit voice recorder (CVR) - operating principles / characteristics / testing
PLT194 Recall collision avoidance - scanning techniques
PLT195 Recall collision avoidance - TCAS
PLT196 Recall communications - ATIS broadcasts
PLT197 Recall Coriolis effect
PLT198 Recall course / heading - effects of wind
PLT199 Recall cyclic control pressure - characteristics
PLT200 Recall dead reckoning - calculations / charts
PLT201 Recall departure procedures - ODP / SID
PLT202 Recall DME - characteristics / accuracy / indications / Arc
PLT203 Recall earth's atmosphere - layers / characteristics / solar energy
PLT204 Recall effective communication - basic elements
PLT205 Recall effects of alcohol on the body
PLT206 Recall effects of temperature - density altitude / icing
PLT207 Recall electrical system - components / operating principles / characteristics / static bonding and shielding
PLT208 Recall emergency conditions / procedures
PLT209 *Removed by the FAA*
PLT210 Recall engine shutdown - normal / abnormal / emergency / precautions
PLT211 Recall evaluation testing characteristics
PLT212 Recall fire extinguishing systems - components / operating principles / characteristics
PLT213 Recall flight characteristics - longitudinal stability / instability
PLT214 Recall flight characteristics - structural / wing design
PLT215 Recall flight instruments - magnetic compass
PLT216 Recall flight instruments - total energy compensators
PLT217 Recall flight maneuvers - quick stop
PLT218 Recall flight operations - common student errors
PLT219 Recall flight operations - maneuvers
PLT220 Recall flight operations - night and high altitude operations
PLT221 Recall flight operations - takeoff / landing maneuvers
PLT222 Recall flight operations - takeoff procedures
PLT223 Recall flight operations multiengine - engine inoperative procedures
PLT224 Recall flight plan - IFR
PLT225 Recall flight plan - requirements
PLT226 Recall fog - types / formation / resulting weather
PLT227 Recall FOI techniques - integrated flight instruction
PLT228 Recall FOI techniques - lesson plans
PLT229 Recall FOI techniques - professionalism
PLT230 Recall FOI techniques - responsibilities
PLT231 Recall FOI techniques / human behavior - anxiety / fear / stress
PLT232 Recall FOI techniques / human behavior - dangerous tendencies
PLT233 Recall FOI techniques / human behavior - defense mechanisms
PLT234 Recall forces acting on aircraft - 3 axis intersect
PLT235 Recall forces acting on aircraft - aerodynamics
PLT236 Recall forces acting on aircraft - airfoil / center of pressure / mean camber line
PLT237 Recall forces acting on aircraft - airspeed / air density / lift / drag
PLT238 Recall forces acting on aircraft - aspect ratio
PLT239 Recall forces acting on aircraft - buoyancy / drag / gravity / thrust
PLT240 Recall forces acting on aircraft - CG / flight characteristics
PLT241 Recall forces acting on aircraft - drag / gravity / thrust / lift
PLT242 Recall forces acting on aircraft - lift / drag / thrust / weight / stall / limitations
PLT243 Recall forces acting on aircraft - propeller / torque
PLT244 Recall forces acting on aircraft - stability / controllability
PLT245 Recall forces acting on aircraft - stalls / spins
PLT246 Recall forces acting on aircraft - steady state climb / flight
PLT247 Recall forces acting on aircraft - thrust / drag / weight / lift
PLT248 Recall forces acting on aircraft - turns
PLT249 Recall fuel - air mixture
PLT250 Recall fuel - types / characteristics / contamination / fueling / defueling / precautions
PLT251 Recall fuel characteristics / contaminants / additives
PLT252 Recall fuel dump system - components / methods
PLT253 Recall fuel system - components / operating principles / characteristics / leaks
PLT254 Recall fuel tank - components / operating principles / characteristics

PLT255 Recall fueling procedures - safety / grounding / calculating volume
PLT256 Recall glider performance - effect of loading
PLT257 Recall glider performance - speed / distance / ballast / lift / drag
PLT258 Recall ground reference maneuvers - ground track diagram
PLT259 Recall ground resonance - conditions to occur
PLT260 Recall gyroplane - aerodynamics / rotor systems
PLT261 Recall hail - characteristics / hazards
PLT262 Recall helicopter hazards - dynamic rollover / Low G / LTE
PLT263 Recall hazardous weather - fog / icing / turbulence / visibility restriction
PLT264 Recall helicopter approach - settling with power
PLT265 Recall helicopter takeoff / landing - ground resonance action required
PLT266 Recall high lift devices - characteristics / functions
PLT267 Recall hot air balloon - weigh-off procedure
PLT268 Recall hovering - aircraft performance / tendencies
PLT269 Recall human behavior - defense mechanism
PLT270 Recall human behavior - social / self fulfillment / physical
PLT271 Recall human factors (ADM) - judgment
PLT272 Recall human factors - stress management
PLT273 Recall hydraulic systems - components / operating principles / characteristics
PLT274 Recall icing - formation / characteristics
PLT275 Recall ILS - indications / HSI
PLT276 Recall ILS - indications / OBS / CDI
PLT277 Recall ILS - marker beacon / indicator lights / codes
PLT278 Recall indicating systems - airspeed / angle of attack / attitude / heading / manifold pressure / synchro / EGT
PLT279 Recall Inertial/Doppler Navigation System principles / regulations / requirements / limitations
PLT280 Recall inflight illusions - causes / sources
PLT281 Recall information in an Airport Facility Directory
PLT282 Recall information in the certificate holder's manual
PLT283 Recall information on a Constant Pressure Analysis Chart
PLT284 Recall information on a Forecast Winds and Temperatures Aloft (FB)
PLT285 Recall information on a Height Velocity Diagram
PLT286 Recall information on a Significant Weather Prognostic Chart
PLT287 Recall information on a Surface Analysis Chart
PLT288 Recall information on a Terminal Aerodrome Forecast (TAF)
PLT289 Recall information on a Weather Depiction Chart
PLT290 Recall information on AIRMETS / SIGMETS
PLT291 Recall information on an Aviation Area Forecast (FA)
PLT292 Recall information on an Instrument Approach Procedures (IAP)
PLT293 Recall information on an Instrument Departure Procedure Chart
PLT294 Recall information on Inflight Aviation Weather Advisories
PLT295 Recall instructor techniques - obstacles / planning / activities / outcome
PLT296 Recall instrument procedures - holding / circling
PLT297 Recall instrument procedures - unusual attitude / unusual attitude recovery
PLT298 Recall instrument procedures - VFR on top
PLT300 Recall instrument/navigation system checks/ inspections - limits / tuning / identifying / logging
PLT301 Recall inversion layer - characteristics
PLT302 Recall jet stream - types / characteristics
PLT303 Recall L/D ratio
PLT304 Recall launch / aero-tow procedures
PLT305 Recall leading edge devices - types / effect / purpose / operation
PLT306 Recall learning process - levels of learning / transfer of learning / incidental learning
PLT307 Recall learning process - memory / fact / recall
PLT308 Recall learning process - laws of learning elements
PLT309 Recall load factor - angle of bank
PLT310 Recall load factor - characteristics
PLT311 Recall load factor - effect of airspeed
PLT312 Recall load factor - maneuvering / stall speed
PLT313 Recall loading – limitations / terminology
PLT314 Recall longitudinal axis - aerodynamics / center of gravity / direction of motion
PLT315 Recall Machmeter - principles / functions
PLT316 Recall meteorology - severe weather watch (WW)
PLT317 Recall microburst - characteristics / hazards
PLT318 Recall minimum fuel advisory
PLT319 Recall navigation – celestial / navigation chart / characteristics
PLT320 Recall navigation - true north / magnetic north
PLT321 Recall navigation - types of landing systems
PLT322 Recall navigation - VOR / NAV system
PLT323 Recall NOTAMS - classes / information / distribution
PLT324 Recall oil system - types / components / functions / oil specifications
PLT325 Recall operations manual - transportation of prisoner
PLT326 Recall oxygen system - components / operating principles / characteristics
PLT327 Recall oxygen system - install / inspect / repair / service / precautions / leaks
PLT328 Recall performance planning - aircraft loading
PLT329 Recall physiological factors - cabin pressure
PLT330 Recall physiological factors - cause / effects of hypoxia
PLT331 Recall physiological factors - effects of scuba diving / smoking
PLT332 Recall physiological factors - hyperventilation
PLT333 Recall physiological factors - night vision
PLT334 Recall physiological factors - spatial disorientation
PLT335 Recall pilotage - calculations
PLT336 Recall pitch control - collective / cyclic
PLT337 Recall pitot-static system - components / operating principles / characteristics
PLT338 Recall pneumatic system - operation
PLT340 Recall positive exchange of flight controls
PLT341 Recall power setting - characteristics
PLT342 Recall powerplant - controlling engine temperature
PLT343 Recall powerplant - operating principles / operational characteristics / inspecting
PLT344 Recall precipitation - types / characteristics
PLT345 Recall pressure altitude
PLT346 Recall primary / secondary flight controls - types / purpose / functionality / operation
PLT347 Recall principles of flight - critical engine
PLT348 Recall principles of flight - turns
PLT349 Recall procedures for confined areas
PLT350 Recall propeller operations - constant / variable speed
PLT351 Recall propeller system - types / components / operating principles / characteristics
PLT352 Recall purpose / operation of a stabilizer
PLT353 Recall Radar Summary Chart
PLT354 Recall radio - GPS / RNAV / RAIM

PLT355 Recall radio - HSI
PLT356 Recall radio - ILS / compass locator
PLT357 Recall radio - ILS
PLT358 Recall radio - LOC / ILS
PLT359 *Removed by the FAA*
PLT360 *Removed by the FAA*
PLT361 *Removed by the FAA*
PLT362 *Removed by the FAA*
PLT363 Recall radio - VOR / VOT
PLT364 Recall radio system - license requirements / frequencies
PLT365 Recall reciprocating engine - components / operating principles / characteristics
PLT366 Recall regulations - accident / incident reporting and preserving wreckage
PLT367 Recall regulations - additional equipment/ operating requirements large transport aircraft
PLT368 Recall regulations - admission to flight deck
PLT369 Recall regulations - aerobatic flight requirements
PLT370 Recall regulations - Air Traffic Control authorization / clearances
PLT371 Recall regulations - Aircraft Category / Class
PLT372 Recall regulations - aircraft inspection / records / expiration
PLT373 Recall regulations - aircraft operating limitations
PLT374 Recall regulations - aircraft owner / operator responsibilities
PLT375 Recall regulations - aircraft return to service
PLT376 Recall regulations - airspace special use / TFRS
PLT377 Recall regulations - airworthiness certificates / requirements / responsibilities
PLT378 Recall regulations - Airworthiness Directives
PLT379 Recall regulations - alternate airport requirements
PLT380 Recall regulations - alternate airport weather minima
PLT381 Recall regulations - altimeter settings
PLT382 Recall regulations - approach minima
PLT383 Recall regulations - basic flight rules
PLT384 Recall regulations - briefing of passengers
PLT385 Recall regulations - cargo in passenger compartment
PLT386 Recall regulations - certificate issuance / renewal
PLT387 Recall regulations - change of address
PLT388 Recall regulations - cockpit voice / flight data recorder(s)
PLT389 Recall regulations - commercial operation requirements / conditions / OpSpecs
PLT390 Recall regulations - communications enroute
PLT391 Recall regulations - communications failure
PLT392 Recall regulations - compliance with local regulations
PLT393 Recall regulations - controlled / restricted airspace - requirements
PLT394 Recall regulations - declaration of an emergency
PLT395 Recall regulations - definitions
PLT396 Recall regulations - departure alternate airport
PLT397 Recall regulations - destination airport visibility
PLT398 Recall regulations - dispatch
PLT399 Recall regulations - display / inspection of licenses and certificates
PLT400 Recall regulations - documents to be carried on aircraft during flight
PLT401 Recall regulations - dropping / aerial application / towing restrictions
PLT402 Recall regulations - ELT requirements
PLT403 Recall regulations - emergency deviation from regulations
PLT404 Recall regulations - emergency equipment
PLT405 Recall regulations - equipment / instrument / certificate requirements
PLT406 Recall regulations - equipment failure
PLT407 Recall regulations - experience / training requirements
PLT408 Recall regulations - fire extinguisher requirements
PLT409 Recall regulations - flight / duty time
PLT410 Recall regulations - flight engineer qualifications / privileges / responsibilities
PLT411 Recall regulations - flight instructor limitations / qualifications
PLT412 Recall regulations - flight release
PLT413 Recall regulations - fuel requirements
PLT414 Recall regulations - general right-of-way rules
PLT415 Recall regulations - IFR flying
PLT416 Recall regulations - immediate notification
PLT417 Recall regulations - individual flotation devices
PLT418 Recall regulations - instructor demonstrations / authorizations
PLT419 Recall regulations - instructor requirements / responsibilities
PLT420 Recall regulations - instrument approach procedures
PLT421 Recall regulations - instrument flight rules
PLT422 Recall regulations - intermediate airport authorizations
PLT423 Recall regulations - knowledge and skill test checks
PLT424 Recall regulations - limits on autopilot usage
PLT425 Recall regulations - maintenance reports / records / entries
PLT426 Recall regulations - maintenance requirements
PLT427 Recall regulations - medical certificate requirements / validity
PLT428 Recall regulations - minimum equipment list
PLT429 Recall regulations - minimum flight / navigation instruments
PLT430 Recall regulations - minimum safe / flight altitude
PLT431 Recall regulations - operating near other aircraft
PLT432 Recall regulations - operational control functions
PLT433 Recall regulations - operational flight plan requirements
PLT434 Recall regulations - operational procedures for a controlled airport
PLT435 Recall regulations - operational procedures for an uncontrolled airport
PLT436 Recall regulations - operations manual
PLT437 Recall regulations - overwater operations
PLT438 Recall regulations - oxygen requirements
PLT439 Recall regulations - persons authorized to perform maintenance
PLT440 Recall regulations - Pilot / Crew duties and responsibilities
PLT441 Recall regulations - pilot briefing
PLT442 Recall regulations - pilot currency requirements
PLT443 Recall regulations - pilot qualifications / privileges / responsibilities / crew complement
PLT444 Recall regulations - pilot-in-command authority / responsibility
PLT445 Recall regulations - preflight requirements
PLT446 Recall regulations - preventative maintenance
PLT447 Recall regulations - privileges / limitations of medical certificates
PLT448 Recall regulations - privileges / limitations of pilot certificates
PLT449 Recall regulations - proficiency check requirements
PLT450 Recall regulations - qualifications / duty time
PLT451 Recall regulations - ratings issued / experience requirements / limitations
PLT452 Recall regulations - re-dispatch
PLT453 Recall regulations - records retention for domestic / flag air carriers
PLT454 Recall regulations - required aircraft / equipment inspections

PLT455 Recall regulations - requirements of a flight plan release
PLT456 Recall regulations - runway requirements
PLT457 Recall regulations - student pilot endorsements / other endorsements
PLT458 Recall regulations - submission / revision of Policy and Procedure Manuals
PLT459 Recall regulations - takeoff procedures / minimums
PLT460 Recall regulations - training programs
PLT461 Recall regulations - use of aircraft lights
PLT462 Recall regulations - use of microphone / megaphone / interphone / public address system
PLT463 Recall regulations - alcohol or drugs
PLT464 Recall regulations - use of safety belts / harnesses (crew member)
PLT465 Recall regulations - use of seats / safety belts / harnesses (passenger)
PLT466 Recall regulations - V speeds
PLT467 Recall regulations - visual flight rules and limitations
PLT468 Recall regulations - Visual Meteorolcgical Conditions (VMC)
PLT469 Recall regulations - weather radar
PLT470 Recall rotor system - types / components / operating principles / characteristics
PLT471 Recall rotorcraft transmission - components / operating principles / characteristics
PLT472 Recall rotorcraft vibration - characteristics / sources
PLT473 Recall secondary flight controls - types / purpose / functionality
PLT474 Recall soaring - normal procedures
PLT475 Recall squall lines - formation / characteristics / resulting weather
PLT476 Recall stabilizer - purpose / operation
PLT477 Recall stalls - characteristics / factors / recovery / precautions
PLT478 Recall starter / ignition system - types / components / operating principles / characteristics
PLT479 Recall starter system - starting procedures
PLT480 Recall static/dynamic stability/instability - characteristics
PLT481 Recall student evaluation - learning process
PLT482 Recall student evaluation - written tests / oral quiz / critiques
PLT483 Recall supercharger - characteristics / operation
PLT484 Recall symbols - chart / navigation
PLT485 Recall taxiing / crosswind / techniques
PLT486 Recall taxiing / takeoff - techniques / procedures
PLT487 Recall teaching methods - demonstration / performance
PLT488 Recall teaching methods - group / guided discussion / lecture
PLT489 Recall teaching methods - known to unknown
PLT490 Recall teaching methods - motivation / student feelings of insecurity
PLT491 Recall teaching methods - organizing material / course of training
PLT492 Recall temperature - effects on weather formations
PLT493 Recall the dynamics of frost / ice / snow formation on an aircraft
PLT494 Recall thermals - types / characteristics / formation / locating / maneuvering / corrective actions
PLT495 Recall thunderstorms - types / characteristics / formation / hazards / precipitation static
PLT496 Recall towrope - strength / safety links / positioning
PLT497 Recall transponder - codes / operations / usage
PLT498 Recall Transportation Security Regulations
PLT499 Recall turbine engines - components / operational characteristics / associated instruments
PLT500 Recall turboprop engines - components / operational characteristics
PLT501 Recall turbulence - types / characteristics / reporting / corrective actions
PLT502 Recall universal signals - hand / light / visual
PLT503 Recall use of narcotics / drugs / intoxicating liquor
PLT504 Recall use of training aids - types / function / purpose
PLT505 Recall use of training aids - usefulness / simplicity / compatibility
PLT506 Recall V speeds - maneuvering / flap extended / gear extended / V_1, V_2, r, ne, mo, mc, mg, etc.
PLT507 Recall VOR - indications / VOR / VOT / CDI
PLT508 Recall VOR/altimeter/transponder checks - identification / tuning / identifying / logging
PLT509 Recall wake turbulence - characteristics / avoidance techniques
PLT510 Recall weather - causes / formation
PLT511 Recall weather associated with frontal activity / air masses
PLT512 Recall weather conditions - temperature / moisture / dewpoint
PLT513 Recall weather information - FAA Avcams
PLT514 Recall weather reporting systems - briefings / forecasts / reports / AWOS / ASOS
PLT515 Recall weather services - TIBS / TPC / WFO / HIWAS
PLT516 Recall winds - types / characteristics
PLT517 Recall winds associated with high / low-pressure systems
PLT518 Recall windshear - characteristics / hazards / power management
PLT519 Recall wing spoilers - purpose / operation
PLT520 Calculate density altitude
PLT521 Recall helicopter takeoff / landing – slope operations
PLT522 Recall helicopter – Pinnacle / Ridgeline operations
PLT523 Recall vortex generators – purpose / effects / aerodynamics
PLT524 Interpret / Program information on an avionics display
PLT525 Interpret table – oxygen / fuel / oil / accumulator / fire extinguisher
PLT526 Recall near midair collision report
PLT527 Recall BASIC VFR – weather minimums

CROSS-REFERENCES TO THE FAA LEARNING STATEMENT CODES

Pages 457 through 464 contain a listing of all of the questions from our private pilot knowledge test bank. Non-airplane questions are excluded. The questions are in FAA Learning Statement Code (LSC) sequence. To the right of each LSC, we present our study unit/question number and our answer. For example, note that in one instance below, PLT003 is cross-referenced to 1-35, which represents our Study Unit 1, question 35; the correct answer is B.

Pages 451 through 456 contain a complete listing of all the FAA Learning Statement Codes associated with all of the private pilot questions presented in this book. Use this list to identify the specific topic associated to each Learning Statement Code.

The first line of each of our answer explanations in Study Units 1 through 11 contains

1. The correct answer and
2. A reference for the answer explanation, e.g., *AFH Chap 1.* If this reference is not useful, use the following chart to identify the learning statement code to determine the specific reference appropriate for the question.

FAA Learning Code	Gleim SU/ Q. No.	Gleim Answer
PLT002	5–28	C
PLT003	1–35	B
PLT003	5–51	C
PLT003	5–52	A
PLT005	5–16	C
PLT005	5–18	C
PLT008	5–35	B
PLT008	5–36	B
PLT008	5–37	C
PLT008	5–38	B
PLT008	5–40	B
PLT008	5–41	C
PLT008	5–42	B
PLT008	5–43	B
PLT008	5–44	B
PLT008	5–45	A
PLT011	5–9	C
PLT011	5–19	A
PLT011	5–20	B
PLT011	5–21	B
PLT011	5–22	A
PLT011	9–29	B
PLT012	5–23	B
PLT012	5–24	B

FAA Learning Code	Gleim SU/ Q. No.	Gleim Answer
PLT012	5–25	B
PLT012	9–16	B
PLT012	11–25	C
PLT012	11–26	A
PLT012	11–27	A
PLT012	11–31	A
PLT012	11–32	A
PLT012	11–33	B
PLT012	11–37	C
PLT012	11–39	C
PLT012	11–40	A
PLT012	11–41	B
PLT012	11–42	B
PLT012	11–43	C
PLT012	11–44	C
PLT012	11–45	B
PLT012	11–46	B
PLT012	11–47	C
PLT012	11–48	B
PLT012	11–49	A
PLT012	11–50	A
PLT012	11–51	A
PLT012	11–52	C
PLT012	11–53	A

FAA Learning Code	Gleim SU/ Q. No.	Gleim Answer
PLT012	11–54	B
PLT012	11–55	A
PLT012	11–56	C
PLT012	11–57	C
PLT012	11–58	B
PLT012	11–59	C
PLT012	11–60	B
PLT012	11–61	A
PLT013	5–29	A
PLT013	5–30	B
PLT013	5–31	C
PLT013	5–32	C
PLT013	5–33	C
PLT013	5–34	B
PLT015	5–27	C
PLT019	5–13	A
PLT019	5–15	A
PLT019	5–17	B
PLT021	5–47	C
PLT021	5–48	C
PLT021	5–49	B
PLT021	5–60	B
PLT021	5–61	B
PLT021	5–62	B

FAA Learning Code	Gleim SU/ Q. No.	Gleim Answer	FAA Learning Code	Gleim SU/ Q. No.	Gleim Answer	FAA Learning Code	Gleim SU/ Q. No.	Gleim Answer
PLT021	5–63	A	PLT059	8–16	B	PLT064	9–60	C
PLT021	5–64	A	PLT059	8–17	B	PLT064	9–61	C
PLT021	5–65	A	PLT061	8–18	A	PLT064	9–62	C
PLT021	5–67	B	PLT061	8–19	C	PLT064	9–63	B
PLT023	2–33	B	PLT061	8–20	A	PLT064	9–64	A
PLT023	2–34	A	PLT061	8–21	C	PLT064	9–65	A
PLT023	2–35	B	PLT061	8–22	C	PLT064	9–66	B
PLT023	2–36	B	PLT064	4–82	C	PLT064	9–68	A
PLT023	2–38	B	PLT064	4–144	C	PLT064	9–69	B
PLT023	2–40	B	PLT064	9–1	B	PLT064	9–70	A
PLT023	2–46	A	PLT064	9–2	B	PLT064	9–71	B
PLT025	1–13	C	PLT064	9–3	A	PLT064	9–72	B
PLT026	8–12	B	PLT064	9–4	A	PLT064	9–74	A
PLT039	3–31	B	PLT064	9–5	B	PLT064	9–75	C
PLT039	3–32	A	PLT064	9–6	C	PLT064	9–76	C
PLT039	3–33	C	PLT064	9–9	A	PLT064	9–77	C
PLT039	3–34	C	PLT064	9–10	B	PLT064	9–88	C
PLT039	3–35	A	PLT064	9–11	A	PLT064	11–23	B
PLT040	3–73	C	PLT064	9–13	A	PLT064	11–24	C
PLT040	9–14	C	PLT064	9–17	A	PLT068	8–56	B
PLT040	9–30	C	PLT064	9–18	B	PLT068	8–57	A
PLT040	9–39	A	PLT064	9–27	B	PLT068	8–58	C
PLT040	9–41	A	PLT064	9–28	C	PLT068	8–59	A
PLT040	9–45	C	PLT064	9–31	B	PLT068	8–60	B
PLT040	9–52	A	PLT064	9–32	B	PLT071	8–40	B
PLT040	9–54	C	PLT064	9–33	B	PLT072	8–31	A
PLT040	9–58	B	PLT064	9–34	B	PLT072	8–32	A
PLT041	2–25	C	PLT064	9–35	C	PLT072	8–33	A
PLT041	2–26	A	PLT064	9–37	C	PLT072	8–34	C
PLT041	2–27	B	PLT064	9–38	B	PLT072	8–35	B
PLT041	2–28	C	PLT064	9–40	C	PLT072	8–36	B
PLT041	2–29	A	PLT064	9–42	A	PLT072	8–37	B
PLT041	2–30	C	PLT064	9–44	B	PLT072	8–38	B
PLT041	2–31	B	PLT064	9–46	B	PLT075	8–43	C
PLT041	2–32	C	PLT064	9–47	A	PLT075	8–44	A
PLT041	2–37	C	PLT064	9–48	B	PLT076	8–50	B
PLT044	3–69	A	PLT064	9–49	C	PLT076	8–51	C
PLT044	3–77	A	PLT064	9–50	A	PLT076	8–52	B
PLT044	3–99	B	PLT064	9–51	C	PLT076	8–53	A
PLT059	8–13	A	PLT064	9–53	B	PLT076	8–54	C
PLT059	8–14	C	PLT064	9–57	C	PLT077	3–1	B
PLT059	8–15	A	PLT064	9–59	A	PLT077	3–2	B

FAA Learning Code	Gleim SU/ Q. No.	Gleim Answer
PLT077	3–3	A
PLT077	3–4	C
PLT077	3–29	A
PLT078	9–7	B
PLT078	9–8	C
PLT078	9–55	C
PLT078	9–83	A
PLT078	9–84	B
PLT078	9–85	C
PLT078	9–86	A
PLT078	9–87	B
PLT078	9–89	A
PLT078	9–90	C
PLT078	9–91	B
PLT078	9–92	B
PLT078	9–94	A
PLT078	9–95	C
PLT081	8–27	B
PLT081	8–28	C
PLT081	8–29	A
PLT081	8–30	A
PLT088	2–14	C
PLT088	2–15	C
PLT088	2–16	A
PLT088	2–17	C
PLT090	10–5	B
PLT090	10–6	C
PLT090	10–7	A
PLT090	10–14	A
PLT091	10–8	C
PLT091	10–9	C
PLT091	10–11	B
PLT091	10–12	C
PLT091	10–13	C
PLT092	5–50	C
PLT092	5–53	B
PLT092	5–54	B
PLT092	5–55	B
PLT092	5–56	A
PLT092	5–57	A
PLT092	5–58	B
PLT092	5–59	A
PLT097	6–20	B
PLT097	6–21	A
PLT097	6–22	C
PLT097	6–23	A
PLT099	3–61	C
PLT099	6–16	C
PLT099	6–17	C
PLT099	6–18	B
PLT099	6–19	A
PLT101	9–36	C
PLT101	10–10	A
PLT101	11–30	C
PLT103	6–25	A
PLT103	6–26	A
PLT103	6–27	A
PLT103	6–28	A
PLT103	6–29	A
PLT103	6–30	C
PLT103	6–31	C
PLT103	6–32	B
PLT103	6–33	B
PLT103	6–34	C
PLT103	6–35	C
PLT103	6–37	C
PLT104	2–55	B
PLT104	6–36	C
PLT112	11–15	A
PLT112	11–16	B
PLT112	11–17	A
PLT112	11–18	C
PLT115	2–82	C
PLT115	2–83	A
PLT115	2–84	B
PLT116	9–78	B
PLT116	9–79	B
PLT116	9–80	C
PLT116	9–81	A
PLT116	9–82	B
PLT116	10–18	B
PLT118	2–49	C
PLT118	2–50	A
PLT119	3–56	A
PLT119	3–57	A
PLT119	3–58	C
PLT119	3–67	B
PLT119	4–166	C
PLT121	5–66	C
PLT123	4–13	A
PLT124	5–2	B
PLT124	5–6	C
PLT124	5–12	A
PLT124	5–14	C
PLT125	3–63	A
PLT127	5–5	B
PLT127	5–8	A
PLT128	1–24	C
PLT131	1–26	A
PLT131	1–27	A
PLT131	1–28	B
PLT131	1–29	B
PLT131	1–30	B
PLT132	1–38	A
PLT132	2–18	C
PLT132	2–19	B
PLT132	2–20	C
PLT132	2–21	C
PLT132	2–22	B
PLT132	2–23	C
PLT132	2–52	C
PLT133	4–12	C
PLT134	1–23	A
PLT136	2–68	A
PLT140	3–115	C
PLT140	3–116	A
PLT140	3–118	A
PLT140	3–119	A
PLT140	3–120	B
PLT141	3–5	C
PLT141	3–6	C
PLT141	3–7	B
PLT141	3–8	C
PLT141	3–9	C
PLT141	3–10	C
PLT141	3–11	C

FAA Learning Code	Gleim SU/ Q. No.	Gleim Answer
PLT141	3–12	A
PLT141	3–13	A
PLT141	3–14	A
PLT141	3–15	B
PLT141	3–16	A
PLT141	3–18	B
PLT141	3–20	A
PLT141	3–21	A
PLT141	3–22	B
PLT141	3–23	B
PLT141	3–24	B
PLT141	3–25	B
PLT141	3–30	C
PLT141	3–105	A
PLT141	3–106	C
PLT147	3–36	C
PLT147	3–37	B
PLT147	3–39	B
PLT147	3–40	B
PLT147	3–41	B
PLT147	3–42	B
PLT147	3–44	B
PLT147	3–45	B
PLT149	2–94	C
PLT150	3–79	C
PLT150	3–110	A
PLT150	9–73	A
PLT161	3–74	B
PLT161	3–76	C
PLT161	3–78	C
PLT161	3–81	B
PLT161	3–82	B
PLT161	3–83	C
PLT161	3–84	A
PLT161	3–85	C
PLT161	3–89	B
PLT161	4–66	C
PLT161	4–69	C
PLT161	4–84	B
PLT161	4–110	B
PLT161	4–112	A
PLT161	4–129	B

FAA Learning Code	Gleim SU/ Q. No.	Gleim Answer
PLT161	4–130	A
PLT161	4–132	A
PLT161	4–152	B
PLT161	4–155	C
PLT161	4–169	A
PLT161	9–12	B
PLT161	9–15	C
PLT161	9–21	C
PLT161	9–22	A
PLT161	9–25	B
PLT161	9–93	C
PLT162	3–75	C
PLT162	4–83	A
PLT163	4–67	A
PLT163	4–71	B
PLT163	4–73	B
PLT163	4–79	B
PLT163	4–80	B
PLT163	4–81	B
PLT163	4–135	B
PLT163	4–136	C
PLT163	4–137	A
PLT163	4–138	C
PLT163	4–141	A
PLT163	4–142	B
PLT163	4–143	A
PLT163	4–145	B
PLT163	4–146	C
PLT163	4–147	B
PLT163	4–148	A
PLT163	4–149	A
PLT163	4–150	C
PLT163	4–151	B
PLT163	9–43	C
PLT165	2–47	A
PLT165	7–2	A
PLT166	2–41	C
PLT166	2–51	C
PLT167	2–42	C
PLT167	2–44	B
PLT167	2–45	C
PLT167	4–156	A

FAA Learning Code	Gleim SU/ Q. No.	Gleim Answer
PLT168	1–14	A
PLT168	1–15	A
PLT168	1–16	A
PLT168	1–17	B
PLT168	1–18	B
PLT168	1–19	C
PLT170	11–66	B
PLT172	3–88	A
PLT173	2–43	C
PLT173	7–46	A
PLT173	7–53	B
PLT173	7–54	A
PLT187	2–48	A
PLT189	2–75	A
PLT189	2–76	B
PLT189	2–77	B
PLT190	2–69	C
PLT190	2–70	A
PLT190	2–71	C
PLT190	2–72	C
PLT190	2–74	C
PLT191	2–73	B
PLT192	7–23	C
PLT192	7–24	B
PLT192	7–39	B
PLT192	7–40	B
PLT192	7–41	B
PLT192	7–42	B
PLT192	7–43	C
PLT192	7–47	A
PLT192	7–48	C
PLT194	2–53	B
PLT194	2–54	C
PLT194	3–59	C
PLT194	3–60	B
PLT194	3–62	B
PLT194	3–64	B
PLT194	3–66	A
PLT194	3–100	B
PLT194	3–101	A
PLT194	3–102	C
PLT194	3–103	C

FAA Learning Code	Gleim SU/ Q. No.	Gleim Answer
PLT194	6–15	A
PLT196	3–71	C
PLT196	3–72	C
PLT200	11–29	A
PLT200	11–34	C
PLT200	11–35	B
PLT200	11–36	A
PLT200	11–38	B
PLT201	3–27	C
PLT204	3–87	C
PLT204	3–96	A
PLT204	3–97	A
PLT204	3–98	C
PLT206	5–3	B
PLT206	5–7	C
PLT207	2–95	A
PLT207	2–96	B
PLT207	2–97	C
PLT207	2–98	C
PLT208	5–39	B
PLT208	11–12	A
PLT208	11–13	C
PLT213	1–32	B
PLT213	1–33	A
PLT215	2–1	C
PLT215	2–2	A
PLT215	2–3	C
PLT215	2–4	B
PLT215	2–5	B
PLT215	2–6	B
PLT215	2–7	C
PLT215	2–8	C
PLT215	2–9	B
PLT219	11–63	A
PLT220	11–14	C
PLT221	3–28	B
PLT221	3–38	B
PLT221	3–43	B
PLT222	3–80	C
PLT225	11–1	A
PLT225	11–3	B
PLT225	11–6	B

FAA Learning Code	Gleim SU/ Q. No.	Gleim Answer
PLT226	7–35	C
PLT226	7–36	B
PLT226	7–37	A
PLT226	7–38	C
PLT235	1–11	A
PLT235	1–12	A
PLT236	1–34	C
PLT242	1–10	A
PLT242	1–31	A
PLT243	1–39	A
PLT243	1–40	B
PLT243	1–41	B
PLT245	1–21	C
PLT245	1–22	A
PLT248	11–62	C
PLT249	2–79	B
PLT249	2–80	A
PLT249	2–81	B
PLT250	2–85	C
PLT250	2–87	A
PLT250	2–89	C
PLT250	2–91	A
PLT251	2–88	C
PLT253	2–78	A
PLT253	2–90	B
PLT258	11–64	B
PLT258	11–65	B
PLT263	7–25	A
PLT263	11–11	C
PLT271	6–24	C
PLT271	7–19	C
PLT274	7–20	C
PLT274	7–21	C
PLT274	8–24	A
PLT278	2–24	C
PLT278	5–26	C
PLT279	10–17	C
PLT281	3–113	B
PLT281	9–23	B
PLT281	9–24	B
PLT281	9–56	B
PLT284	8–49	C

FAA Learning Code	Gleim SU/ Q. No.	Gleim Answer
PLT284	8–55	B
PLT289	8–39	A
PLT289	8–41	B
PLT289	8–42	A
PLT290	8–61	C
PLT290	8–62	B
PLT290	8–63	B
PLT290	8–64	A
PLT290	8–65	C
PLT291	8–25	C
PLT291	8–26	C
PLT300	10–3	C
PLT301	7–22	C
PLT301	7–56	A
PLT301	7–57	C
PLT301	7–58	A
PLT309	1–43	B
PLT309	1–45	C
PLT309	1–46	C
PLT309	1–47	B
PLT309	1–48	A
PLT309	1–49	C
PLT309	1–50	B
PLT311	1–42	B
PLT312	1–44	A
PLT320	11–22	B
PLT322	11–28	A
PLT323	3–17	C
PLT323	3–19	C
PLT323	9–96	A
PLT323	9–97	B
PLT324	2–56	A
PLT328	1–37	A
PLT328	5–46	A
PLT330	6–1	A
PLT330	6–2	C
PLT330	6–3	A
PLT332	6–4	B
PLT332	6–5	A
PLT332	6–6	A
PLT332	6–7	A
PLT332	6–8	A

FAA Learning Code	Gleim SU/ Q. No.	Gleim Answer	FAA Learning Code	Gleim SU/ Q. No.	Gleim Answer	FAA Learning Code	Gleim SU/ Q. No.	Gleim Answer
PLT334	6–9	B	PLT369	4–172	A	PLT393	4–131	B
PLT334	6–10	B	PLT369	4–173	B	PLT393	9–19	C
PLT334	6–11	A	PLT369	4–174	B	PLT393	9–20	B
PLT334	6–12	A	PLT369	4–175	B	PLT393	9–26	C
PLT334	6–13	A	PLT370	3–86	C	PLT395	4–3	C
PLT334	6–14	B	PLT370	4–6	C	PLT395	4–35	C
PLT335	10–4	B	PLT370	4–125	B	PLT399	4–23	C
PLT337	2–10	C	PLT371	4–1	B	PLT399	4–24	B
PLT337	2–11	C	PLT371	4–2	B	PLT399	4–25	C
PLT337	2–12	B	PLT371	4–4	A	PLT399	4–26	C
PLT337	2–13	C	PLT371	4–5	A	PLT400	4–161	C
PLT342	2–57	B	PLT372	4–186	B	PLT401	4–76	C
PLT342	2–58	C	PLT372	4–187	C	PLT401	4–89	B
PLT342	2–59	C	PLT372	4–189	B	PLT402	3–111	B
PLT342	2–61	A	PLT372	4–192	B	PLT402	3–112	C
PLT342	2–62	A	PLT372	4–193	C	PLT402	4–162	B
PLT343	2–60	C	PLT373	4–87	B	PLT402	4–163	C
PLT343	2–93	B	PLT373	4–88	A	PLT402	4–164	B
PLT345	2–39	C	PLT373	4–178	B	PLT402	4–165	A
PLT345	5–1	A	PLT374	4–22	B	PLT403	4–122	A
PLT346	1–3	A	PLT374	4–180	B	PLT405	4–176	C
PLT346	1–4	A	PLT374	4–181	A	PLT405	4–177	A
PLT346	1–5	B	PLT374	4–182	A	PLT407	4–51	B
PLT346	1–6	A	PLT374	11–9	B	PLT407	4–52	C
PLT346	1–7	B	PLT375	4–17	B	PLT411	4–43	A
PLT346	1–8	A	PLT375	4–183	A	PLT413	4–133	C
PLT346	1–9	A	PLT375	4–184	B	PLT413	4–134	B
PLT350	2–63	A	PLT375	4–185	B	PLT414	4–102	A
PLT351	1–36	B	PLT376	4–153	B	PLT414	4–103	C
PLT351	2–64	B	PLT377	4–14	C	PLT414	4–104	A
PLT351	2–65	B	PLT377	4–195	C	PLT414	4–105	C
PLT351	5–4	B	PLT378	4–16	C	PLT414	4–106	B
PLT354	10–15	C	PLT381	4–118	A	PLT414	4–107	B
PLT354	10–16	B	PLT381	4–119	B	PLT414	4–108	B
PLT366	4–199	A	PLT381	4–120	B	PLT414	4–109	B
PLT366	4–200	B	PLT383	4–111	B	PLT425	4–194	A
PLT366	4–201	A	PLT383	4–179	B	PLT426	4–15	B
PLT366	4–202	C	PLT384	4–196	A	PLT426	4–188	A
PLT366	4–203	B	PLT387	4–50	A	PLT426	4–190	C
PLT366	4–204	C	PLT391	3–114	A	PLT427	4–30	C
PLT366	4–205	C	PLT393	4–113	A	PLT427	4–31	C
PLT369	4–171	B	PLT393	4–128	C	PLT427	4–32	B

FAA Learning Code	Gleim SU/ Q. No.	Gleim Answer
PLT427	4–33	C
PLT430	4–114	A
PLT430	4–115	C
PLT430	4–116	B
PLT430	4–117	A
PLT431	4–101	C
PLT434	4–127	A
PLT435	9–67	C
PLT438	4–167	C
PLT438	4–168	C
PLT439	4–18	B
PLT440	4–96	A
PLT440	4–121	C
PLT441	4–49	A
PLT442	4–39	C
PLT442	4–40	A
PLT442	4–41	C
PLT442	4–44	C
PLT442	4–46	B
PLT442	4–47	A
PLT442	4–48	C
PLT443	4–72	C
PLT444	3–65	B
PLT444	3–117	A
PLT444	4–85	B
PLT444	4–86	B
PLT444	4–123	B
PLT444	4–124	C
PLT444	4–126	B
PLT444	4–197	B
PLT444	4–198	B
PLT444	11–8	A
PLT445	4–93	C
PLT445	4–94	C
PLT445	4–95	B
PLT445	8–5	C
PLT445	8–6	B
PLT445	11–10	B
PLT446	4–19	C
PLT446	4–20	A
PLT446	4–21	B
PLT447	4–29	B

FAA Learning Code	Gleim SU/ Q. No.	Gleim Answer
PLT448	4–34	C
PLT448	4–38	B
PLT448	4–53	B
PLT448	4–54	B
PLT448	4–55	B
PLT448	4–56	C
PLT448	4–57	A
PLT448	4–58	C
PLT448	4–59	B
PLT448	4–60	A
PLT448	4–61	B
PLT448	4–62	C
PLT448	4–63	B
PLT448	4–65	C
PLT448	4–68	C
PLT448	4–70	C
PLT448	4–74	A
PLT448	4–75	C
PLT448	4–78	A
PLT449	4–42	C
PLT451	4–36	B
PLT455	11–2	C
PLT455	11–4	C
PLT455	11–5	C
PLT455	11–7	B
PLT457	4–37	B
PLT457	4–45	C
PLT462	3–26	C
PLT463	4–27	A
PLT463	4–28	B
PLT463	4–90	C
PLT463	4–91	A
PLT463	4–92	A
PLT464	4–97	C
PLT465	4–98	B
PLT465	4–99	B
PLT465	4–100	A
PLT466	4–7	A
PLT466	4–9	C
PLT466	4–11	A
PLT467	4–64	B
PLT467	4–139	B

FAA Learning Code	Gleim SU/ Q. No.	Gleim Answer
PLT467	4–154	B
PLT467	4–157	C
PLT467	4–158	C
PLT467	4–159	B
PLT467	4–160	B
PLT468	4–140	B
PLT473	1–1	A
PLT473	1–2	C
PLT475	7–10	B
PLT477	1–20	C
PLT478	2–66	A
PLT478	2–67	B
PLT478	2–86	B
PLT479	2–92	A
PLT485	11–20	A
PLT485	11–21	A
PLT486	11–19	C
PLT492	7–55	A
PLT493	1–25	A
PLT493	7–33	B
PLT494	7–4	C
PLT495	7–9	B
PLT495	7–11	A
PLT495	7–12	B
PLT495	7–13	A
PLT495	7–14	B
PLT495	7–15	B
PLT495	7–16	A
PLT495	7–17	A
PLT495	7–18	B
PLT497	3–90	C
PLT497	3–91	B
PLT497	3–92	A
PLT497	3–93	A
PLT497	3–94	A
PLT497	3–95	A
PLT497	4–77	A
PLT497	4–170	A
PLT502	3–70	B
PLT502	3–104	B
PLT502	3–107	B
PLT502	3–108	A

FAA Learning Code	Gleim SU/ Q. No.	Gleim Answer
PLT502	3–109	B
PLT506	4–8	A
PLT506	4–10	A
PLT507	10–1	C
PLT507	10–2	C
PLT508	4–191	C
PLT509	3–46	C
PLT509	3–47	C
PLT509	3–48	A
PLT509	3–49	C
PLT509	3–50	C
PLT509	3–51	B
PLT509	3–52	B
PLT509	3–53	A
PLT509	3–54	A
PLT509	3–55	A
PLT511	7–6	C
PLT511	7–7	A
PLT511	7–8	A
PLT511	7–49	A
PLT511	7–50	C
PLT511	7–51	C
PLT511	7–52	A
PLT512	7–1	C
PLT512	7–29	C
PLT512	7–30	C
PLT512	7–31	B
PLT512	7–32	A
PLT512	7–34	A
PLT512	7–44	B
PLT512	7–45	C
PLT514	8–1	C
PLT514	8–2	C
PLT514	8–3	C
PLT514	8–4	A
PLT514	8–7	A
PLT514	8–8	C
PLT514	8–9	A
PLT514	8–10	A
PLT514	8–11	B
PLT514	8–23	A
PLT514	8–45	B

FAA Learning Code	Gleim SU/ Q. No.	Gleim Answer
PLT515	8–46	A
PLT515	8–47	A
PLT515	8–48	A
PLT516	7–3	B
PLT516	7–5	C
PLT518	7–26	C
PLT518	7–27	C
PLT518	7–28	B
PLT520	5–10	A
PLT520	5–11	C
PLT526	3–68	B

INSTRUCTOR CERTIFICATION FORM
PRIVATE PILOT KNOWLEDGE TEST

Name: ____

I certify that I have reviewed the above individual's preparation for the FAA Private Pilot—Airplane knowledge test [covering the topics specified in 14 CFR 61.105(b)(1) through (13)] using the *Private Pilot FAA Knowledge Test* book, software, and/or online course by Irvin N. Gleim and find him/her competent to pass the knowledge test.

______________	______	______________	__________	______________
Signed	Date	Name	CFI Number	Expiration Date

* *

INSTRUCTOR CERTIFICATION FORM
RECREATIONAL PILOT KNOWLEDGE TEST

Name: ____

I certify that I have reviewed the above individual's preparation for the FAA Recreational Pilot—Airplane knowledge test [covering the topics specified in 14 CFR 61.97(b)(1) through (12)] using the *Recreational Pilot FAA Knowledge Test* book, software, and/or online course by Irvin N. Gleim and find him/her competent to pass the knowledge test.

______________	______	______________	__________	______________
Signed	Date	Name	CFI Number	Expiration Date

GLEIM®

Aviation

ABBREVIATIONS AND ACRONYMS IN *PRIVATE PILOT FAA KNOWLEDGE TEST*

AAH	*Advanced Avionics Handbook*
AC	Advisory Circular
ACL	Aeronautical Chart Legend
AD	Airworthiness Directive
AFH	*Airplane Flying Handbook*
AFSS	Automated Flight Service Station
AGL	above ground level
AIM	*Aeronautical Information Manual*
AIRMET	Airmen's Meteorological Information
AME	aviation medical examiner
ANDS	accelerate north, decelerate south
AOE	airport of entry
ARTS	Automated Radar Terminal System
ASEL	airplane single-engine land
ATA	actual time of arrival
ATC	Air Traffic Control
ATIS	Automatic Terminal Information Service
AvW	*Aviation Weather*
AWBH	*Aircraft Weight and Balance Handbook*
AWS	*Aviation Weather Services*
CDI	course deviation indicator
CDT	central daylight time
CFI	Certificated Flight Instructor
CFR	Code of Federal Regulations
CG	center of gravity
CH	compass heading
CT	control tower
CTAF	Common Traffic Advisory Frequency
DME	distance measuring equipment
DT	daylight time
DUATS	Direct User Access Terminal System
EFD	Electronic Flight Display
ELT	emergency locator transmitter
ETA	estimated time of arrival
ETD	estimated time of departure
FA	area forecast
FAA	Federal Aviation Administration
FAR	Federal Aviation Regulations
FB	winds and temperatures aloft forecast
FBO	Fixed-Base Operator
FCC	Federal Communications Commission
Fl Comp	Flight Computer
FL	flight level
FSDO	Flight Standards District Office
FSS	Flight Service Station
GPH	gallons per hour
Hg	mercury
HP	horsepower
IAS	indicated airspeed
ICAO	International Civil Aviation Organization
IFH	*Instrument Flying Handbook*
IFR	instrument flight rules
IR	instrument route
ISA	International Standard Atmosphere
LLWAS	lowlevel wind-shear alert system
mb	millibar
MB	magnetic bearing
MC	magnetic course
MEF	maximum elevation figure
METAR	aviation routine weather report
MFD	Multi-Function Display
MH	magnetic heading
MOA	Military Operations Area
MSL	mean sea level
MTR	Military Training Route
MVFR	marginal VFR
NFCT	nonfederal control tower
NM	nautical mile
NOTAM	notice to airmen
NPRM	Notice of Proposed Rulemaking
NTSB	National Transportation Safety Board Regulations
OAT	outside air temperature
OBS	omnibearing selector
PAPI	precision approach path indicator
PCL	pilot-controlled lighting
PFD	Primary Flight Display
PHAK	*Pilot's Handbook of Aeronautical Knowledge*
PIC	pilot in command
PIREP	Pilot Weather Report
RB	relative bearing
SFC	surface
SIGMET	Significant Meteorological Information
SM	statute mile
STC	supplemental type certificate
SVFR	special VFR
TACAN	Tactical Air Navigation
TAF	terminal aerodrome forecast
TAS	true airspeed
TC	true course
TH	true heading
UHF	ultra high frequency
UTC	Coordinated Universal Time
V_A	maneuvering speed
VASI	visual approach slope indicator
V_{FE}	maximum flap extended speed
VFR	visual flight rules
VHF	very high frequency
VHF/DF	VHF direction finder
V_{LE}	maximum landing gear extended speed
V_{NE}	never-exceed speed
V_{NO}	maximum structural cruising speed
VOR	VHF omnidirectional range
VORTAC	Collocated VOR and TACAN
VOT	VOR test facility
VR	visual route
V_{S0}	stalling speed or the minimum steady flight speed in the landing configuration
V_{S1}	stalling speed or the minimum steady flight speed obtained in a specific configuration
V_X	speed for best angle of climb
V_Y	speed for best rate of climb
WCA	wind correction angle
Z	Zulu or UTC time

AUTHORS' RECOMMENDATIONS

The Experimental Aircraft Association, Inc., is a very successful and effective nonprofit organization that represents and serves those of us interested in flying, in general, and in sport aviation, in particular. We personally invite you to enjoy becoming a member. Visit their website at www.eaa.org.

Types of EAA Memberships:

- $40 - Individual (includes subscription to *EAA Sport Aviation* magazine)
- $50 - Family (extends all benefits to member's spouse and children under 18, except for an additional EAA magazine subscription)
- Free - Student (for those ages 8 to 18 who have completed the EAA Young Eagles program)
- $1,295 - Lifetime

Sign up online at www.eaa.org/en/eaa/eaa-membership/types-of-memberships, email membership@eaa.org, or call 1-800-JOIN-EAA.

The annual EAA Oshkosh AirVenture is an unbelievable aviation spectacular with over 10,000 airplanes at one airport and virtually everything aviation-oriented you can imagine! Plan to spend at least 1 day (not everything can be seen in a day) in Oshkosh (100 miles northwest of Milwaukee). Visit the AirVenture website at www.airventure.org.

Convention dates: 2017 -- July 24 through July 30
2018 -- July 23 through July 29

The annual Sun 'n Fun EAA Fly-In is also highly recommended. It is held at the Lakeland, FL (KLAL), airport (between Orlando and Tampa). Visit the Sun 'n Fun website at www.sun-n-fun.org.

Convention dates: 2017 -- April 4 through April 9
2018 -- April 10 through April 15

AIRCRAFT OWNERS AND PILOTS ASSOCIATION (AOPA)

AOPA is the largest, most influential aviation association in the world, with two thirds of all pilots in the United States as members. AOPA's most important contribution to the world's most accessible, safest, least expensive, friendliest, easiest-to-use general aviation environment is their lobbying on our behalf at the federal, state, and local levels. AOPA also provides legal services, advice, and other assistance to the aviation community.

We recommend that you become an AOPA member to get the most out of AOPA's resources. To join, call 1-800-USA-AOPA or visit the AOPA website at www.aopa.org.

LEARN TO FLY – AOPA

AOPA hosts an informational web page on getting started in aviation. "Learn To Fly" contains information for those still dreaming about flying, those who are ready to begin, and those who are already making the journey. At this site, you can see at a glance what your options are, including approximate costs and how long it will take you. You can also learn more about the types of certificates available for new pilots and about additional ratings for current pilots. In addition, you can find information about FAA medical certification, passing knowledge tests, and choosing a flight school and instructor. Visit www.aopa.org/learntofly today!

INDEX OF LEGENDS AND FIGURES

The FAA legends and figures are contained in a book titled *Airman Knowledge Testing Supplement for Sport Pilot, Recreational Pilot, and Private Pilot*, which you will be given to use at the time of your test. For the purpose of test preparation, all of the applicable FAA legends and figures from this supplement are reproduced in color in this book. The legends and figures not included in this book, which are indicated by an "N/A" in this index, pertain to military topics, helicopters, gyroplanes, gliders, and/or topics the FAA removed from the test in 2015 and 2016. Gleim does not believe you will be tested on these figures and legends on your Private Pilot Knowledge Test.

INDEX